A HISTORY OF EASTERN CHRISTIANITY

Detail from the Bawït Icon. *Reproduced by courtesy of the Musée du Louvre.*

A History of Eastern Christianity

Aziz S. Atiya
Distinguished Professor of History,
University of Utah

Enlarged and Updated by the Author with
New Preface
Supplement to Part I
Supplementary Bibliography

KRAUS REPRINT
Millwood, N.Y.

First published 1968
by Methuen and Co Ltd. and
*by University of Notre
Dame Press*

Library of Congress Cataloging in Publication Data

Atiya, Aziz Suryal, 1898–
A history of eastern Christianity.

Bibliography: p.
Includes index.
1. Eastern churches. I. Title.
BX103.2.A8 1980 281'.5 80-232
ISBN 0-527-03703-6

Reprinted with the Permission of the Author
KRAUS REPRINT

A U.S. Division of Kraus-Thomson Organization Limited
Printed in the United States of America

CONTENTS

Errata

Page 14	note 3, line 2: for *19th* read *20th*
Page 133	note 3, line 1: for *Chassinuî* read *Chassinat*
Page 133	note 3, line 2: for *Baonta* read *Baouit*
Page 379	line 21: for *Norton's* read *Munro's*
Page 482	Index: for *Munro* . . . add *p. 379*
Page 483	Index: for *Norton* . . . omit *p. 379*

PREFACE TO ENLARGED AND UPDATED EDITION

The older editions of the present work, published almost simultaneously by Methuen in London and by University of Notre Dame Press in the United States during 1967/1968, have both been out of print for a few years. Nevertheless, it is felt that the book has never ceased to be in demand, and its seekers had to depend on the second-hand book market for the rather rare appearance of an occasional copy for sale. This seems to be sufficient justification for contemplating a new edition in which the bulk of the original text has been retained with little or no change, but enriched with a limited measure of additional material. Moreover, we have seized this opportunity to make a few minor corrections. In the meantime, it was thought expedient to add a new supplement to Part I on a novel development in the story of the Copts during the last few decades. Although known to have been confirmed in their sedentary way of life, the Copts suddenly embarked on an unusual immigration movement which carried thousands of them to new homes in the Old World and the New. Under the title of ". . . The Copts Abroad," we have tried to make a quick survey of this novel feature in Coptic annals. This has not been an easy task on account of two factors. In the first place, Coptic immigration from Egypt has proved to be a continuing process and it becomes rather hard to define its dimensions with precision at any given moment. In the second place, the data pertaining to that movement are as yet unavailable in printed records and hard to be gleaned from private sources in other parts of the world. Consequently, the figures quoted in our accounts must of necessity appear somewhat arbitrary, but they remain on the whole a reasonable approximation to the changing scene in the immigration process.

Furthermore, we have deemed it appropriate to update our bibliographical material by listing all or most of the relevant works of scholarship which have seen the light since the completion of the book, beginning with the year 1967 as our starting point. However, a few older works which do not appear in the previous editions have been included in this additional bibliography owing to their importance. This new listing should complement the general list of sources and works of reference cited in the footnotes of the original text and enumerated in the selected bibliography of our older work. The composite body of all those sources taken together, should provide future scholars with an adequate basis for further researching any given segment of the vast areas which we have tried to cover within the space of a single volume. Please note that the new material added to the first edition is not represented in the reprinted index.

In conclusion, it is our duty to express our personal appreciation to all the distinguished colleagues who have given this work a favourable reception and encouraged us to reissue this new edition. Our thanks are also due to the scholars who have taken the trouble to translate portions of our work into a number of Eastern languages and particularly to those who have thought it worthy of rendering into the Polish language.

ACKNOWLEDGEMENTS

Professor Kurt Weitzmann of Princeton University, Dr Wachtang Djobadze of the University of Utah, Mr Fred Anderegg of the University of Michigan, Mr Anis Rizkallah of the Institute of Coptic Studies and Dr Otto Meinardus of the American University at Cairo have generously supplied me with much of their photographic material from which I made a selection of some of my illustrations. I am truly thankful to all of them for their immediate response to my request. Acknowledgement should also be made to the authorities of the Louvre, the Metropolitan Museum of Art in New York City and the Coptic Museum in Cairo for permission to reproduce some of their valuable art objects.

A. S. ATIYA

ACKNOWLEDGMENTS

PREFACE TO FIRST EDITION

The present volume, though the fulfilment of a lifelong vow, saw its beginnings only during the academic year 1956–7 when I had the privilege of occupying the Henry W. Luce Visiting Professorship of World Christianity at Union Theological Seminary in New York City. It was then that I delivered a course of lectures in which I tried to outline the essentials of the extensive and complex but highly interesting subject of the Eastern Christian churches. From the very start I limited my thesis to the ancient non-Greek family of churches. Those were the Coptic and Ethiopic, the Jacobite, Nestorian, Armenian, Indian, Maronite, and the vanished churches of Nubia and North Africa.[1] As will be seen, the major churches of the Christian East were of Apostolic origin, and they invariably sprang into existence within living memory of the Ascension of Our Lord. Thus their importance in the early formative years of the faith, and their unbroken succession throughout the centuries leave no room for doubt as to the paramount value of this chapter

[1] It has been suggested that the Georgian Church might have been included in our survey. But, though closely associated with Armenia in its earliest Christianity, Georgia chose the Western road from Chalcedon in 451 and became a member of the Greek family. Consequently, it has been considered outside our designated field. However, for reference, the following is a short bibliographical notice on Georgia and its Church: W. A. Allen, *A History of the Georgian People* (London, 1932); M. F. Bosset, *Histoire de la géorgie*, 3 vols. (Sainte-Petersbourg, 1849–58); E. T. Dowling, *Sketches of Georgian Church History* (London, 1912); P. Joselian, *A Short History of the Georgian Church*, tr. from Russian by S. C. Malan (London, 1866); J. Karst, *Littérature géorgienne chrétienne* (Paris, 1934); D. M. Lang, *Lives and Legends of the Georgian Saints*, selected and tr. from original texts (London, 1956); ibid., *A Modern History of Georgia* (London, 1963); Jurgis Paltrusaitis, *Études sur l'art médiéval en Géorgie et en Arménie* (Paris, 1929); M. Tamarati, *L'église géorgienne dès origines jusqu'à nos jours* (Rome, 1910).

Some original source material has been published in the *Scriptores Iberici* series by M. Tarchinisivli and G. Garitte as part of the *Corpus Scriptorum Christianorum Orientalium*. Other material is still unpublished and in some cases unknown, such as the *Codex Georgianus*, which I discovered in the library of the Monastery of St Catherine on Mount Sinai in 1950. This is the oldest Georgian psalter inscribed on Egyptian papyrus which I showed to Mr Garitte during the Mount Sinai Expedition conducted by the Library of Congress and Alexandria University for microfilming its manuscripts. Since that time, I returned to the monastery to mount the fragile leaves under glass for preservation. The monastery also possesses a number of icons of Georgian provenance which have been photographed by the second Mount Sinai Expedition of Princeton and Michigan.

in Christian annals. I have tried to see and to judge the bare facts of the primitive Christianity of the East apart from the later accretions, and the barriers of mediæval and modern polemics. Indeed, well-meaning theologians and brilliant interpreters of Christian sects and churches seem by their argument, to have caused the Western mind to become oblivious to much of the purity and simplicity of the Christian origins of the East.

It was on the occasion of those lectures that Mr Melvin Arnold of Harper and Row approached me with the suggestion that I might formulate and elaborate my notes for publication in a single volume under the auspices of his house. The attraction of the proposal was overpowering in spite of my awareness of the magnitude of the task. Fortunately, a year of complete freedom of action spent at the Princeton Institute for Advanced Study afforded me the time to accumulate the essential data of my theme from the wealth of material in the seminary collections and splendid libraries of the eastern states. Yet this proved to be merely one stage in the fulfilment of a difficult and almost forbidding project. But my hand was already on the plough, and it was not possible for me to look behind. It is my hope that the years I have since devoted to this work have not been spent in vain.

The material presented in the following pages must necessarily be regarded as a modest beginning, and not the end. My primary aim has been to make a brief survey of the story of each church from its foundation until approximately our own times, with emphasis on the historical factors at play in the genesis of world religious events. Often, as in the case of the disputed œcumenical movement of the fourth and fifth centuries, I have felt that the elements of secular politics were drowned in an ocean of theological polemics. It will be noted that some churches of lesser importance in our day once had a most glorious ecclesiastical career. Thus the accomplishments of the Alexandrine divines, and the vast missionary enterprises of the Copts in the West and of the Nestorians in the East are objects of wonder and admiration.

The danger of reading the past through the present must be averted if we are to paint a true picture of the Eastern churches whose claim to Apostolic succession is their pride and glory. Nothing is as distasteful to the Eastern mind as the allegations reiterated in numerous writings by responsible coreligionists that the Christians of the East are schismatics, worse than heretics. Those bearers of the fire of the faith in untold and distant terrains of bygone days question the theory of schism on the basis that the early churches of primitive Christianity had developed in the spirit of harmonious brotherhood and parallelism. In reality, the need for amending a multitude of such unilateral verdicts is nowadays increasingly felt in most camps.

For a fuller understanding of each church, I have concluded my accounts with an enquiry into the institutional and cultural aspects and habits of every community, summarizing the hierarchical organization of the various churches, their rites and ceremonials, ecclesiastical art and architecture, and religious music and literature.

Since all these accounts are in the nature of general background rather than detailed and intensive studies, it has been my policy to supplement them with comprehensive bibliographical footnotes. These are intended as a guide to future researchers in the vast labyrinth of sources both ancient and modern. Thus, while the Select Bibliography incorporates the major collections and the works of a universal character dealing with numerous churches and various movements, the footnotes are devoted to the sources of special topics within the framework of each church.

Hitherto, literature on the Eastern churches could be classified under two categories. The first comprises the Roman Catholic authors, usually men of great learning and erudition who viewed the East from the narrow angle of their own profession with sectarian vehemence and considerable lack of understanding. Works of scholars such as Adrien Fortescue, Raymond Janin and Donald Attwater, have continuously come in for due appraisal in the course of our discussions. The second category consists of a group of well-meaning and sympathetic Protestant writers who, nevertheless, failed to come to grips with the essence of Eastern Christian primitivism. Among the older members of this class are J. M. Neale, Mrs E. L. Butcher, O. H. Parry, J. W. Etheridge, G. P. Badger and many others whose names appear in the relevant sections of this study. Outside those categories, a small school of modern thought has been growing slowly around the names of some church historians such as A. P. Stanley, W. F. Adeney and B. J. Kidd. It is noteworthy, however, that all of them have treated both the Greek and the non-Greek family of churches in the same volumes, and invariably the space allotted to the latter was insignificant. Thus in spite of the scholarly qualities of their attempts, their works have remained as a whole inadequate.

It is hoped that this volume may help in filling that lacuna in Eastern church history. As will be seen, a meticulous effort has been made to abide by the canons of historical research through the use of as many original documents as might be expected in a work of general character. The fruit of research accomplished by numerous scholars in many fields has been utilized to the full. However, the events here put forward, have been viewed from a somewhat different angle. It must be stated that I, a historian by vocation, am also a member of the Coptic Church by birth and upbringing. Consequently, the reader may be able to sense the deeper feeling with which the work is written from within the fold of the Churches of the East. As a matter of fact, I allowed myself to be persuaded into shouldering this arduous task, partly as a modest work of scholarship, and partly as an act of faith.

My notes bear sufficient testimony of my debt to the innumerable Eastern and Western authors whose monographs have enriched our library. Without these, it would have been impossible for me to complete my assignment. A preface is no place for a parade of such names. Reference is made to those innumerable monographs of masters, old and new.

Though conscious of the controversial character of some of my arguments, I have decided not to relinquish even the most provocative amongst them so long as they have any foundation in available source material. My sole ambition has been to establish a base from which others can take over with some measure of confidence. In sum, if this work proves to be a modest counterweight to the galaxy of standard manuals of the history of Western Christianity, I shall be more than rewarded. At any rate, an attempt is here offered in prayerful hope that future generations of interested scholars may carry the torch until the whole truth and wisdom of the great fathers of the faith are fully revealed to all congregations throughout the world.

A. S. ATIYA

MAPS

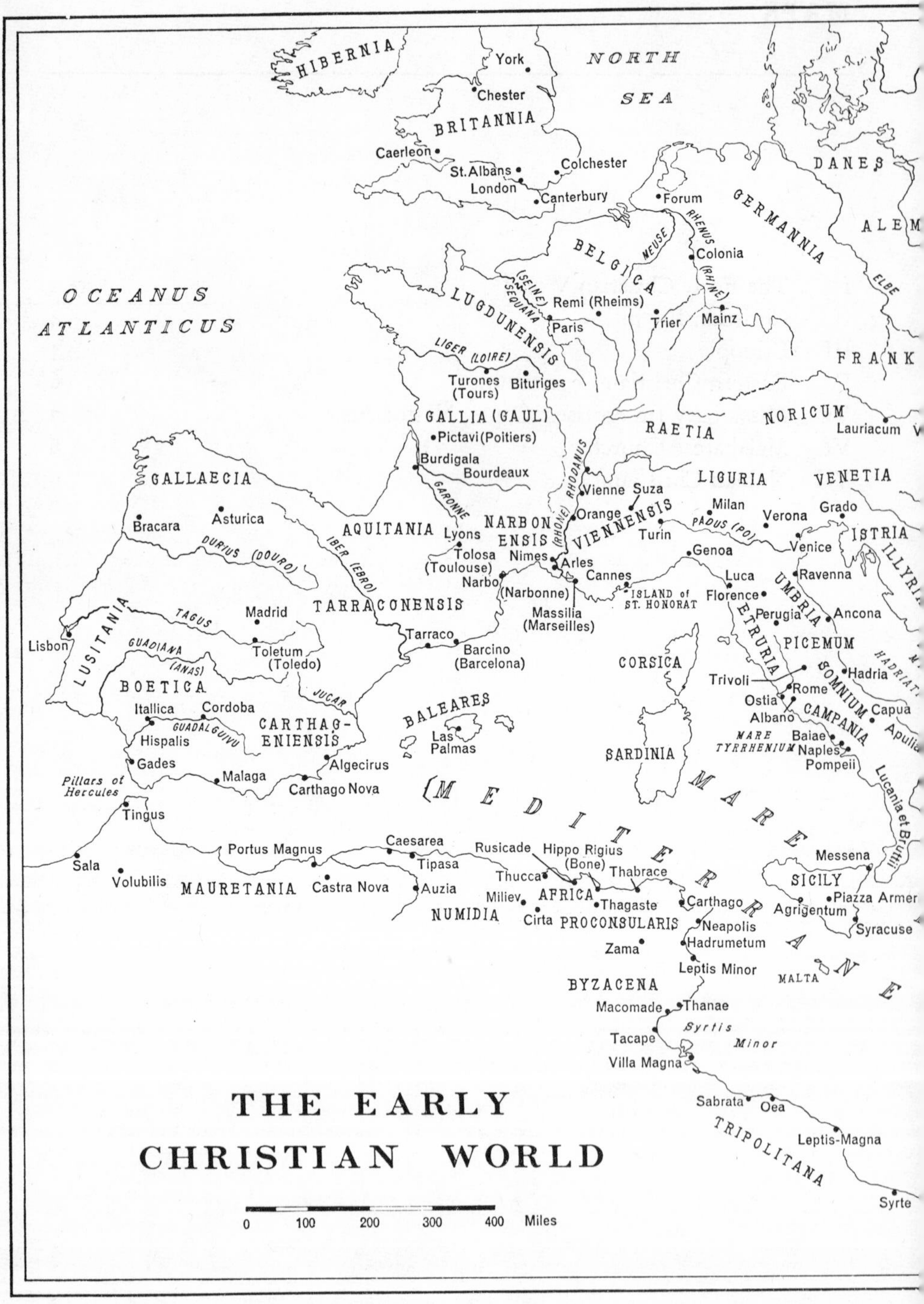
THE EARLY CHRISTIAN WORLD
HIBERNIA
York
NORTH SEA
Chester
BRITANNIA
Caerleon
St. Albans
London
Colchester
Canterbury
DANES
Forum
GERMANIA
ALEM
OCEANUS ATLANTICUS
BELGICA
MEUSE
RHENUS
(RHINE)
Colonia
ELBE
LUGDUNENSIS
(SEINE) SEQUANA
Remi (Rheims)
Paris
Trier
Mainz
FRANK
LIGER (LOIRE)
Turones (Tours)
Bituriges
GALLIA (GAUL)
Pictavi (Poitiers)
NORICUM
Lauriacum
RAETIA
Burdigala
Bourdeaux
GARONNE
RHODANUS
(RHONE)
GALLAECIA
Vienne
Suza
LIGURIA
VENETIA
Bracara
Asturica
Orange
VIENNENSIS
Milan
Verona
Grado
AQUITANIA
NARBONENSIS
Lyons
Turin
PADUS (PO)
ISTRIA
DURIUS (DOURO)
IBER (EBRO)
Tolosa (Toulouse)
Nimes
Arles
Genoa
Venice
ILLYRIA
Narbo
(Narbonne)
Cannes
ISLAND of ST. HONORAT
Luca
Florence
Ravenna
UMBRIA
LUSITANIA
TAGUS
Madrid
TARRACONENSIS
Massilia (Marseilles)
ETRURIA
Perugia
Ancona
Lisbon
GUADIANA (ANAS)
Toletum (Toledo)
Tarraco
Barcino (Barcelona)
CORSICA
PICEMUM
HADRIATICUM
BOETICA
JUCAR
Trivoli
Rome
SOMNIUM
Hadria
Ostia
Albano
CAMPANIA
Capua
Itallica
Cordoba
GUADALGUIVU
Hispalis
CARTHAGENIENSIS
BALEARES
Las Palmas
MARE TYRRHENIUM
Baiae
Naples
Pompeii
Apulia
Gades
SARDINIA
Lucania et Bruttii
Pillars of Hercules
Malaga
Algecirus
Carthago Nova
MEDITERRANE
MARE
Tingus
Sala
Volubilis
MAURETANIA
Portus Magnus
Caesarea
Tipasa
Castra Nova
Auzia
Rusicade
Hippo Rigius (Bone)
Thucca
Thabrace
Messena
SICILY
Milieu
AFRICA
NUMIDIA
Cirta
Thagaste
PROCONSULARIS
Carthago
Agrigentum
Piazza Armer
Syracuse
Neapolis
Zama
Hadrumetum
Leptis Minor
MALTA
BYZACENA
Macomade
Thanae
Syrtis Minor
Tacape
Villa Magna
Sabrata
Oea
TRIPOLITANA
Leptis-Magna
Syrte
0 100 200 300 400 Miles

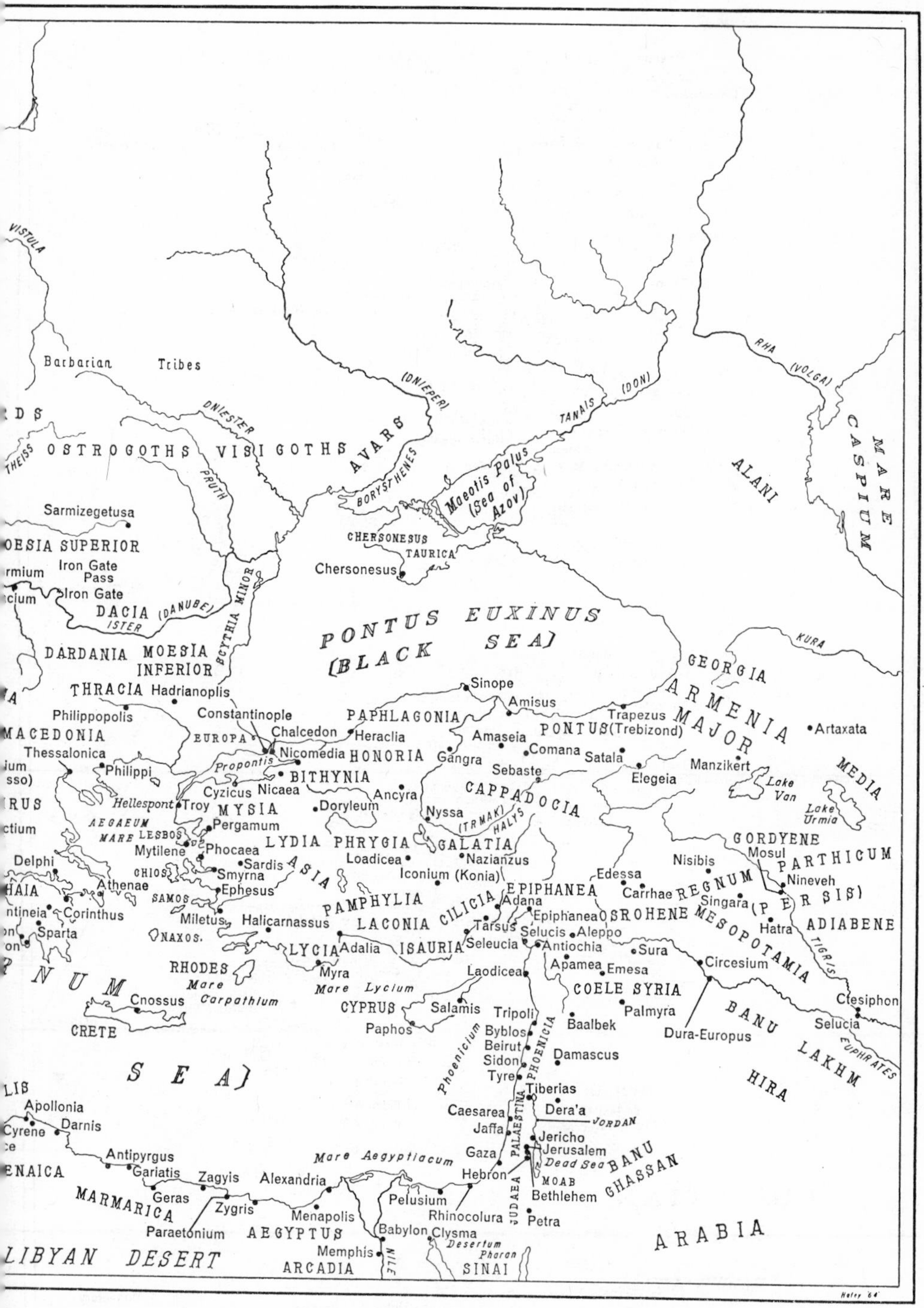
VISTULA
Barbarian Tribes
DNIESTER
(DNIEPER)
TANAIS (DON)
RHA (VOLGA)
MARE CASPIUM
ALANI
OSTROGOTHS
VISIGOTHS
AVARS
PRUTH
BORYSTHENES
Maeotis Palus (Sea of Azov)
Sarmizegetusa
MOESIA SUPERIOR
Iron Gate Pass
Iron Gate
DACIA
(DANUBE)
ISTER
SCYTHIA MINOR
CHERSONESUS TAURICA
Chersonesus
PONTUS EUXINUS (BLACK SEA)
KURA
GEORGIA
ARMENIA MAJOR
DARDANIA
MOESIA INFERIOR
THRACIA
Hadrianoplis
Philippopolis
Constantinople
EUROPA
Chalcedon
Sinope
Amisus
PAPHLAGONIA
Heraclia
Trapezus
PONTUS (Trebizond)
Artaxata
MACEDONIA
Thessalonica
Philippi
Propontis
Nicomedia
HONORIA
Amaseia
Comana
Gangra
Satala
Manzikert
MEDIA
BITHYNIA
Sebaste
Elegeia
Lake Van
Hellespont
Troy
Cyzicus
Nicaea
Ancyra
CAPPADOCIA
Lake Urmia
MYSIA
Doryleum
Nyssa
(IRMAK)
HALYS
AEGAEUM MARE
LESBOS
Pergamum
GORDYENE
Mytilene
Phocaea
LYDIA
PHRYGIA
GALATIA
Mosul
PARTHICUM
Delphi
Sardis
ASIA
Loadicea
Nazianzus
Nisibis
CHIOS
Smyrna
Iconium (Konia)
Edessa
Nineveh
Athenae
Ephesus
EPIPHANEA
Carrhae
REGNUM
SAMOS
PAMPHYLIA
Adana
Singara
(PERSIS)
Corinthus
Miletus
Halicarnassus
CILICIA
Epiphanea
OSROHENE
MESOPOTAMIA
Hatra
ADIABENE
Sparta
NAXOS
LACONIA
Tarsus
Selucis
Aleppo
TIGRIS
Adalia
ISAURIA
Seleucia
Antiochia
Sura
RHODES
LYCIA
Apamea
Emesa
Circesium
Mare Carpathium
Myra
Laodicea
Mare Lycium
COELE SYRIA
Cnossus
CYPRUS
Salamis
Palmyra
Ctesiphon
CRETE
Paphos
Tripoli
Baalbek
Dura-Europus
BANU LAKHM
Selucia
Byblos
Phoenicium
PHOENICIA
EUPHRATES
Beirut
Sidon
Damascus
SEA)
Tyre
HIRA
Tiberias
Apollonia
Caesarea
Dera'a
Darnis
Jaffa
JORDAN
Cyrene
Jericho
Antipyrgus
PALAESTINA
Jerusalem
Gariatis
Zagyis
Alexandria
Mare Aegyptiacum
Gaza
Dead Sea
BANU GHASSAN
MARMARICA
Geras
Hebron
MOAB
Zygris
Pelusium
Bethlehem
Menapolis
Rhinocolura
JUDAEA
Petra
Paraetonium
AEGYPTUS
Babylon
Clysma
Desertum Pharan
ARABIA
LIBYAN DESERT
Memphis
NILE
ARCADIA
SINAI

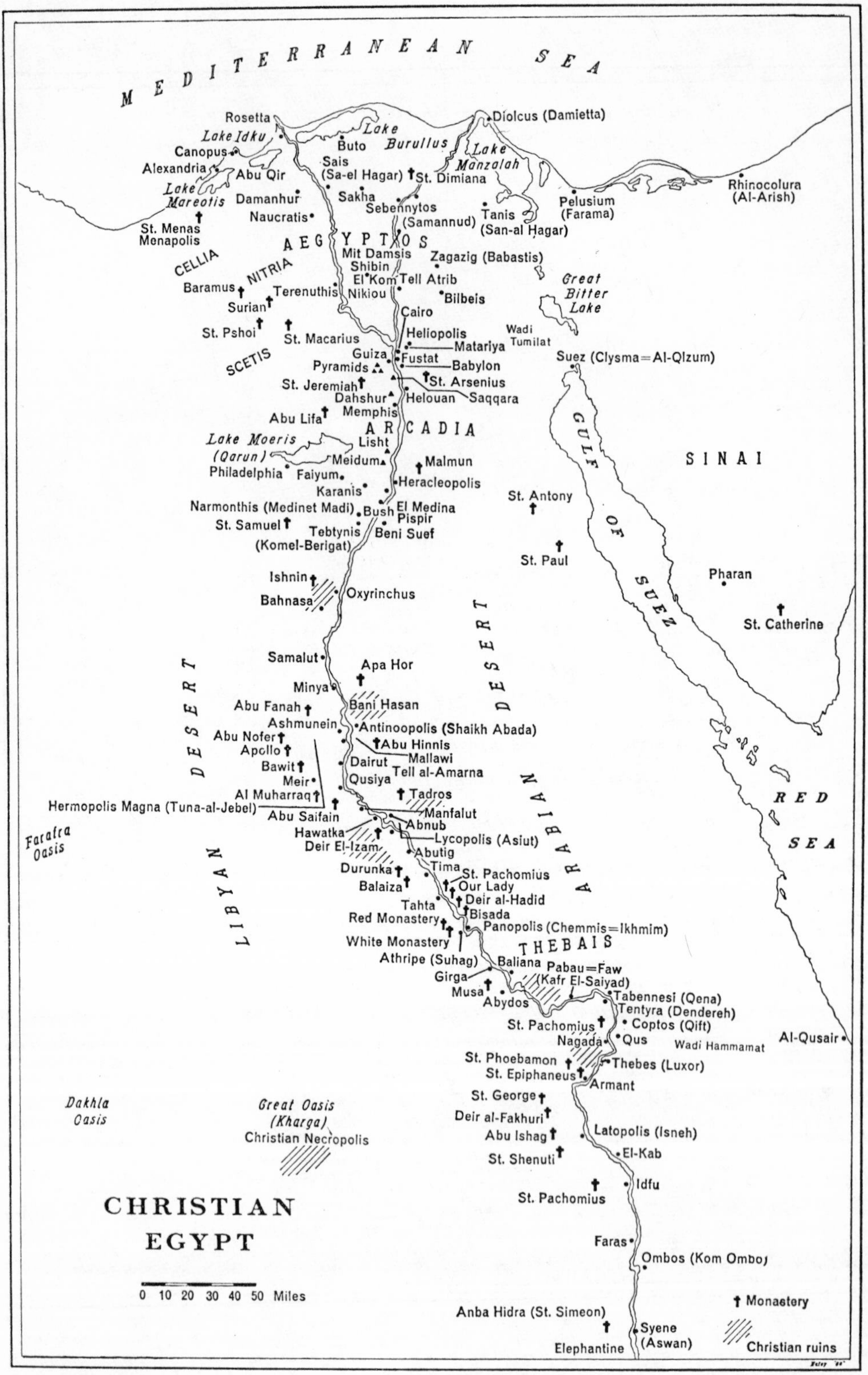

MEDITERRANEAN SEA
Rosetta
Lake Idku
Canopus
Alexandria
Abu Qir
Lake Mareotis
St. Menas
Menapolis
Damanhur
Naucratis
Buto
Lake Burullus
Sais (Sa-el Hagar)
St. Dimiana
Sakha
Sebennytos (Samannud)
Diolcus (Damietta)
Lake Manzalah
Tanis (San-al Hagar)
Pelusium (Farama)
Rhinocolura (Al-Arish)
AEGYPTOS
Mit Damsis
Shibin
El Kom
Tell Atrib
Zagazig (Babastis)
Great Bitter Lake
CELLIA
NITRIA
Baramus
Terenuthis
Nikiou
Surian
Bilbeis
Cairo
St. Pshoi
St. Macarius
Heliopolis
Matariya
Wadi Tumilat
SCETIS
Guiza
Fustat
Babylon
Pyramids
Suez (Clysma=Al-Qlzum)
St. Jeremiah
St. Arsenius
Dahshur
Helouan
Saqqara
Memphis
Abu Lifa
ARCADIA
Lake Moeris (Qarun)
Lisht
Meidum
Malmun
Philadelphia
Faiyum
Heracleopolis
Karanis
GULF OF SUEZ
SINAI
Narmonthis (Medinet Madi)
Bush
El Medina
Pispir
St. Antony
St. Samuel
Tebtynis (Komel-Berigat)
Beni Suef
St. Paul
Ishnin
Bahnasa
Oxyrinchus
Pharan
St. Catherine
LIBYAN DESERT
ARABIAN DESERT
Samalut
Apa Hor
Minya
Bani Hasan
Abu Fanah
Ashmunein
Antinoopolis (Shaikh Abada)
Abu Nofer
Abu Hinnis
Apollo
Mallawi
Bawit
Dairut
Tell al-Amarna
Meir
Qusiya
Al Muharraq
Tadros
Hermopolis Magna (Tuna-al-Jebel)
Abu Saifain
Manfalut
Abnub
Farafra Oasis
Hawatka
Deir El-Izam
Lycopolis (Asiut)
Abutig
RED SEA
Durunka
Tima
St. Pachomius
Balaiza
Our Lady
Deir al-Hadid
Tahta
Bisada
Red Monastery
Panopolis (Chemmis=Ikhmim)
White Monastery
THEBAIS
Athripe (Suhag)
Baliana
Pabau=Faw (Kafr El-Saiyad)
Girga
Musa
Abydos
Tabennesi (Qena)
Tentyra (Dendereh)
St. Pachomius
Coptos (Qift)
Nagada
Qus
Wadi Hammamat
Al-Qusair
St. Phoebamon
Thebes (Luxor)
St. Epiphaneus
Armant
Dakhla Oasis
Great Oasis (Kharga)
Christian Necropolis
St. George
Deir al-Fakhuri
Abu Ishag
Latopolis (Isneh)
St. Shenuti
El-Kab
Idfu
St. Pachomius
CHRISTIAN EGYPT
Faras
Ombos (Kom Ombo)
0 10 20 30 40 50 Miles
Monastery
Anba Hidra (St. Simeon)
Syene (Aswan)
Elephantine
Christian ruins

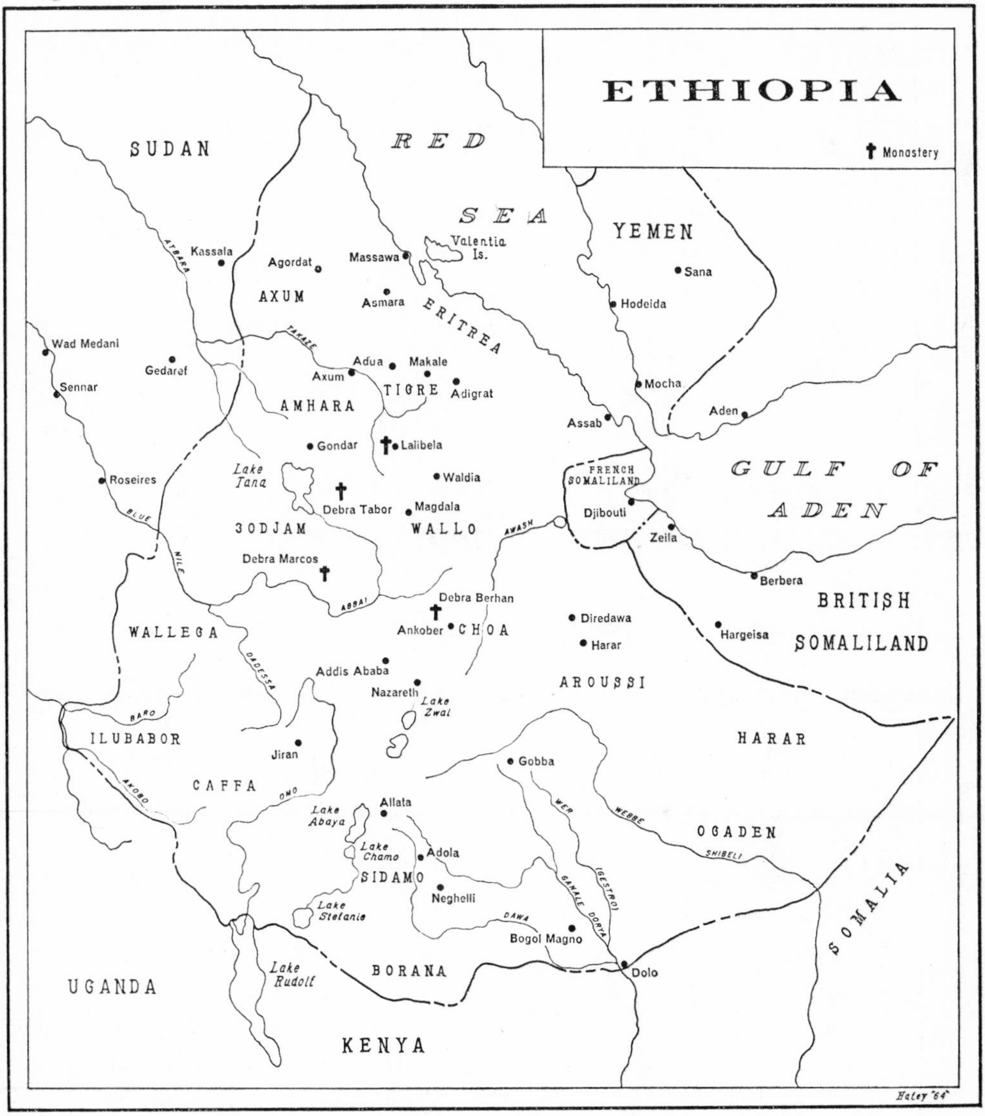

ETHIOPIA
† Monastery
SUDAN
RED
SEA
YEMEN
Sana
Hodeida
Mocha
Aden
GULF OF
ADEN
Kassala
ATBARA
Agordat
Massawa
Valentia Is.
AXUM
Asmara
ERITREA
TAKAZE
Wad Medani
Gedaref
Sennar
Adua
Makale
Axum
TIGRE
Adigrat
AMHARA
Assab
Gondar
Lalibela
Roseires
Lake Tana
Waldia
FRENCH SOMALILAND
Djibouti
Debra Tabor
Magdala
BLUE
GODJAM
WALLO
AWASH
Zeila
NILE
Debra Marcos
Berbera
ABBAI
Debra Berhan
BRITISH SOMALILAND
Diredawa
Hargeisa
WALLEGA
Ankober
CHOA
Harar
DADESSA
Addis Ababa
AROUSSI
Nazareth
Lake Zwai
BARO
ILUBABOR
Jiran
HARAR
Gobba
CAFFA
AKOBO
OMO
Allata
WER
WEBBE
Lake Abaya
OGADEN
Lake Chamo
Adola
SHIBELI
SIDAMO
Neghelli
GANALE DORYA
(GESTRO)
SOMALIA
Lake Stefanie
DAWA
Bogol Magno
Lake Rudolf
BORANA
Dolo
UGANDA
KENYA
Haley '64

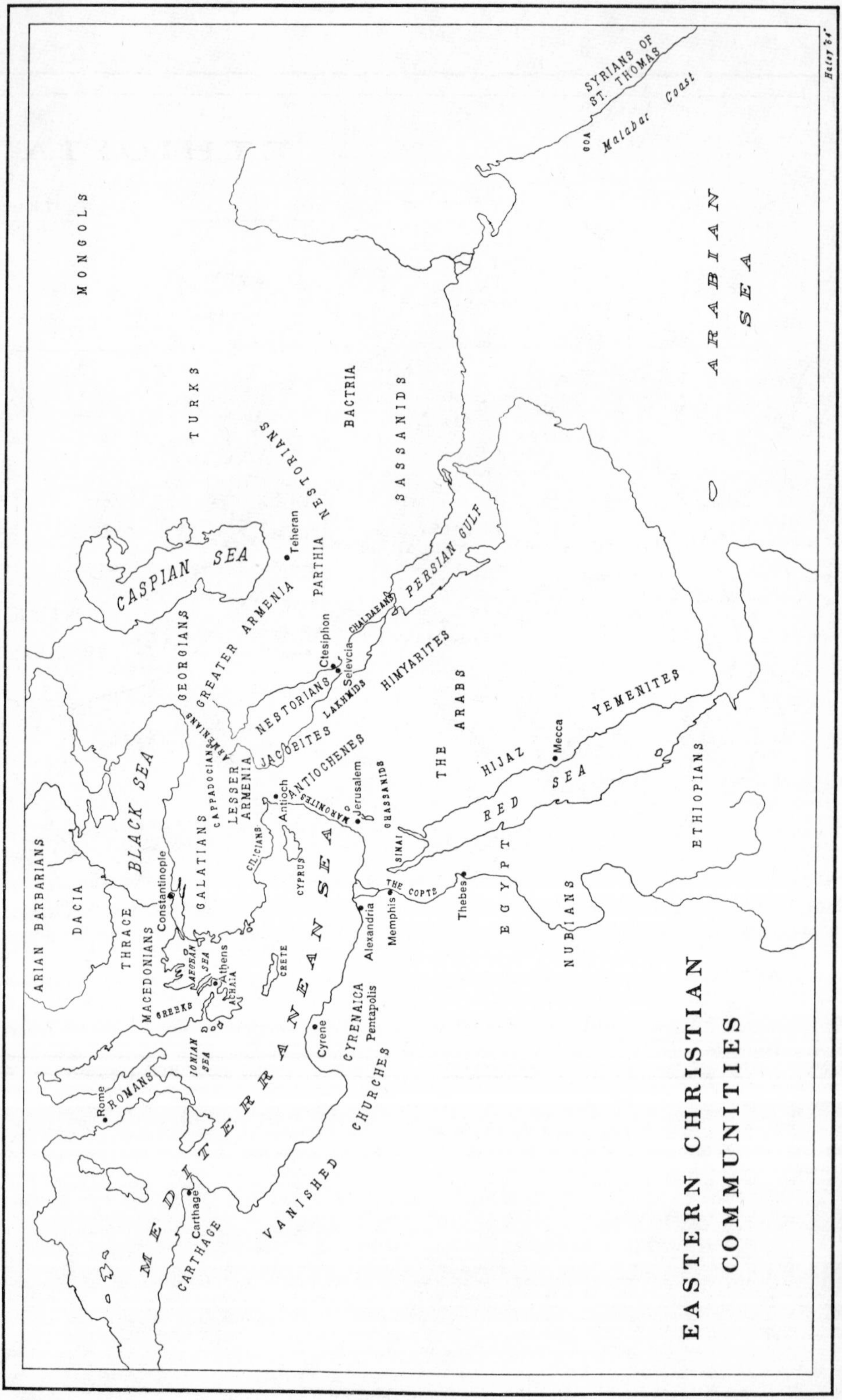

EASTERN CHRISTIAN COMMUNITIES

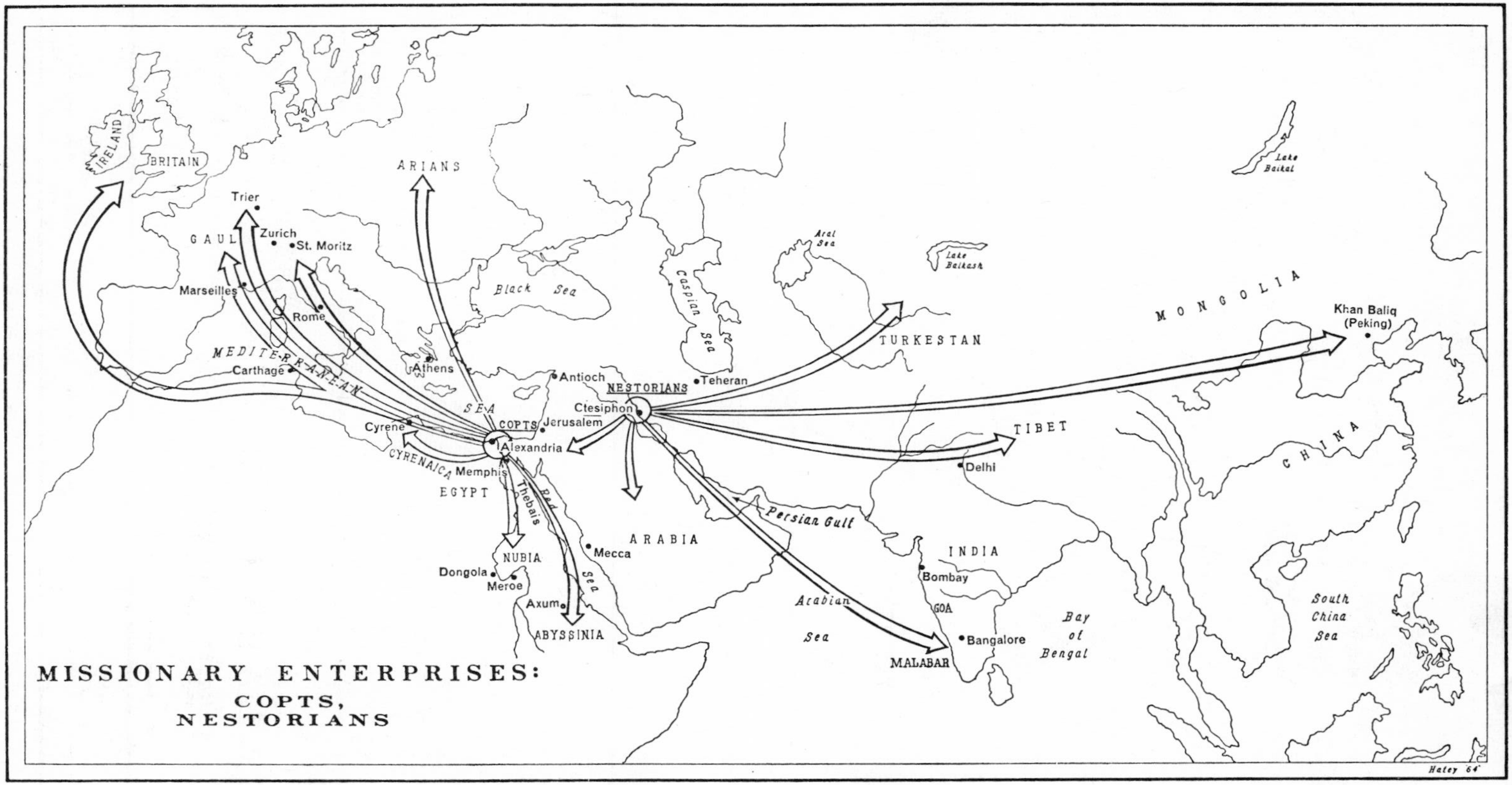

MISSIONARY ENTERPRISES:
COPTS, NESTORIANS

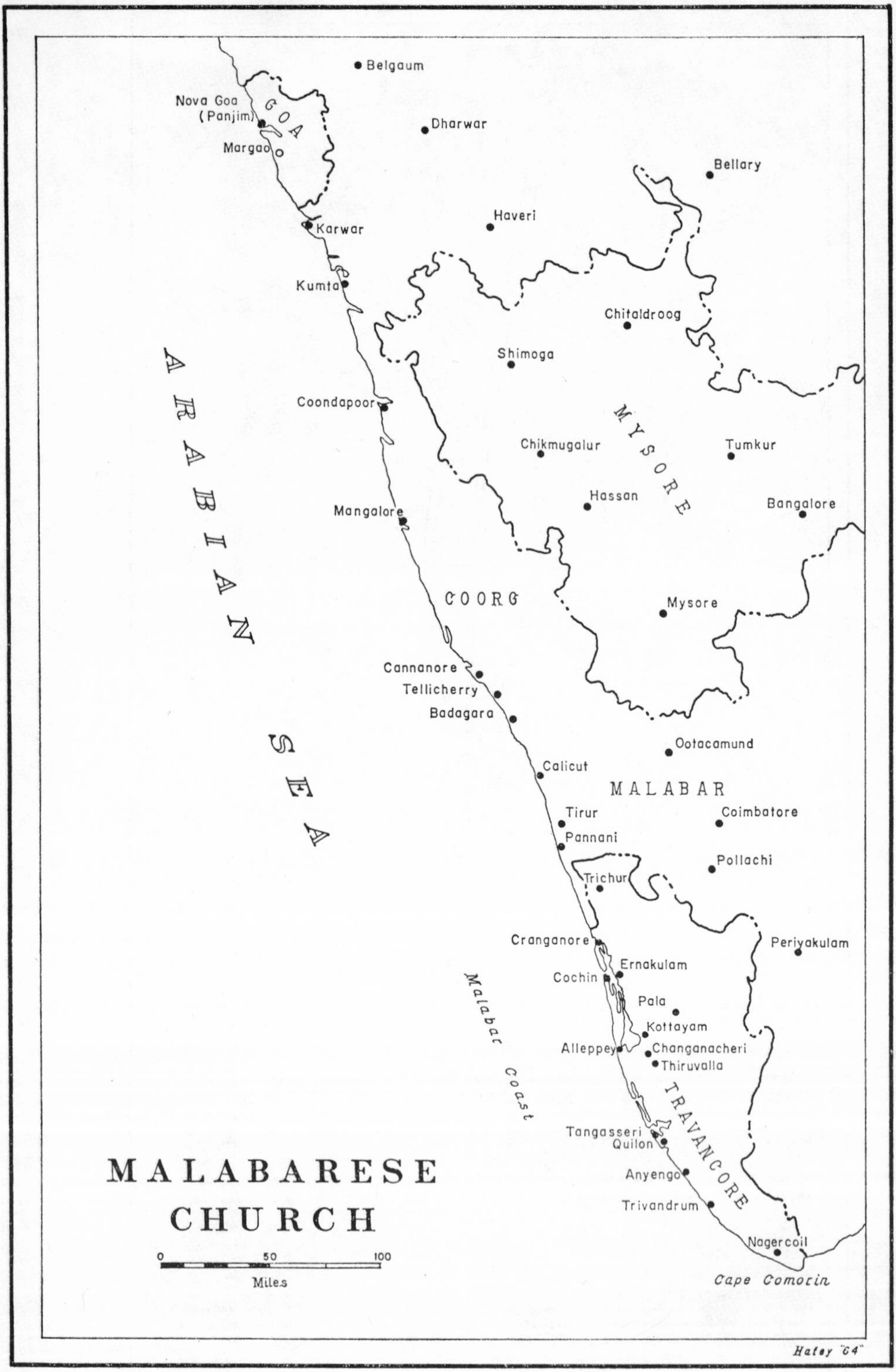

Belgaum
Nova Goa
(Panjim)
GOA
Margao
Dharwar
Bellary
Haveri
Karwar
Kumta
Chitaldroog
Shimoga
ARABIAN SEA
Coondapoor
MYSORE
Chikmugalur
Tumkur
Hassan
Bangalore
Mangalore
COORG
Mysore
Cannanore
Tellicherry
Badagara
Ootacamund
Calicut
MALABAR
Tirur
Coimbatore
Pannani
Pollachi
Trichur
Cranganore
Periyakulam
Ernakulam
Cochin
Malabar Coast
Pala
Kottayam
Alleppey
Changanacheri
Thiruvalla
TRAVANCORE
Tangasseri
Quilon
MALABARESE
CHURCH
Anyengo
Trivandrum
0
50
100
Miles
Nagercoil
Cape Comorin
Hafey '64'

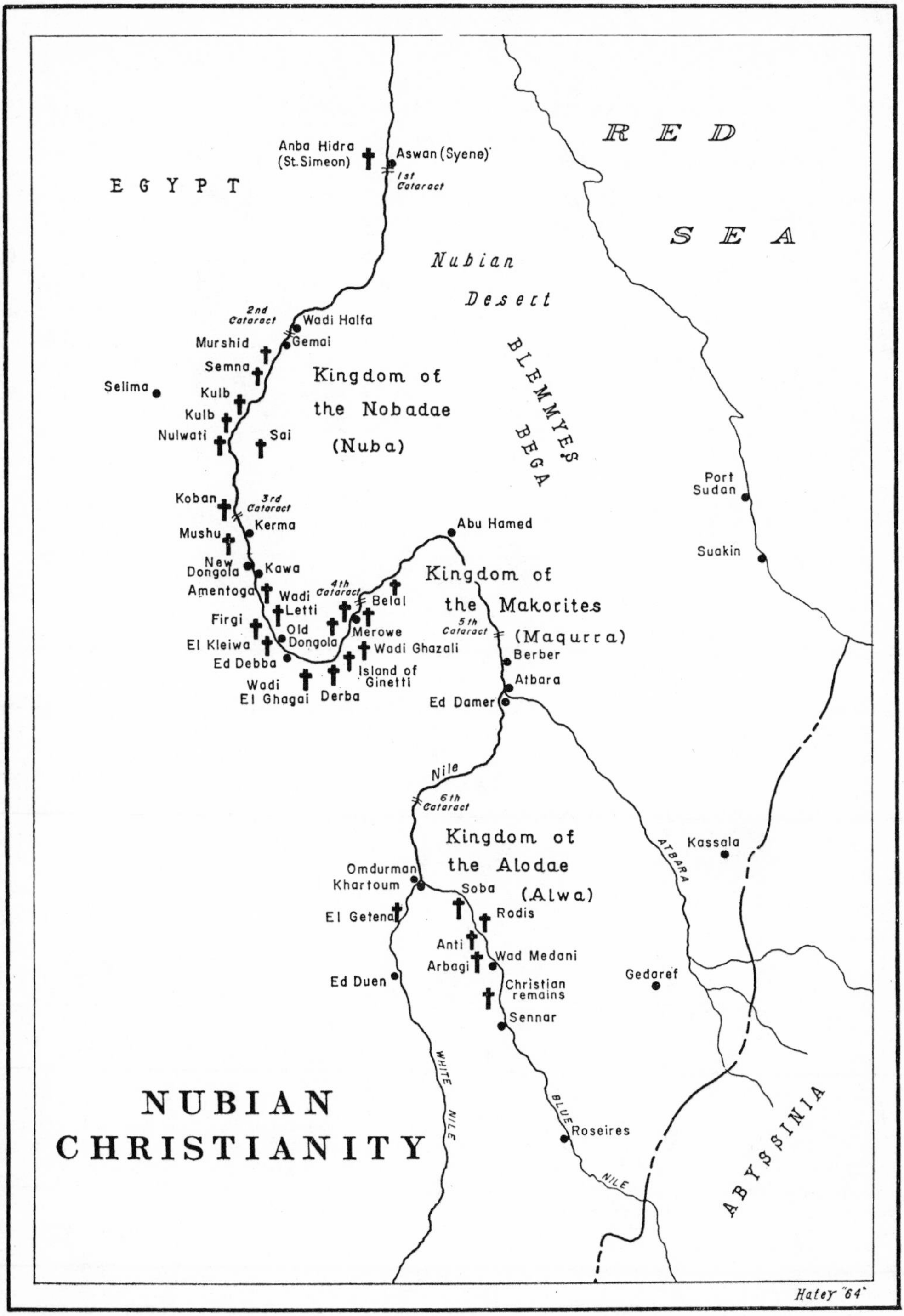
NUBIAN CHRISTIANITY
EGYPT
RED SEA
Nubian Desert
BLEMMYES
BEGA
Anba Hidra (St. Simeon)
Aswan (Syene)
1st Cataract
2nd Cataract
Wadi Halfa
Gemai
Murshid
Semna
Selima
Kulb
Kulb
Nulwati
Sai
Kingdom of the Nobadae (Nuba)
Koban
3rd Cataract
Kerma
Mushu
New Dongola
Kawa
Abu Hamed
Amentoga
Wadi
4th Cataract
Letti
Belal
Firgi
Old Dongola
Merowe
El Kleiwa
Wadi Ghazali
Ed Debba
Island of Ginetti
Wadi El Ghagai
Derba
Kingdom of the Makorites (Maqurra)
5th Cataract
Berber
Atbara
Ed Damer
Port Sudan
Suakin
Nile
6th Cataract
Kingdom of the Alodae (Alwa)
Omdurman
Khartoum
Soba
Rodis
El Getena
Anti
Arbagi
Wad Medani
Ed Duen
Christian remains
Sennar
Kassala
Atbara
Gedaref
White Nile
Blue Nile
Roseires
ABYSSINIA
Hatey "64"

PART I

ALEXANDRINE CHRISTIANITY
THE COPTS AND THEIR CHURCH

1 • INTRODUCTORY

The place of the Copts in the general history of Christianity has long been minimized, sometimes even forgotten, because the Coptic people themselves had voluntarily chosen to live in oblivion. After having led the way for centuries, they decided to segregate themselves from the growing ecclesiastical authority of the West in order to guard their way of worship and to retain their national pride. The beginning of this unfortunate chapter in Christian separatism took place at the Œcumenical Council of Chalcedon in 451 A.D. The details of the Chalcedonian polemic will be treated later in these pages. It is sufficient to note here that by repudiating the Romano-Byzantine Christology and all the other political factors at play behind the Council's decisions, the Copts became acrimoniously self-centred in their own religious nationalism. Then with the advent of the Arab in the seventh century, the whole of Egypt began to turn its face altogether from the West to the East; and the progress of the new religion of Islam in the Middle East gradually dwarfed the Eastern Christian communities. Thus the world increasingly forgot their original role in the development of the Christian faith in its formative years.[1]

This was the situation until the rediscovery of the ancient Eastern Christians in the course of the nineteenth century. Unlike the Nestorians and the Indian Christians of St Thomas, the Copts were not completely lost to the external world. Like the Jacobites and the Armenians, they were mentioned in the works of mediæval European travellers in the Middle East. But they were not as well-known as the Maronites, who were in direct contact with Rome during the age of the Crusades. On the other hand, the Copts were regarded as an insignificant minority of schismatic monophysites, a lingering shadow from the remote past. Indeed, it was only lately that Western scholarship was attracted by the Coptic Christian heritage and consequently inaugurated a systematic enquiry into the vast and rich world of Coptic sources. The

[1] For bibliographical reference, see W. Kammerer (with the collaboration of Elinor M. Husselman and Louise A. Shier), *A Coptic Bibliography* (Ann Arbor, Mich., 1950); J. Simon, *Bibliographie Copte*, Orientalia, 18–26 (1941–56); G. Graf, *Geschichte der christlichen arabischen Literatur*, 5 vols. (Vatican City, 1944–53) esp. Vol. II, pp. 294–475; and *A Bibliographical Guide to the History of Christianity*, ed. S. J. Case (Chicago, 1931).

results have been bewildering and revealing, though we still have only a bare outline of Coptic history. The real significance of Alexandrine Christianity is only just dawning.

Three schools of thought have evolved from this steady increase in the awareness of Coptic sources. The first is the Protestant school,[1] sympathetic authors who wrote about the Coptic church with great affection but limited understanding. The second consists of Roman Catholic scholars[2] whose attitude has invariably been hostile to, and at best unappreciative of, the so-called 'dissident' Copts. The third is a more modest school of native writers[3] side by side with a number of Western scholars concerned with dispassionate research based on original sources.[4] On the whole, it may be said at this

[1] J. M. Neale, *A History of the Holy Eastern Church: General Introduction*, 2 vols. (London, 1896); ibid., *Patriarchate of Alexandria*, 2 vols. (London, 1897); E. L. Butcher, *The Story of the Church of Egypt*, 2 vols. (London, 1897); M. Fowler, *Christian Egypt – Past, Present and Future* (London, 1901); and S. H. Leeder, *Modern Sons of the Pharoahs* (London, 1918).

[2] J. M. Vansleb, *Histoire de l'église d'Alexandrie* (Paris, 1677); E. Renaudot, *Historia patriarcharum Alexandrinorum jacobitarum* (Paris, 1713); M. Lequien, 'Patriarchate of Alexandria', in *Oriens Christianus*, Vol. II (Paris, 1740), 329–666; S. Chauleur, *Histoire des Coptes* (Paris, 1960).

See also the more comprehensive works by R. Janin, *Les Églises orientales et les Rites orientaux*, 3rd ed. (Paris, 1935); A. Fortescue, *The Lesser Eastern Churches* (London, 1913); D. Attwater, *The Dissident Eastern Churches* (Milwaukie, Wisc. 1935); ibid., *The Christian Churches of the East*, 2 vols. (Milwaukie, Wisc., 1947–9).

[3] Essentially in Arabic, see Tewfik Iscarous, *Nawābigh al-Aqbāṭ wa-Mashāhīruhum fī al-Qarn al-'Ishrīn* (Biographies of Famous Copts in the 19th Century), 2 vols. (Cairo, 1910–13); Yūsuf Minqariūs, *Tārīkh al-'Umma al-Qibṭiya* (History of the Coptic Nation, in the Years 1893–1912), (Cairo, 1913); Ramzy Tadros, *Al-Aqbāṭ fī al-Qarn al-ʿIshrīn* (The Copts in the 20th Century), 5 vols. (Cairo 1910 ff.); Yaʿqūb Nakhla Rufaila, *Kitāb Tārīkh al-'Umma al-Qibṭiya* (History of the Coptic Nation), (Cairo, 1898); *Tārīkh al-Baṭārikah*, anonymous History of the Patriarchs by a monk of the Monastery of Baramous, (Cairo, 1897); Bishop Isodoros, *Al-Kharrīdah al-Nafīsah fī Tārīkh al-Kanīsah* (History of the Church), 2 vols. (Cairo, 1923; 2nd. ed., 2 vols., Cairo, 1964); *Tārīkh al-'Umma al-Qibṭiya* (Summary of the History of Christianity in Egypt), by Lajnat al-Tārīkh al-Qibṭi (Commission of Coptic History), 3rd ed. (Cairo, 1925); Jacques Tagher, *Aqbāṭ wa-Muslimūn mundh al-Fatḥ al-ʿArabi ilā ʿĀm 1922* (Copts and Muslims from the Arab Conquest to 1922) (Cairo, 1951); Iris Habīb al-Maṣry, *Qiṣṣat al-Kanīsah al-Qibṭiyah* (Story of the Coptic Church, to 435 A.D.), (Cairo, n.d.); Zaki Shenūda, *Tārīkh al-Aqbāṭ* (History of the Copts), Vol. I (Cairo 1962).

[4] E. Amélineau, *Étude sur le christianisme en Égypte au septième siècle* (Paris, 1887); A. Macaire, *Histoire de l'église d'Alexandrie depuis Saint Marc jusqu'à nos jours* (Cairo, 1894); J. Maspéro, *Histoire des patriarches d'Alexandrie depuis la mort de l'empereur Anastase jusqu'à la reconciliation des églises jacobites* (518–616) (Paris, 1923); A. Heckel, *Die Kirche vonÄgypten, ihre Amfänge, ihre Organisation und ihre Entwicklung bis zur Zeit des Nicänum* (Strassburg, 1918); R. Strothmann, *Die koptische Kirche in der Neuzeit* (Tübingen, 1932); W. L. Westermann et al., *Coptic Egypt* (Brooklyn, N.Y., 1944); W. H. Worrell, *A Short Account of the Copts* (Ann Arbor, Mich., 1945); E. R. Hardy, *Christian Egypt, Church and People* (New York, 1952); Maria Cramer, *Das christlich-koptische Ägypten, Einst und Heute, Eine Orientierung* (Wiesbaden, 1959); E. Wakin, *A Lonely Minority, The Modern History of Egypt's Copts: The Challenge of Survival for Four Million Christians* (New York, 1963).

See also chapters on Copts in general works on Eastern Churches cited in Selected

juncture that the definitive and comprehensive history of the Coptic church is still pending. Its source material[1] is only partly published, and Coptic archæological research is in its infancy. The field of 'Coptology' has long been in a state of abeyance in relation to those of 'Egyptology' and 'Islamology'. Though a central link of the highest importance between the ancient and the Islamic stages in Egyptian civilization, Coptism has undoubtedly suffered between those two monolithic structures, and considerable effort is needed to rectify the picture of the place of the Copts both in Egyptian history and in Christian annals.[2]

In the light of recent discoveries, the feeling prevails that many facets of the general history of Christianity will have to be rewritten in order to incorporate the monumental and sometimes turbulent contributions of the Copts. Substantial sections of the patristic studies must be amended or even recast, while the story of church relations and of the early missionary enterprise must be reconsidered. The outstanding role of the Copts in the Catechetical School of Alexandria and the development of the Monastic Rule, although not unknown, must be subjected to a fresh appraisal. Our knowledge of Coptic biblical literature, both canonical and apocryphal, together with so much of the so-called heretical documents of earliest Christianity, is still very limited. Coptic art and architecture have attracted much attention and interest in recent years, but the last word in these domains is still unsaid.

It is my task to introduce all this and many other phases of Coptic history with the inevitable passion of one who writes from within the Coptic world and yet who must view events dispassionately with the mind of a historian from outside.

Bibliography and including Adeney, Kidd, Rondot and Spuler. References to works mentioned in Bibliography will be limited to names of authors.

[1] For further sources on the Copts consult bibliographies cited in above notes as well as bibliographies of the aforementioned works. See also major collections such as the three Patrologies (Græca, Latina and Orientalis), the Corpus Scriptorum Christianorum Orientalium (Scriptores Coptici), the collection of the Ante-Nicene Fathers, the library of the Nicene and Post-Nicene Fathers (esp. the 2nd series), and the library of Christian Classics (esp. first 4 vols.). The publications of the Society of Coptic Archæology in Cairo contain valuable additions which are growing in quantity and quality.

[2] Other monographs and articles include A. S. Atiya, 'Al-Kanīsah al-Qibṭiyah wal-Rūḥ al-Qaumī fī Miṣr fī al-ʿAṣr al-Byzanṭi' (The Coptic Church and Nationalism in Byzantine Egypt), *Bulletin of the Egyptian Historical Association*, III, 1 (1950), pp. 1–14; Francis al-ʿItr, *Al-'Ummah al-Qibṭiyah wa Kanīsatuha al-Orthodoxiyah* (The Coptic Nation and its Orthodox Church), (Cairo, 1953); Ḥilmi Guirguis, *Al-Aqbāṭ* (The Copts), (Cairo, 1956); S. Chauleur, *Les Coptes* (Alexandria, 1949); J. Murtagh, *The Copts* (Cairo, 1949); A. de Vlieger, *The Origin and Early History of the Coptic Church* (Lausanne, 1900); Ibrahim Noṣḥy, *The Coptic Church, Christianity in Egypt* (Washington, D.C., 1955). See also articles on Copts and on Egypt in the various encyclopædias cited in the Bibliography as well as Gaston Wiet's article 'Qibṭ' in the *Encyclopedia of Islam*.

The Term 'Copt'

The words Copt and Egyptian are identical in meaning, and both are derivatives from Greek '*aigyptos*', which the Hellenes used for both Egypt and the Nile. This in turn was a phonetic corruption of the ancient Egyptian for Memphis, which was *Hak-ka-Ptah*, that is, the house or temple of the spirit of Ptah, who was one of the most highly revered deities in Egyptian mythology. He was the god of all creation, to be worshipped before all others in Memphis. With the suppression of the prefix and the suffix of the Greek word, the stem *gypt* has remained to give us in all European languages the modern words 'Egypt' and 'Copt', in Arabic *Qibṭ* or *Gybṭ*[1] with numerous minor variations.

Other traditions state that the word is derived mainly according to Arabic and Semitic sources, from 'Kuftaim' son of Mizraim, a grandchild of Noah who first settled in the Nile valley and imparted his name to the old town of 'Qufṭ' or 'Gufṭ' in the neighbourhood of Thebes, ancient capital of Egypt. The Arabs called Egypt 'dār al-Qibṭ', home of the Copts, and since the original natives of the land were Christians, the words Coptic and Christian became interchangeable in the Arab mind. Nevertheless, it must be remembered that the original connotation of Copt is not religious, and that Coptic should be considered as being strictly synonymous with Egyptian, and the Coptic Church should therefore be defined as merely the Egyptian Church.

Ethnically, the Copts are neither Semitic nor Hamitic, but rather Mediterranean. They have been described as the direct descendents of the ancient Egyptians[2] and some attempts have been made to prove their similarity to those distant dwellers on the Nile. Whatever the truth may be, it is clear that their religion kept them from mixing with the successive waves of invaders from other faiths. Hence their purity of race is not sheer legend. To the Copt, religion proved to be the cementing factor of the community, and orthodoxy was as much a way of life as a mode of worship. Habitually the Copts kept together in the same villages or the same quarters of the larger towns down to the end of the eighteenth century. With the dawn of modern democracy in the Middle East during the last century then came the movement of enfranchisement which rendered segregation meaningless. In our day, the Copts live everywhere side by side with their Muslim neighbours without discrimi-

[1] Original Coptic pronunciation is 'Keft' or 'Kepto'. It was sacked by Diocletian in the third century, fell to the Persians about 715, and became a centre of commerce with Arabia under Muslim rule. Quft revolted against Arab rule under Saladin, who crushed the rebels by massacring three thousand people. Consequently it began to dwindle, and Qūṣ replaced it in importance. See E. Amélineau, *La Géographie de l'Égypte à l'époque copte* (Paris, 1893), pp. 213–15.

[2] See *Modern Sons of the Pharaohs.*

nation, either political or racial; they enjoy their religious freedom, and their churches increase throughout Egypt. In sum, the Copts have survived as a religious entity, otherwise completely integrated within the body politic of the Egyptian nation, sharing the privileges and responsibilities of all citizens irrespective of faith or creed.

Coptic Language

To this day, the Copts, who are Arabic speaking, have retained the use of the Coptic language in their churches. Coptic is the last phase in the evolution of the language of the ancient Egyptians. The earlier phases are represented in the hieroglyphic, hieratic and demotic scripts. The first was the sacred form used on temple walls, in tombs and on papyri with representations from the Book of the Dead. The second was a less formal and relatively more simplified script employed by the priests in the redaction of official and royal documents, though it was later reserved almost solely for the liturgies. As time passed both these forms became so difficult that the common man became unable to correlate their phonetics with his own. Hence arose the third demotic phase, a much less pictographic form than its two predecessors, but still too complex and inaccessible to the growing needs of daily life. With the coming of the Greeks and the introduction and spread of Christianity in Egypt, demotic[1] was found inadequate for the reproduction of the Christian Scriptures, and thus Egyptian scholars and scribes started a new system of transliterating purely Egyptian texts in the Greek alphabet. They soon realized that that alphabet could not cope with all the native sounds, and solved the problem by means of adopting the last seven additional letters of the Coptic alphabet from their own original demotic script.

The Coptic language may therefore be defined as the late Egyptian vernacular inscribed or transliterated in the Greek alphabet, to which are juxtaposed seven additional characters from demotic. It is very difficult to fix a precise date for the emergence of this new system. It must have been a rather long and gradual process before its final systematization. Illustrating this phenomenon, it may be interesting to note that the first known Egyptian document to be transliterated into Greek characters was written a century and a half before Christ.[2] Though we cannot generalize on the basis of such

[1] H. I. Bell, *Egypt from Alexander the Great to the Arab Conquest* (Oxford, 1948), pp. 112–13.

[2] Discovered by the eminent Egyptologist F. L. Griffith and cited by Wahīb ʿAṭalla Girgis (now Father Bakhom – i.e. Pachomius – of the Muḥarraq Monastery of Our Lady near Asiūṭ in Upper Egypt), 'The Copts', in Alfred Nawrath, *Egypt, The Land between Sand and Nile* (Bern, 1962), p. 132.

isolated instances as this one, it can be regarded as indicative of future practices. In the course of the latter half of the second century A.D., and with the steady progress of Christianity in Egypt, it may be assumed that Coptic was invariably used alongside demotic, which it was destined to replace altogether. The priests of Isis were probably the last remnant of the old order to use the demotic script in their graffiti of Philæ as late as 452 A.D., though it had long been dying out of public usage elsewhere.

It is interesting to note that the Coptic language reflected the old Egyptian local dialects. Consequently, we can distinguish in Coptic the following dialects: Bohairic or Lower Egyptian, Sahidic or Upper Egyptian, Faiyumic, Akhmimic and Bashmuric. Sometimes these overlap to give birth to even more localized forms such as the Sub-Akhmimic. The dialect used in the present-day Church liturgies is the Bohairic, which presumably antedates all others, since Lower Egypt appears to have been susceptible to Greek influences earlier than Upper Egypt, owing to its proximity to Alexandria and Naucratis, both staunch strongholds of Greek culture.

It is possible that by the end of the second and the beginning of the third century most of the books of the Bible had been rendered into Coptic. The oldest Biblical codex hitherto discovered contains extensive portions of the Epistles of St Paul[1] in Coptic on papyrus and estimated to have been written around 200 A.D. In fact, immense treasures have been found in Coptic between the second and fifth centuries, essentially, though not exclusively, Biblical and religious in charater.

Coptic survived the shock of the Arab conquest of Egypt in the seventh century and necessarily continued to be the official language in state affairs and book-keeping used by the native functionaries employed by the unlettered Arab rulers. In 706 the Umayyad Viceroy ʿAbd-Allāh ibn ʿAbd-al-Malik issued the hazardous and untimely decree substituting Arabic for Coptic in all state affairs.[2] Though his injunction could not be carried out in practice, it proved to be an incentive for the native scribe to learn the language of the conqueror, and this resulted in the appearance of many bilingual documents in subsequent centuries.

In those tempestuous times of changing Muḥammadan dynasties, Coptic persisted as a spoken and liturgical language until approximately the thirteenth century which was marked by the emergence of native scholars who com-

[1] J. Finegan, *Light from the Ancient Past* (Princeton, 1951), pp. 332 et seq. Eighty-six leaves of this codex survive, of which 53 are in the Chester Beatty Collection and 30 in the library of the University of Michigan. This was part of some eleven papyrus codices dating from the second to the fourth cent. and comprising nine Old Testament and fifteen New Testament books together with the Book of Enoch and a homily by Melito of Sardis. They constituted what was probably part of an early church collection.

[2] Jacques Tagher, *Aqbāṭ wa-Muslimūn*, pp. 300–8, is a rather indecisive but interesting account of the fate of Coptic in the Islamic period.

posed Coptic grammars in Arabic as well as Arabic-Coptic dictionaries to help in the preservation of that tongue. Among these were the reputed Aulād al-ʿAssāl and Abu al-Barakāt ibn Kabar who flourished under the rule of the Fatimid and Ayyubid dynasties. Nevertheless, Coptic was steadily pushed back into Upper Egypt, and the German traveller Vansleb,[1] who visited Egypt first in 1664, asserted that he had then seen the last Copt named Anastase who really spoke Coptic. Vansleb's remark, however, could not have been the whole truth, since subsequent travellers indicated that they had met Coptic-speaking Copts.

Is Coptic altogether defunct? This is a debatable question. Apart from the use of Coptic in church service, there are still said to be isolated villages in Upper Egypt with 'family tradition about the pronunciation of Coptic'.[2] On the other hand, it would be an error to describe Coptic as a living language. What is certain is that Coptic has left its mark on the spoken Arabic of Egypt in two ways: first, in the residue of a vocabulary that is peculiar to Egyptian Arabic;[3] and secondly, in the nature of the grammar of the vernacular which the early bilingual Copts carried over with them. Currently, the Sunday School movement[4] under Church sponsorship has been active in reintroducing classes in Coptic in order to familiarize the Coptic youth with liturgical terminology and all manner of rituals derived from Coptic. The response to these efforts has exceeded expectation and reduced the incomprehensible formalism of Coptic offices.

[1] Also known as J. M. Wansleben, whose 'Ungedruckte Beschreibung von Ägypten in Jahre 1664' was published in H. E. G. Paulus, *Sammlung der merkwürdigsten Reisen in dem Orient* (Jena, 1792–1803), Vol. III, pp. 1–122. Apparently Vansleb returned to Egypt and wrote a new account which was translated into other languages, of which English is one: *The Present State of Egypt, or, A New Relation of a Late Voyage into that Kingdom, performed in the years 1672 and 1673*, tr. M.D. (London, 1678). Vansleb also wrote the aforementioned early history of the Copts entitled: *Histoire de l'église d'Alexandrie fondée par S. Marc, que nous appelons celle des Jacobites-Coptes d'Égypte, Écrites au Caire même en 1672 et 1673* (Paris, 1677).

[2] W. H. Worrell, *Short Account of the Copts*, p. 51; idem, 'Popular Traditions of the Coptic Language', in *American Journal of Semitic Languages and Literatures*, No. 54 (1937), pp. 1–11; this is a synopsis of material collected by Werner Vycichl in Zēniya and other Coptic communities.

[3] G. P. Sobḥy, 'The Survival of Ancient Egypt', in *Bulletin of the Society of Coptic Archæology*, No. 4 (1938), pp. 59–70.

[4] The Coptic Sunday Schools at Gīza have already published a series of three brochures in Coptic and Arabic entitled *Al-Ṭuqūs al-Qibṭiya* (Coptic Rites). These are anonymous, though special mention is made that the texts were revised by the late Yassa ʿAbd-al-Massīḥ, former librarian of the Coptic Museum and perhaps the most learned Egyptian in the Coptic language in recent years.

Ancient Egyptian Religion

From the earliest times the Egyptian is known to have been religiously minded by nature and upbringing. His profound reverence toward the deities of ancient mythology is matched only by his devotion to the faiths of Christianity and Islam in subsequent ages. In fact, his religious curiosity led to the revelation of many things which seemed to have a bearing on all faiths. This can be very clearly seen in the transition between his old pagan beliefs and Christianity. His familiarity with the basic ideas of the old faith prepared his mind for the acceptance of the dogma of the other without tremendous difficulty or spiritual anguish. Let us tabulate some of the major parallelisms between the old and the new which paved the way to a speedy spread of the teachings of Christ in Egypt.

First, the idea of the oneness of godhead was not novel to the mind of the Egyptian who lived through the great unitarian revolution of King Ikhnaton (1383–1365 B.C.) in the eighteenth dynasty. This was of course a distant event yet it constituted a stage in religious thought. The divinity and humanity of Jesus had their equivalent in the person of Osiris, who was both god and man. In reality, all pharaohs were deified humans.

The conception of the Trinity in the new faith must have seemed to the Egyptian a mere duplication of his own triads. Practically every important town in ancient Egypt possessed some kind of a triad of its own. The most famous of all was of course the triad of Osiris, Isis and Horus. The resurrection of Osiris was similar to the rise of Jesus after his Passion and entombment. Isis and Horus also recalled the position of the Mother and Child. In fact, the early representation of a Coptic Madonna is a true reproduction of Isis suckling the baby Horus. This became an established feature in Coptic iconography.

The story of the Annunciation, the Holy Ghost and the miraculous birth of Jesus from the Virgin Mary was not new to the Egyptian mind. A virgin cow in whom Ptah, the god of creation had breathed his holy spirit gave birth to the god Apis. Other instances are also known for example the story that the last Egyptian pharaoh, Horemheb was conceived by the spirit of the god Amon and born of a virgin.

The question of life after death, which is an integral part of Christian teaching, was the kernel of Egyptian thought and indeed a vital factor in the development of Egyptian civilization. To the ancient Egyptian, resurrection was a physical process whereby the spirit of the dead (Ka) would return to reside in the body of its semblance. To achieve eternity, therefore, the Egyptians strove to preserve their bodies intact and invented the art of embalming, perfecting it to a degree unknown either before or after them. Should the mummy for some unforeseen and untoward circumstance be marred or disappear, a substitute of the likeness of the deceased had to be found and identified by the Ka in order to occupy it. On this account, the Egyptians perfected the arts of painting and sculpture. They also excelled in funerary architecture, pyramids, tombs and temples of great magnificence and solidity built to stand the ravages of time.

Furthermore, the Egyptians seem to have identified the Cross with their own sign of life eternal, the 'Ankh' which only the immortals such as gods and pharaohs held in their hands on all monuments and in records. The Ankh sign was cruciform with a rounded top which the Christians readily adopted from the earliest times, and reproduced on all manner of engravings, paintings, carvings, illuminations, wall decorations, objects in clay such as lamps, and even in polychrome and monochrome textiles.[1] For Christianity as a whole the Cross became the true symbol of the new religion only from the time of Constantine the Great, after his famous vision on the eve of battle. But it is almost certain that the Copts had used the sign of life as their Christian symbol at a much earlier date.

Of iconographic interest, too, was the identification of Horus and his struggle against the god of evil, Seth, with St George and the Dragon.[2] The scene was reproduced in stone carving, painting and woven material.

To spread the new faith through song, St Menas, the third-to-fourth-century saint and martyr, substituted the persons of the Trinity for those of an old triad in some of the most popular hymns in Egyptian mythology and folklore, thereby adapting the old familiar tunes to a new purpose.

The decay and corruption of the old mythology in the late Egyptian period together with the growth of superstition and mystical occult contributed no mean share to the waning of the ancient Egyptian religion. The coming of the Greeks into Egypt had a curious impact on Egyptian religion. In an effort to unify the East and West under their hegemony, the Ptolemies attempted to recast the old religion into a common model acceptable to both Greek and Egyptian. This led to a process of syncretism which complicated a number of vital issues for both sides. The most striking instance was the creation of a new universal deity in Serapis, who was an anthropomorphic representation of Osiris and Apis, and at the same time somehow identified with, or related to, the Greek gods Zeus and Pluto. Between the Hellenized Egyptian and

[1] Maria Cramer has collected the most extensive variety of the *Ankh* sign in the early Coptic period; see her *Das altägyptische Lebenszeichen in christlichen-Koptischen Ägypten—Eine kultur-und religionsgeschichtliche Studie auf archäologischer Grundlage* (Wiesbaden, 1955). Another interesting selection from the western oases where Christianity struck root in the early centuries is presented in Aḥmad Fakhry, *The Necropolis of El-Bagawat in Kharga Oasis* (Cairo, 1951), pp. 36–7.

[2] P. D. Scott-Moncrieff, *Paganism and Christianity in Egypt* (Cambridge, Eng., 1913), pp. 137–40.

the Orientalized Greek, the native mind wandered and wondered where to find the true faith.

Combined with these religious upheavals was the ensuing hopelessness and dire poverty of the Egyptian under Roman rule, when he became a mere tool in the granary of Rome.[1] Life was aimless and dull. Only future comfort and spiritual solace in the next world remained, and this Christianity amply promised. Thus, the stage was set for Christianity, which spread like fire throughout the valley of the Nile.

Flight of the Holy Family

The Copts today cherish the memory of the flight of the Holy Family[2] from its persecutors in Palestine to safe refuge in the land of Egypt. Indeed they take pride in that event, which their writers have commemorated on every possible occasion. In a Coptic doxology for the Feast of the Entry of Our Lord into the land of Egypt, read on the twenty-fourth day of the Coptic month of Bashons, the faithful express their gladness in these words: 'Be glad and rejoice, O Egypt, and her sons and all her borders, for there hath come to Thee the Lover of man, He who is before the ages.'[3]

The appeal which the advent of the Lord to the banks of the Nile had for the imagination of the Egyptian Christian became evident in Coptic literature. The episode appeared in the early translations of the apocryphal Gospels and Coptic Synaxarium. The historic moral of the event could well have been the attraction of more converts to the new faith in the formative years of the primitive church.

It would be interesting to pursue the romantic progress of the Holy Family

[1] Bell, pp. 65–100; J. G. Milne, *Egypt under Roman Rule*, 3rd edn. (London, 1924), pp. 151 et seq., 226–7; W. L. Westermann, 'On the Background of Coptism', in *Coptic Egypt* (Brooklyn, N.Y., 1944), pp. 7–19. More special readings in M. Rostovtzeff, *The Social and Economic History of the Roman Empire* (Oxford, 1926); P. Jouguet, *La domination romaine en Égypte aux deux premiers siècles après Jésus-Christ* (Alexandria, 1947); H. I. Bell, 'Roman Egypt from Augustus to Diocletian', in *Chronique d'Égypte*, XIII (1938), 347–63; S. L. Wallace, *Taxation in Egypt from Augustus to Diocletian* (Princeton, 1938); J. G. Milne, 'The Ruin of Egypt by Roman Mismanagement', in *Journal of Roman Studies*, XVII (1927), 1–13.

[2] The story of this flight appears in practically every history of the Copts. But the best single study is by O. E. A. Meinardus, *In the Steps of the Holy Family from Bethlehem to Upper Egypt* (Cairo, 1963), which uses the apocryphal Gospels of Pseudo-Matthew and St Thomas as well as several other Infancy gospels in Arabic and Armenian. A touristic manual has recently been published on the subject by Samīr William Farīd, *The Flight into Egypt* (Cairo, 1965).

[3] Meinardus, p. 15, quotes the original text in Coptic and offers the English translation quoted here.

from Bethlehem to the furthest point of their itinerary in Upper Egypt. It is possible that Our Lady, with the Infant Jesus in her arms, travelled riding an ass while Joseph walked by the side. The sight is not unfamiliar to those acquainted with the countries of the Middle East even in our day. The group must have crossed the Sinai Peninsula by the northern caravan route alongside the Mediterranean littoral from Gaza to Raphia (the Arab Rafaḥ) and then forded the insignificant frontier brook known as the 'River of Egypt' and come to Rhinocolura,[1] the present al-ʿArīsh, where the Romans exiled criminals and cut off their noses. From there they went to Ostrakini, later the seat of a Christian Bishop Abraham, who participated in the Œcumenical Council of Ephesus in 431 A.D. Their last station in Sinai was Pelusium, the modern al-Farama (from the Coptic 'Pheromi'), regarded as the Eastern key city to Egypt. This was the route followed by the Persians in the sixth century B.C. and later by the Arabs in the seventh century A.D.

Although the course of the flight after that point is drowned in apocryphal tales of wonder and miracle, one may deduce that the refugees probably pursued the same beaten path of both Persian and Arab to the interior of Egypt. The traditional stations of their progress seem to confirm this assumption. The historic interest of pilgrims and travellers of all ages in this subject offers sufficient justification for an enumeration of those stations.

Having crossed the isthmus of Suez below Lake Manzaleh, the group must have passed by the city of Bubastis, the twenty-second dynasty capital of Egypt which Herodotus had visited in the fifth century B.C., on the way to Bilbais in the southern region of the Sharqiya (i.e. eastern) province. This was recognized as the first station where the Family took shelter under a tree which is said to have survived until 1850. The second and better-known station, long frequented by mediæval pilgrims and modern tourists, is the village of Maṭariya where the group rested beneath a sycamore tree in the neighbourhood of an eighteenth dynasty obelisk still standing on the same spot. According to tradition, that sycamore tree has been preserved by pious generations, possibly through transplanting, until our own time, and the existing one could be traced to the year 1672.[2] Under the weight of great age, it collapsed in 1906, though green shoots still keep sprouting from its venerable branches.

The third station is commemorated by the Copts in the Church of the Blessed Virgin and a nunnery at Ḥāret Zwayla in Cairo. But the most attractive landmark on the way further south is probably the cave or perhaps a small subterranean temple within the precincts of Babylon where the Family sojourned for a little time. Over this fourth station, the Copts constructed

[1] The identification with the Coptic *Rinocouroura* is accepted on sufferance by Amélineau, *Géographie*, p. 404.

[2] Meinardus, p. 35; on Maṭariya, see Amélineau, *Géographie*, pp. 246–7.

the fourth-century church of Abu Sarga (St Sergius), while the underground structure was carefully preserved as a special chapel with an altar and a wall niche where the infant Jesus was probably laid to rest.

Afterwards the stations of the Holy Family included a Jewish temple on the Nile south of Old Cairo where the Copts again built another of Our Lady's churches at Maʿādi. The present structure with its attractive triple granary domes is known to date from the thirteenth century. It was here that the travellers crossed the Nile and penetrated Upper Egypt as far as Meir and Qūṣiya in the province of Asiūṭ. Again they hid in a cave for approximately six months, and it was on that site that the pious natives later established Our Lady's Monastery, popularly known as Dair al-Muḥarraq and enriched beyond all other Pachomian monasteries in Egypt by the offerings of an endless stream of pilgrims until the present. One early Muslim writer, namely Muḥammad al-Bāqir[1] (676–731) recorded the passage of the Family through Dair al-Gānūs and al-Bahnasa in Middle Egypt and embellished his story by the reiteration of miracles that were current in the century of the Arab conquest of Egypt.

It is difficult to unravel the legend from the reality and the orthodox from the apocryphal in the romantic accounts of the flight into Egypt. But the Coptic susceptibility to local tradition has survived with the blessings of the hierarchy. Egypt has always abounded in wondrous tales of piety and miracles, but nothing equals the veneration which the earnest and simple believers entertain in the steps of the Holy Family.

The length of their sojourn in Egypt is unknown and not easy to define with precision. It is true that Herod, the instigator of the massacre of the innocents, appears to have died in the same year as that of the birth of Jesus, and the Holy Family could not have found it necessary to prolong their refuge abroad. On the other hand, we must bear in mind the atrocious conditions of travel in those times, as well as the extent of their journeyings, which must have lasted a considerable period. Moreover, the Infancy Gospel of St Thomas quotes the miracle of a revived dead fish as having occurred while Jesus was a boy of three. It is not, therefore, inconceivable that they retraced their steps to Nazareth in Palestine after that age. The flight of the Holy Family continued to appeal to the imagination of later preachers of Christianity and helped to spread the new faith in Egypt.

[1] Meinardus, pp. 41–3.

2 • ORIGINS OF COPTIC CHRISTIANITY

St Mark the Founder

The Copts pride themselves on the apostolicity of their national church, whose founder was none other than St Mark, one of the four Evangelists and the author of the oldest canonical Gospel used by both St Matthew and St Luke, probably also by St John. John Mark is regarded by the Coptic hierarchy as the first in their unbroken chain of 116 patriarchs. He is also the first of a stream of Egyptian saints and glorious martyrs. *The History of the Patriarchs of the Coptic Church of Alexandria*,[1] compiled in Arabic from ancient Coptic sources and continued by Sawīris (Severus) ibn al-Muqaffaʿ, bishop of al-Ashmunain in Middle Egypt, begins with an elaborate biography of the Evangelist and first patriarch.

St Mark's parents were both Jews who had resided in Cyrenaica until they were attacked and their landed property raided by the Berber tribes. Consequently, they decided to move to Jerusalem, where their son was probably born shortly after the Nativity of Jesus. Apparently he was given a good education and became conversant with both Greek and Latin in addition to Hebrew. His family was extremely religious, and he reflected the spiritual fervour of his day. He received his Christian initiation from his older cousin St Barnabas; but he also knew St Peter and St Paul well. Above all, he soon became associated with Jesus, who frequented his home more than once and

[1] Kitāb Siyar al-Ābā' al-Baṭārika, Arabic text first ed. by C. F. Seybold, Severus Ben El-Moqaffaʿ, 'Historia Patriarcharum Alexandrinorum', in *Corpus Scriptorum Christianorum Orientalium, Scriptores Arabici*, Series Tertia, Tomus IX (Beirūt and Paris, 1906); Arabic text with English tr. begun by B. T. Evetts, 'History of the Patriarchs of the Coptic Church of Alexandria', in *Patrologia Orientalis*, 2 vols. in 4 fasc. (Paris, 1907–15), and continued by Yassa ʿAbd-el-Massīḥ, O. E. H. Burmester and Aziz S. Atiya in *Publications of the Society of Coptic Archæology*, 3 parts (Cairo, 1943–59). The last fascicle stops in the year 1102 A.D. The Seybold edition stops much earlier at 567 A.D.

For St Mark, see Evetts, I, pp. 37–50. The orthodox Coptic version of St Mark's biography is compiled by Kāmil Ṣāliḥ Nakhla, *Tārīkh al-Qiddīs Mar Morqos al-Bashīr* (History of St Mark the Evangelist), (Cairo, 1952). The Catholic view of the saint's life may be found in Paul Cheneau, *Les Saints d'Égypte*, 2 vols. (Jerusalem, 1923); for St Mark, see I, 494–509. See also J. J. L. Bargès, *Homélie sur Saint Marc Apôtre et Évangéliste*, Texte arabe et traduction et notes (Paris, 1952).

chose him as one of the Seventy. Even after Our Lord's ascension, the Disciples met at Mark's home, and it was there that the Holy Ghost descended upon them.[1] The room where the monumental event occurred, became the first Christian chapel in history. St Mark was therefore one of the closest witnesses of Our Lord's life, and this fitted him most admirably to write his basic Gospel. Papias (ca. 60–130), bishop of Hierapolis in Asia Minor, made a first-century reference to the Gospel, but he casually ascribed the Marcan material to Peter. Internal evidence, however, renders this allusion a highly debatable question.

It is true that Mark, the enlightened and able scholar, interpreted for Peter, the simple fisherman, when they were together in Rome.[2] But this does not imply that he recorded solely for him, though it is conceivable that all the Disciples pooled details of oral information about the Lord's sayings and acts. The Gospel contained eye-witness source material incorporating both Petrine and Pauline reports. That St Mark wrote his Gospel in Latin or in Greek or in both is probable. St John Chrysostom (ca. 347–407) states that it was originally composed in Egypt in the Greek language. The idea is also advanced that it was written only after the martyrdom of both Peter and Paul, but this is questionable because the Gospel is said to have appeared twelve years after the Crucifixion, that is, in the year 45; and the martyrdom took place in Nero's reign (54–68), possibly in 64 A.D. Whatever the truth, it is certain that St Mark brought his Gospel with him to Alexandria; and though the Greek version could have fulfilled his purpose in that city, the suggestion is made that another version in the Egyptian language was prepared for the benefit of native converts who were not conversant with Greek.[3]

St Mark was indefatigable. He travelled with Paul and his cousin Barnabas to Antioch, then returned to Jerusalem, and later accompanied his cousin to Cyprus. In Italy and Rome he was close to Peter who styled him lovingly as 'my son'. But Mark's real labour lay in Africa. First, he crossed the Mediterranean to Cyrenaica – the Pentapolis which had been his parents' residence in bygone days. This country was colonized by Greeks and many Jews who offered his zeal a ripe and hopeful harvest. After performing many miracles and sowing the seeds of his faith, he went to Alexandria by a circuitous route through the oases and Babylon, or Old Cairo. Alexandria was the Eastern counterpart of Rome both in importance and in being a stronghold of paganism, and it was imperative that Christianity should win the two. The task was as worthy as it was hazardous.

Here we face the important problem of dates. The *History of the Patriarchs*[4]

[1] Acts xiv, 12.

[2] Cheneau, op. cit., I, 497, describes St Mark as St Peter's secretary and interpreter for evident reasons.

[3] Kāmil Ṣāliḥ Nakhla, pp. 86–92.

[4] Fasc. I, 44.

mentions explicitly that the revelation to Peter and Mark that they should advance on Rome and Alexandria came in the fifteenth year after the Ascension of Christ, that is, 48 A.D. Other sources[1] put his entry into Alexandria in 55, 58 and 61 A.D. Whatever the right date of Mark's appearance in the city, the consensus of opinion is that he was martyred in 68 A.D. Between those two dates he was able to fulfil his mission and to win many converts.

The story runs that on entering the city by the eastern gate, he broke the strap of his shoe. So he went to a cobbler to mend it. When the cobbler took an awl to work on it, he accidentally pierced his hand and cried aloud: 'Heis ho Theos' (God is one). Mark rejoiced at this utterance and, after miraculously healing the man's wound, took courage and gave the lesson to the hungry ears of his first convert. This happened to be Anianus, Mark's successor as the second patriarch of Alexandria. The spark was fired, and the cobbler took the Apostle home with him. He and his family were baptized, and many others followed. So successful was the movement that the word spread that a Galilean was in the city preparing to overthrow the idols. Popular feeling began to rise, and men sought him everywhere. Scenting danger, the Apostle ordained Anianus bishop, with three priests and seven deacons to watch over the congregation in case anything befell him. Afterwards, he seems to have undertaken two voyages. First he sallied into Rome where he met Peter and Paul, and he left the capital only after their martyrdom in 64 A.D. He then stayed at Aquilea, near Venice, before his return to Alexandria. On finding his flock firm in the faith, he decided to visit the Pentapolis, where he spent two years performing miracles, ordaining bishops and priests, and winning more converts. When at last he reached Alexandria, he was overjoyed to find that the brethren had so multiplied that they were able to build a considerable church in the suburban district of Baucalis, where cattle grazed by the seashore.

Spreading rumours that the Christians threatened to overthrow the pagan deities infuriated the idolatrous populace. The end was approaching, and the saint was unremittingly hunted by the enemy. In the year 68 A.D., Easter fell on the same day as the Serapis festival. The furious mob had gathered in the Serapion and then descended on the Christians while they were celebrating Easter at Baucalis. St Mark was seized, dragged with a rope around his neck in the streets, and then incarcerated for the night. In the following morning the same ordeal was repeated until he gave up the ghost. His flesh was torn and bloody, and it was their intent to cremate his remains. But the wind blew and the rain fell in torrents, and the populace dispersed. Thus the Christians

[1] Enumerated by Kāmil Ṣāliḥ Nakhla, pp. 57–8. Bishop Isodorus, I, 64–5, adopts 58 A.D. for the decision to go to Alexandria and the rendering of the Gospel into Greek as a preparatory measure, the actual entry into the city being 61 A.D. Iris El-Maṣry, p. 19, quotes the years 55 and 61.

stealthily carried off his body and secretly buried it in a grave which they had carved in the rock under the altar of the church.

In subsequent centuries the body of St Mark did not remain intact. During the later times of schism between the Copts and the Melkites, who were in authority, the church where the body was kept remained in the hands of the latter. At the time of the Arab storming of Alexandria in 642, that church was pillaged and the vestments and the head of the Apostle were stolen. With the establishment of peace in the city, that church together with the body remained in Melkite hands. But the head somehow was returned to the Arab governor, who ceded it to the Coptic Patriarch Benjamin, the only ecclesiastical leader left after the departure of the Greeks. According to their own story, Venetian merchants stole the headless body of St Mark in 828. They smuggled it in a tub of pickled pork to evade Muslim inspection. In this wise, Venice earned its other title of the Republic of St Mark.[1]

Age of Persecution

Though condoned by the Roman authorities in Alexandria, the martyrdom of St Mark was in fact a spontaneous act of violence committed by the enraged pagan populace. To the Greek citizens Mark was a hateful Jew, and his new and obscure sect was regarded as irreligious, immoral, unpatriotic and disloyal to both society and the state. A Christian was a conspiring rebel against time-honoured polytheistic tradition and against the established divinity of the imperial dignity. He was something of a nihilist to be nipped in the bud. To him all the misfortunes of latter day Rome were ascribed, from famine and pestilence to drought and floods. He antagonized the mighty deities, broke up families, and corrupted the old Roman virtues and the Greek mind. Christianity was generally misunderstood and maligned; and the ranks of the people called for its extermination. Thus it can be safely said that the age of persecution was, as in Mark's case, inaugurated by the people, and the state became instrumental in the execution. The Neronian theory of the origins of the age of persecution cannot be applied to all the subsequent waves of terrorization under other emperors. At any rate, during the first century of Christian history, most emperors appeared to reflect the voice of the people in the literal application of the laws by disbanding Christians. Even the saintly

[1] E. M. Forster, *Alexandria – A History and a Guide* (Paperback ed., Garden City, N.Y., 1961), pp. 86–7; Kāmil Ṣāliḥ Nakhla, pp. 110, 114–23. Cheneau, I, 509, explains the lifting of St Mark's body by the Venetians as an attempt to save it from Saracen desecration and mentions that the church of Limours near Paris possesses one of his arms while Soissons has the head.

philosopher, Marcus Aurelius (161–80) found the policy of persecution inescapable.

The community of Alexandrine Christians lay low after Mark and appeared to bide its time. It acted without noise or ostentation in order to avoid further calamities. The sources are almost silent on the events of the following century. In fact, the *History of the Patriarchs* merely lists the consecration and decease of the next ten patriarchs (68–188 A.D.)[1] and provides no details until the reign of the twelfth patriarch, Demetrius I (188–230),[2] the contemporary of Origen, whose reign witnessed the first state-sponsored persecution of Egyptian Christians. Emperor Septimius Severus (193–211)[3] decreed that Christian conversions must be stopped at all costs, and his edict of 202 to that effect was stringently enforced in Egypt without regard to racial differentiation of Greek, Jew or Egyptian. The Catechetical School of Alexandria was closed, though its members continued to meet elsewhere. The Christians were denied the privilege accorded to the Jews of being exempted from the duty of burning incense before an imperial statue; and those who refused to comply with this sign of allegiance to the emperor were conducted to Alexandria from all parts of the country, where a grim fate awaited them. Some martyrs were beheaded, others cast to the lions, still others were burnt alive, but all in common were subjected to sordid torture regardless of age or sex. Origen lost his father, Leonidas,[4] in this massacre, but he himself was saved by his mother, who hid his garments to prevent him from facing his accusers. Yet imperial efforts proved to be without avail. The number of bishops, once restricted to three, had increased to twenty by the end of the reign.

Then followed a short lull when an indifferent emperor became heedless of religious differences, though Christian persecution became invariably the accepted official policy of the rulers. The next massive wave of persecution touching Egypt in particular occurred in the short reign of Decius (249–51).[5] The emperor was troubled by the menacing pace at which Christianity was spreading, and he issued an edict in 250 enjoining every citizen to procure a certificate (*libellus*) from his local magistrate testifying that he had offered sacrifice and libation to the gods. Those who refused to conform were tortured with unprecedented ferocity. Thousands of martyrs perished in many cities and villages besides Alexandria. Grief, terror and despair swept all over Egypt. The persecution went on unabated under his successor, Valerian (252–60),[6] and some Christians recanted to save their lives. The Patriarch Dionysius

[1] Evetts, I, 51–6.
[2] Ibid., 56–75.
[3] Milne, pp. 59–62, 218–19.
[4] Cheneau, I, 483–86. He is cited by Eusebius, Rufinus and Jerome. A short appendix (loc. cit., 486–93) on Origen is also provided.
[5] Milne, pp. 69–72, 219; Bell, pp. 86–90; Scott-Moncrieff, pp. 85–199 ff.
[6] P. J. Healy, *The Valerian Persecution – A Study of the Relations between Church and State in the Third Century* A.D. (Boston, 1905).

(246–64), who had been a fugitive all the time, was constrained for reasons of wisdom and expediency to use a more lenient policy than his predecessors by readmitting the secessionists on mere evidence of penitence. It was not, however, until the year 262 that the Christians began to have a peaceful existence under Emperor Gallienus (253–68), whose own troubles and the futility of a hopeless situation led him to issue an edict of religious tolerance. Perhaps for the first time, Christianity was recognized and its practice permitted on sufferance, churches were allowed to open, and confiscated Christian property was restored.

This momentary relief uplifted the broken hearts of the Christians and aroused their zeal to rebuild their ruined churches and to add more magnificent ones. Official distrust was again aroused and even aggravated by the intensification of Roman despotism. Thus the scene changed during the reign of Emperor Diocletian (284–305), considered in Coptic opinion to this day as the consummation of the age of persecution.

Nevertheless, in fairness to Diocletian, we have to remember that he began his reign with unusual magnanimity *vis-à-vis* Egypt and especially the city of Alexandria. He fortified the southern gate of the country, Syene (modern Aswān), to protect Upper Egypt from the destructive inroads of the Blemyes from Nubia. In Alexandria a Roman legionary called Lucius Domitius Domitianus, nicknamed Achilleus, revolted and declared himself emperor. At once Diocletian personally descended on the Egyptian coast and took the city by storm after a siege of eight months. Parts of the city were ruined in the onslaught, while its trade declined owing to instability.[1] Disease and famine were imminent in the impoverished city until Diocletian saved the situation of its inhabitants by deflecting part of Egypt's corn harvest to Alexandria instead of Rome. This magnanimity was gratefully commemorated by the erection of a stupendous red granite pillar on the capital of which stood a bronze statue of the emperor. The pillar still stands, but the statue has gone.[2]

Diocletian wanted more. His autocracy aimed at the unification of every corner of the empire under his absolutism. Christianity was the most serious hurdle to the realization of his policy, and the Christians had been multiplying to the point of danger. It was in the year 302 that he started by the dismissal of every soldier in his legions who refused to conform in sacrificing to the Roman gods. In the following year he issued more edicts whereby Christian churches and Christian literature should be destroyed, Christian property confiscated, and all Christians be dismissed from all state offices throughout

[1] Milne, pp. 79–82, 219.

[2] Forster, pp. 51, 157–63. Known as 'Pompey's Pillar', 84 ft. high and 7 ft. in diameter. Its granite base (10 ft. high) has an almost illegible inscription in Greek which has been deciphered with difficulty and translated as follows: 'To the Most just Emperor, the tutelary God of Alexandria, Diocletian the invincible: Postumus, prefect of Egypt.'

the empire. Communal meetings of Christians were forbidden, and he who broke the order must be put to death.

But the Christians were no longer a mere handful of nonconformists. They were now sufficiently numerous to retaliate; and when they did, the Roman law was inflicted upon them without compassion. The result was a most formidable wave of persecution and martyrdom. The intensity of the movement varied from country to country, and Egypt appears to have fared worse than many or all. Maiming and mutilation, blinding, slow diabolical torture and burning were amongst the barbarous savageries which the imperial agents employed in the destruction of their victims. Outright decapitation was an unusual act of mercy and a privilege rarely granted. Under duress of sheer human mortification, some recanted, though apparently not as many as in former persecutions. It is a galling experience to read the description of some of those brutalities in works like the *Ecclesiastical History*[1] of Eusebius or the *History of the Patriarchs*.[2] The number of martyrs was legion. The dungeons were full of men and women of all classes and stations in life, awaiting their turn for the rack and the gallows. It is difficult to conceive the official Church estimate of 144,000 to 800,000 martyrs.[3] On the other hand, we must remember that the persecution inaugurated by Diocletian was sustained by Maximinus Daia (305–13), his successor in the East. It is said that the massacre was well-nigh ten years of systematic killing, and this could account for tremendous numbers. Amongst Maximinus' victims was the seventeenth patriarch, Peter I (302–11), known as the 'Seal of the Martyrs'.

It would be impossible to enumerate even a reasonable selection of the martyrs of that era. The Coptic 'Synaxarium'[4] and the 'Lives of Saints' are full, and yet they represent only a fraction of that roll of heroic sacrifice. A few examples may, however, be illuminating. St Sophia, a native of ancient Memphis, in Middle Egypt, succumbed in the reign of the seventh patriarch, Eumenios (129–51), a contemporary of Emperors Hadrian (117–38) and Antonius Pius (138–61). Her body was later removed to Constantinople by

[1] For example, see VI, 39; VII, 11; VIII, 7 and 12.

[2] Evetts, II, 119–36.

[3] The first number is quoted by Fowler, p. 19, and Forster, p. 51; the second by Wahīb ʿAṭalla Girgis, p. 135. The latest Coptic writer in Arabic, Zaki Shenūda, gives the global figure of a million without stating his authority, op. cit., p. 109.

[4] Traditionally known to be compiled by Michael, bishop of Athrīb and Malīg in the fifteenth century, or (according to O. H. E. Burmester, 'On the Date and Authorship of the Arabic Synaxarium of the Coptic Church', in *The Journal of Theological Studies*, T. 38, pp. 240–53) by Peter, bishop of Malīg in the twelfth century. The Coptic Synaxarium is a set of homiletic biographies of saints and martyrs for all the days of the year. For lives of Coptic saints, see Kammerer's *Coptic Bibliography* nos. 1283–1409; Graf, *Gesch. d. Christ. Arab. Lit.*, I, 531–40, J. Balestri and H. Hyvernat, 'Acta Martyrum', in *Corpus Scriptorum Christianorum Orientalium*, *Scriptorus Coptici*, 2 vols. (Paris, 1907–24); W. Till, *Koptische Heiligen- und Martyrerlegenden*, 2 vols., Orientalia Cristiana Analecta, nos. 102 and 108 (Rome, 1935–6); DeLacy O'Leary, *The Saints of Egypt* (London, 1937).

Emperor Constantine I the Great (313–37), and the famous cathedral of Haghia Sophia was dedicated to her. The Holy Damiana, daughter of a governor of the northern Delta, retired to a nunnery with forty virgins, and all were massacred by Diocletian. The site of her retirement and martyrdom is still a favourite pilgrimage centre for the Copts. St Catherine of Alexandria was martyred at the early age of eighteen by Maximinus in 307, and the famous monastery on Mount Sinai still bears her name. St George, the famous Roman legionary, who was probably a noble of Cappadocia in Asia Minor, defied Diocletian and was martyred. It is possible that he was buried in Palestine, and his remains are said to have been brought to Egypt by the Coptic Patriarch Gabriel II (1131–45). St Mercurius, surnamed 'The Two Sworded', another Roman legionary, succumbed in 250 under Decius and was buried in Palestine. A fifteenth-century Coptic patriarch transferred his remains to Old Cairo, where a nunnery and a church are still dedicated to him.

So profound was the impression of the persecution of Diocletian on Coptic life and thought that the Copts decided to adopt for church use a Calendar of the Martyrs – the Anno Martyri, which meant to them as much as the Anno Domini. The first year of that Calendar was 284, the disastrous year of the accession of Diocletian. The months they use with their own Calendar are those inherited from their distant forebears of the dynastic period of ancient Egypt. The farmers of the Coptic period used them, and so do the Muslim farmers of present-day Egypt. This tendency betrays the nationalist temper of the Egyptians even in religion and at that early date.

After Diocletian and Maximinus Daia, the tide of Christian persecution receded. The next phase was inaugurated by the issue of the famous 'Edict of Milan' in 313 by Constantine the Great, even before he became sole ruler of the Roman empire, thereby enforcing religious toleration in the wider sense. After 323, the position was reversed when he forbade pagan practices in favour of Christianity, which had become the state religion. Thus came the turn of the Christian majority to persecute the pagan minority. In Egypt, Patriarch Theophilus (385–412) in person led the local rioting against the temples of Serapis. The one at Canopus (Abu Qīr) fell in 389, and the chief temple in the capital was taken by storm in 411. With its fall a major part of the Ptolemaic Library, or Museion, was destroyed. Armies of Christian monks now camped in Alexandria, ready to attack the remnants of the pagan population. In 415 they intercepted the last of the pagan neo-Platonist philosophers, Hypatia, a woman of great dignity, while she was driving back from a lecture at the Museion. They dragged her to the Cæsareum, now a Christian church, and there stoned her to death.[1]

[1] Bell, pp. 112, 115; Hardy, pp. 104–5; Milne, pp. 98–9; Forster, pp. 55–6; M. Fowler, *Christian Egypt* (London, 1901), pp. 33–4. Charles Kingsley's novel, *Hypatia* (London, 1833) dramatizes her story. Socrates (*Hist. Eccles.*, VII, 15) is the chief contemporary

Hypatia's violent death closed a chapter in the story of persecution. She was a faint glimmer of the ancient Greek culture, now formally extinguished. Egypt and the civilized world were won by Christ. Idolatry had no official status, and there were no more pagans to persecute. Whose turn was coming? As will be seen from the story of Chalcedon and its lamentable aftermath, the answer is that the time of Christians persecuting other Christians had arrived.

For the time being, Alexandrine Christianity became the light of the world. The venerable fathers of the Coptic Church, the great theologians of the Catechetical School of Alexandria, the Coptic saints and heretics, the founders of monasticism, all these and numerous other illustrious Copts made permanent contributions to the establishment of the new faith. Throughout the age of Christian persecutions, the Copts fought fearlessly for the faith and worshipped, not in concealed catacombs or subterranean hiding, but openly on the face of the earth and invited the crown of martyrdom. They had won many spiritual battles in the past, but the future held for them many more fateful battles of a dogmatic or doctrinal nature with other Christian sects.

The Catechetical School

The Catechetical School of Alexandria was undoubtedly the earliest important institution of theological learning in Christian antiquity. Its members were responsible for the formulation of the first systems of Christian theology and for some of the most monumental works of exegesis. Yet it would be an error to limit its curriculum to theology. It was a college in which many other disciplines were included from the humanities, science and mathematics, although its chief function in the age of faith was religion. Its origins are shrouded in the mist of time, and our knowledge of its existence must be associated with the well-known scholars who presided over it, although there is no reason to believe that it very long predated them. But the native orthodox assumption[1] that St Mark was its founder must belong to the realm of legend. The earliest known reference to it occurred in the life of Pantænus, who died about 190 A.D. From that time on it was conducted parallel to the older but pagan Museion, until the latter began to dwindle and was ultimately liquidated after the assassination of Hypatia in 415.

Most of the eminent leaders of Alexandrine Christianity are known to have been connected with it either as teachers or students. In fact, the history of

---

source to mention her story. She was a Neoplatonist and a mathematician of no mean stature. She taught both pagans and Christians. One of her eminent Christian pupils was Synesius, bishop of Cyrene, who commemorated her highly in his epistles.

[1] Wahīb 'Atalla Girgis, p. 136; Zaki Shenūda, p. 120; Iris Ḥabīb El-Maṣry, p. 35.

that school may be summed up in the biographies of those personalities who headed it, and whose contributions to theological scholarship still constitute the solid basis of any study of Christian divinity.

The first great name to emerge at the head of the school was Pantænus.[1] In all probability he was a native of Sicily, although there is no proof as to his origin. The Copts describe him as a citizen of Egypt.[2] Certainly he was an inhabitant of Alexandria. Apart from being a great teacher, he is credited as one of the early architects of the adoption of the Greek alphabet in the Coptic script. His works of exegesis have been lost. At some time in the course of his service, Partiarch Demetrius I elected him for the Christian mission to India, and this he is known to have undertaken after seeking a worthy substitute as head of his school.

His choice of a successor fell upon Clement of Alexandria.[3] Clement was the most illustrious of the pupils of Pantænus and was probably an Athenian born of pagan parents about 150 A.D. He died around the year 215. He became head of the school before 190, and in the time of severe persecution by Septimius Severus, he fled from Alexandria. He studied Gnosticism, which seemed to have had many exponents and followers in his day. It is interesting to note that his outlook on this much-debated subject was not altogether hostile. He seemed to agree that *gnosis*, that is, religious knowledge or illumination, was the essence of Christian perfection. Like Socrates, Clement considered ignorance as worse than sin. He even promoted the idea of the divine origin of philosophy. His aim was to prove that the very constitution of the Church and Scriptures was not incompatible with Greek philosophy. Catechumens should not be discouraged from the pursuit of Greek learning. Thus we find Clement zealously teaching philosophy side by side with theology, although at times he found himself in the embarrassing position of labouring to establish the theory that the Greeks plagiarized Moses and the Old Testament. At any rate, Clement wrote abundantly, though much of his work is lost. His chief works are *An Exhortation to the Greeks*, the *Pedagogus* on

[1] J. Quasten, *Patrology*, 3 vols. (Westminster, Md., 1951–60), II, 4–5; A. von Harnack, *Geschichte der altchristlichen Litteratur bis Eusebius*, 3 vols. (Leipzig, 1893–1904), I, 291–6; G. Bardy, 'Aux origines de l'école d'Alexandrie', in *Recherches de science religieuse*, XXVII (Paris, 1937), 65–90.

[2] Zaki Shenūda, pp. 121–2. In support of this was his zeal for writing the Coptic language in Greek characters.

[3] J. E. L. Oulton and H. Chadwick, *Alexandrian Christianity* (The Library of Christian Classics, Philadelphia, 1956), pp. 56 ff.; Quasten, II, 5–36; Scott-Moncrieff, pp. 53 ff., 78 f.; Bell, pp. 90–1; Hardy, pp. 13–16. See also G. Bardy, *Clément d'Alexandrie* (Paris, 1926); É. de Faye, *Clément d'Alexandrie*, 2nd edn. (Paris, 1906); F. R. M. Hitchcock, *Clement of Alexandria* (London, 1899); J. Patrick, *Clement of Alexandria* (Edinburgh, 1914); R. B. Tollinton, *Clement of Alexandria—A Study in Christian Liberalism* (London, 1914); idem, *Alexandrine Teaching on the Universe* (New York, 1932); J. Munck, *Unterschungen über Klemens von Alexandria* (Stuttgart, 1933); G. Catalfamo, *S. Clemente Alessandrino* (Brescia, 1951).

Christian life and ethics, and his 'Miscellaneous Studies' (*Stromateis*) in which he compiled numerous treatises of varied character somewhat difficult to construe. His erudition is seen especially in the series of discussions whereby he attempted to reconcile Greek culture and Christianity. He is rightly regarded as one of the earliest apostles of Christian liberalism.

Origen[1] followed Clement about the year 215. A true son of Egypt, Coptic to the core, Origen had been born of ardent Christian parents around 185, either in Alexandria or somewhere else in Egypt, and died about 254.[2] He was Clement's most brilliant pupil. As a child he had lived through the anguish of his father's martyrdom for the Christian faith. As a young man he was extremely ascetic by nature, observed the most rigorous vigils, and carried the word of the Gospel literally to the extent of mutilating himself, thus becoming a eunuch,[3] a fact which contributed to his future troubles with the imperious Patriarch Demetrius I. His education was enriched by the knowledge he readily absorbed from his learned master Clement. He also studied pagan philosophy and literature under Ammonius Saccas (174–242), the real founder of Neoplatonism whose directive influence captivated Plotinus. He must have attended Saccas' lectures with Plotinus at the Ptolemaic School of Alexandria. He also travelled widely and became acquainted with most of the eminent scholars and prelates of his day. His wanderings extended from Arabia and Syria to Greece and Rome, where he attended sermons by St Hippolytus. Origen was destined to become one of the world's greatest exegetical scholars of all time.

As a biblical scholar and philosopher, his erudition was massive and his creativity was colossal. There is hardly a single book in the Old and New Testaments on which he did not write a lengthy commentary. His amazing

[1] Probably derived from the ancient Egyptian god Horus.

[2] Oulton and Chadwick, pp. 171 ff; Quasten, II, 37–101; Bell, pp. 90–1; Hardy, pp. 13–14, 16–18, 91–2, 95–7. See also R. Cadiou, *Introduction au système d'Origène* (Paris, 1932); idem, *La jeunesse d'Origène—Histoire de l'école d'Alexandrie au début du IIIe siècle* (Paris, 1935); J. Daniélou, *Origène* (Paris, 1948); J. J. Denis, *De la philosophie d'Origène* (Paris, 1884); É. de Faye, *Origène—Sa vie, son œuvre, sa pensée*, 3 vols. (Paris, 1923–8), English tr. F. Rothwell, *Origen and His Work* (London, 1926); R. P. C. Hanson, *Origen's Doctrine of Tradition* (London, 1954); A. von Harnack, *History of Dogma*, tr. from 3rd German edn. by N. Buchanun, 7 vols. (Boston, 1895–1900); idem, *Der kirchengeschichtliche Ertag der exegetischen Arbeiten des Origenes* (Leipzig, 1919); J. Tixeront, *History of Dogmas*, 3 vols. (St. Louis, Mo.), tr. from 5th French edn. by H.L.B., I, 256 ff.; A. Lieske, *Die Theologie der Logos-Mystik bei Origenes* (Münster, 1938); H. de Lubac, *Histoire et Esprit – L'intelligence de l'écriture d'après Origène* (Paris, 1950); E. R. Redepenning, *Origenes, eine Darstellung seines Lebens und seiner Lehre* (Bonn, 1841); W. Volker, *Das Vollkommenheitsideal des Origenes* (Tübigen, 1931); W. E. Barnes, 'The Third Century Greatest Christian – Origen', in *The Expository Times*, No. 44 (Edinburgh, 1932–33), pp. 295–300; W. R. Inge, *Origen*, British Academy Annual Lectures on a Master Mind (London, 1946); J. Champonier, 'Naissance de l'humanisme chrétien', in *Bulletin de l'Association G. Budé* (1947), pp. 58–96.

[3] Matthew xix, 12: 'There are eunuchs which made themselves eunuchs for the kingdom of heaven's sake.'

critical edition of the Old Testament, the *Hexapla*,[1] combined in six parallel columns all the available texts in both Greek and Hebrew scripts. This was the work used by St Jerome in Cæsarea. His monumental exegetical commentaries, entitled *Scholia*,[2] were partly put into Latin by Rufinus. Only fragments of both have survived. Origen's homilies are reputed to be amongst the most ancient specimens of Christian preaching. In the realm of theology, his most important work was the *De Principiis*,[3] in which he systematized the whole of the Christian doctrine in four books: on God and the celestial world, on man and matter, on free will and its impact, and on the Scriptures. Though the original of that ambitious project perished almost completely, its purport has survived in rather inadequate Latin renderings by Rufinus and St Jerome. In a treatise called *Contra Celsum*[4] Origen defended Christianity from attacks by the second-century pagan philosopher Celsus. He wrote a number of ascetic works, of which two have come down to us. The *Exhortation to Martyrdom*[5] was composed in 235 during Emperor Maximinus' persecution. His more extensive work *On Prayer*[6] had a great appeal to the mind of the early Christians.

His troubles started again during his first visit to Palestine when he was invited by the bishops of Ælia and Cæsarea to preach in their dioceses. It was unthinkable in Alexandrine ecclesiastical discipline that a layman could preach in the presence of bishops. Demetrius was an authoritarian cleric, who was unconsciously pushing patriarchal prerogative to the edge of a monarchical system unable to accept uncontrolled initiative, even if it came from so great a personality as Origen. Demetrius at once recalled him to Alexandria around the year 218. For some twelve years he sustained the gathering storm and buried himself in writing and teaching. The 'winds of wickedness' were blowing hard against him, and synods started discussing his life and dissecting his thought. Finally the hour of deliverance came when he fled back to Palestine in 230. There he was honoured and promptly ordained to the priesthood. It is said that he was even considered for the episcopate. As expected, this action provoked Demetrius, who hastened to nullify the ordination and excommunicate his unbending adversary, whom he also dismissed from

[1] H. H. Howorth, 'The Hexapla and Tetrapla of Origen', in *Proceedings of the Society of Biblical Archæology*, No. 24 (1902), pp. 147–72; H. M. Orlinsky, 'The Columnar Order of the Hexapla', in *The Jewish Quarterly*, XXVII, n.s. (1936), 137–49; W. E. Staples, 'The Second Column of Origen's Hexapla', in *Journal of the American Oriental Society*, LIX (1939), 71–80.

[2] C. Diobouniotis and A. von Harnack, *Der Scholienkommentar des Origenes zur Apokalypse Johannis*, Texte und Untersuchungen, Bd. 38, Heft 3 (Leipzig, 1911); C. H. Turner, 'The Newly Discovered Scholia of Origen on the Apocalypse', in *Journal of Theological Studies* (1912), pp. 386–97; idem, 'Scholia in Apocalypsin', in *Journal of Theological Studies* (1924), pp. 1–16.

[3] G. W. Butterworth, *Origen on First Principles* (London, 1936).

[4] See H. Chadwick, *Origen – Contra Celsum* (Cambridge, 1953).

[5] Oulton and Chadwick, pp. 388–429; Quasten, II, 69–73.

[6] Oulton and Chadwick, pp. 180–387; Quasten, II, 66–9.

the Catechetical School. Origen became an exile, and in 231 he settled in Cæsarea, where a new school arose around his person with more distinguished candidates. Some of his pupils, such as Gregory Thaumaturgus, bishop of Neocæsarea in Pontus, rose to key positions in the hierarchy. He arbitrated in doubtful cases of theology inside and outside Palestine. But the real glory of his calmer life at Cæsarea was the accomplishment of his immense literary work.

During the Decian persecution of 250, however, the great master suffered tremendously but with fortitude. He was imprisoned and tortured. Though he survived the horrors of his ordeal and regained his freedom, his health began to decline, and he died at the city of Tyre in 255, at the age of sixty-nine.

Origen, like most universal thinkers and prolific writers,[1] became a controversial figure both in his lifetime and after his death. The term Origenism was freely accepted in the realms of theology[2] and philosophy as a formidable institution with a supporting school of Origenists and an equally ardent school of anti-Origenists.[3] It is impossible in these pages to embark on even the briefest analysis of Origenist theories about such subjects as the unity of God, its relation to the Trinity, the doctrine of subordinationism, his audacious theory about souls and their prenatal existence and destiny after death, and numerous other physical and metaphysical controversies of almost unfathomable depth. Suffice to mention that many of the greatest names of his day and even afterwards joined the fray for or against Origen. In his defence we may read St Pamphylius (martyred in 209), St Athanasius the Apostolic, St Basil, St Gregory Nazianzen, Didymus the Blind and others. In the hostile camp we meet St Epiphaneus, bishop of Salamis in Cyprus, and both St Jerome and Theophilus of Alexandria, who turned against Origen in later times. In the fifth century, Church councils were convened solely to discuss Origen's views. After a short lull, the Origenist controversy flared up again in the sixth century, and Origen was repeatedly condemned by two councils, held at Constantinople in 542 and 553, with the connivance of the Emperor Justinian himself.

Until the discord between Demetrius and Origen, and the decision of the latter to quit Egypt for Cæsarea in Palestine, the Catechetical School of Alexandria, though closely associated with the Church, succeeded in retaining at least in theory, and to a considerable extent in practice, its academic freedom

[1] Wahīb ʿAṭalla Girgis, p. 138, states that 'Origen wrote more than 6000 books' in the authorship of which his pupils contributed. But even so, there is exaggeration in the statement, and I do not know its origin. However, Origen was surely one of the most prolific writers of any age.

[2] W. Fairweather, *Origen and Greek Patristic Theology* (New York, 1901); F. Prat, *Origène, le théologien et l'exégète*, 3rd edn. (Paris, 1907); cf. Quasten, II, 75 ff.; Harnack, *History of Dogma*, IV, 340 ff.; Tixeront, *History of Dogmas*, II, 331 ff., and III, 129 ff.

[3] L. B. Radford, *Three Teachers of Alexandria – Theognostus, Pierius and Peter: A Study in the Early History of Origenism and Anti-Origenism* (Cambridge, 1908).

and independence. After Origen's flight to Palestine and his dismissal from office at Alexandria, the School came under the direct control of patriarchal and Church authority. His immediate successor was Heraclas,[1] his former pupil and assistant who later followed Demetrius in the episcopate from 230 to 246. One of his first acts was to lift his predecessor's sentence of excommunication from Origen and to urge the return of the great master to Alexandria, but in vain. His reign is of interest on another account. It is said that when he increased the number of local bishops to twenty, the presbyters of the Church decided to distinguish him from the rest of the bishops by calling him 'Papa'. If this is true, then the first prelate in Christendom to bear the title of pope was Heraclas the Copt in the early part of the third century, long before it was known to Rome.[2]

The next head of the School, another famous pupil of Origen, was Dionysius of Alexandria, later surnamed the Great.[3] He occupied that post until he became patriarch (246–64). His reign was full of troubles. In 250 the Decian persecution drove the patriarch into secret hiding, though he was once arrested but escaped. In 257 another persecution was conducted by the Emperor Valerian. The country was harassed from the south by barbarian tribes. In Alexandria, Æmilianus, prefect of Egypt, declared himself emperor, and civil war broke out which ended in his capture by the imperial general Theodotus, who sent the rebel in chains to Rome.[4] The war, however, devastated the city and depleted the population. Plague was imminent and famine at the

[1] Evetts, II, 76–9. Thin biography with little on him in current historical literature. Iris El-Maṣry, pp. 72–5, accounts for the shortage of material on him by the loss of his ancient biographies rather than the lack of energy or enthusiasm which produced an eventless reign.

[2] B. Labanca, 'Del nome Papa nelle chiese cristiane di Oriente ed Occidente', in *Actes du Douzième Congrès International des Orientalistes*, Rome, 1899, III, ii (Florence, 1902), 47–101, with bibliography. Cf. F. L. Cross, 'Pope', in *The Oxford Dictionary of the Christian Church* (London, 1957). Gregory VII limited the use of the title solely to the bishop of Rome in the Council of Rome in 1073. Wahīb 'Aṭalla Girgis, p. 134, determines the emergence of the title in the reign of Heraclas, and Iris El-Maṣry, p. 73, no. 1, ascribes this fact to the authority of the tenth-century Coptic historian Sa'īd ibn Baṭrīq, though she contends that the title was used as early as Ænianus, the second patriarch, as is cited by the historian Maqrīzi in his *Geschichte der Copten*, Arabic edn. with German tr. F. Wüstenfeld (Göttingen, 1845), p. 8. Worrell (*Short Account of Copts*, p. 17) uses the term Papa or 'Pope' in relation to Alexandros at the Council of Nicæa in 325.

[3] Evetts, I, 80–93; C. L. Feltoe, *The Letters and Other Remains of Dionysius of Alexandria* (critical edn. with introduction and notes; Cambridge, 1904); idem, *St Dionysius of Alexandria: Letters and Treatises*, English tr. (London, 1918); F. C. Conybeare, 'Newly Discovered Letters of Dionysius of Alexandria to the Popes Stephen and Xystus', in *English Historical Review*, XXV (1910), 111–14; J. Burel, *Denys d'Alexandrie – Sa vie, son temps, ses œuvres* (Paris, 1910); P. S. Miller, *Studies in Dionysius the Great of Alexandria* (diss. Erlangen, 1933); F. Dittrich, *Dionysius der Grosse von Alexandrien* (Freiburg, 1876); P. Morize, *Denys d'Alexandrie* (Paris, 1881); T. Panaitescu, *Das Leben und literarische Tätigkeit des hl. Dionysius von Alexandrien* (Bucarest, 1905).

[4] Milne, *Egypt under Roman Rule*, pp. 73–4.

door. At the end of every persecution, Dionysius was faced with the problem of the apostates. But he was broad-minded enough to readmit them, and he moreover forbade the rebaptism of returned heretics and schismatics. It is a wonder that he had time to compose a number of theological works, where he displayed an independent but rather controversial mind. He was accused of tritheism by his namesake at Rome, was defended by Athanasius, and opposed by Basil. In regard to the Trinity, however, he himself rejected the heretical innovations of Paul of Samosata, bishop of Antioch and wealthy procurator of Queen Zenobia of Palmyra.[1]

At a later date Athanasius entrusted Didymus[2] the Blind with the headship of the School from about 315 to 398. He lived during the tempestuous age of Arianism and the Council of Nicæa. Among his pupils were St Gregory Nazianzen, St Jerome and the historian Rufinus. He was a man of erudition, but his works are almost all lost. It is said that the treatise entitled *Against Arius and Sabellius*, preserved under Gregory of Nyssa's name, was dictated by him. It is interesting to know that he cared for the welfare of the blind – he had been blind since the age of four – by promoting for the first time in history a system of embossed or engraved writing for them. After Didymus we enter the obscure period in the history of the School. It had done its share in shaping Christian doctrine and theological scholarship in those formative years. Then the zeal and the knowledge began to fade, and with them a great institution.

Saints and Heretics: Age of Athanasius and Cyril

The reign of Constantine the Great ushered in the triumph of Christianity over paganism and the reversal of the policy of persecution in which the Church Militant began to bait those who still adhered to the old idolatry. Save for its temporary recurrence during the rule of Julian the Apostate (332–63), paganism proved to be gasping its last breath. In the province of Egypt, the reaction to Julian's relapse turned out to be increasing violence. The regimented monks of Mareotis and Nitrea intimidated the aristocratic remnants of the worshippers of Serapis in Alexandria, while the battalions of St Shenūte of Panopolis (the modern Akhmīm) set out to wipe away paganism

[1] Hardy, pp. 23–9.

[2] G. Bardy, *Didyme l'Aveugle* (Paris, 1910). Edition of works by J. A. Mingarelli (Bologna, 1769), reproduced in Migne, *Patrologia Græca T. 39*, col. 131–1818. Among later and less famous names at the leadership of the School toward the end of the third and the beginning of the fourth centuries were Theognostus, who directed it from about 265 to 282; his follower Peirius, noted for poverty and for learning in philosophy; Peter, about 300; and Hesychius in the fourth century. Quasten, II, 109–18, and III, 85–100.

from the Thebaïd and destroy or transform the old pagan temples into Christian churches.

During the early persecutions, converts to the new faith were necessarily driven into a united front and had no time to dwell on or rather bicker about details of doctrine. With progressive relief from external brutal pressures, the Christians began to weigh all manner of emerging theological problems and argue about doctrinal differences. The outcome was the rise of heresy, which may be defined as divergence from the formal orthodox doctrine accepted by Church authority. It would of course be a grave error to describe a heretic as an irreligious person. On the contrary, some of the early heretics were deeply attached to the faith and often combined great erudition with profound piety or even self-inflicted asceticism. This was the age of saints and heretics, and both were well-meaning Christians, each in accordance with his creed or sect.

The patristic period in Church history is marked by the appearance of numerous heresies. In Egypt, two major heresies in succession gained considerable ground throughout the country and accordingly deserve an attempt at a brief analysis. One was Gnosticism, which struck root in the second century, and the other was Arianism, which disturbed the peace of Egypt and the whole empire in the fourth.

The historic background of Egyptian Gnosticism[1] was closely associated with two second-century Alexandrine teachers, namely, Valentinus and Basilides. They developed an elaborate religious order based on a multitude of pre-Christian and even pagan antecedents and gave it a Christian setting by trying to combine their tenets with the terms of the Holy Scriptures. The result was a system in which both syncretism and symbolism prevailed. In a society where paganism and late Egyptian magic were still a living memory, Gnosticism developed into a kind of esoteric cult of a mystic and mysterious character.

The central factor in the redemption of man was the Greek *gnosis*, or the revealed knowledge of God which was reserved for the spiritual élite. The privilege of this revelation was attained by the *illuminati* through the medium of complex esoteric practices with obscure occult incantations and metaphysical speculation. They recognized the existence of a Supreme Being or God of unknowable and unfathomable nature beyond human comprehension. From that remote Being descended vast numbers of 'æons', angelic forms or emanations which in turn gave rise to the Demiurge, who was the immediate creator

[1] For the literature on Gnosticism, see Kammerer's *Coptic Bibliography*, nos. 1596–1664, pp. 91–5. See also R. M. Grant, *Gnosticism and Early Christianity* (New York, 1959); Jean Doresse, *The Secret Books of the Egyptian Gnostics – An Introduction to the Gnostic Coptic manuscripts discovered at Chenoboskion, with an English translation and critical evaluation of The Gospel according to Thomas* (New York, 1960). This latter was originally published in French in Paris, 1958.

of the world. That Demiurge ruled the terrestrial spheres, which were evil and devoid of spirituality. Then Jesus, whom Gnostics recognized as the Logos and the representative of the Supreme Being, came down with the light of the *gnosis*, whose spark was apostolically transmitted to future generations of spiritual élite. The *Pistis Sophia*[1] and the books of *Jêu*,[2] original monuments of Gnostic operations known for over a century, provide the details of a fantastic apocalyptic cosmology with various stages through which the chosen and illuminated souls might ascend towards perfection and beatific bliss.

According to Gnostic teachings, Christ had only an illusory human appearance and did not assume any tangible or material fleshly frame. When it came to the Crucifixion and death, they assert that he was either miraculously saved from that agony or that he had a substitute in the person of Judas Iscariot or Simon of Cyrene. This is identical with the main substance of another, less widespread but slightly older, first to second-century heresy known as Docetism,[3] which bears a striking resemblance to the Qur'ānic[4] theory of Jesus in Islam.

Both heresies were condemned by the Church and attacked by the early Fathers from their very inception. Docetism with its phantasmal thesis of Jesus was attacked by St Ignatius (ca. 35–107), bishop of Antioch, as he was ready to enter the Roman arena for martyrdom. Gnosticism was forcefully bombarded by St Irenæus (ca. 130–200), bishop of Lyons, and Tertullian (ca. 160–220) of Carthage, and the Roman doctor and theologian St Hippolytus (ca. 170–236). The irregularity of those heresies, however, should not delude us from the intense piety and asceticism of their followers. Gnosticism apparently survived until it became merged in Egypt with the Manichæan doctrine of the dual godhead.

[1] E. C. Amélineau, *Pistis-Sophia, Ouvrage gnostique de Valentin, traduit du Copte en français avec une introduction* (Paris, 1895); G. W. Horner, *Pistis Sophia*, with introd. by F. Legge (London, 1924); G. R. S. Mead, *Pistis Sophia, A Gnostic Gospel* . . . (London, 1896); M. G. Schwartze, *Pistis Sophia, Opus gnosticum Valentino* . . . (Berlin, 1851); C. Schmidt, *Pistis Sophia, neu herausgegeben mit einleitung nebst griechischem und koptischem Wort- und Namenregister* (Hauniae, 1925); idem, German tr. (Leipzig, 1925).

[2] Scott-Moncrieff, pp. 148–97; Grant, p. 41; Doresse, p. 77.

[3] Discussed in most of early Christian histories and religious dictionaries and encyclopædias. See also Oulton and Chadwick, pp. 23, 32–3, 88, 163; H. Bettenson, *The Early Christian Fathers* (Oxford, 1956), pp. 5, 60, 241; R. M. Jones, *The Church's Debt to Heretics* (New York, 1924), pp. 41, 53–8. On Marcion, famous advocate of Docetism, see A. von Harnack, *Das Evangelium von fremden Gott* (Leipzig, 1924) and *Neue Studien zu Marcion* (Leipzig, 1924); idem, *History of Dogma*, I, 222 ff.; Tixeront, *History of Dogmas*, I, 183 ff.; R. S. Wilson, *Marcion* (London, 1933); E. C. Blackman, *Marcion and His Influence* (New York, 1950); J. Knox, *Marcion and the New Testament* (Chicago, 1942); Doresse, pp. 24–6; F. C. Conybeare, *The Origins of Christianity* (New York, 1958), pp. 329–46.

[4] Sūrah IV: 157 reads as follows: 'And because of their saying: We slew the Messiah Jesus son of Mary, Allah's messenger – They slew him not nor crucified, but it appeared so unto them; and lo! those who disagree concerning it are in no doubt thereof; they have no knowledge save pursuit of a conjecture; they slew him not for certain.'

It is to be remembered that our acquaintance with the Gnostic heresy has come chiefly through its enemies, for the usual practice in the Church was the complete destruction of all heretical material whenever that was condemned by the authorities. In recent years, however, a discovery of no less consequence than that of the Dead Sea Scrolls took place in the field of Gnostic sources in Upper Egypt. This is the Chenoboskion collection of Coptic papyrus codices containing 'The Secret Books of the Egyptian Gnostics', found in the neighbourhood of Nagʿ Ḥamādi, north of Luxor. These manuscripts are presumably fourth-century Coptic translations of second-century Greek originals. Apart from demonstrating the extent of the spread and the survival of Gnostic teachings within Egypt, these codices will undoubtedly throw a flood of light on the original nature of the heresy. Already they have revealed for the first time the existence of a considerable number of apocryphal Biblical texts which were either unknown or known only by name.[1]

Gnosticism was ultimately superseded in the public eye by another, much more menacing heresy in which emperors, patriarchs, and whole hierarchies became involved for more than half a century. In fact, this proved to be the greatest metaphysical battle of the fourth century. The issue at stake was Christological – in other words, the question of the Trinitarian unity and the relation of Jesus to God, of the Son to the Father, and the place of the Holy Ghost in the whole thesis. At the crucial juncture in the development of the Creed for all time, the faithful found themselves torn asunder between two schools of thought. Whereas one party followed the patriarch Alexander, or rather the Athanasian principle of consubstantiation, of the *homoousios*, signifying the Son and the Father to be one and the same essence, another dangerously large group accepted the Arian *homoiousios*, indicating that the Son even with his divine origin was only of *like* essence, begotten of the Father as an instrument for the creation of the world and consequently His unequal in eternity.[2]

[1] Doresse, pp. 142–5, lists 49 texts contained in the 13 codices preserved in the Coptic Museum from the Nagʿ Ḥamādi Papyri together with the Jung Codex now in Zurich. Two of the texts have already been published: (1) *Evangelium Veritatis* (Jung Codex), ed. and tr. M. Malinine, H.-C. Puech and G. Quispel (Zurich, 1956); (2) *The Gospel according to Thomas*, Coptic text established and tr. A. Guillaumont, H.-C. Puech, G. Quispel, W. Till and Yassa ʿAbd al-Massīḥ (Leiden and New York, 1959). See also *The Gospel of Truth – A Valentinian Meditation on the Gospel*, tr. from the Coptic and with commentary by K. Grobel (London, 1960); *The Gospel of Philip*, tr. from the Coptic with introduction and commentary by R. McL. Wilson (London, 1962).

[2] Chief sources included in Patrologias, Nicene and Post-Nicene Fathers Library, and Mansi and Hefele for Councils. See Athanasius, Epiphaneus, Rufinus, Socrates, Sozomen, Philostorgius, Theodoret, Eusebius of Cæsarea, Eusebius of Nicomedia, Gregory of Nazianzus, Gregory of Nyssa, St Basil of Cappadocia. There is a vast array of secondary sources. Some of the older standard works still stand including monumental church histories and special monographs. In addition to the general works, the following is a useful selection: G. Hermant, *La vie de saint Athanase, patriarche d'Alexandrie*, 2 vols. (Paris, 1671–79); L. Maimbourg, *Histoire de l'Arianisme* (Paris, 1675; English tr. 1728–29);

Here we are treading on tender soil, and it might be a treacherous venture to delve too deeply into the endless outpour of theological arguments of the age. But since the central battlefield was Alexandria and Egypt, a brief treatment of some of the broader elements of the subject seems inevitable in any outline of Coptic history.

Although the outbreak of the universal controversy began in the reign of the aged Bishop Alexander (d. 328), the two chief actors in the drama were Arius (ca. 250–336) and Athanasius (ca. 296–373). The latter was the patriarchal secretary and the power behind the throne of Alexander until he succeeded him in 328. Both Arius and Athanasius were learned theologians, ascetic in temperament, irreproachable in character, with infinite zeal, determination and extraordinary ability in preaching. Arius was probably a Lybian by birth, educated in the Antiochian School under Lucian (ca. 312), and he approached the problem with simplicity from the sharp angle of dialectic. Athanasius was an Alexandrian, who attended the Catechetical School of his native city, and grew up with a mystic outlook on matters of faith. Whereas Arius drew his support essentially from Greek or pro-Greek elements, Athanasius had Egypt and the Fathers of the Desert solidly behind him. Arianism seemed to enjoy a more universal appeal at the beginning, notably beyond the confines of Egypt, and thus Athanasius found himself standing against the world (*Athanasius contra mundum, et mundus contra Athanasium*).

The story started with Alexander's nomination of Arius as presbyter of the historic and rather important Church of Baucalis. The Arian system of Christology had already been laid out in Antioch on the basis of the subordinationist theology expounded by Lucian. Hitherto subordinationism

---

G. Bull, *Defensio Fidei Nicænae* (Oxford, 1703; English tr., 1851); J. A. Möhler, *Athanasius der Grosse* (Mainz, 1844); H. Voigt, *Die Lehre des Athanasius* (Bremen, 1861); F. Böhringer, *Athanasius und Arius* (Leipzig, 1874); W. Kölling, *Geschichte der arianischen Häresie bis zur Entscheidung in Nicäa*, 2 vols. (Gütersloh, 1874–83); J. H. Newman, *The Arians of the Fourth Century* (London, 1876); A. P. Stanley, *The Council and Creed of Constantinople in Christian Institutions* (London, 1881); H. M. Gwatkin, *Studies of Arianism* (Cambridge, 1900); E. Fialon, *St Athanase, Étude littéraire* (Paris, 1877); L. Atzberger, *Die Logoslehre des Athanasius, ihre Gegner und Verläufer* (Munich, 1880); W. Bright, *Lessons from the Lives of Three Great Fathers* (New York, 1891); P. Lauchert, *Die Lehre des heiligen Athanasius*, (Leipzig, 1895); K. Hoss, *Studien über Schrifttum und Theologie des Athanasius* (Freiburg, 1899); Quasten, *Patrology*, III, 7–13 (Arius), 13–19 (Alexandrus), 20–79 (Athanasius); L. L. Paine, *Critical History of the Evolution of Trinitarianism* (Boston, 1900); W. F. Frazer, *Against Arianism, St Athanasius* (London, 1900); L. H. Hough, *Athanasius the Hero* (Cincinnati, 1906); P. Snellman, *Der Anfang des arianischen Streites* (Helsingfors, 1904); A. Rogala, *Die Anfänge des arianischen Streites* (Paderborn, 1907); F. Haase, *Altchristliche Kirchengeschichte nach orientalischen Quellen* (Leipzig, 1925); G. Bardy, *Saint Athanase* (Paris, 1914); K. F. Hagel, *Kirche und Kaisertum in Lehre des Athanasius* (Leipzig, 1933); A. E. Burn, *The Athanasian Creed* (Oxford, 1912); F. L. Cross, 'The Study of St. Athanasius' (lecture, Oxford, 1945); R. M. Jones, *The Church's Debt to Heretics*, pp. 85–103. From the Coptic side, see bibliographical listing in Kammerer, nos. 1112–30, 1280–81, 2435–37.

was a relatively obscure heresy which placed Jesus and the Holy Ghost in a subordinate position relative to the Father. Alexander did not realize the seriousness of the situation until the fiery Arius set Baucalis ablaze with his unorthodox teachings. The alarmed patriarch sought to put a stop to this new wave by summoning a local synod of some hundred bishops at Alexandria about 320, and he secured their condemnation of Arius, whom he consequently suspended from service and excommunicated.

In the meantime, the defeated but undaunted Arius continued to bring pressure to bear upon the orthodox party from two sides. A poet and a musician of fair stature, he versified his theology in a collection of hymns known as *Thalia*[1] (banquet), on models of popular folk songs, and the ruse worked with the populace, who sang Arian Christology everywhere. Arius also had access to the imperial palace in Constantinople through his former fellow-student Eusebius, bishop of Nicomedia, a friend of Emperor Constantine, whom he later baptized. The emperor was interested in unity above all considerations, and was thus prevailed upon to write both contestants to refrain from their 'incomprehensible logomachy' and to terminate their differences. He also commissioned Hosius (ca. 257–357), the aged and celebrated bishop of Cordova, to mediate and report on the situation. The *impasse* was found to be insurmountable, and the Emperor yielded to the recommendations of both Hosius and Alexander by summoning an Œcumenical Council to meet at Nicæa[2] in Bithynia in the summer of 325.

Thus for the first time in history, representative bishops of all Christendom – Western, Byzantine, African and Eastern – traditionally numbering 318, convened to settle all outstanding dogmatic and doctrinal differences. The Nicæan deliberations gave Christianity a Creed which has survived to this day. Arianism was condemned and Arius together with four bishops who refused to sign the text of the Creed were deposed and banished. This was perhaps the first instance in which civil punishment was imposed for religious heresy. Behind the Nicæan triumph stood the persuasive eloquence of Athanasius, still a young deacon, who came to the Council in the train of his old bishop, Alexander.

[1] G. Bardy, 'La Thalie d'Arius', in *Revue de Philogie*, LIII (1927), 211–33.

[2] Present day Isnik in Turkey. For sources, see P. Batiffol, 'Les sources de l'histoire du Concile de Nicée', in *Echos d'Orient*, XXVIII (1925), 385–402, and XXX (1927), 5–17; Kammerer, *Coptic Bibliography*, nos. 1256–73. Also G. D. Mansi, *Sacrorum Conciliorum Nova et Amplissima Collectio*, 59 vols. (Florence etc., 1729–1927), Vol. II, pp. 635 ff.; C. J. Hefele on Councils, see standard augmented French translation by H. Leclercq, *Histoire des conciles*, 8 vols. (Paris, 1907–21), T. I, pt. 1, pp. 442 ff. and T. I, pt. 2, pp. 633 ff., 1139 ff.; J. Chrystal, *Authoritative Christianity: Decisions of the Six Sole Ecumenical Councils*, 6 vols. (Jersey City, 1891), Vol. I, pt. 1 (Nicæa). Also E. Revillout, *Le Concile de Nicée, d'après les textes coptes*, 2 vols. (Paris, 1873–98); F. Haase, *Die koptischen Quellen zum Conzil von Nicäa* (Paderborn, 1920; A. F. Burn, *The Council of Nicæa: A Memorial for its 16th Centenary* (London, 1925); A. d'Alès, *Le dogme de Nicée* (Paris, 1926); A. von Harnack, *History of Dogma*, IV, 1 ff.; Tixeront, *History of Dogmas*, III, 2 ff., 34–75.

With the death of patriarch Alexander in 328, Athanasius succeeded him to a stormy reign during which he had to sustain the fighting with Arians and semi-Arians. He suffered exile from his see five times. Even before Constantine's death, the imperial hero of Nicæa withdrew his support and exiled the champion of orthodoxy to Trier in 336. He was allowed to return only after the emperor's death in 337. The second exile (339–46), also due to Arian intrigue, he spent in Rome, where he resided at the curia of Julius I and introduced Coptic monasticism into the Roman church. The importance of the third (356–61) and the fourth (362–63) exiles was due to the fact that Athanasius spent those years with the Fathers of the Desert, thereby giving the monastic movement the impetus of high office while gaining the monks' total support against Arianism and schism. The fifth exile (365–66) was short, and the Emperor Valens found the patriarch's return necessary to reconcile the angry Orthodox Alexandrine population. Athanasius was the image of a militant churchman throughout the whole of his career and although the cinders of Arianism were still smouldering at the hour of his death in 373, he did everything in his power to prepare for its total rout and final destruction at the Council of Constantinople of 381.[1] Only then was the Nicene Creed safeguarded for all history.

When one looks back upon the heroic and poignant years of the life of Athanasius, his wanderings across Europe and western Asia and the African deserts, the councils he attended, the conspiracies he had to weather, and the day-to-day onus of a prelate's endless duties, one wonders how and where he found time to write books.[2] In his youth, he composed two apologetic treatises entitled *On the Incarnation of the Divine Word* and *A Discourse Against the Greeks* which may well support the thesis of his Coptic origin. His dogmatic works are too numerous to be considered here, but they were mostly on the subject of Arian heresy and include *A History of the Arians*, prepared between 358 and 360 for the edification of the monks, as well as *Against Apollinarius*—two books in defence of the full humanity of Christ. In exegesis he wrote a *Commentary on the Psalms*, with an allegorical touch, and made a synoptic compendium of the Bible. His ascetic compositions are many, but the most famous of all is of course his *Life of St Anthony*.

The problems of Christology, inaugurated at Nicæa with a resounding din that filled Christendom, were to be resumed in the following century by another peer of Athanasius, a learned graduate of the monastery of St Macarius, already known as a centre of theological scholarship. He was the imperious Saint Cyril (412–44), surnamed the Great[3] and a man of unusual ability.

[1] Mansi, III, 521 ff.; Hefele, II, 1, 1–48.

[2] St Athanasius, *Werke*, ed. H. G. Opitz (Berlin and Leipzig, 1934); idem, *Select Works and Letters*, ed. A. Robertson (Nicene and Post-Nicene Fathers, IV; London, 1892).

[3] Apart from the old ecclesiastical historians mentioned in previous notes as well as the conciliar collections of Mansi and Hefele, the works of Cyril himself are a primary source

As soon as he succeeded Theophilus (385–412), his own uncle, he declared a spirited warfare on many fronts. At home, he had under his command an army of dedicated followers known as *parabolani*, that is, 'those who disregarded their own lives' in serving the cause of the Church. The patriarch inspired them with mortal hatred for the remnants of Neoplatonism in Alexandria. Although there is no evidence to prove that he had a direct hand in Hypatia's massacre in 415, there is hardly any doubt that the act was a by-product of Cyril's war against Neoplatonists. The Jews were equally subjected to the same treatment by his monastic bodyguard. All this brought him into immediate strife with the imperial prefect Orestes, whose authority in Alexandria was in jeopardy. The ill feeling between the patriarch and the prefect was further intensified by Orestes' high regard for Hypatia. Outside Egypt, he attacked the Novatianist schism of a few isolated communities of Roman origin. Their founder, Novatian,[1] was a contemporary of the Decian persecution of 249–50; and he initially supported the adoption of a lenient policy towards readmission of apostates. But in the course of complicated papal elections in which he was a losing candidate, Novatian reverted to a reigourist stand, became rival pope, and was martyred by Valerian in the persecution of 257–8. He and his scanty followers, although perfectly orthodox, were of course under sentence of excommunication until the fifth century, when Cyril aimed at their destruction.

The greatest conflict of Cyril's life, however, was with the formidable patriarch of Constantinople, Nestorius,[2] over a new phase in Christology. The subject of Nestorianism has been treated elsewhere, and it may suffice here

of his biography. The old edition of his works, ed. J. Aubert, 6 vols. (Paris, 1638), appears in Migne, *P.G.*, LXVIII–LXXVII, with additions. P. E. Pusy also re-edited many of his works in 7 vols. (Oxford, 1868–77); and E. Schwartze edited many epistles by Cyril in the *Acta Conciliorum Œcumenicorum* (Berlin, 1922 ff.). See also Evetts, II, 166–179. Studies on the age of Cyril: LeNain de Tillemont, *Mémoires pour servir à l'histoire ecclésiastique des six premiers siècles*, Vol. XIV (16 vols., 1693–1712); idem., *History of Arians and Council of Nice*, English tr. T. Deacon, 2 vols. (London, 1721); S. Kopallik, *Cyrillus von Alexandrien, Eine Biographie nach den Quellen bearbeitet* (Mainz, 1881); A. Rehrmann, *Die Christologie des hl. Cyrillus von Alexandrien* (Hildesheim, 1902); T. Weigl, *Die Heilslehre des hl. Kyrill von Alexandrien*, 2 vols. (Mainz, 1902); biographies: in Russian by T. Liastsenko (Kiev, 1913) and in Greek by C. Papadopoulos (Alexandria, 1933); H. du Manoir de Juaye, *Dogme et spiritualité ehez saint Cyrille d'Alexandrie* (Paris, 1944); A. von Harnack, *History of Dogma*, Vol IV, pp. 164 ff.; Quasten, *Patrology*, III, 116–42; Kyrilliana, *Études variées à l'occasion du XVe centenaire de saint Cyrille d'Alexandrie*, A.D. 444–1944 (Cairo, 1947); R. M. Jones, pp. 104–30.

[1] Words ed. J. Jackson (London, 1728); also critical ed. in 'Cambridge Patristic Texts' by W. Yorke Fausset (Cambridge, 1909); English tr. H. Moore (London, 1919); A. d'Alès, *Novatien, Étude sur la théologie romaine au milieu du IIIe siècle* (Paris, 1925); M. Kriebel, *Studien zur älteren Entwicklung der abendländischen Trinitätslehre bei Tertullian und Novatian* (Marburg, 1932).

[2] See the chapter below on the Nestorian Church for sources; Quasten, *Patrology*, III, 514–19.

to point out that the use of the term *Theotokos*, or the Mother of God, was rejected by Nestorius in regard to the Virgin Mary, whom he wanted to be called Mother of Christ. This led to the inference of the dual nature of Jesus and to another round of metaphysical warfare between the rival patriarchs. Cyril wrote a corrective letter to Nestorius without avail. So he wrote to Emperor Theodosius II, to Empress Eudocia, and to the emperor's sister Pulcheria. The imperial family was in fact displeased with these quarrels within the Church and spoke about the possibility of an œcumenical council to restore order. Cyril meanwhile addressed himself to Celestine, bishop of Rome, on Nestorian irregularity; and since Nestorius had received the Pelagian[1] enemies of Celestine with honour, the Roman bishop was more willing to lend ear to Cyril against the patriarch of Constantinople. Celestine readily condemned Nestorianism in council at Rome, while Cyril hurled twelve anathemas against Nestorius from Alexandria. Nestorius answered by casting twelve counter-anathemas at his adversary. The stage was again set for another œcumenical council, this time at Ephesus in 431,[2] and the summons was issued jointly by Theodosius II in the East and Valentinian III in the West.

This was the third œcumenical council, the other two being Nicæa (325) and Constantinople (381). Nestorius arrived at Ephesus with sixteen bishops and an armed bodyguard headed by no less a personality than the commander of the imperial guard. Cyril came by sea with fifty bishops and an army of devotees, retainers and a few monks, who were said to have included the great Shenūte in their number, though this report is unconfirmed and rather doubtful. On Cyril's side was Memnon, bishop of Ephesus, who mustered forty suffragans from Asia and twelve from Pamphilia. Celestine I of Rome sent two bishops and a priest who upheld Cyril's cause. With that host of allies, Cyril decided to inaugurate the session, while Nestorius abstained from attending because he still awaited the Antiochene contingent under his old comrade Bishop John. Two hundred bishops then unanimously condemned and anathematized Nestorius. A little later, on the arrival of Bishop John of Antioch with forty-two bishops, Nestorius held his own rival-council which also unanimously deposed and anathematized both Cyril and Memnon. The two parties rushed their verdicts to the emperor, who unwittingly signed both edicts and all the leaders found themselves under arrest. After much intrigue, the Cyrillian party was freed, Nestorius imprisoned at his old cloister, and for the next two years the exchange of dispatches continued between the

[1] The Pelagian heresy is so named after its originator, Pelagius, of British or Irish origin. Pelagius expounded the view that man was his own instrument of salvation, irrespective of divine grace. He visited Rome in the reign of Bishop Anastasius (399–401 A.D.). Later, he escaped to Africa when Rome fell to Alaric in 410.

[2] E. Schwartze, *Acta Conciliorum Œcumenicorum*, Vol. I (Berlin and Leipzig, 1927) pts. I–V (Concilium Universale Ephesenum); Mansi, IV, 569 ff.; Hefele, II, pt. i, 219 ff.; Chrystal, I, pt. ii, and II–III (Ephesus).

hostile churches. Then at last a *rapprochement* was reached, and Nestorius was left a solitary victim to face a grim fate. The year 433 saw Nestorius a sorry figure, manhandled in his forced retirement, then carried into exile first to Petra then to the oasis of the western desert, where probably he died in oblivion and tragedy after the year 439. Cyril was at the height of his own power in that year.

Cyril left behind him a tremendous number of works in theology, exegesis, homiletics and apologetics. As a meticulous theologian he seems, however, to have devoted more attention to the essence of an argument than to the external elegance of style. Yet it must be noted that his almost indiscriminate use of the words *physis* and *hypostasis*[1] led to the Chalcedonian confusion which resulted in the establishment of the so-called 'Monophysite' doctrine. Cyril's apology against the Emperor Julian the Apostate is a document of historical interest. His numerous epistles are documents of importance for the ecclesiastical historian. His twenty-nine Paschal Homilies defined the date of Easter. On the whole, his theology was regarded by all future sects as the key to orthodoxy, though subsequent theologians differed on its interpretation. At the time of his death, the Alexandrine Church occupied the position of undisputed leadership in the whole Christian world.

[1] Literally in Greek means 'substance', also 'person' more frequently used in Latin. It was the ambiguity between the two words that led to confusion.

3 • THE COPTS AND THE WORLD

Missionary Enterprise

From its very beginning, Christianity had been a missionary religion; and the early Coptic converts were not behind other nations in their evangelizing labours. Although the absence of contemporary documentary material limits our knowledge of the role they played in this field, there is unmistakable evidence that they spread the faith in every direction beyond their geographical frontiers. Since Ptolemaic times, Alexandria had been the crossroads of the ancient world. As a trade centre, it was frequented by merchants from all nations, and its Catechetical School was attended by theological scholars from most Christian communities. Thus the natives of Egypt became acquainted with men of every race, and the ascetic sons of the Nile found all doors opened to them. In fact, there is reason to believe that the Christian emissaries from Egypt reached all three continents known to Christian antiquity, though Africa was the field in which their propagation of the faith was most successful.

It is not inconceivable that Coptic relations with North Africa, notably with Cyrenaica or the Pentapolis, took place with the introduction of Christianity. In his visitations from Alexandria, St Mark must have been accompanied to the Pentapolis by Alexandrine helpers. Educationally, the natives of the Pentapolis looked towards Egypt. Synesius (ca. 370–414),[1] bishop of Ptolemais, received his instruction at Alexandria in both the Catechetical School and the Museion, and he entertained a great deal of reverence and affection for Hypatia, the last of the pagan Neoplatonists, whose classes he had attended. Synesius was raised to the episcopate by Theophilus, patriarch of Alexandria, in 410. Since the Council of Nicæa in 325, Cyrenaica had been recognized as an ecclesiastical province to the see of

[1] H. I. Marrou, 'Synesius of Cyrene and Alexandrian Neoplatonism', in *The Conflict between Paganism and Christianity in the Fourth Century*, ed. A. Momigliano (Oxford, 1963), pp. 126–50; Synesius of Cyrene, *Letters*, English tr. A. Fitzgerald (Oxford, 1926); idem, *Essays and Hymns*, 2 vols. (London, 1930). For biographies of Synesius, see C. Lacombrade (Paris, 1951), G. Grutzmacher (Leipzig, 1913), W. S. Crawford (London, 1901), J. C. Pando (Washington, 1940).

Alexandria, in accordance with the ruling of the Nicæan Fathers. The patriarch of the Coptic Church to this day includes the Pentapolis in his title as an area within his jurisdiction. It is doubtful, however, whether Coptic influence extended further west in North Africa, where Carthage and Rome held greater sway.

The area where Egyptian Christianity had its most direct impact was probably in the upper valley of the Nile, by the southern gate of Egypt at Syene (modern Aswān). The ancient Egyptians had known those parts since the eighteenth dynasty, some fifteen hundred years before Christ, and their magnificent temples and monuments are spread all over Nubia. Two factors helped in the steady flow of Christian missionaries south of Syene. First, the persecutions gave the initial incentive to Christians to flee from the face of their oppressors to the oases of the western desert and beyond the first cataract into Nubia. Secondly, the rise of ascetic monasticism furnished the new religion with pious emigrants who penetrated the southern regions as soldiers of Christ. Recent archæological excavations in the lower Sudan prove that Christianity had struck root in those distant regions by the fourth century.[1] In the fifth century, good relations are recorded between the monastic order of the great St Shenūte and the Nubian and Baga tribes of the south. At the beginning of the sixth century, there was a certain Bishop Theodore of Philæ, apparently a Christian substitute to the Isis high priesthood established on that island from Roman times. In the same century, Justinian (527–65) issued a command that all the pagan tribes on the periphery of the Byzantine empire should be converted to Christianity. The imperial order accelerated a process already taking place in Nubia, though as a consequence, the monophysite Copts had to combat paganism and the Chalcedonian profession of faith at one and the same time. It would appear that the Coptic victory was complete by 559, and through the sympathy and connivance of Empress Theodora, and in defiance to court injunctions, a monophysite bishop, Longinus,[2] was consecrated for the see of Napata, capital of the Nubian kingdom. The ancient temples were progressively transformed into Christian churches, and new churches were constructed. Furthermore, monasticism was introduced among the Nubians, who founded numerous monasteries on the edge of the valley. The most outstanding example is that of St Simeon, which stood at a small distance across the Nile

[1] D. Dunham, 'Romano-Coptic Egypt and the Culture of Meroë', in *Coptic Egypt* (Brooklyn, N.Y., 1944), pp. 31–3; C. P. Groves, *The Planting of Christianity in Africa*, 4 vols. (London, 1948–58), I, 46–9; S. Clarke, *Christian Antiquities in the Nile Valley* (Oxford, 1912).

[2] He appears to be the true apostle of Nubian Christianity, though it is said that he was preceded by another named Julian, who seems to have converted the king and the court of the tribe of the Nobadæ. C. P. Groves, I, 49–50; Zāher Riāḍ, *Kanīsat al-Iskandariyah fī Ifrīqiyah* (*The Church of Alexandria in Africa*), (in Arabic; Cairo, 1962), 159–65.

from modern Aswān. Though raided by Saladin's Islamic armies in the year 1172, its imposing ruins are still a testimony of architectural, artistic and spiritual solidity.

Even more romantic than the conversion of the Nubian kingdom to Christianity in the late antiquity, was that of the more distant and isolated kingdom of Abyssinia. According to an apocryphal tradition, the Ethiopian court at Axum had long been acquainted with monotheism. The story of the journey of the Queen of Sheba[1] to the court of King Solomon in the tenth century B.C., their marriage, and the subsequent birth of Menelik I of Ethiopia, though probably legendary, has given the Ethiopian monarch the title 'Lion of Judah'.[2] Menelik's visit to his father in Jerusalem, and his return with the Ark of the Covenant, said to be enshrined in the cathedral of Axum, belongs to the same tale.[3] The next contact with monotheism occurred when the eunuch in the service of 'Condace, Queen of the Ethiopians', encountered the Apostle Philip on his return from Jerusalem by way of Gaza.[4] Here, however, the Nubian queen is confused with the Ethiopian. Historic evidence shows that Ethiopia remained pagan until the fourth century A.D. when the authentic evangelization of the kingdom took place. Two brothers, Frumentius and Aedesius, residents of Tyre but originally from Alexandria, boarded a trading ship going to India and were shipwrecked on the Red Sea coast near Abyssinia. They were picked up by the men of the Ethiopian monarch, probably Ella Amida,[5] who took them into his service. Aedesius became his cup-bearer, and Frumentius his secretary and tutor to the young crown prince, Aeizanas (Ezana), to whom he doubtless gave a Christian education. When Aeizanas became king, he, together with his courtiers and retainers were converted, and Christianity was declared the official religion of the state. Afterwards Aedesius was allowed to return to Tyre, while Frumentius went to Alexandria to convey the news to the Patriarch Athanasius and to plead with him to consecrate a special bishop to watch over the spiritual welfare of those distant Christians. The meeting with Athanasius was presumably between 341 and 346.[6] The patriarch appointed Frumentius himself

[1] Meaning 'Queen of the South'.

[2] The lion is still the arms of the kings of Ethiopia. The emperor always keeps a lion at the palace entrance.

[3] The story is derived from a fourteenth century MS., said to have been translated from an Arabic version of an original Coptic in Egypt, and promoted by the Zaguē dynasty, which ascended the throne in 1270 A.D., in an attempt to establish the continuity of the Solomonian line in Ethiopia. A. H. M. Jones and E. Munroe, *A History of Ethiopia* (Oxford, 1960), pp. 10–21; J. Doresse, *Ethiopia*, English tr. Elsa Coult (London, 1959), pp. 13 ff.

[4] Acts of the Apostles viii, 26–40.

[5] His reign was about the years 320 and 325 A.D. Archæological evidence shows his inscriptions to retain the pagan character, whereas his son's refer to a monotheistic deity. Further, numismatic evidence is decisive. Early coins of Aeizanas' reign bear the pagan symbols, later replaced by a Cross. Jones and Monroe, pp. 26–31; Doresse, p. 30.

[6] Doresse, p. 62.

under the name of Anba Salāma, that is, 'the father of peace'.[1] The new bishop of Axum finally returned to his see in or before 356, no doubt accompanied by presbyters to help in the evangelization of the kingdom and the establishment of churches in the country.[2] In 356 the Emperor Constantius, an Arian, wrote to Aeizanas to withdraw the Orthodox Frumentius, but without avail. After the Council of Chalcedon in 451, the Ethiopians adhered to the Coptic profession.

The winning of Ethiopia for the Gospel must have been regarded as one of the most spectacular events of the century and a crowning to the labours of the Copts in Africa.[3] Further east, the Copts emerged in the missionary field in Asia, though of course on a more modest scale. It is very difficult to generalize on the basis of isolated instances, but there is no doubt that the Egyptians moved freely to many parts of Palestine, Syria, Cappadocia, Cæsarea and to some extent Arabia. Origen, it will be remembered, was invited to Bostra to arbitrate in doctrinal differences. Mar Augin of Clysma (the modern Suez) was the founder of monasticism in Mesopotamia and the Persian empire, making a considerable impact on both Syrian and Assyrian Christianity.[4] As early as the second century the great Pantænus (about 190), who presided over the Catechetical School of Alexandria, was chosen by Demetrius I to preach the Gospel in India.[5] After accomplishing his mission, he visited Arabia Felix (the modern Yemen) where he must have continued his missionary enterprise. Unfortunately our information on this fascinating subject is extremely limited. In the sixth century there was a further Indian adventure by another Alexandrine, Cosmas Indicopleustes,[6] who later became a monk and left an account of his travels. He speaks of Christian communities with their own bishops on the Persian Gulf, the existence of

[1] Called *Abūna* (Our Father), also *Casate Berhan Salāma* (Revealer of Light).

[2] The Abyssinian tradition mentions Nine Saints. Groves, I, 53; Doresse, p. 81.

[3] It is interesting to note that there is a growing tendency among present-day African Christians towards affiliation with the Coptic Church. The *Arab World*, No. 110 (30 July 1962), p. 53, published an article entitled 'African Christians Returning to Church which Originated in Africa', in which Mr S. K. Kassassa, of Kampala (Uganda), is reported to have asked (as early as 1958) permission for his group to join the Coptic Church and to send students to the Coptic Ecclesiastical College. Father Makary El-Souriani (now Bishop Samuel) was sent to Kenya and Uganda in 1961 to make an enquiry and report to Pope Kirollos VI. When interviewed on this, the pope replied: 'I have found out that there are nearly five million Christians in Uganda and several millions in the neighbouring countries, the majority of whom would like to join the Coptic Church.' How realistic this is, remains to be seen.

[4] See sections below dealing with Jacobite and Nestorian monasticism.

[5] The geographical situation of India was rather confused in those days with Southern Arabia and Abyssinia, but it is quite possible that Pantænus reached India proper. On his return journey, Eusebius (*Hist. Eccles.*, V, 10–11) tells us, he recovered the original Gospel of Matthew in Hebrew which had been brought to the East by the Apostle Bartholomew.

[6] Critical edition of his *Christian Topography* by E. O. Winstedt (Cambridge, 1909).

Christians in the island of Socotra, and the yet more numerous Christians of St Thomas in India. He is reputed to be one of the first to travel to Ceylon.

The role of the Copts in Europe may be illustrated from the first two exiles of the great Alexandrine patriarch, Athanasius. The first exile began in Constantinople and ended in Trier, where the saint spent parts of 336 and 337, and it is difficult to believe that he did not preach during all that time in his new environment. Most of the second exile, from 339 to 346, was at the Roman curia as the guest of Julius I. Apart from establishing good relations between Alexandria and Rome, Athanasius carried out some missionary work by introducing into Roman religious life the highly developed monastic rule of the Fathers of the Egyptian deserts. This was an important event in view of the magnitude of the contributions of the rising monastic orders in the preservation of culture, and in the progress of European civilization.[1]

In those days the stream of pilgrims who came from the west to visit the Egyptian wilderness with its hermits and monks included many who may well be regarded as missionaries of Coptic religious culture, since they transplanted Coptic teachings to their native countries. The most eminent of these was John Cassian (ca. 360–435), a native of southern Gaul and the son of rich parents who gave him a good education. He and an older friend named Germanus decided to undertake a pilgrimage to the Holy Land, and in Bethlehem they took monastic vows. Then they went to Egypt, where they spent seven years visiting the solitaries and holy men of the wilderness of Scetis in the Nitrean valley as well as the Thebaïd during the fourth century. It was on that occasion that John Cassian collected the material for his two famous works, the *Institutes*[2] and the *Conferences*.[3] These books deal with the life and habits of the Egyptian monks as well as their wisdom and institutions, and both were widely read in mediæval Europe. St Benedict of Nursia used them when he codified his rule in the sixth century. After spending some time with St John Chrysostom in Constantinople on his return journey, John Cassian was ordained priest, probably in Rome, before settling down in the neighbourhood of Marseilles, where he has been accredited with the introduction of Egyptian monasticism into Gaul. At Marseilles, above the shrine of St Victor, who was martyred by the Emperor Maximian (286–305) in the last Christian persecution, John Cassian founded a monastery and a nunnery on the model of the Cœnobia, which he had witnessed in Egypt.[4] In

[1] See above notes pp. 39 ff. in previous chapter on Athanasius.

[2] *De institutis cœnobiorum et de octo principalium vitiorum remediis libri XII.*

[3] *Collationes Patum*, XXIV; both works tr. into English by E. C. S. Gibson in the Nicene and Post-Nicene Fathers, Ser. 2, Vol. XI (1894), 161–641. Cassian wrote another less important work against Nestorius entitled *De Incarnacione Domini*.

[4] H. I. Marrou, 'Jean Cassien à Marseille', in *Revue du Moyen Âge Latin*, I (1945), 5–26; O. Chadwick, *John Cassian, A Study in Primitive Monasticism* (Cambridge, 1950); L. Cristini, *Jean Cassien, ou la spiritualité du désert*, 2 vols. (Paris, 1946); A. Hoch, *Die Lehre des Johannes Cassianus von Natur und Gnade* (Freiburg, 1896).

the catacombs below the present day fort of St Victor, will be found numerous archæological remains, including sarcophagi with stone carvings and sculpture which betray in animal and plant motifs the direct influence of early Coptic art. On the island of St Honorat, off the coast at Cannes, there is an old monastery where the monks explain to visitors that they use the rule of St Pachomius of the Thebaïd.

Wherever the Roman legions went, they were apparently followed by Christian missionaries. To Switzerland a mission from Thebes, according to local legend or tradition, arrived in the year 285 with the Theban legion. It was led by St Mauritius, who seems to have earned martyrdom for refusing to sacrifice to the heathen gods. His statue stands today in one of the public squares of St Moritz, and his body was enshrined in what later became the chapel of an abbey of Augustinian canons at Saint Maurice in Valais. His companions, a legionary named Felix, his sister Regula and a third called Exuperantius, hid themselves in the dreary wastes of the land of Glarus, and ultimately reached the Lake of Zurich, where they baptized converts until they were seized by the emperor's men and led before Decius, the Roman governor of the region. On refusing to sacrifice to the gods they were tortured. Legend says that as they were beheaded a voice from heaven called to them: 'Arise, for the angels shall take you to Paradise and set upon your heads the martyr's crown.' Thus the bodies arose, and, taking their heads in their hands, walked forty ells[1] uphill to a prepared ditch, where they slept underneath what is now the crypt of the Zurich *Grossmünster*. On the spot of their martyrdom arose the *Wasserkirche*. The *Fraumünster* cloister across the Limmat River has eight famous mediæval frescoes representing every stage of their story. The three headless saints with heads in hand are the subject of the arms of the city of Zurich. A parallel story with some variation has been recounted about the town of Solothurn, and the name of St Victor (the Coptic *Boktor*) is mentioned as its hero.

There is little doubt that the Coptic missionaries reached as far as the British Isles on the edge of mediæval Europe. Long before the coming in 597 of St Augustine of Canterbury, Christianity had been introduced amongst the Britons. The eminent historian Stanley Lane-Poole says: 'We do not yet know how much we in the British Isles owe to these remote hermits. It is more than probable that to them we are indebted for the first preaching of the Gospel in England, where, till the coming of Augustine, the Egyptian monastic rule prevailed. But more important is the belief that Irish Christianity, the great civilizing agent of the early Middle Ages among the northern nations, was the child of the Egyptian Church. Seven Egyptian monks are buried at Disert Uldith, and there is much in the ceremonies and

[1] A measure of length varying in different countries but approximately averaging one yard or a little more.

architecture of Ireland in the earliest time that reminds one of still earlier Christian remains in Egypt. Every one knows that the handicraft of the Irish monks in the ninth and tenth centuries far excelled anything that could be found elsewhere in Europe; and if the Byzantine-looking decoration of their splendid gold and silver work, and their unrivalled illuminations, can be traced to the influence of Egyptian missionaries, we have more to thank the Copts for than has been imagined.'[1]

Even when we review Coptic heresies and heretics, it behoves us to consider how these ardent sons of the Nile, when forbidden from practising the beliefs of their sects within the Pax Romana, crossed the frontiers of the empire to the unknown realms of the barbarians, where they freely preached Christianity in accordance with their convictions. Perhaps the most striking feature in the history of the barbarians as they descended on the Roman Empire was the spread of Arianism in their midst. It is true that the Goths, Visigoths, Vandals, Burgundians and Lombards must have had their apostles of Arian Christianity. Perhaps the best-known is Ulphilas (ca. 311–83), apostle to the Goths, who was probably of Cappadocian birth but who knew their language as well as Greek and translated the Bible into the Gothic tongue for the first time. But Arianism, it must be remembered, was purely an Alexandrine creation, and its founder was the heresiarch Arius, a Libyan native of Alexandria. It is only logical to assume that the followers of Arius or their disciples were responsible for the spread of that heresy from Egypt to the Germanic and barbarian tribes beyond the Danube and Rhine.[2]

Œcumenical Movement

Few topics in religious history have aroused such endless and ardent controversy as the œcumenical movement, beginning with Nicæa in 325 and

[1] *Cairo – Sketches of its History, Monuments and Social Life* (London, 1898), pp. 203–4. Bishop Samuel of the Coptic Church, who visited that area, tells me that the 'Book of Leinster' in the Royal Irish Academy, Dublin, contains a litany which says 'Seven Egyptian monks in Disert Ullaigh, I invoke unto my aid through Jesus Christ.' Three other MSS. include similar supplications, and a fourth contains a guide to Irish pilgrims to the desert of Scetis in the Nitrean Valley. He further assures me that one MS. placed the apostolic sees in the following order: Jerusalem, Alexandria, Antioch and Rome. It would be interesting systematically to carry the enquiry further. The initials and miniatures still show the influence of Coptic art on Irish art; see F. S. Henry, *Irish Art in the Christian Period* (London, 1939). Kenneth Mildenberger, 'Unity of Cynewulf's Christ in the Light of Iconography', in *Speculum*, XXIII, no. 3 (July, 1948), 426–32, reveals the influence of Coptic iconography on Northumbrian monastic art and religious culture, and accidentally provides us with another milestone in construing the Egyptian missionary enterprise in Ireland and Britain, which is the only explanation to his interesting thesis.

[2] E. A. Thompson, 'Christianity and the Northern Barbarians', in *The Conflict between Paganism and Christianity in the Fourth Century*, pp. 56–78.

ending with Chalcedon in 451. The attempt to eradicate heresy and doctrinal differences from the various centres of Christianity was accomplished in the first three councils, of Nicæa (325), Constantinople (381) and Ephesus (431). The formulation of the Nicæan Creed, that enduring charter of the faith, became universally accepted, and the christological definition and relation of the divine and human natures in the person of Jesus by Cyril the Great was sanctioned at Ephesus. From the standpoint of a historian of the Coptic Church, the important feature of those councils was the fact that they were dominated by the spiritual and intellectual leadership of Alexandria. Home of the Catechetical School and chief centre of theological discourse, Alexandria proved to be the fountain-head of Christian scholarship and subsequently of Christian authority. The position imparted by that pre-eminence gave the patriarchs of the Egyptian Church enormous power both within their own country and in the Christian world at large. They became what has been ingeniously described as 'the pharaohs[1] of the Church', a status which alarmed the bishops of Rome and Constantinople. It was at this point that the heritage of Athanasius and Cyril fell into the hands of Dioscorus, who was not their equal in tact and diplomacy.

The increasing doctrinal differences between East and West were limited to a mere interpretation of the degree of unity of the divine and human natures in the person of Christ. As a reaction to Nestorianism, Eutyches (ca. 378–454), a pious archimandrite of a Greek monastery in Constantinople, espoused the view of the unity of the two natures in one solely divine nature since the Incarnation. Flavian, bishop of Constantinople, immediately excommunicated and deposed him in a local synod. But Eutyches had influence in the imperial palace through a highly placed eunuch named Chrysaphius, who succeeded in persuading Theodosius II to call a general council to reconsider his case under the leadership of Dioscorus. Dioscorus accepted the invitation, and the second meeting at Ephesus[2] took place in 449. It is fitting here to give up the Coptic view of the council's transactions. Representatives of Rome, Antioch, Constantinople and most of the other Christian bishoprics of both East and West in addition to the Egyptian delegation of ten bishops converged on Ephesus in response to an imperial request. Eutyches was summoned to speak for himself. Moving from his earlier position of incorporating the human entirely in the divine nature, he proclaimed the Nicæan Creed and the formula of St Cyril, both recognized as the orthodox doctrine. Thus he was acquitted and reinstated in his former position by the council. The result of the verdict was the deposition of Bishop Flavian and his supporters and their abuse by the imperial guard, probably through the influence of Chrysaphius.

[1] Term used by some historians; see, for example, Hardy, pp. 79 ff.
[2] Mansi, VI, 503 ff.; Hefele, II, pt. 1, 555 ff.

This further step in the assertion of Alexandrian supremacy, perhaps indiscreetly flaunted by Dioscorus, incurred the abusive description of the whole meeting as a *Latrocinium* ('highway robbery') in a letter sent by Pope Leo to the emperor. Dioscorus was probably unwise to overlook the 'Tome of Leo', which the Roman delegates brought with them. However, it must be remembered that the change of emperors at this very moment worked miracles. The death of Theodosius II and the succession of Marcian (450–7) and his wife Pulcheria, a former nun and sister of the deceased emperor, reversed the imperial ecclesiastical policy. The Council of Chalcedon[1] was consequently summoned in 451, not to discuss the unity or duality of the natures of Christ, but to try Dioscorus for what was regarded as a conciliatory attitude toward the initial Eutychian thesis, in spite of the legality of the Ephesian procedure and the adherencce of the Copts to Cyril's formula of the unity of the two natures. Politics played a prominent part in regard to the expanding and menacing influence of Alexandria, and imperial authority brought together in 451 more than six hundred bishops at Chalcedon, across the Bosphorus from Constantinople. The Tome of Leo was read, Dioscorus was summarily condemned even without a hearing, then deposed and in 454 exiled to the island of Gangra in Paphlagonia. Even the bishops who had signed the verdict of the second Council of Ephesus were constrained to sanction the Chalcedonian decision, save for the Copts, who abstained in fear of their congregations on their return home.

The council then issued twenty-eight canons, the last of which was the most significant, since it decreed 'that the city which was honoured with the sovereignty and the senate, and which enjoyed equal privileges with the elder royal Rome, should also be magnified, like her, in ecclesiastical matters, and be second after her'.[2] Thus the sixth canon of Nicæa which insisted on 'the preservation of the rights and privileges of the bishops of Alexandria, Antioch, and other provinces',[3] was abrogated in the favour of Constantinople.

Dealing with the œcumenical movement William Worrell points out: 'The See [of Alexandria] was the most important in the Church, as the city was the most important in the whole of the East. To the prestige of ancient Egypt and Hellenistic Alexandria were added the reputation for Christian learning and the power of leadership.'[4] As to Chalcedon, he adds: 'It was

[1] Schwartze, II (Concilium universale Chalcedonense); Mansi, VI, 528 ff.; Hefele, II, pt. 2, 649 ff.; R. V. Sellers, *The Council of Chalcedon* (London, 1953); A. Grillmeier and H. Bacht, *Das Konzil von Chalcedon*, 3 vols. (Würzburg, 1951–4); Tixeront, III, 76–123.

[2] E. H. Landon, *A Manual of Councils of the Holy Catholic Church*, 2 vols. (Edinburgh, 1909), Vol. I, p. 197. This was presumably rejected by the Catholic delegates, and the pope later did not sanction so great an advancement for Constantinople; A. Fortescue, *Lesser Eastern Churches*, pp. 180–1.

[3] Landon, I, p. 408.

[4] *A Short Account of the Copts* (Michigan, 1945), p. 17.

here that the Egyptian church lost its leadership. The action taken at Chalcedon was chiefly due to Pope Leo I (440–61). The Alexandrines were used to having their way, and would not be governed by the Council. Native Egypt was united behind the Patriarch of Alexandria. National feelings were involved. Thus the national church of Egypt began.'[1]

The Copts believe[2] that behind the triumph of the West was a great deal of political manœuvring and personal interest. As Rome leaned toward the two natures, the Nestorian bishops, including the Antiochenes, were won over. The relatively new see of Constantinople, supported by the emperor for obvious reasons, assumed the next place to Rome by humiliating Dioscorus. To this day the Copts remember the tragedy of Chalcedon with acrimony, and protest against the assumption that they are Eutychians; many of their prelates, old and new, reject the basic elements of Eutychianism as much as they attack the doctrines of Nestorianism. They never denied the existence of the two natures, but insisted on their unity. It is difficult even to see the shadowy differences between the varied interpretations of Cyril's accepted authority. The Copts deny the œcumenicity of Chalcedon and all subsequent councils. They reject the Chalcedonian profession as a breach of faith contrary to the spirit of the Nicæan Creed and the decisions of Ephesus. They never called themselves 'monophysite', a spiteful term more fitting for Eutychianism which the Greeks and Romans invented for the humiliation of the Copts and their allies, the Jacobites, the Ethiopians and the Armenians. Strangely enough, the Copts refrained from fighting that novel epithet, but seemed rather ready to accept it as a sign of distinction from the 'diophysite' Christians.

The net result of the decisions taken at Chalcedon was irreparable schism. And since the Copts hold that they had never been subject to Rome, but only parallel, the terms 'schismatic' and 'dissident', often used by the Roman Catholic historians to describe the sister Coptic church, are repudiated by the so-called 'monophysites' as objectionable allegations. To the Coptic mind, the apostolic sees of Alexandria, Antioch and Rome were of equal status, and as such had all lived in perfect harmony and sustained mutual regard toward each other, even in the days when Alexandria was beyond a shadow of doubt pre-eminent.

If Chalcedon had another result beyond schism, this was to accelerate the nascent Egyptian nationalism within the pale of the native Coptic Church. Contemporary with the œcumenical movement was the spreading of the monastic rule within Egypt and beyond its frontiers. Monasticism, a purely

[1] Op. cit., p. 18.

[2] The Coptic view is expressed in a work in Arabic on 'The Age of Councils' published by Kirollos al-Anṭūni (Cairo, 1952), then a monk of the Monastery of St Antony near the Red Sea and now assuming the name of Basileus, Coptic archbishop of Jerusalem.

Egyptian creation with world potential, proved in the century after Chalcedon to be a potent factor fanning the flame of nationalism.

Of both nationalism and monasticism in the social and religious life of the Copts, more must be said. It would however be wrong to end this sad chapter in the story of Christian disunity on these depressing notes, when two august modern prelates of the Roman Catholic Church, John XXIII and Paul VI, have openly promoted the cause of reconciliation of the churches of Eastern Christendom in the present Vatican Council. Pope Paul's address of 30 September 1963 to the second Vatican Council seems to arouse greater expectations of reunion of the sister churches than anything since Chalcedon. Indeed, if a Paul VI had been present at Chalcedon in 451, the stream of history might have been deflected into the direction of bridging rather than unbridging gaps. His impressive appearance in the Council, with the episcopal mitre rather than the papal tiara, is a significant act of humility that impels admiration and recalls to mind the constitution of primitive apostolic churches, where the *Episcopus Romanorum* stood before the throne of Jesus Christ in line with the other bishops of the great cities of antiquity.

Monastic Rule

Coptic monasticism[1] was truly the gift of Egypt to Christendom. Like all movements of universal importance, that religious system evolved over a period of time and in successive stages. From its modest beginnings on the edge of the desert, it developed into a way of life the wonder of Christian antiquity. Most writers ascribe the origins of monasticism to St Antony (ca. 251–356), who is supposed to have been the first to retire to the eastern desert of Middle Egypt and whose fame was spread by his famous biography written by St Athanasius. Without minimizing the place of Antony in the story of monachism, there is reason to believe that organized flights to the

[1] For the sources and general history of Coptic monasticism until the year 1950, see Kammerer's *Coptic Bibliography*, nos. 2476–2569, also nos. 1202–1340, 1620, 2674–75, and 3108. Special reference to particular studies will be made in the following notes with regard to material subsequent to 1950. Most important Arabic source ed. and tr. by B. T. A. Evetts, *The Churches and Monasteries of Egypt and Some Neighbouring Countries, attributed to Abu Ṣāleh the Armenian* (Oxford, 1895). A. M. J. Festugière, *Historia Monachorum in Aegypto* (Subsidia hagiographica No. 34; Brussels, 1961). Of general interest is the selection made by R. Draguet, *Les pères du désert* (Paris, 1949), which superseded Helen Waddell, *The Desert Fathers* (London, 1936). For origins see W. H. Mackean, *Christian Monasticism in Egypt to the Close of the Fourth Century* (London, 1920); J. M. L. Besse, *Les Moines d'Orient antérieurs au Concile de Chalcédoine* (Paris, 1900); Jules Leroy, *Moines et monastères du Proche-Orient* (Paris, 1958), pp. 32–62; K. Heussi, *Der Ursprung des Mönchtums* (Tübingen, 1936); J. Brémond, *Les pères du désert*, 2 vols. (Paris, 1927); Quasten, *Patrology*, Vol. III, pp. 146–89; Otto F. A. Meinardus, *Monks and Monasteries of the Egyptian Deserts* (Cairo, 1961).

desert must have been coterminous with the age of persecution. An instance is cited in the reign of Emperor Antoninus Pius (138–61), when a certain Frontonius decided to reject the world and was able to persuade seventy others to follow him to the Nitrean desert. It is said that St Antony himself, as he went deeper and deeper into the eastern desert around the middle of the fourth century, discovered by accident St Paul the Hermit, aged 113 years and about to die. Since his early youth, he had found the perfect life in the solitude of the desert. We must assume that he was one among many others unknown.

Nevertheless the first definable stage in the genesis of Coptic monasticism may be described as 'Antonian monachism', whereby a pious recluse or anchorite took to a solitary life of asceticism and austerity, torturing his body in order to save his soul. The example of St Antony was the most famous, though by no means the only one of his age. An orphan of wealthy Christian parentage from the village of Coma,[1] in the territorial division of Heracleopolis, at the age of twenty, he renounced the world, selling his estate and distributing the proceeds to the poor,[2] keeping back only what was necessary for the subsistence of a younger sister, whom he entrusted to a community of virgins before crossing the Nile to the eastern desert. Apparently he received his first lessons in ascetic devotion from other hermits in the neighbouring desert caves and discarded ancient tombs overlooking the valley. For well-nigh eighty-five years he kept pushing further and further into the desert, and his austerities grew greater, his fasts longer, his combats with the demons more spectacular, according to the reports of his biographer[3] and in keeping with the spirit of the times. A true 'athlete of Christ' his fame spread far and wide, and Athanasius himself came to sit at his feet, while the Emperor Constantine wrote asking for his spiritual support. Antony descended from his cave overlooking the Red Sea into the valley only on two occasions – once in 311 to fortify the faithful during the last persecution of Maximinus, and again in 338, to uphold the Athanasian cause against the seething remnants of Arianism.

Fame brought Antony many disciples who sought his spiritual guidance,

[1] District of Būsh in the province of Beni Suef.

[2] On hearing in church the words of the Gospel of St Matthew (xix, 21): 'Sell that thou hast . . .'

[3] Athanasius, *Vita Sancti Antonii* (Migne, *P.G.* XXVI, 835–976) – numerous editions, translations and selections in various languages, considered spurious by H. Weingarten ('Der Ursprung des Mönchtums in nachconstantinischen Zeitalter', in *Zeitschrift für Kirchengeschichte* (Gotha, 1877), Vol. I, pp. 1–35 and 545–74, but authenticity since established by A. Eichhorn, *Athanasii de Vita Ascetica Testimonia Collecta* (Halle, 1886); R. Meyer, *St Athanasius – The Life of St Anthony* (Westminster, 1950); G. Garitte, *Un témoin important du texte de la Vie de saint Antoine par saint Athanase* (Brussels and Rome, 1939); Meinardus, pp. 17–21. An Arabic translation of the *Vita* with introductory remarks and epilogue is made by Fr. Markus Dawūd (Cairo, 1950).

but they continued to lead solitary lives in the neighbourhood of his cave. Thus we begin to witness the development of numerous settlements of anchorites around the dwelling-places of men of great holiness. These included those driven either consciously or unwittingly by natural impulse toward the gregarious life for self-defence against the hazards of wild beasts, malevolent marauders, or illness without care or assistance. A disabled anchorite alone was doomed, for usually he had to walk in the blistering sands for a day or two to replenish his stock of food and water. In this way, and during Antony's lifetime, there developed the second stage of monastic life, which may be called 'collective eremitism'. These settlements multiplied, the oldest growing around Antony's towering personality in the district of Pispir and spreading eastward into the outer mountains of what is known now as the Arabian desert in the direction of the Red Sea, approximately where the Monastery of St Antony stands to the present day. Another community arose at Chenoboskion, in the Thebaïd near the hermitage of St Palæmon, from whom St Pachomius the Great received his initiation into monastic life. This is roughly the area where the treasure of the Gnostic papyri was discovered, not far from the modern city of Nagʿ Ḥamādi. Finally, there were three settlements in the western desert within a day's journey of Alexandria, namely, Nitrea, Cellia and Scetis. The Nitrean colony was founded by Amoun, who is said to have espoused secretly the cause of monasticism after his marriage. For eighteen years he persuaded his young wife to meet him at night but only for watching and praying, and in 325 he retired completely to Nitrea for the next twenty-two years, where monks congregated around him. Cellia, slightly north of Nitrea, was the home of Macarius the Alexandrian, who had spent some years almost naked in the mosquito-infested marshes of Mareotis. His feats of austerity astounded his contemporaries. He died in 393 at the age of one hundred years. It was in Cellia that Arsenius, master of Constantine, came to live. The third settlement was in Scetis, south-east of Nitrea and a forbidding wilderness where St Macarius the Great founded another monastery about 330.[1]

Originally a disciple of St Antony, this second Macarius performed superhuman feats of austerity. The *Paradise* of Palladius furnishes the incredible story of Macarius' visit at a later date to a Pachomian monastery in Tabennesis for the forty days of Lent. The abbot admitted the stranger on sufferance owing to his great age. Lent began and the younger brethren vied with one another in fasting, some until vespers, others for two days, others for five. But Macarius stood alone in a corner, plaiting palm-fibres and praying for

[1] Most impressive on this area is the monumental work by H. C. Evelyn-White, *The Monasteries of Wādi 'n Naṭrūn*, 2 vols. (New York, 1926–33). See also C. Martin, 'Les Monastères du Ouadi Natroun', in *Nouvelle Revue Théologique*, LXVIII (1935), 113–34, 328–52.

forty days without touching bread or water, though he ate a few raw cabbage-leaves on Sundays so as not to seem ostentatious. He neither slept nor knelt nor spoke. The humiliated brethren thus approached the abbot, rebelliously asking the expulsion of that strange creature on the threat of leaving themselves. When Pachomius heard their story, he realized who the visitor was. Then he sped to his oratory and kissed him and thanked him for exposing the conceit of his youngsters and for edifying his congregation. Before allowing him to leave, he asked for his prayers; then Macarius departed.[1]

Other less imposing settlements of hermits emerged in various parts of the country, such as those at Babylon, Memphis, Heracleopolis and Oxyrynchus. But, in the meantime, a new chapter in the story of monasticism was beginning at Tabennesis. This was associated with the name of Pachomius. Born a pagan and serving as a youth in the armies of Constantine and Licinius, Pachomius[2] was exposed to the communities of Christians during his campaigns. The goodness of those Christians who came to wash the soldiers' feet and offer them food in spite of their harsh treatment of the poor villagers seems to have impressed the young Pachomius who resolved to join them as soon as he was released. Later he was converted to Christianity and, in the zeal of a new convert, followed the famous hermit Palæmon, who trained him in the art of self-inflicted torture. In the process his mind was opened to a new revelation. He perceived that solitary life and torture and famine were not the only possible roads to heaven; and if he were to inaugurate a combination of asceticism and cœnobitic, or communal, life, he might recruit a greater number of pious men with a useful purpose. Thus was born the rule of St Pachomius (ca. 290–346), surnamed the Great. This was the third and last stage in the development of the monastic ideal. Contemporary ecclesiastical historians declared that he received a tablet with the rule inscribed on it from an angel's hands. That rule, however, like all enduring institutional achievements, was not merely a codified set of regulations but an evolutionary process in which the saint devised solutions to meet emerging

[1] Story quoted by Helen Waddell, pp. 14–16.

[2] L. Th. Lefort, *Les vies coptes de saint Pachôme et de ses premiers successeurs* (Louvain, 1943); idem, *Œuvres de S. Pachôme et de ses disciples* (Corpus Scriptorum Christianorum Orientalium, Vol. 100; Scriptores Coptici, T. 24; Louvain, 1956); *Pachomiana: Commémoration du XVIème Centenaire de St Pacôme l'Égyptien* (348–1948) (Publications du Centre d'Études Orientales de la Custodie Françiscaine de la Terre-Sainte, Coptica 3; Cairo, 1955); F. Halkin, *S. Pachomii Vitæ Graecæ* (Brussels, 1932); E. Amélineau, *Histoire de St Pakhôme et de ses communautés, Documents coptes et arabes inédits* (Annales du Musée Guimet, 17; Paris, 1889); P. Ladeuze, *Étude sur le Cénobitisme pakhômien pendant le quatrième siècle et la première moitié du cinquième* (Louvain, 1898); G. Grutzmacher, *Pachomius und das älteste Klosterleben, Ein Beitrag zu Mönchsgeschichte* (Freiburg and Leipzig, 1896); A. Boon, *Pachomiana Latina, Règle et épitres de St Pachôme, épitre de St Théodore et Liber de St Oriesius* (Louvain, 1932); J. Doresse, 'Monastères coptes thébains', in *Revue des Conférences Françaises en Orient* (Novembre, 1949), pp. 3–16.

problems. St Pachomius presents us with all the qualities of his own life and experience: as a soldier who knew discipline, an educator who appreciated knowledge, an administrator who organized his communities with a practical dexterity, and a holy man who appreciated the virtues of prayer and a perfect life. When he died in 346, he left behind him a large number of monasteries teeming with formidable communities, and his system spread from Tabennesis to all the other monastic centres. Figures are always deceptive when we deal with those remote annals. One modest record, however, states that the Pachomian foundation in Tabennesis housed 7,000 monks, Mount Nitrea 5,000, and Arsinoë over 10,000.[1] Another report in 394 said that the dwellers of the desert equalled the populations of the towns, and enthusiasm ran high everywhere.

A brief analysis of the rule of St Pachomius may be given as one of the great landmarks in the history of Christianity. The general trend of the Pachomian system showed the soldier and the holy man combined in one person. Every detail of the monk's activity by day and night was prescribed by the legislator: the brother's dress, his food, the hours and manner of his sleep, his travels, his hours of worship, and a penal code to be rigorously enforced against all defaulters. Yet Pachomius was no inhuman giant who imposed a merciless regime on his followers. As he watched the ghastly practices of the Antonian and Palæmonian anchorites during his early days, his heart was moved toward the humanization of monasticism. A monk must curb the body, but it was unnecessary for him to destroy it in pursuit of

[1] Waddell, pp. 7–8; Hardy, p. 92, on the authority of Palladius quotes the number of 7,500 monks for the districts of Alexandria and Nitrea and an equal number for the Thebaïd and other places that he visited. The figure of 10,000 monks and 20,000 virgins who took the veil in Oxyrynchus alone on the authority of the *Historia Monachorum* by Rufinus and quoted unquestioningly in Butcher's *Story of the Church of Egypt*, Vol. I, p. 195, is questioned by Hardy (loc. cit.), though he estimates the total of the monastic profession at its height loosely between 100,000 and 200,000 out of a population not exceeding 7,500,000, which Josephus recorded in the first century. Hardy mentions the existence of a hundred bishoprics in Egypt at the time. Meinardus (*Monks and Monasteries*, p. 380) estimates the highest figure to have been more than half a million and quotes 10,000 in the Faiyūm according to Rufinus (p. 372), 5,000 in the Nitrean wilderness by Palladius (p. 387). The Thebaïd had 3,000, Bawīṭ 5,000. According to John of Petra (p. 550), Scetis had 3,500, and Cassian's earlier figure is 5,000, but St Jerome's 50,000 is an exaggeration. On the eve of the Arab Conquest, Nikiou in the Delta is reported to have had 700 hermits. The Islamic historian al-Maqrīzī (ca. 1442), writing about the Arab Conquest in the seventh century, mentions that there were 100 monasteries in Wādi al-Naṭrūn alone, though only seven survived in his day, and that 70,000 monks, each carrying his staff, went out of that valley to welcome the conqueror ʿAmr ibn al-ʿĀṣ on his return from Alexandria and to seek his safe-conduct; see his *K͟hiṭaṭ*, 2 vols. (Bulāq, 1270 A.H.), Vol. I, p. 186; cf. ʿUmar Ṭoussoun, *Wādi al-Naṭrūn* (in Arabic; Alexandria, 1935), p. 39, but this number is a clear exaggeration. Other numerical estimates of the Nitrean monks are given as 737 for the year 1075 A.D. and 201 for the year 1924 (ibid., 45, 168). The leaflet of Deir-el-Sourian of 1959 mentions 45 monks in that monastery. Bishop Samuel tells me that its present 1962 number is 30 out of a total of 300 monks in all the Egyptian monasteries.

heaven. While providing for the needs of the life of a brother, the new rule also watched over the salvation of his soul. Celibacy, chastity, devotion, poverty, and obedience were among the prerequisites of a good monk. Perhaps the most revolutionary features in the system were the introduction of manual labour, and a considerable measure of education in the cenobitic life of the monks. During the probationary period of one to three years a novice had to prove the seriousness of his intention before acceptance. Apart from sharing in the ways of the community, he was requested to learn how to read and write, and also to memorize twenty psalms and two epistles of the New Testament. Illiteracy was banned in Pachomian cœnobitism.

The monk had to be a useful human being and must labour for his daily bread and enrich his mind, without neglecting his spiritual duties. A customary occupation was basket-weaving and rope-making, though the monastery was usually a self-contained unit with its bakers and cooks, weavers and tailors, farmers and millers, masons and carpenters, smiths and mechanics, even scholars and copyists of manuscripts. Bishop Palladius tells us that he saw at the monastery of Panopolis fifteen tailors, seven smiths, four carpenters, fifteen fullers and twelve camel drivers. The Pachomian monastery had the appearance of a vast Roman fortification surrounded by a high and massive wall, on the fringe of the valley or some way within the desert. Next to the great portal was a guest house, within the walls, but outside the inner courtyards reserved for regular monks. Chapels, a community hall, library (or *scriptorium*), refectory, hospital, mill, bakery, kitchen, vestry, shop, varied stores and all manner of buildings clustered around a central keep, or fortified tower, with a drawbridge leaning on to a nearby roof to which the brethren resorted whenever attacked by marauding bedouin tribes. The monastic cells lined the walls. The Pachomian rule placed three monks in a cell, except in the case of recluses who led a solitary life in their own quarters, though the practice was usually discouraged but not completely eliminated by the abbot. A corner was reserved for burial. The rest of the open space was kept for gardening, and open-air labour, which comprised work at the water-wheel, wells and stable.[1]

[1] Apart from gleanings about the structure of a Pachomian monastery, the accounts of some modern travellers are helpful in this regard. In Arabic see the account by two Coptic archæologists, Labīb Ḥabashy and Zaki Tawaḍros, of a 1927 visit to the Eastern Monasteries of St Paul and St Antony, publ. Cairo, 1928; see also ʿUmar Ṭoussoun's work cited in the note above. Most useful among older publications are A. J. Butler, *The Ancient Coptic Churches of Egypt*, 2 vols. (Oxford, 1884); H. G. Evelyn-White, op. cit.; H. E. Winlock, *The Monastery of Epiphaneus at Thebes*, 2 vols. (New York, 1926); U. Monneret de Villard, *Les couvents près de Sohâg*, 2 vols. (Milan, 1925–6); idem, *Il Monastero di S. Simeone presso Aswan* (Milan, 1927); C. M. Kaufmann, *Die Ausgrabung der Menasheiligtümer in der Mareotiswuste*, 3 vols. in 1 (Cairo, 1906–8). The last is a typical early Christian pilgrim city. For modern travellers, see Jules Leroy, op. eit., J. Doresse, 'Deux monastères coptes oubliés: Saint Antoine et Saint Paul dans le désert de la Mer Rouge',

Pachomius aimed at a closely knit government of all his foundations, in order to guard against corruption and material or moral deterioration. Every three or four monasteries within easy reach of one another were united in a clan, with a president elected from among their abbots, and the monks met periodically to discuss their local problems. The clans were united under a superior-general, who was head of the principal monastery. A general assembly was convened twice every year: on the twentieth of the Coptic month of Mesuri (12 August) in the summer for administrative purposes after the harvest; and at Easter when annual reports were given, new superiors were announced and finally, in an impressive scene, a mutual forgiveness of sins was made by the whole brotherhood.

Within the monasteries, in addition to the bulk of Coptic cenobites, there were monks from different nations – Greeks, Romans, Cappadocians, Libyans, Syrians, Nubians, Ethiopians and others. To each nation was accorded a special ward, under the leadership of a fellow citizen who acted for the abbot.

The fathers of the Church from numerous parts of the world flocked to those religious houses for apprenticeship in the art of monasticism. An immense traffic of pilgrims was conducted to the caves of holy men and to regular monasteries in the Egyptian wilderness. Some of the greatest personalities of the age joined this stream of pious men who came to the school of the desert from all countries. Emperors sent representatives, and the great Patriarch Athanasius has already been mentioned. St John Chrysostom (ca. 347–407), bishop of Constantinople, stayed under the Pachomian rule in the Thebaïd from 373 to 381. St Jerome (ca. 342–420)[1] and Rufinus (ca. 345–410),[2] the ecclesiastical historian, came from Italy and spent time in Egypt. St Basil (ca. 330–79),[3] the Cappadocian Father and author of the famous Liturgy bearing his name and still in use in the eastern churches, introduced monasticism into Byzantium on the basis of his Pachomian apprenticeship. St John Cassian (ca. 360–435) passed seven years in the Thebaïd and the Nitrean

in *Revue des Arts* (March, 1952); idem, *Recherches d'archéologie Copte: les monastères de Moyenne Égypte* (Comptes rendus de l'académie des Inscriptions et Belles-Lettres; Paris, 1952). Two small but interesting guides are noteworthy: O. H. E. Burmester, *A Guide to the Monasteries of the Wādi n'Naṭrūn* (Cairo, 1956) and a leaflet entitled 'The Monastery of the Holy Virgin and St John Kané known as Deir-el-Sourian', prepared by the monks in English (Cairo, 1959); cf. Otto Meinardus, *Monks and Monasteries of the Egyptian Deserts* (Cairo, 1961); J. Simon, 'Le monastère copte de Samuel de Kalamon', in *Orientalia Christiana Periodica*, I (1935), 46–52.

[1] *Nicene and Post-Nicene Fathers*, 2nd ser., Vol. III; L. T. Lefort, *Un texte original de la règle de Saint Pachôme* (Paris, 1919).

[2] Rufinus Tyrannius Aquileiensis, *Historia Monachorum, seu, Liber de vitis patrum*, in Migne, *P.L.*, XXI, 389–462; cf. *Nicene and Post-Nicene Fathers*, 2nd ser., Vol. III.

[3] See *Nicene and Post-Nicene Fathers*, 2nd ser., Vol. VII; cf. W. K. L. Clarke, *St Basil the Great: A Study in Monasticism* (Cambridge, 1913); E. F. Morison, *Basil and His Rule: A Study in Early Monasticism* (London, 1912).

desert before introducing monasticism into Gaul and writing his *Institutes* and *Colloquies* from personal experiences with the desert fathers.[1] Palladius (ca. 365–425), bishop of Helenopolis in Bithynia, compiled the lives of the Egyptian saints in his *Lausiac History*,[2] sometimes described as 'The Paradise of the Fathers'.[3] Even women came; among them 'Etherea', the fourth-century Spanish abbess, and Melania (ca. 345–410), the aristocratic Roman widow.[4]

The rule of St Pachomius, which took the lead in the world, and the Pachomian community which became so international in character, strangely enough gave rise to a stricter rule of national importance in the fifth century. This rule was associated with the name of St Shenūte of Atripe,[5] who succeeded his uncle Pgol, founder of the White Monastery, across the Nile from the ancient city of Panopolis and just outside the new city of Sūhāg, in 383. He died either in 451 or 466,[6] showing at any rate that he held the helm for more than sixty-five years, during which time he developed his own rule of more austerity and intense manual labour. He accumulated enough wheat in his granaries to feed armies of refugees[7] from the Blemye invaders of Upper Egypt. He lived at one of the most critical moments in Egyptian history, when paganism lost its last round with the destruction of the *Serapeum* and the massacre of Hypatia in 415. In Upper Egypt, he responded by leading an army of his monks in wrecking the ancient pagan monuments and temples. This was also the age of the œcumenical councils, and Shenūte presumably accompanied Cyril the Great to Ephesus in 431. The tragedy of Chalcedon occurred in 451, followed by the rise of the so-called Coptic 'monophysitism', which intensified the nationalist temper of Shenūte, and he then started a deliberate movement to purge both the Coptic liturgies and literature of

[1] See note above.

[2] C. Butler, *The Lausiac History of Palladius*, 2 vols. (Cambridge, 1898–1904). See also Kammerer's *Bibliography*, nos. 1179–81, 2530, 2557, 2565.

[3] This is really an old compilation from Palladius and other Fathers. E. A. T. Wallis Budge, tr., *The Book of Paradise* . . ., 2 vols. (London, 1904); idem, *The Paradise of the Fathers* . . ., 2 vols. (London, 1907; rev. edn. Oxford, 1934); idem, *The Wit and Wisdom of the Christian Fathers of Egypt* (Oxford, 1934).

[4] See articles on Etherea and Melania in *The Oxford Dictionary of the Christian Church*, ed. F. L. Cross (Oxford, 1957).

[5] Atripe, or Atribe, is situated on the west bank of the Nile by the modern Sūhāg, facing Panapolis, or Ikhmīm.

[6] On the problem of dates, see J. Leipoldt, *Schenute von Atripe und die Entstehung des national ägyptischen Christentums* (Leipzig, 1903), pp. 44 ff.; J. F. Bethune-Baker, 'The Date of the Death of Nestorius, Schenute, Zacharias, Evagrius', in *Journal of Theological Studies*, IX (Oxford, 1908), 601 ff.; K. H. Kuhn, *Letters and Sermons of Besa* (Corpus Scriptorium Christianorum Orientalium, 158, Scriptores Coptici, 22; Louvain, 1956), p. 1. Besa was the immediate successor of Shenūte as abbot of the White Monastery, and his work illustrates the austerity of the new rule.

[7] Milne, *Roman Egypt*, pp. 223–25, cites 20,000 men, women and children for three months and the use of 85,000 artabas of wheat besides other material.

every element of Greek. He was a tireless preacher and a prolific writer whose works made Sahidic Coptic the elegant language of writing, as against the I<u>kh</u>mīmic, which became that of colloquial speech. He was not a theologian of consequence, but rather a moralist, an administrator, and an inveterate enemy of heathenism and Hellenism. His followers numbered more than two thousand monks and a couple of thousand nuns,[1] all of purely Coptic origin; which fact accounts for the absence of his name from all the European literature of the time concerning the Fathers of the Desert.[2] From the Coptic standpoint, however, if we accept the authority of Worrell, he was 'the most remarkable man whom the Copts ever produced, the founder indeed of Coptic Christianity':[3] a verdict to be accepted only with reservations, though his further remark that 'Shenūte was also the greatest of all writers in the Coptic language'[4] is indisputable.

Monasticism has survived in Egypt, and has given the Coptic Church an unbroken line of 116 patriarchs beginning with St Mark around the middle of the first century. Though the Copts have been preyed upon by the Greeks and Romans, and in modern times by all manner of Protestant missionaries, they are still a standing monument to primitive apostolic Christianity. It is true that most of their monasteries have disappeared, and that the Pachomian rule has lost its ancient fire; but there is a revival in the surviving monasteries with their modern recruits from the educated class. Of the monasteries still intact and inhabited by groups of Coptic monks, there are four in the Nitrean Valley in the western desert, two in the eastern desert bearing the names of St Paul the Hermit and St Antony the Great, and the Monastery of Our Lady, known as al-Muḥarraq, on the western edge of the valley in the neighbourhood of the city of Asiūṭ. They are all monuments of Christian antiquity. The White Monastery and the Red Monastery[5] stand where they were in the age of Shenūte, in tolerably good condition, but are now used only as churches with no resident monks.

Recent attempts have been made, notably under the sponsorship of the present 'Pope' and Patriarch Kirollos, or Cyril VI, both before and after his consecration, to restore St Samuel's monastery in the wilderness of Antinoë. He has also aimed at re-establishing the cathedral of St Mena, built by Emperor Arcadius (395–408). Both sites have been excavated. Other monastic

[1] Hardy, p. 102; Meinardus, p. 380, mentions 2,200.

[2] *Sinuthii Archimandritæ vita et opera omnia*, ed. J. Leipoldt and tr. H. Wiesmann, 4 vols. (Paris, 1906–31). See Kammerer, nos. 1195–1206, 1557–8, 1564–5, 2480, 2526–7, 2537, 2710.

[3] Worrell, *Short Account of Copts*, p. 22. The founder of Sahidic literature was presumably Pachomius (ibid., p. 16), for he and his Coptic disciples did not write in Greek, but Shenūte was much more prolific than all his predecessors in that dialect.

[4] Ibid. l.c.

[5] Not far from the White Monastery, built in red brick, under the abbacy of Apa Pshai; Worrell, p. 20.

sites excavated, with important artistic yields, include the fifth-century St Jeremias' at Saqqāra;[1] Bawīṭ[2] founded in the western desert by Apa Apollo, who died in 315; and St Simeon's at Aswān. The Metropolitan Museum has conducted excavations at St Ephiphaneus, near Thebes, and at the monasteries of Wādi al-Naṭrūn.[3] The Coptic Archæological Society explored the area where once St Phœbamon's Monastery stood, also near Thebes.[4] Moreover, a whole monastic settlement must have been located at the distant El-Bagawat necropolis in the Kharja Oasis in the western desert. This has already been excavated, and a remarkable description of the findings published.[5]

In Wādi al-Naṭrūn alone, the older histories mention fifty monasteries, and the late Prince ʿUmar Toussoun[6] seems to have identified at least twenty-five of them in the unexcavated mounds within the valley. In the fifteenth century, Maqrīzi[7] enumerated eighty-six monasteries in the whole of Egypt, but the original number must have been much greater. Some Coptic archæologists[8] estimate them at 365, for both monks and nuns. Five nunneries survive, and all are situated in the region of Cairo.[9] The task of bringing the ruins of those still unknown or unidentified establishments to the light of day is in its infancy, but the enduring impact of the Coptic Fathers of the Desert on world history is a living reality.

[1] Now mostly in the Coptic Museum; M. H. Smaika, *A Brief Guide to the Coptic Museum* (Cairo, 1938). The earlier Arabic edition in 2 vols. (Cairo, 1930–2) is fuller.

[2] See above note on Bawīṭ treasures in Coptic Museum, also some articles in the Louvres: J. des Graviers, 'Inventaire des objets coptes de la salle de Baouit au Louvres', in *Rivista di Archeologia Cristiana*, IX (1932), 51–103; G. Mounereau, 'La Salle copte de Baouit', in *Chronique d'Égypte*, V, 9 (1930), 115–16, repr. from *Écho de Paris*.

[3] See above notes 1, p. 61, and 1, p. 64, on the works of both Winlock and Evelyn-White.

[4] Publications of the Coptic Archæological Society (Cairo).

[5] Aḥmad Fakhry, *The Necropolis of El-Bagawāt in Khargo Oasis* (publ. Service des Antiquités de l'Égypte; Cairo, 1951).

[6] *Wādī al Naṭrun: Its Monks, Monasteries and Summary of the History of the Patriarchs* (in Arabic), pp. 48 ff.; he estimates an average of 100 monks per monastery.

[7] Macrizi, *Geschichte der Kopten*, ed. and tr. F. Wüstenfeld (Göttingen, 1846); see tr., pp. 85–117 on monasteries.

[8] Zaki Tawaḍros and Labīb Ḥabashi, p. 28. This figure is the one accepted by most Copts. Many ancient ruins are seen on the edge of the desert plateau in Upper Egypt. They are little known and may be remains of monastic cenobia.

[9] Listed by Wahīb ʿAṭalla Girgis, pp. 140–1, as follows: first, two convents of St Mary and St George at Ḥāret Zuwaila in Cairo; secondly, Convent of Ḥāret El-Roum in Cairo; thirdly, Convents of Abu El-Seyfein (St Mercurius) and of Mari Girgis (St George) in Old Cairo.

4 • AFTERMATH OF CHALCEDON

Monophysitism *versus* Diophysitism

The immediate outcome of the Chalcedon decisions in 451 was the first great schism of the Apostolic Church. The East was branded by the West as Monophysite, while the West was described by the East as Diophysite. The rise of the so-called 'Monophysitism' in the East was of course led by the Copts of Egypt. This must be regarded as the outward expression of the growing nationalist trends in that province against the gradual intensification of Byzantine imperialism, soon to reach its consummation during the reign of Justinian (527–65). Interesting as they may be to the student of divinity, the theological controversies between the 'Monophysites' in Alexandria and the 'Diophysites' in Rome and Constantinople have been unduly overrated as the root of the cleavage between the Eastern and Western Churches. Consequently the historical factors in this intricate picture have suffered and some facets of the real issue have been overshadowed by purely religious considerations. To this day the Copts hold the view that the differences magnified at Chalcedon and after never justified a widening doctrinal gap between sister sees.

The Copts consistently repudiate the Western identification of Alexandrine Christianity with the Eutychianism which originated in Constantinople, and which they have always regarded as a flagrant heresy, since it declared the complete absorption of Christ's manhood in His single divine nature, whereas the Copts clearly upheld the doctrine of the two natures – divine and human – mystically united in one, without confusion, corruption, or change. As a strictly traditional church, its religious leaders have sought biblical justification for this interpretation of the Nicæan Creed and the Cyrillian formula, but meanwhile have restricted the substance of their variance to interpretation. Those who can read the Coptic sources,[1] both in

[1] The official Coptic interpretation has been made by Wahīb A. Girgis (now Fr. Pakhoum A. El-Moḥarraḳy), *The Christological Teaching of the Non-Chaldedonian Churches* (in Arabic and English; Cairo, 1962); Kirollos El-Anṭouny (now Archbishop Basileus of Jerusalem), *The Age of the Œcumenical Councils* (in Arabic; Cairo, 1952), pp. 172 ff. See

Coptic and in Arabic, rather than study their doctrinal outlook through secondary works by members of the opposite camp,[1] are left wondering whether political and ecclesiastical authority was not behind the unnatural exaggeration of existing differences between the two professions.

In fact, unless we study the main events more deeply the real issues at stake will continue to be drowned in vociferous arguments and mutual accusations on both sides. That the East, or more precisely, the Alexandrine Fathers of the Coptic Church, had led the way in the first three crucial œcumenical councils, seems to be a foregone conclusion which needs no elaboration. That a fourth meeting, at Ephesus, should again be dominated by the Coptic element appeared to strike a note of alarm in the imperial cities of Rome and Constantinople. The subsequent fury of the West over the second Council of Ephesus was demonstrated in its rather impulsive description of it as a 'robber council'. This may help to explain the unusual efforts exerted by the empire and the Western Church to assemble so great an army of bishops (approximately six hundred) as was convened at Chalcedon to reverse the decisions made in 449 and to re-assert the religious supremacy of the seat of empire over provincial insubordination. Parallel to its doctrinal decisions, Chalcedon generated a historic by-product of very grave character. The first defeat sustained by Egypt in the œcumenical field, and the humiliation, deposition and exile of its native Patriarch Dioscorus, were followed by the installation of a successor in the see of Alexandria in the person of Proterius (452–7), a docile friend of Byzantine imperialism, by means of brutal military force. The Egyptians immediately responded by the election of a rival native patriarch Timothy Aelurus. Consequently, the hitherto united bishopric of Alexandria was split between two lines of patriarchal succession. The Melkite, or royalist, line was Greek and originated from Constantinople while obeying Chalcedon. The other, described as 'Monophysite', was native and stood fast by the national cause of the Egyptian people while repudiating Greek hegemony and the Chalcedonian profession. It was thus

---

also below under the Jacobites, ch. 9, n. 26, reference to the Indian Fr. V. C. Samuel, who wrote a Yale thesis on the Christology of Severus of Antioch and suggested the term 'Meaphysitism' to convey the sense of union rather than the misnomer of 'Monophysitism'. A secular writer in Arabic, Fransis El-ʿItr, voices the same traditional Coptic view but selects his supporting documents from purely Roman Catholic sources; cf. his *The Coptic Nation and its Orthodox Church* (Cairo, 1953), pp. 39–63.

[1] The Western outlook on 'Monophysitism' appears in most of the Roman, Greek and even Protestant works, both theological and historical; e.g., A Fortescue, *The Lesser Eastern Churches* (London, 1913), pp. 163 ff.; A. A. Luce, *Monophysitism, Past and Present: A Study in Christology* (London, 1913); J. Maspéro, *Histoire des patriarches d'Alexandrie* (Paris, 1923), pp. 1 ff., 182 ff.; W. A. Wigram, *The Separation of the Monophysites* (London, 1923).

within the pale of the Church that the already-emerging Egyptian nationalism became accelerated in its progress.[1]

At the beginning, the central secular authority took the movement rather lightly and thought that sectarian heterodoxy could easily be mended. But the seriousness of the position became clear when the Alexandrian populace seized the opportunity presented by the Prefect's entanglement in the wars with the Vandals in North Africa and the Blemyes in the Thebaïd, to pounce on the unguarded and unhappy Proterius, assassinate him, drag his body through the city streets, burn it, and cast his dust to the winds. Timothy became momentarily the sole patriarch, and his position was strengthened in 475, when the Emperor Zeno was ousted from the capital by Basiliscus, who had strong leanings towards Monophysitism. This situation did not last long. Shortly afterwards Zeno was reinstated, but Timothy Aelurus died in time to escape imperial deposition. Zeno's new candidate was Timothy Salophaciolus in opposition to the nationally elected Peter Mongos. This Timothy died in 481, and the Copts pleaded for their own Peter Mongos as sole patriarch. The unwilling emperor gave them instead a strongly orthodox bishop named John Talaia, who enjoyed support from Rome. The ensuing confusion was even more intensified by the popular choice of another candidate, John of Tabenna, to succeed the deposed Peter. But neither John Talaia nor his new opponent John Tabenna was able to retain favour with the court of Constantinople. The first committed acts of imprudence and fled to Rome, while the other was disregarded by Zeno. At that moment Peter Mongos was in the capital while Acacius (471–89) was bishop of Constantinople. *Rapprochement* between the two leaders was engineered while Zeno began to feel the hopelessness of winning the Monophysites in Alexandria by force. A new device had to be found for the restoration of peace and unity to Church and empire.

The Henoticon

The new device to solve the religious problem was known as the *Henoticon*,[2] that is, Act of Union. In their earlier leanings, both the Emperor Zeno and

[1] E. L. Woodward, *Christianity and Nationalism in the Later Roman Empire* (London, 1916); A. S. Atiya, 'The Coptic Church and the Nationalist Trend in Byzantine Egypt' (in Arabic), in *Bulletin of the Royal Society of Historical Studies*, III, 1 (Cairo, 1950), 1–14; E. R. Hardy, *Christian Egypt*, pp. 111 ff.; Worrell, pp. 26 ff.; Milne, *Egypt under Rome*, pp. 100 ff.; A Fortescue, p. 182; Maria Cramer, *Das Christlich-Koptische Ägypten, Einst und Heute* (Wiesbaden, 1959), pp. 6–15.

[2] S. Salaville, 'L'affaire de l'hénotique ou le premier schisme byzantin au Ve siècle', in *Échos d'Orient*, XVIII (1918), 255–66, 389–97, and XIX (1920), 49–68; A. A. Vasiliev,

the Patriarch Acacius of Constantinople were distinctly Chalcedonian. But the rebellion of Basiliscus, temporary as it was, proved to both beyond doubt the strength of the Monophysites and the importance of pacifying them. It was therefore essential to find a formula that would be acceptable to them in place of the Chalcedonian profession. In fact Peter Mongos and Acacius, the architects of the *Henoticon*, aimed at taking the Church back to pre-Chalcedonian theology, and in 482, without great difficulty they prevailed upon Zeno to approve the new attempt. The text of the *Henoticon* recognized the decisions of the first three œcumenical councils. Both Nestorius and Eutyches and their followers were categorically anathematized. Christ was declared to be of the same nature as the Father, though He combined the human nature therewith. In phrasing the *Henoticon* care was taken to avoid explicit mention of one nature and two natures. An anathema was imposed on 'all who have held, or hold now or at any time, whether in Chalcedon or in any other synod whatsoever, any different belief'.[1] Although Chalcedon was not repudiated outright, the terms of the Act of Union provided an immense step toward Monophysite thinking. The immediate result was a *rapprochement* between the churches of Alexandria and Constantinople, though Rome was extremely unhappy about the whole arrangement.

As soon as people had time to consider these developments, however, it became clear that the official position was not completely representative of both congregations. The Greeks fell somewhat under the spell of decisions made by Pope Felix in a Roman synod of 484 excommunicating Acacius, though the papal delegates to Constantinople were man-handled and imprisoned by Zeno. It was hard for the Greeks to swallow the concessions made to the Monophysites, while the Alexandrians in turn considered that Chalcedon was not openly reversed. Acacius in the meantime reacted by ordering the omission of the Roman bishop's name from the Greek Diptychs, or Eucharistic Liturgies. A breach between Constantinople and Rome—technically known in Roman Catholic literature as the Acacian Schism[2]—followed and lasted for some thirty-five years. In spite of the deaths of Acacius in 489, Peter Mongos in 490, and Zeno in 491, the *Henoticon* was still upheld by the new emperor, Anastasius I (491–518). Successive bishops of Constantinople were made to sign the *Henoticon* on their nominations, and Monophysite leanings remained the order of the day until Timothy of Constantinople and Emperor Anastasius died in 518. This was precisely the period in

---

History of the Byzantine Empire, 224–1453 A.D. (Madison, Wisc., 1952), pp. 107 ff.; Fortescue, pp. 193 ff.; Hardy, pp .118–19; C. Lagier, *L'Orient Chrétien*, 2 vols.: (1) *dès Apôtres jusqu'à Photius, 33–850* A.D., (2) *de Photius à l'Empire Latin de Constantinople, 850–1204* A.D. (Paris, 1935–50), Vol. I, pp. 284–5.

[1] Cf. Vasiliev, p. 108.

[2] Fortescue, pp. 193–9.

which Severus of Antioch (512–18) became the eloquent exponent of Monophysitism in his famous theological discourses.

A reaction took place on the accession of Emperor Justin I (518–27), assisted by his nephew Justinian, both of whom were Chalcedonians. Severus was deposed in Antioch, and saved his life only by becoming a hunted fugitive at Alexandria. Reunion with Rome was arranged by Pope Hormisdas, who sent delegates to the imperial court in Constantinople with yet another formula in which he cursed and condemned Eutyches and Nestorius equally, as well as Dioscorus, Acacius, and all the other Monophysites.

Justinian[1] (527–65), on succeeding to the throne, assumed the responsibility for action in the religious disputes. The new emperor represented the consummation of Byzantine imperialism. A great lawgiver, he was also a theologian of no mean merit. He was determined to restore unity in the Church as a fundamental step toward the realization of his theocratic aspirations and authority. From the beginning he leaned toward Chalcedon, though he refrained from quarrelling with Monophysitism. One very important factor in the picture was Empress Theodora, who was secretly a Monophysite, and who defended Monophysitism and its upholders with every possible means in her power without openly antagonizing the Emperor. Though Procopius of Cæsarea, who wrote the secret history of the imperial court at the time, provides a most scandalous portrait of the empress, Theodora must have been profoundly interested in religion, a trait she shared with her husband. Her influence was considerable in shaping the religious policy of the empire. She persuaded Justinian to attempt a theological reconciliation of the hostile groups, and in 533 Severus felt safe enough to come to Constantinople at the head of a strong delegation from Egypt for that purpose, but nothing decisive was accomplished.

To please the Monophysites and attract them to unity, Justinian issued an edict in 544, in which three pillars of Nestorianism were condemned. These are known as the Three Chapters[2] (*Tria Kephalaia*), namely, Theodore of Mopsuestia, Theodoret of Cyrus and Ibas of Edessa. The East readily accepted their condemnation, while the West oscillated between condoning or rejecting the edict. Vigilius, bishop of Rome (540–55), happened to be the scapegoat in the ensuing muddle. He was raised to the papacy by Theodora's machination through the agency of the famous general Belisarius, while he was fighting the Goths in Italy. The price of his elevation, after much vacillation and frustration, was his signature on the condemnation of the Three Chapters; an act which infuriated the Roman bishops, and even created a schism in the Roman hierarchy. Vigilius, virtually a captive in

[1] Vasiliev, pp. 148–54; L. Bréhier, 'La politique religieuse de Justinien', in *Histoire de l'Église depuis les origines jusqu'à nos jours* (ed. A. Fliche and V. Martin, IV, Paris, 1948), pp. 437 ff.; Lagier, I, 291 ff.

[2] Fortescue, pp. 199–208.

Constantinople for most of the time, was set free, to die of exhaustion at Syracuse on his way to Rome. His successor, Pelagius I (555–61), was forced to confirm his acceptance of Justinian's edict. As a result, the western schism persisted in Africa, Illyricum, Milan and Tuscany. It was not completely mended until 606. In fact, the whole issue of the Three Chapters began to quieten down only after Justinian's death and the accession of Emperor Justin II (565–78), who published another *Henoticon* in 571.

The conditions and policies within Egypt during that period were marked by the complete disorganization of administration, furthered by religious differences that ultimately became identified with the political rifts. The Melkites were supported by imperial forces, whereas the Monophysites had their own armies of monks. The monasteries gradually came into possession of vast property in land, and the monks were dedicated producers and farmers. The imperial prefects were harassed from within by the nationalist Monophysites, while the Persians, the barbarians and the Blemyes hovered like vultures on the frontiers. To relieve the prefects from the resultant confusion, Justinian divided the country into two sections, entrusting the north (Alexandria and the Delta) to one prefect, and Upper Egypt, or more precisely the Thebaïd, to another. His aim was to lighten the burden of administration on a single prefect. Instead he sowed the seeds of local rivalry and civic disorganization between two governors of one province. But this was not the end of his innovations. When he nominated Apollinarius to the see of Alexandria in 541, he invested him concurrently with prefectural military powers to enable him to enforce religious policies by arms without dependence on secular authority. Furthermore, the Melkite patriarch was given the right to collect direct taxes for the maintenance of churches and for pastoral care. In addition to causing increased confusion in the administration of Egypt, these changes set a dangerous precedent for subsequent emperors. They gave the Church authorities the tools by which they could renew a fresh phase in the age of persecution, this time between Christian and Christian, with immeasurable consequences. The native Monophysites were embittered by this new policy. Actually it is said that that tragedy was inaugurated in the lifetime of Bishop Apollinarius, who attempted to curb the turbulent Monophysite elements by means of a public massacre.[1]

Justinian's role in the history of Egyptian Christianity was not altogether of a dubious character. In keeping with his policy of putting an end to paganism, surviving in the fringes of the empire, he encouraged the missionary enterprise to Nubia, though here Theodora seems to have foiled his plans by advancing the Monophysite mission as against the Melkite. He also closed the pagan temples of Isis in Philæ and of Amon in the Sīwa Oasis, replacing them with Christian churches. Justinian is reputed to have been one

[1] Milne, pp. 108–11; Vasiliev, pp. 148–54; Fortescue, pp. 199–208.

of the greatest builders of Christian antiquity. Though most of the Coptic monasteries in the Egyptian wilderness were prior to his reign, it is possible that he made some additions to them. But Egypt owes to him the Monastery of St Catherine, previously known as the Monastery of Transubstantiation, on Mount Sinai.

Monotheletism

The remaining years of Byzantine rule in Egypt constitute one of the saddest periods in the history of that country. Not only did the problems of imperial succession and the usurpation of authority at Constantinople reflect themselves in the administration of a much-coveted province, but also the innovations made by Justinian in the creation of rival prefectural powers produced a chaotic state of affairs. Thus Egypt was exposed to the forces of evil from within and to the covetous invader from without. Local adventurers found it possible to lead organized bands and plunder such towns as Busiris and Kinopolis, within reach of the seat of authority in Alexandria, while one prefect was busy deposing another in that great city. The shaky throne of Phocas (602–10) was tottering at this time, to fall at the feet of a new usurper of the imperial crown in the person of Heraclius, a Byzantine general of the African armies who crossed the Mediterranean and deposed his adversary in 610. While all this was happening, the Persian armies under Chosroes Parviz were on the march into the Byzantine Asiatic provinces of Syria and Palestine. At the moment of the accession of Heraclius (610–41), Chosroes was within sight of the great city of Antioch. In 613 he entered Damascus, and in 614 he seized Jerusalem and carried away the Holy Cross and the instruments of the Passion, which he presented to his Christian Jacobite queen, Shīrīn, in his capital Ctesiphon. In 619, while one of his contingents was forging ahead toward the Bosphorus, another invaded Egypt, which the Persians retained for well-nigh ten years.

The state of the empire was pitiful, and all seemed lost. While Heraclius was contemplating flight to Carthage, the Byzantine Patriarch Sergius placed his Church treasure at the disposal of the emperor for conducting the first pre-crusading war of the Cross. By a daring strategy Heraclius led his armies across the Mediterranean to land on the shores of the Gulf of Alexandretta in 622, intercepting the Persian armies from that point. And in the following year, he sailed the Black Sea to Trebizond, from which he surprised the Sassanian headquarters at Ganzak. The Persians were thus forced to withdraw from Egypt in 627, and the fame of Heraclius was enhanced by the recovery of the Holy Cross, which was triumphantly re-instated in the Holy Sepulchre at Jerusalem.

Egypt was thus returned to Byzantium, but Heraclius learned nothing from the bitter lesson. Not merely did he revive Justinian's policies in Egypt, but intensified them. He appointed a Melkite patriarch who became simultaneously prefect of the whole of Egypt, with vast religious, military, financial, administrative and judicial powers. In his eagerness to win the strong Monophysite party in Egypt without losing the western Chalcedonians, he hit upon a new device to replace the former unsuccessful *Henoticon*. In conjunction with Sergius, patriarch of Constantinople (610–38), he declared in 622 the new doctrine of Monotheletism,[1] in the hope that it might replace Monophysitism in the vocabulary of the turbulent provinces of Syria and Egypt.

Without touching the burning question of the one and the two natures of Our Lord, Monothelete theology dwelt on the oneness of His human and divine wills, which were identical, unchanging and harmonious. It was hoped that the new formula would be readily accepted by the Monophysites, while to the Western supporters of Chalcedon it did not conflict with the two natures, with which the Lord simply combined a unique will. At the outset, this ingenious device seemed to please some of the prelates on both sides. Most noteworthy amongst those who accepted it were Athanasius (621–9), patriarch of Antioch, and Honorius I (625–38), the Roman pope. It is interesting to note, however, that Antiochene acceptance survived only amongst the Maronites of Lebanon,[2] whereas Honorius met stubborn resistance from his bishops in the West. In 638, Heraclius published his edict, the *Ecthesis*, intended to force all to accept Monotheletism. Without dwelling on the opposition to that doctrine at the Roman curia after Honorius, it must be noted that the chief stronghold of hostility was in Alexandria, where the Copts repudiated every Greek solution, from Chalcedon to the *Henoticon* and Monotheletism. Suspicion of Greek manœuvres, the fear of departing from the dogmatic theology of Athanasius and Cyril, and the nationalist awareness of the Copts rendered them most reluctant to move from established tradition and meet the imperial authority half-way in matters of faith.

But Egypt, the granary of the empire, was too precious for Heraclius to surrender to religious and civil separatism. He was determined to impose uniformity on that province by fair means or foul. The first step came in the

[1] Fortescue, pp. 209–13; Vasiliev, pp. 222–4. See also below under Maronites. L. Bréhier and R. Aigrin, 'Grégoire le Grand et les États barbares et la conquête arabe (590–757)', in *Histoire de l'église*, ed. Fliche and Martin (Paris, 1947), Vol. V, pp. 131 ff., 151 ff.; Lagier, I, 377–86; Harnack, *History of Dogma*, Vol. IV, pp. 252 ff.; Tixeront, *History of Dogmas*, Vol. III, pp. 153 ff.

[2] See elsewhere, Part VI, Chapter XXIV, on origins and development of Maronite doctrine.

year 630, when he recollected that one of the early supporters of his Monothelete creation was a certain bishop of Phasis, in the Caucasus near the Black Sea, whose name was Cyrus, whose leanings were originally Nestorian, and whose national origin was doubtful. But he was astute enough to mirror imperial thinking and to reflect its religious policies. Thus Heraclius decided to elevate him to the joint function of Melkite patriarch of Alexandria and imperial prefect of Egypt on condition that he should bring the Copts to the faith of Chalcedon and of Monotheletism by hook or crook. Cyrus, later known in the Arab sources as al-Muqauqus, probably reached Alexandria early in 631, and set to work out his own plans without mercy. For ten years he was one of the most hateful tyrants in Egyptian history. He used the Cross as an iron mace to club native resistance.

The popularity of Heraclius, the hero who rescued the Cross from Persian captivity, soon sank to a low ebb. Every vestige of loyalty to Constantinople was obliterated by the behaviour of the imperial patriarch, who pursued Coptic prelates and Coptic nationalists until they paid lip service to his imperial faith or lost their lives. The new Coptic patriarch Benjamin I[1] (633–62) was a fugitive in obscure and remote monasteries in the Thebaïd throughout the last years of Byzantine rule in Egypt and until the advent of the Arabs. The patriarch's own brother, Menas, was martyred by Cyrus in the new wave of persecution which swept over the country. According to the *History of the Patriarchs*, Cyrus 'seized the blessed Menas, brother of the Father Benjamin, the patriarch, and brought great trials upon him and caused lighted torches to be held to his sides until the fat of his body oozed forth and flowed upon the ground, and knocked out his teeth because he confessed the faith; and finally commanded that a sack should be filled with sand, and the holy Menas placed within it, and drowned in the sea'.[2] Cyrus's visitations of the cities and villages in the Delta and the Valley left behind a trail of terror. Flogging, imprisonment and killing were coupled with confiscation of property and of sacred church utensils. He even went to the monasteries to hunt out his enemies, and the monks either fought a losing battle or singly fled from their impious persecutor. Even hermits and ascetics were seized for trial and tortured to death. The story of Samuel, ascetic at the monastery of Qalamon,[3] in the wilderness of Arsinoë, is an example of the steadfast defiance of the Copt in the face of terrorization by a fellow-Christian,

[1] The only biography of Benjamin in book form is in Arabic by Kāmel Ṣāliḥ Nakhla (Cairo, 1946).

[2] Evetts, II, 227. Presumably the author substituted the emperor's name for that of his patriarchal prefect.

[3] E. C. Amélineau, *Monuments pour servir à l'histoire de l'Égypte chrétienne aux IVe, Ve, VIe, et VIIe siècles*, 2 vols. (Paris, 1888–95), Vol. IV, pt. 2, 774 ff.; idem, 'Samuel de Qualamoun', in *Revue de l'Histoire des Religions*, XXX (1894), 1–47; A. J. Butler, *The Arab Conquest of Egypt and the Last Thirty Years of Roman Dominion* (Oxford, 1902), pp. 185–8.

who was then a patriarchal prefect. Dragged from his hermitage in chains, with an iron collar round his neck like the worst of criminals, he was taken to the city of Piom (modern Faiyūm), where he was abused, scourged, smitten on the mouth, subjected to all manner of diabolical tormenting, and ordered in the end to be slain by the soldiers, though he was saved under cover of night by his devoted pupils, who stole his mutilated body still wavering between life and death. Attempts at the assassination of Cyrus were craftily detected by his agents and followed by mass murder of all conspirators and suspects.

The Copts were humiliated as never before, and the Coptic Church suffered the tortures of the damned at the hands of the Melkite colonialist. The wonder is that their communities were able to bear the brunt of such travesties and survive. It is conceivable, of course, that some members should feign conformity to escape indignity, flagellation and the rack. Examples cited by the *History of the Patriarchs*[1] include such illustrious names as Victor, bishop of Piom, and Cyrus, bishop of Nikiou. But the bulk of the Coptic nation remained faithful unto the last, and harboured a deep-seated hatred of the Byzantine oppressors and all things Byzantine, which found natural expression not only in the so-called Monophysite doctrine but also in the Coptic language, Coptic literature, and above all in Coptic art.[2] The gap which separated these ancient brethren widened, and could never be bridged. The differences went beyond all reasonable or unreasonable compromise. The stage was set for imminent change, whatever the change might be. It was at this moment that there came the Arab Conquest, and the Copts could do little more than stand aside and watch an inveterate and impious enemy crumble to the ground. A new leaf was about to be turned in their record of suffering and fortitude, and what could anyone do in the circumstances?

[1] Evetts, II, 227.

[2] See below, Chapter VIII.

5 • THE COPTS UNDER ARAB RULE

The Arab Conquest

The coming of the Arabs to Egypt,[1] like that of St Mark to Alexandria, was an event of immeasurable consequence in the shaping of history in that crucial spot of the ancient and mediæval worlds. Egypt, the granary of first Rome and then Byzantium, was not unknown to the Arabs during pre-Islamic days. ʿAmr ibn al-ʿĀṣ, its conqueror, appears to have led Arab trade caravans to the Nile Valley and even to have visited Alexandria and gazed on its splendour and untold wealth with bewilderment. It is no wonder, then, that during the Syrian campaign after the battle of Yarmūk (20 August 636) and the seizure of Jerusalem in 638, he approached the second Orthodox Caliph ʿUmar (634–44) and pleaded for permission to invade Egypt, the fairest of all Byzantine provinces, with whose passages and fortifications he was familiar. If the Persians were able to seize it twice, surely the Arab victors over the Persians in the battle of al-Qādisiya (636) could do the same and more. The invincibility of the Byzantine army had become a myth after the Syrian campaign. The caliph, who seems to have yielded reluctantly when in Jerusalem, revised his fears about a set-back when he returned to Medina. He rushed a message to his general to turn back if his letter should reach him before crossing the Egyptian frontier. If, however, the message reached him afterwards, then he should proceed, and the Muslims would implore heavenly aid for the invaders. The suspecting ʿAmr did not open the letter until he and

[1] The fullest and most authoritative work on this subject is still that of A. J. Butler, *The Arab Conquest of Egypt and the Last Thirty Years of the Roman Dominion* (Oxford, 1902). All standard histories of Egypt under the Arabs have devoted adequate space to this chapter, and the following are quoted for reference: S. Lane-Poole, *A History of Egypt in the Middle Ages* (London, 1925), pp. 1–58; G. Wiet, *Histoire de la Nation Égyptienne*, IV: *L'Égypte arabe* (Paris, 1937), pp. 1–80; idem, *Précis de l'Histoire d'Égypte*, II, pt. 2: *L'Égypte musulmane dès la Conquête arabe à la Conquête ottomane* (Cairo, 1932), pp. 109–53; P. K. Hitti, *History of the Arabs* (London, 1958), pp. 160–77. All histories of the Copts enumerated elsewhere devote sufficient attention to this capital event. Of the Arabic studies, see biography of Patriarch Benjamin I by Kāmel Ṣāliḥ Makhla (Cairo, 1946), and Jacques Tagher's work on Copts and Muslims up to 1922 (Cairo, 1951), pp. 11–111. Chief original sources and authorities are cited by Butler.

his four thousand Arab horsemen reached the Egyptian frontier town of al-ʿArish. They thus pursued their route through northern Sinai to Pelusium (al-Farama), the north-eastern stronghold, long regarded as the gate to the Delta. It fell into their hands after one month, early in 640. Another month saw the capture of Bilbais, east of the Delta. Its Byzantine garrison lost 1,000 slain and 3,000 captives. Soon after, the Arabs stood before the strategic fortress of Babylon,[1] at the apex of the Delta, and from which the Byzantines ruled Lower Egypt on one side and Upper Egypt on the other. But here they could do nothing beyond a prolonged siege while they sallied into the surrounding country to subjugate the adjacent provinces. Reinforcements came from Arabia under al-Zubayr ibn al-ʿAwwām to raise the thin contingent to an army of 20,000. The village of 'Um Dunain[2] to the south was occupied and a Byzantine garrison was routed at the battle of Heliopolis (ʿAyn Shams)[3] in the north while an Arab column reached Memphis and raided the province of Faiyūm in Middle Egypt, all in the course of 640.

The beleaguered Cyrus, whom the Arabs called al-Muqauqus[4] and mistook for a Copt, chose to negotiate the surrender of the fortress, which took place on Good Friday, 6 April 641. The self-seeking Cyrus attempted to secure privileges from the invaders, who were adamant in their usual offer of three alternatives: adoption of Islam and sharing with the faithful, unconditional surrender and payment of tribute, or the sword until Allah decided the fate of the belligerents. The fall of that stronghold was a great shock to both the native Copt and the foreign Byzantine. Minor encounters followed on the road to Alexandria, the capital. Nikiou,[5] on the Rosetta branch, was taken by storm and its garrison slaughtered in May. The siege of Alexandria promised to be a rather prolonged affair. The city had fortified walls and strong towers, a garrison of 50,000 armed with engines of war and the fearful Greek fire, and having free access by sea to the empire for purposes of reprovisioning. The Arabs, on the other hand, inexperienced in siege warfare, excelled only in open battle. Alexandria could have held out indefinitely had it not been for the duplicity of Cyrus, whom Heraclius withdrew from Egypt and whom

[1] Built by Trajan (98–117 A.D.) on a Persian foundation, this has nothing to do with the Assyrian Babylon, but is rather an Arabic corruption (*Bab-al-yun*) of the Græcized Egyptian *Pi-Hapi-n-On* or *Per-Hapi-n-On* (that is, 'The Nile City of On'), which was the island of Roḍah opposite the fortress. Lane-Poole, p. 3, n. 2. In Arab times, it has been called 'Qaṣr al-Shamʿ' (that is, 'Castle of the Candles') because it was lit at night by candles or torches.

[2] The old Tendunias, to the south, not the north, of Babylon; Butler, p. 231 n.

[3] The old Egyptian City of 'On'.

[4] His problematic personality was discussed in detail and identified as Cyrus by Butler, Appendix C, pp. 508–26. He was no Copt and that name is probably derived from the region of the Caucasus where he originated.

[5] Within the boundaries of Menūfiya Province, an old Roman station on the road from Babylon to Alexandria, identified by Butler (pp. 16–17 n.) on the authority of Quatremère as the modern Shabshīr.

Constans II reinstated only after his father's death in February 641. The usual policy of negotiation with the Arabs was reopened by Cyrus, who probably hoped against hope to retain the leadership of the Egyptian Church under the sponsorship of the invaders. The predicament of the native Alexandrian included not merely the surrender of the city to the Arabs in September 642, but also Cyrus' approval that all able-bodied adults should pay the new master a poll tax of two gold dinars per head. It was possibly on this account that Alexandrians conspired with the Byzantine emperor, who responded by sending a fleet of 300 sail under the Admiral Manuel. The Greeks were able to recapture the city temporarily, but were soon driven out of it by treachery from within. The Arabs dismantled its walls to prevent repetition of similar untoward events, and the fate of all Egypt was sealed under the Arab rulers. ʿAmr prided himself on having crowned his invasion by the seizure of Alexandria's 4,000 palaces, 4,000 public baths, 400 theatres, and 40,000 rich poll-tax paying Jews out of a total population estimated at 600,000 men, not counting the women and children.[1]

The Arab invasion of Alexandria included the distressing episode of the burning of its great library by ʿAmr[2] who is said to have been only executing an order from Caliph ʿUmar. This romantic story, however, belongs to the realm of legend. It occurs first in the works of the Persian traveller ʿAbd al-Latīf al-Baghdādi[3] (d. 1231 A.D.) and the Jacobite Syrian prelate Bar Hebræus[4] (d. 1286), that is, about six centuries after the invasion. They contend that on consultation with the Commander of the Faithful in Mecca, ʿUmar supplied his general with the famous verdict that if the contents of the library agreed with the Qur'ān, they were unnecessary, hence superfluous; and if they disagreed, they should be eliminated as dangerous to the spirit of Islam. In either case, the books had to be burnt. On receipt of this message it took ʿAmr the incredible period of six months to dispose of the immense contents of the library as fuel for the public baths of Alexandria. None of the contemporary chroniclers makes any reference to that story. Moreover, it is doubtful whether any traces of the Ptolemaic library survived until the advent of the Arabs. A major part of it is known to have been destroyed in the Alexandrian wars of Julius Cæsar in 48 B.C. Later, in the fourth century A.D., the triumphant Christians are known to have committed many acts of systematic arson to obliterate the vestiges of pagan institutions, which must necessarily have touched the Museion or what remained of it. The nature of the papyrus scrolls and codices accumulated in the library was such that, from centuries of use they must have disintegrated long before the Arab Conquest.

[1] Butler, p. 360; Lane-Poole, p. 12. The latter quotes 70,000 Jews.
[2] Butler, pp. 401–26.
[3] *Historia Ægypti Compendiosa*, ed. J. White (Oxford, 1800), p. 114.
[4] *Historia Dynastiarum*, ed. E. Pococke (Oxford, 1663), p. 114 Latin, p. 180 Arabic text.

In other words, the story of firing the public baths with the Alexandrian library should be repudiated as a baseless and unhistoric invention.

As to the position of the Copts in those troubled times, the rather confused contemporary material seems to show that they adopted a neutral policy. In spite of the fact that the Arabs were acquainted with the caravan routes on the edge of the desert, those in the interior of Egypt necessitated local guides, and these are said to have been the Jews and not the Copts. Nevertheless, the Coptic communities were totally estranged from any sympathy with their relentless Melkite persecutors and were consequently unwilling to offer them solace and aid. Since Justinian, the Byzantine armies had been divided into separate local units, and lacked the means for unified action. This fact and the hostile attitude of the native Copt demoralized the garrisons at the time of the great crisis. The obnoxious personality of Cyrus not only rendered positive resistance impossible but also prepared the way for speeding the imminent catastrophe. In those trying moments in Egyptian history, the Copts could not lose by the change of rulers. The Byzantines had tried to efface both religious and political liberty in Egypt, whereas the early Arabs came at least with the prospect of religious enfranchisement for the Copts, who were destined to lose political independence anyway. The attitude of the Muslims toward the people of the Book or Dhimmis would ensure under the Covenant of ʿUmar such religious status for the Copts as they had not enjoyed under the Byzantines for a long time.

This new attitude became clear after the establishment of Arab rule. The monophysite patriarch Benjamin, for ten years a hunted fugitive from his Melkite pursuers, reappeared on the scene, and was revered by ʿAmr, who granted him safe conduct to discharge his church affairs in peace. The Patriarch forgave those of the clergy who had apostatized under duress to Monotheletism and restored many churches and monastic establishments. In his reign as well as in those of his successors, the Copts witnessed an unprecedented revival of their national religion, literature and art with their complete and undisturbed liberation from Greek influences. In the government they were substituted for the many Greek functionaries badly needed for running the administration of the new province. On the other hand, it would be an error to assume that the Arabs favoured the Copts or that the Copts went out of their way to help the conquering Arabs. The truth appears to be that the Arabs did not make any sectarian distinction between Monophysite and Monothelite or Melkite, which alone was a tremendous relief to the Coptic community. The Copts, who had been living under religious terrorization and civil disability, then found themselves treated as the equals of the Melkites. It is noteworthy, however, that the Arabs did not oust leading Greek personalities in the administration simply to please the Copts. The Arabs were interested in the smooth levy of the taxation irrespective of any consideration. For instance, they retained three principal officers for whom the Copts harboured a great deal of hatred as former instruments of the Heraclian regime. These were Menas, prefect of Lower Egypt, and Sanutius, prefect of the Rif, and Philoxenus, prefect of Arcadia or the Faiyūm.[1] The historian of the Arab Conquest, Alfred J. Butler, gives the impression that the three were renegades, and even makes this amazing statement: 'One almost begins to wonder whether the conduct of al-Muqauqus (Cyrus) himself could not be explained on the theory that he was a secret convert to the religion of Mohammed.'[2] Apparently the local employees, tax collectors and provincial magistrates were Copts, and the Coptic language replaced the Greek in normal transactions until Arabic made its appearance in bilingual papyri.

The Arabs were essentially interested in the state revenues, which consisted of a general tribute, known as the *kharāj*, and the poll-tax, or *jizya*, to be levied per capita on all able-bodied adult Christians, who were barred from Muslim military service and had to offer a substitute in cash. ʿAmr raised a total of twelve million gold dinars.[3] His tyrannical successor, ʿAbd-Allah ibn Saʿad ibn al-Sarḥ, increased this already formidable amount by two more millions. This precipitated a series of local rebellions. The bloodiest of them was the Bashmuric uprising, which occurred in 829–30 in the marshlands of the lower Delta. The senseless obstinacy of the rebels ended with their removal beyond the sea to Syria after their inevitable defeat. The point is that Coptic complacency toward Arab dominion was not absolute, though on the whole there was a sense of relief from Byzantine religious brutality. General revenues kept declining under the Umayyad and Abbasid viceroys until they were standardized at three million dinars in the ninth century. This decline was partly the result of frequent conversion to Islam in order to escape the taxes on Christians. Such conversion became so frequent that at one point the Muslim governors seemed to discourage steady conversion in order to protect the state revenue. Gradually the Copts adapted themselves to the new circumstances and survived all further vicissitudes in a way which is in contrast to North African or Nubian Christianity.

[1] Butler, pp. 362–3. It has been asserted that Sanutius was a Copt and not a Greek as his name Shenūda or Schenūte suggests (Kāmel Ṣāliḥ Nakhla, pp. 106–7), and that he played an important part in the establishment of relations between his patriarch, Benjamin, and ʿAmr.

[2] Butler, p. 263.

[3] To this must be added the taxes in kind, including grain, cattle, cloth, hospitality and all manner of daily articles needed by the Arab army. For any special study of this early Arab period in Egyptian history, it will be inevitable to consult the Arabic papyri, which contain innumerable specific details of social and economic life. The most important contribution in this field is Adolf Grohmann's monumental publication *Arabic Papyri in the Egyptian Library*, 6 vols. (Cairo, 1934–62). Other more limited works are extant, such as: A. Dietrich, *Arabische Briefe aus der Papyrussammlung der Hamburger Staats und Universitats-Bibliothek* (Hamburg, 1955); Nabia Abbott, *The Monasteries of the Fayyūm* (Chicago, 1937). For more material, see works listed by Grohmann in his brief but excellent manual of papyrology *From the World of Arabic Papyri* (Cairo, 1952).

In summing up the benefits which the Copts reaped from the Arab Conquest, we see that the first was perhaps religious enfranchisement. They were also able to appropriate many Melkite churches and religious establishments vacated by the Greeks. In the local administration they monopolized the government offices. They became the only scribes, tax collectors and magistrates. A revival of Coptic culture also filled the vacuum created by the sudden disappearance of Byzantine influence. The flow of capital outside the country under the governors of the Orthodox caliphate and the Umayyad dynasty was checked by the rise of independent local dynasties, including the Ṭūlūnids (868–905) and the Ikhshīdids (935–69), who wrested Egypt from the Abbasid caliphate in Baghdad. These were followed by the even more independent Fatimid caliphate (969–1171). Christian disabilities, such as the imposition of a distinctive dress or the prohibition from horse riding, were rarely enforced. When the Umayyad governor ʿAbdallah ibn ʿAbd al-Malik issued his edict of 705 making Arabic the official language in all state transactions, this measure only resulted in an attempt by the Copts to master that tongue in addition to their own, which survived for some centuries in daily use. As a spoken language Coptic was discontinued some time in the late Middle Ages, though it is still used as a liturgical language in Coptic churches to the present day. The troubles in store for the Copts were largely due to individual royal whims rather than to a set policy of whole dynasties. It will be noticed that at times the Copts flourished considerably under Muslim domination. As a matter of fact, the miracle of their survival must be ascribed to two essential factors. In the first place, the calamities sustained by them under Arab rule were not continuous, and sporadic pressures upon them often gave way to periods of peace and understanding between the members of the conflicting faiths. Except in cases of madness, as in the reign of al-Ḥākim, a Muslim ruler never attempted complete annihilation of his Christian subjects. On the contrary, the Copts were preserved as a fine source of revenue. In the second place, the racial characteristics of the Copts themselves, their unwavering loyalty to their church, their historic steadfastness toward the faith of their forefathers, and the cohesive elements in their social structure combined to render their community an enduring monument across the ages. Their special qualities were invariably appreciated even by their Muslim neighbours and by their rulers. Further, the Copts developed a certain ability for integrating themselves within the body politic of the Islamic state, but without losing their inner way of life and their religious identity. They survived all the hazards of a tumultuous life, and are still safe and strong, indeed an imperturbable minority.

First Five Centuries

With the re-establishment of peace and the declaration of religious liberty – or at least the equality between Monophysite and Melkite Christians in Arab eyes – the ostensible lowering of the Byzantine tribute of twenty million to the Arab kharāj of twelve, and the considerate attitude of the Arab governor toward the Coptic patriarch Benjamin, the rule of the Arabs augured well under ʿAmr ibn al-ʿĀṣ. In those days of drastic changes, the Copts must have had an exciting time with the withdrawal of the hateful Melkite authorities, both religious and military, as well as with the opportunities for appropriating the lands, homes and churches vacated by the Greeks. Except for a few loitering Greek renegades, the bulk of the administration fell to the Copts. The first serious setback occurred during the administration of ʿAmr's successor, ʿAbd-Allah ibn Saʿad, who exacted two millions more than his predecessor and undoubtedly enriched himself by other unknown extortions. In fact, this seems to have become the established pattern for the next two centuries under Umayyad and Abbasid rule. The caliphs made a habit of curtailing the periods of their governors' tenure in order to prevent them from striking root and gaining independence in that rich province. According to the tables compiled by Stanley Lane-Poole,[1] Egypt had at least as many as 108 governors during the first 226 years of Arab rule, that is, up to the year 868, when the Ṭūlūnids succeeded in founding the first independent Muslim dynasty in Egypt. Consequently, none of those governors, who averaged about two years each in office, could have the interest of the country and the population at heart. In spite of their rapacity, the tribute kept falling steadily a fact which needs some explanation. If we overlook the occasional low Niles and plagues, the absence of a central policy of care for the canals, dykes and irrigation system resulted in irreparable damage to agriculture and reduced the paying capacity of the farmers. This took place despite the increasing financial imposts, the extension of the poll-tax to the monks and priests (who had hitherto been exempt from it), a new register[2] which brought more landed property under taxation, and the use of the shorter Muslim lunar calendar year[3] instead of the Coptic solar calendar as the basis of computation.

The imposition of a much higher tribute at a time when personal income

[1] *Egypt in the Middle Ages*, pp. 45–58.

[2] That is, cadastre or '*rōk*' ordained by the governor, 'Ubayd-Allah ibn al-Aḥdath, in the years 724–5, thus raising the tribute to four million dinars in spite of the low price of grain at the time. The contemporary papyri show that the surveyors oftentimes exaggerated their estimates on the government side. An example is quoted of an estate of 139 acres estimated to be 200 and, on complaint, the revised figure was decided at 148; Jacques Tagher, *Aqbāṭ wa-Muslimun*, p. 89.

[3] Tagher, p. 89.

was declining incited a rebellious temper among the natives. But this was suppressed with ferocity. Between 739 and 773 five rebellions flared up, and it is noteworthy that some Muslims joined the Coptic rebels in protesting against the financial oppression which befell both elements of the population. The most serious of all the uprisings was the Bashmuric rebellion of 831, during the caliphate of al-Ma'mūn, already mentioned. After the return to peace, the Caliph visited Egypt and conciliated its inhabitants. But the pressures were renewed until 869 when the last Abbasid governor, Aḥmad ibn al-Mudabbir, resorted to making an accurate census of all the ecclesiastical hierarchy and the monks in their monasteries, and enjoined the reigning Patriarch Sanutius to pay a lump sum for the lot. In desperation the Patriarch appointed two delegates from among the leading Copts, Sawīris and Ibrāhīm[1] by name, to submit to the Caliph al-Muʿtazz (866–9) in Baghdad a petition pleading for relief. This seems to have been granted. Exemption of men of religion from capitation and safeguards of religious tolerance were again confirmed by his successor al-Muhtadi (869–70). It was in the reign of the latter that the Ṭūlūnids (869–905), followed by the Ikhshīdids (935–69), declared their independence in Egypt. Apparently, the Copts as a whole fared well with those non-Arab rulers, who refused to replace ibn al-Mudabbir with an Arab after his withdrawal, but used the native Copts in key positions under their own direct surveillance. This step proved to be beneficial to both the Copts and the new rulers; and the only serious trouble which befell the patriarch personally was the result of a conspiracy within the Church by an excommunicated bishop.[2] Ibn Ṭūlūn owes the two greatest structures of his reign to a Christian architect called ibn Kātib al-Firghāni. These are the Nilometer at the southern tip of the Rawḍa island and the great mosque bearing his name. Both are still among the greatest Islamic monuments in Cairo. It may be mentioned that for the mosque ibn Kātib devised the use of the pointed arch about two centuries before its prototype appeared in Gothic architecture in Europe.[3]

[1] Yaʿqūb Nakhla Rufaila's *Arabic History of the Coptic Nation* (Cairo, 1898), p. 94.

[2] The reigning Patriarch was then Khā'īl III, and the bishop in question was the bishop of Sakha in Lower Egypt. The mediators on behalf of the patriarch included two clerks in the administration, both sons of Mūsa, who was ibn Ṭūlūn's secretary. Also two other clerks in the office of the Wazir Aḥmad al-Mārdīni named Yūḥanna and Makārius pleaded with their chief to speak to ibn Ṭūlūn, which he did. The patriarch was accordingly released from prison upon signing a debt warrant of 20,000 dinars, which sum the latter clerks guaranteed as the price of his freedom from arbitrary imprisonment. Apparently he paid the first half and re-entered prison for the second half until Aḥmad's son Khumārawayh set him free; ibid., pp. 98–100. It is interesting to know that in the attempt to raise the money, the patriatch sold church property, including a Fusṭāṭ church, to the Jews, who still hold it as a synagogue to this day; ibid., p. 100, n. 1.

[3] Ibid., pp. 101–2; S. Lane-Poole, *Cairo* (London, 1898), pp. 20–4. The devout Christian architect used new material and built brick columns to avoid the usual system of taking marble columns from existing churches. The minaret has an outer staircase identical with

The real grandeur and subsequent decline of the Coptic nation in Islamic times took place under the Fatimed caliphs,[1] who invaded Egypt from Tunisia in 969 and held it till 1171. They founded the city of Cairo,[2] which became the centre of an empire extending from Morocco to Syria. There they accumulated immense riches and fostered cultural activities until Cairo became the great peer of Baghdad in the Islamic world. The early Fatimid caliphs were extremely tolerant toward the Christians and the Jews. One of the key personalities in the administration of the first Fatimid caliph to take residence in Cairo, al-Muʿizz (952–75), was a Copt by the name of Quzmān ibn Mīna, surnamed abu al-Yumn, who remained a faithful Christian. He became the caliph's viceroy in Syria and displayed great ability, dexterity and integrity in the discharge of his duties during the difficult wars with the Turks. He died a celibate and placed his immense wealth in the hands of the Coptic patriarch for the benefit of the Church and of the poor in his nation.[3]

Al-Muʿizz appears to have favoured the Copts to such an extent that a considerable legend about his sympathies was woven by some Christian writers.[4] His son and successor, al-ʿAzīz (976–96), continued his father's

---

another in Sāmarra on the Upper Tigris. Whether the architect was Christian Coptic or Armenian is not easy to say with precision, though the Coptic historians describe him as a Copt.

[1] Descendants of Fāṭimah, daughter of the Prophet Muḥammad and wife of ʿAli, his cousin and fourth successor. They were Shiʿite believers in their divine right of succession as against the Sunnite or Orthodox caliphs. At present, the sect resides mainly in Iran. On the Fatimids see DeLacy O'Leary, *A Short History of the Fatimid Caliphate* (London, 1923); Ḥassan Ibrāhīm Ḥassan, *Al-Fāṭimiyūn fī Miṣr* (Cairo, 1932).

[2] From the Arabic *al-Qāhirah* (The Victorius), Cairo is the last phase in the development of the mediæval city. The other phases are al-Fusṭāṭ (The Pavilion), established by ʿAmr on the edge of the desert near the Fort of Babylon; al-ʿAsākir (The Camp), developed by the Umayyad and Abbasid governors as a royal residence north of Fusṭāṭ or Old Cairo; al-Qaṭāiʿ (The Wards, or Fiefs), established further north-east by Ibn Ṭūlūn and kept by the Ikhshids; and at last al-Qāhirah al-Maḥrūsah (Cairo The Guarded), still further beyond al-Qaṭāiʿ where al-Azhar Mosque still stands; see Lane-Poole, pp. 2–6.

[3] Rufaila's *History*, pp. 108–11; Jacques Tagher, p. 123.

[4] One legend states that ibn Killis, in an attempt to embarrass the Copts, brought to the attention of the Caliph al-Muʿizz the verse where Matthew (xvii, 20) records Jesus' saying, 'If ye have faith as a grain of mustard seed, ye shall say unto this mountain, Remove hence to yonder place; and it shall remove; and nothing shall be impossible unto you.' The caliph thus called the patriarch, who confirmed the verse, and consequently the caliph commanded him to perform the miracle to prove the truth of his religion. The patriarch and the community then kept vigil and prayer for three days and three nights, and as he dozed inside the sanctuary, the virgin directed him in a dream to a humble and unlettered tanner at a given spot. In this wise he found his man of faith, and in a picturesque performance the Muqaṭṭam hill was moved while the hierarchy and the community chanted a hymn of mercy behind the poor and unassuming tanner.

Another legend is that the caliph was so impressed by the performance that he began a systematic enquiry into the Christian religion, until he became convinced of its truth and was baptized and spent the latter part of his life in Christian meditation at a monastery after abdicating in favour of his son. The story was revived by the late Morkos Smaika

policy of religious tolerance and married a Melkite Christian under whose influence he appointed Arsenius and Aristides, his brothers-in-law, as Melkite patriarchs of Alexandria and Antioch. He suppressed all social distinctions between Muslims and D͟himmi Christians, and appointed Christians to high places in the administration. He excused the Copts from all extraordinary taxes and permitted the patriarch to restore old churches and even to build new ones. When the infuriated Muslim populace attacked the churches, he granted the patriarch armed protection and a decree to complete the restoration with an offer of financial reparations. The patriarch gratefully accepted all but the monetary aid, which was returned to the treasury. He permitted those who went over to Islam under compulsion and full liberty to return to Christianity and is said to have refrained from punishing a Muslim who became a Christian convert.[1] Both measures were strictly contrary to the spirit of Islamic jurisprudence.

The Copts were allowed at that time to carry the highest honours and titles of state.[2] Their technicians received every encouragement and excelled in the delicate arts and crafts for which the age has been known. Jewellers, cabinet-makers, fullers, dyers, smiths, builders, painters, engineers, archi-

---

Pasha, former director of the Coptic Museum, but was vehemently rejected by the noted Muslim writers Aḥmad Zaki Pasha and Md. ʿAbdallah ʿEnān; cf. Jacques Tagher, pp. 120–2.

The former story is elaborated in the *History of the Patriarchs* (II, pp. 93–6 Arabic; pp. 140–5 English), but there is no mention of the second. The said vigil was kept in the Muʿllaqa Church of Our Lady in Old Cairo, and the patriarch was Ephraem the Syrian (975–8 A.D.), originally a rich layman of great piety.

[1] Jacques Tagher, p. 125, on the authority of Quatremère, quotes the name of a Christian convert from Islam as 'Vasah' and retranscribes it into Arabic as 'Wasāʿ' in the reign of al-Muʿizz. Tagher probably means Ét. Quatremère, *Mémoires géographiques et historiques sur l'Égypte et sur quelques contrées voisines*, 2 vols. (Paris, 1811) without mentioning the exact reference. A whole chapter on the same episode appears in Neale's *History of the Eastern Church: Patriarchate of Alexandria*, Vol. II, pp. 15, 193–6, but he does not mention his source for 'The History of Vasah'. It is possible that this is al-Wāḍiḥ ibn al-Rajā', who became a Christian in the patriarchate of Philotheus (979–1003) and in the reign of al-Ḥākim (996–1020), not the reign of al-Muʿizz. The details of his story are given by his friend and contemporary, the historian Sawīris ibn al-Muqaffaʿ, bishop of al-Ashmunein, author of the *History of the Patriarchs*, Vol. II, pt. 2, pp. 100–15.

[2] Rufaila, p. 142, mentions the following: 'al-Ra'īs, Hibat Allah, al-Amgad, al-Asʿad, al-shaik͟h, Nagīb al-Daulah, Tāj al-Daulah, and Fak͟hr al-Daulah.' All these titles are reserved for Wazirs and high functionaries. Here are some other famous names of Copts under the Fatimids: Master Surūr al-Jūlāl, Intendant of Caliph al-Mustanṣir; Abu al-Fak͟hr ibn Sa'īd, and his children, Chiefs of Personnel; Abu al-Ḥasan al-Amaḥ, Caliph al-Ḥāfiẓ's private secretary; al-Asʿad ibn al-Mīqāt, wealthy notable accused by Shawar of relations with the crusaders; Abu al-Futūḥ ibn al-Mīqāt, head of military personnel; Abu al-Yumn ibn Makrāwah ibn Zanbūr, treasurer and prefect of al-Rīf; Abu Saʿad Manṣūr ibn Abi al-Yumn, wazir of Caliph al-Mustanṣir; Abu al-Faḍl ibn al-Usquf, secretary of Badr al-Jamāli; Master Zuwayn, Caliph al-Ḥāfiẓ's intendant; Shaik͟h Aḥzam, state auditor; etc.; cf. Rufaila, pp. 162–9.

tects, manufacturers of plain and stained glass, and other workmen flourished in those times and produced objects of art which are still the pride of both the Coptic Museum and the Museum of Islamic Art in Cairo as well as the surviving churches and mosques of that century. The Copts produced many famous physicians, scribes and writers, although their most prolific literary productivity seems to have been concentrated in the following Ayyubid period. In Fatimid times, however, the Copts could justly pride themselves on the outstanding *History of the Patriarchs of the Egyptian Church*,[1] compiled from old Coptic sources in various monasteries, especially the Monastery of St Macarius in the Nitrean Desert, by Sawīris ibn al-Muqaffaʿ, bishop of al-Ashmunain, a contemporary of the infamous Caliph al-Ḥākim bi-Amr Allah (996–1021). Sawīris left behind him other minor works on theological subjects.[2] Even more picturesque, are the theological discourses by a convert from Islam named al-Wāḍiḥ ibn al-Rajā',[3] the personal friend and contemporary of Bishop Sawīris, as well as those of another convert from Judaism called ʿAbd al-Massīḥ al-Isrā'īli,[4] who wrote in the eleventh century. Contemporary patriarchs,[5] including Christodoulus (1047–77), Cyril II (1078–92) and Gabriel ibn Tarīk (1131–45), composed various sets of canons and encyclicals to define facets of the faith and to reform the morals of the Copts who had taken to the notorious habit of keeping concubines. Other eminent social and religious reformers of this age were Abu Yāsir ibn al-Qasṭāl and the writer Marcus ibn al-Qunbar.[6]

The glory of the Copts under Fatimid rule was darkened by one of the most senseless persecutions in mediæval times by the Caliph al-Ḥākim,[7] presumably a schizophrenic maniac who set himself to the bloodthirsty torture and killing of Christians, Jews and Muslims in turn. First he enforced distinctive dress on Christians, whom he commanded to wear a five-pound cross, and on Jews, who had to hang a heavy bell round the neck. Christians were dismissed from the administration, and their churches were ordered to be demolished by letting loose the mob on them. Most serious was probably his levelling the Holy Sepulchre to the ground. Confiscation of property, pillage, humiliation, imprisonment, executions and all manner of diabolical terrorization became the order of the day. A Jewish street was blocked and all its inhabitants perished. The entrance to a public bath for women was walled up and the bathers were entombed alive within. Orders banning women from appearing on the streets were issued, and certain food prescriptions were forbidden on pain of death. Toward the end of his reign he

[1] See above Chapter 2, p. 25, n. 1.
[2] Graf, *Geschichte der Christlichen arabischen Literatur*, Vol. II, pp. 295–318.
[3] Ibid., II, 318–19.
[4] Ibid., II, 319–20.
[5] Ibid., II, 321–7.
[6] Rufaila, pp. 149–57; Graf, II, 327–32.
[7] Contemporary of the Patriarchs Philotheus (979–1003) and Zaccharias (1004–32); see *History of the Patriarchs*, Vol. II, pt. 2, pp. 100–51 (Arabic) and pp. 150–228 (English).

fell under the spell of some Christian monks and was a frequent visitor to a monastery south of Cairo in the Ḥelouan desert. The immediate outcome was some relief for the Christians and more stringency against the Sunnite Muslims. Finally he followed the Isma'ilite doctrines as preached by a certain al-Darazi (d. 1019), who imparted his name to the Druze sect, and al-Ḥākim declared himself the incarnation of Allah on earth and expected to be worshipped by his subjects. His mysterious disappearance while practising astrology on the Muqaṭṭam hills was explained in different ways. Some said he retired to a life of oblivion in a Christian monastery, while his followers decided that he survived in a divine form until his next return. The truth is probably that he was killed in a conspiracy organized by his own sister, Sitt al-Mulk, whose own life was endangered by the Caliph's disapproval of her character and morality.

The subsequent story of the Copts under the remaining Fatimid caliphs is a mixed one. Religious liberty was restored together with most of the destroyed churches. The Church of the Holy Sepulchre was rebuilt by al-Ḥākim's immediate successor, al-Ẓāhir (1020–36). A major event for Coptic history was the transfer of the patriarchal seat from Alexandria to Damrū,[1] which the historian of the patriarchs called a second Constantinople, with its seventeen imposing churches. Ultimately the patriarchate was settled in Cairo, nearer the caliph's court and under his protection. All this happened in the reign of Christodoulus (1046–77), whose successor, Cyril II, took residence in the keep of St Michael's Church on the island of Rawḍa, near the thickly populated Coptic district of Old Cairo. Coptic public festivities,[2] suspended by al-Ḥākim, were again resumed and the state officially participated in them. The Wazir Badr al-Jamāli, of Christian Armenian origin, favoured the Copts and imported thousands of Armenian families to live with them in Egypt. Excellent relations were established with the Christian

[1] An ancient city in the Gharbiya Province in the Delta, mentioned in pre-Islamic sources with its early martyrs. E. Amélineau, *La Géographie de l'Égypte à l'Époque Copte* (Paris, 1893), pp. 505–6.

[2] The chief public festivities of the Copts which have been described by most mediæval writers and travellers such as Mas'ūdi, Musabbaḥi, Qualqashandi, Maqrīzi, ibn Iyās and the rest are: (*a*) The Epiphany, celebrated with great pomp. The torches on the banks of the Nile, the lighted boats and the crowds having the annual 'health-giving' dip in the River made a very picturesque scene at night. The caliph, his court and harem attended. (*b*) The Naurūz or Coptic New Year's day, observed with renewed clothing, lavish banquets, lots of fruit. The day was a general public holiday and the state distributed money to the employees on the occasion. (*c*) Christmas was the time when lanterns were hung above all doors, fish and sweetmeats were distributed everywhere, and everybody high or low bought candles, toys, candy and new clothing for the children. (*d*) Feast of St George the Martyr, during which the relic of his finger was dipped in the Nile water with a religious service so that the flood might take place. As a rule the government minted special gold coins for distribution to its employees on this occasion. Cf. Jacques Tagher, pp. 146–50.

kingdoms of Nubia and Abyssinia through the good offices of the patriarch. Differences within the Church were settled in a synod[1] convened by order of Badr al-Jamāli. The synod is revealing since it showed the extent of the episcopate in Egypt at the time. Coptic troubles in the later Fatimid era were only a phase of the great confusion and revolt within the court as well as famine and plague that prevailed in the country. The Turkish and Sudanese divisions in the caliph's bodyguard fought an internecine battle of extermination, to the detriment of the palace. Then national disaster befell Egypt, and the weakened caliphs were caught between the crusader, their own Wazir Shāwar, and the incoming Sunnite Turkmans of Shirkūh, who brought with him a young nephew by the name of Saladin (Ṣalaḥ al-Dīn). In this situation, where conflicts of race, religion, sect and interest played havoc before the dwindling and powerless throne of the caliphs, the logical result was attained when the Sunnite wazir suppressed the potent Shiʿite caliphate. Thus Saladin was able to inaugurate the Ayyubid sultanate (1169–1250), which coincided with the age of the Crusades.

Age of the Crusades

At the time of the First Crusade (1096–9) and the establishment of the Latin kingdom of Jerusalem in the last decade of the eleventh century, Fatimid power was vested in the hands of the Wazir al-Afḍal, son and successor of the famous Badr al-Jamāli, a Muslim convert of Christian Armenian extraction, who had followed a lenient policy toward the Copts. In fact, Fatimid policies on the whole *vis-à-vis* the Copts since the disappearance of al-Ḥākim were shaped by two main factors: the undying popular hostility of the lower Muslim classes, who thirsted for pillage and hated the Christian tax-collector, and the persistent need of the central administration for funds. The caliphs often failed to bridle the Muslim mob and resorted to pacifying

[1] Rufaila, pp. 147–8, mentions that forty bishops attended besides five absentees for great age or great distance. Bishop Isodorus, in his Arabic *History of the Church*, 2 vols. (Heliopolis, 1915–23), II, 313–15, gives details of 22 names from Lower Egypt and an equal number from Upper Egypt in addition to five absentees, making a total of 49 bishops for the whole of Egypt in Fatimid times. Numerous lay archons were also present. The authoritative lists compiled by H. Munier (*Recueil des listes épiscopales de l'église copte*, pub. Société d'Archéologie Copte in the series 'Textes et Documents', Cairo, 1943) on p. 27 cites 47 bishops in addition to three from the metropolitan area (miṣr, Gīza and al-Khandaq) who were summoned by Badr al-Jamāli to the synod, besides others who were unable to attend. It is interesting to note that Munier listed 66 episcopal dioceses at the peace of Constantine besides Philae, created later by Athanasius (p. 1). He also quotes a John Ryland MS R53, dated 1853 and probably based on the fourteenth-century list of Abul-Barakāt ibn Kabar naming 99 bishoprics in Lower and Upper Egypt (pp. 53–7). Pococke's list of 1722 mentions 83 sees (pp. 58–62).

the populace by wholesale dismissal of Copts from the administration. But they soon found out that good government could be conducted only with the help of the unpopular Copts, who were consequently restored to office. However, the patriarch was not always seized or imprisoned in response to popular Muslim outcry. On numerous occasions such violence was precipitated from within the church by a vicious monk or bishop. The worst example occurred in the reign of Christodoulos (1047–77),[1] when a monk named Colluthos submitted a calumnious report against his superior, who had refused him preferment. Consequently the authorities arrested Christodoulos at Damrū and confiscated six thousand dinars from the Church treasury. His successor, Cyril II (1078–1102), was maligned by Yuḥanna, bishop of Sakha,[2] and only a synod of forty-seven bishops saved him from ruin.[3]

The personal tolerance of the majority of the Fatimid caliphs did not lessen their desire to raise funds under any pretext from their Coptic subjects. This lust for, or perhaps lack of, funds increased the rate of ordinary or extraordinary taxes, while the wars of the Franks in Syria called for more expenditure. The nation had to bear the brunt of the added burden, and the Copts were always the first victims. It was only normal at the outbreak of the Crusades for Muslim rulers to suspect Coptic sympathies with their co-religionists who descended from western Europe on the Holy Land. What did they know about Chalcedon, Monophysitism and Diophysitism? All were Christians, and the Muslim ruler of Egypt had to keep watch and impose more exactions. This was the attitude adopted in official circles throughout the disastrous era of the Crusade.

On the other hand, from the Coptic point of view the Crusades proved to be one of the greatest calamities which befell the communities of Eastern Christians. It is true that they had never lived on a bed of roses under the rule of Muḥammadan dynasties, and they never expected to receive the full measure of equality with their Muslim neighbours. That had to wait until the dawn of liberty and democracy came in our own times. The Copts realized that they had to give up many material privileges in order to retain their spiritual heritage. Before the Crusades, however, they adapted themselves to the conditions of Islamic rule without the loss of their way of life, and were generally accepted and often very highly revered by the caliphs. They were the clerks, tax-collectors and treasurers of the caliphate. Heads of state always trusted their deftness and integrity, and they seemed somehow to be able to

[1] *History of the Patriarchs*, Vol. II, p. 180 (Arabic), pp. 274–5 (English).

[2] In the Gharbiya Province inside the Delta, mentioned frequently in the Coptic Synaxarium and the Chronicle of John of Nikiou at the time of the Arab Conquest; Amélineau, *Géographie*, p. 410.

[3] *History of the Patriarchs*, Vol. II, pp. 213–16 (Arabic), pp. 333–7 (English); Rufaila, pp. 146–9.

make themselves indispensable in public service. The Crusades, being the Holy Wars of the Cross, antagonized the followers of Muḥammad toward all 'worshippers of the Cross', whether Latin, Greek or Coptic, and so a new agonizing chapter began in the Copts' unending patience. From the opposite side, the catastrophe was even more disastrous, for the Latins looked upon the Eastern Christian Monophysites as outcasts and schismatics, worse than heretics. Copts, Jacobites and Armenians alike fell in that category, and the Maronites of Lebanon were saved only by submitting to the authority of Rome, though they clung to their eastern ecclesiastical customs. Latin hostility toward the eastern Christians showed itself in prohibiting them from performing the annual pilgrimage to Jerusalem and the Holy Sepulchre. The devout nature of Coptic pilgrims made the visit to the Holy Places a binding duty on all who could undertake it. To be deprived of kneeling at the Lord's Sepulchre and earning the blessings of walking in the steps of the Master was a tremendous disability which shocked Coptic imagination and piety.

An interregnum of more than two years in the patriarchate after the death of Macarius II in 1128 can be partly explained by two factors. In the first place, the community was so impoverished that it found great difficulty in raising the three to six thousand dinars to pay the state treasury for the issue of the decree of nomination of the new patriarch. This was essentially due to the burden of extraordinary taxation for the war with the Franks. In the second place, the Coptic leaders were afraid that the wazir might refuse to sanction any Christian election at all because of the state of international affairs. Furthermore, the situation was made still more difficult by two principal functionaries who harboured great hatred for all Christians: one a Muslim, the other a Sumerian named Ibrāhīm, who misled the caliph into believing that the Copts collected the Church income and sent it to aid the Franks.[1] The caliph immediately ordered the confiscation of all available Coptic funds, whether ecclesiastical or secular. The harrying of the Copts continued until these two men were removed from the scene by assassination during a revolt of the armed forces. They were replaced by a Melkite Christian through whose intercession the Wazir Aḥmad, grandson of Badr al-Jamāli, allowed the Copts to submit a nomination for patriarch. The choice fell upon a scribe in the Diwan by the name of Abul-ʿAlā', a celibate whose career and character were above reproach. The new Patriarch Gabriel ibn Tarīk (1131–45), this being his name after consecration, steered his ship well in those tempestuous days.[2]

Fatimid rule ended with a calamity that affected the Copts more than the

[1] Rufaila, pp. 158–9.

[2] Kāmil Ṣāliḥ Nakhla wrote the only full-volume biography in Arabic of this patriarch (Cairo, 1947). See pp. 37 and 44 for confiscations and increased poll-tax.

Muslims. This was the burning of the ancient capital of al-Fusṭāṭ in 1168 by Shāwar, the wazir of the last caliph al-ʿĀḍid (1160–71), in order to save it from falling into the hands of Amalric, the Latin king of Jerusalem, who aimed at using it as a base for the conquest of the whole of Egypt. Shāwar decided to cut short the prospects of a crusading victory by pouring twenty thousand barrels of naphtha on the strategic city of Fusṭāṭ, and his men used ten thousand torches to set it ablaze. The massive conflagration lasted fifty-four days, and the population fled.[1] Coptic historians[2] give the impression that the Copts were a majority at Fusṭāṭ, and all became destitute overnight. This was another calamitous by-product of the Crusades in the story of the Copts.

At that time, a tremendous change occurred in Egyptian history. While the Shiʿite Fatimids were imperilled by crusading inroads, the armies of the Sunnite Sultan Nūr-al-Dīn in Syria came under his general Shirkūh to assist in the defence of Egypt against their Christian common enemy. After the withdrawal of the Crusaders, however, they stayed under the pretext of protecting the Caliph. Shortly afterwards, Shāwar was assassinated, and the Caliph paradoxically named the Sunnite Shirkūh as his wazir. In Shirkūh's train was his young nephew Saladin, who took the reins of the wazirate on his uncle's demise. A change of dynasty became imminent and, upon the death of the last Fatimid, he at once suppressed their shadowy caliphate and acceded to power in Egypt. The transitional period between the Fatimids and Ayyubids was a very sad one of confusion and insecurity for all. Saladin inaugurated his rule as wazir by the dismissal of the Copts from office, a measure which he had to repeal in the interest of good administration after the stabilization of affairs. The humiliation of the Copts was made public by the enforcement of distinctive dress and the prohibition from riding horses. Heavy fines were imposed on them and they had to sell most of their property to meet the new exactions. Many surrendered their lands and liberties to the Arabians for protection, and others professed the faith of Islam and were saved. In particular, those in high offices chose the latter means to retain their positions and their lives. The outstanding example was that of an old and influential Coptic family from Asiūt. Its head, Zakariya ibn Abi al-Malīḥ ibn Mammāti, pleaded in vain for relief from the obnoxious disabilities and taxes. Finally he changed his first name and became a Muslim along with all his family. Thus he was able to keep his high offices of war secretary and treasurer of the kingdom, honours which he transmitted to his son. He was a contemporary of the last Fatimid caliph and of Sultan Saladin. He was a poet of no mean merit and a writer of unusual distinction, best known for a

[1] Lane-Poole, *Egypt in the Middle Ages*, pp. 184–5; DeLacy O'Leary, pp. 240–2; Rufaila, pp. 159–60, contends that the majority of the inhabitants of Fusṭāṭ were Copts.

[2] See, for instance, Rufaila, p. 159.

treatise on the state of Egypt[1] in Saladin's time, including one of the oldest mediæval registers of the country. He died at Aleppo in 1209.

Saladin's most enduring monument was the Cairo Citadel, built for him on the Muqaṭṭam hills by two Coptic architects, Abu Manṣūr and Abu Mashkūr.[2] In Alexandria, however, the Ayyubid authorities decided to pull down St Mark's Cathedral,[3] overlooking the two harbours of the city, on the pretext that it was by nature a great castle where the Crusaders might fortify themselves should they descend on Alexandria. Saladin also sent an expedition to chastise the Christian kingdom of Nubia as well as the unruly Coptic elements in remote parts of Upper Egypt. The year 1173 saw the first serious and destructive Muslim invasion of Nubia, where the fortified monastery of St Simeon near Aswan and another at Ibrīm were destroyed and many inhabitants including the Monophysite bishop were imprisoned and sold in the slave market. The prosperous Coptic city of Quft was also levelled to the ground and has ever since remained a poor village.

With the victory of Saladin over the Crusaders, culminating in the fall of Jerusalem in 1187, the Ayyubids became composed and their policy of intolerance toward the Copts changed. The sultan granted them a monastic establishment adjacent to the Holy Sepulchre, which they own to the present day. Some regained their high offices in the state and many recaptured their lost wealth and prosperity. Saladin selected a Copt – Ṣafiy al-Dawla ibn Abi al-Maʿāli, surnamed ibn Sharāfi – as his private secretary; and ibn al-Mīqāt, another Copt, rose to the headship of the war office in the reign of al-ʿĀdil Sayf-al-Dīn (1199–1218), known as Saphadin in Western chronicles. In the Crusade of Damietta (1218), its Christian inhabitants suffered much at the hands of the Latins; while in the fighting of 1249–50 against Louis IX's invasion of Egypt, names of notable Copts were found on the side of the Sultan.[4]

Until the age of the Ayyubids, the Coptic language was still in use, though it was felt that Arabic was a serious menace to its survival. During this period,

[1] *Kitāb Qawāwīn, al-Dawāwīn*, ed. A. S. Atiya (Cairo, 1943); for ibn Mammāti's biography, see pp. 8–28; for the '*rōk*' or cadastre of Egypt, see pp. 85–231. The book also includes chapters on the Nile, irrigation, canals, dykes, agriculture, survey, state offices, minerals, weights and measures, finance, customs forests, seasons and the agricultural calendar, etc. The book shows great learning and authority. The original copy prepared for Saladin with all the details of land acreage and taxation is lost, but what remains in other ancient manuscripts is invaluable. This is one of ibn Mammāti's numerous works.

[2] Rufaila, p. 170.

[3] Built by Patriarch Agathos (662–80 A.D.), who succeeded Benjamin I (623–62 A.D.) within sight of the Arab Conquest. It was situated on the ancient site of Baucalis and was of imposing dimensions. The Copts are said to have made an offering of 2,000 dinars to save it from destruction, but in vain.

[4] Rufaila, pp. 183–9, reports a great number of names of people who distinguished themselves either in the administration or by the acquisition of vast fortunes or by their great learning.

therefore, a class of Coptic scholars arose who wrote some of the most important Coptic grammars and compiled admirable dictionaries to help preserve the language. The Copts had their schools attached to the churches, and manuscripts were deposited there for the use of their children.[1] Amongst those who particularly distinguished themselves were Aulād (= sons of) al-ʿAssāl, who flourished around the first half of the thirteenth century.[2] Three of them rose to high office in the Ayyubid administration, and all were highly educated writers with a profound knowledge of Coptic and Arabic in addition to Greek. Among the works of other writers of the period, the history of the churches and monasteries of Egypt and neighbouring countries, attributed to Abu Ṣāliḥ the Armenian[3] but probably written by Abu al-Makārim Saʿad-Allah ibn Girgis ibn Masʿūd, is invaluable. The world history of al-Makīn Girgis ibn al-ʿAmīd[4] (d. 1273), long known in Europe where it has been translated into various languages since the seventeenth century, had already served mediæval Islamic chroniclers such as the eminent al-Maqrīzi (1364–1442). Yūsāb, bishop of Fuwwah,[5] who died after the year 1257, wrote a worthy continuation to the *History of the Patriarchs*. Though it would be impossible to include all the writers of this era, we cannot overlook the name of Kirollos ibn Laqlaq, patriarch of the Church from 1235 to 1243. He was a rather controversial figure who left behind him numerous legal, liturgical and religious works.[6]

At the time of the outbreak of the Crusades, the Copts appear to have adopted a position of complete neutrality between the Latins and Saracens. Their involvement in their own local troubles left them on the defensive,

[1] Graf, II, 333–445, enumerates a considerable number of writers, including historians, exegetes, commentators, grammarians, and other categories.

[2] These were al-Ṣafiy Abu al-Faḍā'il, al-Asʿad Abu al-Faraj Hibat-Allah, and al-Mu'taman Abu Isḥāq Ibrāhīm. All seem to have died before 1260. The varied nature of their writings in the field of religion and of philology calls for special research. They were the founders of Coptic linguistic studies, though it must be remembereed that they were not alone in this field. See Graf, II, 398, 403, 407 respectively.

[3] Ibid., II, 338–40. B. T. A. Evetts, *The Churches and Monasteries of Egypt and Some Neighbouring Countries attributed to Abu Ṣāliḥ the Armenian* (text, Oxford, 1894; trans. 1895).

[4] Graf., II, 348–51. Thomas Erpenius, *Historia Saracenica* (Leiden, 1625); Samuel Purchas, 'The Saracenical Historie . . . written in Arabike by George Elmacin', in *Purchas, His Pilgrimage* (London, 1626); Pierre Vattier, *L'histoire mahométane ou les quarante-neuf Chalifes du Macine* (Paris, 1657). There are two fragments of that chronicle in manuscript in the Coptic Museum; see Marcus Smaika, *Catalogue of the Coptic and Arabic Manuscripts in the Coptic Museum, the Principal Churches of Cairo and Alexandria and the Monasteries of Egypt*, 2 vols. (Cairo, 1939–42), Vol. II, nos. 610 and 613, pp. 275–6.

[5] Graf, II, 369–71. Also known as ibn al-Mubārak, whose history has not yet been systematically published. It is still in manuscript in Dair al-Suryān and the private ownership of the heirs of the late Hegomenos Filutheus ʿAwaḍ and Girgis Filūtheus ʿAwaḍ. Kāmel Ṣāliḥ Nakhla used the first manuscript in compiling an Arabic biography of Pope Cyril III ibn Laqlaq (publ. at the Syrian Monastery of Our Lady, 1951). For Fuwah or Fouah, see Amélineau, *Géographie*, pp. 244–5, 484.

[6] Graf, II, 360–9; see also note above.

with only enough energy to meet the pressures of a whimsical ruler, or to raise the funds demanded of them. Then in moments of tolerance, they soon became reanimated and demonstrated an extraordinary power for quick recovery. This is evident from considering their lot under the Ayyubids. As the early persecutions subsided, they regained their former position in the administration and were able to accumulate lost wealth. Their vitality was demonstrated in literary productivity, and they even found it possible to participate in the defence of their Egyptian homeland against the Latin invaders, side by side with the Muslim neighbour. Unfortunately that healthy attitude did not last long after the change of dynasties. It has been said that Mamlūk rule from 1250 was merely a continuation of the Ayyubid system. This may be true in certain aspects, such as their counter-crusading expansionist policy or the development of international trade. Otherwise the Mamlūks were literally a dynasty of enfranchised slaves whose Islamic background was only skin-deep. They did not share the aspirations or even speak the language of their subjects. Assassination followed assassination in their internecine wars, and their unity only became a reality in the face of a common enemy from the outside. Insecurity and increasing poverty under their rule drove the natives into reckless desperation. Whenever the Copts rose to wealth and power for the simple reason that they developed a genius for the management of state finance, the destitute populace clamoured for their dismissal from office. Mob fury became too overpowering even for the Mamlūk despots to keep it under control. Destruction of Coptic churches became so serious a menace that in 1320 some Coptic monks retaliated by secret arson, and many mosques with hundreds of houses were thus burnt to the ground. In addition to the sporadic cases of violence and popular persecution, the records show that repeated dismissals of the Copts took place during the period from 1279 to 1447. Every time this happened, complete paralysis in the machinery of the state ensued, and the ruler had to resort to the only segment of Egyptian society that could mend the deteriorating position. It was a vicious circle, and the Crusades merely intensified Mamlūk hatred of the indispensable Copt. In the Cairo region alone fifty-four churches are reported as having been destroyed during that period, in addition to a number of monasteries. Several Christians nominally professed Islam and are said to have persecuted the Muslims under cover of conversion.[1]

In the fourteenth century the difficulties of the Copts remained acute. In 1365 the Crusaders of Alexandria plundered both Muslim and Copt with

[1] Macrizi, *Geschichte der Copten*, ed. F. Wüstenfeld (Göttingen, 1845), pp. 29–33 (Arabic), 70–81 (German); Rufaila, pp. 204–61; Jacques Tagher, pp. 172–206; A. S. Atiya, *The Crusade in the Later Middle Ages* (1st ed., London, 1938; 2nd ed., New York, 1965), pp. 272–8; W. Muir, *The Mameluke or Slave Dynasty of Egypt, 1260–1517* A.D. (London, 1896), passim; S. Lane-Poole, *Egypt in the Middle Ages*, pp. 242 ff.; G. Wiet, *L'Egypte arabe*, pp. 383 ff.; M. Fowler *Christian Egypt*, pp. 96 ff.

equal ferocity. The trustee of a Coptic church, the crippled daughter of a priest named Girgis ibn Faḍā'il, had to surrender all her own fortune in order to rescue the church in spite of asserting her Christianity by signing the Cross. On the Muslim side, the authorities dragged the Coptic Patriarch Yuhannes X (1363–9) to the court, where he and his community were subjected to all manner of humiliation and confiscation of property. In later mediæval times, however, a small measure of relief was caused by foreign intervention from three sources. The first was the emperor at Constantinople, himself harassed by the Ottoman Turks, who pleaded with the Mamlūks on behalf of the Melkite minority in Egypt. The second was the king of Aragon, whose country was on good terms with Egypt, and who urged the reopening of churches in Egypt and the Holy Land. The third and most important was the *negus* of Ethiopia, who, to obtain relief for his co-religionists in Egypt, bargained with the sultan over retaliation against Abyssinian Muslims and the menace of deflecting the course of the Nile water.

In the fifteenth century occurred the abortive attempt to bridge the gap between Rome on one side and the Copts and Abyssinians on the other at the Council of Ferrara-Florence (1438–9). Yuhannes, the Coptic abbot of St Antony, and Nicodemus, the prior of the Abyssinian Convent of Jerusalem, represented their respective nations on the council. Union was published and Yuhannes appears as a signatory of the *Decretum pro Jacobites* issued by Pope Eugenius IV. But the act of union remained in abeyance, and the popes continued without avail to write urging the Copts to unite with Rome, even after the Turkish Conquest of 1516–17. In 1586 a strong delegation descended on the docile Patriarch Yuhannes XIV (1571–86) from Rome. A synod was convened to discuss union once more, and the patriarch prevailed upon many bishops for approval. Another act of union was ready for signature, when Yuhannes died overnight before putting his seal on it, and the movement was buried with him.

6 • MODERN TIMES

The Ottoman Turks

The disappearance of the Mamlūk sultanate after the Turkish Conquest of Egypt by Selim I in 1517 did not mean the extermination of the Mamlūks as a clan. In the reorganization of the state under the new sultan there was a twofold objective: first, to eliminate the possibility of any adventurer wresting the valuable province from the sultan's hands, and second, to squeeze a rich annual tribute from the population. Thus Selim divided authority among three rivals in order to keep the balance of power in his own hands. The viceroy, or pasha, was charged with collection of the tribute, and his tenure was usually a short one to prevent him from striking root in the country. Then, the powerful army garrison had its own independent council. Lastly, the Mamlūks were entrusted with the local government of the provinces. The system achieved the sultan's principal aim admirably, but it also in the meantime brought about the political and financial ruination of Egypt. Without entering into the constitutional details of Ottoman governance, it may be sufficient here to note that the country became prey to three taxing agencies instead of one, and Mamlūk misrule persisted with its usual brutality. Though Islamic in character, the administration cared little for religious considerations in matters of finance. In this respect, there was no distinction between Muslim and Copt; both were equally subject to a triple system of impositions at a time when Egypt had lost a chief source of income by the steep decline in its international mediæval trade. Thus the country entered one of the darkest periods of its long history with the advent of the Ottoman Turk.

The people of Egypt fell into a state of lethargy, and the Copts were no exception to the rule, save that they were destined by nature and upbringing to play the prominent role in administering Mamlūk estates and handling finance and taxation. It would be a mistake to contend that they suffered no pressures, but the period was, on the whole, one of miserable respite in comparison with the murderous persecutions of later mediæval Mamlūks. In common with all other Egyptians, the Copts were depleted in numbers by plagues and poverty. Cairo lost its glamour and became a secondary town. It is difficult to obtain a clear picture of Egypt from the exceptionally meagre sources of that period. In 1769, the Mamlūk ascendancy ended in the expulsion of the Turkish pasha by ʿAli Bey al-Kabīr and the declaration of Egyptian independence. ʿAli's meteoric empire soon comprised Syria and Hijāz. Finally his downfall was precipitated in 1773 by Mamlūk conspiracy and secret Turkish intrigue.

In the course of these upheavals, a number of Copts were advanced in the train of their Mamlūk masters. Muʿallim, or Master Rizq,[1] became ʿAli Bey's chief of the mint and principal adviser in matters of finance. Other names following other Mamlūk dignitaries were the illustrious Gauhari brothers,[2] Ibrāhīm and Girgis, who accumulated fabulous wealth and commanded universal respect from both Muslim and Coptic contemporaries. Ibrāhīm, who was bereaved of his only son, donated most of his wealth to the Coptic Church. A list of 238 indentures[3] bearing his name show the extent of his gifts to monasteries and individual pious foundations of the community. He also hired scribes to copy older theological works for distribution among the churches in order to increase religious knowledge, perhaps the first serious attempt to revive the dormant Coptic theological studies in modern times. He procured a special *firman*, or decree, from Istanbul for the erection of the present Cathedral of St Mark at Ezbekieh, since then the new seat of the patriarchate. Through his influence, legal dispensations were granted for the restoration of numerous churches and monasteries. Both Muslim and Coptic writers of his time praised his generous behaviour toward all Egyptians without religious discrimination. He died on the eve of the French Expedition in 1797, and his brother and successor, Girgis al-Gauhari,[4] became the chief of the *diwans* of the last two great Mamlūks, Ibrāhīm Bey and Murād Bey. He witnessed the decline of their power and lived through the tempestuous years of French rule, to become Muḥammad ʿAli's finance secretary. He was probably the only man of his age who commanded confidence from Mamlūks, French and Turks alike. His leniency in taxation endeared him to all Egyptians though it brought down disfavour from the rapacious Muḥammad ʿAli, who, after exiling him for four years, was constrained to reinstate him in 1809 because of his indispensable knowledge and ability. But soon after this he died (1810).

Toward the end of the Ottoman period, two facts stand out from the confusion and misrule of the time. The invincibility of the Turk became a clear myth, and external forces were made aware of the extraordinary strategic

[1] Rufaila, pp. 270–3. [2] Ibid., pp. 273–87.

[3] Tewfīq Iscarous, *Nawābigh al-Aqbāṭ* etc. (Arabic Biographies of Famous Copts in the 19th Century), 2 vols. (Cairo, 1910–13), I, 281 ff.

[4] Rufaila, pp. 273–87; Iscarous, II, 280–312.

position of Egypt, so long forgotten. This explains the forthcoming rise and fall of Napoleonic imperialism in the Middle East. Meanwhile, a new orientation in Coptic annals occurred when the long-standing barriers between Copts and Muslims began to disappear in contemporary history.

The Copts under the French

Of short duration, the French Expedition (1798–1801) proved to be a monumental event in the history of Modern Egypt. For the first time since the Crusades, Egypt had intercourse with a European country. Now Napoleon Bonaparte came for the establishment of a Middle Eastern empire under the pretext of the defence of, rather than the attack on, Islam. In so doing, however, he exposed Egypt to Western thought and Western politics. Every phase of Egyptian life was affected in varying degrees of intensity by that movement, and Egypt also became a factor in international affairs. The rise of Muḥammad ʿAli and the establishment of his dynasty in Egypt may even be regarded as a by-product of the expedition. In those days of turmoil and change, Coptic society did not remain passive. In 1798, Girgis al-Gauhari wrote an appeal to Napoleon, the true son of the French Revolution and the exponent of the principles of liberty, equality and fraternity, to lift the disabilities of the Copts and grant them a full measure of equality with their Muslim brethren. Napoleon's initial response was favourable, though he never sacrificed the interest of the Muslim majority for the sake of the Coptic minority; and we have to remember that numerous French soldiers, including Napoleon at the head of the list, posed as Muslims.

The Copts, however, were widely used in the administration, and some of them rose to high office. Girgis al-Gauhari was again appointed to a key position in control of taxation, after the flight of the Mamlūk Amīrs from the French. In a commission of twelve instituted for local justice, six were Muslims and the other six were Copts. The president of the commission, too, was Muʿallim, or Master Malaṭi,[1] who happened to be a Copt. Though the Copts were not in any way favoured by their French co-religionists, the fact remains that they were not subjected to repression.

Perhaps the strangest and most romantic figure in the Coptic history of that period was General Yaʿqūb[2] (1745–1801), whose career was a prelude to an

[1] Iscarous, II, 313 ff.

[2] Older studies of Yaʿqūb's career by such writers as Rufaila (pp. 289–91) have been superseded by the discovery of a set of official documents in London by the late Professor Shafīq Ghorbāl, published in Arabic under the title of 'General Yaʿqūb and the Chevalier Lascaris' (Cairo, 1932), as well as more documents found in Paris by G. Douin, 'L'Égypte indépendante, Projet de 1801', in *Publications of the Egyptian Geographical Society* (Cairo,

independent Egypt neither French nor Turkish. Owing to the importance of the subject in both Coptic and Egyptian annals, a summary of his life and work may be included in these pages.

In Mamlūk days, Muʿallim Yaʿqūb Ḥanna was in charge of the province of Asiūṭ under Amīr Suleiman Bey. As a young man, he had to develop a police system of his own in his insecure province. He learnt from his Mamlūk friends the equestrian art as well as the methods of warfare. He fought side by side with Suleiman Bey and later joined Murād Bey in the battle of Manshiya near Asiūṭ, where the Turks were defeated on the eve of the coming of the French. During the bitter years of fighting between Turk and Mamlūk, he began to realize the stark reality that the people of Egypt were a victim to the rapacity of both foreign elements, from whose yoke there seemed to be no means of escape. Then the advent of the French and the displacement of the Turk and the Mamlūk before their irresistible modern arms, gave Yaʿqūb an idea about a possible outlet. Since the position of the country could not be any worse, he decided to try his luck with the new invader. His acquaintance with the Egyptian roads and means of communication as well as the methods of army provisioning rendered his services invaluable to the French army. When Napoleon sent Desaix to complete the conquest of Upper Egypt, he appointed Yaʿqūb as his adjutant. Yaʿqūb fought valiantly and on one occasion managed alone to keep the Mamlūks at bay until the French main army appeared in the rear. Desaix gave him an inscribed sword to commemorate the victory. His cooperation made it possible for the French to subdue the whole of Upper Egypt as far as Aswān, with Asiūṭ as the central headquarters. His ingenious organization of the postal service (*barīd*) closely knit the distant garrisons by swift dromedaries, which proved invaluable for the conveyance of despatches, provisions and wounded soldiers to hospital concentrations.

While Yaʿqūb was stationed in Upper Egypt, events were moving fast against the French in the north. They lost their fleet at Abuqīr, and Nelson was in command of the sea. Napoleon returned home, and Kléber succeeded him with an empty treasury, while the Muslims were suspicious about French policies. The French were in dire need of men like Yaʿqūb. While Kléber was fighting the Turks at the battle of Heliopolis (March 1800), Yaʿqūb strove to quell a revolt incited by Turkish infiltration within the City. It was in those untoward circumstances that he was able to persuade the French to help him in the realization of an old dream. Egypt had long been

---

1924). See also Gaston Ḥomṣy, *Le Général Jacob et L'Expédition de Bonaparte en Égypte* (Marseilles, 1921). The Coptic Historical Commission republished the same documents in a separate Arabic brochure (Publication No. 3; Cairo, 1935). The views of the contemporary annalist al-Jabarti should be revised in the light of the official documents.

deprived of a national army of its own, and he was firmly convinced that there could be no rehabilitation of the nation without an army. But since the Turks played on religious sentiments in order to break the unity of the Egyptian people, Yaʿqūb conceived the idea of trying the experiment on his own co-religionists. After the battle of Heliopolis, French authorities approved his plan for a Coptic Legion to consist of two thousand recruits, mainly from Upper Egypt. These were trained by professional officers, and Kléber appointed Yaʿqūb their commander with the rank of colonel in May 1800, ultimately promoting him to general in March 1801.

When the treaty of 27 June 1801 was signed by the French, relinquishing Cairo to the Turks, it was stipulated that those of the natives who wished to depart with them should be allowed to do so. Accordingly, Yaʿqūb decided to leave with his family, a group of loyal friends and a small bodyguard which fought later in the Napoleonic campaigns. They embarked on the British battleship Pallas, under the command of Captain Joseph Edmonds, from Alexandria on 10 August 1801. Soon afterward Yaʿqūb became seriously ill and died on 16 August. Owing to his position, his body was preserved in 'a case of spirits' until it was laid to rest on French soil at Marseilles in a military funeral on 18 October 1801.

The truth about Yaʿqūb's controversial career and his secret mission to Europe has been uncovered in the memoirs of Lascaris, chevalier of the Order of Malta, who travelled on the *Pallas* and interpreted for him in his deliberations with Captain Edmonds, prior to his illness. He wanted the captain to carry a message from him in the name of the Egyptian people to the British government to the effect that the only solution to the Egyptian question was Egyptian independence. The message was transmitted to the Lord of the Admiralty, the Earl of Saint-Vincent, with a covering letter dated 4 October 1801 from Minorca. Similar appeals dated 23 September 1801 were later submitted by the other members of the Egyptian delegation to Bonaparte as First Consul and to Talleyrand, his Foreign Secretary. In this way the dawn of Egyptian nationalism broke forth from the shattered life of General Yaʿqūb.

Age of Cyril IV, Father of Coptic Reform

Marcus VIII, the contemporary Coptic patriarch of the French Expedition, was succeeded by Peter VII (1809–52),[1] surnamed al-Gauli, whose long reign coincided with that of Muḥammad ʿAli. The viceroy's appreciation for the patriarch was enhanced by his refusal to accept an invitation of the tzar of

[1] Iscarous, I, 58 ff.

Russia for the Coptic Church to regard him as its defender and liege lord. He extended the Church's influence by consecrating the first bishop of the Sudan after its conquest in 1823, and by the despatch of a monk of St Antony by the name of Dāwūd on a diplomatic mission to Ethiopia. That very Dāwūd was destined to succeed him as patriarch under the name of Cyril IV. Peter's frugality resulted in the accumulation of an immense fortune which made his successor's reforms possible.

Cyril IV (1854–61) has been universally acknowledged as the father of Coptic reform.[1] Born of farmer stock about 1816 in an obscure village in the province of Girga, Dāwūd (as he was then named) shared in the tilling of the soil with his father and befriended the neighbouring Arabs from whom he learned the equestrian art and camel riding and was admired for his skill in chivalry. At twenty-two he joined the monastic order at the Convent of St Antony and soon distinguished himself for piety, enlightenment and administrative skill. On the death of the abbot, his colleagues unanimously elected him to that dignity. His reforming spirit was immediately shown in combating illiteracy and promoting theological studies amongst the monks, whom he also persuaded to observe the ancient rule of their profession. He doubled the monastery resources by his vigilance, and used part of his funds for the establishment of the first elementary school at Būsh, where he offered free instruction to the children on and around the monastery estates.

After the accomplishment of his patriarchal mission to Ethiopia and upon his return in July 1852, Dāwūd found that the patriarch had died in April; and the consensus of public opinion favoured his election against the will of a conservative hierarchy. The bishops were pious but uneducated old people, not easily reconciled to the idea of advancing a younger man with modernizing tendencies. So the Coptic archons, or community leaders, decided to proceed toward his preferment in stages. The synod of 17 April 1853 was persuaded to nominate him metropolitan of Cairo under the name of Cyril, and to entrust him with the affairs of the patriarchate. In that probationary capacity he proved himself worthy of the patriarchal dignity in about a year. It was then that he started the foundation of the Coptic Orthodox College, next to the new cathedral and the patriarchal palace, which owe their inception in the district of Ezbekieh to the *firman* procured by the older Gauhari brothers. The project was acclaimed by the community and the nation. The reform movement thus won its initial battle, and he was finally installed as patriarch under the name of Cyril IV in June 1854. His election was sanctioned by the Khedive ʿAbbās I toward the end of his reign.

[1] Rufaila, pp. 305–24; Iscarous, II, 60–197; Bishop Isodorus' Arabic *Coptic Church History*, Vol. II, pp. 506–12. The need is pressing for biographical study of each name cited here, especially Cyril IV. The present is a short organized summary of an interesting subject. See also R. Strothmann, *Die Koptische Kirche in der Neuzeit*, pp. 24–31; Fowler, *Christian Egypt*, pp. 131–3; Maria Cramer, *Das Christlich-Koptische Ägypten*, pp. 93–4.

Cyril's short reign (1854–61) abounded in reforms. His first target was education, and he spent no less than six hundred thousand piastres, then an enormous sum of money, to complete his exemplary college, where instruction was free. He even distributed books and stationery without charge. Outstanding professors were appointed to teach Coptic, Arabic, Turkish, French, English and Italian, as well as the usual subjects of an academic curriculum. His devotion to the project was such that he spent all his spare time in classes and preferred to make the school his meeting place with visitors whose advice he sought on matters of instruction. The college gained so much prestige that the Khedive Ismā'īl, in the reign of Cyril's successor, Demetrius II, donated fifteen hundred acres of arable land in perpetuity to help the patriarch in meeting the expense of its expanding enrolment. An additional annuity of two hundred pounds in cash was granted but not paid owing to the insolvency of the Egyptian treasury at that time.

Two other schools were also established in distant quarters of the city, and what was even more impressive, he opened the first girls' college in Egypt and became the great pioneer in female education. He was alarmed at the shortage of printed literature, both Arabic and Coptic, since Egypt possessed only the government press at Būlāq. So he hastened to purchase a printing press from Europe and obtained the Khedive Sa'īd Pasha's permission to send four young Copts to learn the art of printing at Būlāq. On the arrival of the press at Alexandria, Cyril, who was at St Antony's, ordered an official reception for it with an imposing procession of deacons in ecclesiastical vestments chanting hymns all the way from Cairo station to the patriarchate. When criticized about the performance, he retorted by saying that if he had been present at that great event, he would have danced before it as David did before the tabernacle.

His religious reforms included reparation of old churches and the building of new ones. Perhaps the completion of the present Basilica of St Mark in Ezbekieh was his greatest feat in this field. Realizing how the Coptic clergy had long been a prey to ignorance, he summoned all priests within reach of the capital to a regular Saturday assembly at the patriarchate for systematic readings and theological discussions, himself participating in their edification. He enforced church discipline, more especially in regard to sacred music and vestments on old models. Father Takla, noted for his mastery of ancient traditional vocal music, was commanded to offer classes to the deacons. The liturgies, hymnals, synaxaria, eucologia, lectionaries, texts of church offices, and even biblical literature, hitherto of limited accessibility in manuscript, were printed for free distribution to churches and even Coptic homes.

In the reorganization of the administration of church property, he eradicated the informality of personal handling which caused confusion and loss of revenue. Orderly book-keeping, and standard registers for property, marriages, births, deaths and similar affairs were inaugurated in the new patriarchal archives.

Cyril also brought foreign prestige to the Church. He was sent by Saʿīd Pasha, Khedive of Egypt, on a hazardous mission of political mediation with Theodor, *negus* of Ethiopia, when war was imminent between the two countries. Starting on 4 September 1856, he returned as late as 13 February 1858[1] after settling the differences of both monarchs with tact and skill. Theodor showed his esteem by meeting the patriarch at a three days' journey from the capital.

In the sphere of external church diplomacy, the visionary Cyril entertained dreams of pan-orthodoxy. He cultivated sympathies with the Melkite Greek patriarch to the point that the latter entrusted him with surveillance over his church affairs during his absence in Constantinople. His policy was one of forgiveness and forgetfulness, even of the fearful memories of Chalcedon and Cyrus. But the peculiar position of Egyptian politics under the khedives made the realization of his new venture a very dangerous one. When Cyril envisaged wider contacts beyond the frontiers of Egypt, notably with the Russian Orthodox Church and the Church of England, he incurred the khedive's tacit ire and suspicion, fearing foreign interference in the realm through such religious associations. The rumour was circulated by word of mouth, but never put in writing before Farouk's abdication for self-evident reasons, that Saʿīd summarily poisoned[2] the illustrious and ambitious patriarch. He completed his course on 30 January 1861, immediately after an audience with the khedive, and the Copts have never forgotten him to this day.

The age of Cyril was rich in outstanding names in the hierarchy. Foremost in sanctity and primitive austerity, reminiscent of the early days of the fathers of Coptic antiquity, was Anba Abraam,[3] bishop of Faiyūm (1829–1914), who freely gave all he had to the poor and the needy of his diocese without distinction between Muslim and Copt. Anba Basileus[4] (1818–99) was consecrated archbishop of Jerusalem by Cyril IV in 1856. His personality rendered him the official representative of the Copts and the unofficial representative of all Egyptians in that international centre. Endowed with unusual administrative ability, he extended Coptic property in the Holy Land, built imposing hostels for pilgrims and, what is more, established the unique and fascinating diminutive chapel at the head of the Holy

[1] It is interesting to realize that Cyril used the time of his long journeying learning Turkish from two Aghas whom Saʿīd delegated as members of his court; Rufaila, p. 315.

[2] Fowler, pp. 132, 133; he wrote at the turn of the century and openly records the murder of the patriarch by order of the khedive.

[3] Strothmann, p. 118; Isodorus, II, 521.

[4] Iscarous, II, 198–279; Strothmann, pp. 116–17; Isodorus, II, 521.

Sepulchre under the great central dome. A story is current among the Copts that the tzar of Russia offered him its volume in gold to buy it, but the wary archbishop gently said that it was not his own to sell. Though somewhat unrealistic, this episode is significant. Through his offices, Sultan Abdul-Hamid issued the *firmān* confirming Coptic possession of Dair al-Sulṭān, which Saladin had given the Coptic community and where the pious Abyssinians craved and still crave a footing within its precincts.

The personality of Cyril's own successor, Demetrius II (1862–70),[1] was dwarfed by the achievements of the preceding reign. Under the successive patriarchs, the graduates of Cyril's college continued to throng the departments of state, and some reached the highest posts in the administration, the example of Bouṭros Ghāli Pasha, who became premier of Egypt, is well known. Others distinguished themselves in all fields in the service of their country and people. A new generation of illuminated priesthood was also budding, though not at the same rate as the Coptic laity. The Hegomenus Fīlūtheus Ibrāhīm ʿAwaḍ (1837–1904)[2] is an instance of progressive learning, eloquence, and public service. In 1874 he became rector of a new school for the education of monks, the class of divines from whom the prelates and patriarchs were selected. He combated the novel inroads of both the Catholic and Protestant missionaries who arrived at this time. He compiled the Coptic canon law which governed family relationship. His homiletics compare favourably with the finest. The fact remains that the impetus given by Cyril IV produced the most felicitous results in building up an enlightened and progressive laity, whereas the clergy unfortunately lagged behind the flock. Thus we begin to perceive a kind of imbalance within Coptic society, which explains the gathering clouds of a new battle between constitutionalism and conservatism. The echo of its din still resounds in our ears to this day.

Cyril V: Clerical Conservatism *versus* Popular Constitutionalism

Born in 1824, Cyril V died in 1927[3] after a tumultuous reign in which he oscillated between clerical conservatism and the aspirations of a progressive

[1] Strothmann, pp. 31–3; Fowler, pp. 133–5. Rufaila, p. 323, records that the khedive summoned the patriarch and warned him against acting like his predecessor, saying that if he wanted something he should do it through the khedive's offices. The warning is of course significant. Bishop Isodorus in his history, II, 508, states that he was poisoned on account of the project of union with the English and Russian churches.

[2] Iscarous, II, 85; Isodorus, II, 520–1.

[3] Rufaila, pp. 329 ff.; Yūsuf Minqarious, *History of the Coptic Nation, 1893–1912* (in Arabic; Cairo, 1913), pp. 59 ff.; Strothmann, pp. 33–5; Fowler, pp. 135–43.

community. His outlook on life had the limitations of his past. His early life was sorrowful. As a young man, Ḥanna Maṭar lost his parents and remained in the care of a modest older brother. In his twenties he took the monastic vow, first at the Monastery of Our Lady of the Syrians (Dair al-Suryān), and afterwards at the poorer Monastery of Baramous, both in the Nitrean Valley. There he lived in poverty and privation. His chief vocation, apart from a share in the religious and domestic service, was the copying of manuscripts for a living. After years of austerity, Demetrius II summoned him for service at St Mark's Cathedral, where he was exposed to contacts with the community. In answer to supplications from his brethren in the wilderness, the patriarch released him for a return to the monastery, where he stayed until 1875. Demetrius died in that year, and the prelates and archons unanimously recalled Father Ḥanna to assume the patriarchal dignity as Cyril V. He occupied the throne for well-nigh fifty-three years. His loyalty, piety and good intentions were above reproach. But he combined with imperturbable obstinacy, the narrowness of an honest man whose education was limited to the knowledge that he had gathered as a simple copyist. This limitation he shared with the hierarchy, which was generally recruited from the uneducated ranks of simple folk. After Cyril IV, the position was thus reversed and the torch of reform was carried alone by lay members of the community. The new age was one of political enfranchisement, parliamentary government and advisory committees. Cyril V came from a different world and was unable to cope with these progressive methods. Hence arose decades of strife between the old order and the new.

It would be unjust to accept the verdict of the anti-patriarchal group which maligned Cyril V as a giant of iniquity. The constructive side of his career was seen in the restoration of many churches, monasteries and nunneries.[1] He also built new churches throughout Egypt and consecrated one at Khartoum in the Sudan. A Coptic technical school for boys and another of home economics for girls were inaugurated in his early years, but it is difficult to define his contribution to their promotion. He bought a spacious house at Mahmasha in Cairo, where he was persuaded to start a new clerical seminary for religious education. In 1896 he issued an encyclical[2] enjoining the clergy to abide by stricter rules of organized religious life. If we can believe his enthusiastic court biographer, he increased patriarchal revenue from five thousand pounds at his accession to forty-three thousand pounds in 1913 through frugality and wise administration.[3] It was in his reign that the 'tribute', a relic of the mediæval Islamic system, the old *jizya* levied from

[1] It is interesting to note Minqarious's enumeration (pp. 63–4) of thirteen monasteries and nunneries in or around Cairo in addition to the patriarchate and one monastery at Faiyūm. The churches restored numbered four and the newly built were ten.

[2] Full text published by Minqarious, pp. 69–73.

[3] Ibid., p. 65.

dhimmi subjects, was completely abolished by Sa'īd Pasha, and all Egyptians became liable to uniform taxation.[1] Subsequent constitutions, though insisting on Islam as the state religion, proclaimed equality of all citizens irrespective of religious beliefs or ethnic origins.

The critical group, on the other hand, indicated that Cyril surrounded himself by a multitude of reactionary clerics and listened to their advice and evil counsel.[2]

During the interregnum between Demetrius II and Cyril V, a number of fervent Copts established a reform association[3] which surveyed the social, cultural and religious state of the Copts and found it lamentable in comparison with other communities. So they approached Anba Marcus, archbishop of Alexandria, who acted for the patriarch, and proposed that he should apply to the government for the creation of a Coptic council of twenty-four members, to be elected by the people with powers of participation in the management of Church property on a sound and profitable basis. The archbishop acquiesced, and a decree was issued on 3 February 1874 initiating the first Community Religious Council (*Maglis Milli*)[4] under the chairmanship of the patriarch or his deputy. Cyril found the Council in office at his accession, and their collaboration augured well by their joint approval of the foundation of the Coptic Theological Seminary. The bone of contention emerged later, when budgetary appropriation was discussed and the members wished to interfere directly in organizing the proceeds of religious property (*Waqfs*). The Patriarch automatically refused to attend the council sessions or even to appoint a deputy for the next seven years, and the legislature became powerless. Still more alarming was his unilateral decision to close the clerical college and a girls' school. This aroused public opinion, and enthusiastic reformers responded to the hardening patriarchal stand by forming scores of benevolent societies in most cities to look after Coptic schools and social work among the poor without resorting to the ecclesiastical authorities or church funds. But the suspension of the council had other detrimental consequences which could not come within the jurisdiction of private associations. Legal cases of marriage, divorce, inheritance and other personal affairs were either retarded or mishandled by the clergy in a way which incited widespread disaffection.

Delegations to the government brought forth in 1883 the reissue of a decree[5] ordering the resumption of the council. The stubborn patriarch

[1] S. Chauleur, *Histoire des Coptes d'Égypte*, p. 161; Jacques Tagher, pp. 238, 254–5. In Muḥammad 'Ali's reign the Copts still paid the *Jizya* amounting to £3,000, but they received some £60,000 in salaries for service in the state. John Bowring, 'Report on Egypt and Candia, addressed to Viscount Palmerston' (London, 1840), pp. 44–5.

[2] Rufaila, pp. 329 ff.

[3] Jam'iyat al-Taufīq; Rufaila, pp. 343–4.

[4] Rufaila, pp. 330–1.

[5] Ibid., p. 335.

protested to the khedive personally, but his appeal was rejected. When the new council was convened the patriarch again abstained from attending its sessions over a technicality. A third council was elected in 1891, and it suffered the fate of its predecessor. Further negotiations were without avail. The new Taufīq Association was formed for reconciliation, as its name indicated, and for the pursuit of reform. Attacks between the ecclesiastical and secular parties became scandalous in the press and in government circles. Patriarchal pleas to the khedive were ignored, and the request for an audience was flatly refused by the palace. The khedive instructed Premier Bouṭros Ghāli Pasha to ask the patriarch to refrain from addressing the court directly. Meanwhile, Council members, in the face of his unflinching obstinacy and disregard for official injunctions, petitioned for his suspension from patriarchal affairs and the appointment of a deputy from the hierarchy to act for him. The bishop of Ṣanabu was mentioned. On hearing this, the infuriated patriarch threatened the candidate with excommunication and approached foreign diplomats to intercede with the khedive on his behalf. Alarmed by the irregularity of this step, Bouṭros Pasha made a final attempt to bridge the dispute by holding a hurried meeting with the patriarch. Though he succeeded in wresting a written agreement from him,[1] it came to nothing.

Finally, in September 1892, the khedive exiled him to the Baramous Monastery, and his aide, the archbishop of Alexandria, was ordered to retire to St Paul's on the Red Sea. This measure aroused popular sympathy for him, more especially as no one doubted his sanctity and good intentions. Efforts by both his friends and foes were exerted at the palace for his return, which was granted in February 1893.[2] He was given a royal welcome by Cairenes, and was accompanied by a state representative and the city governor, who officially reinstated him in the patriarchal palace. The council was accepted, the bishop of Ṣanabu forgiven, the seminary reopened, and a new secondary section in the Coptic college was created. A proclamation was made for expansion in religious education by the inauguration of branch seminaries at Alexandria, Būsh in Beni Suef, and the Muḥarraq Monastery in Asiūṭ. In spite of the rebuffs of conservatism, the modern elements of constitutionalism won the day, and the Community Council became an accepted reality in Coptic public life.

With the settlement of the constitutional crisis within the Church, the Copts became free to deal with other problems originating in Cyril's long reign. One of these touched the Syrian Jacobite Church, which was identical with the Coptic Church in rites, dogmas and doctrines to the extent that both found it normal to exchange prelates and monks in the course of their long history. The situation was momentarily clouded by an untoward incident.

[1] Text published by Minqarious, pp. 304–6; Rufaila, pp. 351–3.

[2] Rufaila, p. 363.

Cyril V, in keeping with older tradition, welcomed a Syrian by the name of Nāʿūm to the fold of Coptic monasticism and later in 1897 raised him to the bishopric as Isodorus.[1] He then appointed him abbot of the Baramous Monastery. Isodorus was an author and church historian of no small merit, but he apparently deviated from tradition on certain topics and was accused of heresy. As administrator, he antagonized his direct superior, the archbishop of Alexandria. Inside the monastery, his policy led to the ruin of the Baramous brotherhood. Some monks discarded Coptic orthodoxy altogether, and the rest deserted the convent. The Holy Synod, under Cyril's presidency, tried him, found him guilty, and degraded him. He resorted to the patriarch of Antioch, who disregarded the sentence and again made him bishop as Cyril Isodorus. He further nominated him as his representative with powers to recover some churches and convents in Egypt for Syrian authority. These decisions were communicated in writing to Cyril V and the Egyptian government. The Coptic patriarch in turn refuted those claims by similar letters to Antioch and the authorities. Happily the incident soon passed and the authorities gave it no particular attention.

The other problem assumed greater dimensions, and, though it finally subsided, evoked national uproar for a time. This was the movement of the Coptic Congress[2] held in 1911 at Asiūṭ for requesting fuller Coptic civic enfranchisement and complete equality of all Egyptians in opportunities and duties, irrespective of religious profession. A counter-movement was the establishment of a Muslim Congress simultaneously held in Alexandria to confound Coptic claims. The khedive was displeased with both movements, and the patriarch tried to persuade the Coptic Congress leaders to transfer their meetings to Cairo in compliance with the government's wishes. After a period, however, the movement subsided; and eight years later the leading members of the Coptic Congress were among the foremost nationalist delegates of the Wafd party in the great struggle for independence of their common fatherland. At a later date, the Muslim Brothers tried to revive sectarian nationalism, which proved to be an unnatural imposition contrary to progress, and the Egyptian revolution had no difficulty in suppressing the whole Brotherhood with its reactionary and disruptive policies. Even the incidents of the sack of a Coptic church at Zagazig in March 1947 and the burning of the Suez church by incendiaries in January 1952 were discounted by the Copts as criminal acts punishable by the public law and without

[1] Full report with documents to be found in Minqarious, pp. 88–111; Rufaila, pp. 369–71. Bishop Isodorus' own point of view in the matter is summarily presented in his own *Coptic Church History*, Vol. II, p. 513. But he provides the details of what he calls his tragedy later in the supplement, II, 563–99. However, he makes a generally favourable account of Cyril V's reign and the Coptic personalities of the time; cf. II, 513–25.

[2] Kyriacos Mikhā'īl, *Copts and Moslems under British Control* (London, 1911), pp. 19 ff.; Minqarious, pp. 422 ff.

general significance or national consequence. Perhaps the most remarkable outcome of the succession of events from the days of Cyril V is that national unity has come to stay, that religion belongs to God and the homeland to all.

Coming of the Missionary

The advent of the European missionary, both Catholic and Protestant, and the Coptic counter-movement took concrete shape in the reign of Cyril V. Catholic attempts at conciliation, however, go further back into history. The first endeavour at the Council of Ferrara-Florence in 1438–45 was followed by another in 1597, without avail. Then in 1630 a Capuchin friar of Paris, Joseph Leclerc du Tremblay, founded a modest religious centre in Cairo which another Father Agathangelo of Vendôme inherited, but evidently he failed to impress the Copts. In the end, he migrated to Abyssinia, where he was killed. In 1675, the Franciscans came to Upper Egypt and the Jesuits settled in Cairo. Both missions had no response whatever until, in 1741, Anba Athanasius, bishop of Jerusalem, became a Catholic with two or three ineffectual successors. It was at that time that Rūfa'īl al-Ṭūkhi, a learned Coptic convert to Catholicism, had to flee to Rome, where he spent the years 1736–49 editing the Copto-Arabic *Eucologion* and other prayer books of the Coptic Church. The French expedition of 1798–1801 offered the Latin missionary more freedom of movement in the country, and a few Copts seem to have had no objection to union with Rome, until the bishop of Girga, Anba Yūsāb al-Abaḥḥ, known for his sanctity and eloquence, rose to defend Coptic doctrine and silence Roman propaganda.

In fact, the introduction of Catholicism into Egypt came more through politics and expediency than through candid conviction. The story runs that the French consul-general approached Muhammad ʿAli requesting that he might issue a summary invitation, or rather order, to the Coptic patriarch to offer ecclesiastical allegiance to Rome. The khedive, in acquiescence, told his Coptic secretary, Muʿallim Ghāli, to act accordingly on his behalf; but knowing Coptic obstinacy in matters of creed, the resourceful Ghāli suggested proselytizing himself with his family and dependents as a first step, and having an example, the rest would follow him. The result was disappointing, though Catholicism came to stay.

Rome put into force its pretensions of superiority over the Coptic Church in 1895 by the elevation of a Uniate Catholic priest named Cyril Macarius as Coptic papal nuncio to the whole diocese of Egypt, together with two suffragan bishops for Lower and Upper Egypt. Instead of quietly acting within his jurisdiction over the strict Catholic minority, Cyril Macarius[1] began to issue encyclicals addressed to members of the Coptic congregation and their priests, inviting them to offer allegiance to the pope at Rome. The Coptic liturgy was adopted *verbatim* and the Coptic hymnal chanted in a similar fashion in all Catholic Coptic churches in Coptic and Arabic with the necessary interpolations concerning the pope. People did not distinguish differences and the whole scheme looked like a conspiracy, which Cyril V firmly met with a long and forceful encyclical read by Coptic bishops and priests in all Coptic churches. Coptic preachers and theologians thundered from every pulpit in defence of the faith of their fathers, and the Hegomenos Filūtheus ʿAwaḍ played a decisive role in the ensuing controversy.

Protestant missionary activity in Egypt was inaugurated by the United Presbyterians of America in 1854, and the Church Missionary Society of England supplemented that work in 1882. Launched primarily to work amongst non-Christians, they soon took the shorter road of proselytizing the Copts through the medium of excellent educational offerings and fine social service, and the Copts reacted with some vigour.[2]

The result of both endeavours was the establishment of two small but active minorities of Catholic and Protestant congregations. The impact of their dynamism on the Coptic Church saw its modern awakening from centuries of lethargy. The challenge shook the ancient church to its very foundations and inspired its sons to rekindle the dimmed flame of a glorious past.

[1] Minqarious, pp. 74–88. For the Catholic outlook on the subject, see M. Khuzām, *The Catholic Coptic Mission* (Cairo, 1929). Works by Catholic scholars such as Adrian Fortescue, Donald Attwater and R. Janin contain useful background material. See also S. Gaselee, *The Uniates and their Rites* (London, 1925); V. Buri, 'L'unione della Chiesa Copta con Roma sotto Clemente VIII', in *Orientalia Christiana* (Rome, 1931), XXIII, 2, no. 72; *Le problème de l'union des églises d'Orient et d'Occident, Essai historique et pastoral*, par les Missionnaires de St Paul (Harissa, Liban, 1939); Centro Francescano di Studi Orientali Cristiani, *Il primato e l'unione delle chiese nel Medio Oriente*, in Studia Orientalia Cristiana, Collectanea No. 5° (Cairo, 1960): Chiesa Copta (pp. 1–181), La Chiesa Siriana (pp. 183–214), Chiesa Armena (pp. 215–353), Chiesa Caldea (pp. 355–438, followed by some documents; Fowler, pp. 231–4, 270–1.

[2] For background material on the Protestant missionary work in Egypt, the following is a useful selection: R. Anderson, *History of the American Board of Commissions for Foreign Missions to the Oriental Churches* (Boston, 1872); J. Batal, *Assignment, Near East* (New York, 1950); A. J. Dain, *Mission Fields Today: A Brief World Survey* (London, 1956); A. Dempsey, *Mission on the Nile* (London, 1955); M. Fowler, *Christian Egypt* (London, 1901); *Handbook of Foreign Missions* of the United Presbyterian Church of North America (Philadelphia) and the Board of the Women's General Missionary Society (Pittsburgh); A. H. Hourani, *Minorities in the Arab World* (Oxford, 1947); C. R. Watson, *Egypt and the Christian Crusade* (Philadelphia, 1907). For further references, see K. E. Moyer, *A Selected and Annotated Bibliography of North Africa and the Near and Middle East* (New York, 1957); Fowler, pp. 235–69 on Anglican mission, 274–9 on American Presbyterian mission, 280–2 on other Protestant missions.

An Innovation

After the decease of Cyril V in August 1927, the Coptic hierarchy made a new departure from the accepted tradition of patriarchal elections. Hitherto the patriarch-elect had been chosen from the ranks of simple monks by the archons or notables of the community in collaboration with the leading church dignitaries and in accordance with the time-honoured terms of the *Didascallia* and the interpretation of its contents by mediæval writers. During the early decades of the twentieth century, the equilibrium between the clergy and the laity in matters of progress and education was shaken. While members of the Coptic community were advancing by leaps and bounds socially and professionally, the clerical positions were filled essentially by men whose education was defective. Secular apathy grew in regard to the clergy with serious consequences. Thus we find that bishops and archbishops began to covet the patriarchal throne for themselves, while the community remained passive and disinterested in ecclesiastical developments. It was in this atmosphere that the last three patriarchs were elected. The first was the veteran archbishop of Alexandria and Beḥaira Province, Joannes XIX (1927–42). The second was the archbishop of Asiūṭ who succeeded as Macarius III (1944–5). The third was the archbishop of Girga, Yūsāb II (1946–56), then considered by some as a better candidate since he had partial theological training in Greece. But the apparent sterility and absence of constructive policies in Church affairs during the first two reigns only gave way to simony and corruption in the third. The reaction to that lamentable state was a violent reawakening of the Copts.

The quarrel between the patriarch and the people over the influence of his servant in the administration of Church finances and episcopal nominations became one of the worst public scandals in Coptic history. Finally came the dismissal of his temporizing Community Council and the appointment by decree of an independent commission of twenty-four Coptic leaders[1] to handle the deteriorating position. The unprecedented abduction of the patriarch by the extremists of a 'Society of the Coptic Nation'[2] was one demonstration

[1] Having been one of the nominees to that Council, I had the opportunity to witness the workings of the patriarchal machinery from within. The present account is given from memory rather than memoirs. I participated in numerous sub-committees of enquiry into some facets of emerging situations. Members of the clergy testified and the *procès-verbaux* of the meetings were compiled, and, if saved in the patriarchal archives, they should provide future scholars with revealing details. Our *liaison* with the government was the Coptic member of the Cabinet, the late Guindy (Bey) ʿAbd al-Malik, a former supreme court judge and a man of great integrity. His personality was above reproach and his courage was tremendous.

[2] 'Jamāʿat al-Umma al-Qibṭiya.' A modern author, Edward Wakin in his *A Lonely Minority, the Story of Egypt's Copts, the Challenge of Survival for Four Million Christians*

of the rising feelings among the Copts and the gravity of public opinion. The new commission was universally welcomed, but its members soon came to clash with the simoniacal patriarch and his corrupt retinue. Meanwhile, under the influence of evil advisers, he antagonized his own bishops through excessive extortions and threats of degradation. Hence the hierarchy swung to the side of the Council and formed a united front. After several enquiries into the patriarch's behaviour, a joint decision was reached by the Holy Synod and the Community Council to relieve Yūsūb of Church administration. A request to that effect was granted by the state in a decree dated September 1955, and the unhappy patriarch was escorted by the authorities into exile at the Monastery of Our Lady, known as Dair al-Muḥarraq, in Asiūṭ. His spiritual prerogative was entrusted to an ecclesiastical commission of three archbishops of recognized piety. He died on 14 November 1956, and a saintly recluse named Mena was elected to succeed him and was consecrated under the name of Cyril, or Kirollos VI, on 10 May of the same year. Consequently, all Copts rejoiced at the breaking of dawn again.

Modern Reform

Even in its darker moments, the Coptic Church has always found reforming and progressive personalities in its membership. The educational limitations of its priesthood began to give way to university graduates who came to enroll in the hierarchy, both monastic and secular, during the reign of Yūsāb II. This movement has been rapidly growing since the accession of Cyril or Kirollos VI, who has surrounded himself with advisers of a much higher calibre than his predecessors, and the Coptic Holy Synod has incorporated a major section of its membership from the highly qualified younger ranks of the community – men who combine commendable education and learning with piety, integrity, and unswerving dedication to the cause of service.

With the extension of religious liberties under the Constitution and the National Charter, the Copts have been able to build numerous churches to cope with their increasing numbers throughout the country and in the big cities. The ancient models of Coptic architecture have been revived by men

(New York, 1963), pp. 93 ff., has lightly touched the periphery of the subject as a whole. Of course it is extremely difficult to give details, since the sources are unpublished and the process is still current history. The writer of these pages, who happened to be a modest factor in the events of the period, has prepared a fuller account under a Rockefeller grant to the Egyptian Historical Association for research on the subject of 'Modernization in the Arab World'. Since the lamentable death of the chief editor, Shafīq Ghorbāl, it has been difficult to know the fate of that material.

of vision and unusual skill. The Zamalek Church of Our Lady[1] is the last word in this renewal of the old and the adaptation of the modern. The rebuilding of the Cathedral of St Mark in Alexandria has given the old capital a worthy house of worship. More than a score of churches have emerged throughout Cairo, notably in the thickly populated district of Shubra. The historic churches have received national attention, and contributions from the public funds have helped in their restoration and preservation, through the good offices of the Commission for the Conservation of Arab Monuments in the Department of Antiquities.

The multiplication of Coptic benevolent societies in every corner of the country, now under close control by the Ministry of Social Affairs, has given to the country a variety of foundations, of which the Coptic college for girls and the Coptic hospital in Cairo are the most important. The Coptic hospital has proved to be one of the finest in Egypt, and its services are extended to all patients, regardless of faith or creed. It was inaugurated by a benevolent Coptic association in the reign of Cyril V, and it has been enlarged since then with state aid. Because of its importance to the public, it has lately been nationalized by the state, together with other similar hospitals, both Coptic and Muslim alike.

With the nationalization of educational institutions in recent years, the innumerable Coptic private schools have been ceded to the Ministry of Education, but Coptic theological training has remained the chief concern of the Community Council. The Coptic clerical college which Cyril V was persuaded to start as a small and rather insignificant institution, has been moved from its antiquated quarters at Mahmasha to the imposing Anba Ruweis building, and it has been supplemented by a fine annexe on its extensive grounds. Now it comprises three divisions: an intermediate, with a five-year curriculum for young folk holding a primary school certificate only; an advanced section, with a three-year programme for graduates of secondary education; and evening classes open to students of all description who are interested in divinity without intention to join the priesthood. Its present principal[2] is a doctor of philosophy in Coptic studies from Manchester and a monk of Dair-el-Muḥarraq. A special branch of the college, St Didymus Institute for the Blind, sponsors the instruction of chanters, who constitute an important element in the celebration of Coptic liturgies. There is a tacit recognition from the bishops that no priest may be ordained before gradua-

[1] Its architect-artist is Ramses Wiṣṣa Wāṣef, a graduate of the Paris Polytechnic and the son of a former president of the Egyptian parliament. His imagination and skill extended from architecture to stained glass, painting and coloured tile. His school of folk-weaving will be mentioned later.

[2] Dr Wahīb ʿAṭallah Girgis, now Father Bakhūm al-Muḥarraqi, is a former pupil of the eminent Coptologist the late Professor Walter Till. He has written several brochures in Arabic and in English, of which some have been cited already.

tion from that college. Of late years, its student enrolment has included numerous graduates from the faculties of letters, law, science, agriculture and engineering of the Egyptian universities. At long last, the infiltration of real scholars into the hierarchy may be regarded as an auspicious beginning of a Coptic religious renaissance. Young men of the same calibre have also joined monastic foundations with sure prospects of candidacy to the episcopate. Already a number of them have succeeded the deceased bishops and archbishops of the old school.

Partly inspired by the progress of religious education, and in collaboration with a number of ordained university graduates, the Coptic youth have constituted a Sunday School organization to instruct young Copts in matters of religion and the Church. Centuries of pressure and seclusion had produced a priestly class which, while retaining traditions of piety and spirituality, fell under the yoke of ignorance. Methods of worship among the Copts became mere forms with little life or even intelligibility. The first task of the Sunday School leaders has been the eradication of this danger through voluntary instruction. From modest subscriptions, too, they have been able to establish a great many elementary schools in remote regions, and to start homes in the metropolitan areas for students with religious inclinations.

In the religio-cultural field, three noteworthy features have aroused considerable appreciation in scholarly circles. These are the Coptic Museum, the Society of Coptic Archæology, and the Institute of Coptic Studies.

The Coptic Museum was founded by the late Morkos Smaika[1] (Pasha) in 1910 in a single hall near the Muʿallaqa Church, within the precincts of the Fort of Babylon in Old Cairo, with the approval of Cyril V. Armed with a patriarchal charter, Morkos (Pasha) combed all the historic monasteries and churches to collect objects of archæological interest for the Museum. He also used his personal influence to acquire important articles from old Coptic homes. The state became interested in it, and finally it was incorporated in the Department of Antiquities and given a fine home built in Coptic style on the same spot. Monuments of Coptic provenance in the Egyptian Museum were transferred to it, including the magnificent collections from Bawīṭ and St Jeremias. Whole painted roofs from older foundations were transported to it, and stained glass windows helped to embellish the atmosphere of the building. The museum soon overflowed with precious contents. Halls were devoted to stonework, stelæ and tombstones, woodwork, furniture, metalwork, textiles and embroideries, pottery, porcelain and glass, engraved ivory, icons, frescoes and wall paintings and domestic articles of all kinds.

[1] Later he inaugurated a museum publication series with profusely illustrated guides in English, French and Arabic. The Arabic guide appeared in 2 vols. (Cairo, 1930–2). The French and English are smaller brochures which appeared also in Cairo in 1937 and 1938 respectively.

The museum has grown to be a precious link between the Egyptian Museum and the Museum of Islamic Art. Its library, too, has been developed into a true repository of Coptic source material, both published and in manuscript. It contains one of the finest collections of Coptic papyri, ostraca, manuscripts and all manner of inscribed material. The Gnostic papyri of Chenoboskion found at Nagʿ Ḥamādi are among its most prized acquisitions of recent years. Numerous Christian Arabic manuscripts have been accumulated in it from varied sources.[1]

The Society of Coptic Archæology was started by Mr Mirrit Ghāli, a grandson of Bouṭros Ghāli Pasha, in 1934 under the original name of the Society of the Friends of Coptic Art. It assumed its present title in 1938. Its *Bulletin*[2] has attracted contributors of profound Coptic scholarship from all parts of the world, and its publications as a whole have multiplied.[3] In recent years, the Society undertook a Coptic excavation on the site of St Phœbamon's Monastery in the Thebaïd near Luxor.[4]

In a sense the Institute of Coptic Studies[5] may be regarded as a natural corollary to the development of the foregoing foundations. The need had long been felt for an educational institution in Egypt where instruction, training and research might be conducted in the field of Coptic studies. With limited funds and unlimited dedication, a small group of specialized scholars was able to make the new foundation a reality in the spacious Anba Ruweis Building, the use of which was granted by the Coptic Community Council. The Institute was conceived for the study of every facet of Egyptian civilization in what is known as the Coptic period, the millennium of transition between the dynastic and Islamic eras. The plan comprised some twelve departments, not all functioning then or as yet, but representing Coptic

[1] Marcus H. Smaika (sic), *Catalogue of the Coptic and Arabic Manuscripts in the Coptic Museum, the Patriarchate, the Principal Churches of Cairo and Alexandria and the Monasteries of Egypt*, 2 vols. (Cairo, 1939–42).

[2] Fifteen volumes of the *Bulletin* had already appeared from 1935 to 1959, of which the first three or four are already out of print.

[3] The Society publications consist of four categories: (1) Art and Archæology, (2) Excavations, (3) Texts and Documents, and (4) Miscellaneous. A total of 22 volumes are in print.

[4] The results of this excavation are planned in three volumes under the title, *Le Monastère de Phœbamon dans le Thebaïde:* (1) Archæology by Ch. Bachatly, (2) Texts by R. Rémondon, W. C. Till and Yassa ʿAbd al-Masīḥ, and (3) Analysis of Vegetals and Materials by E. A. M. Greiss, A. K. El-Duweini and Z. Iskander. Tome II only published (Cairo, 1965). The death of some of the above-mentioned writers has delayed publication of further volumes of this important work.

[5] A parallel Catholic 'Institut Copte' was founded in 1952 by a Franciscan, Père Sylvestre Chauleur. It has published a series of brochures on Coptic subjects called 'Les Cahiers Coptes', about ten in number. Another Catholic foundation was started by another Franciscan, Father Martiniano Roncaglia, under the name 'Centro di studi orientali della Custodia Francescana di Terra Santa'. It publishes a series called 'Coptica'. Both are in Cairo. M. Cramer, *Das Christlich-Koptische Ägypten, Einst und Heute*, p. 95.

language and linguistics, history, social studies, archæology, art, canon law, church music, theology, Ethiopian and African studies, and Semitics and Christian Arabic letters. It was made clear from the beginning that the project, though sponsored by the Church and its Community Council, was not a sectarian or a religious affair but a school geared to the study of a phase of Egyptian civilization which happened to be Coptic and Christian. It was open to scholars of all faiths and all sects without the slightest discrimination. There was reassuring response to the idea within Egypt and outside its frontiers. The growth of its library resources has been spectacular, and the enrolment has been on the ascendant.

A mutual alliance of the three afore-mentioned organizations will undoubtedly yield results of importance to the Egyptian humanities and also elevate clerical standards.

Internationalism and Œcumenicity

Like a great and solitary Egyptian temple sorrowfully standing on the edge of the desert and weathering sandstorms over the years until it became submerged by the accretions of time, the ancient Coptic Church led its lonesome life unnoticed on the fringe of Christian civilization and was buried in the sands of time and oblivion. Like the same massive temple, too, it has proved itself to be indestructible though battered by the winds of change. As an organism, its potential vitality, though enfeebled by sustained fighting, has survived in a latent form under the weight of accumulated rubble. In the last few decades, with increasing security and liberty from within and support and sympathy from without, its sons have started removing the sands of time from around its edifice, which has shown modest signs of shining again. The task is a joint effort in which all the aforementioned institutions must join hands with a hierarchy that is gradually shaking off the dust of ignorance and formalism, and those international organizations of religion which have nurtured a growing interest in its historic heritage.

The Coptic Church, which had chosen the solitude of its own primitiveness, its peculiar spiritualism, and the rough road of its so-called Monophysitism since the black days of Chalcedon in 451, is now steadily recapturing its faith in old friends and foes overseas and in distant climes. The aloofness and traditional suspicion of the patriarchs towards other Christians of different sects is gradually being replaced by a sense of mutual regard and a measure of cooperation with other churches and other nations in the realm of œcumenicity. With the Eastern and African brethren, the Coptic Church has of course been conducting many visitations and contacts beyond its older frontiers, thus increasing the awareness of that historic kinship in many areas. In Asia, apart from amicable contacts with the Syrians as well as the Armenians and Indians, the project of consecrating a Coptic bishop of Kuwait in 1963 was an event not to be underestimated. Activities in Africa have been more intense, and the *rapprochement* of the nations of that continent must necessarily reflect itself in the religious exchanges with Egypt, both Christian and Muslim. Ethiopian relations with the Copts are indeed paramount in the general picture. It has been thought by some that the decision to relieve the Ethiopian Church from an Egyptian archbishop, a tradition dating from the days of Frumentius in 340 A.D., meant that schism had set in. This is a serious mistake. The consecration of the first Ethiopian patriarch-catholicus in the person of the Ethiopian Anba Basilius on 28 June 1959, has been a wise step in keeping with the growing sense of nationalism. Hitherto the tie between the two Churches had been the person of the ethnically foreign Anba Salāma. Now the bond is not personal but doctrinal, since the document of consecration has rendered the relation much deeper, clearer and healthier. The 'pope of Alexandria and the patriarch of the see of St Mark' has become the accepted and direct head of all sister churches under his obedience. This recognition was demonstrated in concrete form during the recent visit of Pope Cyril, or Kirollos VI, to Ethiopia. The total number of bishops now in Ethiopia is twenty-four.

In Africa, moreover, the Coptic Church has two archbishops in the Sudan, one for Khartoum and another for Omdurman. South Africa has had a Coptic bishop. Ghana's former President Nkrumah, who is wedded to a Coptic woman, opened the door to Coptic ecclesiastical service in his own country. However, the staggering news of the projected affiliation of some five million African Christians from Uganda and the neighbouring countries with the Coptic Church awaits further confirmation, though it must seem natural that those nations so recently liberated from the colonialist yoke should look to Egypt for religious leadership and spiritual guidance from the only indigenous African church.

Acrimonious feelings toward the Western churches in Europe and America have been fast disappearing with the growing recognition of the Coptic Church as a living reality. The first demonstration of a spontaneous approach toward the Christian West took place when the Copts decided to send a delegation of three members[1] to represent the Coptic Church officially in the World Council of Churches held at Evanston, Illinois, in the summer of 1954. Those Copts protested vehemently against the gracious welcome accorded them as newcomers to œcumenicity. They had been here, they said,

[1] These were Father Makary El-Souriany (now Bishop Samuel), a monk of Dair al-Suryān, and Father Ṣalīb Souriāl (a former attorney and now secular priest at Guiza), and the writer of these pages.

up to 451, when they decided to retire from the earliest phase of that world movement after the iniquities and humiliation of Chalcedon. With the rebirth of Christian fellowship, understanding and mutual forgiveness, the Copts have relinquished their established policy of seclusion in order to play again their part in the commonwealth of the churches after a break of fifteen centuries. Since Evanston, they have undoubtedly made themselves felt in the general deliberations of the Council and in its Central Committee. Pope Cyril, or Kirollos VI, found it a worthy proposition to consecrate a special bishop of œcumenical and social service. The Copts have not missed one meeting since 1954. They also despatched their own observers to the Second Vatican Œcumenical Council.[1]

At long last, the retiring Coptic Church has emerged once more into œcumenicity. But this is not the end. The spring of 1954 witnessed a further step when the Coptic Church sent three representatives, a monk and two laymen,[2] to the Muslim-Christian Convention at Bḥamdoun, Lebanon. About eighty spiritual leaders, half Muslim and half Christian, drawn from many churches and about thirty countries, met in solemn convocation to 'pledge that under God we will work unceasingly, with mutual confidence and regard for the rights of others, to promote understanding and brotherliness between the adherents of Islam and Christianity'.[3] The Copts, who had co-existed with the Muslims in Egypt for thirteen centuries, were an important factor in that international and interreligious movement, with the fundamentals of which they had not been unfamiliar. Nothing could be more acceptable to the mind of the Copt than the aforementioned pledge, again affirmed by the Alexandria Declaration of 14 February 1955, 'to do all within our power to further the spirit of friendship between the people of our respective faiths, to eradicate prejudice and misunderstanding, and to create brotherhood and mutual understanding in every possible way.'[4] This is perhaps the consummation of Coptic aspirations on the road of internationalism.

[1] Father Bak͟hūm al-Muḥarraqi (Dr Wahib 'Aṭalla Girgis attended as observer at the Council.

[2] Father Makary (Bishop Samuel), the late Alexandre Asabgi (former judge of the Mixed Courts) and the writer of these lines.

[3] *Handbook for Fellowships of Muslims and Christians*, 'The Bhamdoun Covenant', pp. 22–3.

[4] Ibid., The Alexandria Declaration', pp. 23–9.

7 • COPTIC FAITH AND CULTURE

The Hierarchy

From its very foundation, the backbone of the Coptic Church was its hierarchy.[1] Throughout their long history the Copts regarded their prelates with the highest deference. To them they looked for spiritual leadership and personal guidance, especially in the days of great trial, which were not infrequent in Coptic annals. Neither massacre, nor persecution, nor dismissal from office, nor confiscation of property could exterminate the Copts as a community, and the hierarchy stood in the midst of all movements to fortify the faithful through times of storm. Faith and fortitude were their means of survival, and their rallying point was the patriarch, whom they feared and revered, not on account of the legal powers accorded to his office, but because of his piety and godliness. If not the earliest, the Coptic Church was at least one of the earliest on record to boast a truly established Church with a complete hierarchical framework. Even in the time of St Mark, the first patriarch of Alexandria, the Church seems already to have had a bishop, presbyters and deacons.

Until the present reign of Cyril or Kirollos VI, the patriarch's full title, indicating his wide ecclesiastical jurisdiction, was as follows: 'Most holy Pope and Patriarch of the great city of Alexandria and of the places subject to Egypt, of Jerusalem the holy city, of Abyssinia, Nubia, the Pentapolis, and of all the places where St Mark preached.'[2] With variation of wording rather than meaning, that title has been resolved under the terms of the decree of 10 May 1959 for the present patriarch, Cyril VI, as simply 'Pope of Alexandria

[1] A good source is to be found in Ṣafiy ibn al-ʿAssāl's Arabic compilation of the Coptic Laws, the 'Nomcanon' written in 1238, published several times. The edition used here is that of Murqus Girgis (Cairo, 1927). For literature on the 'Nomcanon', see Graf, II, 401–3. A. Fortescue, *Lesser Eastern Churches*, pp. 252–9, gives an old but still useful account with the usual reservations to be taken with a Catholic writer of great prejudice. M. Cramer, *Das Christlich-Koptische Ägypten*, pp. 95–6, gives some curt notes of limited usefulness.

[2] Fortescue, p. 255. In note 3 he fails to appreciate the use of the word 'Pope' in the Coptic Church; see above.

and Patriarch of the See of St Mark'.[1] Though more curtailed than any preceding descriptions, this title is at the same time more general and comprehensive enough to cope with the new situation in Ethiopia, where there is a new patriarch-catholicus obedient to the see of Alexandria. The said pope is one of four principal Apostolic patriarchs, the other three being those of Rome, Antioch and Ephesus; and the last was translated to the royal city of Constantinople. Three other subsidiary patriarchs are recognized in Jerusalem, owing to its sanctified position, in Seleucia-Ctesiphon, on account of its distance from the mother see of Antioch, and in Ethiopia. The four principals alone have jurisdiction to ordain archbishops and bishops, to hold great, or general, synods for doctrinal considerations, and to consecrate the holy chrism. The Copts do not entertain the idea of infallibility in regard to their pope and patriarch, but they recognize his supreme authority over the whole church, and no power can dethrone him, once he is duly elected and consecrated. The patriarch is expected to convene the general synod once a year, and the archbishops should summon their own bishops twice a year for the local synod, which is authorized to make minor decisions on matters of local interest.[2] The epithet 'judge of the world' has been used in speaking of the Coptic patriarch.[3]

The manner of his election is of interest. In theory, the whole nation participates. In practice, three candidates are chosen by the joint deliberations of the members of the Holy Synod, the Community Council, and the Coptic archons or leading personalities. Each candidate must be a monk of lifelong celibacy, the son of first-wedded parentage, and at least fifty years of age. He should be known for his sanctity, learning and great wisdom, without bodily defect or chronic disease that might interfere in the discharge of his public and religious duties. Before the final selection is made by lot, continuous services are held for three days in succession and a complete vigil is observed on the eve of the third. Names of the three candidates on little scrolls are enclosed in a sealed envelope with a fourth scroll on which is written, 'Jesus Christ the Good Shepherd'. This is deposited on the altar and opened before the congregation after the final Holy Communion by the celebrant, who is usually the oldest interim archbishop acting for the patriarch. Then an infant of about eight picks out the winning name, unless the fourth scroll emerges to indicate that none of the three is acceptable to the divine will and thus the whole operation must be repeated until the issue is resolved. The idea behind this method is to remove from the human electorate all personal responsibility

[1] Most of the recent developments here outlined have been supplied by Bishop Samuel during his episcopal visitation to the Copts in America in September 1963.

[2] Ibn al-ʿAssāl's *Laws*, pp. 21–8.

[3] Fortescue, loc. cit., points out that that epithet is assumed by both Greek and Coptic patriarchs of Alexandria in succession to St Cyril the Great, who presided over the Œcumenical Council of Ephesus in 439.

for the patriarch-elect and to render him patriarch by the grace of God, answerable to Him alone. Afterward, he is ordained in stages by all the archbishops and bishops, who lay hands on him first as deacon and priest, then as archpriest (*Hegomenos* or *Qummuṣ*) and abbot, then bishop while he kneels before them. In the end, he is enthroned and crowned as patriarch, and in turn they kneel before him and offer him allegiance while the congregation acclaims him and he imparts his blessing to all.

In history, it may be noted that this dignity had never been coveted by pretenders. The burdens and hazards, both spiritual and physical, associated with that great office made those selected for it very reluctant to accept it. Candidates are known to have been occasionally dragged in chains from monastic seclusion to the seat of authority. But once elected, they met the demands of office with great dedication and diligence. They continued to dress in black with the distinctive episcopal black turban, though some were reported to have worn underneath the regular outer clothing of black cloak and tunic a rough woollen shirt next to the skin. They led a severely abstemious life, and some slept on beds only within sight of a witnessing servant, but lay down on rough matting on the floor when left to themselves. Their income consisted of free offerings in addition to revenues from property given by the faithful for religious purposes.

Strictly speaking, the total number of archbishops and bishops consecrated by patriarchs and under their jurisdiction, direct or indirect, is fifty-seven. These may be classified under five categories. The first category comprises nineteen archbishops of sees within Egypt.[1] The second, seven abbots of the great monasteries[2] hold the rank of bishop. Thirdly, two new bishops have recently been installed by Cyril (Kirollos) VI, one for public, œcumenical and social services,[3] the other in charge of theological and educational institutions,[4] both stationed in Cairo and without regular sees. Fourthly, four archbishops and bishops reside in foreign countries – one at Jerusalem, two in the Sudan[5] and Uganda, one in South Africa, and one newly created bishop

[1] These are the Archbishops of al-Sharqiya, al-Gharbiya (including al-Beḥaira and Kafr al-Shaikh), al-Minūfiya, al-Daqahliya, al-Qaliūbiya, al-Gīza, al-Faiyūm, Beni Suef, Dayrūṭ, Manfalūṭ, Asiūṭ, Abu Tīg (including Ṭaḥṭa and al-Marāgha), Sūhāg, Akhmīn, Girga, al-Balyana, Qena (including Qūṣ and Naqāda), and Luxor (including Isna and Aswan).

[2] Al-Suryān, Anba Bshoi, Abu Maqār, al-Baramous, Anba Bula, Anba Antonius and al-Muḥarraq. St Samuel, sparsely inhabited, does not have a bishop.

[3] Bishop Samuel, a graduate in law from Cairo University, of education from the American University at Cairo, of theology from the Clerical College and a Master of Arts from Princeton. He is a member of the Central Committee of the World Council of Churches.

[4] Bishop Shenūda, a graduate from the English Department of the Faculty of Letters in Alexandria University and of the Clerical College in Cairo.

[5] For the north or Nubia, his title is archbishop of Omdurman, ʻAṭbara and Nubia; the other, archbishop of Kharṭoum, the south and Uganda.

of Kuwait.[1] Fifthly, Ethiopia has twenty-four bishops and archbishops, including Patriarch-Catholicos Anba Basilius, whom the pope of Alexandria consecrated at Cairo in the presence of Emperor Haile Selassie on 28 June 1959. This came as the result of a treaty whereby the primacy of Alexandria over Ethiopia has been recognized in perpetuity. The number of bishoprics has varied from time to time in accordance with the expansion or shrinkage of population, reaching a maximum of approximately one hundred prior to the Arab Conquest.

The Church has three vicars-general. Two of these are priests, one in charge of the patriarchal administration in Cairo, and another in Alexandria. The third, in Jerusalem, is always the archbishop[2] of that important see. Under the bishops and archbishops – all monks of course – are the secular priests, who are all married men. These may be ordinary priests (presbyters) or archpriests by rank of *Hegomenos* or *Qummuṣ*. A priest must marry before his ordination; otherwise he remains celibate. If he loses his wife, he may remarry only after withdrawing from the priesthood. There is absolutely no marriage after ordination. Tacit agreement among the bishops has been reached on the educational standards of priests, and the condition of graduation from the clerical college is now in force. Priests are subsidized by a small stipend in addition to free offerings and voluntary fees for marriages and other functions.

The class of deacons in the Coptic Church in modern times has consisted mainly of children assisting in the service as a chorus. Efforts have been made, however, to revive the older and more important position of the deacon and archdeacon in the Church. Originally, both were parallel to the priest and archpriest, and their task in helping with a religious service was extended to the faithful outside the church. Deacons marry after ordination, and if they lose a wife they can remarry as simple laymen. On the other hand, they may remain celibate and live in the world on a voluntarily monastic basis. As such, they are eligible to the highest Church office in the hierarchy, including the episcopate and even the patriarchate. Athanasius was raised from the diaconate to the patriarchate in the fourth century. It would seem from the early records of the Church that in reality most of the first patriarchs had been deacons or archdeacons. The idea behind that system may have been that monks and hermits had lost touch with the world, whereas celibate deacons and archdeacons qualified for more effective service in the patriarchate. The mediæval custom of reserving the patriarchal throne for a regular monk from the wilderness may have been an innovation of later times.

The chanters amongst the Copts are usually blind singers found in most

[1] Stationed at Johannesburg; created in the summer of 1963.

[2] The present archbishop, originally a monk of Anba Antonios, is Basileus II, who has a doctorate in theology from Thessalonica and has written books in Arabic and in Greek.

churches. Nevertheless, chanters in some of the churches nowadays are not blind at all. A special section of the clerical college at present provides them with the training required for their office. A fine chanter can always make a splendid contribution to the liturgies.

The monastic rule in the Coptic Church is still important. Each of the seven remaining inhabited monasteries is a separate entity under a bishop or an abbot nominated directly by the patriarch and always under his personal jurisdiction with no obligation to the local archbishop. From the community of monks, totalling about three hundred in the aforementioned monasteries, are elected all bishops, archbishops and the patriarch.

In and around Cairo, we find several nunneries, already enumerated in our survey of monasticism. The total number of Coptic nuns at present is about 150, and a change in their status seems imminent. Previously, nuns were retiring, old and disabled maidens or widows. They are now being encouraged by Pope Cyril (Kirollos) VI to assume some measure of social service to the community. One nun, a former employee in an oil company, made a tour of centres of social service in Europe and is now engaged in the creation of a new order for public service, – a commendable revolution in a neglected corner of Coptic life.

Finally, it must not be forgotten that the whole monastic order in the Coptic Church came into existence at first as a separate religio-secular entity without ecclesiastical status in the hierarchy. The incorporation of the monastic order within the body politic of the Church gradually took place later.

Rites and Ceremonials

The consensus of opinion about the rites and ceremonials of the Coptic Church has been one of universal reverence and profound spirituality. Even those with a consistently prejudiced outlook are stricken with awe at the sight of the Coptic religious performance in its primitive setting. 'Perhaps nowhere in the world', writes an eminent Catholic historian of the Eastern churches, 'can you imagine yourself back in so remote an age as when you are in a Coptic church. You go into a strange dark building; at first the European needs an effort to realize that it is a church at all, it looks so different from our usual associations. But it is enormously older than the clustered columns, moulded arches and glowing clerestory, than the regular aisles and balanced chapels to which we are accustomed. In a Coptic church you come into low dark spaces, a labyrinth of irregular openings. There is little light from the narrow windows. Dimly you see strange rich colours and tarnished gold, all mellowed by dirt. In from the vault above hang ropes bearing the white ostrich eggs,[1] and lamps sparkle in the gloom. Before you is the exquisite carving, inlay and delicate patterns, of the *haikal*[2] screen. All around you see, dusty and confused, wonderful pieces of wood carving. Behind the screen looms the curve of the apse; on the thick columns and along the walls under the low cupolas are inscriptions in exquisite lettering – Coptic and Arabic.'[3] In this inspiring atmosphere, the ancient Coptic liturgy offers one of the most impressive scenes of Christian antiquity.

The divine liturgy or mass is the central function in all Coptic sacramental offices. Indeed, all the numerous offices connected with baptism, matrimony, extreme unction and the rest converge upon the Mass and should end with Holy Communion. At present, the Copts use only three liturgies, those of St Basil the Great, St Gregory Nazianzen and St Mark. The last was recorded and perfected by St Cyril the Great, whose name is usually associated with it. The Basilian Liturgy is habitually used throughout the year, while the Gregorian Anaphora is reserved for the festive occasions of Christmas, the Epiphany and Easter. The Cyrillian Anaphora of St Mark is rather long and little known, and apparently it is used chiefly in the monasteries on account of the purity of its Egyptian texture and sound. All three liturgies have their counterparts in the Greek originals, but they are not the only ones in Coptic history. The Ethiopians have conserved fourteen liturgies, and at least some of these must be ascribed to lost Coptic originals.

Although only a brief account of the Basilian liturgy will be given here, it is necessary to say that the Canonical Hours of the Coptic Church are a different set of prayers, of which some usually precede, some succeed the normal liturgy.[4] Whereas the liturgy cannot be celebrated without an ordained

[1] Regarded as a symbol of steadfast watchfulness from the way the ostrich buries her eggs in the sand and stays at a distance with her eyes fixed on that spot.

[2] Arabic word for sanctuary, the area behind the screen or iconostasis. It also applies to the altar specifically.

[3] Fortescue, *Lesser Eastern Churches*, pp. 288–9.

[4] For the Coptic Liturgy, apart from the numerous Copto-Arabic editions in Cairo, the following works may be quoted for reference in English: *The Coptic Liturgy, Authorized by His Holiness Abba Kirollos VI* (pub. Coptic Orthodox Patriarchate; Cairo-U.A.R., 1963); *The Coptic Morning Service of the Lord's Day*, tr. John, Marquis of Bute (London, 1908); *Coptic Offices*, tr. R. M. Woolley (London, 1930); *The Liturgies of St Mark, St James, St Clement, St Chrysostom, St Basil*, ed. (in Greek) J. M. Neale (London, 1875); J. Garrido, *La Messe Copte* (Cairo, Institut Copte, n.d.). The older works are still invaluable, such as E. Renaudot, *Liturgiarum orientalium collectio, Accedunt dissertationes quatuor:* (I) *De Liturgiarum orientalium origine et autoritate*, (II) *De Liturgiis Alexandrinis*, (III) *De Lingua coptica*, (IV) *De patriarcha Alexandrino cum officio ordinationis ejusdem*, 2 vols. (Paris, 1706; 2nd edn. Frankfurt, 1847); F. E. Brightman, *Liturgies Eastern and Western* (Oxford, 1896), one vol. only. See also P. Alfonso ʿAbdullah: *L'Ordinamento Liturgico di Gabriele V, 88° – Patriarca Copto* (1409–27), (Studia Orientalia Cristiana, Centro Francescano di Studi Orientali Cristiani), (Cairo, 1962). A meticulous analytical study of the *Coptic Liturgy of St Basil* has recently been made by Munīr Barsoum (Cairo, 1964) in Coptic and Arabic. In English, see survey by O. H. E. Burmester in a number of extensive articles in *Eastern Churches*

priest, the hours are prayers open to all. They were practised in the earliest Pachomian monasteries in the fourth century, and the monks and most abbots, including St Pachomius himself, were rarely ordained when the cenobitic movement began. Nevertheless, each member of the order religiously recited the seven hours every day and night. These seven hours consisted of the Morning Prayer, Terce, Sext, None, Vespers, Compline and the Midnight Prayer, to which the monks usually added a 'prayer of the veil' (i.e., the veil of darkness) before going to bed.

An altar or even the vessels and instruments of Holy Communion may not be used a second time on the same day for the Eucharistic Liturgy. The liturgy may, however, be repeated on a second of the three altars within the majority of Coptic sanctuaries. The holy bread, leavened but not salted, is baked by the priest or an authorized person in the morning of the day it is to be used. The small and rather flat round cakes are stamped with a cross surrounded by twelve smaller crosses and an inscription from the Coptic *Trisagion*: 'Agios O Theos, Agios Ischyros, Agios Athanatos.'[1] The wine used in the offices is unfermented grape juice. The main utensils of the Eucharistic celebration include the chalice, paten,[2] asterisk,[3] spoon, and ark.[4] On the altar may be found also a gospel, cross and a fan for keeping flies and insects from touching the chalice, in addition to four candlesticks on the four corners.[5] The vestments and insignia for the solemn occasion are the sticharion,[6] amice,[7] sleeves, epitrachelion,[8] orarion,[9] girdle, phelonion, crown or

---

Quarterly (pub. Exeter), VII, 6 (1948), 373–403; VIII, 1 (1949), 1–39; VIII, 5 (1950), 291–316; IX, 1 (1951), 1–27, under the title of 'Rites and Ceremonials of the Coptic Church'. Burmester's articles are supplemented by comprehensive bibliographies. Some useful gleanings are to be found in Dom Gregory Dix, *The Shape of the Liturgy* (Westminster, 1954). See pp. 162 ff. under 'The Egyptian Tradition' and 'Prayer of Oblation of Bishop Sarapion'. See also pp. 217 ff., 446 ff., 504 ff.; references to St Mark's Liturgy.

[1] 'Holy God! Holy and strong! Holy and immortal!' From a hymn sung by Nicodemus and Joseph at the Lord's entombment. The cakes are pierced five times around the central Cross, symbolizing the nails, crown of thorns and spear used in the Passion. The chosen cake is called *Ḥamal*, i.e. the 'Lamb'.

[2] Silver flat dish, 23 cm. in diameter and 3·5 cm. deep, for the *Hamal*.

[3] Two half-hoops of silver or metal, 13 cm. high, riveted together at right angles; to be placed over the paten to prevent the cover from touching the *Ḥamal*.

[4] Cubical box, 25 cm. wide and 29 cm. high, with paintings of the Last Supper, Our Lady, angel and church patron saint on the four sides; intended to hold chalice until Communion.

[5] Other implements inside the sanctuary include censer, incense box, ewer and basin for washing priest's hands before touching the *Ḥamal*, cruets for the Myron, or chrism, and an *artophorion*, or small silver box for conveyance of part of the Precious Body moistened with the Precious Blood to those who want Communion but cannot attend the Liturgy.

[6] Arabic *tunyah*, white robe reaching feet with long sleeves, embroidered with Crosses, worn by officiating priest or prelate as well as deacons.

[7] Arabic *ṭailasān*, wide strip of embroidered linen hanging down the back and ending up with hood worn by officiating priest.

mitre, onophrion,[1] cap and pastoral staff. The Copts prefer the colour white for the vestments as a sign of purity and chastity, and the officiating priest and his aides wear no shoes inside the sanctuary. Fasting is a binding condition for the celebrant and participants as well as those intending to take Communion.

Strictly speaking, the preparatory prayers for the Eucharistic Liturgy begin on the eve of the day of its celebration with the Service of the Offering of the Evening Incense, usually after the Ninth Hour. This is resumed in the Midnight Hour with a series of set readings from the Psalter, prayers, hymns and commemoration of a saint. The Copts always remember their saints and martyrs. Next morning, another Service of the Offering of Incense is repeated. This is followed by an introduction of the liturgy and the presentation of the 'lamb'.[2] Thus the solemn liturgy proper is inaugurated with the Nicæan Creed, hymns, Gospel readings, and a long series of responses in which the priest, the deacons and the congregation become so involved that the visitor may be prone to dismiss the whole affair as sheer confusion. The reality is that this is the core of the Coptic service, when all seem to engage in a ruthless struggle for the sanctification of the occasion. The Copts deeply feel the real Presence and unreservedly lift their voices to Heaven in exactly the same way as did their unsophisticated, perhaps primitive, ancestors. Their litanies, or intercessory prayers, encompass almost everything and everybody. They pray for the dead, the sick and those who are travelling, for the offerings, for the Nile, the fish and all things living, for priests, prelates and rulers, for security and mercy, for the winds and all the good things of the earth, and for total reconciliation.

The Liturgy is actually officiated in three main stages. The first is the Liturgy of the Catechumens,[3] reminiscent of the days when intending but unbaptized would-be Christians were allowed to attend church up to the point where the mystery of the Sacrament began. After the dismissal of the catechumens, the Liturgy of the Faithful[4] is conducted, with prayers for the peace of the Church, for the saints and martyrs whom the Copts never seem to forget, for the patriarch, and for the congregation. Its consummation is the Kiss of Peace, and all are 'exalted beyond all power of Speech' while the choir sings to the accompaniment of cymbals. The final phase is the Ana-

[8] Arabic *baṭrashīl*, band richly embroidered with Crosses and twelve Apostles, reaching feet from breast with opening to pass the head, worn by higher prelates.

[9] Arabic *Zunnār*, narrow strip embroidered with Crosses, worn by deacons, who pass it under right arm with ends hanging over left shoulder.

[1] Arabic *burnus*, similar to Latin cope, without hood for ordinary priest, but with one for higher prelates.

[2] The Arabic *Ḥamal*.

[3] Burmester, op. cit., VIII, 1, 9–14.

[4] Ibid., 14–20.

phora[1] proper, where the 'mystery of godliness' is accomplished by sanctifying the Holy Body and the Precious Blood.

By way of example let us quote one edificatory prayer from this phase of the Anaphora for the interested souls. It runs like this: 'Master, Lord Our God, the great and eternal, Who art wondrous in glory, Who keepeth His covenant and His mercy with them who love Him with all their heart. Who hath given to us redemption of sins through His only-begotten Son, Jesus Christ Our Lord, the Life of all, the Help of those who flee to Him, the Hope of those who cry unto Him. Before Whom stand thousands of thousands and myriads of myriads of holy angels and archangels, the cherubim and the seraphim, and all the innumerable host of heavenly powers. God, Who hath sanctified these gifts which are set forth, through the coming down upon them of the Holy Spirit, Thou hast purified them. Purify us also, Our Master, from our sins, the hidden and the manifest; and every thought which is not pleasing to Thy goodness, God the lover of man, may it be far from us. Purify our souls and our bodies and our spirits and our hearts and our eyes and our understanding and our thoughts and our consciences, so that with a pure heart and an enlightened soul and an unashamed countenance and a steadfast faith and a perfect love and a firm hope we may have courage with fearless boldness to pray to Thee, God, the Holy Father Who art in the heavens, and to say: Our Father which art in heaven,' etc.[2]

The central event in the remaining part of the Anaphora is the Holy Confession, which is recognition of 'The Holy Body and the Precious Blood and True Blood of Jesus Christ, the Son of Our God. Amen.' This is repeated and confirmed by the congregation. 'The Holy Things to the holy,' and the Communion follows while the deacon exclaims: 'Pray for the worthy communion of the Immaculate, Heavenly and Holy Mysteries,' to which the congregation responds: 'Kyrie eleison!' After thanksgiving, the inclination of heads, and the priestly dismissal of the faithful with a blessing hand over each head, the drama of the liturgy is ended.

[1] Burmester, op. cit., VIII, 1, 17–37.

[2] Ibid., 25–6. I have a personal incentive for the choice of this particular prayer. As a child, I remember my own father repeating it amongst his many religious recitations in his prayers. I was deeply impressed by the text in the original version, and the sound of its beautiful phrases still ring in my ear after the passing of so many decades. I thought the reader might be entitled to one of the reminiscences of my own childhood in my Coptic atmosphere.

Coptic Art

The discovery of Coptic art,[1] which is a relatively recent event, has aroused a great deal of interest and excitement among specialists in the fields of general art, archæology and historical studies. At present, all the major museums of many countries have devoted one or even several halls to exhibits of purely Coptic provenance. The Coptic Museum itself had emerged as a separate entity only in 1908. Before that date, its nucleus had been merely a secondary department within the Egyptian Museum. There may be some variance of opinion as to the importance of the place which Coptic art occupies in the universal scheme of man's artistic achievement. But there is unanimity amongst all as to the superior qualities which have given it a distinctive character of its own. In originality, depth of feeling, and unusual vigour, Coptic art has earned for itself a position of independence in Christian antiquity. At one time, it was summarily dismissed as a ramification of Byzantine art. At another, it was regarded as a minor outgrowth from dynastic archæology. It was not long, however, before both propositions were found inadequate, since Coptic art betrayed a multitude of influences arising from waves of foreign invasions, all of which left their mark on Egyptian culture. Another factor in the artistic orientation of Coptic Egypt was the substitution of Christianity for the ancient Egyptian mythology. Thus Greek, Roman, Persian, Byzantine and even Palmyrian artistic influence can be traced at various times in Egypt, though it would be a grave error to contend that Egyptian art became subject to any of these varied disciplines at any one time.

In Coptic art certain considerations are inevitable. That all the aforementioned influences converged in the art of Egypt and contributed to the mainstream of Coptic art cannot be denied. But it must be remembered that their impact was felt more in Lower than in Upper Egypt. The Greek trends were essentially aristocratic in character and accordingly centred on the capital Alexandria, the Greek towns in the Delta and the Faiyūm oasis. Strictly speaking, these influences were never able to reach the common man. While the mummy portraits of the Faiyūm and the exquisite bone and ivory carvings

[1] J. Strzygowski, *Koptische Kunst* (Vienna, 1904); Al. Gayet, *L'art Copte–École d'Alexandrie, architecture monastique, sculpture, peinture, art somptuaire* (Paris, 1902); Brooklyn Museum, *Pagan and Christian Art, Egyptian Art from the First to the Tenth Century* A.D. (Brooklyn, N.Y., 1941); idem, *Late Egyptian and Coptic Art* (Brooklyn, N.Y., 1943); idem, *Coptic Egypt* (Brooklyn, N.Y., 1944); A. Badawy, *L'art copte – Les influences égyptiennes* (Cairo, 1949); idem, *L'Art copte – Les influences hellenistiques et romaines* (Cairo, 1953); Olsen Foundation, *Coptic Art* (Guildford, Conn., 1955); G. Duthuit, *La sculpture copte* (Paris, 1931); V. de Grüneisen, *Les caractéristiques de l'art copte* (Florence, 1922); C. Mulock and M. T. Langdon, *The Icons of Yuhanna and Ibrahim the Scribe* (London, 1946). Separate articles on the subject have also appeared in journals; cf. Kammerer, *Coptic Bibliography*, nos. 2787–2823.

of Alexandrian craftsmanship never became part of the art of the common man, the less sophisticated Roman way appeared to strike deeper root with Egyptian folks in stonework and clay. The religious factor, of course, was paramount in Coptic art, as may be witnessed in the evolution of the stone stelæ, from the pagan figure with a bunch of grapes in one hand and a dove in the other to the Christian with hands raised in a posture of prayer to the Cross. After the spread of Christianity, the Egyptian artist abhorred the dynastic heritage of his forebears as pagan and strove to dissociate himself from the older tradition. But that process led to the debasement of the ancient Egyptian art. Nevertheless, pagan symbolism persisted in Coptic art even after Christianity became the official religion of the state. Moreover, the repercussions of Egyptian apocryphal literature and Gnosticism were clearly felt amidst the artistic representations of the early centuries of our era. In all religious paintings of the time, however, the Coptic artist continued the traditions of his ancestral system in the use of bold colouring with astonishing effect. He did not know the half-tone in his paintings.

It was this composite background which gave birth to a new school of art. Roughly, the first three centuries of our era saw the development of what might be termed 'proto-Coptic' art, a fluid term still hard to define with archæological precision. It could even antedate Egyptian Christianity, occurring in the later Ptolemaic period and the early Roman period when the country was impoverished by heavy taxation and neglect of its irrigation system. Popular art found its expression in clay and textiles, which were within reach of the humble folks' limited means. Objects of terra-cotta are abundant from that period, and fragments of more perishable material survive in smaller amounts in burial grounds. The prevailing feature in both is the Roman religious syncretism where Egyptian, Oriental and Græco-Roman deities together with mythological scenes are profusely represented for votive purposes. 'Coptic art' *par excellence* with ostensible Christian influence began to flourish in the fourth century, and it endured even beyond the Arab Conquest of the seventh century. This was pre-eminently the age of the great christological quarrel between the Greeks and the Egyptians culminating in Chalcedon (451) with its aftermath of persecutions which intensified the nationalist trends in Egypt and the general purge of Greek influences from native art and literature. It was in this manner that the Egyptian artist finally came into his own, and the standard decorative motifs of Coptic art emerged in stonework, painting, woodwork, terra-cotta, ivories and the renowned monochrome and polychrome fabrics from Coptic looms.

Although the ravages of time have reduced the archæological and artistic remains of the Coptic age to a negligible fraction, and although that minor residue suffered still further at the hands of the earlier Egyptologists and Islamologists who aimed at saving their own domains by looking askance at the Coptic material intermingled with their findings, it has at least been possible to accumulate enough material to construe the salient characteristics of that humble but most remarkable art. The older monasteries in the wilderness behind the sands of the desert, a number of ancient churches nestled beyond sight in the obscure alleys of Old Cairo, the White and Red monasteries near Sūhāg, and a few sites of Coptic excavations, notably at Abu Mīna,[1] Ahnās,[2] Bāwīṭ,[3] St Jeremiah,[4] St Shenūte[5] and St Simeon's[6] near Aswān, together with many others explored throughout Egypt, have yielded artistic and architectural treasures of which the best specimens are displayed in the Coptic Museum.[7]

It would be presumptuous within our limitations to attempt to formulate the fruits of Coptic excavations or to present a comprehensive picture of Coptic archæological and artistic research. Such studies are still in their infancy when compared with other similar fields. Nevertheless, it will be illuminating here to offer a brief outline of one site by way of illustration, namely, Bāwīṭ, where treasures of Coptic art have been buried under mounds of sand for centuries. The monastic settlement of Bāwīṭ owed its origin to Apa Apollo, a holy man and a disciple of St Pachomius the Great, who retired to a cave near the town of Meir, where the Holy Family is said to have taken refuge during the flight to Egypt. When that saint died in 395, he already had three hundred followers in what seemed like an unusual beginning for a monastery. With increasing numbers the area grew to formidable dimensions in subsequent centuries. New churches and buildings were constructed, and monastic artists embellished them with paintings of the highest importance in the history of Coptic art. Several frescoes, graffiti and inscriptions remain intact and have been dated. Some of its churches, in common with those at Sūhāg, Isneh and Aswān, were built in the reign of Justinian. An inscription shows that the monastery was inhabited as late as the eleventh century under Arab

[1] C. M. Kaufmann, *Die Ausgrabung der Menas-Heiligtümer in der Mareotiswsüte*, 3 vols. in 1 (Cairo, 1906–8).

[2] U. Monneret de Villard, *La scultura ad Ahnas, Note sull'origine dell'arte copta* (Milat, 1923).

[3] J. Clédat, *Le monastère et le necropole de Baouît*, 2 vols. (Cairo, 1904–16); E. Chassinuî, *Fouilles à Baouît* (Cairo, 1911); G. Schlumberger, 'Les fouilles de Jean Maspéro à Baonta en 1913', in *Comptes-rendus, Académie des inscriptions et des belles-Lettres de l'Institut de France* (Paris, 1919), pp. 243–8.

[4] J. E. Quibell, 'The Monastery of St Jeremias at Saqqara', in *Comptes-rendus* of the 2nd International Congress of Archæology (Cairo, 1909), pp. 268–70; idem, *Excavations at Saqqara*, 4 vols. (Cairo, 1907–13). (Inscriptions ed. Sir Herbert Thompson.)

[5] U. Monneret de Villard, *Les couvents près de Sohâg* (*Deyr el-Abiad et Deyr el-Ahmar*), 2 vols. (Milan, 1925–6).

[6] Idem, *Description générale du monastère de St Siméon à Aswân* (Milan, 1927).

[7] Such as the monasteries of Wādi al-Naṭrūn and St Epiphaneus at Luxor; see Evelyn-White and Wenlock, op. cit.; U. Monneret de Villard, *Les églises du monastère des Syriens au Wâdî en Natrûn* (Milan, 1928). See also Ch. Bachatly, *Le monastère de Phœbammon dans la Thébaïde* (Fouilles de la Société d'Archéologie Copte), 3 vols., in progress.

rule. Then, in the course of the Nubian campaign organized by Shirkūh during the twelfth century, we may assume that Bāwīṭ, together with other Christian monuments of Upper Egypt at Quft, Isneh and Aswān, must have suffered the first of a series of ruinous attacks by Muslim foreign rulers. In the following, or at the very latest in the fourteenth century, the monastery was completely discarded, and as usual the sand crept over it and filled the whole area. Bāwīṭ thus became one of those *kōms*, or mounds, which are found as archæological sites in Egypt. In 1900, the French archæologist M. Clédat, a member of the French Institute of Cairo, was commissioned to chart the Necropolis of Meir. During his exploration, he was attracted by the extraordinary colouring of the sand of Kōm Bāwīṭ and voluntarily made some soundings which revealed the existence of structures within. He could not return to the site for two years, when he succeeded in obtaining authorization to excavate Bāwīṭ with the ridiculous fund of five hundred francs. He did enough with that money to show the magnitude of the discovery, which brought M. Chassinat, his chief at the Institute, to the project in 1911, and M. Maspéro came in 1913.[1] The harvest of Christian antiquities from the area exceeded the wildest expectations, and special accommodation had to be made for it both in the Louvre and in the Egyptian Museum.[2] In fact, the themes of the paintings of Bāwīṭ represent all three stages of Coptic art: the classical with its mythological figures, the transitional with its apocryphal characters and finally the Coptic Christian. The glorious apse of the principal church, with its striking frescoes in two registers, now in the Coptic Museum,[3] is a remarkable composition in theme and simple colouring. The lower register consists of a central seated Madonna with the infant Jesus in typically Coptic attire, and a row of six apostles and a local saint on each side – including, of course, Apa Apollo. The upper register has the figure of the Semite, beardless young Jesus seated on a jewelled chair, the open Gospel with 'O Agios' (Oh! Holy!) thrice repeated in inscription under His left hand and the right hand raised in benediction. His head has a halo with inset Cross, and round Him are the four symbols of the four Evangelists and two full angels. The primitive purity of the Bāwīṭ paintings is overpowering.

The stonework from St Jeremiah's Monastery at Saqqārah contains capitals of Corinthian style with the acanthus leaf, palm, vine and cruciform ornamentation. Front-facing angels with the Cross in a crown of laurel, geometrical interlacing, animal and bird motifs, and hunting scenes are also

[1] See summary in chapter on Coptic Art in S. Chauleur, *Histoire des Coptes d'Égypte* (Paris, 1960), pp. 181–6.

[2] J. des Graviers, 'Inventaire des objets coptes de la salle de Baouît au Louvre', in *Rivista di archeologia cristiana*, IX (1932), 51–103; G. Mounereau, 'La Salle copte de Baouît', in *Chronique d'Égypte*, V, 9 (1930), 115–16.

[3] All recent guides to the museum in English or French contain a full reproduction of the apse here described. See also Plates III and IV in this volume.

represented. The woodcuts on ebony panels at the Church of St Sergius representing the Annunciation and other biblical themes and mounted saints from the tenth century are dwarfed by the magnificent fourth-century sycamore gate of St Barbara with its exquisite panels, of which the one depicting the entry of Jesus into Jerusalem riding an ass on Palm Sunday leaves the spectator speechless. The superb figurines and decorated clay lamps fill museums and are the joy of the modest collector. Carved bones and ivories are also to be found everywhere with their interesting themes, both pagan and Christian. Articles of domestic use such as combs, plates and jewel boxes are either painted or carved with interesting scenes. Icons, stained glass, metalwork and jewellery are among the accomplishments of Coptic craftsmanship. The bronze Roman eagle excavated in the Museum grounds within the precincts of Fort Babylon is an impressive work of art which adorns one of the Coptic Museum halls, together with a multitude of metal crosses and censers.

The Coptic textile industry has been attracting a great deal of attention in recent years, and the accumulation of specimens of embroidered fabrics of astounding beauty are on display in many museums.[1] The Coptic weaver's dexterity produced fantastic scenes from classical antiquity, which were replaced by Christian themes from the fourth century. His material consisted usually of linen and wool, and some of the polychrome portraits can match any painting in beauty. The textile colours were usually subdued, and brown embroidery was much used. Shrouds, tunics, head-dresses, church hangings, and table covers of varied sizes, sometimes inscribed but generally embroidered, have been found in both monochrome and polychrome, with human, animal and plant motifs as well as a wide variety of crosses. Rug material with loop stitch is not uncommon. The Faiyūm, al-Bahnasa and Akhmīm were noted as great centres of *ṭirāz*, or weaving, although other smaller towns of many districts have their own workshops. Figures became increasingly stylized in the early centuries of the Islamic period, and the use of more geometrical designs became customary. Nevertheless, the feeling of movement and the sense of liveliness in the stylized human and animal figures

[1] A. F. Kendrick, *Catalogue of Textiles from Burying Grounds in Egypt*, Victoria and Albert Museum, 3 vols. (London, 1920–2); A. Wulff and W. F. Volbach, *Spätantike und Koptische Stoffe aus Ägyptischen Grabfunden in den staatlichen Museen* (Berlin, 1926); idem, *Catalogo del Museo Sacro della Biblioteca Apostolica Vaticana*, III, 1, Tessuti (Vatican, 1942); A. J. B. Wace, *Exposition d'art copte – guide* (Société d'Archéologie Copte; Cairo, 1944); *The Dumbarton Oaks Collection Handbook* (Washington, D.C., 1955), pp. 155 ff.; L. M. Wilson, *Ancient Textiles from Egypt in the University of Michigan Collection* (Ann Arbor, 1933); N. P. Britton, *A Study of Some Early Islamic Textiles in the Museum of Fine Arts* (Boston, 1938); A. C. Weibel, *Two Thousand Years of Textiles*, Detroit Institute of Arts (New York, 1952). See brochures issued by the Textile Museum, Washington D.C.; also Kammerer's *Coptic Bibliography*, nos. 2853–2992. The newly issued *Textile Museum Journal* was inaugurated in 1962 with the study 'A Coptic Tapestry of Byzantine Style', by R. Berliner.

became a source of inspiration for some of the most notable modern masters, including Matisse, Derain and Picasso. When the American painter Marsden Hartley discovered Coptic textile portraiture, he set out to build up a collection of his own, and his style was affected by this contact.[1] The creative nature of the ancient Coptic weaver's product is another subject for more detailed study. The hereditary, latent skill in the handling of the loom among village youths has recently been the object of a new school, with remarkable results.[2]

Coptic Architecture

Occasional reference has been made to the subject of Coptic ecclesiastical architecture, and here it is planned to cast a quick glance at its early development. Though many ancient Coptic monuments suffered greatly from hostile incursions and many more fell into disuse and were ruined, a representative number of monastic and church structures have survived in their early original forms. Consequently, the archæologist has been able to construct a fair picture of the essentials of Coptic architecture. Literature on this interesting facet of Coptic history has been growing steadily,[3] but much remains to be done on the sites and mounds which fill the length and breadth of the Nile valley. Some of these are known, but unexcavated, while innumerable others are still undiscovered and untouched.

It is not inconceivable, however, that the oldest forms of Coptic churches were derived from their ancestral places of worship, that is, the ancient Egyptian temples. In fact, the spread of the earliest Christianity in Egypt resulted at first in the conversion of the pagan temples into churches. More-

[1] N. B. Rodney, in *Coptic Art* (Olsen Foundation), p. 5.

[2] The idea of the spontaneity of art coming from within was the underlying principle in a school of popular art started by a great Egyptian educationist and artist, the late Ḥabīb Gorgi, whose work was displayed in London and Paris under U.N.E.S.C.O. auspices. The works of art produced in his school were sculpture and textile weaving. Finally he relegated the weaving to his gifted son-in-law, Ramses Wiṣṣa Wāṣef, who established a special school for that purpose at the village of Ḥarrānia, in the shadow of the pyramids of Gīza. The results, exhibited in numerous European art centres, were fantastic and may be seen from a sumptuous publication entitled *Tapestries from Egypt, Woven by the Children of Ḥarrānia*, by W. and B. Forman and R. W. Wāṣef (London, 1961).

[3] A. J. Butler, *The Ancient Coptic Churches of Egypt*, 2 vols. (Oxford, 1884); Somers Clarke, *Christian Antiquities in the Nile Valley, A contribution towards the Study of Ancient Churches* (Oxford, 1912); see also Evelyn-White, Winlock, and Monneret de Villard, op. cit. For small but useful guides, see O. H. E. Burmester, *A Guide to the Ancient Coptic Churches of Cairo* (Cairo, 1955); A. Badawy, *Guide de l'Égypte Chrétienne* (Cairo, 1953); both in the publications of the Société de Archéologie Copte. Cf. Kammerer's *Coptic Bibliography*, nos. 2652–2735.

over, numerous instances are reported of Christian ascetics who sought seclusion by living in ancient tombs and funerary shrines.[1] Later when the Copts began to erect their own chapels independently, it was normal for their architects to copy the existing temple models of the master builders of antiquity, more especially as these seemed to fulfil the requirements of the new faith during the first four centuries of transition between paganism and Christianity.

The topography of the ancient Egyptian temple had already been shown to have consisted of three main divisions. First, the outer gate led into an open court surrounded by two rows of columns with a narrow stone roofing. Secondly, beyond that huge quadrangle devoted to general worshippers, the hypostyle hall followed. This space was filled with crowded columns in close rows supporting a massive stone roof and reserved for the royal family and the aristocracy. The third section of the temple, at the end, was a closed and rather dimly lit small chamber, wrapped in great mystery. This constituted the inner shrine, the *sanctum sanctorum* or holy of holies, where the deity resided, and which was accessible only to the high priest or pharaoh.

The primitive Coptic churches appear to have retained this triple division, which may still be witnessed in some of the chapels of the ancient monasteries. The innermost part behind the iconostasis was the sanctuary (*haikal*) where the priests and deacons alone were admitted to officiate the mystery of the Holy Sacrament. Outside the sanctuary, the central part of the church was reserved for baptized Christians, while a third section at the narthex or entrance was left open for the unbaptized catechumens. As already shown, the Coptic liturgy is divided into three corresponding stages, namely, the Liturgy of the Catechumens, the Liturgy of the Faithful, and the Anaphora. Whereas the Catechumens were expected to depart after the first stage, the screen is later drawn to conceal the mystery of sanctification of the Precious Body and Blood before Holy Communion.

At an unknown date, the distinction between the baptized Christian and the Catechumen began to disappear, and with it the divisions of the church gave way to the perpendicular triple sections of nave and aisles. In this way, the basilica style began to assert itself in Coptic ecclesiastical architecture. St Mena's cathedral built by Arcadius (395–408) in the district of Mareotis near the Delta, the ruins of the magnificent cathedral at Ashmunain, and the Red and White Monasteries of St Shenūte at Sūhāg are fourth and fifth-century examples of that imminent change. On the other hand, the irregularity of church forms in Old Cairo indicates that the basilica style was only slowly adopted as the accepted standard. Here we find churches consisting of the

[1] A. Badawy, *Les premiers établissements chrétiens dans les anciennes tombes d'Égypte*, Publications de l'Institut d'Études Orientales de la Bibliothèque Patriarcale d'Alexandrie, No. 2 (Alexandria, 1953).

sanctuary and a single enclosure for the congregation, while others have an additional side aisle usually reserved for women worshippers. A few have a gallery over the narthex also devoted for women.

As a rule the choir area is one step higher than the church floor, and the sanctuary one more step above the choir. A wooden screen beautifully carved and richly inlaid with ivory and mother-of-pearl in cruciform or geometrical shapes conceals the sanctuary, which comprises three altars for alternate use in case of the celebration of several masses on the same day. Some ancient churches have apses and domes but no belfry. The domes are occasionally granary-shaped, as in the Church of Our Lady at Maʿadi on the bank of the Nile. The Copts use painted icons but no statuary. Few churches have side chapels, and the older ones usually contain saintly relics.

In Old Cairo and many historic places, several churches originated in the fourth century, but most of them were destroyed and rebuilt during subsequent ages, invariably on the original foundations. Though each church has a charm all its own, perhaps the most widely frequented ones are the churches of Abu Sarga and the Muʿallaqa, or Suspended Church of Our Lady, so named since it was built on one of the towers of Fort Babylon, probably for defensive purposes against mob rioting. The first was dedicated to two saints martyred in Syria, Sergius and Bacchus, and it stands over a subterranean crypt where, according to tradition, the Holy Family rested at Old Cairo during the flight to Egypt. The other is much richer in objects of art. It became the seat of the patriarchate during the reign of Christodoulos in the eleventh century. Equally historic churches may be found in the provinces, many of them still unknown to archæologists.

Coptic Music

In spite of the antiquity of Coptic religious music,[1] the science of Coptic musicology is still very young and none can speak with final authority of its specific details. Although the present account is no place for a specialized survey of all the data of a difficult subject, it may be helpful to note that there are two schools of thought on the status of Coptic music. The first school holds that Egyptian music was swamped by Byzantine music after the introduction of Christianity into the valley of the Nile. The arguments for this thesis are extant in standard works, which have long been accepted by unsuspecting students of music who had no other alternative. The second school

[1] A. S. Atiya, *Coptic Music*, brochure accompanied by a recording of selections from the Coptic Liturgy, prepared by the Institute of Coptic Studies, and published by Folkways (New York, 1960); H. Hickmann, *45 siècles de musique dans l'Égypte ancienne à travers la sculpture, la peinture, l'instrument* (Paris, 1956).

of thought is recent and still relatively unknown, but its exponents are ardent enthusiasts with a touch of nationalism. Their chief merit is their concentration on the human sources of Coptic melodies in remote areas where external influences were unlikely. It will be illuminating to summarize their views.

The historic factors in support of an independent Coptic musical heritage are multiple. That the Copts are the descendants of the ancient Egyptians is now generally recognized by most archæologists. Bohairic Coptic is still essentially the language of the liturgy, though Arabic has been the spoken language of Egypt for approximately six centuries. The assumption, therefore, that ancient Egyptian vocal music has been preserved by the Copts in their religious chants has appeared to some as a plausible thesis, worthy of a serious enquiry. The most ancient music of the Copts was entirely vocal until the introduction of the cymbal and triangle in the course of the Middle Ages. It may be assumed, however, that Byzantine, Arabic and Oriental accretions were superimposed on the Coptic chants of urbanized churches; but the purer forms of primitive Coptic melodies were handed over from generation to generation in secluded monasteries and isolated country churches at inaccessible spots in Upper Egypt and on the fringe of the desert. Furthermore, it must be remembered that after Chalcedon in 451, the Copts systematically set out to purge their literature, language and liturgy of all vestiges of Greek influence, and there is no reason to think that they made an exception of Byzantine music against their own native chants.

Since all the aforementioned data were confined to the realm of theorizing, it was necessary that someone should undertake serious research on the subject. A Copt of some wealth, namely Ragheb Moftāḥ, decided to devote his time and fortune to the recording and analysis of Coptic offices from the most authoritative chanters of the day. In 1927, he invited an English musicologist, Ernest Newlandsmith of Oxford and London Universities, to spend winters as his guest in a houseboat on the Nile with the sole obligation of listening to old native chanters and reducing their tunes to notation. Newlandsmith compiled thirteen large folio volumes, and declared that the results exceeded his wildest expectations. Let us hear his final verdict, since we can do little more in a work of this nature. 'What we understand today as Oriental music,' he proclaimed, 'appears simply a degradation of what was once a great art. This music, which has been handed down for untold centuries within the Coptic church, should be a bridge between East and West, and place a new idiom at the disposal of the Western musicians. It is a lofty, noble, and great art, especially in the element of the infinite which is lacking today.' Newlandsmith is apparently of the opinion that, to use his own words, 'Western music has its origin in ancient Egypt.'[1]

[1] Quotations from *The Morning Post*, 22 April 1931.

Whether or not this school is destined to gain future universal acceptance remains to be seen. However, it must be remembered that the whole Coptic service is vocal and choral; and the actors in that divine drama are the priest, the master chanter with his choir of deacons, and the congregation which plays a vital role in the responses, in contrast to the Greek and Roman traditions. The fervour with which the performance of the Coptic liturgy is conducted rises to great spiritual heights, and its chanting is occasionally pervaded by unusual vigour. The vast range of Coptic hymns and offices for all seasons is impressive in richness and variety.

Since its foundation in 1954, the Institute of Coptic Studies in Cairo has been sponsoring the registration on tape of the Coptic music notated by Newlandsmith. This has been accomplished by the oldest traditional chanters of a dying generation. Again according to the English musicologist: 'Such a basis of music opens up a vista quite undreamt of by the ordinary musicians of the Western world.' The moral of this rather unorthodox verdict from a western mind can only open the road to reconsideration and revision of the established views of the Byzantinist school in Coptic music in the light of the findings now in progress at the aforementioned institute.

Coptic Literature

Projects of a comprehensive history of Coptic literature have been recurring for almost a century and are still unfulfilled.[1] Here our task will be limited to a matter of classification and the outlining of general trends in a fascinating field. We have already touched on salient facets of literature in the course of this brief survey of the march of events in Coptic annals. Of necessity, Coptic literature was born with the emergence of the Coptic language[2] and Coptic script from a happy compromise between Demotic, or the last phase in the evolution of ancient Egyptian, and the adoption of the archaic Greek alphabet in order to cope with the needs of daily life and the rendering of the new Christian Scripture. The debate as to when this system was accepted as a *fait accompli* may still be raging among specialists. But the fact remains that the earliest phase in Coptic literature as represented by Scriptural translation and the famous Gnostic texts must have occurred between the second and fourth centuries of our era. Coptic letters were necessarily, though not exclusively, religious in character.

The struggle for pre-eminence among the five established dialects of

[1] R. de Rustafjaell, *The Light of Egypt* (London, 1909), pp. 100–38, contains an interesting chapter on Coptic MSS., with specimens of religious literature and good reproductions from originals.

[2] See above, Chapter 1.

Coptic (Bohairic, Sahidic, Akhmīmic, Faiyūmic and Bashmuric) was fanned by localized interests in the various provinces of Egypt throughout the centuries. In fact, there were other dialectal sub-divisions such as sub-Akhmīmic, and some recent discoveries in the realm of ancient Coptic papyri indicate even the existence of other subsidiary dialects hitherto unknown and still undefined. On the whole, the two predominant dialects were the Sahidic and the Bohairic; and the struggle was eventually narrowed down to those two dialects. St Shenūte the Great's prolific literary output and his eloquence rendered the White Monastery a stronghold of Sahidic letters. In the meantime, the Monastery of St Macarius the Great in Wādi al-Naṭrūn near the Delta became the centre of a flourishing Bohairic literature. Here the factor of age could not be overlooked and, contrary to prevalent impressions, Bohairic must have pre-dated Sahidic owing to the fact that the adoption of the Greek alphabet by the Egyptians must have started in the Delta in the neighbourhood of Alexandria and other Lower Egyptian Greek urban centres rather than the remote terrains of Upper Egypt. But the truly decisive factor in the picture must be tied to patriarchal influence. Since the popes and patriarchs of the Coptic Church took to the habit of making the monastery of St Macarius their favoured quarters under early Arab rule, the Bohairic texts used there were eventually accepted as the official ones for general use in the Coptic Church toward the beginning of the eleventh century or perhaps earlier.

The adoption of Bohairic as the official liturgical language of the whole church, however, did not eliminate the progress of Sahidic literature, which owed its efflorescence to the influence of the great Shenūte and his successors from the fifth century. After Chalcedon, the nationalizing of Egypt swept off the vestiges of Greek from Sahidic offices. This was a purifying literary element not to be slighted. The Copts apparently had a preference for the forceful texts of the apocryphal Gospels and Acts, the violent tenor of the lives of their martyrs, and all manner of works of magic and miracle in their Sahidic sacred letters. It is still hard to assess the impact of that tremendous literature on the formative years of primitive Christianity. Yet some of the known samples in the field are impressive beyond description. The hair-raising account of St Paul's descent into the abyss and his encounter with Judas Iscariot has been made popular by Worrell[1] in an English version of the apocryphal Acts of the Apostles Andrew and Paul. The Nagʿ Ḥamādi Gnostic papyri, discovered in 1946, have yielded some forty-four treatises, including such apocryphal Biblical literature as the Secret Book of John, and the Gospel to the Egyptians, otherwise known as the Sacred Book of the Invisible Grand Spirit, the Apocalypse of Paul, and the Apocalypse of James, the Acts of Peter, the Gospel of Thomas, the Gospel of Philip, and other

[1] *A Short Account of the Copts*, p. 21.

mystifying material, all in the Coptic Museum. The Codex Jung, which found its way to Zurich, contains the famous *Evangelium veritatis*, a fourth-century version of a text ascribed to Valentinus, who might have written it while in Rome between 140 and 150 A.D.[1]

It begins thus:[2]

> The Gospel of Truth is joy for those who have received the grace of knowing from the Father of Truth, Him through the power of the Verb come forth from the Pleroma who is immanent in the Thought and in the Mind of the Father who [and] who is He whom they call 'The Saviour', for that is the name of the work which He is to accomplish for the Salvation of those who were ignorant of the Father, since this name . . . the Gospel is a revelation of Hope, since it is a discovery of Him. Indeed the All was searching for Him from whom it came forth. But the All was inside of Him, that Incomprehensible, Inconceivable [one], who is superior to all thought. It was this ignorance concerning the Father which produced Anguish and Terror. And Anguish became dense like a mist, so that no one could see. For this reason, Error was strengthened. It elaborated its own matter in emptiness, without knowing Truth . . . Oblivion did not exist close to the Father although It came into existence because of Him. On the contrary, that which comes into existence in Him is Knowledge [The Gnose], which appeared in order that Oblivion should be abolished in order that they might know the Father.

The same trend of Gnostic thinking re-emerges in the Gospel according to Thomas:[3] 'Jesus said: If those who lead you say to you: "See, the Kingdom is in Heaven", then the birds of the heaven will precede you. If they say to you: "It is in the sea", then, the fish will precede you. But the Kingdom is within you and it is without you. If you [will] know yourselves, then you will be known and you will know that you are the sons of the Living Father. But if you do not know yourselves, then you are in poverty and you are poverty.' This impressive language in its naïveté seemed to have a tremendous appeal to the Egyptian mind, just emerging from idolatry, in its search for a religious haven. The same search also opened the same mind to the inroads of Manichæan thought during the third century. The Coptic Manichæan papyri discovered in 1930 in the Faiyūm must be tied to the

[1] See above on Gnosticism under Chapter 2.

[2] *Evangelium Veritatis*, ed. M. Malinine, H.-C. Puech and G. Quispel (Zurich 1956), pp. 88–90.

[3] *The Gospel According to Thomas*, ed. A. Guillaumont, H.-C. Puech, G. Quispel, W. Till and Yassah ʿAbd al-Masīḥ (New York, 1959), pp. 2–3.

refutation of Manichæism in a fourth-century treatise by Serapion, bishop of Thmuis.[1]

Nevertheless, it would be a mistake to assume that the whole of Coptic literature was religious in character. The Coptic *Chronicle* of John of Nikiou was terminated with the advent of the Arabs in Egypt. Medical tests, confused with magical formulæ, also survived the Coptic period. Business transactions and private letters are extant on papyrus as well as ostraca. In fact, the momentum of purely literary writing in Sahidic continued beyond the Arab invasion, and we find even then as late as the eighth century new Sahidic tales which enlisted Coptic nationalistic sentiments. Let us take the story of Theodosius and Dionysius. These were two Egyptians, one of whom had made his way to Byzantium and somehow risen to the imperial throne. Then he suddenly remembered his old colleague and caused him to be called to the capital, where he installed him as archbishop of Constantinople. Such wishful fiction bespoke nationalism. Another tale is the Cambyses romance which, though incomplete in the original and full of confusion in names and data, appears to underline the same trends as the former. Both stories are written in naïve pseudo-biblical style, and both are of course in prose.[2]

Poetic literature, though somewhat rare in Coptic, nevertheless exists. One of the best examples is the story of Archellites and his mother, Synkletike, of which only two leaves have survived. Of Roman Christian origin, Archellites was sent by his wealthy widowed mother for an education overseas at Athens or Beirūt. He ended as a monk in the Convent of Apa Romanus, where he attained such sanctity that he performed the miracle of healing. His mother lost track of him and thought him dead. She used her great wealth in the establishment of a pious hostel for stray travellers. One day she overheard some merchants talking about a saint Archellites in the Convent of Apa Romanus who was endowed with the gift of healing. The mother recognized her son and at once went for a glimpse of him to cure her grief. Here the tragedy began. The saint had vowed never to set eyes on a woman, and he would never break his oath even for the supplications of his mother or the intercession of the archbishop. He thus prayed for death to keep his word before admitting his mother to his presence. On witnessing his face in death, the mother died too, and both were buried side by side.[3]

At that time, the intellectual life of the Arabs was almost at its zenith under the Abbasid caliphate. Baghdad was the great centre of world culture and all the subject nations looked up to it. In order to have some place in the

[1] Chauleur, p. 172.

[2] Worrell, 31–4. For other stories, see E. Amélineau, *Contes et romans de l'Égypte chrétienne*, 2 vols. (Paris, 1888).

[3] Worrell, pp. 37–43.

new world régime, the Copts were fast learning and using Arabic, probably at the cost of Coptic. During the eleventh century a significant event took place. Bishop Athanasius of Qūṣ[1] in the midst of the Thebaïd found it fitting to compose the first grammar on record in Arabic for the Bohairic and Sahidic dialects of the Coptic language. This appeared to be a necessary measure for the preservation of Coptic among the natives. It was also in that century that Patriarch Christodoulos (1047–77), who moved the seat of the patriarchate from Alexandria to Cairo, also ruled that the official language of the Church should be Bohairic. This proved to be the final knell for Sahidic literary productivity. By the thirteenth century, Bohairic Coptic was the liturgical language, though most Copts remained bilingual in speech for some time yet. The great avalanche of Coptic grammars and lexicons in Arabic which saw the light at that time might provide strong testimony as to the need for them in order to preserve the old tongue among the natives. These authors have been reviewed elsewhere.[2] Most famous among them were Aulād [sons of] al-ʿAssāl. The last Coptic work of any importance to appear was the *Triadon*,[3] a fourteenth-century didactic poem in Sahidic probably written by an unknown monk in praise of the Coptic language, which he considered to be a miracle even though its use was declining. It is to be noted, however, that the author accompanied his Coptic text with an Arabic version to make it comprehensible to his readers. Coptic literature became defunct, though Coptic has remained the language of the liturgy to our own time.

From the later middle ages to modern times, the cultured Copt made his contribution to Arabic literature in Arabic, and it has become increasingly difficult nowadays to distinguish between writings which are of Coptic origin and others which are purely Islamic, except when it comes to works of a religious character. Although the Copt has retained his religious personality within the framework of his Church, his social and political integration in the body politic of the whole nation has reflected itself in the nature of his literary accomplishment, more especially in the contemporary period. In recent decades, we find Copts writing in every conceivable field on the same footing as their Muslim fellow-citizens without any distinction whatsoever. Their Arabic poets, orators, political thinkers, jurisconsults, scientists, historians, journalists, and all manner of scholarly and literary writers have attained universal recognition side by side with their Muslim neighbours and colleagues in the Arab world. Even in their own communal and

[1] Worrell, p. 45; Graf, II, 445, refers to the same Athanasius, but does not give a definite date, though he states that Abul-Barakāt includes him in his thirteenth-century list of Coptic philologists.

[2] See above on Arab rule, Chapter 5.

[3] Worrell, p. 47.

religious poetry, we find superior examples of forceful and artistic writing which has entitled the Coptic men of letters to a place in the sun.[1]

[1] The subject of Coptic literature as a whole and more especially from the Arab period to our day has not yet been studied with sufficient care. The only comprehensive, though extremely modest, attempt to compile the Arabic phase of Coptic letters appeared at Cairo only in 1962 by a Muslim scholar, Muḥammad Sayyid Kīlāni (*Al-Adab al-Qibṭi qadīman wa-ḥadīthan*). Though this work must be regarded as only a beginning, and though we cannot agree with many of the author's interpretations, he succeeded in assembling a variety of samples of original material which should leave us in no doubt about the heights attained by Coptic writers in the world of Arabic belles-lettres.

Since this work was prepared, the first volume of a new book has appeared on Coptic history by Martiniano Roncaglia: *Histoire de l'église copte* (Vol. I: *Les origines du Christianisme en Égypte, Du Judéo-Christianisme au Christianisme hellénistique, Ier et IIe siècles*), Dar Al-Kalima (Lebanon), 1966. Other volumes are planned as follows:

Vol. II, *L'Égypte Chrétienne, Le Didascalée: Les hommes et les doctrines* (IIIe *s.–451*)
Vol. III, *L'église d'Égypte à la recherche de sa personnalitè 'Copte'* (*451–642*)
Vol. IV, *Coptes et musulmans* (*642–1801*)
Vol. V, *Les coptes dans l'Égypte moderne et contemporaine* (*1801–*)
Vol. VI, *Bibliographie, Index, Appendices et Additions.*

8 • THE ETHIOPIANS

Introductory

The modern Empire of Ethiopia,[1] situated west of the 'Horn of Africa' and the Red Sea, covers the enormous area of about 400,000 square miles of mountainous country sometimes rising to an altitude of 15,000 feet and descending into the lower plains of Eritrea, which has been one of its provinces since 1952. It has a population of approximately eighteen millions, of whom at least eight are Coptic Christian and eight are Muslim, the rest being a mixture of animistic pagans and primitive Africans on its southern periphery. The Christians form the governing class; they speak Amharic and are warlike by nature and upbringing. They represent an ethnic mixture of Semitic and African stocks, and are usually tall, with refined features, dark skin, and curled hair. Their proud character is matched by a deep sense of piety and attachment to their church.

Ethiopia comprises thirteen provinces, each an episcopal diocese, with a total of thirteen *rases*, or kings and governors. In addition to the thirteen provincial prelates, there are eleven other metropolitan bishops. At the head of the state is the Emperor of Ethiopia – King of Kings, Lion of the tribe of Judah, supposedly a descendant of King Solomon and the Queen of Sheba, who bore for him Menelik I in pre-Christian times. During the centuries, the capital of Ethiopia has kept moving in a southerly direction, but has remained always in the midst of the interior mountains. Axum, the first imperial and ecclesiastical metropolis, was replaced by Gondar, on the northern shore of Lake Tana, and this again was replaced by the present

[1] For general accounts of Ethiopian history, culture and church, see J. Doresse, *Ethiopia*, tr. Elsa Coult (London, 1956); A. H. M. Jones and Elizabeth Monroe, *A History of Ethiopia* (Oxford, 1935); H. M. Hyatt, *The Church of Abyssinia* (London, 1928); Delacy O'Leary, *The Ethiopian Church, Historical Notes on the Church of Abyssinia* (London, 1936); J. S. Trimingham, *Islam in Ethiopia* (London, 1952); Sir E. A. Wallis Budge, *A History of Ethiopia*, 2 vols. (London, 1928); R. Strothmann, 'Die Koptischen Metropoliten der abessinischen Kirche', in *Theologische Blätter*, IX (1930), 225–33. On the interesting subject of Ethiopic religious literature, see J. Guidi, *Storia della litteratura etiopica* (Rome, 1932); and J. M. Harden, *An Introduction to Ethiopic Christian Literature* (London, 1926).

Addis Ababa, that is, 'New Flower', founded by Menelik II (1889–1913), surnamed the Great after the defeat of the Italians at the battle of Adowa in 1896. Addis Ababa has almost a million inhabitants at present and is the seat of the emperor, the legislature, the centre of the United Nations Economic Commission for Africa, a new and thriving state university, a theological seminary and the headquarters of the Ethiopian Coptic Orthodox Church with its new patriarch-catholicos Anba Basileus, the first native *abuna* of the Ethiopians. This is the land where the torch of Christianity was kept lighted in Africa without interruption throughout the centuries while in others it was either totally extinguished or engulfed in the surging sea of Islam, whose waves of invasion drowned the countries of the Middle East on both continents of Asia and Africa. Nevertheless, the unswerving adherence of the Ethiopians to Coptic doctrine can be matched only by their inborn national sentiments.

Historical Background

Any history of the Abyssinian Church must take into account the background of the political history of Ethiopia. It is often hard to separate the ecclesiastical from the secular events in that country. We must at least attempt a simple enumeration of the main historical landmarks in order to be able to understand developments within the Church. However, owing to the very nature of Ethiopian history, which is still obscure and involved because of the shortage of its material, the danger of elaboration should be avoided.

In ancient times, little is known about this area beyond the meagre details to be gleaned from the Egyptian Queen Hatshepsut's naval expedition to the land of Punt in eastern Africa about the year 1520 B.C. Apparently the kingdom of Axum remained pagan until we next hear of the legendary bond of union between King Solomon and the Queen of Sheba[1] in the tenth century before Christ, giving rise to the apocryphal line of succession to the throne of Ethiopia from Solomon. This was the first contact between what might have been Ethiopia or Yemen and Judaistic monotheism. It was also on that occasion that the Ark of the Covenant is supposed to have been removed by the Queen's retinue from the Temple of Solomon in Jerusalem to Axum, where it was treasured, though all archæological evidence points to the survival of paganism until the introduction of Christianity in the fourth century of our era.

During the Christian era, Abyssinia emerges in first-century descriptions of the coasts of the Red Sea and the Indian Ocean, known as the 'Periplus

[1] I Kings x, 1–13.

of the Erithrean Sea'. It reappears in the fourth century in the Frumentius episode, and again in the sixth-century *Christian Topography* of Cosmas Indicopleustes. Hitherto, the primitive civilization of the kingdom was one of barbaric splendour where Christianity and paganism left their impressions. To that period belongs the erection at Axum of those gigantic monolithic obelisks,[1] whose purpose is still a mystery and a source of curiosity to the archæologist.

Prior to the coming of Islam, Ethiopia witnessed an expansion of the kingdom beyond the Red Sea into Yemen. The aim of the campaign undertaken by the Axumite King Caleb was to chastise Dhū Nuwās, who persecuted the Christians of Najrān in 522 and installed the son of al-Ḥārith (Aretha), the martyred tribal shaikh, on the throne of Ḥimyar.[2] Tradition has it that an Ethiopian viceroy, Abraha al-Ashram, was preparing to attack Mecca almost on the eve of the birth of the Prophet Muḥammad, when the Arabs resorted to the Persians for help, those being the inveterate enemies of the Byzantines, who were Ethiopian allies. The Battle of the Elephant (al-Fīl), mentioned in the Qur'ān,[3] took place and Ethiopian rule was ended in Yemen. These events show that pre-Islamic Arabs were acquainted with the kingdom of Ethiopia. During the early Quarayshite persecution of the followers of Muḥammad, the Prophet advised them to flee to the court of Axum, where they would find 'a king under whom no man is persecuted' and where 'God will bring you rest from your afflictions'.[4]

Here we enter one of the darkest periods in Ethiopian history, when the line of kingship from Solomon was lost, and then restored towards the end of the thirteenth century by the extermination of the Zagwé dynasty. The lure of Ethiopian isolation in that era was associated with the Prester John tales of wonder and fabulous wealth which circulated throughout Christendom. To this obscure period, however, belongs the well-known series of ten rock-hewn churches of King Lalibela. These monumental structures are said to have been inspired by Coptic architects. Meanwhile, the return of the original kings of Judah was ascribed to the influence of one of the greatest saints of Ethiopian history, Tekla Haymanot, on whose account the new king, Yekuno-Amlak, granted the Church one-third of the kingdom in perpetuity, a fact which explains the great ecclesiastical wealth in Ethiopia to this day.

During the next age, Ethiopia becomes better known through a native

[1] In size they surpass the known obelisks of Egypt. Jones and Monroe, p. 33.

[2] The Syriac sources of this episode are the *Book of the Himyarites* (Lund, 1920–21) and a 'Letter of St Simeon of Beth Arsham' (*Analecta Syriaca* III, 235), and a Greek narrative entitled 'Martyrdom of St Arethas' (Migne, *P.G.*, CXLVII, 301–4); cf. DeLacy O'Leary, *Ethiopian Church*, pp. 35–7; Doresse, *Ethiopia*, p. 86–8.

[3] Sūra CV. J. S. Trimingham, *Islam in Ethiopia*, p. 41.

[4] Cf. Doresse, p. 88; Hitti, *History of Arabs*, p. 121.

literary renaissance. Considerable translation of works from Coptic and Arabic included books on history, hagiography, homiletics and all manner of religious subjects. It was then that the famous universal *History* of John of Nikiou was rendered into old Geʿez. Original chronicals were compiled for the reigns of ʿAmda Seyon (1314–44) and Zarʿa Yakob (1438). That was the age of the Crusade and Counter-Crusade, during which the Mamlūk Sultans of Egypt abused the Copts and consequently aroused their Ethiopian co-religionists to relieve their distant brethren from increasing pressures. Whenever the news of fresh persecutions reached the Ethiopian monarch, he resorted to one or more of three retaliatory measures. First, he threatened to deflect the course of the Nile and turn Egypt into a desert. Secondly, he employed the means of negotiation and exchange of presents, as in the case of King David I, whose twenty-two camel-loads of gifts to Sultan Barqūq appear to have been sufficiently conciliatory. Thirdly, in case of failure, he simply took severe reprisals against the Abyssinian Muslims, whom he regarded as hostages, and even expressed the intention to invade Egypt from the south, as in the reign of Zarʿa Yakob[1] (1438–68). Relations with western Europe also became more frequent in that time. An envoy of King Weden Arʿad (1299–1314) appeared at the papal curia of Clement V in Avignon, but the object of his mission is unknown. Zarʿa Yakob appointed Nicodemus, prior of the Abyssinian Convent at Jerusalem, and another unnamed Ethiopian delegate to participate with Johannes, Coptic abbot of St Antony, in the Council of Ferrara-Florence (1438-9) in order to seek the peace of all churches and unity in the face of a common enemy.[2] The Abyssinian chronicles do not refer to these representatives, but mention the advent of a Frank, perhaps the first Frank in history to enter Ethiopia. In the following reign, a Venetian artist named Nicholas Brancaleone resided and painted in Ethiopia for almost forty years. His painting of the infant Jesus resting on the left hand of the Virgin once caused an uproar from the Abyssinian clergy, who considered it a grave sin to have the Lord on a lesser arm, and only the king could quell the ecclesiastical protests.[3]

The closing years of Zarʿa Yakob's reign witnessed the beginning of a mortal struggle with the Muslim neighbours, who defeated his successors and the fate of the empire was left in the balance. To save the situation, the hard-pressed monarchs asked the Portuguese to help them. This was the age of Portuguese exploration, and Prince Henry the Navigator seized upon the idea of using 'Prester John' to accomplish his Indian venture. Outside the Coptic Church and the advent of one *abuna* after another, the door of Ethiopia was for the first time set slightly ajar to foreign influence. One

[1] A. S. Atiya, *The Crusade of Nicopolis* (London, 1934), pp. 167–8 and n. 17.
[2] Idem, *Crusade in Later Middle Ages*, pp. 277–8.
[3] Jones and Munroe, p. 58.

Portuguese embassy followed another. These were begun by Pedro de Cavilham and Alphonso Payo in 1490, who came by way of the Levant and the Red Sea; they were followed by the more formal embassy of Francis Alvarez in 1520, who journeyed from the Indies, since the route of the Cape of Good Hope had linked India directly with Portugal since 1498. These embassies were on the whole of little help, and sometimes even a burden to the suspicious Ethiopians. The Jesuits, a newly founded company, came with other missions for purely proselytizing purposes. They had some measure of success under royal patronage as is demonstrated by the missions of Oviedo, Pæz and Mendez in 1557, 1595 and 1624 respectively. But this remained only an outward triumph without reaching the hearts of the people at all.[1]

At the time of the Portuguese mission, the Turks had occupied Yemen in 1538, and their forces began to pour across the Red Sea on the African coast. Soon Muslim Harar became the centre of their reconnaissance against Ethiopia, and the rise of the fearful Aḥmad Grañ wrecked the Portuguese garrison and defeated the Abyssinian forces, while the Gallas at the other end were pouring into the country. The damage done to the churches, monasteries and Ethiopian cultural treasures at the hands of the invaders was irreparable. Finally the Ethiopians had to fall back on their own resources for defence. Thanks to the rainy season, the nature of the physical configuration of the country, Ethiopian tenacity in guerilla warfare, and above all, the spirited leadership of a new young king in the person of Claudius, Aḥmad Grañ's men were routed and he himself killed in 1542.[2] The war with the Muslims, though persisting on the eastern periphery of Ethiopia, never again assumed the dimensions of Grañ's ravages.

Of the Portuguese mission, perhaps the only enduring outcome was the birth of Ethiopian studies in Europe. When Mendez assumed his shadowy patriarchal dignity with imperial approval, he inaugurated his reign with a pastoral visitation to Tigré, where two of his priests celebrated mass in an Ethiopian church and were found slain the following morning. Though this was a definitive sign of failure of the mission, Mendez had sent four Ethiopians to Rome for indoctrination as a preliminary measure for planting Catholic doctrine amongst the natives by means of educating groups of preachers and future priests. The four natives were placed in the care of Job Ludolf,[3] a superior German scholar who was able in three years to learn both Amharic and the old Geʿez from his pupils. Ludolf further prepared a grammar, a lexicon and a history of Ethiopia. In Ethiopia, Mendez

[1] Idem, pp. 76 ff.

[2] Idem, pp. 83 ff.; Doresse, pp. 146–9; Trimingham, *Islam in Ethiopia*, pp. 85–91. Grañ's full name is Imām Aḥmad ibn Ibrāhīm al-Ghāzi (1506–43). The nickname Grañ given him by the Abyssinians means 'the left-handed'.

[3] DeLacy O'Leary, pp. 67–8.

and his companions managed with difficulty to reach the port of Suakin and sail to Goa in 1636, and the Portuguese Jesuit mission came to an inglorious end. Louis XIV wished to renew the enterprise and by way of exploration despatched a French physician by the name of du Roule. He went to Sennar on the Sudanese border of Ethiopia and applied to Emperor Tekla Haymanot (1706–8) for an entry visa, but was dead before he received the imperial reply.

Another era of complete isolation in Ethiopian history began. The intrigues, assassinations and local unrest during the next century are of little importance to this study. External concern for the Ethiopian empire came from the two neighbouring countries – the Sudan, now occupied by Egypt in the west, and Eritrea, in the hands of the Italians in the east. To settle their differences on the western border, the khedive sent the Coptic patriarch Cyril IV[1] on a peace mission, which he accomplished with difficulty on account of the suspicious nature of the Ethiopians. The Italians, on the other hand, under the delusion of building a colonialist empire in Africa, took to the risky road of their own defeat at Adowa[2] in 1896, which they were determined to vindicate when Mussolini pounced on the old and relatively defenceless empire with all his accumulated arms in 1935. The temporary occupation of the country by the Italians (1936–41) and its inglorious end in the course of the Second World War are chapters in contemporary history. Perhaps the staggering outcome of the war was the annexation of Eritrea by the empire and the recovery of the long-lost shores of Ethiopian access to the sea. More than any other Ethiopian monarch in history, Haile Selassie has worked to relieve his country of the dead-weight of conservative stagnation, to educate his people, and to cope with the forward march of modernizing influences, though without breaking away from time-honoured tradition.[3] His task has only been partly accomplished owing to the nature of the Ethiopians, whose love for their own way of life is proverbial.

Church Origins and Development

The historic origins of Ethiopian Christianity have already been outlined under the Coptic missionary enterprise.[4] This romantic episode was repeated by most of the ancient ecclesiastical historians,[5] mainly on the authority

[1] See above.

[2] D. Mathew, *Ethiopia, The Study of a Polity (1540–1935)*, (London, 1947), pp. 224–34.

[3] Doresse, pp. 201 ff.; Jones and Monroe, pp. 159 ff.

[4] See above. For the lives of Ethiopian saints, see E. A. Wallis Budge, *The Book of the Saints of the Ethiopian Church*, 4 vols. (Cambridge, 1928).

[5] For example, Socrates (I, 19), Sozomenos (II, 24) and Theodoret (I, 22); cf. *Nicene and Post-Nicene Fathers*, Vol. II, pp. 23, 274 and III, 58.

of Rufinus,[1] who is said to have recorded it from the mouth of Aedesius as an old man, long after his return from his joint Ethiopian adventure with his brother Frumentius. The Abyssinians would like to remind us of earlier Israelite and Christian Ethiopian traditions in spite of their legendary character. The first apocryphal contact with monotheism goes back to Solomon's marriage to the Queen of Sheba. Again, within sight of the ascension of our Lord, the somewhat mythical tale of St Matthew's sermon to the Ethiopians,[2] they contend, was the foundation-stone of the new faith in Abyssinia. Another story, from the Acts of the Apostles,[3] mentions that the Apostle Philip baptized 'a man from Ethiopia, an eunuch of great authority under Candace queen of the Ethiopians, who had the charge of all her treasure, and had come to Jerusalem for to worship'. In this way, it is assumed that the Axumite Church had its beginnings. Candace, however, was the title of the Meroïtic queens of Nubia rather than those of Abyssinia, and the word 'Ethiopian' in the Semitic tongues signified one 'dark-skinned' (the Arabic *Ḥabashi*) but not utterly black. The historic date of the Christianization of Ethiopia, on the other hand, has been fixed approximately as 340 A.D.[4]

The tradition of placing a Coptic monk from Egypt at the head of the Ethiopian Church started when Frumentius was consecrated for the new diocese by Athanasius the Great in Alexandria. He became *Apa Salama*, or Father of Peace, otherwise *abuna* – a word which means 'Our Father'. This custom remained in force until the agreement of July 1948 liberated the Ethiopians from the bond of an Egyptian *abuna*, and the present Abyssinian patriarch-catholicos, Anba Basileus, was consecrated at Cairo on 28 June 1959 by Pope Cyril (Kirollos) VI in the presence of Emperor Haile Selassie.

The next event of consequence in Ethiopian church history was the introduction of monasticism in accordance with the rule of St Pachomius before the end of the fifth century and within memory of the saint's lifetime. Though individual monks came to Ethiopia from the Thebaïd at one time or other, the most important landmark in the propagation of both monasticism and Christianity was the advent of the Nine Saints[5] about the year 480 A.D. The central figure in the group was Apa Michael Aragawi, the founder of the famous monastery of Debra Damo on a Pachomian model at a forbidding height in the neighbourhood of Axum. Other monastic fathers include Apa Johannes, founder of the monastery of Debra Sina, and Apa Libanos, founder of Debra Libanos, later associated with the name of the national

[1] Migne, *P.L.*, XXI, 478–80 (*Hist. Eccles.* I, 9); text trans. quoted Jones and Monroe, pp. 26–7, Rufinus mentions India instead of Ethiopia.

[2] Doresse, p. 62.

[3] VIII, 26–39. Reference is made to this story by Eusebius (II, 1), in *Nicene and Post-Nicene Fathers*, Vol. II, p. 105, nn. 30–31.

[4] Doresse, p. 62, places it between 341 and 346 A.D.

[5] Hyatt, pp. 31–32; Doresse, pp. 64–81.

Abyssinian, St Tekla Haymanot, who was instrumental in bringing great wealth to his organization. Ethiopia did not lack mountainous sites, and the saints usually looked for the most inaccessible among them to ensure the seclusion of their brotherhood.

To the influx of the highly lettered monks we owe the emergence of religious literature in translation from Coptic, Greek and Syriac into the old liturgical language of Geʿez. Though Amharic has replaced it as a spoken language, Geʿez is still the language of the liturgy in much the same way as Coptic in the Egyptian church. The Geʿez Bible was completed between the fifth and seventh centuries, together with the Liturgy of St Cyril the Great and a few apocryphal books such as *The Ascension of Isaiah*. The number of churches multiplied with great rapidity throughout the country.[1]

The fifth century witnessed the Chalcedonian rift between East and West, and almost immediately Ethiopia declared its adherence to Coptic Monophysitism. This period is also marked by the leadership which the Ethiopian Church demonstrated beyond its frontiers during the Yemenite wars in pre-Islamic Arabia. After the coming of Islam, the relations between the Ethiopian Christians and the Prophet Muḥammad as well as his early caliphs appear to have been quite friendly. Hostility began later when the Arabs attempted to settle on the African shores of the Red Sea and the Indian Ocean.[2] With the spread of Islam in Ethiopia, it may be assumed that the Muslims remained in the lower plains while the Amharic Christians retired to the higher plateaus of the interior and grew more and more invincible and inaccessible. For six centuries, roughly from 650 to 1270, Ethiopia and the Abyssinian Church were shrouded in one of the darkest epochs of their history. Practically all external relations were limited to the Copts of Egypt, and these almost ended with the consecration of one metropolitan *abuna* after another, perhaps even with an occasional interregnum, where only the unenlightened but natural piety of the Ethiopian helped in the survival of Christianity in those isolated mountain fastnesses. The great monolithic rock churches of Lalibela (1190–1225) are impressive monuments of Abyssinian devotion of which the records are silent during that dark period. Only occasional reports of the fabled land of Prester John reached the outer world. Ethiopian delegates came to the Council of Ferrara-Florence[3] with their Coptic co-religionists and were an object of great interest and curiosity; but as has been noted, no positive results ensued from the undertaking, and only the Muslim peril which was menacing within the Ethiopian borders could again draw the Abyssinian Church toward the west.

The conflict of Islam and Christianity during the Zagwé period in Abyssinia had, however, been growing on account of the strengthening of

[1] Doresse, pp. 82 ff.

[2] Trimingham, *Islam in Ethiopia*, pp. 42 ff.

[3] See above.

Muslim infiltration. Muslims could be found in the Christian interior of the country. In Tigré an Islamic necropolis has been discovered with stelæ inscribed in Arabic, and bearing dates as early as 1006. A Muslim sultanate was established at the end of the ninth century under the Makhzūmi dynasty in the district of Shoa. Mention of it continues in Arab sources until the year 1285, when it was succeeded by another called the Walashma from a neighbouring and more redoubtable state in the district of Ifat, all in the southeast of Ethiopia.[1] The Coptic sources[2] themselves confirm these facts.

The struggle between Muslims and Christians in the interior smouldered until the great conquest of the sixteenth century, which was associated with its parallel on the sea between Ottoman[3] and Portuguese, and the Ethiopian monarch was constrained by Aḥmad Grañ's ravages to solicit Portuguese support. The impact of this step on Ethiopian church history was colossal, since for the first time the Roman Catholic missionary came in the steps of the rather meagre Portuguese contingents. In reality, the legacy of the Islamic conquest with all its devastating effects in Ethiopia was ironically the coming of the Latin mission to the scene. By the year 1578, the Muslim period was ended, but the process of latinization in Ethiopia persisted until approximately the middle of the seventeenth century.

The first real apostle of Latin Christianity in Ethiopia was Bermudez, who clamoured at the court of King Claudius for obedience to Rome, but the king retorted quietly by sending word to Gabriel, patriarch of Alexandria, for one bishop after another. Bermudez was incarcerated for months, then deported to Goa. The Society of Jesus had just been founded in 1558, and Ignatius Loyola pleaded with the reigning pope for permission to inaugurate his New Life with an Ethiopian mission. Though Ignatius himself was not allowed to go, the pope consecrated Nuæs Baretto as new patriarch of Ethiopia, with two suffragan bishops, Andrew Oviedo and Melchior Carneiro. Only Oviedo reached Ethiopia. The others remained at Goa, where Baretto died in 1562. Oviedo promptly assumed the patriarchal dignity, and finding the Ethiopians averse to submission to Roman obedience, he requested the superior-general of the Jesuits to mediate with the papacy for Portuguese troops to be dispatched to impose his will on the Ethiopian people. The Portuguese Cardinal Don Henry acquiesced; but the curia wisely translated the impulsive Oviedo and his company from Ethiopia to

[1] It would be tedious to attempt a complete enumeration of the Muslim principalities within Ethiopia. Trimingham, pp. 62–3, mentions Adal, Mora, Hobat, Jidaya, Hadya, Fatajar, Dawaro, Bali and Mara extending from the interior to the east and south of the Ethiopian *massif* in the Harar and Arusi territories.

[2] See, for instance, Abu Ṣāliḥ, *The Churches and Monasteries of Egypt*, tr. B. T. A. Evetts (Oxford, 1895), p. 290.

[3] The Ottomans inherited the legacy of the Indian maritime war with the Portuguese from the Egyptian Mamlūks after the downfall of their last sultan Qanṣūh al-Ghauri in 1516.

China and Japan in 1567. Oviedo died shortly afterwards at Fremona. His companions in the Jesuit mission followed him to the grave one after the other, Francesco Lopez being the last to be buried in 1597. With his death the Jesuit mission ended in complete failure.[1]

It is interesting, however, to note that two more Jesuits, Pedro Pæz and Antonio de Monserrate, attempted to revive the Roman claim over Ethiopia. Shipwrecked on the Arabian coast, they were enslaved for seven years by the Arabs. The history of the mission becomes somewhat confused at this point. We read of a Maronite Jesuit sent by Dom Alexo de Menezes, archbishop of Goa, to pursue the work of proselytizing the Ethiopians, but he was intercepted and murdered at Massowah. Then we hear of Bishiop Jean-Baptiste, ordained by Pope Gregory XVIII and commissioned to confer with John XIV, patriarch of Alexandria, for reconciliation of the Copts. He failed in the task and proceeded further on the road to Ethiopia but met the same fate as the Maronite, also at Massowah. Meanwhile, the archbishop of Goa selected an Indian Brahmin convert to Catholicism, da Sylva by name, to revive the Jesuit cause in Ethiopia. A disguised Indian had a better chance in the Turkish and Arab realms, and he accordingly reached his destination in safety. In 1604 the Spanish Jesuit Pedro Pæz, who had obtained his freedom, joined the Indian missionary and managed to work his way amidst the conflicting local policies into the good graces of one of the ambitious Ethiopian princes, Jacob, or Za Dengel, who had seized the throne from Malak Sagad I. Jacob thought he could obtain military support from the pope and the Portuguese by feigning conversion to the Roman rite, and Pæz was his instrument. On the other hand, the bulk of the people remained immutably behind the Coptic *abuna*. The same politico-religious manœuvre was regularly repeated until the autocratic Malak Sagad III took the whole matter in hand and summarily ordered obedience to Rome. Alphonso Mendez, consequently, was made patriarch of Ethiopia in 1624 and, on reaching the country, became confirmed by the king while hastening to issue a sentence of formal excommunication against the Coptic *abuna* and all his followers. The Latin prelate then began his aforementioned patriarchal visitation to the province of Tigré with tragic consequences. Revolt broke out, and Mendez opened an inquisition in which he started burning the nationalists alive. Feeling in the country ran high, and even the emperor turned against the patriarch. Finally, the accession of Fasildas (Basilides) to the throne on his father's death in 1632 tolled the knell of the Jesuit mission. The new king was a staunch supporter of the national church, and Mendez had to flee for his life. With only two survivors, he was able with difficulty to sail to Goa after having been plundered by the Turks.

[1] Delacy O'Leary, pp. 60–7; Groves, *Planting of Christianity in Africa*, Vol. I, pp. 138 ff.; C. F. Rey, *The Romance of the Portuguese in Abyssinia* (London, 1929), passim.

Though the bankruptcy of the Jesuit mission was self-evident, a group of Capuchins insisted on the resumption of the Roman venture and took the road to Abyssinia. They succeeded in reaching Axum, but on their arrival they were immediately seized by the Abyssinian authorities and condemned to death. All were hanged, and a ban was issued by the government against the entry of Roman Catholics into the country. Neither the zeal of Philip II of Spain for Catholicism nor even the weight of the French monarchy under Louis XIV could resuscitate the defunct cause for which the Jesuits stood, though the tenacity and determination of the Roman see persisted in its interest in Ethiopia. Thus in 1702, with the blessings of Pope Clement XI, three Franciscans reached Gondar and reported a somewhat doubtful submission to Rome. In 1846, the country was divided into two zones of Roman influence: the vicariate of Abyssinia, headed by M. de Jacobus and the Lazarists, and that of the Galla, where the future Cardinal Guglielmo Massaia led the Capuchins. In 1904, quiet conversions took place in the Tigré, Amhara and Gondar, which had half a dozen chapels; but the harvest was greater amidst the pagan Gallas, where eighteen thousand turned to Rome and some twenty Catholic chapels were founded. In 1950, a native Ethiopian was consecrated by Rome as a titular bishop of Suzusa and combined with that dignity the title of 'Apostolic Administrator for Catholics of the Ethiopian Rite'.[1]

In the nineteenth century, the Protestant missionaries Samuel Gobat and Christian Kugler were despatched to Ethiopia by the Church Missionary Society. By 1838 the mission had come to nothing, since Kugler died and Gobat was exiled. Protestant missions in those days were a mixed affair, and German, Polish, Swedish, French, British and Swiss names keep flickering on the scene of events from the middle of the century without concrete results. The young theologians of the St Chrischona Institute in Basel are mentioned together with a western educated Abyssinian guide named Mader-akal, who later became Emperor Theodore's interpreter. The Ethiopians tolerated the coming of the Protestants since they needed them as technicians and some were gunsmiths. However, the British group under Stern was imprisoned after its arrival in 1860, and it took Lord Napier's expedition to regain freedom for them in 1868. They were expelled in due course. The American missionary emerged later in the century. He concentrated on medical service at the new capital of Addis Ababa and in the midst of the Galla tribes.[2]

It must be stated, however, that in principle neither the Coptic *abuna* nor the Ethiopian people nor even the imperial court favoured the missionary,

[1] Groves, IV, op. cit., 305.

[2] Hyatt, pp. 41–3; Groves, IV, 305 ff.; J. Richter, *A History of Protestant Missions in the Near East* (Edinburgh and London, 1910), pp. 371–90.

who was regarded with great suspicion. Ecclesiastically, Ethiopia has been impervious to foreign influence, and the suspicious nationalism of the Abyssinians has demonstrated itself of late in claiming the right to their own native archbishop and bishops. In 1959, the Ethiopian Church won its first native *abuna* in the person of Anba Basileos, catholicos-patriarch of all Ethiopia, who has his own native suffragan bishops. At present the empire has twenty-two bishops, one for each of the thirteen provinces and others in the cities and monasteries, especially the long-disputed Dair al-Sultan in Jerusalem. It is here, and not in matters of doctrine, that the rift has widened between the Copts and the Ethiopians, who claim a footing on that holy soil in the neighbourhood of the Holy Sepulchre. The grant of Dair al-Sultan dates from the reign of Saladin, after his conquest of Jerusalem in 1187, when he allowed the Eastern Christians to re-enter the Holy City from which the Latin Crusader kingdom had banned them as schismatics. The tendency in Ethiopia at present is one of personal but not doctrinal independence from the Copts. Their clerical college for religious instruction of future priests, formerly headed by a Coptic ecclesiastic, has been ceded to a Malabarese priest or scholar from the Syrian Orthodox Church of St Thomas, who acts as principal. Nevertheless the ties with the Coptic Church are cherished by the Ethiopians, who send their promising young scholars to both the Coptic Theological College and the Institute of Coptic Studies in Cairo. The recent visit of the Coptic Pope Cyril (Kirollos) VI to the Empire of Ethiopia has been a demonstration of the strength of the enduring links which have bound the Coptic mother Church of Alexandria to its daughter Church of Ethiopia.

Ethiopian Faith and Culture

In matters of dogma and doctrine the Ethiopians have faithfully adhered to the Alexandrine teachings of the Coptic Church. A survey of Ethiopian ecclesiastical usage would therefore be somewhat redundant. The salient features of Ethiopian faith – Monophysitism, church order, eschatology, biblical and hagiographical literature, liturgies, and even their monastic rule – stem from Coptic origins. Nevertheless, it would be a grave error to describe the Ethiopian Church as a mere replica of the Coptic Church. The native traditions, whether Jewish or pagan, have given the Ethiopian Church a distinct colour of its own, and here will be mentioned the main variants which give that church its own special personality.[1]

[1] G. A. Lipsky, *Ethiopia – its people, its society, its culture* (New Haven, 1962), pp. 100 ff.; Sylvia Pankhurst, *Ethiopia, A Cultural History* (Woodford Green, Essex, 1955), pp. 111 ff.;

Without unduly exaggerating the Jewish influences in the country, it may be noted that the Ethiopians observe the Sabbath on Saturday, practice male circumcision, and shun numerous items of food as unclean – all of which are customs of Judaic origin. Judaism in Ethiopia is still represented by the powerful Falasha tribe, whose advent presumably antedates Christianity. Tradition tells us that an Israelite tribe accompanied the infant Menelik I in the reign of the Queen of Sheba. The famous dance of the *dabteras* with their T-shaped crutch or staff in the left hand and the jingling sistrum[1] or rattle in the right during religious processions on certain days is said to be an ancient custom inherited by the Ethiopians from the Levites, who danced before the Ark inside Solomon's Temple in Jerusalem. However, the T-shaped crutch was used by the Antonian monks in Egypt during their long prayers, while the sistrum was employed by the priests of the Egyptian goddess Isis in pre-Christian times. The accompaniment of the drum for keeping the rhythm is another usage which can be traced only to pagan African origins. The *dabteras*, often mistaken for priests, are unordained chanters and psalmists, without whose participation a church service cannot be celebrated. They are also known as church scribes, and they hold a place in Ethiopian folklore as the writers of popular charms for guarding bearers against demons and for healing the sick.[2]

Their church music, far from being of modern creation, is ascribed to a sixth-century deacon named Yared, who, according to a native legend, heard it from a chorus of angels in heaven and immediately recorded it for his countrymen. Like the Copts, who still use ancient Coptic liturgies, the Ethiopians read their services in the old Geʿez instead of the modern Amharic language. This imposes considerable rigorous training on their priests before ordination. The church order and canon law are in the main those of the Coptic Church, with a few additional elements. On the other hand, the Coptic Church has no *dabteras*, and one of the high offices peculiar to the Ethiopian Church is that of the *echage*, who has no equivalent among the present-day Copts, though his position could be identified with that of superior-general in the early Pachomian monasteries. The *echage*[3] is regarded as the head of all Abyssinian monastic brotherhoods, and he is customarily the abbot of Debra Libanos, the true successor of the great Tekla Haymanot. As the leader of a powerful army of monastic communities and the

---

Doresse, *Ethiopia*, pp. 205 ff. See also pamphlet prepared by Ethiopian delegation for distribution to members of the World Council of Churches in the session of 1954 held at Evanston, Ill., and written by K. M. Simon, *The Ethiopian Orthodox Church*, and giving a summary of the official church views (pp. 24).

[1] See illustration in Hyatt, p. 135. The sistrum was used in the mystical music at the worship of Isis and mentioned by Ovid; cf. ibid., p. 145.

[2] Hyatt, p. 59.

[3] Ibid., pp. 50–1.

dispenser of vast monastic property, he ranks next to the *abuna* in the hierarchy.

Ethiopian prelates must receive imperial sanction before their preferment. The Church and empire are the true sources of power and authority as well as national culture in Ethiopia. They are not unlike the two swords, the spiritual and the temporal, in European mediæval thought. Until recent times, in one of his pronouncements, the emperor, as defender of the faith, declared that the Church was like a sword and the imperial government like an arm, and thus 'the sword cannot cut by itself without the use of the arm'.[1] Both institutions are clothed in a garb of awe, and are universally respected and feared.

It may be of interest here to note the enormous size of the clerical profession as a special class. The travellers' assertion that Abyssinia has more churches than any other part of Christendom is perhaps an exaggeration.[2] However, the country is estimated to have about 20,000 churches. Some villages have more than one church, and each of them must have two ordained priests in addition to numerous *dabteras* and deacons. On this assumption, the number of ecclesiastics throughout Ethiopia has been estimated at approximately twenty-five per cent of the whole male Christian population. The priest is a principal personality in his congregation, and his offices extend from the church to the homes of his flock, indeed to every phase of individual and family life from birth to death. The strength of Ethiopian piety is demonstrated, not merely by profound deference toward the priesthood and by the resounding religious processions to the awesome beat of the great drums, but more particularly in the strict observance of the sacraments and the long seasons of fasting, which amount to some 250 days every year. Besides abstaining from meat and all forms of animal products in their meals, the devout Ethiopians usually refrain from touching food before the third hour of the afternoon on fast days, except Saturdays and Sundays. As a mark of adherence to the faith, young girls often tattoo themselves with the Cross on the forehead. Education starts amongst the younger generation as a church affair, since the traditional elementary school is an adjunct to the village church. Besides reading and arithmetic, the central theme in education consists mainly of the Psalms of David, the praises of Jesus and the Virgin Mary and a series of closely knit prayers[3] in the old Geʿez.

In ecclesiastical architecture, although the original basilica or rectangular and cruciform styles have been preserved in a multitude of ancient churches, the Ethiopians have developed their own peculiar octagonal or round churches, which may have been inspired by their conception of the Temple of

[1] Cf. Lipsky, p. 101.

[2] Hyatt, p. 109. Alvarez records that the Portuguese were stunned when they were met on their arrival by a procession of 20,000 clerics preceded by mitred prelates carrying gold Crosses; cf. Doresse, p. 207.

[3] Pankhurst, pp. 234 ff.; Lipsky, pp. 107 ff.

Solomon in Jerusalem. On the other hand, it has been asserted that this may have been purely a reproduction of the customary southern Ethiopian habitation, which was circular.

The oldest Ethiopian church is of course the Cathedral of Axum, dedicated to Our Lady of Zion, in whose sanctuary the Mosaic Ark is enshrined and where the imperial coronation takes place. Though the church itself has been burnt to the ground many times and its present structure dates only from 1854, the ancient rectangular form of its building has been preserved. Erected on a raised platform with an impressive façade, three main entrances, some side chapels and a forbidden sanctuary, the Cathedral is lavishly decorated with paintings from biblical scenes in the traditional Ethiopian style in which the artist has concentrated on the theme and the bright colour rather than the proportion. The central objects are the coming of the Ark, the Virgin and the Infant Jesus, St George and the Dragon, and a pictorial record of the Nine Saints. As a rule, paintings were made on canvas which was then pasted to the walls, in accordance with Abyssinian artistic techniques. During the succession of invasions, the emperors craftily concealed the treasured Ark, or *Tabot*, and later reinstated it. Since no one is allowed within the Holy of Holies, the Ark and its contents have never been described in an official Christian source. But we are told by the Muslim chroniclers that the hidden treasure is a large white stone inlaid with gold.[1] Although all Ethiopian churches are normally open to both sexes, the Cathedral of Axum is an exception, since women are not permitted to set foot on its floor. This rule dates from the time when a former empress is said to have desecrated the building.

The more familiar form of the Ethiopian church is either octagonal or circular. The countryside is spotted with such churches, usually built on an elevation and with thatched roofs. Invariably, they consist of three concentric rings; a square sanctuary is situated in the middle of the circle and is screened. This is followed by an area reserved for the choir and those receiving Holy Communion, while the rest of the congregation stands in the outer ring, always barefooted on the floor covered with matting. Men and women are separated by partitions. Priests circulate in their midst while praying, blessing and swinging their censers until the interior is filled with clouds of incense. The interior is decorated with wall paintings and the usual icons.[2]

The third type of Ethiopian church is the historic rock-hewn group founded by the pious monarch Lalibela (1181–1221), of the Zagwé dynasty. Because of their monolithic character, architectural skill, massive dimensions, carefully carved colonnades, arcades and vaulted ceilings, these churches are considered by archæologists to rank amongst the finest achievements in

[1] Doresse, p. 206.

[2] Pankhurst, pp. 167 ff.; Lipsky, p. 109.

ecclesiastical architecture of any age throughout Christendom. Apparently King Lalibela re-established a firmer relationship with Egypt and undertook a pilgrimage to the Holy Places. He was thus able to invite skilled Coptic and Syrian architects to come to Ethiopia to help in this monumental project. The Lalibela churches, eleven in number, possess the general air of ancient Egyptian temples. They form three groups with intercommunication at varying levels by trenches and subterranean tunnels, which are engineering feats of no mean stature. In fact, the Lalibela churches have often been compared in their grandeur to the rock-hewn temples of Abu Simbel in Nubia, of Petra in Jordan, and of Ellora in the Indian state of Hyderabad – all monuments of singular exotic beauty. Though carved from the live rock in the mountain side, these monolithic structures were detached from the body of the mountain by excavating deep trenches around each of them. After separating the massive rock formation from the surrounding fastness by that deep trench, the exterior of each church was fashioned in a manner to give the impression of buttressed walls with bays and colonnades. The roof was gabled or carved flat, cruciform or simple, invariably with an attractive cornice. Afterwards, the craftsmen set themselves to hollow the interior and to design extraordinary forms of architecture which could never have been accomplished by normal building processes and techniques. Some churches had three naves, others five, with rows of impressive columns and capitals. Arches, windows, niches, colossal crosses and swastikas in bas-relief and haut-relief, decorative rock mouldings and friezes of geometrical shapes, apses and domes – all these and other features have truly rendered the Lalibela churches enduring monuments of Christian architecture in the heart of the African continent.[1]

Monastic architecture, too, deserves at least some notice here. The Ethiopian monastic system follows rather closely the Coptic. While the latter aimed at the wilderness of the eastern and western deserts, the Ethiopians established their cenobia in the complete seclusion of mountain peaks. Illustrative of the fact is Debra Damo,[2] a monastery built probably as early as the seventh century by Emperor Gabra Maskal and still standing atop a plateau, or rather mountain peak, accessible only by means of the rope. After building it, the emperor ordered the connecting staircase to be demolished. The centre of the monastery is occupied by a church that is a

[1] The latest and most impressive work on the rock-hewn churches is sumptuously published with colour plates and detailed plans by Imgard Bidder, *Lalibela, The Monolithic Churches of Ethiopia* (Cologne, 1958). All works on Ethiopian history and culture devote space to this subject. Pankhurst, pp. 151 ff.; Hyatt, pp. 110 ff.; Doresse, pp. 93 ff.; T. Pakenham, *The Mountains of Rasselas* (New York, 1959), pp. 171–6. The last is only a travel account. Other works on these interesting churches include A. A. Monti della Corte, *Lalibela, le chiese ipogee e monolitiche* (Rome, 1940); A. Raffray, *Les églises monolithes de la ville de Lalibela* (Paris, 1882).

[2] Pakenham, pp. 78–90.

jewel of Abyssinian ecclesiastical architecture.[1] Its stone and wood carving is exquisite. The panels of animal haut-relief and the geometrical friezes are reminiscent of specimens to be found in early Coptic art. Its mural structure has the obelisk patterns of Axum. The use of massive wooden beams and stone in alternating horizontal tiers lends an unusual charm to its outward appearance. Round the church, the monastic cells spread out in greater intimacy than in most other monasteries. As a rule, Ethiopian monasticism is marked by severe austerity and a tendency toward eremitism.

Another notable type of Ethiopian mediæval ecclesiastical architecture is the cave church pattern. Of this type, the most famous examples are Imrahanna Kristos and Jammadu Mariam. The first was built inside a tremendous cave in the Lasta Mountains by the Emperor who imparted his name to it after deciding to retire from the throne to monasticism. He died and was buried in that church about the middle of the twelfth century. The second was built by Emperor Yekuno-Amlak about 1268, also in the Lasta Mountains, to commemorate the restoration of the line of Solomon with the support of the great saint, Tekla Haymanot.[2]

All these and other similar monuments were probably built by anonymous monastic architects as an act of faith. Perhaps a better known contribution of the Ethiopian monks lies in their formidable manuscript heritage. Undoubtedly the followers of St Pachomius, of whom the Nine Saints were the most eminent disciples of Ethiopian monachism, carried with them the teachings of their superior, who insisted on education and manual labour side by side for a healthy life of the monks under his rule. It was in this way that many Abyssinian cenobites became accomplished copyists. Others developed the art of the miniature, and their illustrations of Geʿez codices reached a degree of perfection that places their work on an equal footing with the similar great arts of other lands.

Ethiopian literature[3] in the old Geʿez seems to have arisen simultaneously

[1] For description and plan of the church, see Pankhurst, pp. 141–5.

[2] Ibid., pp. 146–9.

[3] Pankhurst, pp. 177 ff.; Hyatt, pp. 243 ff.; Doresse, pp. 217 ff.; Lipsky, pp. 121–35. Comprehensive works on literature are few. See J. M. Harden, *An Introduction to Ethiopic Christian Literature* (London and New York, 1926); E. Littmann, *Geschichte der äthiopischen Litteratur* (Leipzig, 1907); J. Guidi, *Storia della Litteratura Etiopica* (Rome, 1932). On the subject of Ethiopic liturgies see A. B. Mercer, *The Ethiopian Liturgy – Its development and Forms* (Milwaukee and London, 1915). A complete tr. into English and Arabic of the fourteen Ethiopian Anaphoras has been made by a Coptic priest Father Marcos Daoud and revised by Blatta Marsie Hazen under the title of *The Liturgy of the Ethiopian Church* (Cairo, 1959). It would be interesting to enumerate those anaphoras which include some from ancient Coptic sources now unknown to the Copts: (1) Anaphora of the Apostles; (2) Anaphora of the Lord; (3) Anaphora of John, Son of Thunder; (4) Anaphora of Holy Mary; (5) Anaphora of the Three Hundred [Bishops at Nicæa, more correctly 318]; (6) Anaphora of St. Athanasius; (7) Anaphora of St Basil; (8) Anaphora of St Gregory; (9) Anaphora of St Epiphaneus; (10) Anaphora of St John Chrysostom; (11) Anaphora of St Cyril;

with the introduction of Christianity into the Axumite kingdom. At some unknown date around the dawn of modern history it gradually fell into disuse and was replaced by the more recent Amharic style, though the conservative Ethiopian has hitherto retained Geʿez as the liturgical language of the church. The original Geʿez literature was pre-eminently biblical and religious. Its general substance was translated from Coptic, Syriac, some Greek and at a later date from Arabic. The Ethiopic Bible contains the major Apocrypha; and the liturgies, besides the standard Coptic Gregorian, Basilian and Cyrillian texts, preserved others that have since disappeared in Egypt and still others of purely Abyssinian origin. Though the Geʿez Bible is said to have been started by Frumentius, the surest data point to the age of the Nine Saints, toward the end of the fifth century, as that of the rendering of the earliest biblical books for the Ethiopians. The golden age of the Geʿez letters is coterminous with the great awakening associated with the restoration of Solomon's line of succession in 1270, though it is very difficult to construct a complete picture of the literary and artistic excellence of mediæval Ethiopia. The reason for this obscurity is the destructive Islamic invasion of the sixteenth century, when Aḥmad Grañ systematically desecrated Ethiopian churches. He left them in ruins after looting their treasure and putting every available ancient codex to the flame. Ethiopia has never fully recovered from the barbarous descent of the Turks on its cultural heritage. Had it not been for the physical inaccessibility of some churches and monasteries, the world might have completely lost contact with that glorious literature. More opportunities may still be offered by further discoveries in the twenty island monasteries in the waters of Lake Tana, though numerous manuscripts have already found their way to European repositories.[1]

The Ethiopian scribe used vellum or parchment in the redaction of his codices. The binding was either simple wooden boards or embossed leather. A treasured Gospel, Bible or Psalter was carefully encased in a leather container with a strap so that it could be carried around the shoulder. Apart from the predominant religious literature – biblical, liturgical and hagiographical treatises, mainly derived from the Coptic Synaxarium, or Lives of the Saints – the Ethiopians developed a marginal, quasi-religious and secular set of

(12) Anaphora of St John of Serough; (13) Anaphora of St Dioscorus; (14) Anaphora of St Gregory II.

[1] The strongest Ethiopic manuscript collections appear to be 688 in Poland (1952), 500 in the British Museum (1928), 170 in the Bibliothèque Nationale (1877) with later expansions, and about 100 in the Bodleian Library at Oxford (1951); cf. Pankhurst, pp. 88–90. It would be interesting to estimate the Italian acquisitions after the Ethiopian conquest, which came to an end in May 1941. A. Dillman catalogued 82 MSS. in the British Museum in 1847, and these were supplemented by 408 by William Wright in 1877. Of these, at least 122 are biblical and apocryphal. With the exception of 32 secular treatises, the rest of the codices are on religious matters.

writings covering various fields. These comprised law, which was essentially canon law derived from the Coptic Didascallia, history, some Greek science, magic and quack medicine, and tales of Abyssinian folklore.[1] The *Kebra Nagast* (Glory of Kings) is the outstanding native classic, where the legend of the Queen of Sheba's betrothal to King Solomon and the birth of Menelik I is still cherished by the Ethiopian people. The *Physiologus*, from the Greek, is a natural history. A multitude of chronicles have survived, together with a translation of John of Nikiou from Coptic and the *Historia Saracenica* of ibn al-Makīn[2] from Arabic. The *Story of Barlaam and Yewasef* as well as the *Romance of Alexander*[3] have enjoyed a special place in Abyssinian belles-lettres, to be surpassed only by the prolific literature on the Virgin Mary.[4] Like the Copts, whose deeply seated affection for the Virgin may have been a continuation of their pre-Christian intense regard for Isis, the Ethiopians have inherited Coptic mariolatry and accentuated it even beyond the parent church.

A fine Ethiopian school of painting has evolved from the illustrative miniatures with which their artists decked the majority of the aforementioned classics. Radiant colours, including red, azure, gold and some brown, predominate in the Abyssinian miniature. The faces of the blessed and the holy are painted in full and are invariably in light colour, while the unholy appear in dark profile. Though the native artist displayed no sense of perspective, his work was full of vigour. To him a painting was the representation of a given theme, and this he managed to accomplish in primitive purity and without affectation. On the whole, Ethiopian art imparts a feeling of originality and freshness which, in spite of its modest qualities, assures it of some place in the general framework of the religious arts.

The Ethiopians have retained the elaborate paraphernalia demonstrated in the scenes of their older paintings, as may be witnessed to this day in their religious functions. The richly embroidered vestments of the clergy, the colourful ceremonial umbrellas, the gold or silver gilt crosses, the jewelled implements of the liturgy, the sistrum, staff, censer, and a multitude of other

[1] Abyssinian folklore is essentially preserved in Amharic. See R. Davis and B. Ashabranner, *The Lion's Whiskers, Tales of High Africa* (Boston and Toronto, 1959).

[2] See above.

[3] The Ethiopian Alexander is represented as a saint and Philip his father as a martyr. Sir E. A Wallis Budge, ed., *The Life and Exploits of Alexander the Great*, Ethiopic text and English tr. and notes, 2 vols. (1896); cf. Pankhurst, pp. 218–31.

[4] Pankhurst, pp. 192–200. The Lady Meux Ethiopic MSS., purchased in a Quaritch sale in 1897, were first acquired by a British officer during the Magdala Expedition of 1867. They are profusely illustrated with some of the most magnificent specimens of the Ethiopic miniature in bright colours. The collection has been sumptuously edited by Sir E. A. Wallis Budge and includes *Legends of Our Lady Mary, the Perpetual Virgin* (London, 1900) as well as *The History of Hanna, the mother of the Blessed Virgin Mary* and the *Lives of Maba Sion and Gabra Chrestos* (London, 1899).

items render their services or processions picturesque events which are further dramatized by the exotic dancing of the *dabteras*, the rhythmic handclapping of the congregation to the exciting beat of the great drums.[1] The priests are dressed in white in daily life, and only the *shama*, thrown over their shoulders, has an embroidered edge of subdued colours. Their turbans are also white, unlike those of the bishops, whose robes are identical with those of their Coptic peers in Egypt – that is, entirely black. When officiating, however, the Ethiopian bishop uses a snow-white silk turban decorated with crosses in gold thread, whereas the Copt wears the mitre or a jewelled crown.

In matters of faith and culture, the Ethiopians as a whole have retained the older piety and the Church its traditional conservatism. Contacts with the foreign missionary have always been overshadowed by fear and suspicion of his real motives. Even with the Copts, their lifelong companions since antiquity, they seem to have grown impatient. The departure from former obedience to a Coptic *abuna*, the consecration of their own native bishops and the establishment of a local native synod for Ethiopia are modern nationalist trends which the pope of Alexandria and patriarch of the see of St Mark honoured with all the concessions which left no room for doctrinal aberrations or dogmatic cleavage between the two great native churches of Africa.

In the meantime, the survival of the ancient scenes and habits, at times within hearing distance of the roaring of lions and whining of hyenas, at others in the neighbourhood of thundering jet planes, has brought both the Ethiopian Church and the Ethiopian society of a bygone era face to face with the stark realities of a new and changing world. This is the great challenge with which both Church and empire must cope. The country has taken considerable strides in religious and secular education as a solution to the problems of progress, but much still remains to be done. The ways of reform are indeed multiple, and the Church needs all of them. After its newly acquired hierarchical independence, and with its presumably legendary wealth, the Church is expected by many Ethiopians to share more actively in the realization of national aspirations. In spite of the limitations imposed upon the religious activity of foreign missionaries,[2] both Protestant and Roman Catholic, their very existence within the country has aroused the request of the Ethiopian youth for ecclesiastical reform. It is difficult as yet to estimate the impact of those foreign elements on the native church. In Egypt, as has

[1] A fine photographic record of Ethiopian church and monastic life and religious ceremonial has appeared in no. 225 of *Vivante Afrique* (Paris, March-April 1963). The photographs are unequalled, but the text of the explanatory remarks, though sympathetic with Ethiopian Christians, is critical of Ethiopian and Coptic Christianity and strongly leans towards purely Roman Catholic propaganda.

[2] The missionary activities are regulated by special decree no. 3 (27 August 1944), which narrows them down to medical and educational services. Groves, IV, 249; Lipsky, p. 120.

already been said, the Church owed the first sparks of its awakening to the missionary. Perhaps the day is not far when the same episode will repeat itself in Ethiopia. The Church is slowly coming out of its isolation, and one of the signs of this new trend is its enrolment in the universal family of the World Council of Churches, where it was represented by Anba Theophilus, archbishop of Harar, and a few younger Ethiopians. The same prelate consecrated an Ethiopian branch of the Church in America in December 1959. But its real function has remained nearer home where, as the truly Christian outpost in the African continent, it has established a more effective branch in Trinidad. The present emperor has encouraged the translation of the Bible into the more intelligible Amharic[1] and despatched more theological scholars to Coptic institutions in Egypt. The Theological College at Addis Ababa, founded towards the end of 1944, has been enlarged under government auspices. More than a thousand students are said to attend its classes, and the Church seems to have expanded its educational service to some 100,000 boys throughout the country, according to a census of 1960.[2] Progress has been made, and there is no doubt that dawn is breaking on the Ethiopian horizon. But a great deal of adjustment and labour are still necessary to bring this ancient and august Church into line with the swift pace of modern developments.

[1] This translation was done at the initiative of Emperor Haile Selassie. Before the issue of an authorized version in Amharic, other versions by both the Protestant and Catholic missionaries had been in use, but none were recognized by the Ethiopian Church authorities (Pankhurst, pp. 282–3). Amharic has been declared by Article 126 of the Constitution of 4 November 1955 as the state language. The same Constitution devotes Articles 127, 128 and 129 to the organization of the Church. Article 10 enacts that the head of the Church should be in the Regency Council. Zāhir Riāḍ, *The Ethiopian Constitution* (in Arabic), pp. 19–41.

[2] Ibid., pp. 98, 112. According to Zāhir Riāḍ (*Church of Alexandria in Africa*, p. 132, in Arabic), the year of its founding was 1941–2 and it was completely from the private imperial coffers, with 200 students increasing to 600 in 1961.

9 • SUPPLEMENT TO PART I: THE COPTS ABROAD

Introductory

The exodus of immigrants from the Middle East to the United States may have started at an early date rather modestly by a couple of Armenians in 1653,[1] although the real flight of the Armenian people from Turkish genocide must have taken place only in later centuries. In the meantime, the Christians of Greater Syria (including the mountains of Lebanon) began to make their escape to the United States from Turkish oppression and the Druze Massacres of the Sixties (1860)[2] in the course of the latter decades of the nineteenth century. This movement became intensified at the turn of the century, and currently the number of Arabic-speaking residents in the United States is estimated at about one million strong.[3] However, the Copts, although forming part of that total, were much later newcomers to the New World than the Syrians and Lebanese. Unlike those neighbours, they had no pressing need to leave the land of their forebears. In fact, Coptic immigration from Egypt came rather as an unusual phenomenon during the last few decades. Habitually the Copts are known as a sedentary race who, throughout their history, detested quitting their historic homeland which they firmly regarded as their birthright, even at times when their horizon was darkened by an oppressive ruler.

Coptic immigration in relatively large numbers began only as late as the sixties of this century, although numerous isolated cases could be traced to earlier dates. In reality, the restrictions on personal liberties and the economic hardship associated with the rather despotic reign of Gamal Abd-el-Nasser over Egypt may have sparked the immigration movement to the Western democracies. The Egyptian intelligentsia, partly Muslim but predominantly Coptic, seriously contemplated leaving for other terrains with prospects of freedom and economic prosperity. Perhaps the Copts had one more reason for leaving their native country. Contrary to the policy of tolerance established by the higher political échelons of Egypt, the

[1] Kenonian et al. 'The Armenians,' in *The New Jersey Ethnic Experience* (ed. B. Cunningham), page 41.

[2] See p. 407–8.

[3] P. M. Kayat, "Arabic-Speaking People" in *The New Jersey Ethnic Experience,* p. 27.

bigotry of local Muslim functionaries in state offices could not be stopped from discriminating against the Copts, which rendered government service unattractive to them. Thus lines of Copts were continuously seen at the American Embassy soliciting immigration visas to the United States as a first preference.

The United States and Canada

The early bands of immigrants appear to have settled mainly in the east and partly in the west of the United States. The United States census of the year 1970 indicates that the foreign-born Egyptians in the country numbered 20,666 of a total Egyptian population of 31,358 souls. Of these, at least 80 percent were Copts. By 1976, Coptic immigrants, including children born in the United States reached forty-five thousand according to local Coptic church sources.[4] Again the same source indicates that by 1979, the number rose to about seventy-five thousand.[5]

In the meantime, Coptic immigrants to Canada may be reckoned in excess of thirty thousand. Such figures are not stationary, although somewhat arbitrary. In spite of the economic difficulties facing both the United States and Canada, the tide of immigrants continues, but at a much slower pace, and those progressive numbers cannot be fixed at any level at any given time.

On the whole Coptic immigrants to the New World consisted of an educated élite and university graduates. They were predominantly professional young people in the fields of medicine, engineering, architecture, business, and education. Many of them have distinguished themselves in their fields with their proficiency and their industry. The Coptic population of the United States is largely concentrated in the East and West together with a sprinkling in between, though a growing minority is gradually penetrating the North, South and Mid-West. The density of Coptic families may be gauged by the distribution of their churches in the country. At present, the United States has fifteen churches, and Canada has five. New York and New Jersery alone have six Coptic churches, and California has three together with a projected Coptic monastery in the neighbourhood of Los Angeles. Again single churches may be found in Houston (Texas), Cleveland (Ohio), Chicago (Illinois), Detroit (Michigan), Philadelphia (Pennsylvania), and Washington (D.C). In Canada, Toronto and Montreal each has two churches, while the capital, Ottawa has one. It is noteworthy that the Coptic residents of Toronto have built the first Coptic-owned church in purely Coptic style. A more ambitious project is envisioned

[4] G. Abdelsayed, "The Coptic-Americans, A Current African Contribution," in *The New Jersey Ethnic Experience,* pp. 122–23.

[5] Figures like this which are not from a certified census are gathered from the church authority. This applies to other figures mentioned below.

on Long Island (New York), where six acres have been donated for the construction of a Coptic center, now in progeress. Growing Coptic concentrations in other areas of the United States are striving to open new churches in future, and all of them persist in keeping the Coptic rites of the mother Church. Coptic and Arabic are used in the celebration of the divine liturgy with some adaptation in English to suit the rising needs of the Americanized congregation. It is understood that there are as many Coptic priests in the New World as the existing churches, and His Holiness Pope Shenouda III generally sanctions the opening of a new church only after ascertaining the availabilty of a suitable priest who can conduct the church offices with dignity in his foreign environment. Accompanied by a delegation of bishops, His Holiness made an extensive visitation tour of all Coptic churches in the United States which lasted from April 14 to May 22, 1977. He was able to meet the dignitaries of all other churches and even held an audience with the president of the United States in the company of the ambassador of Egypt to Washington. That visit proved to be a landmark in arousing interest in this ancient form of Christianity and made people more aware of the Coptic Americans than any time before.

Australia

Second to the United States in the strength of the communtiy of Coptic Orthodox immigrants is the distant continent of Australia whose Coptic population numbers in excess of forty thousand. Although immigration has been tapering off lately on account of economic stringency, it is inconceivable to think that it has stopped altogether. Australia prides itself on having six Coptic churches in the populous districts of Sydney and Melbourne where the main concentration of the community lies. Nevertheless, it is known that isolated Coptic families have established homes in the captial Canberra and other towns in more remote regions.

Europe: Great Britain

Again within the pale of Western civilization, Coptic immigrants have made their way to numerous European countries, notably Great Britain, Germany and France together with a sprinkling in Switzerland, Austria, and the Low Countries. In Great Britain, Copts are to be found essentially in England, though some families are encountered in Scotland and Ireland. Here they rank highly in the medical profession where a few Copts occupy pivotal places in some hospitals. Probably London has the heaviest concentration of Copts whose community was able to establish the first Coptic-owned church in Britain, recently consecrated by no less a dignitary than His Holiness Pope Shenouda III whose visit to England lasted from January 27 to February 7, 1979. His presence caused a stir in the religious circles of Great Britain, thus increasing British awareness of the Copts and Coptic Christianity. The London church has been the object of public attention owing to its peculiar adaptation of Coptic rites and its Coptic iconographical and stained glass motifs designed and executed by a Coptic artist from Cairo.

One feature which Egypt has in common with other countries where the Copts are sparsely spread is the practice of the itinerant priest. Owing to the adherence of the Copts to their church, appeals are extended to the priests of populous regions to keep moving among isolated small communties of Copts for the celebration of the divine liturgies either in borrowed churches, preferably Armenian or Greek, or even at homes of the faithful. Those priests also hold the functions of baptism, marriages, and funerals of Copts deceased away from the central churches of the larger cities.

Europe: The German-Speaking Countries

In the German-speaking world, Copts are encountered in Austria, Switzerland and the Federal Republic of Germany.[6] Though the first two countries depend on the visits of itinerant priests, West Germany possesses a number of established Coptic churches and a vicarage stationed at Frankfurt. The Coptic Church in Germany came into existence by a papal decree of March 1977 in response to the call of some five hundred families living in that country. Soon afterwards, the Copts were able to secure a regular church of their own dedicated to St. Mark, originally a historic foundation built at Frankfurt in 1799. They also purchased an adjacent hall for Coptic meetings on special occasions. Another church followed at Stuttgart with St. George as its patron. At present West Germany has a total of seven Coptic churches including, besides the above-mentioned two, others at Dusseldorf and Munich (gifts from the Catholics), Hanover (gift from the Evangelical Protestants dedicated to St. Athanasius the Apostolic), Berlin (Protestant gift dedicated to St. Antony and St. Shenoute), and Hamburg where the use of an imposing Evangelical church is arranged on loan whenever a Coptic priest comes to hold offices for the Coptic residents of that region.

Although it is somewhat difficult to present precise figures of the Copts in Germany owing to their dispersion in distant towns such as Bremen and

[6] Most of the information on the subject is drawn from a report by Father Salib Suryal, in *Watani Weekly*, July 9, 1978.

Kiel, the growing population has rendered it necessary to engage another priest, a monk from the fourth-century monastery of Baramous in the Nitrean valley. The monk, Palladius, originally was a law graduate who took residence at the town of Linzburg from where he ministers in all directions to relieve the older father at Frankfurt. The Copts in the German-speaking areas comprise successful members in the medical profession as well as some engineers, business men and educators.

Europe: France

The tradition of Coptic presence in Western Europe is nowhere more historically felt than in France. Without dwelling on Christian antiquity in Gaul and the Frankish Kingdom in the Middle Ages, a subject already treated in this book under the heading of Missionary Enterprise,[7] it would seem that the first Coptic family to set sail from Egypt to France in modern times was that of General Ya'qūb[8] in 1802. The familiarity of the Copts with French culture since the French Expedition of 1798–1801 appears to have established a bridge between the Copts and France in the realm of education. Ultimately this led to a continuous stream of educational missions from affluent Coptic families in Egypt to all manner of French institutions of higher learning. French was freely spoken with Arabic by educated Coptic families. Hence, crossing the Mediterranean to French shores became a familiar practice throughout the century.

During the later decades of our time, however, and for the same circumstances which precipitated the Coptic exodus to the New World, that movement assumed the form of immigration and became accelerated although at a slower pace. It is extremely difficult to give any precise estimate of the Coptic community in France. Copts with long-standing residence in that country have been assimilated and are hard to distinguish from native Frenchmen. On the other hand, Coptic immigrants and permanent residents in France may be estimated in the neighbourhood of five thousand. In Paris, the Copts have their own church with a Coptic priest in residence.

Perhaps the most picturesque and unique feature in the structure of Coptic Christianity in France is the consecration of Coptic bishops of French extraction. Two French monks were elevated to that dignity by Pope Shenouda III on June 2, 1974. One was named Monseigneur Marcos, Bishop of Marseilles, Toulon and the whole of France. The second was Monseigneur Athanasios, Suffragan Bishop (Chorepiscopos) of Paris. The first took residence in a hermitage he founded at the old Provençal village of Revest-les-Eaux (Var) with a simple but impressive chapel in Coptic style dedicated to Our Lady of Zeitoun. Monseigneur Athanasios established his headquarters

[7] See pp. 49 ff.
[8] Ibid., pp.101–103.

at the Priory of St. Mark at Plessis l'Evêque (Seine and Marne) with a chapel dedicated to Our Lady and St. Mark the Evangelist. Apparently both chapels in the North and the South have been the object of visits by considerable groups of believers of both Coptic and French origins. Monseigneur Athanasios states that in the summer of 1976,[9] more than eight hundred pilgrims of the Coptic and the Catholic professions performed the pilgrimage to the Hermitage and participated in the celebration of the Coptic divine liturgy in its chapel.[10] The Coptic community itself in the French capital has a Coptic church with a Coptic priest who officiates regularly for the Coptic congregation.

Europe: Other Countries

On the periphery of all these concentrations of Copts amidst the English-speaking people, the German-speaking countries, and France, we meet Copts in most countries of Europe, even in distant places like Portugal at one end and Poland at another. But these are isolated instances which call for no special treatment except perhaps in the case of the Low Countries. Here, the Copts are estimated at a couple of thousand which is substantial for two little states such as Holland and Belgium.

Conclusion

If we add up the numbers quoted in this paper, a conservative estimate of the total population of Copts living abroad as immigrants to other countries could be placed between 165,000 and 170,000. Approximation is a necessary factor in this estimate since more Copts, especially among the youth, continue to contemplate immigrating as soon as they complete their higher education and graduate from the Egyptian universities. Meanwhile, younger Copts who study in foreign countries end up by seeking employment there, and finally become permanently settled in their new homelands.

Outside the countries of Western Civilization, Copts are known to have penetrated segments of Africa and Asia in the Old World. In Africa, the majority of Ethiopians have been followers of Alexandrine Christianity from 340 A.D., Ethiopia, therefore, used to harbour a continuous stream of Egyptian Copts; but these have tapered off since the Communist Revolution and the downfall of the Empire. To the northwest, the Sudan has retained its

[9] *Le Monde Copte,* Ed. P. de Bogdanoff, No. 2, p. 30.
[10] Ibid., no. 2, p. 42.

Coptic colonies whose spiritual welfare is guarded by the two Coptic archbishops of Khartoum and of Omdurman. The Sudanese Copts, however, are not recent immigrants, and most of them have lived in the upper reaches of the Nile valley for more than a century. Africa has a third Coptic archbishop in residence at Nairobi with a number of Coptic monks who labour among the Christian natives. Left without a shepherd since the withdrawal of the white missionary, those natives sought affiliation with the mother African church, and the Coptic Patriarch responded to the call by nominating Anba Antonios as Bishop of the Africans. As he was also a graduate in medicine, he was able to combine religious duties with medical service. Numerous Coptic educators, technicians and business people are found in the oil-rich country of Nigeria and some can be seen in Ghana, whose former president Nkrume was married to a Copt. Libya, too, has quite a few Copts. Other oil-rich states in Asia such as Saudi Arabia, Kuwait and even Iraq employ numerous Copts in many fields. But all of these are temporary employees and workers with no intention to strike root in these countries. On the other hand, small Coptic community has existed in Jerusalem from time immemorial and is found around Dair al-Sultan, an area granted to the Coptic Church by Saladin in the twelfth century. The Copts in the Holy Land have an archbishop in residence at the Holy Sepulchre with the title of Vice-Patriarch of Jerusalem and the Whole East. But none of those colonies enter into the category of immigrants in the same way as the Copts who adopted new homes in the countries of Western Christendom.

PART II

ANTIOCH AND THE JACOBITES

10 • ORIGIN AND DEVELOPMENT

Historical Setting

The setting of the city of Antioch undoubtedly gave it a special place in the early annals of the rise of the Christian faith. Accordingly, the Church of Antioch, long in exile, proved to be one of the central and dynamic forces in the formative centuries of primitive Christianity; indeed a worthy peer to the great ancient sees of Alexandria and Rome. Favoured by a fine geographical position in the valley of the Orontes, at the crossroads of the Euphrates and the Mediterranean as well as Asia Minor and Palestine, the prosperity of Antioch was assured by the continuous flow of commerce from the countries of the north, south, east and west. Greek, Egyptian, Syrian and Asiatic merchants met in its marts, and its population is said to have numbered about half a million souls towards the fourth century A.D.[1] Its prosperity under the Seleucids was confirmed by the Romans, who granted it the status of a *civitas libera*, a privilege the Antiochenes managed to retain until the close of the fourth century. It was then that the Emperor Theodosius I (379–95) decided to chastise them for rebellion against his excessive measures of taxation by the removal of that privilege. Nevertheless, it was that same monarch who embellished the Daphne Gate of the city with a layer of glittering gold that could be seen from a considerable distance.[2] The development of the city and its opulence made it one of the greatest artistic centres of the ancient world, with its magnificent temples, forums, theatres, baths, palaces, and its historic aqueduct together with all the pompous features of a Roman settlement. At one time, it ranked as the third city in the whole empire. Such was the Antioch which received from the very beginning Apostolic visitations and became one of the earliest strongholds of Christianity. Although it suffered greatly in the period of Roman persecution of Christians, it

[1] E. S. Bourchier, *A Short History of Antioch, 300* B.C. – *1268* A.D. (Oxford, 1921), pp. 77–8, also states that the city had 100,000 households within a circumference of about fifteen miles. The *Encyclopædia Britannica* mentions only a quarter million as the fourth century population.

[2] Bourchier, loc. cit. The city had been known in antiquity as 'Antioch the Golden'.

remained the object of imperial attention, and even Diocletian built a tremendous palace in it. Christian Byzantine emperors continued to patronize Antioch until it became torn by schism and revolt, especially against the Chalcedonian profession in the fifth century. Constantine the Great was the first Christian emperor to build an official church in the city, and his example was followed by his successors and by the rich citizens and prelates who made it a real metropolis of eastern Christendom. Then sectarian quarrels ushered in disaffection and disunity among its inhabitants, leading to a steady decline of the flourishing city. In fact, the decline of Antioch, thus begun by religious strife, was strongly accelerated by three momentous factors in its history: first, a series of earthquakes, of which the last on record in antiquity occurred during the year 526 and ruined many of its notable buildings; secondly, the Persian invasion of 538, in which the Sassanid Emperor Chosroes almost completed the destruction of the city; and thirdly, the Arab conquest in 638, whereby Antioch was engulfed in an alien Islamic empire and separated for ever from the Christian world with the exception of the ephemeral and rather unwelcome occupation by the Crusaders. With the extermination of the Latin kingdom of Jerusalem from the Asiatic mainland, Antioch reverted to the Mamlūk sultanate of Egypt towards the end of the thirteenth century and became a satellite city of secondary importance to the amirate of Aleppo. Handed from Muslim to Muslim, the august city was next captured by a new Turkish empire builder, Selim I, who seized the whole of Syria and Egypt in the years 1516–17. In modern history, the Egyptian forces managed to capture Antioch twice: first under the Khedive Muḥammad ʿAli during his famous march to Istanbul in 1840, and secondly under General Allenby in 1918 at the end of the First World War. Afterwards the city and the whole of the Syrian province wrested from the Turks by the Allies were put under the mandatory power of France by the League of Nations in 1920. In 1939, when the mandate was lifted from Syria, the French authorities arbitrarily returned the city together with the whole Sanjaq of Alexandretta to the new Turkish Republic. The 1950 census showed its population to have been 30,385, a sorry picture compared with its glorious past.

From this brief survey, it is evident that the days of true greatness in the history of Antioch were more or less limited to the ancient period extending roughly to the sixth century of our era. The patriarchs of Antioch, whose see flourished in those few centuries within the city itself, were doomed to exile from their hereditary metropolis, as will be seen in the following pages. The importance of early Antiochene history becomes increasingly dim and its sources grow more meagre with its steady decline in later ages. With the passing of time, the original patriarchate of Antioch, that is, the Monophysite and subsequently the Jacobite patriarchate, gave rise to others appropriating the same title. These included a Greek Orthodox patriarchate, the Monothelite Maronite patriarchate now in communion with Rome, the Catholic Uniate, or Melkite patriarchate, the Nestorian, or East Syrian, catholicate, and both the Armenian and Georgian patriarchates within the confines of the Soviet Union. Yet none of the patriarchs of all these offshoots from Antioch now resides in the city of Antioch.[1] Their historic terrain has spread in successive ages over Syria, Asia Minor, Arabia, Persia, Turkey, Russia, Central Asia, India and even China – in a word, the whole of the vast Asiatic continent.

Apostolic Visitations and Early History

The patriarchate of Antioch rightfully claims greater antiquity and fuller apostolicity than all the other ancient Christian churches. In fact, there can be no doubt as to the venerable age of that church, mentioned so many times in the New Testament, notably in the Acts of the Apostles.[2] The new religion was first preached to the gentile Greeks in Antioch, and it was there that the

[1] The definitive history of the patriarchate of Antioch, or more specifically, the Jacobite Church, is still unwritten. The chapters in Kidd, *Churches of Eastern Christendom*, pp. 436–438; Adeney, *Greek and Eastern Churches*, pp. 500–9; J. W. Etheridge, *The Syrian Churches*, pp. 135–49; Bourchier, op. cit., pp. 129–50; O. H. Parry, *Six Months in a Syrian Monastery*, pp. 279–355; A. Fortescue, *Lesser Eastern Churches*, pp. 323–52; and D. Attwater, *Christian Churches of the East*, Vol. II, pp. 255 ff., are all inadequate. De Lacy O'Leary, *The Syriac Church and Fathers* (London, 1909) – brief review to rise of Islam. More substantial general literature on the subject includes J. M. Neale, *A History of the Holy Eastern Church: The Patriarchate of Antioch*, ed. G. Williams (London, 1873); R. Devreesse, *Le patriarcat d'Antioche depuis la paix de l'église jusqu'à la conquête arabe* (Paris, 1945); G. W. Elderkin, R. Stillwell and others, *Antioch on the Orontes*, 3 vols. (Princeton, 1934–41); G. Downey, *Ancient Antioch* (Princeton, 1963); idem, *A History of Antioch in Syria from Seleucus to the Arab Conquest* (Princeton, 1961); R. Duval, *Histoire politique, religieuse et littéraire d'Édesse jusqu'à la Première Croisade* (Paris, 1892). Illuminating articles on various facets and personalities of this church may also be found in such famous encyclopædic works as the *Dictionnaire d'Histoire et de Géographie Ecclésiastiques*, ed. A. Baudrillart and others; the *Catholic Encyclopedia*; the *Encyclopedia of Religion and Ethics*; the *Dictionnaire de Théologie Catholique*, ed. A. Vacant, E. Mangenot and E. Amann; and the *New Schaff-Herzog Encyclopedia of Religious Knowledge*, to cite only a few. For more general works in other languages, see the *Oxford Dictionary of the Christian Church*, ed. F. L. Cross, pp. xiii–xix. The chief ancient sources are found in Eusebius, *Historia Ecclesiastica*; J. S. Assemani, *Bibliotheca Orientalis*, Vol. II; Michael the Syrian's *Chronicle*, ed. with French tr. J. B. Chabot, 4 vols. (Paris, 1899–1910); and Bar Hebræus (Gregorius Abul-Faraj, Ar. ed. A. Ṣalḥāni, Beirūt, 1890). Two recent Arabic works from two different angles are of value: the first is *History of the Syrian Church of Antioch* (4–518 A.D.) by Severius, Syrian metropolitan of Beirūt and Damascus (2 vols., Beirūt, 1953–57). The author is a 'Jacobite' archbishop, and his work represents the eastern point of view. The second is *The Church of the City of God – Great Antioch* by Asad J. Rustum, 3 vols. (Beirūt, 1958). It represents the Melkite or Greek Orthodox offshoot in the East.

[2] Some of the References in Acts are xi, 19–27; xiv, 21, 26; xv, 22–3, 30–5; xviii, 22.

Apostles were first called Christians.[1] Moreover, Eusebius[2] asserts that the church of Antioch was founded by St Peter, who became its first bishop even before his translation to the see of Rome. According to tradition, he presided for seven years over the newly established Antiochene church, from 33 to 40 A.D., when he nominated St Euodius as his vicar before departure to the West. While the circle of preaching the Gospel was widened towards the East in Edessa, Nisibis and distant Malabar by the Apostle Thomas and Mar Addai (St Thaddæus), the fall of Jerusalem in the year 70 A.D. could only have increased the number of Christian Jewish emigrants to Antioch.[3] For those days of remote antiquity, the historical data present only a general outline without any certainty as to minute details. We may assume that Antioch became the object of Apostolic visitations from the very beginning and suffered from Roman persecutions equally with Alexandria and Rome. St Euodius is said to have earned the crown of martyrdom in the reign of Emperor Nero (54–68 A.D.), and he was succeeded by another glorious martyr, St Ignatius, who may have been consecrated by the hands of St Peter, St Paul, or at any rate by an Apostolic prelate.[4] The story of St Ignatius, who suffered martyrdom in the reign of Trajan (98–117), is interesting as it is representative of the spirit of the times. The saint was first subjected to a personal inquest by the emperor himself. On finding him so defiantly firm in the faith, the emperor ordered him after removal from Antioch to be thrown to the wild beasts in the arena at Rome, perhaps in the early part of the second century. He was escorted to Rome by the imperial guards, and the saint was apparently permitted to address the faithful everywhere and to visit fellow Christians in spite of his complaint of cruelties committed against his person by his armed companions. In his train was a deacon by the name of Philo who followed him through Syria, and at Smyrna he was received by Polycarp as well as Onesimus, bishop of Ephesus. Afterwards, he sent epistles to the faithful of Ephesus, Philadelphia and Smyrna which are regarded as a monument of the literature of the sub-apostolic age. He was followed by pious priests during his march from place to place. In Rome, he consoled those among the brethren who were moved with grief for his imminent death. His Roman journey must have appeared like the triumphant march of a spiritual athlete.[5] Finally, he was devoured by the wild beasts before eighty-

[1] Acts xi, 26.

[2] Eusebius, III, xxxvi. St Jerome refers to the fact; cf. Neale, p. 3, n. 2.

[3] S. G. F. Brandon, *The Fall of Jerusalem and the Christian Church – A Study of the Effects of the Jewish Overthrow of* A.D. *70 on Christianity* (London, 1951), is dubious about the impact of the dispersion of the Jews on the spread of the new faith, but the fact remains that Antioch rather than Jerusalem became the centre of Apostolic Christianity henceforward. See also Bourchier, pp. 133–4.

[4] Neale, pp. 11–12.

[5] Eusebius, III, xxi, xxxvi; Neale, pp. 19–21.

seven thousand spectators, whose savage exaltation compared only with the compassion of his fellow Christians. The legend runs that his scanty remains were taken to his native city, and enshrined there until in the fifth century the Empress Eudocia ordered them to be transferred to the old temple of Fortune, then a church.[1] So revered was the saint in Syrian history that the later Jacobite patriarchs invariably adopted the name Ignatius on the occasion of their consecration.

The early Bishops of Antioch were Jewish Christians, certainly until the reign of Judas in 135 A.D. He is described as the last of the Bishops of the Circumcision.[2] The next landmark in Antiochene church history was the bishopric of Theopilus, a highly lettered prelate and a prolific author, who undertook the task of combating pagan ideas and the heretical teachings of the early Syrian Gnostics. His best-known work is the *Treatise to Autolycus*, an eloquent defence of Christianity and a vehement refutation of Marcion's views. The author's knowledge of the ancient religions as well as the Old Testament and the Gospels is formidable. His mystical interpretation of theological themes renders his discussions more appealing to the contemporary mind. This is one of the earliest works of Christian theology on record. Of great interest is the fact that the term 'Trinity' may be traced as far back as this treatise, thus indicating that Theophilus was the first to employ it.[3] Apparently the book was published at the beginning of the reign of Emperor Commodus (180–92), while Christianity was still a persecuted religion.

It seems that Antioch was steadily becoming a real stronghold of orthodoxy. In the following decade, another Antiochene theologian emerged in the person of Serapion, who became bishop in 199 and died in 211. He also wrote a series of epistles and works addressed to the Greeks and certain persons, namely Caricus, Pontius and Domninus. He is said to have combated chiefly the heresy of Montanus of Phrygia, but since most of his literary work was lost, little could be deduced from fragmentary remains.[4]

A succession of bishops filled the rest of the third century, and we must confine this survey to the less obscure amongst them. St Babylas ruled the see of Antioch for nearly a decade, between 240 and 250. He was immortalized by St John Chrysostom, who stated that he fearlessly denied entrance to the church to a Roman emperor with anti-Christian leanings, probably Philip the Arabian (244–9) until he atoned for his crimes. He lost his life in

[1] Bouchier, pp. 136–7, doubts whether the relics of St Ignatius ever reached Antioch and contends that they must have been buried in an obscure church in Rome.

[2] Neale, p. 22.

[3] Theophilus was the sixth from the Apostles. He also wrote another treatise: 'Against the Heresy of Hermogenes' (Eusebius, IV, xix, xxiv); Neale pp. 26–9, contains an analysis of the work. The Church celebrates his day on 18 October.

[4] Eusebius, V, xviii, xxii; VI, xi–xiii; and Neale, pp. 35–6.

the persecutions of Decius (249–51), and a special cult was developed around his name in Antioch which found its way to the West in an eighth-century Latin translation by Aldhelm, the poet bishop of Sherborne.[1]

In contrast to the life of Babylas was that of Paul of Samosata,[2] the well-known heresiarch who became bishop of Antioch from 260 to 270. Of humble birth, he amassed great wealth which he used to raise himself to that key position in the Church. He was a protégé of Zenobia, queen of Palmyra, to whom he had been tutor in her youth. As the forerunner of Nestorius, he was the first to lay the foundations of the Christology of the dual personality of Jesus, and it was he who used the celebrated term *Homoousios* in the course of his dispute with other bishops who condemned his teachings. It took two Councils of Antioch to dislocate the notorious Paul from the see of Antioch. The first was convoked by Dionysius of Alexandria in 264, and after heated discussions in which Paul saw no way of escape, he pretended conviction and seemingly rejected his doctrine of consubstantiality. Later he reverted to his heterodoxy and combined with it immorality, thus calling for the irrevocable decision of deposition by the Second Council of Antioch in 269.

The career of Paul of Samosata stands outside the Antiochene traditions of the first three centuries, which may rightly be described as the age of persecution and martyrdom for the faith. In fact, the roll of martyrs of the church of Antioch was one of the most glorious. Few of its partriarchs died peacefully in their beds, the majority earned the martyr's crown. We read of thousands of martyrs of the church of Antioch, from the reign of Nero onwards. Perhaps the most conspicuous example was that of the eleven thousand martyrs, soldiers who espoused Christianity wholesale in the reign of Trajan (98–117), and were banished by the emperor to the wilds of Armenia, to be massacred in the reign of his successor, Hadrian (117–38). The steadfastness of Antioch, though broken in the infamous reign of Bishop Paul was again resumed by other saintly followers, of whom one presbyter must be cited as the founder of the great theological school of Antioch. This is Lucian, the theologian and martyr who perished in 312 at Nicomedia on the eve of the issue of the 'Edict of Milan' which enfranchised all Christians. He was a great biblical scholar, and revised both the Septuagint and the Gospels. The contention that he had been a pupil of Paul of Samosata has been undermined, though it is said that some of the seeds of Arianism can be traced to his school, since Arius had once been one of its active members.[3] Lucian's school played its role in the movement for the settlement of Christian dogma and Christian doctrine. It also produced a number of the historic personalities

[1] Eusebius, VI, xxxi, xxxix; Neale, pp. 41–3.

[2] Eusebius, V, xxviii; VII, xxvii, xxx, xxxii; Neale, pp. 45–52; Duchesne, *Early History of the Christian Church*, Vol. I, pp. 337–44.

[3] Eusebius, VIII, xiii; IX, vi; G. Bardy, *Recherches sur Lucien d'Antioche et son école* (Paris, 1936), passim; Neale, pp. 71–3; Bourchier, pp. 140–3.

associated with Antioch. Diodorus, Lucian's successor, in turn taught John Chrysostom and Theodore of Mopsuestia, while the latter instructed the famous Nestorius, patriarch of Constantinople, and Theodret, bishop of Cyrrhus in Syria, theologian and historian of note.

Nicæa to Chalcedon

Under this heading, our chief task is to show the place held by Antioch rather than reiterate the whole general history of the councils treated in some detail elsewhere.[1] At the first œcumenical council of Nicæa in 325, Antioch was strongly represented with a formidable delegation of bishops.[2] Eustathius its chief bishop and representative, ranked in the same category as Hosius, bishop of Cordova, who was special consultant to Emperor Constantine on matters of religion, as well as Alexander, the patriarch of Alexandria, who presided over the Council. In fact, those three are said to have participated in a kind of co-presidency at Nicæa, and hence the world looked for leadership to Alexandria, Antioch and Constantinople. It would, however, be wrong to contend that Antioch had been unwavering in its loyalty to orthodoxy. On the contrary, one may easily sense the signs of imminent schism in the course of the Nicæan deliberations. Arius had attended the School of Antioch with Bishop Eusebius of Nicomedia, his fellow disciple who submitted to the Council an initial creed with Arian leanings, which the majority of bishops rejected outright. After Nicæa, three parties began to emerge in Antioch. The first, or Eusebian, party followed the order of Nicomedia and Cæsarea; in other words, without demonstration of open hostility to the Council decisions, which the Emperor Constantine would not allow, they continued quietly to work at undermining the Nicæan doctrines. This policy gained more ground with the ascendancy of Eusebius, who baptized that emperor (d. 337) in his last illness, and then again caught the ear of his successor Constantius (d. 361) leading to the exile of Athanasius from Alexandria. The next party was identified with Eustathius (d. 330) who adamantly stood for the Nicæan Creed and Canons, thus representing the official and orthodox position until Arianism became more popular at the imperial court and the bishop was subsequently deposed and sent to Thrace, where he died in exile. Then a third party consisted of pious and law-abiding people who espoused the Nicæan rule but obeyed the bishop in office, caring

[1] See Part I (Alexandrine Christianity), Chapter 3, section 2 (Œcumenical Movement).

[2] Devreesse, pp. 1–16, 124–8; Neale, pp. 85 et seq.; Duchesne, II, 98 et seq.; Fliche and Martin (ed.), *Histoire de l'église*, Vol. III, p. 69 et seq. Downey's works on Antioch (see above p. 171. n. 1) provide indispensible historical background for church development up to the Arab Conquest.

little for difference on minutiæ and objecting to schism in principle. Strictly speaking, it would be difficult to find any outspoken theologian of the time in whose words the germs of some kind of heretical thought could not be held in suspicion. Even Eustathius[1] was charged with Sabellianism[2] and his Christology was regarded as foreshadowing that of Nestorius.

What is clear is that Arianism was not stamped out during the post-Nicene age, and both the emperors and the hierarchy in Constantinople and in Antioch, the great sees of the Orient, continued to sway between Arius and Athanasius. The accession of Bishop Meletius[3] at Antioch in 360 was heralded by both Nicæans and Arians who looked to him for support. He was temporarily deposed by the Emperor Constantius for his orthodoxy, while unable to obtain the support of Athanasius for his heterodoxy. Twice deposed by Emperor Valens, again to be reinstated in 378, he presided over the Council of Constantinople of 381, the year of his death. A saintly man, he left behind a schism within the orthodox party itself, since the followers of Eustathius suspected his theology and consecrated as anti-bishop a certain Paulinus in 362.

This was the age of St John Chrysostom (ca. 347–407), who was educated in the Antiochene School under Diodorus and elevated unwillingly to the see of Constantinople, where his virtues and tactless criticisms antagonized the imperial court and ultimately led to his deposition. Even the 'Golden Mouth' could not escape the iron hand of the time. The age abounded in great names of bishops and theologians. St Gregory of Nazianzen (329–89), St Gregory of Nyssa (330–95) and St Basil the Great (330–79) were known as the 'three Cappadocian Fathers'. In Jerusalem, St Cyril (ca. 315–86) reigned as bishop, and in Nisibis and Edessa the great St Ephraem (ca. 306–73), the Syrian Biblical exegete, enriched the literary heritage of Eastern Christianity. The Fathers of the Egyptian Church, so numerous and so great, form a special chapter of their own. In spite of the swelling tide of heresy and schism, Antioch retained its ecclesiastical authority over all the province of the Orient. Nicæa had confirmed its rights over Syria, Palestine, Cyprus, Arabia and Mesopotamia including Persia and India. The churches of Cæsarea, Edessa, Nisibis, Seleucia-Ctesiphon and Malabar looked to Antioch for spiritual leadership, at any rate, in the early centuries. That authority was again ratified by the Council of Constantinople in 381. Antiochene jurisdiction in the period from the fourth to the seventh century has been cal-

[1] M. Spanneut, 'Recherches sur les écrits d'Eustathe d'Antioche', in *Mémoires et Travaux Facultés Catholiques de Lille*, Fasc. LV (Lille, 1948), followed by the edn. of the Greek fragments of the works of Eustathius, pp. 95–131.

[2] From Sabellius, obscure Roman theologian of the third century, who gave a new interpretation of the earlier heresy of Monarchianism, a movement attempting to safeguard Monotheism in the unity, or 'monarchy', of the Godhead, and failing to give full recognition to the Son.

[3] Devreesse, pp. 17–38.

culated to embrace eleven metropolitan provinces and one hundred and twenty-seven episcopal dioceses.[1]

The accession of John of Antioch to the bishopric in 429 seemed to reunite the factions within the church for a brief period. The new, real upheaval within the church was forthcoming from another centre by an old Antiochian on the subject of Christology. This was Nestorius, a famous pupil of Theodore of Mopsuestia in the School of Antioch and later patriarch of Constantinople, whose expostulations about the two natures of Jesus Christ gave rise to the summoning of the third œcumenical council of Ephesus[2] in 431 by order of the Emperor Theodosius II. His great antagonist was the formidable patriarch of Alexandria, Cyril, who had wrested a decision condemning Nestorius for heresy and deposing him just as the belated Antiochian delegation was entering the city of Ephesus under Bishop John. Though the latter held a separate synod vindicating Nestorius, his efforts remained without avail and he was reconciled with Cyril two years afterwards. That reconciliation had far-reaching results in both East and West. Since Antioch conformed with Alexandria on the Monophysite Christology, the East Syrians chose to take the side of the deposed Nestorius, and their church ultimately became identified with him. In Rome, the predominance of Alexandrine theology was viewed with alarm, and steady manœuvres were taken for its reversal. The quarrel of the churches thus assumed gigantic dimensions.

The appearance of another heresiarch, Eutyches (ca. 378–454), an archimandrite of one of the monasteries of Constantinople, inflamed even more the discussion over Nestorian Christology, which he opposed with great vehemence. Eutyches was led to complete confusion of the two natures of Jesus, and in vain did Patriarch Flavian of Constantinople try to deter him from his error. Meanwhile, the great actors in the drama of the First Ephesus had died: John of Antioch and Sixtus of Rome in 440 and Cyril of Alexandria in 444. These were succeeded by Domnus II of Antioch, who seemed to be at one with Leo I of Rome against the fiery Monophysite Dioscorus of Alexandria, who supported Eutyches, then deposed and condemned by Flavian of Constantinople. The Second Council of Ephesus was summoned in 449 by Theodosius II (408–50), who was under the influence of the Eutychian party through the sympathies of his chamberlain the eunuch Chrysaphius. The Council acquitted Eutyches, and both Flavian and Domnus were reviled in that stormy meeting, since known as the *Latrocinium*, or 'Robber Council'. But that was an ephemeral success destined to change with the accession of another emperor, Marcian (450–7), who lent his ear to the 'Great Tome', an epistle whereby Leo I, bishop of Rome (440–61), renounced the findings of that council.

[1] Ibid., pp. 305–12.

[2] Ibid., pp. 39 et seq.; Fliche and Martin, IV, 211–24.

In 451, the emperor summoned the fourth œcumenical council of Chalcedon,[1] which in turn denounced and anathematized Dioscorus and Eutyches, deposed and exiled them both, and adopted Leo's pronouncements as the standard form of orthodox Christology, with immeasurable consequences for the relations between East and West. It is true that the emperor gained full recognition for the patriarchal status of the see of Constantinople, the 'New Rome', by the twenty-eighth canon of Chalcedon. But the rupture with the East was complete without hope of repair. The attempt of the imperialist, or 'Melkite', clerics to impose the Council decisions on Alexandria, Jerusalem and Antioch resulted in bloodshed and the identification of nationalist awakening with Monophysite tendencies. The paradox of Chalcedon is that it praised Cyril though it denounced his theology, whereas it condemned Nestorius while supporting Diophysitism.

The next serious step in the development of events came in the reign of Emperor Zeno[2] (474–91), whose eagerness to bring unity to the Church made him accept a formula devised by Acacius, patriarch of Constantinople, and Peter Mongus, patriarch of Alexandria. This is the famous *Henoticon*, or 'Act of Union,' which he ratified in 482 and which, though anathematizing both Nestorius and Eutyches, avoided the mention of 'one nature' and 'two natures' as well as any coercive phraseology towards either orthodoxy or Monophysitism. There was no doubt a certain measure of rehabilitation of the Monophysites by this act, but it was far from satisfactory to either party as a whole. Further, the infuriated Romans hastened to excommunicate Acacius, who retaliated by the omission of the name of the Roman pontiff from the Byzantine liturgy. This was probably the only immediate outcome of the new situation.

Where does Antioch stand in this universal tumult? At first, its leading hierarchy aimed at conforming with the official position. On the other hand, the Antiochian clergy together with the majority of the laity did not conceal their increasing traditional leanings towards Monophysitism, and they ultimately succeeded in forcing the elevation of Monophysite candidates to the patriarchal throne. The identification of these religious tendencies with the rising feeling of nationalism rendered the movement more and more popular in the East. The life of Peter the Fuller, who became patriarch of Antioch in 465, represents this restless mood of the times. Twice deposed for his Monophysitism, he was finally able to regain his throne by a show of acceptance of Emperor Zeno's *Henoticon*. Nevertheless, Peter is remembered

[1] Bishop Severius Samuel, *History of the Syrian Church of Antioch*, Vol. II, pp. 155 ff.; Asad Rustum, *Church of . . . Antioch*, Vol. II, pp. 328 ff.; Devreesse, pp. 60 ff., 136–40; R. V. Sellers, *Council of Chalcedon* (London, 1953), pp. 158–81; Duchesne, III, 219–315; Fliche and Martin, IV, 228–40; Downey, *Antioch in Syria*, pp. 461 ff.

[2] Devreesse, pp. 65 ff.; Vasiliev, *History of the Byzantine Empire*, pp. 107–9; Duchesne, III, 337–59; Fliche and Martin, IV, 287–97.

mainly by the introduction of the Monophysite clause 'who was crucified for us' into the *Trisagion*, or 'thrice holy', of the ancient eastern liturgy where the chant runs: 'Holy God, Holy and Mighty, Holy and immortal, have mercy upon us.' He is also responsible for the commemoration of the *Theotokos* in every service.

The greatest exponent of Monophysite doctrine at Antioch was the Patriarch Severus (ca. 465–538).[1] He was closely connected with Alexandria, where he had studied in his youth, and later took refuge whenever he fled from his persecutors or when he was deposed. His patriarchate coincided with the reigns of Emperors Anastasius, Justin and Justinian. At first he was in favour with Anastasius (491–518), who gave protection to the Monophysites. In 518, Justin I reversed his predecessor's policy, and Severus accordingly fled from Antioch to Alexandria, where the Patriarch Timothy IV offered him shelter. Under Justinian, he was excommunicated by a Synod of Constantinople in 536. Until his death in 538, however, Severus remained strongly anti-Chalcedonian. He was a great theologian and left behind him a number of works of the highest interest, mostly available in the Syriac versions. His death turned a new leaf in the annals of the see of Antioch. From then onwards up to the present day the double succession to that see has been maintained. Severus' rival successors represented the Synodite, or Melkite, Greek Orthodox line on the one hand, and on the other, the Syrian Monophysite line, soon to be identified as Jacobite, from Jacob Baradæus, one of the greatest saints of that church. While the one line looked westward to Byzantium, the other looked eastward in search of independence from the Greeks.

The two legacies of that age were probably the double hierarchy and the doctrine of tritheism.[2] While the one became a permanent feature of Antiochian history, the other proved to be ephemeral, though not devoid of interest. The invention of this curious heresy which appears to be distinctly polytheistic in character could, according to the Syriac chronicle of the

[1] Devreesse, pp. 69–71; E. Honigmann, *Évêques et évêchés monophysites d'Asie antérieure au VIe siècle* (Corpus Scriptorum Christianorum Orientalium, 127: 2; Louvain, 1951), pp. 142–54; Bishop Severius, II, 253, 266. Father V. C. Samuel of the ancient Church of South India composed a thesis at the Yale School of Divinity on 'The Council of Chalcedon and the Christology of Severus of Antioch' (May 1957) in which he gave an extensive definition of a difficult problem and its terminology. Apparently he objects to the use of the term 'Monophysitism', invented in the West for purposes of reviling the East, and he suggests the substitution of the term 'Meaphysitism' (cf. below Epilogue, p. 442 ff.), which implies the sense of union of the human and the divine rather than the misleading one-ness of nature which never strictly occurred with the orthodox Fathers of the so-called Monophysite Church. The thesis is still unpublished. The author made extensive use of the Greek and Syriac material in building his arguments.

[2] Devreesse, *Patriarcat d'Antioche*, pp. 76–94; Adeney, p. 504; Fortescue, *Lesser Eastern Churches*, p. 208.

Jacobite Patriarch Michael the Syrian,[1] be traced to the imagination of a little-known monk of Constantinople by the name of John 'Asquçnâgès' in the reign of the Emperor Justinian. By rejecting the factor of unity in the three constituent elements of the Trinity, he was led to the supposition that there were three separate divine Persons. Though silenced for the rest of his life, his heretical teachings somehow found several strong supporters at a later date among philosophers and theologians. John Philoponus, the Aristotelian commentator, was one of them. Others were Photinus (a priest of Antioch), Athanasius (a relative of Empress Theodora), and Sergius (a priest of Tella who became patriarch of Antioch). The tritheistic school was short-lived, but it was symptomatic of the state of an imminent breakdown of Syrian Monophysitism.[2] None but a new apostle could save it from destruction, and that apostle was near at hand.

Jacob Baradæus

At a time when the Syrian Monophysite hierarchy was dwindling and its clergy hunted by Justinian's agents, the church was salvaged from foundering by the appearance of the immortal personality of Jacob Baradaeus.[3] In reality the survival of that Church may be ascribed to two main factors: first, the connivance of the Empress Theodora, who is said to have been the daughter of a Syrian priest with strong secret sympathies for the eastern Monophysite churches in general; and secondly, the unremitting and indefatigable efforts of Jacob Baradæus, whose ventures in its behalf have become legendary. Justinian's determination to have one universal church in his unified empire was rigorously pursued with a policy of suppression of Monophysitism and the imprisonment and exile of its leaders, including so high prelate as Theodosius, patriarch of Alexandria. He and three hundred of his clergy were imprisoned in the fortress of Derkos near Constantinople for many years.[4] The empress, according to John of Ephesus,[5] put the palace

[1] *Chronique de Michel le Syrien, Patriarche Jacobite d'Antioche, 1166–1199* A.D., ed. and tr. J. B. Chabot, 3 vols. (Paris, 1899–1905), II, 251–3.

[2] Adeney, p. 504, refers to yet another heresy called 'Tetratheism' accruing from the teachings of Damianus, a Syrian who recognized God himself as one entity in addition to the three Persons constituting the Trinity.

[3] Monograph in Dutch on Jacob's life: H. G. Kleyn, *Iacobus Baradæus – de stichter der syrische monophysietische Kerk* (Leiden, 1882); Assemani, *Bibl. Orientalis*, Vol. I, pp. 255–6.

[4] Honigmann, pp. 158–9. Later Theodora succeeded in providing the old patriarch with a special refuge in the city for the years 539–48. He remained in favour with Theodora until her death (548), and afterwards he still commanded the respect of the emperor despite differences with him. Justinian even allowed him to preach in Constantinople, and the old patriarch wrote a treatise on the Trinity in which he refuted Tritheism and the Sabelian heresy. He died in Constantinople in 566 after thirty-one years of exile.

[5] His Syriac *Vita Baradæi*, ed. J. P. N. Land, in *Analecta Syriaca*, Vol. II (Leiden, 1862–

of Hormisdas at the disposal of some five hundred Monophysites from many parts of eastern Christendom. Monophysite resistance at home was concentrated in the monastic centres of the Wilderness of Scetis in Egypt, as well as on the fringe of the Arabian peninsula under the loyal Ghassānid princes, and at various places in North Syria, Osrohene and Mesopotamia. The use of Coptic in Egypt and of Syriac in Asia rendered the opposition inaccessible to the imperial Greek officers who ignored those languages. The decisive date in the revival of Syrian Monophysitism was the year 542, when, at Theodora's instigation and the debatable request of the Arab King al-Ḥārith ibn Jabalah, the old Coptic patriarch consecrated two metropolitans for the regions of Asia: Jacob, who became metropolitan of Edessa, and Theodore, bishop of Bostra.[1]

Born around 500 at the village of Gamāwā, north of Tellā (Constantina) in the upper reaches of the Euphrates, Jacob took holy orders at the Monastery of Phasīlthā (i.e., the Quarry) on Mount Izala. He received his religious education at the College of Nisibis, where, from the year 527, he resided for nearly fifteen years until his consecration as bishop. He came to Constantinople with another monk by the name of Sergius, whom he later consecrated as patriarch of Antioch in succession to Severus, probably in 543. The sources are full of apocryphal details concerning the saint, though most of the historic particulars of his life and work have been established and compiled by various authors.[2] His real career began in 542 after his ordination, when he is said to have been smuggled out of the Byzantine capital by the Arab King al-Ḥārith.[3] At that time the Monophysite clergy in Asia were

---

1875), pp. 364–83; see also E. W. Brooks, *Lives of the Eastern Saints* (Patrologia Orientalis, XVII–XIX; Paris, 1923–6). Frequent references are also made to Jacob's activities in Michael the Syrian's Syriac *Chronicle*, Bk X (see Chabot, II, 285 et seq.); Bar Hebræus' *Universal History* is poor on the subject, but his *Chronicon Ecclesiasticum* is essential. On John of Ephesus, also surnamed 'of Asia', and his *Ecclesiastical History and Lives of Oriental Saints*, see J. M. Schönfelder, *Die Kirchengeschichte des Johannes von Ephesus* (Munich, 1862); R. Duval, *Littérature Syriaque*, pp. 191–5, 364.

[1] Otherwise the city of Baṣrah. He was a Monophysite monk from Arabia who was imprisoned for several years in Constantinople. He became associated with Jacob Baradæus as the metropolitan of Arabia and resided mainly in the district of al-Ḥīrah, between Mesopotamia and Arabia. Honigmann, pp. 161–64.

[2] Perhaps the best life of Jacob is in E. Honigmann, op. cit., pp. 157–60, 163–5, 178–81, and passim. Next in importance is R. Devreesse, pp. 75–92. The older work in Dutch by H. G. Kleyn (see above p. 180 n. 3) is of course still useful. Other shorter biographies are O. H. Parry, *Six Months in a Syrian Monastery*, pp. 291–5; Adeney, pp. 500–3; Kidd, *Eastern Christendom*, pp. 436–7; Fortescue, pp. 323–6; E. Venables in *Dictionary of Christian Biography*, Vol. III, pp. 328–32; M. A. Krugener in *Revue de l'Orient Chrétien*, VII (1902), 196–217. See also Assemani, *Bibl. Orient.*, II, 62–9. Bishop Severius, *History of the Syrian Church*, Vol. II, pp. 255–7, indicates his ability as a prolific poet; idem, 'The Syrian Church Yesterday and Today', in *Orthodoxy*, VI (1956), 227–9.

[3] Written in Western documents as Aretas or Arethas. He is the son of King al-Mundhir of the Ṭayy tribe. Asad Rustum, I, 277, quotes the older historian and Orientalist Theodor

pursued by imperial agents who either disbanded or imprisoned them as enemies of the state. This was done in accordance with Justinian's strict orders as an essential measure to eradicate disunity from his realm. We are told that only two Syrian bishops were able to retain a precarious freedom and that Syrian congregations were left without shepherds in most districts. The church was in serious danger of extinction until it found its true restorer in the person of Jacob Baradæus[1] – Ya'qūb al-Barda'i. He dressed himself in shabby vestments made of old saddle cloth, not only for austerity, but also as a measure of disguise from his imperial prosecutors.

Jacob had no fixed headquarters as his residence.[2] His vast journeys from country to country in western Asia as well as Egypt are almost incredible for any man who travelled mainly on foot. He is said to have traversed the whole of Syria, Armenia, Cappadocia, Cilicia, Isauria, Pamphylia, Lycaonia, Lycia, Phrygia, Caris, Asia and the 'Islands of the Sea', that is, Cyprus, Rhodes, Chios, Mytilene or Lesbos, as well as the royal city of Constantinople.[3] To these we must add the whole of Mesopotamia, Arabia, Sinai and Egypt. Nothing could be more reminiscent of the memorable voyages of St Paul in the Apostolic age. Everywhere the great saint defended the persecuted Monophysite doctrines, strengthened the faithful, and ordained new bishops and priests to replace those who died without successors and those who were kept in captivity. Probably no prelate in history ordained as many clergymen as Jacob and although it is difficult to believe the number of 102,000 priests quoted in his apocryphal biographies, his ordinations must be numbered in thousands. The same apocryphal lives of the saint also state that he consecrated 87 or 89 bishops, but the number of 27 prelates can be justified from the official records.[4]

Nöldeke, who contends that al-Ḥārith's visit to Constantinople and his role in the story of Jacob's exit from the city are apocryphal. On Arab Christianity, see also Asad Rustum, I, 390–402.

1 The Latinized form of the Syriac Bard'āya or Bard'anā, in Arabic Barda'i; that is, originating from a beast of burden's saddle, implying that his tattered clothing was made from old animal covers, whether donkeys or mules.

2 As a rule his hiding place was a monastery and he is known to have frequently sojourned at the Convent of Bēth Aphthoniā (Honigmann, p. 174).

3 Cf. Honigmann, p. 168.

4 Since no less than three bishops could consecrate other new bishops, it must be assumed that Jacob sought at first collaboration from Theodore of Arabia (Honigmann, pp. 158–64), who was ordained with him by Patriarch Theodosius and Bishop John of Hephaistou (ibid., pp. 165–7). Other bishops from Egypt may also have assisted him, but there is no concrete evidence for the fact. The names and distribution of the new bishops enumerated by Honigmann, pp. 172–3, are as follows: Dometius of Laodicia, John of Seleucia in Syria, Conon of Tarsus, Eugenius of Seleucia in Isauria, John of Chalcis, Sergius of Carrhes, John of Soura, Eunomios of Amid, John of Ephesus, Peter of Smyrna, John of Pergamus, Peter of Tralles, John of Chios, Paul of Aphrodisias, Julian of Alabanda, and twelve unnamed bishops for the provinces of Egypt whom he consecrated by mandate from Patriarch Theodosius in the royal city of Constantinople itself.

Jacob, who literally became the spiritual leader of his Church, was never elevated to the patriarchal throne, but he himself consecrated two patriarchs. One was Sergius of Antioch (ca. 542–62),[1] his old companion in captivity at Constantinople. The other was Paul the Black (564–81), an Egyptian born in Alexandria who spent part of his monastic life in some of the Syrian monasteries. His career was stormy, and, like the rest of the patriarchs of Antioch since Justinian, he was never able to attain that city as a Monophysite. He was pursued by the emperor's men and had to take refuge at the court of the Ghassānid Arab kings, al-Hārith ibn Jabala and his successor al-Mundhir, and sometimes in the Mareotis desert south-west of Alexandria. Apparently he at one time feigned conversion to the Chalcedonian profession of faith and was welcomed by the Byzantine emperor in Constantinople, where he spent a few years and where he died after a chequered reign of schisms within his church and the taint of tritheism of which Sergius was also accused.[2]

The latter phase of Jacob's life is wrapped in obscurity. In 570, the emperor summoned him with Theodore of Arabia to a council in Constantinople. Theodore went, but Jacob was forced by the monks of Syria to remain in the East, which offended the emperor. In 575, Jacob presided over an Eastern council where Paul the Black was received in the hope of ending a local schism. Owing to the split between Peter of Alexandria and Paul of Antioch, a new menace of a greater schism between the two sister churches of Egypt and Syria loomed on the horizon. To prevent this, Jacob had to accept Paul's deposition by Peter, after which Paul retired to die in Byzantium. Jacob then planned to visit Alexandria with a delegation of eight, amongst whom were some bishops, in order to cement the traditional union between the two great Monophysite churches. But he and three other members died mysteriously towards the end of July 578 at the Monastery of St Romanos on Mount Casion near the Egyptian eastern frontier. The Coptic patriarch Damianos, who succeeded Peter, sent a letter of condolence to the clergy of the East on the occasion of this irreparable loss. Later, in the year 622, Jacob's remains were transferred to his old monastery of Phasīlthā, in the neighbourhood of Tellā.[3]

The vast efforts of the great saint who imparted his name to the Jacobite Church, lasting for more than thirty-five years, ended in the consolidation of its tottering structure. It is interesting to know that he also left his impression in Persia. He is said to have visited the court of Chosroes I (the famous Arabic Kisrā Anū Sharwān) at Seleucia in 559 to gain tolerance for the Christian Jacobites. While there, he raised the bishop of Beth ʿArabāye, by name Aḥūdemmeh, for the first time to the dignity of 'metropolitan of the East', thus

[1] Devreesse, p. 119, fixes his accession in 538, but this could not be the case since Jacob escaped from Constantinople only in 542. For the certain date of his life, see Honigmann, pp. 192–5.

[2] Honigmann, pp. 195–205.

[3] Ibid., pp. 176–7, 243–5.

laying the foundation for the Jacobite Maphrianate, or catholicate, of Persia.[1] The new metropolitan was active in preaching the Gospel according to his creed and ended by earning the crown of martyrdom in 575 at Chosroes' hands for converting a member of the imperial family to Christianity. In Persia, however, the Jacobites and Nestorians survived side by side until the coming of the Arabs, under whose rule both their churches attained a status of legality which they had never enjoyed with Byzantium.

Jacob's life began like a flaming torch and ended in the gloom of schism and persecution. He was a holy man and a great evangelist. He was unassuming and lived in strict poverty and austerity, yet fame pursued him in spite of his own will. At the time of his death the Monophysite Church of Syria had an assured existence, thanks to his tireless and tenacious efforts and devotion. He was also a man of considerable theological and scriptural knowledge and could defend the teachings of his church in Greek, Syriac and Arabic, which he spoke with equal facility. On the whole, he must be regarded as one of the most remarkable figures of his age.

Ascetics and Stylites

The development of the Jacobite monastic ideal was pre-eminently one of very great austerity.[2] From the beginning it fell under the influence of ascetics and stylites. It must, however, be noted that the story of early monasticism in the Asiatic regions of the Middle East could not be designated as Jacobite or Nestorian, Syrian or East Syrian, Monophysite or Diophysite. These distinctions became sharply defined when the rupture with Antioch reached its consummation with Babai II's assumption of the patriarchal title in 498. Until then, therefore, the first stages in the introduction and progress of monastic teachings from Egypt must be studied in common between Edessa and Nisibis, Antioch and Seleucia-Ctesiphon, with St Augin of

[1] John of Ephesus calls Aḥūdemmeh 'Catholicos of the Orthodox', a title which appears for the first time with the Monophysites of Persia. Cf. Honigmann, *Le Couvent de Barṣaumā et le Patriarcat Jacobite d'Antioche et de Syrie* (Louvain, 1954), pp. 94–5. The title of 'Maphrian of Tekrit' first appeared in 629 and was suppressed in Persia as late as 1859, although in recent years it has been revived in an honorary capacity for the Jacobite metropolitan of Jerusalem. See Bishop Severius Jacob, 'The Syrian Church', in *Orthodoxy*, p. 228; Fortescue, p. 340.

[2] A. Vööbus, *Celibacy – A Requirement for Admission to Baptism in the Early Syrian Church* (Papers of the Estonian Theological Society in Exile; Stockholm, 1951). This interesting thesis which demonstrates this tendency from Syriac, Armenian and Arabic sources is based mainly on the homilies of Aphrahet, written between 336 and 345, where he expresses his antipathy to marriage as a mere means of procreation without ethical or spiritual value. He even puts it that celibacy and asceticism are requirements for admission to baptism.

Clysma as the historic initiator of the movement in Upper Mesopotamia in the course of the fourth century.[1] Although differences had existed between Antiochian orthodoxy and Nestorian heterodoxy from the early decades of the fifth century, the co-operation of the two schools of thought remained effective in both church and monastic life. The great Rabbula (d. 435), staunchly orthodox in character, was succeeded by the unorthodox Ibas (d. 457) in the bishopric of Edessa. It would be erroneous to label the earlier foundations as solely belonging to the one camp or the other, except, of course, in very special cases. This distinction took shape gradually in later times as a natural result of the intensification of the differences between the Western and Eastern Syrians with a host of historic factors at work in the background. On the whole, however, the thesis that the Jacobites were essentially identified with the monastic establishments to the north of Baghdad around Tekrit, whereas the Nestorians occupied the foundations south of Baghdad with Seleucia-Ctesiphon (the Arab al-Madā'in or twin cities) as the seat of their religious activities, is acceptable.[2] Baghdad itself appears to have remained mainly under Nestorian predominance.

There is little doubt that the cenobitic life was adopted by the Syrian monks in the course of the fourth and fifth centuries. Evidence shows that at least thirty-five fully fledged monasteries had come into being during those two centuries in Mesopotamia and its adjacent territories.[3] The tendency towards rigorous asceticism in the monastic ranks of the Syrian church is apparent in every phase of its early annals. Syrian hagiography teems with those self-mortifying spiritual athletes from St Augin (d. ca. 363) to St Jacob Baradæus (d. 578) and beyond. But perhaps the most striking and peculiarly distinctive feature in the story of Syrian asceticism is the emergence of that class of saints who retired from the world to complete seclusion on top of ancient pillars or pillars which they erected for themselves. They became known as 'stylites'.[4] The inventor and promoter of this mode of life is said

[1] See the section below on Nestorian monasticism.

[2] This is the view advanced by Bahīja Fattūḥi Lovejoy, member of the Jacobite church, of Iraqi birth and American citizenship, in her unpubl. diss. (Harvard, 1957) 'Christian Monasteries in Mesopotamia'. The thesis is the most comprehensive record of the monasteries in this area, most of which have disappeared. The author was able to compile and identify 163 monasteries from the Arabic and Syriac sources. The material is preceded by a chapter on Christianity in Mesopotamia (pp. 2–41) and another on the sources, notably the tenth-century Arabic al-Shābushti and his *Kitāb al-Diyārāt* (pp. 43–67). The monasteries themselves are enumerated under two sections: the first based on al-Shābushti and other writers (pp. 69–169), and the second containing monasteries mentioned by mediæval and modern Christian and Muslin writers (pp. 171–272).

[3] Ibid., pp. 282–90. In his indexes, Vööbus (see note 1, p. 186) under *Dairā* (monastery) enumerates 113 in his first two volumes, where he has not yet used al-Shābushti (*Kitāb al-Diyārāt*). In Vol. II, pp. 224–55, Vööbus gives a repertory of the more outstanding monasteries.

[4] From the Greek στῦλος, pillar.

to have been St Simeon Stylites (ca. 389–459), some of the details of whose career seem to be pure legend on account of their superhuman character. Nevertheless, the Greek, Syriac, Coptic, Georgian, Armenian and Arabic hagiographies are in agreement about the sum total of his biography, which forms a luminous chapter in the story of the Syrian church and of the Syrian monastic ideal.[1]

Born of devout Christian parents at Sīs, in the borderland of Syria and Cilicia, he spent his childhood as a shepherd and received no education. In the mountain solitude he had visions of a holy and constructive life. Around the age of sixteen he joined a neighbouring community of monks, with whom he spent the first ten years of his ascetic life. Even in his early youth he performed such feats of asceticism and self-torture as to frighten and even alienate his older colleagues. Whereas other monks broke their fast every two days, he ate only once a week. Then he tied a rough rope made of rough palm-tree fibre on his flesh underneath his garment and his secret was revealed when his fellows saw a trail of blood trickling from his body. He refused to accept a healing ointment for his ulcer, and the superior decided to expel him from the monastery. So he fled to the mountain and hid himself in a dry cistern for five days, until his old superior regretted his guilt and sent his men to scour the countryside to bring him back to the fold. Yet he did not stay with them long, for his soul aspired to greater austerities. When he retired to the wilderness of Tellneshin, some leagues from Antioch, he asked a certain Bassus to build a wall over the entrance of his cell and leave him

[1] The Greek lives of some of the famous Stylites have been edited by the Bollandist Hippolyte Delahaye, *Les Saints Stylites*, Subsidia Hagiographica XIV (Brussels and Paris, 1923), The book includes a fine introduction on the life of St Simeon Stylites (pp. i–xxiv); but the Greek texts published in it are those of St Daniel (pp. 1–147), St Alypius (pp. 148–95), St Luke (pp. 195–237) and St Simeon the Younger (pp. 238–71), all stylites. The best life of St Simeon the Elder has been preserved by his contemporary the Antiochene bishop of Cyrrhus, Theodoret (c. 393–c. 458), noted theologian and historian (cf. *Hist. Relig.*, 26). See also *Acta Sanctorum*, Jan. 1 (Antwerp, 1643), pp. 261–86; the Greek life ed. A. Papadopoulos-Keramaes (St Petersburg, 1907); the Syriac life ed. H. Leitzmann, 'Das Leben des heiligen Simeon Stylites', in *Texte und Unterschungen zur Geschichte der altchristlichen Literatur*, ed. O. von Gebhardt and A. von Harnack (Leipzig, 1882), XXXII, 4, 1908; P. Peeters, *S. Simeon Stylite et ses premiers biographes*, Analecta Boll., LXI (1943), pp. 29–71. The Arabic life may be found in the Sinai Arabic MSS. nos. 352, 406, 445, 448 and 571; see Atiya, *Arabic MSS. of Mt Sinai*, pp. 9, 11, 13–14, and 23. Assemani, *Bibl. Orientalis*, I, 254–5. On Syrian asceticism in general, see the most elaborate work in recent years: A. Vööbus, *A History of Asceticism in the Syrian Orient: A Contribution to the History of Culture in the Near East*, 2 vols. (Corpus Scriptorum Christianorum Orientalium, Nos. 184, 197; Louvain, 1958–60). The work is planned in five volumes: (1) The Origin of Asceticism, Early Monasticism in Persia; (2) Early Monasticism in Mesopotamia and Syria; (3) Monasticism among the Monophysites, Blossoming and Fate under Arabs to 10th Century; (4) Monasticism among the Nestorians; and (5) Aftermath of Syrian Monasticism, Breakdown of Arab Empire to Timur Lenk. Only Vols. I and II have appeared. On St Simeon Stylites see II 208–23. References to other stylites are scattered and so far somewhat inadequate.

without provisions for forty days, since it was Lent. Bassus blocked the entrance but insisted on leaving ten loaves and a pitcher of water with the saint to prevent a suicidal project. When he reopened the enclosure at the end of Lent, he found the provisions intact and the saint prostrate between life and death. Simeon was nursed back to health. Theodoret, his authoritative biographer, says that the saint repeated this frightful experience twenty-eight years in succession.[1] No wonder his fame spread far and wide through Christendom and pilgrims began to frequent his hermitage. He wrought miracles of healing the paralytic and the sick, and of blessing sterile wives who bore children. The growing reverence to his person disturbed him, and men and women sought to touch him or take clippings of his leather tunic as a holy relic. It dawned upon him that he might solve his problem by mounting a column for complete segregation. So he built himself a pillar eleven cubits high, later raising it to seventeen and twenty-two, on which he lived for seven years. The new idea apparently appealed to the saint, who finally raised the pillar to forty cubits[2] and spent his remaining thirty years standing on it exposed to the elements with nothing but a hood to cover his head. Once a visitor from Ravenna, watching the saint in that superhuman posture without food or sleep, asked him whether he was man or angel. The saint ordered a ladder to be brought for the pilgrim to come to him and made him feel his flesh. He preached twice a day and at night raised his hands in prayer until dawn. He performed miracles and converted the heathen. A whole settlement arose around his pillar, with a continuous stream of pilgrims from every corner of Syria, from Armenia, Georgia, Persia and Arabia as well as Spain, Britain, Gaul and Italy. The Emperor Theodosius II and his sisters sent a delegation of bishops to ask him to come down from his pillar and come to court to heal the sick at the capital. They were unable to persuade him.

When he died, his body was closely guarded by six bishops and six hundred soldiers under the command of Ardaburius, head of the militia. His precious remains, placed in a lead sarcophagus, were carried in procession to the church of Cassianus and a month later transferred to the cathedral church of the city of Antioch. Around his column arose a great octagon with a magnificent dome flanked by four church buildings in the shape of a cross. The art and architecture of the now ruined Qalʿat Samʿān leave the spectator speechless with admiration for the immensity of those structures as well as the beauty of their stone carving and elegant soberness.[3]

[1] Cf. Delahaye, p. xxvi.

[2] Approximately sixty feet, according to the above-mentioned 'Lives'. Other accounts of his life reduce it to thirty cubits, that is to forty-five feet. Vööbus, II, 214, estimates about fifteen metres.

[3] Downey, *Antioch in Syria*, pp. 459–61, discusses St Simeon's spiritual impact on the political government of the city.

The deceased saint unwittingly inaugurated a new mode of ascetic life.[1] His example was followed by scores of stylites, members of the Syrian church, throughout the Middle Ages, and the movement extended even beyond the frontiers of that church to Egypt and Greece. St Daniel of Samosata in Syria (d. 502) spent forty-two years on his pillar, and St Simeon the Younger (d. 592) of Edessa occupied another pillar near Antioch for some forty-five years and performed innumerable miracles.[2] St Michael, a pupil of St Acha, after founding a monastery at the ancient town of Nineveh, retired to the top of a pillar where he remained until his death in 556 at the advanced age of 105 years.[3] Even under the rule of the Arabs, stylites were to be found. St John of Litharba (al-Athārib, near Aleppo), who was an exegete, astronomer and historian of no mean merit and whose lost chronicle was used by the famous historian, Michael the Syrian, spent the concluding years of the seventh and the opening years of the eighth centuries perched on a column. Pilgrims from distant regions in Europe saw stylites during their eastern peregrinations. St Willibald records (723) two cases, and the Russian priest Daniel (1106–7) found one at Bethlehem. Thomas of Marga mentions a ninth-century Jacobite stylite at Beth Kardagh who succumbed in a hail-storm and was ridiculed by the Nestorian metropolitan of Adiabene. Basil II, who became Jacobite catholicos in 848, had previously been an inmate of the Monastery of Beth Bottin in Mesopotamia, where he was known as Lazarus the Stylite.[4]

Notable examples outside Syria include St Alypius of Adrianople, in Paphlagonia, who died in the reign of Emperor Heraclius (610–41). He spent many years on a pillar and was endowed with the gift of prophecy.[5] St Luke of Anatolia lived in the tenth century, and died a centenarian on a pillar near historic Chalcedon.[6] Egypt, too, had its first stylite in the person of Theophilus the Confessor, cited by the chronicler John of Nikiou in the reign of Heraclius. Both the Coptic and Ethiopic Synaxaria quote the name of St Agathon the Stylite without fixing the years of his life.[7] Ancient columns

[1] It is interesting to know that the unknown precursor of St Simeon's is a former prefect of Constantinople under Emperor Theodosius II by the name of Theodolus, who, it is asserted, spent years of his later life of penitence on a column near Edessa, but the historicity of that episode is questioned. Delahaye, pp. cxviii–cxx. Delahaye refutes the authenticity of the 'Chronicle of Joshua the Stylite', supposed to be written at the unlikely date of 507 A.D., and whose provenance is said to have been the Monastery of Zouqnin near Amida or Diyarbekr (see P. Martin, *Chronique de Josue le Stylite* [Leipzig, 1878] and W. Wright, *The Chronicle of Joshua the Stylite* [Cambridge, 1882]). Delahaye asserts that there is confusion between this chronicle and the life of St Daniel, the earliest stylite after St Simeon. On 'Josue Stylites', see also Assemani, *Bibl. Orient.*, I, 260–82.

[2] Delahaye, pp. lvi–lvii, lxiv–lxxi.

[3] Ibid., p. cxxi.

[4] Ibid., pp. cxxv et seq.

[5] Ibid., pp. lxxvi–lxxxv (introduction), 148–94 (Greek lives).

[6] Ibid., pp. lxxxvi–cv (introduction), 195–237 (Greek life).

[7] Ibid., pp. cxxxv–cxxxvi.

were sometimes occupied by stylites. Two columns erected by Theodosius and Arcadius in Constantinople were found to serve this purpose in the thirteenth century when two stylites replaced the fallen imperial statues.

That mode of life, though demanding the fortitude of a spiritual athlete, was not altogether impossible. If taken as an example, the capital of Pompey's Pillar in ancient Alexandria is nearly ten feet wide and has a considerable hollow where the base of Diocletian's statue was fitted. From the existing stump of St Simeon's Pillar at Qalʿat Samʿān, it can be deduced that each side of the square capital was about six feet. The stylite was not completely segregated from the rest of humanity. A hanging ladder served his disciples and admirers for the purpose of carrying the scanty provisions to their master. In some cases a support was planted on the column against which the stylite leaned, since most stylites spent their lives in a standing posture. Modern times have seen occasional stylites. The last was mentioned about 1848 by the traveller Brosset at Djqondidi in Georgia, where a recluse built a tiny cell for himself on a column in the Caucasian Mountains.[1]

We should not, however, regard the rise of the stylites as a separate movement which developed independently of Syrian monasticism. The two were often linked together, since in many cases the stylites came from already existing monasteries, and the reverse occasionally happened: a monastic settlement was built up around a saint's column. Planted in eastern Asia by an Egyptian – Mar Augin, or St Eugenius of Clysma[2] – in the fourth century, monasticism flourished in the Syrian church on a cenobitic pattern and discipline in accordance with the new and elaborate rule of St Pachomius the Great (ca. 290–346) in the Thebaïd.[3] The first of these monasteries was naturally that of Mar Augin himself, founded towards the end of the fourth century

[1] Ibid., pp. cxxxv, cxlvii, cl.

[2] This is al-Qulzum of the Arab Middle Ages situated at the head of the Gulf of Suez, roughly where modern Suez stands.

[3] Sources of Syrian monasticism and monastic establishments are enumerated by Vööbus (see note on p. 186), Mrs Lovejoy in her unpubl. diss. (see p. 185, n. 2) and Paul Krüger in his diss., *Das syrisch-monophysitische Mönchtum im Tur-ʿAb(h)din von seinem Anfängen bis sur Mitte des 12. Jahrhunderts* (Munster i. W., 1937). The chief Arabic source is Abul-Ḥasan ʿAli b. M. Al-Shābushti (d. 998 A.D.), (Book of the Monasteries), ed. by Gurgis ʿAwwād (Baghdad, 1951). The editor provides an extensive bibliography including practically all the sources and secondary materials existing in Arabic. Al-Shabushti used earlier Arabic works on monasteries, all lost, notably those by Hishām b. M. b. al-Sā'ib al-Kalbi (d. 819 or 821 A.D.) and Abul-Faraj b. ʿAli b. Al-Ḥasan al-Iṣfahāni (d. 966), author of the famous *Kitāb al-Aghani*. In turn al-Shābushti's work was utilized by subsequent Arab writers such as Abu Ṣāliḥ al-Armanni (d. 1172), the geographers Yāqūt (d. 1228), Qazwīni (d. 1283) and ibn ʿAbdul-Ḥaqq (d. 1338), the encyclopedist ibn Faḍl-Allah al-ʿUmari (d. 1348), and the historians ibn Shaddād (d. 1234), al-Maqrīzi (d. 1441) and ibn Ṭūlūn (d. 1546). Al Shābushti's work is pre-eminently literary, but contains numerous authentic references of historical and geographical interest. He surveys a total of fifty-three monasteries distributed as follows: thirty-seven in Iraq, four in al-Jazīra (upper Mesopotamia), three in Syria and nine in Egypt. Apparently these were

on the original mountain of his retirement overlooking the plains of Nisibis. It was seized by the Nestorians in the sixth century, and it flourished under the caliphate. An old Chaldæan Nestorian calendar states that at one time it housed 160 monks and owned 400 heads of sheep, five mills and five villages. Moreover, it enclosed a school for the edification of both ecclesiastical and secular scholars. In the sixteenth century the number of its Chaldæan occupants dwindled, and the Jacobite Syrians in turn revived monastic life in it. In 1909 an abbot and eight hermits resided there, and after the First World War only one inmate was left in all its vast establishments.[1]

In the fifth century the monastery of Mar Barṣaumā came into existence.[2] Its founder played some role in the controversy over the Eutychian heresy, and attended the Council of Ephesus of 449 by special invitation from the Emperor Theodosius II. He was the only participant below the rank of bishop, since he remained an archimandrite to the end. He died in 457. The importance of his monastery, which was situated in the mountains between Samosata and Melitene (Malaṭiya), is due to the fact that it became the chief seat of the Jacobite patriarchs under Arab rule from the eighth or ninth centuries until the middle of the fourteenth, when it was destroyed by the Kurds. It has been in ruins ever since. It was in this monastery that the greatest literary monuments of Jacobite church history saw the light. Here Michael the Syrian (1166–99) resided and wrote his famous chronicle. His tomb stood amidst those of other Jacobite patriarchs in one of its churches. The anonymous Syriac *Chronographia* of 1234 was also recorded within its precincts, and at least a major part of the renowned *Histories* of Bar Hebræus (1226–86) before his preferment to the maphrianate of Tekrit and all the Orient. Afterwards, the patriarchs apparently chose as a new seat the Monastery of al-Zaʿfarān (Saffron), otherwise known as the Monastery of Mar Ḥanānia, the active archbishop of Mardin who built it in 793–800 on the basis of a more ancient foundation and enriched it with a great library. Eighty monks flocked to it in his own lifetime, and the patriarchs actually lived there from 1293. It has been in continuous use ever since. It is a strongly fortified establishment on the mountain overlooking Nisibis on the caravan

still in use in the tenth century, but the list is incomplete, especially in connection with Syria and Egypt. The editor, however, supplemented the text with additional material from other sources on thirty-one more monasteries. Some of his information is furnished by the Jacobite patriarch Ephraem I Barṣūm of Ḥomṣ, whose erudition and first-hand knowledge add weight to these statements. Al-Shābushti's section on Egyptian Monasteries is edited by A. S. Atiya in *Bulletin de la Société d'Archéologie Copte*, T. V (1939), pp. 1–28.

[1] Al-Shābushti, pp. 121, 238–41; Lovejoy, pp. 123–7.

[2] Honigmann, *Le Couvent de Barṣaumā et le Patriarcat Jacobite d'Antioche et de Syrie*, Corpus Scriptorum Christianorum Orientalium, Vol. 146, Subsidia Tome 7 (Louvain, 1954); Vööbus, *Asceticism*, II, 196–208.

route between Moṣul, Mardin and Damascus, in an area rich with vineyards, fruit trees and attractive vegetation. Of its monks twenty-one became patriarchs, nine maphrians, and 110 bishops.[1] It is the most frequented of Jacobite monasteries by pilgrims, visitors and travellers from East and West.[2]

The next important Jacobite monastery is that of Shaikh Mattai (Matthew), as it has been called in the Arab period. It is situated, fortress-like and partly hewn in the solid rock on the Maqlūb Mountain, overlooking the plains of ancient Nineveh twenty miles north-west of Moṣul. Mar Mattai, who founded it in the latter part of the fourth century, was originally a native of the district of Amid (Diyarbekr). During the persecutions of Julian the Apostate (d. 363), he fled towards the Persian frontier with three companions – Abraham, Zakki and Daniel – and himself became a hermit in a cave where the monastery now stands. Others soon followed his example by adopting ascetic life in neighbouring caves. This was the modest beginning of one of the most extensive monasteries in history. The Arab geographer Yāqūt, writing in the twelfth and thirteenth centuries, said that it was inhabited by a thousand monks.[3] In the Middle Ages it became a centre of learning and instruction. In a synod of 869 its abbots and monks recognized the authority of the Jacobite maphrian of the East. By the tenth century it was regarded as an equivalent to the patriarchal convent of Barṣaumā, and the maphrians resided in it. Both the cell and the tomb of Bar Hebræus inside one of its chapels are objects of interest to visitors and pilgrims to Mar Mattai. The invaluable chronicles of Bar Hebræus must have been finished here. It is sad to realize that the priceless contents of its famous library are now dispersed abroad between the Vatican, the British Museum and other European manuscript repositories. Its present superior, Bishop Timothy Yaʿqūb, guards closely a handful of unimportant codices and is assisted in the administration of the monastery by four monks who deal with the stream of visitors. The present status of the monastery is that of a hostelry, or summer resort, for wealthy Iraqis and Iranians from Moṣul and elsewhere.[4]

[1] Al-Shābushti, pp. 121–6; also Patriarch Ephraem's notes, on pp. 241–2.

[2] O. H. Parry, *Six Months in a Syrian Monastery* (London, 1895), pp. 103 et seq. For a more recent visit, see Jules Leroy, *Moines et monastères du Proche-Orient* (Paris, 1958), pp. 246–7. It was situated, of course, in the mountainous region famous by the name of Ṭūr ʿAbdīn.

[3] Muʿjam al-Buldān, II, 694. Perhaps the number is exaggerated, but it denotes the size of the community.

[4] Parry, pp. 263–9; Leroy, pp. 228–33. Mrs Lovejoy, a Jacobite herself and a frequent visitor to that monastery since her girlhood, gives a vivid personal picture of it in her thesis, pp. 211–20. She notes the vandalism of the Mongols, Turks and Kurds in regard to the monastery and the dawn of peaceful existence since the declaration of Iraqi independence in 1921. Many native Iraqi Muslims share the reverence of the old Shaikh with their Christian compatriots.

South-west of Moṣul exists another ancient monastery of Mar Behnām, who was converted to Christianity by Mar Mattai. It changed hands several times. First, the Nestorians took it after their breach with the Monophysites. Then in the sixth century, the Jacobites recovered and retained it until 1767, when its Superior Hindi Zora went over to Roman Catholicism with his monastery. It has remained with the Chaldæans, who have been using it mainly as a school. The building, though largely restored in modern times, still has older sections and chapels of pure arabesque style and numerous bas-reliefs of various saints from earlier periods.[1]

Mention is also made of special convents for Syrian and Monophysite nuns from quite an early date. The most famous of them in the district of al-Ḥīrah, is ascribed to Queen Hind, daughter of the Arab King al-Nuʿmān b. al-Mundhir (585–613 A.D.). It repeatedly appeared on the scene of events in Arab history and was mentioned by Arab writers such as al-Iṣfahāni, al-Shābushti, al-ʿUmari and al-Bakri throughout the Middle Ages. Another, located in the Christian quarter of Baghdad, was called the Convent of the Virgins. Both al-Shābushti and Bar Hebræus referred to its existence in the tenth and eleventh centuries, and the latter author named it 'The Sisters' Nunnery'.[2]

Although most of the surviving Jacobite monasteries have disintegrated into hostelries and wine distilleries, Jacobite monasticism unquestionably had a glorious past and played an eminent role in the preservation of culture and the diffusion of education. Cenobitic life was the general pattern, though hermits continued to dwell in caves in complete seclusion. The mountains around famous monasteries were dotted with them. The monastery itself was of necessity a fortified settlement with high walls. It contained chapels, refectories, libraries, mills, bakeries, distilleries, workshops, store-rooms, water wells, stables, gardens and cells for monks. Each monastery was invariably a self-sufficient unit, and many convents were real centres of scholarship.

[1] A good account of a recent visit to this monastery is given in Leroy, pp. 233–43.

[2] Al-Shābushti, pp. 70, 157, 230, 245–6. The same author makes a rather obscene literary reference (p. 69) to another convent of virgins at a place called al-Ḥaḍirah, near Tekrit on the Tigris.

11 • THE JACOBITES IN HISTORY

Under the Caliphate[1]

On the eve of the Arab conquest of Syria and the Middle East, the Jacobite Church, like the Nestorian, had become illegal, and its priesthood had been outlawed. The Greek, or Melkite, Orthodox patriarch of Antioch, the sole church prelate approved by the Byzantine emperor, and his Chalcedonian bishops and clergy were the only clerics authorized by the state. The Nestorians had long disappeared beyond the Byzantine frontiers and were safe from imperial wrath within Persia. The Monophysites, on the other hand, still the majority in Syria, had been rigorously pursued for their activities and driven underground as demonstrated in the story of Jacob Baradæus. With the coming of the Arabs, the picture underwent a complete change. The followers of Muḥammad in those early decades knew little or nothing of the differences of the Christian sects, though they recognized the 'People of the Book', to whom they promised protection and offered safe-conduct as long as they did not interfere with Islam and its invading armies and paid the taxes. The new state's interest in newly conquered Christian territory was chiefly limited to peaceful co-existence with the *Dhimmi* subjects and the regular levy of two forms of taxation: first the *Kharāj*, or land tax, imposed equally on Muslim and Christian subjects without discrimination; and second, the *Jizyah*, or capitation, that is, the poll-tax paid only by the Christians, originally estimated at one gold dinar per head in lieu of military service. This varied at a later date in conformity with the status of the individual, though it was customarily restricted to able-bodied men, and exemptions from it were extended to women and children as well as priests, monks and aged men. Thus Jacobites, Nestorians and Orthodox Christians became one nation subject to the same impositions and enjoying the same privileges without distinction. The Jacobites under Muslim rule attained a degree of religious enfranchisement they had never had with their Byzantine co-religionists. The

[1] L. E. Browne, *Eclipse of Christianity in Asia* (Cambridge, 1933), pp. 44–63, contains an interesting chapter on 'Christianity under the Caliphs'; A. S. Tritton, *Caliphs and Their Non-Muslim Subjects* (Oxford, 1930); P. K. Hitti, *History of Syria*, pp. 517–26.

early annals of Islam were also marked by the spirit of religious tolerance and a strict sense of justice. This was combined with the eagerness of the Arabs to profit from the advanced culture and learning of the old established races within their dominion, irrespective of religious differences. This healthy attitude explains the high place occupied by both Jacobite and Nestorian at the court of the caliphs. Another factor also emerges with the unification of Syria, Mesopotamia and Persia under the same Arab rule. The lifting of the older barriers between the Asiatic territories under Byzantine and Persian domination furnished the Jacobites with the opportunity of missionary expansion eastward in areas where the Nestorians had almost a complete monopoly. It is true that the Jacobites were never able to cover the same ground as the Nestorians in their missionary activities in Central Asia and the Far East. But under the Arabs they undoubtedly began to work with diligence in Mesopotamia and Persia even amongst the Nestorians themselves, as will be seen from the following survey. On the other hand, it would be a mistake to say that the Jacobites had no representation whatever in that area before the coming of the Arabs. The first wife and queen of Chosroes II Parviz (590–628), the famous Shīrīn, was a Jacobite Christian. During the subsequent period of strife, the Jacobite monk Marutha (629–49), who witnessed the end of Sassanid rule, was raised to the metropolitan dignity of Tekrit and had fifteen suffragans in Persia and Mestopotamia. It is true that the Nestorians enjoyed special favour with both the Persian rulers and their Arab successors. Indeed the Nestorian catholicos was the only head of a Christian church to be seated in the capital of that new empire. Nevertheless, the new status of the Jacobite church made it possible for it to flourish and expand under the *pax arabica* beyond the Syrian border into old Persian territories. This is the background against which the long-oppressed Jacobite church functioned under the caliphate. At first it had its brilliant moments of progress and prosperity during the early centuries of Arab rule, until the Crusaders tipped the balance of peace in the Holy Land and the whole Middle East. It would be an error to contend that there had been no Christian persecutions before that time. As a rule sporadic antagonism to the Christians was not a set policy in the early Islamic polity but rather depended on the whim of the ruler in office. The Crusade was possibly the decisive factor in the alienation of the Muslim from the older spirit of fellowship with his Christian neighbour. Following this, the position of the Eastern churches and communities, including the Jacobites, greatly deteriorated. The later Middle Ages proved to be the end of their glory and their ancient vitality. Their theological acumen and the Syriac literary genius disappeared from existence. Henceforward a poor, oppressed and shrinking minority, they lived on memories of their past heritage.

First Three Centuries

From the seventh to the tenth centuries Jacobite history, though not as glowing as that of the Nestorians, whose scholars thronged the Abbasid Academy of *Dār al-Ḥikmah* (House of Wisdom) beginning with Ḥunayn ibn Isḥāq and his family, had its brighter side and new orientations. The need for theological controversy and Biblical exegesis which marked the Byzantine period and the urge to defend Monophysitism against Greek Chalcedonian professions was not pressing under the Arabs. Hence the Jacobites – and this also applies to the Nestorians – could direct their creative writing, whether in Syriac or Arabic letters, to the subjects of hagiography, history, astronomy, science and medicine. It may be noticed, however, that as Arabic gained momentum, Syriac waned until in the end it became more or less a liturgical language.

As will be seen, most of the Jacobite worthies were not patriarchs who were invariably engrossed in schisms and struggles for survival. The first really great Jacobite divine of this period is Marutha,[1] metropolitan of Tekrit and, from 629 to his death in 649 after the Arab conquest, he was the first to bear the title 'Maphrian of the East', whose ecclesiastical jurisdiction covered the area from al-Hīrah in the Arabian Peninsula to Persia and even beyond. The maphrianate, now a titular and honorary vestige of the past, was an important institution in those days when the patriarchs were in no position to care for the distant provinces of the East. The maphrian shouldered the task of working in provinces dominated by the strong Nestorian element. He had to relieve the patriarch of far-flung responsibilities and was empowered to nominate his own suffragans. Marutha was equal to the spirited Nestorian, Barṣaumā, in the defence of Monophysitism in Persia and Mesopotamia. To him is ascribed an epistle he is said to have written at the request of the Jacobite Patriarch John I (631–48),[2] who according to Bar Hebræus translated the first Gospel into Arabic at the instigation of the Arab Amīr ʿAmr b. Saʿad. It was also in John's patriarchate that Bishop Severus Sebokht (d. 667) of the convent of Kenneshrē[3] excelled in the study of

[1] Marūt͟hā, a native of Persia born in the village of Bēth Nuhādrā, became a monk at the Convent of Zakki or Zacchæus at Callinicus (al-Raqqah), where he spent twenty years, then moved to the rich literary and theological centre of the Convent of Mar Mattai at Mosul after a period spent at the Edessene College. W. Wright, *A Short History of Syriac Literature* (London, 1894), p. 136; Assemani, *Bibl. Orient.*, I, 174–95; A. Baumstark, *Geschichte der Syrischen Literatur* (Bonn, 1922), p. 245; R. Duval, *La Littérature Syriaque* (Paris, 1900), p. 375; J. B. Chabot, *Littérature Syriaque* (Paris, 1934), pp. 81–2.

[2] Wright, p. 139; Chabot, p. 82; Duval, p. 374. Often called 'John of the Sedras' owing to the fact that he is better known as the author of several important homilies or 'sedras'. He also planned a Syriac liturgy.

[3] That is, 'Eagle's Nest', situated on the left bank of the Euphrates, founded by John

Hellenistic philosophy, mathematics, astronomy and theology. He was undoubtedly one of the pioneers of Hellenistic-Syriac science. Amongst his works are a treatise on the syllogisms in Aristotle's *Analytica Priora* and others on the astrolabe and on the zodiac. The monastery of Kenneshrē became the real Jacobite centre of learning under Severus Sebokht. Most eminent amongst the Kenneshrē graduates in the seventh century was Jacob of Edessa (633–708) – bishop, theologian, exegete, grammarian, philosopher and historian. He has occasionally been described as the Jerome[1] of the Jacobite church and is reckoned one of its most prolific writers. Apart from a complete revision of the Old Testament and extensive Bible commentaries, he made a tremendous contribution to the stabilization of the Syriac liturgy. After a definitive revision of the ancient Liturgy of St James, he composed a new anaphora, a baptismal rite, the solemnization of matrimony, and the calendar of Church offices. Among his translations from the Greek was one of Severus of Antioch's *Homiliæ cathedrales*. His grammar of the Mesopotamian language embodied extensive research in the reform of Syriac linguistics and orthography. His lost chronicle, planned in continuation to Eusebius of Cæsarea's *Historia ecclesiastica*, was used by both Michael the Syrian and Bar Hebræus. A few disjointed and mutilated sheets are all that remain from a monumental work that would have given us much knowledge of this obscure time.[2] His numerous 'Epistles to John the Stylite of Litharba' (al-Athārib, near Aleppo) and to other contemporary personalities throw much light on the problems of his time. Towards the end of his life, Jacob embarked on a monumental study of the creation and creatures entitled *Hexæmeron*,[3] which he left unfinished. This was conceived as the second part of an encyclopædia of theological knowledge, the first part being a work called *Causa causarum*, attributed to him, though bearing an inscription citing only a bishop of Edessa as author. In its known form, the work is incomplete, but parts of it represent a consensus of all the scientific notions of the age. The author describes a kind of utopia in which people of all faiths are reunited in one universal religion, and he systematically avoids statements which may antagonize either Jew or Muslim. His sympathy with the mystic philosophy of the Arabs is also noticeable.

In addition to his immense literary career, Jacob, was a driving power in the reformist church activities of his day. He tried to enforce rigid discipline in the convents of his diocese. When the monks revolted against him the

Bar Aphthonia, who fled from western Syria at the time of Justin's persecutions in 521; Chabot, pp. 73, 82–3; Baumstark, p. 246; Wright, p. 138, apparently misplaces it.

[1] Wright, p. 143.

[2] Ibid., p. 148; last to be mentioned in the extant folios are Heraclius I of Constantinople, Ardashēr III of Persia and Abu Bakr, the first Orthodox caliph.

[3] The Syriac *Al-Aksamiran*, that is, 'the six days', meaning the Creation.

Jacobite patriarch Julian sided with them. So the bishop took a copy of the old canons and burnt it at the gate of the patriarchal seat, declaring that he would rather destroy what the patriarch regarded as superfluous. He then left his diocese and moved from monastery to monastery for years, teaching, writing and preaching until his death on the eve of his return to Edessa in 708. The Jacobites often call him *philoponus* – the 'laborious' and the 'interpreter'.[1]

It remained for another to complete the *Hexæmeron*. This task was undertaken by George,[2] bishop of the Arabs (686–724) and Jacob's fellow-disciple at Kenneshrē. At his episcopal seat in Akoula (the Arab al-Kūfah) he also wrote numerous theological and philosophical treatises. He defended Monophysite doctrines from Nestorian incursions and wrote epistles on chronology and astronomy. The modern French writer Ernest Renan praises his work on Aristotle's *Organon* as incomparable amongst Syriac commentaries in importance, method, and exactitude.[3]

Apparently the Jacobite Church was making gains in the field of evangelization at that time. Undoubtedly the most important instance was that of Elias, a Syrian orthodox Diophysite converted to Monophysitism after the study of the works of Severus of Antioch. He was subsequently elected as patriarch of the Jacobites (709–24), and wrote an apology in defence of his conversion in response to an epistle from Leo, Melkite bishop of Ḥarran.[4] Another patriarch, Kyriakos of Tekrit (793–817), worked on winning the Julianist Armenians. In the reign of his successor, Dionysius of Tellmahrē (817–45), progress was impeded by a schism arising within the church from an argument over 'the heavenly bread' in which the patriarch's view was contested by the monks. Abraham of the convent of Qarṭamīn, was accordingly elected anti-patriarch by the malcontents, leading to humiliating scenes before the Muslim authorities. When the storm began to calm down, Dionysius embarked on a vast tour of visitations in order to appease the congregation and meanwhile to procure privileges for the church by following the courts of the rulers before whom he wanted to lodge his appeals. Between 825 and 827 he went to Egypt to procure a letter from Caliph al-Ma'mūn's envoy, 'Abdallah ibn Ṭāhir, to his brother Muḥammad, who had ordered the destruction of all newly built religious foundations in Edessa. In 829 he

[1] Baumstark, pp. 248–56. Chabot, pp. 84–8; Wright, pp. 141–54; Duval, pp. 375–8.

[2] Baumstark, pp. 257–8; Wright, pp. 156–9.

[3] Chabot, p. 88.

[4] It is interesting to note that in the interval between Elias and Kyriakos, the Syriac literary activity is represented, according to Bar Hebræus, by Theophilus bar Thomas of Edessa, a Chalcedonian according to Dionysius and a Maronite in Bar Hebræus, but cited under the Jacobites by Wright, pp. 163–4, and Chabot, p. 91. He is known to have been an astronomer of distinction highly esteemed at al-Mahdi's court. He died in 785. References have been made to several astronomical tracts by him, a lost chronicle, and a complete Syriac version of Homer's *Iliad* and *Odyssey*, which seems almost incredible.

went to Baghdad, then to Damascus, in pursuit of an audience with the caliph on behalf of the Bashmuric Copts, who were then in open rebellion against Arab rule. His intercession was in vain, since the caliph and his general, Afshīn, had succeeded in crushing the rebellion. While in Egypt the patriarch visited its antiquities, obelisks, pyramids and the Nilometer. In 835 he revisited Baghdad to render homage to al-Ma'mūn's successor, the new Caliph al Muʿtaṣim, and met the Christian king of Nubia, who was there for the same purpose. During his pontificate the church was torn by internal dissensions and suffered external afflictions from Muslim rulers. Dionysius is known as the author of a universal history of the period from the accession of Emperor Maurice in 582 to the death of Theophilus in 842, a work of capital importance for the events of the Syrian churches, utilized by Michael the Syrian and subsequent historians but unfortunately surviving only in a fraction of its original form.[1]

The period under review closes with a somewhat noteworthy Jacobite, Moses bar Kepha, who died in 903 at the age of ninety. His fields were theology, exegesis, homiletics and philosophy. His *Hexæmeron* was probably inspired by Jacob of Edessa. The *Disputation against Heresies* and a treatise on the sects are interesting. A commentary on the Old and New Testaments, another on the works of Gregory Nazienzen, two liturgies (of which one is apocryphal), and a work of Aristotle's *Dialectics* bear his name.[2]

The church, in spite of its growing burdens under the Muslim rulers, managed to retain a great measure of autonomy. As a rule the caliph's interference ended with the ratification of patriarchal election and the periodic reimbursement of the *Kharāj* and the *Jizya* taxation. The Christians were the educated members of the community and thus made themselves necessary in key positions at the Abbasid court in Baghdad. Their libraries and their schools and their scholars, of whom the above-mentioned Jacobites must be taken into account, were the normal channels through which the fruits of Hellenism found their way to Arabic culture. The Christians as a whole

[1] Baumstark, p. 275; Chabot, pp. 92–3; Duval, pp. 389–90. Wright, pp. 200–3, gives the following details of the 'Annals' of Dionysius known to Assemani (*Bibl. Orient.*, II, 72–7), who had published an extract therefrom. Written after the manner of John of Asia, the work has a longer and a shorter redaction. It is divided into four parts. The first covers the period from the Creation to Constantine and is based on Eusebius, Julius Africanus, the anonymous *Chronicon Edessenum*, the Syriac *Treasure Cave* (German tr. Bezold, *Die Schatzhöhle*, 1883), the *Seven Sleepers* (Guidi, *Testi orientali ined. sopra i Sette Dormienti di Efeso*, R. Acad. dei Lincei, Atti, s. 3, vol. 12, 1884), and Josephus' *Jewish Wars*. The second part, from Constantine to Theodosius II, follows Socrates' *Ecclesiastical History*. The third, from Theodosius II to Justin II, follows John of Asia and incorporates Joshua the Stylite and the Epistle of Bēth Arṣhām on the Ḥimyarite Christians. The fourth part, to 158 A.H./774–5 A.D., is his own from documents, oral reports, and eyewitnesses. Assemani, *Bibl. Orient.*, II, 98–116, sums up the work with an excerpt from the last part known to be in the Vatican.

[2] Baumstark, pp. 281–2; Chabot, pp. 95–6; Wright, pp. 207–11; Duval, pp. 391–2.

enjoyed a fair measure of freedom of thought and action under the early Abbasid caliphs and the Jacobite patriarch became a frequent visitor to the court, though the maphrian of Tekrit took care of the Jacobites of that part of Mesopotamia and the further Middle East. But only the Nestorian patriarch, or catholicos (the Arabic Jat͟hlīq), was allowed to reside in Bag͟hdad. The Christians also handled much of the mercantile activities in the Arab empire, and this increased the wealth of their community and had great effect on the church as well as the monastic foundations with their schools and libraries.

Age of Decline

The clement tolerance of Arab rule did not last forever. Two main circumstances contributed to the imminent change in their dealings with the Christian communities in their dominions. First, the continuous growth in the education of the Muslim rendered the caliphate less and less dependent on Christian functionaries. Thus we find increasing instances of wholesale Christian dismissals from office by the caliphs and sultans, sometimes with and often without any conceivable pretext beyond religion. Secondly, the decline of the pure Arab and the steady weakness of the caliphate against the rise in influence of non-Arab elements became overpowering in the Islamic polity. The origins of this state of things may be traced back to the reign of Caliph al-Muʿtaṣim (833–42), Hārūn al-Ras͟hīd's son from a Turkish slave. In order to relieve himself of the influence of the Arab soldiers of K͟hurāsān to whom the Abbasids owed the caliphate, al-Muʿtaṣim founded a new bodyguard of four thousand Turks and Turcomans from Central Asia. The caliph miscalculated the outcome of his decision. Even in his own lifetime they became so aggressive in the capital that he found it necessary to remove the seat of government north to Samarra,[1] on the Tigris. In the following century their influence kept growing until they literally seized most of the power and wrested the title of sultan from the caliphs, who became figureheads by the end of the eleventh century. Like the Barbarians before the fall of the Roman empire, they barbarized the caliphate with their ignorance and bigotry. Their treatment of the Christians and their behaviour in the holy places helped to precipitate the Crusades. They formed their own dynasties, of which the Saljūq was the most redoubtable, and their unbridled oppression directly affected the life of the Jacobite church in upper

[1] This is an old Assyrian name which was transformed in Arabic to *Surra man raʾa*, that is, 'Pleased is he who sees it'. The contemporary twisted the sense by diverting the pleasure to him who sees Bag͟hdad well rid of the Turks (Hitti, *Arabs*, p. 466).

Mesopotamia. Legal restrictions, overlooked in the early centuries, were frequently enforced from the tenth century onwards.[1] In reality, the tenth, eleventh and twelfth centuries might aptly be described as the age of decline of Syrian Christianity and the fall of Syriac literature.

We look in vain for a great name in the Jacobite church during the tenth century. A certain John son of Maron (d. 1003), a monk of the convent of Gubos near Melitene (Malaṭiya), described as an 'ocean of wisdom', compares badly with the older masters of Syriac learning. He wrote an unimportant treatise on Solomon's Proverbs, and his real contribution was more as a copyist than an author. Still more insignificant and pitiful was the story of Mark bar Kiki, who was elevated to the maphrianate of Tekrit under the name of Ignatius in 991. His diocesans drove him out of that dignity owing to his abusive character, and he apostatized to Islam in 1016. Later, however, he recanted and wrote a poem in debased Syriac on his downfall.[2] Nor did the eleventh century yield any great names. The historians of Syriac literature quote two modest names – Yeshūʿ bar Shūshān (or Jesus bar Susanna) and Ignatius, monk of the convent of Mar Aaron. The first became patriarch in 1058 under the name of John X, was forced to abdicate in the interest of a rival in 1064, but he was re-elected in the same year. He died at Amid in 1072 after a troubled reign which was symptomatic of the times. He engaged himself in a discussion with the Armenians over the use of yeast, oil and salt in the bread prepared for holy communion, wrote some liturgical texts and composed four Syriac poems on the pillage of Melitene by the Turks. Ignatius became bishop of Melitene in 1061 and died in 1095 after writing an obscure chronicle based on Jacob of Edessa and Dionysius of Tellmahrē (known only to Michael the Syrian). One year after his death the city was sacked by the Turks, and his successor, Bishop John (original name, Saʿid bar Ṣabḥūni), was massacred along with other Jacobites.[3]

The sterility of the Jacobite church and of Jacobite Syriac literature continued until the middle of the twelfth century, when suddenly a revival took place with the appearance of three names of universal fame, indeed the last great names to be encountered in their annals. These were Dionysius Bar Ṣalībi, Michael the Syrian and Gregorius Bar Hebræus – the most illustrious in later mediæval Jacobite history.

Dionysius bar Ṣalībi,[4] a native of Melitene, was enthroned as bishop of Marʿash (Germanicia), to which the Jacobite Patriarch Athanasius VIII annexed Mabbog in 1154. Then he was transferred in 1166 by Michael I to the

[1] See note from Browne (pp. 46–7) and al-Māwardi (*Les Statuts Gouvernmentaux*, tr. Fagnan) quoted on Nestorians.

[2] Chabot, p. 115; Baumstark, p. 291; Wright, pp. 222–5; Duval, pp. 396–7.

[3] Baumstark, pp. 291–3; Chabot, pp. 120–1; Wright, pp. 225–7; Duval, pp. 396–7.

[4] His original name was George Bar Ṣalībi, and the new name of Dionysius was given to him when he became bishop.

more substantial diocese of Amid (Diyarbekr), where he remained until his decease in 1171. His works embrace a wide variety of subjects and he wrote at very great length. They include vast commentaries on the Old and New Testaments,[1] and others on the Centuries of Evagrius and on Fathers and Doctors of the church. He compiled a *Compendium of Theology*, wrote a treatise on the providence of God, and a multitude of tracts on the Nicene Creed, the Jacobite confession and many other topics. He left a copious treatise against heresies including the faiths of Muhammadans, Jews, Nestorians and Chalcedonian Diophysites. Apparently, he stabilized the Syriac liturgy with an interpretation, two more anaphoræ and several pre-anaphoral prayers, known as *sedras*. His homilies are quite numerous. In the field of philosophy he was chiefly occupied with a number of books from Aristotle. He composed several poems dealing with the Muslim capture of Edessa by Zangi in 1144, the fall of Marʿash to the Armenians (who seized him therewith as a prisoner of war) in 1156, and on the maphrian who fell and married a Muslim woman. He is said to have written a chronicle of his own times. No wonder he has been described as the star of the twelfth century in Jacobite history.[2]

His other remarkable contemporary was Michael the Syrian, surnamed the Great.[3] Born at Melitene in 1126, he embraced monasticism at an early age in the renowned convent of Barṣuamā in the neighbourhood of his native town. At the age of thirty he became an archimandrite. Then he resisted the temptation of preferment to the bishopric of Amid (Diyarbekr) in 1165 for fear of losing the solitude of contemplation and the freedom to follow his literary pursuits. But destiny had a heavier burden and a greater career in store for him. On the decease of the Jacobite Patriarch Athanasius VIII in the following year, Michael was elected to succeed him at the unusually early age of thirty-one. He remained at the helm until his death in 1199, during a period in which the Middle East was the scene of momentous events. It was the age of Saladin and the Third Crusade (1189–92). Michael appears to have been in amicable relationship with the Latin Kingdom of Jerusalem and the Crusaders; but, unlike the Armenians and the Maronites, he remained impervious to the hazards of proselytizing Rome and of submission to the papacy.

[1] Wright, pp. 246–7; Chabot, pp. 123–4. The order in the O.T. is: Pentateuch, Job, Joshua, Judges, Samuel and Kings, Psalms, Proverbs, Ecclesiastes, Song of Songs, Isaiah, Jeremiah and Lamentations, Ezekiel, Daniel, the Twelve Minor Prophets, and Ecclesiasticus. The order of the N.T. is thus: the four Gospels, St John's Revelation, Acts of the Apostles, the seven Apostolic Epistles, and St Paul's fourteen Epistles. The O.T. books usually have two commentaries: the one material or corporal, and the other spiritual or mystic, otherwise allegorical or symbolic.

[2] Baumstark, pp. 295–8; Wright, pp. 246–50; Chabot, pp. 123–5; Duval, pp. 399–400.

[3] Also known as Michael the Elder, son of the priest Elias, to distinguish him from his nephew Michael the Younger; Wright, p. 250, n. 3.

The patriarch's life had, however, been embittered by the treacherous behaviour of his own disciple Theodore bar Wahbūn[1] in regard to the relations between the Jacobite and Byzantine churches. In 1170 the Emperor Manuel despatched a certain Theorianus with special letters to the Armenian catholicos and the Jacobite patriarch for the reunion of the Eastern churches with Constantinople. Michael objected to granting audience to the imperial emissary and sent John of Kaisun to confer with him in a preliminary way at Qal'at al-Rūm in Cilicia. Apparently it was agreed to hold a conference[2] in which the representatives of the churches might have the opportunity to discuss the problems at issue, and Michael appointed Theodore as the Jacobite delegate. Later, Theodore accused the patriarch of Chalcedonian leanings and ultimately got himself elected anti-patriarch at Amid (Diyarbekr) in 1180. Michael, who happened to be in Antioch at the time, acted swiftly by seizing his opponent, whom he deposed and imprisoned at the convent of Barṣaumā. Theodore managed to flee to Damascus in the hope of placing the case before Saladin. Doubting the sultan's reactions, he decided to change his course to Cilicia, where he joined the Armenian catholicos Gregorios Degha and King Leo, who reinstated him as patriarch of the Jacobites within their realm. Michael's tribulations came to an end only with the death of Bar Wahbūn in 1193. Michael was indeed a fine scholar and a great linguist. He was conversant with Greek, Armenian and Arabic in addition to his own native Syriac. On the authority of Bar Hebræus, he wrote his case against his adversaries in the Arabic tongue.

In spite of all those vexatious occurrences and the weight of his patriarchal duties, Michael must have laboured day and night in writing the admirable works he left to the church.[3] His most valuable and most formidable literary contribution is, of course, his *Chronicle*, long famous in Europe through an abridged Armenian version[4] until the discovery of the complete Syriac text, now in print with a French rendering.[5] The *Chronicle* begins with the Creation and ends with the year 1195. Approximately half of his material was compiled from sources and documents mostly lost. The author cites many

[1] Baumstark, pp. 300–1; Chabot, pp. 127–8; Wright, pp. 253–4; Duval, p. 401.

[2] The Greek Acts of this Conference have been found and published in Migne, *P.G.*, CXXXIII; cf. Chabot, p. 128.

[3] According to the testimony of Bar Hebræus; cf. Chabot, p. 125.

[4] The Armenian version, begun by the Vartabed David, was completed by the priest Isaac in 1248. Sections of it were published by Delaurier in *Journal Asiatique* (1848), pp. 281 et seq., and (1849), pp. 315 et seq. Afterwards the whole translation was made by V. Langlois, *Chronique de Michel le Syrien* (Paris, 1868). Michael's works were popular in Armenia from an early date, and a third person, the Vartabed Vartan, attempted to translate the rest of his works into Armenian. Cf. Wright, p. 252.

[5] The unique Syriac text, dated 1598, was discovered by Mgr. Raḥmāni at Urfa (Edessa). Edited with a French tr. by J. B. Chabot, *Chronique de Michel le Syrien, Patriarche Jacobite d'Antioche*, 1166–99, 4 vols. (Paris, 1899–1925).

of those sources both in his preface and in the course of his text.[1] He intended to follow the example of Eusebius in the original plan of the book by dividing his material into three categories: sacerdotal, temporal and miscellaneous – each in a special column from right to left. But he had to discard that system at a later date in favour of a unique and continuous text where his Syrian and ecclesiastical interests were apparent. In using the sources, his primary task was one of co-ordination rather than critical selection. But he undoubtedly succeeded in handling the material at his disposal with integrity, though it would be unfair to expect of him the critical method of another age. The work ends with a number of appendices[2] in which Michael compiled data pertaining to the Eastern churches and extensive lists of the Jacobite patriarchs, including a note on each of them since Severus of Antioch (512), as well as the bishops consecrated by them since Kyriakos (792).

Apart from the *Chronicle*, Michael wrote numerous other books, mainly of an ecclesiastical character. He prepared a liturgy in which prayers were arranged in alphabetical order, and he revised the Pontifical and ritual of ordinations. He also brought together the scattered and disjointed accounts of the life of Mar Abhai, a legendary fourth-century Nicæan bishop, and re-edited the whole in consecutive form. His aim was probably the defence of the cult of sacred relics. It must be remembered that Michael remained an inveterate enemy of iconoclasm and extolled the reverence of Christians towards icons and relics alike. In common with most notable Jacobite writers, he also left several prayers, (or *sedras*), of which some appear under his name in prayer-books. Among his homilies, one is devoted to John of Mardin and another to St Barṣaumā. He refers in his *Chronicle* to other works, including a *Profession of the Faith* addressed to Emperor Manuel, a *Refutation of the Errors of Mark ibn Qunbar* (a schismatic Coptic priest who is presumed to have fallen under the spell of the Msallian movement). He also wrote a treatise against the Albigenses on the occasion of an invitation to the third Lateran Council held in 1179, as well as a panegyric of Dionysius bar Salībi, and a poem on the constancy of a Christian young woman whom the Muslims failed to convert to their religion.[3]

[1] In the first six books, Michael relied on Eusebius for history from the Creation to Constantine. Then he used Socrates and Theodoret for the years 325–431 A.D., Zaccharias Rhetor for 431–505, Cyrus of Batna for 565–82, John of Asia for 325–582, Jacob of Edessa and John of Litharba for 325–726, Dionysius of Tellmahrē for 582–842, Ignatius of Melitene for 325–1118, Basil of Edessa for 1118–43, and finally John of Kaisūn and Dionysius Bar Ṣalībi for his contemporary history. The whole work comprises thirty-one books divided into many chapters.

[2] A total of six appendices (*Chronique*, IV, 427–524). The episcopal lists contain 950 names, mostly unknown (Chabot, *Litt. Syr.*, pp. 126–7). These lists have been used extensively by Honigmann in his two books (*Évêques et Évêchés Monophysites* and *Couvent de Barṣaumā*.

[3] Chabot, *Litt. Syr.*, p. 127.

As a historian Michael had a thirteenth-century successor who continued his good work. The unique manuscript of that valuable continuation, found in private hands at Constantinople, happened to be a mutilated fourteenth-century copy of a lost original reaching back to 1234. The author was probably a monk of the convent of Barṣaumā, still the seat of the Jacobite patriarchate at that date. He planned his chronicle in two separate sections both as a secular and as an ecclesiastical history.[1]

With the coming of the thirteenth century, it will be noted, the process of Arabicizing the Jacobite people had made such progress that only few felt the need or urge to use Syriac any more as a vehicle for literary writing. Arabic, hitherto confined to official state proceedings, now made its incursions into the fields of the intellect and of literature. The last of the great Jacobite writers, Gregory Abul-Faraj, surnamed Bar Hebræus,[2] wrote both in Syriac and in Arabic with equal facility and felicity. His command of the Arabic tongue was at the opposite pole from his surprising ignorance of Greek.[3] In subsequent ages Syriac was restricted to its present function as the liturgical language of the Church, and its long-standing impact on creative thought faded away.

In conclusion, however, we must outline the life and work of Bar Hebræus, a great Jacobite churchman and the last entitled to claim a lofty place in Syriac science and letters. Born of Jewish ancestry in 1226 at Melitene (Malaṭiya), he died at Marāg͟hah in Azerbaijān in the summer of 1286. As a youth he must have witnessed the horrors of the invasions of Hulagu Khan's Mongol hordes, since his family fled from its native city in 1243, shortly after the fall of Melitene (Malaṭiya). They settled down at Antioch, still in the hands of the Franks during the Crusade period. It was there that he took holy orders and went to Tripoli to study philosophy and medicine. Then the Jacobite Patriarch Ignatius II consecrated him as bishop of Gubos (near his old home town Melitene) in 1246. He was only twenty years old. In the following year he was transferred to the adjoining see of Lacabane (Laqabhīn), also in the Malaṭiya district. In 1252, he became involved in one of the recurring Jacobite schisms: Ignatius II died in that year, and the patriarchate was claimed by two rivals – Dionysius (Aaron Anjur) and John bar Madani.[4] Bar Hebræus espoused the cause of the first, who transferred him to

[1] Chabot, *Litt. Syr.*, pp. 129–30. Both text and French translation of the *Chronique Anonyme de 1234* have been published by Chabot (Paris 1916–20).

[2] The Syriac *Bar ʿIbrāya* and Arabic *Ibn al-ʿIbri*, that is, 'son of the Hebrew', thus denoting his ancestry. His father, a certain Aaron, was a converted Jew who became established as a physician in Melitene.

[3] Wright, p. 266, says that Bar Hebræus devoted his boyhood to learning Greek and Arabic; but Chabot, *Litt. Syr.*, p. 133, rightly notes that all his references to the Greek authors were made second-hand because he did not know any Greek at all. It would appear that by that time, most of the Hellenic heritage had found its way into Arabic.

[4] Bar Madani was maphrian of Tekrit. Owing to his unattractive personality, he was

the diocese of Aleppo in the hope that he might gain its congregation for his cause. But apparently their loyalty to Bar Madani was too great, and they drove Bar Hebræus out of their city, whereupon he retired to the convent of Barṣaumā near his chosen patriarch. Ultimately, however, he returned to Aleppo in 1258, where he stayed until the next patriarch, Ignatius III, elevated him to the maphrianate of the Orient in 1264. This he retained until his death in 1286. For the last twenty years of his life, he dedicated himself with unflinching assiduity to a double cause. In the first place, he committed himself not only to the service of his own community but also to all Christians, irrespective of their profession or their creed. In the second place, he devoted a great deal of his energy to the fulfilment of a literary and scientific project with few equivalents in the history of authorship. His decease was an occasion of public mourning, and we are told that even Greeks, Armenians and Nestorians marched side by side with the Jacobites at his funeral. His remains were later transferred to the monastery of Mar Mattai near Moṣul, where they rest to the present day.[1]

As to his literary output, even a brief survey would leave the mind wondering how a man could cover such a wide range in the span of threescore years of a troubled existence. Bar Hebræus was a man of many-sided interest and encyclopædic knowledge. Historian, Biblical exegete, theologian, canonical jurist, philosopher, grammarian, poet, man of letters and science, astronomer, physician and encyclopædist – he was a true forerunner of the *uomo universale* of the Renaissance. It may be hazardous to contend that he had his own system of philosophy based on the universality of knowledge and, like Ramon Lull and Roger Bacon in mediæval Europe, set himself the task of covering its first and last principles in Syriac and Arabic. But the proposition is nevertheless worthy of consideration.

In the world of scholarship Bar Hebræus' fame chiefly rests on his contribution to historical studies. He attempted the compilation of universal history in three chronicles: the *Chronicon syriacum*[2] and the *Chronicon ecclesiasticum*[3] written in Syriac, and what may be described as the *Chronicon arabicum*,

forced by the people of Moṣul to leave the city. He retired to Baghdad, where he was in favour with three Jacobite brothers, Shams-al-Daulah, Fakhr-al-Daulah and Tāj-al-Daulah, the sons of a certain Thomas – all physicians of influence at the court of Caliph al-Mustanṣir. He returned on his election to the patriarchate, but was never able to reign freely until the Anti-patriarch Dionysius was assassinated at the Convent of Barṣaumā in 1261. He died in 1263. Details of those scandalous events are given by Bar Hebræus; cf. R. Duval, op. cit., p. 407.

[1] Assemani, *Bibl. Orient.*, II, 244 et seq.; Duval, pp. 408–11; Wright, pp. 265–81; Baumstark, pp. 312–20; Chabot, *Litt. Syr.*, pp. 131–7.

[2] Inadequately edited with a Latin translation for the first time by P. J. Bruns and G. G. Kirsch, *Bar Hebræi Chron. Syr.*, 2 vols. (Leipzig, 1789). Syriac text more satisfactorily re-edited by P. Bedjan (Paris, 1890), but without translation.

[3] Edited with Latin translation and notes by J. B. Abbeloos and Th. J. Lamy, *Chron. eccles.*, 2 vols. in 3 (Louvain, 1872–7).

which he composed towards the end of his life in forceful Arabic style under the title *Epitome of the History of Dynasties*[1] (*Mukhtaṣar Tārīkh al-Duwal*). He must have availed himself of a multitude of Syriac, Arabic and Persian sources already assembled by his predecessor Michael the Great, to which he added many acquisitions. The author covered the whole history of mankind from the Creation, and, for all the early annals, he summed up Michael the Syrian's *Chronicle*. The secular history from the Creation to his day is somewhat general in character, and the ecclesiastical history from Aaron to the post-apostolic age is brief, but then it becomes the story of the patriarchate of Antioch up to Severus, being narrowed down to the Monophysite and Jacobite offshoot to the year 1285–86. It ends with an account of the maphrianate and maphrians of Tekrit, with careful notices on the Nestorian patriarchs.[2] The chronicle was continued to 1288 by his own brother Barṣauma, who had succeeded him as maphrian and who compiled a list of thirty monumental works bearing Bar Hebræus' name. An anonymous author of less distinction made a second continuation of the same chronicle to 1496. In the Arabic compendium Bar Hebræus enriched the work with additional data on Islamic dynasties in response to a request from his Muslim friends.[3]

As a Biblical exegete, he compiled a voluminous repertory of glosses and commentaries on the Scriptural texts of the Peshitta, Hexapla and Harklean versions with innumerable quotations from Athanasius, Basil, Gregory Nazianzen, Gregory of Nyssa, Hippolytus, Origen, Philoxenus, Severus of Antioch, Jacob of Edessa, Moses bar Kepha and Yeshudad of Marw the Nestorian. He used all those ecclesiastical sources in Syriac or Arabic, and his erudition was phenomenal. Owing to the decline in the knowledge of Syriac, he enriched the work with many remarks on Syriac grammar and lexicography together with the precise pronunciation of words and dialectic differences between Nestorian and Jacobite. He gave his study the title *Storehouse of Secrets*[4] (*Horreum mysteriorum*) which betrays, like most of the

[1] Arabic text without trans. ed. A. Ṣālḥāni (Beirūt, 1890). Earlier edn. with Latin tr. E. Pococke, *Historia compendiosa Dynastiarum* (Oxford, 1663). See also E. A. Wallis Budge, *The Chronography of Bar Hebræus*, 2 vols. (London, 1932).

[2] Chabot, *Litt. Syr.*, p. 132, states that for his material on the Nestorian patriarchs he used freely a work in Arabic by a twelfth-century Nestorian writer called Māri ibn Sulaimān. This work, *Kitab al-Majdal* (Book of the Tower), extant in two vols. in the Vatican collection, is often wrongly ascribed to ʿAmr ibn Matta of Ṭīrhān. The MS is a copy dated 1401 and is theological, dogmatical and historical; Wright, pp. 255–6.

[3] Bar Hebræus knew the older outstanding Arab historians such as al-Wāqidi (d. ca. 823), al-Balādhuri (d. 892), al-Ṭabari (d. 923), al-Masʿūdi (d. c. 956), al-Kindi (d. 961), al-Quḍāʿi (d. 1062), and probably ibn al-Athīr (d. 1234) who had written in the early decades of the same century.

[4] Preface of work published by Cardinal Wieseman (Rome, 1828), and numerous sections produced as doctoral theses in Germany; see lists in Baumstark, pp. 314–15. Definitive ed. and English tr. by M. Sprengling and W. S. Graham, *Bar Hebræus Scholia on the Old Testament* (Chicago, 1931), based mainly on the oldest text in Florence dated 1278. Cf. Chabot, *Litt. Syr.*, pp. 133–4.

titles of his other books, the influence of the system of Arab authors.[1] He dealt with Monophysite theology at great length in two other books: *Lamp of the Sanctuary* and *Book of Rays*;[2] the latter summing up the basic arguments for popular use. His *Book of the Dove*[3] is an ascetical work intended for the guidance of monks and recluses and is based on his own experience, which he detailed in an autobiography at the end.

Canon law claimed his attention, too, since the church under the caliphate handled the affairs of its own members. Hence the bishops were the sole judges of their congregations in all ecclesiastical matters and to a great extent in cases of civil law. He thus compiled what was invaluable to the clergy – the *Book of Directions*, commonly called *Nomcanon*, which comprised a practical guide for all manner of legal usage.[4]

In the field of philosophy he read the Arabs voraciously and translated into Syriac numerous philosophical treatises, including ibn Sīna's (Avicenna) *Book of Directions and Notifications*.[5] On logic and dialectics, Bar Hebræus wrote a *Book of the Pupils of Eyes*. His compendium entitled, *Book of Speech and Wisdom* is a survey of dialectics, physics and metaphysics (which stands for theology). He confided the completest Syriac Aristotelian discipline to a monumental encyclopædic work called the *Cream of Science*,[6] in which he presented the sum of knowledge from Arab sources in three large parts. The first contained a study of logic, dialectic, rhetoric, art and poetry and all allied subjects. The second dealt with physics, the sky and the universe, meteors, generation and corruption, minerals, plants, animals, and the soul. The third is subdivided into one section devoted to metaphysics (or theology) according to Syrians and another comprising ethics, economic and political sciences. Owing to the vast nature of the work, he composed an abridgement of it called *Trade of Trades* (*Mercatura mercaturarum*).

His knowledge of mathematics and astronomy must have been very considerable. He lectured on Euclid at the school of the Marāghah Convent in 1272. He drew up the *Zīj*, or astronomical tables, much used by the Arabs. Then he wrote his definitive treatise on astronomy and cosmography under the title *Ascent of the Mind*,[7] which he adorned with mathematical figures and numerous illustrations.

[1] The Arabic system of using flowery rhymed titles without denoting the nature of the contents. Another influence of Arabic is the use of the lengthy gloss (*Ar. Ḥāshiya, pl. Ḥawāshi*) so common in Qur'ānic commentaries and jurisprudence (*Fiqh*).

[2] Chabot, *Litt. Syr.*, 134.

[3] *Le Livre de la Colombe*, ed. P. Bedjan (Paris, 1898); English tr. A. J. Wensinck, *Book of the Dove* (Leiden, 1919); cf. Chabot, op. cit., p. 135.

[4] Chabot, *Litt. Syr.*, p. 134; Wright, pp. 276–8.

[5] *Kitāb al-Ishārāt wal-Tanbīhāt*; Wright, p. 270. See also A. Baumstark, *Geschichte der Syrischen Literatur* (Bonn, 1922), p. 317.

[6] Chabot, op. cit., p. 135; Wright, pp. 269–70.

[7] Pub. by F. Nau, *Livre de l'ascension de l'esprit* (Paris, 1899); cf. Chabot, op. cit., pp.

We must, however, remember that the original vocation of Bar Hebræus was medicine, which he apparently continued to practice even as a prelate. He tells us in his ecclesiastical history that he treated in 1263 the Tartar 'King of Kings'. He wrote and translated into Syriac and Arabic many books on medicine and *materia medica*. Into Syriac, too, he made an abridged rendering of Dioscorides' famous treatise *De medicamentis simplicibus*. He summarized in the same language al-Ghāfiqi's Arabic *Book of Simples* (*Kitāb al-Adwiyah al-Mufīdah*). He commented in Arabic on Galen's *De elementis* and *De temperamentis* as well as Hippocrates' *Aphorisms*. He also published a Syriac abridgement and commentary on Ḥunayn ibn Isḥāq's Arabic *Questiones medicæ*. He translated into his native tongue most of ibn Sīna's *al-Qānūm fi al-Tibb* and wrote a comprehensive medical treatise without a special title, also in Syriac.[1]

As a grammarian, his works have long served many generations of Orientalists in the study of the Syriac Language. The most elaborate of his grammatical compendia, entitled *Book of Splendours*, was compiled on the model of extensive Arabic[2] works in the field; and he made a rhymed synopsis of it, possibly in imitation of the famous Arabic *Alfiyat ibn Mālik*. His poetry, too, has attracted much attention for centuries. The *Carmina de divina sapientia* was edited with a Latin rendering as early as the seventeenth century.[3] He tried his pen at all manner of projects, such as the *Interpretation of Dreams* which he composed in his youth and a collection of tales of wit and wisdom.[4] All this together with a complete liturgy and a Profession of the Faith[5] among the long list of his works were accomplished in times of political, ecclesiastical and international unsettlement; and before the age of sixty, Bar Hebræus achieved a glorious finale to the long annals of Syriac letters and learning.

135–6. The work is divided in two books: one on heavenly bodies and another on earth and the relations between the heavenly and earthly bodies, astronomy and astrology being interwoven.

[1] Wright, pp. 271–3; Baumstark, p 318; H. F. Wüstenfeld, *Geschichte der arabischen Ärzte und Naturforscher* (Göttingen, 1840), pp. 145–6 (no. 240).

[2] Paulin Martin, *Œuvres grammaticales d'Abou'l-Faradj, dit Bar Hebreus* (Paris, 1872); Axel Moberg made a German version of the bigger grammar with critical notices (Leipzig, 1907; 1913); cf. Wright, p. 273, and Chabot, op. cit., p. 136. Apparently Bar Hebræus left a third grammar unfinished.

[3] By Gabriel Sionita, *De sapientia divina poēma ænigmaticum* (Paris, 1638); re-issued by Yoḥanna Noṭayn al-Darʿūni, *Carmen de divina sapientia* (Rome, 1880); cf. Chabot, p. 136, and Wright, p. 280.

[4] Published in Syriac and English by E. W. Wallis Budge, *Laughable Stories* (London, 1896); cf. Chabot, p. 136.

[5] Translated into Latin by E. Renaudot, *Liturgiarum orientalium collectio*, 2 vols. (Paris, 1716), II, 455 ff., Duval, p. 410.

Mongols, Turks and Kurds

In spite of elements of decline in so many aspects of Syrian life and literature, the Jacobite church must have continued to thrive under Arab rule sufficiently for its community to produce men like Michael the Syrian, Dionysius bar Ṣalībi, and Bar Hebræus. Indeed it is quite conceivable that the Jacobite church enjoyed one of its best periods of prosperity under Muslim rule towards the end of the twelfth and the beginning of the thirteenth centuries. On the authority of Bar Hebræus,[1] the august historian of that age, the Jacobite patriarchs then ruled over twenty metropolitans and about a hundred bishops in dioceses spread over Syria, Anatolia, upper Mesopotamia and other regions of the western parts of the Middle East, while the maphrianate of Tekrit included eighteen episcopal dioceses in lower Mesopotamia-Persia and lands eastwards. The Jacobites were gaining ground, and in, stances of peaceful conversion to their creed from amongst the Nestorians were not infrequent. On the whole they disliked violence and coerced neither Greek, Latin nor Muslim, though amongst themselves they did not lead a peaceful life. The patriarchal dignity was coveted by rival claimants, and this led to a succession of schisms, the practice of simony, and the bribing of caliphs and the Muslim administration in order to acquire their support for one party against another. Enlightened members such as Bar Hebræus preferred to keep out of these internecine contests for the patriarchate. This lamentable state worsened with the change of rulers and became scandalous under the Turkish sultans.

The real tribulations of the Jacobites began with the Mongol invasions[2] and their indiscriminate ravages in western Asia, of which Bar Hebræus, an eye-witness, gives a vivid picture in his chronicles. The early Mongols, however, favoured the Christians, and some of their great khans were almost Christian converts themselves. Hulagu, the conqueror of Baghdad, city of the caliphs, in 1258 and the founder of the Il-Khanate of Persia, had a Christian wife[3] and he is said to have professed Christianity, though there is no proof that he was baptized. In the sack of the city, where the slain were estimated at 800,000, the Christians survived safely within their own quarters. Further, Christians were allowed to rebuild their churches and practice their faith without restriction or humiliation in Baghdad and Damascus. Bar Hebræus lamented the death of Hulagu and his wife as if they were defenders of the faith. It would be an error to assume that the Christians did not

[1] *Hist. eccles.*, 460; cf. Fortescue, p. 331.

[2] L. E. Browne, *Eclipse of Christianity in Asia*, pp. 147–78; H. H. Howorth, *History of the Mongols*, 4 parts in 5 vols. (London, 1876–1927), III, 141, 154, 170, 247.

[3] Her name was Dukuz Khatun; Howorth, III, 164, 210; L. Cahun, *Introduction à l'histoire de l'Asie* (Paris, 1896), pp. 391 et seq.

suffer at all amidst the din and clamour of those barbarian invasions. The Jacobites who had been living with the rest of the population outside the capital in territories trodden by the Tartar hordes could not be singled out for special treatment. Consequently, they must have shared their compatriots' heavy loss of life and property in the course of the indiscriminate Mongol maraudings, irrespective of the tolerance of the great khan and his court.

The deliberate reversal of Mongol benevolent policy towards the Christians dates from the time of their conversion to Islam. The *History of Yahballaha* and the *Continuation of Bar Hebræus' Chronicle* give a true picture of that sorry chapter. The missionaries of both the East and the West failed to promote the cause of the Gospel at the Mongol court, and ultimately Ghāzān adopted the faith of Islam and made it the official religion of the state from 1295.[1] As a result, the Jacobites together with other Christian communities were subjected to systematic persecution throughout the fourteenth century. The advent of Timur Lane in 1394 meant national disaster for all. Districts pre-eminently Jacobite in character, such as Amid (Diyarbekr), Mardin, Moṣul, Ṭūr-ʿAbdīn and Tekrit, suffered unparallelled devastation at the hands of his hordes. Jacobites were hunted and massacred in al-Jazīrah and upper Mesopotamia. Those who escaped slaughter took refuge in the arid mountains until the storm subsided, only to return home to find their churches and monasteries levelled to the ground. It is to this period that we must date the disappearance of the majority of the hitherto flourishing monastic foundations of the Jacobites. Those ancient seats of light and learning were extinguished forever, and their priceless literary contents were set aflame. The maphrianate of Tekrit was vacant from 1379 to 1404.[2] The morale of the clergy was low, and the patriarchal dignity was coveted by rival parties of a poor quality, which resulted in disunity and frequent schisms. Deprived of strong leadership and beset by one enemy after another, the community dwindled and declined. At first, their civilization was all but wiped out by the Mongols and Timur Lane's hordes. Then the Turks followed, to stay for centuries – the Saljūqs, with their traditional intolerance intensified by the Crusades, were replaced by the Ottomans, who ruled, or rather misruled, loosely the remote *pashaliks* of their Asiatic empire from Istanbul on the European shores of the Bosphorus.

The main interest of the Sublime Porte lay in exacting as much money as possible from the Christian 'millets', and the sultan granted the usual firman or charter confirming a patriarchal election to the highest bidder. In turn Christian prelates resorted to simoniacal practices to fulfil their obligations towards their supporters. The Church became demoralized, and the spiritual

[1] Howorth, III, 384, 396, 427; L. Cahun. *Introduction*, p. 432.

[2] L. E. Browne, *Eclipse of Christianity in Asia*, p. 172.

and educational welfare of the community was no longer of any account. Like the Nestorians, the Jacobites were stricken with phenomenal ignorance and great poverty in modern times. Their ranks were steadily depleted until they numbered from 150,000 to 200,000 in the nineteenth century,[1] mainly in Kurdistan and upper Mesopotamia around Moṣul and in Syria at Ḥomṣ. On the whole, the Jacobites tried to preserve amicable relations with their Muslim neighbours and sought peaceful co-existence with the Kurds. Sir Mark Sykes,[2] who travelled in the area during the early years of this century, noted that it was difficult to distinguish the Jacobites from the Kurds at a first glance either in appearance or language. Though they did not suffer the same fate as the Armenians at the hands of the Ottoman Turks, or as the Nestorians in their strife with the Kurds, it may be assumed that the ugly wave of fanaticism which surged in those regions could not have left them unharmed. It is very difficult to assess with precision the relations between Jacobite, Turk and Kurd in modern times, though certain broad principles are sufficiently clear. In spite of the traditional bigotry of the Kurdish *mullah* and the Jacobite priest, as a general rule their communities appear to have been living together in relative harmony. Only when inflamed by the revival of the spirit of holy war, customarily fanned by the Turkish governors in an attempt to divide and rule, did these relations truly deteriorate. The Jacobites differed from their Armenian and Nestorian co-religionists. While steadfastly retaining their faith and loyalty to their church, the Jacobite people were never averse to social integration within the greater order of all citizens irrespective of religious difference. This normal behaviour, combined with religious tenacity, accounts for their survival in their traditional homeland, unlike the Armenians and the Nestorians, who were either exterminated or dispersed. Instances of Kurdish violence are not wanting. The bishop who accompanied the Rev. Horatio Southgate[3] to the library of the monastery

[1] Minority numbers are very controversial in the area. This estimate is based on O. H. Parry's report (*Six Months in a Syrian Monastery*, p. 346) published in 1895 and adopted by H. B. Tozer (*The Church and the Eastern Empire*, p. 80), F. J. Bliss (*Religions of Modern Syria and Palestine*, pp. 74–5) and B. J. Kidd (*Churches of Eastern Christendom*, p. 438). A. Diomedes Kyriakos, *Geschichte der orientalischen Kirchen von 1453–1898* (Leipzig, 1902), pp. 268–9, cites 50,000 families at the end of the sixteenth century, 30,000 families in the eighteenth, and about 200,000 souls in the nineteenth. Roman Catholic writers cherish a downward estimate. R. Janin, *Églises Orientales* (Paris, 1926), p. 469, mentions 120,000, and D. Attwater, *Christian Churches of the East*, Vol. II, p. 230, quotes 90,000 with 10,000 in Syria and Lebanon. Rondot's table in *Chrétiens d'Orient*, p. 224, provides the thinner total of 40,135, which is highly doubtful. P. Raphael, *The Role of the Maronites in the Return of the Oriental Churches* (Youngstown, Ohio, 1946), p. 99, puts them at 90,000.

[2] *The Caliphs' Last Heritage* (London, 1915), p. 354.

[3] *Narrative of a Visit to the Syrian (Jacobite) Church of Mesopotamia; with Statements and Reflections upon the Present State of Christianity in Turkey, and the Character and Prospects of the Eastern Churches* (New York, 1856), p. 225. The monastery is said to have been twice occupied by the Turks: once for forty years and again for ten; ibid., p. 197. Parry, *Six*

of al-Zaʿfarān in 1841 apologized for its depleted contents, as the Kurds had used most of the ancient codices as wadding for their guns during their last occupation of the establishment. In spite of this vandalism the monastery reverted to the Jacobites.

The modern history of the Jacobite church is very obscure compared with its ancient annals, in part owing to lack of education and national awareness. One of the first signs of awakening occurred in 1838 when the Jacobite patriarch was told by the Armenian patriarch in the course of a visit to Constantinople that people without schools must inevitably decline. The remark sank deep into his mind, and on his return he founded a modest school for twenty-five boys[1] at Deir al-Zaʿfarān. Syriac, Arabic and penmanship taught by defective clerics without text-books was their starting point. Though other schools followed in the remaining four or five Jacobite monasteries, the ecclesiastical impetus was found to lag behind the times by the laity who clamoured for wider reform and, in 1913–14, succeeded in obtaining a new constitution from the sultan whereby an administrative council, or secular assembly, participated with the hierarchy in the control of Church affairs.[2] The council stressed clerical education and the revival of Church discipline in accordance with ancient doctrine in order to arrest the rising tide of proselytizing by the more highly developed systems of Roman Catholic and Protestant missionaries from the West.

In 1920 the Jacobite patriarch deemed it safer to transplant his seat to Ḥomṣ (the ancient Emesa) in Syria as a result of the rising anti-Christian feeling incurred by the sanguine struggle between Kurd and Nestorian. From there he ruled and still rules over a total of sixteen metropolitan and episcopal dioceses. These include seven in South India, three in Syria, two in Iraq, two in Turkey, one in Egypt, and one in the United States of America jointly with Canada.

Missionary Movement

In their desperate struggle against ignorance and stagnation, the Jacobites began to look to the West for co-operative measures, and the coming of the missionary appeared at first to be a sure way of salvation – hence the early acquiescence of the church to the emergence of this new modernizing factor in the educational and spiritual life of the people. The Syrian missions came

Months, pp. 337–8, gives a short description of the contents of the library, with four MSS. dated tenth–eleventh century. Further notices by Ainsworth, II, 345, and Badger, I, 51.

[1] Southgate, p. 202.

[2] Janin, *Églises Orientales*, p. 461.

from three sources: Rome, America and England. All were no doubt well-meaning at the beginning and wished to render much-needed service. The Roman Catholics were the earliest on the scene, and they were followed by many Congregationalists and Presbyterians from the United States as well as more modest numbers from the Church of England. Let us deal briefly with each of the three movements to complete the picture of the modern history of this ancient church and its difficulties with its new helpers.

As has already been stated, the eastern Monophysites, though deploring the Chalcedonian profession of faith in the West, still continued to consider Rome as one of the three leading ancient Apostolic bishoprics with which they had much in common – the others being Alexandria and Antioch. In their days of depression, the eastern Christians were not averse to sending delegations for *rapprochement* with Rome. The earliest of these Syrian missions occurred in 1552 when Moses of Mardin went to Rome for an attempt at reconciliation with Pope Julius III.[1] But neither party seemed to take this approach seriously. Then around the middle of the seventeenth century, one Abdul-Ghal Akhijan of Mardin, a Jacobite, was converted to Catholicism by a Catholic missionary and fled to Lebanon, whence he was sent to the Maronite Seminary in Rome for instruction. Later, on the suggestion of the French Consul François Piquet at Aleppo, the Maronite patriarch consecrated him as Catholic Syrian bishop of Aleppo under the name Andrew in 1656. With the glamour of diplomatics behind him and with what he could offer in the progressive services of the West, as well as his convincing learning versus limited Jacobite aptitudes, he succeeded in building up a following. Then, when the Jacobite patriarch died at Mardin and rival parties contested succession, Piquet and another French diplomat named Baron worked hard to put Andrew in possession of the vacant throne. In the words of the historian of this curious chapter who quoted the official documents, the story reads: 'Spending very much money, he succeeded, due to the official intervention of France, to have the Sultan give in 1662, for the favour of Msgr. Andrew, an imperial commandment, the most ample they ever saw written with gold characters and another order to all the Pashas and Cadis to submit all the Syrian people under the above-said, Msgr. Andrew's jurisdiction, in the whole Empire.'[2] Pope Clement IX ratified the election and sent him the pallium in 1667. Thus was born the Catholic patriarchate of the Syrians, and the Jacobites faced a new crisis in their history. It is beyond the limitations of this work to follow the details of the ensuing struggle, at times both pathetic and even scandalous. But with lavish expenditure, magnificent

[1] Parry, p. 302; Etheridge, p. 149.

[2] P. Raphael, *Role of Maronites*, pp. 104–5; see p. 105, no. 1, for reference to unpublished material and dispatches from the diplomatic correspondence from Turkey in the Ministère des Affaires Étrangères in Paris (T. XXXVIII, f. 209).

churches in key towns such as Mosul, profound learning, well-knit propaganda, ecclesiastical discipline, and the benefits of higher education offered by St Joseph's University in Beirūt as well as seminary foundations, the Catholic Church was destined to stay amidst the Syrians and carve a considerable congregation from the body of the old Jacobite community. In recent years their number has ranged between 60,000 and 65,000.[1]

The Romanized Syrians are designated by the firm Jacobite Syrians as *Maghlūbīn*, Arabic for 'vanquished'. At first, the Catholics met with fierce opposition and were actually on the edge of extermination when, in 1783, Michael Jarweh, archbishop of Aleppo, turned Roman Catholic. He was followed by four Jacobite bishops: Abraham, Naʿmeh, Moses and George, who proclaimed him patriarch of Mardin, and Pope Pius VI hastened to his confirmation with the customary pallium in the same year. It happened that the old Jacobite patriarch had died at the time, and the Romanized Jarweh speedily moved to Mardin to seize the vacant see. But the Jacobite bishops had already elected another of their profession, and Jarweh was pursued in flight for his life, first to Baghdad and then to Lebanon, where he died a hunted refugee in a Maronite village in 1800.[2]

Nevertheless, the Catholic succession has been maintained to the present day, and the new line has comprised some notable Syrian scholars. Patriarch Ignatius Ephraem Raḥmāni (1898–1929)[3] was a man of learning who retained lively interest in Syriac letters and theology. During his tenure, he decided to transfer the Roman patriarchal residence to Beirūt amongst the more friendly Maronite co-religionists in order to escape from the hostility of the more numerous Jacobites and the interference of the Turkish authorities. His successor, Ignatius Gabriel Tappuni, was raised to the cardinalate in 1936, and for the first time in history a Syrian became one of the princes of Rome. With assiduousness and tenacity the Catholics instituted missionary organizations to labour amidst the Syrians. In 1882 they created the Missionaries of St Ephraem in Mardin, who dwindled away. The movement was reinvigorated in 1935 by means of the introduction of the Rule of St Benedict at the convent of Sharfeh, from where the Church conducted seminaries, schools, publishing and active propaganda without trespassing on parochial jurisdiction. The more opulent monastery of Mar Behnam, once a Jacobite foundation, has become a stronghold of Catholic influence in the midst of the

[1] Janin, *Églises Orientales*, p. 476, gives an estimate of about 65,000, of whom 6,800 are in the U.S.A. and 8,000 in Canada, South America, France and elsewhere. Attwater, I, 157, cites 60,000 in the patriarchal territory of Syria and Iraq, but in his general table he puts the Catholic Syrians of Syria, Iraq, and the U.S.A. at 74,500.

[2] P. Raphael, pp. 113–15; Attwater, I, 154.

[3] It is interesting to note that the Catholic patriarchs have adopted the name Ignatius, which the Jacobite patriarchs have consistently kept since the reign of Ignatius V (Bar Wahīb) of Mardin in 1292. Fortescue, p. 338.

important Jacobite centre of the Moṣul region. In Beirūt, too, Patriarch Raḥmāni started a convent of St Ephraem for Syrian nuns. The adoption of the Catholic profession was made a simple affair for the Syrians. Submission to Rome was the kernel of the problem. Even since the Council of Sharfeh in 1888, enforcing celibacy on the clergy, the door was kept open with special dispensation to any married Syrian priest (khūri) who wished to turn from the Jacobite to the Catholic rite. The ancient Liturgy of St James has been adopted by Rome for the Syrians in the same original Edessene dialect of Syriac, with minor alterations and interpolations to evade the open repudiation of Chalcedon and to affirm papal supremacy.[1]

The arrival of the Protestant missionary[2] on the scene in the Middle East during the nineteenth century was a different affair. From America the movement was inaugurated by a Congregational committee of the Board of Missions in 1819 at the Old South Church in Boston. Pliny Fisk and Levi Parsons were selected as the first emissaries for labouring in the Turkish Near East without a preconceived plan directed to any given Oriental Church, and it is doubtful whether the Americans had any clear idea about the intricacy of the network of ancient denominations in the East. The initial offering of $290·92, which has increased to a quarter-billion dollars in our day, helped to bring those two pioneers to Smyrna to explore the possibilities of service amidst the poverty-stricken and disease-ridden peoples under the Turkish yoke.[3] The field was found to abound in opportunities. Two others followed when the Rev. Isaac Bird and William Goodell arrived at Beirūt in 1823 to concentrate on Arabic-speaking Syria and Lebanon. The Rev. Justin Perkins was assigned to Persia and devoted himself to working with the Nestorians or East Syrian Christians. In 1836, the Rev. Horatio Southgate was commissioned by the Board to make a fuller investigation of further possibilities of missionary endeavour in Turkey, Persia, Syria and Egypt. His reports commended work amongst the Eastern Christians as a

[1] Janin, pp. 470–7; Parry, pp. 301–5; Raphael, pp. 110–23.

[2] On the American Protestant missionary in this area see: R. Anderson, *History of the American Board of Commission for Foreign Missions to the Oriental Churches* (Boston, 1872); J. Batal, *Assignment – Near East* (New York, 1950); A. J. Dain, *Mission Fields Today* (London, 1956); *Handbook on Foreign Missions of the United Presbyterian Church of North America* (published annually at Philadelphia); O. D. Morton, *Memoir of Rev. Levi Parson – First Missionary to Palestine from the United States* (Burlington, Vt., 1830); J. Richter, *History of Protestant Missions in the Near East* (New York, 1910); P. E. Shaw, *American Contacts with the Eastern Churches, 1820–70* (Chicago, 1937); P. Rondot, *Les Chrétiens d'Orient*, Cahiers de l'Afrique et de l'Asie, No. 4 (Paris, 1955); F. G. Smith, *Missionary Journeys through Bible Lands – Italy, Greece, Egypt, Palestine, Syria, Asia Minor and Other Countries* (Anderson, Ind., 1915). More detailed references may be found in *A Selected and Annotated Bibliography of North Africa and the Near East*, compiled K. E. Moyer (New York, 1957) from the contents of the Missionary Research Library at Union Theological Seminary in New York City.

[3] Shaw, *American Contacts*, pp. 71 et seq.; Batal, *Assignment*, pp. 17 et seq.

preliminary measure towards dealing with non-Christians. Accordingly, the Mission to the Near East came into existence in the following year, and the Rev. John J. Robertson was chosen for the Greeks in Constantinople and Southgate for the Jacobites in Mardin. Their instructions were explicit to keep the unity of the Eastern churches and avert the evils of schism, recognizing their Apostolic character without compromising Protestant principles. When Robertson withdrew to the United States for domestic reasons in 1842, Southgate succeeded him in Constantinople and ultimately became its first Episcopal bishop in 1844. Accordingly, he was diverted from the Jacobites by the work amongst the Armenians in Anatolia; and although he maintained friendly relations with the eastern patriarchs, the nominees of the Board started proselytizing native Christians against his will and the spirit of their original instructions. This led to trouble and the frequent withdrawal of missionaries from the field, ending with the resignation of Southgate himself in 1850.[1]

The failure of Southgate's mission in the capital did not stop missionary expansion from Beirūt, where the Syrian Protestant College was founded in 1866. The main legacy of the Protestant missionary in the Middle East was in the field of education, and we find the mission centres multiplying in Syria side by side with schools. Thus the Protestant Evangelical Church continued to make gains amongst the Syrians and from all the ancient churches, Jacobite and otherwise. On the whole, it was impossible for the American missionary to value the nature and traditions of those churches, which he regarded as mere fossils without hope of revival. To him Church history began with Martin Luther, and many Syrians found in this modern organization a safe shelter from Roman Catholic encroachments. Thus the number of Protestant congregations in greater Syria, comprising Transjordan, Lebanon and Palestine, reached in the end 74,700, almost exclusively drawn from the ancient churches including the Jacobite community.

From the Church of England more modest attempts were also forthcoming, but on a completely different principle. J. W. Etheridge[2] visited the Jacobites around 1840 and later published a lengthy account of the Syrian churches and their liturgies and literature. Then in 1842, G. P. Badger,[3] the representative of the archbishop of Canterbury's mission to the Assyrians or Nestorians, also examined the state of the Jacobite Church and gave an account of his enquiries. The most important of the reports on that Church, however, came towards the end of the century. A Syrian Patriarchate Education Society was founded in England, and in 1892 it selected O. H. Parry,

[1] Shaw, pp. 62–9.

[2] *The Syrian Churches* (London, 1846), pp. 135 et seq., on the Jacobites.

[3] *The Nestorians and their Rituals, With the Narrative of a Mission to Mesopotamia and Coordistan in 1842–44*, 2 vols. (London, 1852). On the Jacobites see I, 44, 59–63, 71–2.

of Magdalen College in Oxford,[1] to travel to the Middle East on its behalf to examine the position of the Jacobite Church and to decide ways in which the English Church could help it. He was expected in particular to inspect the schools founded by the patriarch and to prescribe the means of promoting education among the Jacobites. The outcome of the six months he spent in a Syrian monastery was a masterly account of the first direct contact with the Jacobite people and their historic Church. His outward journey encompassed Aleppo, Urfa (Edessa), Diyarbekr, Mardin, Moṣul, and above all Dair al-Zaʿfarān, the historic seat of the Jacobite patriarchs. In the area of Ṭūr-ʿAbdīn, he noted that a village possessed an average of four books and that the need was pressing for educational help, which the Syrians sought from the West. This was the first element in any stable reform, which had to come from within the community itself. The Jacobite Syrians were a proud and patriotic people who had been crying for disinterested assistance in resisting the inroads made upon their Church, and it was the duty of the English Church to respond to their cry in the spirit of Christian charity without seeking converts of intercommunion. It is difficult to assess the concrete results of his enterprise. The material resources of the project in England were unequal to the goodwill of its mission.

The impact of the Protestant missionary movement in the Near East has meant essentially a remarkable awakening of the ancient churches. At the outset, the American missionary encountered no hostility from either the hierarchies or the communities of Eastern Christians, who witnessed with curiosity his new methods of worship and modern disciplines, as well as the opportunities of admirable service in the educational, medical and social fields. He was also regarded as a new ally and a true helper against the growing menace of Roman inroads. The Jacobites had already been in open warfare with the Catholics at home and entertained visions of aid and solace from the Protestant newcomer. Instead, bitter disillusionment ensued as the Protestant missionary began to change his attitude towards those venerable organizations of which he had no real understanding and which he considered to be beyond reform. Thus he embarked on forming his own Protestant Evangelical Church and took to proselytizing members of ancient congregations with lamentable consequences. The Jacobites, who sought education without the peril of divorce from their traditional churches, accordingly welcomed the disinterested tone of the English missionary. Soon afterwards, in 1874, the Jacobite patriarch Peter III visited England by special invitation from Dr Tait, archbishop of Canterbury, and was honourably received by Queen Victoria.[2] Oswald H. Parry's associations with those friendly Christians together with his six months stay[3] at the monastery of al-Zaʿfarān in the

[1] *Six Months in a Syrian Monastery.*

[2] Ibid., p. 351. [3] Ibid., p. 105.

summer of 1892 gave him an insight into their real needs and turned him against the Protestant activities of his day.[1] His enlightened remarks about the Christian religious tangle in the Middle East at the turn of the century have since been justified. On the other hand, the Protestant challenge gave the hierarchy of the old church a rude awakening to rekindle the flickering flame of a glorious past.

[1] *Six Months in a Syrian Monastery*, p. 309, deprecates the Americans who 'pursue a wrong policy'. Parry, p. 310, gives them credit, for 'the education which they give is the best in Turkey'. With all his understanding, however, Parry (p. 312), stumbles over Chalcedon and cannot see his way to intercommunion with an excommunicated church, although the Bishop of Durham, B. F. Westcott, who introduced the book, notes (p. vii) in speaking of both Jacobites and Nestorians that 'the accusation rests on the misunderstanding of technical terms, and can be cleared away by mutual explanations'.

12 • FAITH AND CULTURE

The Hierarchy

The organization of the hierarchy of the Jacobite Church is elaborate, closely knit together, and has some unique features arising from its peculiar circumstances in history. It comprises both the monastic and secular types of priesthood. The highest authority and head of the church is the patriarch. His official title is 'His Holiness Mar Ignatius . . . Exalted Patriarch of the Apostolic See of Antioch and of all the Jacobite Churches of Syria and in the East.'[1] The title 'Ignatius' has been adopted since 1293, when Bar Wahīb for the first time took the name of Ignatius, the great bishop of Antioch martyred at Rome about 107 A.D. The patriarch is elected by the synod including the maphrian and all the bishops in consultation with the leaders of the Jacobite people. He resides at Ḥomṣ in Syria, previously having lived for some centuries at the monastery of al-Zaʿfarān, near Mardin in Turkish territory. His election was always confirmed by a special firman from the Sublime Porte giving him vast ecclesiastical and civil powers in conducting the affairs of the Jacobite community or 'Millet'. After his consecration, he could be deposed only for heresy or by a unanimous vote of the nation. As a rule, the synod submitted two names to the sultan for him to choose one, and this enabled the Turkish administration to bargain with the highest bidder. The candidate had to be a monk of lifelong celibacy, learning and sanctity. Since the ancient discipline prohibited, as in the Coptic Church, the translation of bishops from one see to another, it became the rule that a bishop could not be elevated to the patriarchal throne. Of course, a number of isolated cases of episcopal preferment to the patriarchate can be found in mediæval times, but these are rare. Perhaps the first instance of that kind on record was that of the Patriarch Severus bar Maske, who had been bishop of Amida in 977. Again Athanasius VI, formerly bishop of Arishmitat (Arsamosata), was elected in

[1] According to Parry (p. 314), who states that sometimes he has been called 'Papa Orientis' and 'Patriarcha theopolis Antiochiæ totiusque Orientis'. Etherdige (pp. 147–8) puts him as 'Patriarch of Antioch, the City of God and of the Whole East', and says that he is described as 'Abo Darishonee', that is, 'Father of the Chiefs'.

1058, but his election caused a schism within the Church. In 1222, Ignatius David was advanced from the maphrianate to the patriarchate, thereby setting a new pattern for a few generations.[1] Though there is no ancient Syrian canon prohibiting this practice, it has never been firmly accepted. In fact, it has been described as a form of ecclesiastical bigamy and the equivalent of re-baptism, since the candidate was bound to undergo a second consecration and assume a new name. Jacobite patriarchs, on the whole, have been men of integrity and steadfast in the faith, though exceptions occur in their crowded annals. Within living memory, the career of Patriarch Ignatius ʿAbdallah Saṭṭūf presents an image of instability and vacillation. Formerly bishop of Ḥomṣ and Ḥamā under the name of Gregory, he later assumed the metropolitan see of Diyarbekr as a Jacobite prelate. He visited England and South India, where he fell under the spell of Protestant ideas and revolted against ikons upon his return to Syria. Curiously, however, he bewildered everyone by a sudden decision in 1896 to become a Uniate, a position he maintained for nine years. In the end, he recanted to the Jacobites, who promised him the patriarchal throne in 1906.[2] Since those days the Church has recovered its prestige only through the accession of other men of weight to the patriarchal dignity. The late Patriarch Mar Ignatius Ephraem I,[3] who resided at Ḥomṣ, was an exemplary personality of considerable erudition and a credit to his venerable church.

Next to the patriarch is the maphrian,[4] a dignitary to be found only in the Jacobite church with the historic title 'Maphrian and Catholicos[5] of the East', signifying the position he once held as primate of lower Mesopotamia, Persia and the lands beyond. The first Jacobite metropolitan of Persia was Ahodame, formerly bishop of the Arabs, whom Jacob Baradæus consecrated during his eastern visitation in 559. The seat of the maphriantate was fixed at Tekrit in 628 with the ordination of Marutha, the great Syrian scholar, as maphrian by Patriarch Athanasius I. Under him the eastern province grew to great strength with 15 bishoprics covering Arabia, lower Mesopotamia, Persia and Afghānistan. The maphrian was possessed of all patriarchal prerogative in the East. He ordained and deposed bishops, consecrated the chrism, and discharged all pontifical functions independently in the same areas within his jurisdiction. A bishop of bishops, or *pater patrum*, the maphrian in modern times became a titular and honorary dignity usually conferred upon the metropolitan of Jerusalem. Since the death of Behnam IV, the eighty-first maphrian, in 1895,

[1] Fortescue, p. 337; Parry, p. 316.

[2] Fortescue, pp. 338–9; Attwater, II, 228.

[3] His additional notes to al-Shābushti's famous work *Kitāb al-Diyārāt* are valuable.

[4] *Maphriono*, or *Maphryānā*, sometimes considered a corruption of *Malphono*, that is, doctor; more correctly it is derived from *aphri*, a word designating fruitfulness or paternity. Etheridge, p. 148; Fortescue, p. 340.

[5] For which we have the arabicized form *Jaṯhlīq* common in Arabic chronicles.

the title has remained in abeyance.[1] One of its most notable mediæval holders was, of course, Bar Hebræus (1264–86), who expressed no desire for preferment to the patriarchal throne.

From monastic ranks, too, are drawn the heads of metropolitan dioceses, sixteen archbishops (*Muṭrans*) distributed in the following manner: seven in India, three in Syria, two in Iraq, two in Turkey, one in Egypt and one in the United States of America and Canada.[2] They have no suffragans and are usually consecrated by the patriarch with the assistance and in the presence of at least two or three bishops. Apparently the new name or title they receive on ordination has been permanently fixed by the diocese. Hence Antioch, the patriarchal province, carries Ignatius; Jerusalem, Gregorius; Urfa (Edessa), Severus; Diyarbekr (Amida), Timotheus; Mardin, Athanasius; Moṣul, Basileus; and Aleppo, Dionysius.[3] Abbots of monasteries bear the title of bishop, though Mar Mattai at Moṣul is cited as archbishop. The Jacobites have five monasteries,[4] but evidently no nunneries. Thirty-five years is the minimum canonical age for episcopal consecration, although there are exceptions such as the case of Bar Hebræus, who became bishop at twenty.

Secular priests, living with the congregations in villages, are married only once before ordination. If any of them loses his wife, he retires automatically to a monastery and becomes eligible to the rank of bishop to enable him to continue living in his original parish, but cannot advance further. A head priest in a large town with several assistant priests may be elevated to the dignity of *chor-episcopos* with responsibilities, both civil and ecclesiastical, of a regular bishop. Under the Ottomans, priests were exempt from certain taxes and services. Hence the priesthood was sought after, and many more were ordained than were needed by parishes. A Jacobite priest as a rule is poor and has to supplement his meagre stipend by working with others in the fields. The congregation of the parish elects its own priests from the multitude of deacons in the area, and the bishops ordained the priests by the laying on of hands. Members of the clergy shave their heads and grow beards. They wear a black cloak and a black turban. Distinction of higher ranks is indicated by the onion-shaped, domelike turban.

The minor orders comprise the singer (*mazmorano*), reader (*kurayo*), subdeacon (*phleguth-mashamshono*), deacon (*mashamshono*), and archdeacon (*rish-mashmashonee*).[5]

The order of deaconesses, though known to have existed in the early

[1] Severius Jacob, Syrian metropolitan of Beirūt and Damascus, 'The Syrian Church Yesterday and Today', in *Orthodoxy*, VI (1954), 228.

[2] List provided in *Orthodoxy*, VI (1954), under 'Our Eastern Brothers'.

[3] Cf. Parry, pp. 321–2.

[4] Parry, p. 323, lists five; Fortescue, p. 341, mentions the same number, but lists only four.

[5] Etheridge, p. 147.

centuries for assisting in the baptism of women, has long since disappeared with the adoption of the system of child baptism and confirmation.

Rites and Liturgy

The rites and liturgies of the Syrians are known for their great antiquity, since Antioch was one of the first places where organized Christian worship was instituted. It is here that one may legitimately trace the origins and parentage of Jacobite practices. The Syrian churches, in their appearance of austere simplicity, not only betray the poverty of the community but also the primitive nature of the place of worship in Christian antiquity. The Jacobites in the past, however, took to building their churches in accordance with the standard traditions of the East. They consisted mainly of a narthex, nave, chancel and sanctuary. The main entrance from the narthex customarily opened out to a courtyard, or atrium, where they were accustomed to officiate in times of excessive summer heat. Otherwise the congregation squatted on matting or stood for the service inside the nave with a special space reserved for women – benches being, of course, a relatively modern improvement. The chancel is a slightly elevated platform frequently surrounded by railings for the deacons and choir. A couple of lecterns stand on either side of the sanctuary door within the chancel for lesson readings. A wall, though usually without pictures, takes the place of the *iconostasis* between the chancel and a sanctuary which is again elevated by one or two more steps. It contains a central high altar and sometimes one, or even two side altars[1] for concelebration. Each altar has an apse, or niche, behind it and an open door leading to the chancel and nave, with a curtain to be drawn at certain moments during the liturgy, or even when there is no liturgy. The chief celebrant at the high altar leads the prayer while the others officiate silently. The altar is either of stone or a wooden construction with a board dedicated at its centre for the Eucharist that is surrounded by Gospels, crosses, candles and other utensils. Relics are kept in oblong cylinders entrusted to the deacons, who lock them safely inside the sanctuary enclosure. The vestments consist of the alb, amice, girdle, stole and chasuble. Priests wear a black skull cap, but bishops use an embroidered large hood (*masnefto*) and an omophorion (*badrashin*) hanging down front and back over the chasuble. Uniate bishops, of course, wear the Roman mitre and ring, both unknown to the Jacobites.[2]

The sacred liturgy of the Jacobites, or West Syrians is one of the oldest

[1] The Copts always have three, the Byzantines only one.

[2] Parry, p. 320; Fortescue, pp. 344–5; *Orthodoxy*, VI (1954), 232–45; Attwater, II, 231–2.

and richest in Christendom. They use essentially the Liturgy of St James[1] in the west Syriac dialect. Dionysius bar Ṣalībi,[2] the greatest of all Syrian liturgiologists of mediæval times, records a tradition that St James celebrated that liturgy for the first time in Jerusalem in conformity with the order which he had heard from the Lord himself. Although the historicity of the story is questionable, the liturgy appears to have been drawn up shortly after the Council of Nicæa[3] in 325 and definitely before Chalcedon in 451. It is possible that its roots are even deeper in antiquity and, at any rate, its main lines must have been laid down much earlier in the patristic age. The background of that liturgy may throw light on its history and development. Coming from Jerusalem to Antioch, it seems to have ousted the old Antiochene rite and was put into Greek and Syriac, both being used at first with little or no discrimination. Antioch, it must be remembered was the centre of that traditional tug-of-war between the forces of Hellenization inherited from the Seleucids on the one side and the native Syrian anti-Hellenism on the other. The first became identified in the Christian period with Byzantine orthodoxy, a kind of 'Cæsaro-papism', as against the growing nationalist Syrian or Semitic divergence destined to lead to the fifth-century Monophysite rupture with the Melkite, or royalist, party. This was reflected in the liturgical metamorphosis. Whereas the Hellenic party was thus steadily byzantinizing the liturgy, the Syrians spontaneously reacted by clinging more and more to the original pure Syriac of St James. In fact, the process of substituting the Greek Liturgy of St Basil for that of St James was complete in Antioch by the thirteenth century, while the Syrians adapted the text of St James to their Monophysite teachings and enriched it with a great many new Syriac anaphoras outside the old capital.[4]

Without going into the details of that great liturgy, it must be admitted that it has all the makings of the early traditions when paganism and Christianity still intermingled. Hence, there is first the Liturgy of the Catechumens, open to the unbaptized as well as those who received baptism. After the dismissal of the catechumens, the celebrant went on with the central liturgy of the Faithful (*Missa fidelium*), intended only for the baptized who could partake of the Eucharist. This contains the *Trisagion*, that is, 'Holy art Thou O Lord, Holy O Mighty, Holy O Immortal', together with the much contended

[1] Etheridge, pp. 188–91, enumerates forty-one Syriac liturgies; and Brightman, *Liturgies Eastern and Western* (Oxford, 1896), pp. lviii–lxiii, mentions sixty-four anaphoras; on Syrian Rite see pp. 4–110. Bishop Severius Jacob, op. cit., in *Orthodoxy*, loc. cit., gives a total of some eighty anaphoras. For Jacobite liturgies rendered into Latin, see Renaudot, *Liturgiarum orientalium collectio*, 2 vols. (Paris, 1716), II 45 ff.

[2] Cf. Fortescue, p. 346.

[3] Etheridge, p. 195, notes that the word 'consubstantial' was used for the first time at Nicæa, thus fixing its date as a starting point for the liturgy.

[4] Dom Gregory Dix, *The Shape of the Liturgy* (3rd impression, London, 1947), pp. 173–207, gives a scholarly exposition of the Syrian tradition.

Monophysite clause, 'Thou who wast crucified for us.'[1] Amongst his interesting Syrian experiences, the traveller Oswald Parry[2] recounts a curious ceremony which he witnessed in the course of the Liturgy of St James on Whit-Sunday. After the sermon, the deacons chanted and abruptly stopped, feigning slumber. Then each man tapped his neighbour on the shoulder as if to wake him, while the priest prayed and sprinkled water on the congregation with an olive branch. This was thrice repeated to signify the gift of the Holy Spirit, symbolized by water, to the sleeping members of Christ's church. The drama of the liturgy seemed very real to those ardent worshippers.

It is beyond our limitations to attempt a full appraisal of the impact of this forceful liturgy on other liturgies of a later date, both Eastern and Western. Nevertheless, an illustration of how far the Syrian influence must have travelled even in the West at an early date may be quoted from the use of the *Trisagion* in Gaul, probably from a Spanish source. Towards the beginning of the seventh century, in the lifetime of St Gaugericus, bishop of Cambrai, the Bobbio Missal plainly implies that this should be recited in the Gallican use with the Syrian Monophysite 'interpolation', 'Who wast crucified for us', to be followed by the threefold *Kyrie eleison* of the Syriac St James.[3]

The Jacobites keep the usual hours from matins to compline, which they describe as the 'protection prayer' (*suttara*) before retiring. Their calendar is based on the old Julian system[4] of reckoning, exactly like the Copts. Also like the Copts, they cross themselves from left to right. Their fasts include, in addition to Wednesdays and Fridays, five others: the 'great fast' of Lent lasts forty-nine days before Easter; the 'little fast' of Advent is forty days before Christmas; the Fast of Nineveh occupies three days from the Monday of the third week before Lent; the Fast of the Apostles totals fifty days after Pentecost; and the Fast of the Virgin Mary is observed for fifteen days from the beginning of August. They strictly enforce the Mosaic food ordinances, forbidding all animal food and its extracts.[5]

The Jacobites do not believe in the doctrine of purgatory, but they pray for the dead and say that the good souls are led by angels to paradise, whereas the souls of sinners are kept by demons until the day of judgment. They have no *filioque* in the Creed. Their agreement with the Copts on the sacraments is complete. They celebrate the eucharistic liturgy only on Sundays and feast days. They are very sparing in the use of icons. Arabic has made its incursions on the liturgy, which has become bilingual except in the Syriac-speaking villages.

[1] Parry, p. 339; Fortescue, p. 348.
[2] *Six Months*, p. 341.
[3] Dix, pp. 466–7.
[4] Except in America, where they have adopted the Western system for reasons of expediency.
[5] Parry, p. 345.

Art and Architecture

The thesis advanced by some scholars that a Jacobite Church has little or nothing of special interest to offer the archæologist[1] or the art historian is undoubtedly based on two false assumptions. The first is that the Jacobite church as an institution begins with Jacob Baradæus in the sixth century and has no roots further in the past, and the second is the imperfect view that the village chapels of the impoverished communities of northern Syria or upper Mesopotamia are the true representatives of the art and architecture of the Syrian Jacobites. This outlook, however, must be repudiated as unhistorical, since the Jacobites are known to be the descendents of the west Syrians whose ancient patriarchate predates Jacob Baradæus at Antioch with roots deep in the Apostolic age. The whole picture accordingly changes and it would therefore be erroneous to detach the Jacobites from their ancestral heritage in the general Syrian framework of the early Antiochene school. The fact that the West Syrian Church with its Monophysite nationalism was outlawed by the Greeks and gradually pushed back by Byzantine imperialism from the shores of the Levant into the mountainous region now known as Ṭūr-ʿAbdīn, should not mislead us into the belief that the Jacobites were a different race from the builders of the monumental Christian heritage of northern Syria in both the spiritual and material domains. Antioch was of course the area where the two schools of thought, Byzantine and Syriac, converged; and one has to be very careful in separating the output of two different viewpoints, both in theology and in art and architecture, both before and after Chalcedon. The theology of Severus of Antioch must be distinguished from Melkite ideas, just as we have to segregate the famous Byzantine mosaics of Antioch from the Syrian stone architecture which filled the countryside between the Mediterranean and the Euphrates with magnificent cities and structures. Indeed, whole cities of singular beauty spotted the North Syrian countryside, the work of the native Syrian master builders which vanished rapidly after the Arab conquest. Discarded by their early Christian inhabitants, they completely fell into ruin and were forgotten. It was not until the last few decades of our time that the attention of the archæologist was drawn to these relinquished areas, and their discovery has been one of the most remarkable events in the history of early Christian architecture.[2] They

[1] See, for example, Fortescue, p. 344.

[2] The father of archæological work in this area is the Marquis Melchior de Vogüé, whose activities there date as far back as 1862. His splendid work *Syrie Centrale: Architecture civile et religieuse du Ier au VIIe siècle*, 2 vols. (Paris, 1865–77), is monumental and still a fundamental reference, especially as some of the structures recorded therein have already disappeared. The archæological work was resumed in expeditions from Princeton, where several relevant publications have appeared by H. C. Butler: (1) *Publications of*

have come to be known as the 'dead cities' of northern Syria. Dispersed in the plains extending east from Antioch towards Edessa and north to the Syrian Gates on the lower edge of the Taurus Mountains, the remains of those silent cities stood with half-ruined walls, towers, arches, vaults, ranges of houses, stone pavements, pillars, carved stone, forums and magnificent church buildings. They flourished roughly from the first to the seventh century and were great monuments of a Christian society which did not hide in catacombs, but developed an ecclesiastical architecture which surpassed anything else in existence before Justinian's St Sophia in Constantinople. The rise and sudden disappearance of those cities are phenomena which may be explained by the trade activities between East and West in later antiquity and the early Middle Ages prior to the Arab Conquest. They are situated at the great juncture of the trade routes from East Asia, India, the Persian Gulf, the upper Euphrates and Arabia converging in the borderland of Anatolia, where the merchants of Europe and the Byzantine empire met the traders of the East. They thus owed their apparent opulence as trade centres to this East–West commerce.[1] When the influx of trade was stopped by the emergence of the Arab empire, and the interchange between East and West was no more possible, these cities were deserted and fell into swift decay. In fact, Antioch itself, the ancient capital of the Seleucid empire and the ecclesiastical capital of the East, fell into a second-rate position and began to shrink with bewildering rapidity.

A survey of the ancient history of Syria shows how much its pre-Christian civilization was under the influence of foreign cultures, from the Egyptian in the south to the Greek from the north. It would appear that the Syrian

---

Expedition to Syria in 1899–1900 (New York and London, 1903); (2) *Syria: Publications of the Princeton Archæological Expeditions to Syria in 1904–5 and 1909* (Leiden, 1910–20); (3) *Early Churches in Syria, Fourth to Seventh Centuries*, ed. E. Baldwin Smith (Princeton, 1929). See also J. Strzygowski, *L'ancien art chrétien de Syrie* (Paris, 1936); A. Mattern, *À travers les Villes Mortes de Haute Syrie*, Mélanges de l'Université Saint-Joseph, T. XVII (Beirūt, 1933); J. Lassus, *Sanctuaires chrétiens de Syrie*, Bibliothèque archéologique et historique, Institut Français de Beyrouth, T. XLII (Paris, 1947); G. Tchalenko, *Villages antiques de la Syrie de Nord – Le Massif de Belus à l'époque romaine*, 2 vols. (Paris, 1953). The more recent traveller Jules Leroy, *Moines et Monastères de Proche-Orient* (Paris, 1958), gives an impassioned account of those sites on pp. 166 et seq. Jules Leroy's work has recently been translated into English by Peter Collin under the title: *Monks and Monasteries of the Near East* (London, 1963). References to it on the following pages are made to the French original. Of a more general nature, the following works include references of interest for various facets of the subject: F. Van Der Meer and Christine Mohrmann, *Atlas of the Early Christian World*, English tr. Mary F. Hedlund and H. H. Rowley (London, 1958); W. Lowrie, *Art in the Early Church* (New York, 1947); *L'Art et l'Homme*, ed. René Huyghe, 2 vols. (Paris, 1958).

[1] Leroy, p. 181, states that those cities owed their wealth to the commerce in the olives of the Lebanese and Syrian mountains. But of course so much wealth could not be forthcoming from this sole produce, and the fact is that all Eastern trade poured from Asia into those terminal trade emporia.

people were able to find themselves only after the dawn of the Christian era, when they developed an architecture of their own which reached its peak in their ecclesiastical establishments. Innumerable churches and basilicas of great size and beauty are still standing almost intact in those extinct Syrian cities. In fact, some of them lack nothing but a roof and minor repairs and restoration to make them again usable. Amongst those splendid specimens are the churches at Serjilla, Kharāb Shams, Qalōṭa, Roueiha and Mshabbak, all from the fourth and fifth centuries. Practically all of them consist of a narthex, nave and aisles separated by two rows of six columns each, and a sanctuary with a splendid apse behind the altar.[1] The immense sixth-century basilicas at Qalb Lōzeh and Roṣāfah[2] are veritable architectural feats with their tremendous semicircular arches supported by columns and supporting domes. All are built of perfectly hewn limestone from the Syrian quarries. The sides of doors and windows are usually fluted, and there are exquisite samples of decorative stonecarving in bas-reliefs. These may be seen on lintels and around entrances and apses at Dair Mishmish, Qalb Lōzeh and elsewhere.[3] Capitals of outstanding beauty in design from the fifth and sixth centuries have been collected from the churches and cathedrals of Brad, Dar Qita, Meʿez, Roṣāfah, Jeradeh, Dana, Kimar, El-Bara and Kokanaya.[4]

With the introduction of monasticism in Syria, many monasteries and monastic settlements and cities arose as a consequence. Names of places indicate their existence in many regions of northern Syria. The words Dair, Qaṣr and Qalʿah, meaning convent, palace and castle, invariably signify the remains of a monastic establishment. Thus we have Dair Mishmish (Apricot Monastery), Dair or Qalʿat Samʿān (St Simeon's Monastery), Qaṣr al-Banāt (Virgins' Palace, i.e., nunnery), Dair Sita and so forth. Undoubtedly the finest achievement in the monastic group of buildings is that of Qalʿat Samʿān situated on a hill bearing the saint's name by the road from Antioch to Aleppo.

That magnificent architectural landmark was begun during the lifetime of the first of the great stylites, St Simeon the Older, that is before 459, the year of his death. The saint's fame spread far and wide throughout the ancient world, and pilgrims from all parts of Syria, Arabia, Persia, Mesopotamia and Egypt as well as the Byzantine empire, Italy, Gaul, Brittany and Spain thronged around his pillar in endless streams to see that spiritual athlete and to receive his blessings. Hostelries were constructed on and at the foot of his mountain for housing those pious wanderers in addition to the monastic settlement of disciples already within reach of the pillar. The influx of visitors continued increasingly even after the saint's death. Though his precious

[1] Lassus, Plates I, VII, VIII, IX and X.
[2] Ibid., Plates XI, XII, XVII.
[3] Ibid., Plates XX, XXXV, XLVI, LIV, LV, LVI.
[4] Ibid., Plates L–LIII.

remains, coveted by all authorities, were transferred to Antioch and subsequently to Constantinople, pilgrims cherished the site and emblem of his sanctity and came to pray around his pillar. In the end, Emperor Zeno (d. 491) rendered the greatest homage to the saint's memory by ordering the construction of a great basilica around the column. Accordingly, the Syrian architects, all anonymous and self-denying, seized the opportunity to give vent to their pious aspirations in the realization and accomplishment of one of the most wonderful and most elaborate architectural enterprises of Christian antiquity before St Sophia in the reign of Justinian. The builders of St Simeon's were the sons and heirs of the men whose genius had earlier produced another miracle in Roman times – the temple of Baalbek. Begun in 476, this new and immense undertaking, comprising more than one hundred thousand square feet of stone buildings, was completed in 490. The outcome surpassed all expectation, both as a work of great skill and as a concrete expression of profound faith. It proved to be the perfect systhesis of all that was beautiful in the creative art and architecture of the old Syrians.[1]

The architects had a dual object. While building a *martyrion* around the saint's pillar, they aimed at the construction of a cathedral or a series of basilicas for the celebration of divine worship. Thus starting with the *martyrion* in the form of a vast octagon around the stylite's column, they decided to erect four rectangular churches springing from the octagon and, together, taking the shape of a monumental Cross. The central octagon was eighty-five feet in width. Its eight sides were topped by considerable arches resting on pink marble columns with Corinthian capitals. In the middle stood the rock-hewn base of the historic pillar, above which was once an impressive dome. Each of the four basilicas is oriented towards one of the cardinal directions. Each consists of a spacious central nave and two aisles, the naves opening into the octagon. The eastern basilica is the largest of the four branches, with nine bays as against seven in the other three. Further, it terminates in a sanctuary with a large central apse behind the high altar and two smaller apses on the sides. Apparently the liturgy was celebrated in that part, while the other three basilicas were used by the pilgrims for individual prayer and

[1] Lassus, pp. 129–37 and Plates XXIV–XXVI; Vogüé, Syrie, pp. 141–53; H. C. Butler, *American Archæological Expedition to Syria* (New York, 1903), 184, and the Princeton Expedition (see above, pp. 225–6, n. 2) II, 281. See also by H. C. Butler, *Early Churches in Syria, 4th to 7th centuries*, ed. and completed E. Baldwin Smith (Princeton, 1949), pp. 100–5; M. Ecochard, *Le sanctuaire de Qalʿat Semʿān*, Bull. d'Études Orientales VI (Damascus, 1937); D. Krencker, *Die Wallfahrtskirche des Simeon Stylites in Kalʿat Simʿān*, Abhandlungen der Preussischen Akademie der Wissenschaften (Berlin, 1939); H. W. Beyer, *Der Syrische Kirchenbau* (Berlin, 1925), pp. 281 et seq. Van Der Meer (pp. 102–3, 171) has reproduced impressive pictures of the ruins of St Simeon's Monastery, followed (pp. 104–5) by others from Dair Turmanin and Qalb Lozeh Basilica as well as Dair Sita's hexagonal baptistry, all not later than the sixth century. The plates in the present book show examples of various churches.

other religious functions. Free access to all parts of the buildings was made possible by twenty-seven entrances on all sides. The four main portals stood within an arched porch, or narthex, to the south rather than the customary orientation to the west, this being dictated by the land configuration of the mountain summit. On the other hand, the architect conformed to the tradition of placing the altar eastward so that worshippers might face the rising sun, emblem of the risen Christ.

The vast floors, it must be assumed, had been laid with Byzantine coloured mosaics and the walls covered with radiant frescoes. But no imagination is needed for an appraisal of the decorative art as represented in the magnificent stone mouldings around the arches and on the cornices. Here the Syrian sculptor adopted foliated and geometrical motifs. The acanthus leaf and the vine, so common in early Christian art, appeared in a multitude of places with exacting accuracy and a lofty sense of beauty.

The area, though much dilapidated, still teems with features and other buildings of archæological and architectural interest. The colonnades, understructures, superstructures, architraves, windows by the score, exterior ornamentation, subsidiary chapels, a convent, residential quarters, domestic buildings and more items complete the picture of a highly cosmopolitan settlement. The influence of Qalʿat Samʿān on the art and architecture of both East and West,[1] though admittedly not inconsiderable, has not been sufficiently assessed as yet. Certain artistic phenomena in many countries leave no doubt as to how far Syrian influence travelled in the world. In the monastery of Our Lady of the Syrians[2] in the Wādi al-Natrūn oasis on the desert road from Alexandria to Babylon (Old Cairo), the stone mouldings in some chapels belong to the same school as that of the great works of art on the walls of St Simeon's and other early churches in Syria. In this particular case, we can of course conceive the Syrian monastic craftsman settling down amongst brother Monophysites and transporting to them the fruit of Syrian accomplishment in the arts. It is hazardous to generalize on the link between the early Romanesque and Syrian architecture, but there are unmistakable parallels. In reality, the influence of Syria appears to have reached Europe at an early date through two channels. First, it must have followed the Syrian merchants of whom numbers are recorded in Italy and Gaul as early as the fourth century.[3] Secondly, certain ritual customs, such as the use of the *prothesis* and *diaconicon* seen at St Simeon's basilica and other Syrian churches, were adopted in Visigothic architecture in Spain, apparently through North Africa. The

[1] Butler, *Early Churches in Syria*, pp. 260–4, gives an interesting though indecisive account of the origins and influence of Syrian art and architecture.

[2] Strzygowski, *Art Chrétien de Syrie*, pp. 161–3, 173–8.

[3] Butler, p. 264, records an even earlier instance of a 3rd-cent. gravestone from Genay, France, with a bilingual inscription stating the death of a Syrian from Kanatha, identified as Ḳanawāt in Ḥaurān.

same feature finally found its way to the early church of Silchester in England.[1] It was natural that at a later date the imagination of the Crusader architects should be fired by the witness of such beauty in Syrian stone, and they must have carried back home with them new ideas which contributed to the development of ecclesiastical architecture, much the same as they did in the better-known field of military architecture. A modern traveller, Jules Leroy,[2] declares that the Western eye, accustomed to the churches of Vézelay, Saint-Benoît-sur-Loire or Moissac, finds itself more at home with St Simeon's than in the Byzantine churches. As to the interaction between Christian Syrian and mediæval Islamic architecture and arabesque designs, the examples are far too numerous to be given here. The variance of scholarly opinion on dating the stone ornamentation of the extraordinary Mchatta frieze from the fifth century to the age of the Umayyad dynasty,[3] to quote just one instance, shows how much the early Christian Syrian art and the purely Islamic arabesque overlapped in character and quality.

It would be interesting to follow the migration of those early Syrian styles from St Simeon's and the dead cities east to the monasteries of Ṭūr ʿAbdīn and upper Mesopotamia. But this is a task which no one can accomplish without excavating and at least partially restoring a few of the scores of ruined establishments in that area. Honigmann's monograph on the historic monastery of Mar Barṣaumā,[4] the home of the mediæval Jacobite patriarchs, including the chronicler Michael the Great, is a work of erudition without archæological background. Some of the wealth of architectural material of Christian origin has been re-used, but mainly in Islamic foundations, as is evident in the magnificent pillars, capitals and friezes of the Great Mosque[5] of Amid (Diyarbekr). In northern Syria around Jabal Samʿān and Jabal Baricha alone there existed towards the end of the sixth century at least eighty

[1] Butler op. cit. The parish and village of Silchester are situated ten miles from the city of Reading, Hampshire, England.

[2] He spent recently two years in the Middle East and visited, amongst other monastic centres, Qalʿat Samʿān. See *Moines et Monastères du Proche-Orient*, p. 193.

[3] This is one of the main items on which J. Strzygowski based his study *L'ancien art chrétien de Syrie*, in which he published a number of plates (I, IV, XIII, XIV, XV) of that frieze preserved in the Berlin Museum. The combination of floral, animal and bird *motifs* in stone sculpture that looks like fine lace is a peerless work of art. The use of the acanthus leaf and the vine branch with bunches of grapes is typically Christian. The animal and bird life is reminiscent of some of the best specimens of designs in the early Coptic textiles, and the borders represent the best forms of ornamentation described as arabesque. Strzygowski sees Iranian influence in this work of art (*Art Chrétien*, p. 89, 94–7); and Lassus (*Sanctuaires Chrétiens*, p. xxi) insists that the work is of Umayyad provenance and date. The fact remains that this was Syrian workmanship of the most exquisite kind, no matter to which century it belonged.

[4] Honigmann, *Le Couvent de Barṣaumā et le Patriarcat Jacobite d'Antioche et de Syrie* (Louvain, 1954).

[5] Strzygowski, pp. 143–5; M. van Berchem and J. Strzygowski, *Amida* (Heidelberg and Paris, 1910), pp. 298 et seq.

monasteries.[1] For Ṭūr ʿAbdīn and upper Mesopotamia it is impossible to furnish exact figures. Only a poor remnant of nine monasteries, reported by Parry[2] during the last decade of the last century, survives. Two of them are worthy of special note: Dair al-Zaʿfarān, until later years patriarchal residence after the end of Mar Barṣaumā's Convent, and that of Shaikh Mattai, once the seat of maphrians of the East and a repository of learning.

Dair al-Zaʿfarān, or the Saffron Monastery, from the yellow tint of its stone walls is originally named after the founder of its present structure, Mar Ḥanānia, bishop of Mardin in 793, though the Jacobites contend that this was only the second founding on a much older institution ascribed to Mar Augin, whose tomb still stands in its fourth-century *martyrion*. It is generally called 'Monastery of Mar Augin and the Twelve Thousand Saints'.[3] It is the only Jacobite monastery which has any considerable body of monks and all the features which ensure self-sufficiency. Enclosed within high walls of massive masonry, it is fortress-like and surrounded by rich orchards. A huge square building on two levels, its cloisters are arched all round. The chief object of archæological interest is its ancient church of Mar Yaʿqūb, probably built in the fourth century and certainly embellished by Emperor Anastasius (491–518), who had Monophysite leanings. It is in the traditional plan with three altars in the sanctuary, and the pillars are enriched with carved capitals and a fine floral frieze runs around the whole building. It has one dome and other semi-domes. Parry[4] records the Syrian custom of burying patriarchs in a sitting posture on their thrones side by side in large recesses, of which he counted eight in 1892. Almost all that remained of the rich library of the monastery was taken with the patriarch when he moved to Ḥoms after the First World War. The Jacobites have introduced the use of the bell for calling to prayer instead of the old wooden *simandron*, which is now reserved for signalling refectory hours.[5]

[1] Leroy, p. 194; cf. maps by Lassus in *Sanctuaires Chrétiens*.

[2] *Six Months*, pp. 139, 186, 198, 201, 215, 323. These are Dair al-Zaʿfaran, Dair Mar Quriaqos, Dair al-Mokhr, Dair al-ʿOmar and Dair Ṣalīb in Jebel Ṭūr, Mar Mattha near Moṣul, Mar Jacob at Ṣalāḥ, Mar Abraham at Midhiat – Ṭur ʿAbdīn, with its ecclesiastical capital Midhiat, has always been a centre of Jacobite monasticism, hence its name, which means the 'Worshippers' Mountain'. P. Krüger, *Das syrisch-monophysitische Mönchtum im Ṭur-ʿAb(h)dīn*, p. 4, cites names of twenty monasteries in this area in addition to the Qarṭamin Monastery (later in the Arab period known as Dair al-ʿOmar), which is the object of his dissertation. The eighteenth-century traveller Niebuhr recorded from hearsay seventy monasteries all in ruins. Some thirty-five villages with a total of about 4,000 families are reported by Jules Leroy (*cum grano salis*), p. 244, according to the Jacobite archbishop of Mardin in the last few years. Ṭur ʿAbdin is reckoned the Mount Athos of the Middle East.

[3] Leroy, p. 246. The fullest description of the monastery and life in it is given by Parry, pp. 103–40. Travellers have been attracted to it; see Gertrude L. Bell, *The Churches and Monasteries of the Ṭur ʿAbdin*, London, 1910.

[4] *Six Months*, p. 108.

[5] Ibid., note.

The monastery of Mar Mattai, though of great antiquity, was systematically harassed by the Kurds and later restored. Thus the older buildings must have been changed considerably and many interesting archæological features lost. It is built mainly of the rough concrete common in Moṣul instead of stone from the mountain. Its outlook on the plains of Nineveh and Moṣul, the size of its terraces, the tremendous dimensions of the building, its semicircular and pointed arches, its plain but ancient church where the remains of Bar Hebræus are interred, its outer walls, retreats and gardens impress the traveller in spite of the absence of any active monastic life within this historic *cenobium*, now administered by a bishop and a few monks as a summer resort. The contents of its vast library are gone, either burnt in the Kurdish wars or stolen and sold to strangers. A limited number of manuscripts are still closely guarded by the bishop – a poor symbol of a glorious literary past.

The Syrian artistic genius found a perfect expression in stone wall sculpture rather than statuary, though specimens of the latter are not entirely wanting. The Syrian Good Shepherd is always represented as a youthful figure with short curly hair. Icons and miniatures have also been made. The Syrians, however, were never great lovers of iconography and preferred to concentrate on the embellishment of manuscripts, which they produced in considerable numbers in the *scriptoria* of their great mediæval convents. Although the wealth of Syrian miniatures extant has been greatly minimized by the successive raids and arson in which heaps of priceless manuscripts in the Jacobite monasteries must have perished, the surviving specimens in the repositories of the East and West are sufficient to enable art scholars to construe the true picture of a hitherto neglected subject. From a recent enquiry into the Syriac manuscript collections, Jules Leroy[1] has published a small but representative number of impressive miniatures from the ancient *Codex Rabulensis* and the later mediæval *evangelia* preserved in the Vatican and in Dair al-Zaʿfarān showing the character and quality of the Syrian miniature.

The *Codex Rabulensis*, since 1476 in the Laurentian collection at Florence, was written and illuminated in 586 by a monk of the North Syrian monastery of St John of Zagba, named Rabbula, that is, less than a century after the completion of St Simeon's monastery and half a century before the advent of the Arabs. Its antiquity and the magnificence of its opening fourteen pages of ornamentation provide one of the most striking examples of the Asian Christian art of the Syrians in its purer form.[2] The Vatican *Evangelion* was

[1] *Moines et monastères du Proche-Orient*, pp. 199–201, 231–2, 251.

[2] Lavishly edited with full-size colour plates and commented upon by Carlo Cecchelli, Giuseppe Furlani and Mario Salmi under the title *Evangeliarii Syriaci, Vulgo Rabbulae, in Bibliotheca Medicea-Laurentiana* (Plut. I, 56) *Adservati Ornamenta Edenda Notisque Instruenda* (Oltun and Lausanne, 1959). The illustrations include Biblical scenes such as the Pentecost (fol. 14b), Christ enthroned (14a), the Ascension (13b), the Crucifixion and the Holy Women at the Sepulchre, Canon Tables from the Old and New Testaments

written on paper in 1220 by a monastic scribe of Mar Mattai called Mubārak and enriched by fifty-two miniatures for the weekly liturgy throughout the year.[1] Though the human figures are somewhat under Byzantine influence, the vivid colours, geometrical designs, ethnic features, brocade vestments, and oriental furniture reproduced by the artist bring those illustrations into perfect unison with the Islamic works of the schools of Baghdad and Moṣul. It is thought that a studio existed at Mar Mattai for the duplication of those works of Eastern art, since a similar but unsigned copy of the same *Evangelion* is also to be found in the British Museum. On the other hand, the manuscript of Dair al-Zaʿfarān completed by the scribe Dioscorus Theodorus between 1222 and 1273, falls entirely under Byzantine influence save for the ethnic features of human representations.[2]

Syrian art found another expression in wall paintings, of which little is left. The monastery of Mar Behnam, several times exchanged between the Jacobites and the Chaledæans, has a row of stucco portraits of the greater personalities in the history of monasticism, including St Antony, St Pachomius, St Daniel and others together with the images of Mar Mattai, Mar Behnam and his sister St Sarahin. An ancient chapel is dedicated to her. This pictorial art side by side with arabesque friezes, engravings and niches of the epoch of the Atabegs of Moṣul offers a novel combination to be found chiefly in Syrian monuments.[3]

On the whole, however, the Syrian contribution was essentially limited to stone work and architectural design, though Syrian artists did not refrain from trying their skill in the minor arts. In this field, it appears that they depended more on their Monophysite neighbours the Copts and the Armenians. Nevertheless, a production such as the great Chalice of Antioch[4] is a magnificent example of their achievements in the lesser crafts. Discovered accidentally by Arabs digging a well in the neighbourhood of Antioch in 1910, this object of singular beauty and archæological importance was acquired in 1950 by the Metropolitan Museum of Art and placed in the Cloisters in New York City after the establishment of its authenticity as an early mediæval work of art. With its twelve human figures seated in the midst of vine branches and

(3b–12b), a letter from Eusebius to Carpianus (3a–2b), Eusebius of Cæsarea and Amonius of Alexandria (2a), the Holy Virgin in a shrine (1b), and the Apostles gathering for the election of a twelfth witness in the place of Judas. All are exquisite examples of the Syrian art of miniature at its best. These are preceded by a multitude of other illustrative material from other sources, both in colour and in black and white, which enhance the value of the work. Lowrie, Pl. 136–7, reproduces six pages reduced in black and white together with a note on the Rabula Gospel, pp. 205–6. We are able here to reproduce a representative sample of this great codex (see Plate XVI).

[1] Leroy, Plate 46, portraits of Ammonius and Eusebuis.

[2] Ibid., Plates 51 and 52, Transfiguration and the Forty Martyrs of Sebastia respectively.

[3] Ibid., Plates 56 and 57, Annunciation and the Resurrection of Lazarus.

[4] Ibid., pp. 239–41, also Plate 54 showing sculptures around entrance and niche.

grape clusters, baskets, birds and animals, this great chalice is an artistic prize of the highest order and a demonstration of skill and exquisite taste.[1] Although the seated figures are similar in body, the faces are distinct and each has its own personality. The central figures on both sides are those of the youthful Christ and of the mature Christ and Saviour.[2] Each of the other ten figures may be identified through a symbol scratched on his chair. Thus St Luke has a tree, the emblem of life; St Mark has the water jug of the Last Supper; St Peter, facing St Paul, has the keys; remaining figures are those St Jude, St James the Lesser and St James the Greater, St Andrew, St Matthew and St John. A Roman eagle with outspread wings stands on a basket of loaves underneath the platform where Jesus is seated, symbolizing the Roman empire partaking of the blessings of Christianity. To the right of the Lord is the Lamb with head turned back to Him. The Star of Bethlehem shines over Christ's extended right hand. Grapes fill the remaining loops harmoniously without show of overcrowding. A dove over Christ's head represents the Holy Ghost. The rabbit so common in early Christian art also appears on the goblet nibbling at a grape cluster. Other items are a butterfly, a grasshopper, two snails and a plate of loaves and fish, with a band of fifty-seven rosettes and a six-pointed star just under the rim. On comparison with similar objects some historians and archæologists have advocated the theory that the Great Chalice of Antioch may belong to the last three decades of the first century of our era, while others more authoritatively place it in the fourth or fifth centuries.[3]

The flourishing of Syrian Christian civilization at the time of the decline and fall of the Roman empire was a natural phenomenon. While the West was trampled under the heels of the barbarian invader, Syria enjoyed a peaceful spell in its history, and except for theological controversies and subsequent

[1] G. A. Eisen, *The Great Chalice of Antioch* (New York, 1933); J. J. Rorimer, *The Authenticity of the Chalice of Antioch*, repr. from *Art and Literature for Belle Da Costa Greene*, ed. Dorothy Miner (Princeton, 1954), pp. 161–8; Bayard Dodge, 'The Chalice of Antioch', in *Bull. of the Near East*, III (May–June, 1950); C. R. Morey, 'The Antioch Chalice', in *Art Studies*, III (1925), pp. 73–80; J. Strzygowski, *Ancien art chrétien de Syrie* (Paris, 1936), pp. 23 et seq. See also Plate XIX in this volume.

[2] Height from base of chalice, 7·26 in., or approx. 19 cm.; diameter of cup about the same. Its capacity is two and a half quarts of liquid, which is the normal volume of a Passover Cup; Eisen, p. 7.

[3] Coloured full-size picture of chalice in Eisen's frontispiece as well as details of each figure in black and white within the text. Christ's figure in both images is young and beardless in accordance with the Syrian tradition. The dual imagery on vessels is Roman in character. Eisen (p. 9) cites an example of 79 A.D. where Augustus appears as a man on one side of the cup and a boy on the other. Fuller portraits of Christ, Apostles and Evangelists are published in a *de luxe* two-volume edition. *The Great Chalice of Antioch* (New York, 1923) was published by the original owner Fahīm Kouchakji. Van Der Meer, p. 104, has reproduced a silver vase of the fifth century from Emesa (Ḥomṣ) in Syria with images of Christ, Peter and Paul inside *clipei*, or shields or medallions, somewhat reminiscent of the work on the Antiochene chalice though not as elaborate; the latter vase is now in the Louvre. See also *L'Art et l'Homme*, II, 96.

schisms, it reaped the bountiful fruits of commerce flowing from East to West. The 'dead cities' of northern Syria arose chiefly as trade centres. The Syrian, like the Phœnician, was noted for his ability in handling commerce and international transactions. The end of antiquity and the birth of the Middle Ages were for Syria, unlike Europe, periods of spiritual, material and artistic progress which were dimmed only by its isolation after the rise of the Arab empire and the decay of its prosperous trade. Even then, the Syrian artist channelled his ingenuity in the service of the Arabs to the development of another great culture and a new civilization.[1]

[1] Eisen, p. 15.

PART III

THE NESTORIAN CHURCH

13 • ORIGINS AND DEVELOPMENT

Introductory

The Nestorian[1] Church, otherwise known as East Syrian, derived its name in mediæval times from Nestorius, who became bishop of Constantinople in the year 428. Strictly speaking, that Church could trace its origins even further back than the reign of Nestorius and the age of the œcumenical councils as a whole. The seeds of Syrian Christianity had been sown in Jerusalem during the Apostolic age, and the contention has been made that the first bishop of the Syrian Church was none other than St James, one of the Twelve Apostles identified as 'St James the Less' and described in the Holy Scripture as a Brother of Jesus. In those early days, primitive Christians had not yet fallen into the nationalist separatism and political disaffection which eventually broke the universal Apostolic church into independent units. It was not until the condemnation of Bishop Nestorius in the course of the fifth century that the East Syrians appeared as one of those emerging units and identified themselves with Nestorian Diophysitism.

As a special community, the East Syrians roughly held their habitat alongside the mobile frontier between the Roman and Persian empires in Asia. This coincided in general terms with the boundaries of modern Turkey, Iraq and Iran, though religiously they remained an integral part of the wider Syrian Church during the first four centuries of our era. The early bishops of that Church were essentially Judaistic, owing mainly to the fact that the heralds of the most ancient Christianity were Jewish. As time went on and the work of evangelization influenced other nations and races, the gentile

[1] The appellation 'Nestorian', though never objectionable to the members of this sect, came to be used in official or semi-official documents of the Church only in the thirteenth century when Mar ʿAbd-Ishūʿ, Metropolitan of Nisibis, formulated 'The Orthodox Creed of the Nestorians' in the year 1298; G. P. Badger, *The Nestorians and their Rituals*, 2 vols. (London, 1852), pp. 49–51. The Arabic mediæval literature of the Abbasid period cited these Christians as *Nasṭūriya* and *Nasāṭirah*. The terms Chaldæans and Assyrians had long been used, although the former is now taken to mean the Uniate branch, while the latter has been brought into prominence by the Anglican missionaries of the nineteenth century to evade heretical incrimination by the use of the word Nestorian.

element soon became preponderant in the Church. Thus, converts from the West, both Roman and Byzantine, began to relinquish the tradition of a Judaistic episcopate and envisaged independent policies which led to a rupture between East and West. The first outcome of the new position was the transfer of the episcopal see to Antioch, where the Byzantines wanted to free themselves from Jewish influence in Jerusalem and transplant the church government to a Greek centre. In this way the Christian church inaugurated those Eastern and Western leanings which reflected themselves increasingly in the lives of the faithful. In Asia, the issue resolved itself at the outset in the freedom of the gentile elements from Judaistic superiority. In regard to Antiochene orthodox Christianity, a number of offshoots arose within gentile ranks. At first the absence of affinity between the Greek and the Syrian resulted in a duality of the episcopate of Antioch. Next, that splintering affected the Syrians, who became sub-divided into two separate denominations: the Syrian Church, comprising the West Syrian clans, and the East Syrian Church, whose membership spread eastward of Syria into eastern Anatolia, Kurdistan, upper Mesopotamia and Persia. While the one became utterly Monophysite and was later identified as the Jacobite Church, the other began to swing towards Diophysitism, or Nestorianism since the first œcumenical council of Ephesus (431), and preferred to be described as Assyrian rather than just Syrian. In this manner, the Assyrian or East Syrian branch of the Church came into being paradoxically as the champion of a heretic doctrine of Greek origin while it was striving to purge itself of all vestiges of Greek ecclesiastical authority. Unlike the Antiochenes who used a Greek liturgy, the Assyrians, or would-be Nestorians, continued to speak a particular dialect of Aramaic known later as Syriac and persisted in the use of their ancient liturgy in the same language. In fact, they were protected from Greek practices and Byzantine encroachments by their very existence within the confines of the Persian empire. Relentlessly pursued by the Greeks, they therefore found their haven of peace in Persia, the inveterate enemy of Byzantium, and so they started looking eastward rather than westward for opportunities. Like the frontiersmen in American history, a whole world lay ahead of them for spiritual expansion. This, together with their austere monastic discipline and an infinite zeal for the propagation of their faith, may help to account for the mediæval glories of their Church throughout the continent of Asia. The flame of their missionary activities was carried far and wide into Persia, Turkestan, China and India at a time when Cathay was as far from Western imagination as the moon. It is no exaggeration to contend that, in the early Middle Ages the Nestorian Church was the most widespread in the whole world. The staggering rapidity of the rise of the Nestorians in Asia is equalled only by the rapid decline of their influence in the later Middle Ages. Their world was drowned in a surging sea of Islam, and the enlightened tolerance of the early caliphate gave way to fierce fanaticism of newly Islamized dynasties under which the Nestorian chance was lost forever. When Nestorians were rediscovered in the last century or two, their villages were clustered in the mountain fastnesses of Kurdistan around Lake Urmia. Their numbers were depleted, their wealth limited, and their ignorance was phenomenal. Yet they represented one of the most enlightened chapters in Christian history, sanctity and scholarship. They had suffered persecution after persecution to the extent that one of their authors, writing in English about the story of his own kinsfolk and church, published his book under the title *Death of a Nation.*[1] Indeed, the systematic extermination of the Nestorians is comparable in a way to that of the Incas, Aztecs or other Indian tribes in the blackest annals of the New World. With these generalizations in mind, let us outline the triumphs and the tribulations of that Church.

Most of our knowledge comes from secondary literature, and it must be remembered that works on the Nestorian Church have been composed by either Catholic or Protestant authors who approach it either as dissident, schismatic and heretic or retrogressive and antiquated. Unfortunately, modern reforming attempts ended in tragedy, and the only way out of the *impasse* of the Nestorians seemed to be through proselytizing either to Catholicism or to Protestantism. As a rule, foreign writers on the subject tended to demonstrate little constructive sympathy for and less understanding of that church; and the literature from within[2] its own ranks is scanty and thin. Nevertheless, numerous works from the patristic age include useful gleanings on its early history,[3] and it is not difficult to construe a reasonably good picture of such items as the Edessene school or the evangelizing impact of the Nestorian missionary in the high Middle Ages. It would, however, seem hard in the earliest records to disentangle the Assyrian church completely from its Syrian sister, identified later as Jacobite in the annals of primitive Christianity. Both shared the same fortunes in antiquity, and the patrology of both was identical at least in their first four centuries. They used the same liturgy and scripture in the same Syriac language without distinction or discrimination. As the Nestorians grew more and more isolated in later times their history was obscured through lack of records and archival material, and their community

[1] Abraham Yuhannan; see following note. The last chapter in Nestorian history has been compiled by a young Nestorian scholar, John Joseph, in his *The Nestorians and their Muslim Neighbors, A Study of Western Influence on their Relations* (Princeton, 1961). See also R. Strothmann, 'Heutiges Orientchristentum und Schicksal des Assyrer', in *Zeitschrift für Kirchengeschichte*, LV (1936), 17–82.

[2] The best-known examples of literature from within are: W. C. Emhardt and George M. Lamsa, *The Oldest Christian People – A Brief Account of the History and Traditions of the Assyrian People and the Fateful History of the Nestorian Church* (New York, 1926); Abraham Yuhannan, *The Death of a Nation, or, The Ever Persecuted Nestorians or Assyrian Christians* (New York, 1916).

[3] Cf. following notes on source material.

became forgotten until their existence was accidentally revealed by the Western missionary in a spectacular manner. Though a fair amount of work[1] has been done to clarify their position in the story of Christianity in Asia, it would appear that the definitive history of the Nestorian Church from its remote origins to the present day still remains to be written. This essay is only a modest attempt to give an abridged account from the available sources and the secondary literature of their involved and long career.

Age of Legend

Assyrian or Syriac traditions link the establishment of Syrian Christianity with the earliest Apostolic age. Some even assert that the evangelization of Edessa occurred within the lifetime of Jesus Christ himself. Accordingly, the Nestorians promoted three legends in support of that contention while relating them to Assyrian origins, namely the episode of the three Magi and their visit to the Infant Jesus, the story of King Abgar of Edessa, and the Acts of St Thomas the Apostle.

In the first place they submit that since the three Magi were apparently Aramaic-speaking, they could have come only from the kingdom of Urhai or Edessa, which alone retained its autonomy and Aramaic language amidst a conglomeration of other principalities with other languages wedged between the two great empires of Parthia in the East and Rome in the West. An even more picturesque episode was recounted by the Assyrians to the effect that, on his retirement from the world to a lonely cave in the seventh century B.C., Zoroaster had a great vision of such divine laws, principles and morals as could be found only in the teachings of the Christian religion. It is said that his prophecy stipulated, amongst other things, that a number of Magi from his priestly caste should proceed under the guidance of divine light to the

[1] Here is a list to be supplemented from following notes: W. F. Adeney, *The Greek and Eastern Churches* (Edinburgh, 1908); D. Attwater, *The Christian Churches of the East*, 2 vols. (Milwaukee, 1947–8); G. P. Badger, *The Nestorians and their Rituals*, 2 vols. (London, 1852); F. C. Burkitt, *Early Christianity* (London, 1904); Mrs C. E. Couling, *The Luminous Religion – A Study of Nestorian Christianity in China with a Translation of the Inscriptions upon the Nestorian Tablet* (repr. from the *Chinese Recorder*, LV [1924], 215–24, 308–17, with inscription tr. Prof. Saeki of Tokyo; London, 1925); R. Etteldorf, *The Catholic Church in the Middle East* (New York, 1959); J. Foster, *The Church of the T'ang Dynasty* (London, 1939); R. Janin, *Les églises orientales et les rites orientaux* (Paris, 1926); B. J. Kidd, *The Churches of Eastern Christendom* (London, 1927); J. Labourt, *Le Christianisme dans l'empire perse sous la dynastie sassanide, 224–632 A.D.* (Paris, 1904); J. Leroy, *Moines et monastères de Proche-Orient* (Paris, 1958); F. Loofs, *Nestoriana* (Halle, 1905); P. Rondot, *Les Chrétiens d'Orient* (Paris, 1955); J. Stewart, *Nestorian Missionary Enterprise – The Story of a Church on Fire* (Edinburgh, 1928); W. A. Wigram, *An Introduction to the History of the Assyrian Church, or The Church of the Sassanid Empire, 100–640 A.D.* (London, 1910); A. C. Moule, *Christians in China before the Year 1550* (London, 1930).

great One who was empowered to rule the whole world. During their captivity, the Aramaic-speaking Jews interpreted Zoroaster's vision as that of the coming of the Messiah who was destined to rule the world as king of the Jews. Those Magi, however, according to Assyrian traditions, were not just three in number, but twelve divided into three groups of four – a gold-bearing group consisting of Arvandid, son of Artiban, Hormsed son of Satros, Cosnasap son of Gonapar, and Arshak son of Mahros; a myrrh-bearing group of Zarandar son of Warzod, Akreho son of Kesro, Arbakchest son of Kolite, and Ashtonkakodon son of Sheshron; and the frankincense bearers, being Mahros son of Kohram, Aksherosh son of Kashan, Sadlak son of Baldan, and Merodak son of Bildad.[1]

The second famous legend is that of Abgar V the Black (*Ukkoma* or *Uchomo*), King of Urhai or Edessa, who exchanged letters with Jesus Christ. Though its historicity is questionable, the Abgar story has made its way to the earliest Christian literature and, as such, it claims a place on these pages. It is said that Abgar dispatched an embassy to Sabinus, the Roman governor of Eleutheropolis in Palestine. The Edessene ambassadors, Mariyab and Shamshagram together with a certain notary called Ḥannān the Scribe, while passing through Jerusalem on their return journey, learned of a new prophet who healed the sick. At once they conceived the idea that that prophet might heal their leprosy-stricken king, to whom they conveyed the good tidings. Abgar would have gone to Jerusalem for this purpose, had not his way been barred by Roman territory extending between Edessa and Jerusalem. So he decided to send a special envoy in the person of Ḥannān with a letter inviting Jesus to come to his kingdom to heal him and to preach the new faith to his people. This apocryphal epistle and Jesus' answer are cited in Greek by Eusebius,[2] bishop of Cæsarea in the fourth century and in Syriac in the work entitled *Doctrines of Addai*[3] by an anonymous author who also wrote towards the end of the fourth century. So famous did this story become throughout Christendom that versions of it have been found not only in Greek and Syriac[4] but also in Latin, Armenian[5] and Arabic.[6] Let us quote the less

[1] Emhardt and Lamsa, pp. 23–5.

[2] Eusebius, I, xiii.

[3] Burkitt, *Early Eastern Christianity*, pp. 11 et seq.

[4] B.M. fifth-century MS. discovered in 1864 and another sixth-century MS. discovered in 1876, first incomplete and second complete, both more elaborate than Greek. W. Cureton, *Ancient Syriac Documents Relative to the Earliest Establishment of Christianity in Edessa and the Neighbouring Countries from the Year after Our Lord's Ascension to the Beginning of the Fourth Century* (London, 1863; posth. ed. W. Wright); G. Phillips, *Doctrine of Addai the Apostle* (London, 1876); L. J. Tixeront, *Les origines de l'église d'Édesse et la légende d'Abgar* (Paris, 1888); J. Quasten, *Patrology*, 2 vols. (Utrecht and Brussels, 1951–53), I, 140–3, with a comprehensive bibliography (p. 143).

[5] Leroubna d'Édesse, *Hist. d'Abgar*, in *Coll. des historiens . . . d'Arménie*, ed. V. Langlois (Paris, 1880), I, 313ff.; cf. Fortescue *Lesser Eastern Churches*, p. 29, n. 1. Assemani, *Bibl. Orientalis*, I, 554–6.

[6] The Mt Sinai microfilming expedition of 1950 has revealed the existence of numerous

elaborate but quite communicative text of the copies of the two epistles as they appear in Eusebius' *Ecclesiastical History*. First, a copy of a letter written by Abgar the Toparch to Jesus and sent to him to Jerusalem by the Courier 'Ananias':

> Abgar Uchama, the Toparch, to Jesus the Good Saviour who has appeared in the district of Jerusalem, greeting. I have heard concerning you and your cures, how they are accomplished by you without drugs and herbs. For, as the story goes, you make the blind recover their sight, the lame walk, and you cleanse lepers, and cast out unclean spirits and demons, and you cure those who are tortured by long disease and you raise dead men. And when I heard all these things concerning you I decided that it is one of the two, either that you are God, and came down from heaven to do these things, or are a son of God for doing these things. For this reason I write to beg you to hasten to me and to heal the suffering which I have. Moreover I heard that the Jews are mocking you, and wish to ill-treat you. Now I have a city very small and venerable which is enough for both.

Secondly, the reply from Jesus to Agbar, the Toparch, by the Courier 'Ananias':

> Blessed art thou who didst believe in me not having seen me, for it is written concerning me that those who have seen me will not believe in me, and that those who have not seen me will believe and live. Now concerning what you wrote to me, to come to you, I must first complete here all for which I was sent, and after thus completing it be taken up to him who sent me, and when I have been taken up, I will send to you one of my disciples to heal your suffering, and give life to you and those with you.[1]

While in Jerusalem, Ḥannān, according to the *Doctrine of Addai*, painted a portrait of Jesus with supernatural qualities to which the king gave a place of honour in his palace. This is said to have been seized by the Muslims when they conquered Edessa, and they later ceded it to the Byzantine emperor in return for a heavy ransom and the liberation of Muslim captives.[2] There the portrait remained until it was taken to the West, possibly after the fourth Crusade, and since then it was lost.

Arabic MSS containing particulars of the Abgar legend and the two epistles in question sometimes incorporated in mediæval Arabic liturgies of the monks of St Catherine's Monastery. The story figures in the Arabic MSS. nos. 232, 445, 448, 485, 514 and 540 which I have microfilmed for the Library of Congress. See Atiya, *The Arabic MSS. of Mt Sinai* (Baltimore, 1955), pp. 7, 13–14, 17, 19, 21–2.

[1] Loeb edn., pp. 89–90.

[2] A Christian Arab writer, Abu Naṣr Yaḥyā b. Jarīr of Takrit, states in his work that he had seen that portrait in St Sophia in 1058 A.D. (450 A.H.); cf. Graf, *Christliche Arabische Lit.*, II, 259–60.

After the Lord's Passion and Ascension, His promise was fulfilled by the Apostles, who sent Addai, one of the seventy-two elect, on a missionary assignment to Edessa. There he resided with one of its Jewish inhabitants called Tobias son of Tobias, before healing King Agbar from his affliction. Subsequently he baptized the king and all his subjects, including a jeweller by the name of Aggai and a certain Palūt. On his deathbed, Addai ordained Aggai as his successor. But the reversion of the new King Maʿnu to paganism brought martyrdom to the second bishop, whose seat was left vacant until Palūt was ordained bishop of Edessa by Serapion, bishop of Antioch. To complete the cycle of Apostolic succession, the Nestorians explain that Serapion was in turn ordained by Zephyrinus of Rome, who had received his episcopate from the hands of St Peter himself.

This historicity of the legend is questionable by reason of numerous anachronisms. Serapion of Antioch is known to have reigned from 190 to about 211. Thus he could not have been consecrated by Pope Zephyrinus, who occupied the Roman see from 202 to 218. Again, the assertion that Zephyrinus had any direct relation with St Peter is a clear myth. From textual and internal criticism, Leclercq[1] arrives at the conclusion that the language of those epistles is derived not from the Gospels, but from Tatian's *Diatessaron*, compiled in the second half of the second century. They could not, therefore, have been written before the third century, though it is possible that they were based on earlier tradition. The modern Nestorians have never doubted their authenticity and continue to demonstrate their reverence to them by citing them on some occasions in the Syriac liturgy. Others in remote territories also defended their veracity, and Cureton states that until the last century, the letter supposedly by Jesus was hung in homes in England as a charm against illness.

The third of these legends is that of the apocryphal *Acts of St Thomas the Apostle* which will be discussed later in relation to the Church of Mar Thoma in southern India. It is sufficient here to register the importance of the tradition prevailing among the Nestorians that after the Apostle's martyrdom, his bones were transferred to Mesopotamia, where they were laid to rest on Assyrian soil.

Whatever the historicity of those legends may be, the moral is that the roots of Assyrian Christianity are deep in antiquity. Though it may be hard to accept the hypothesis of Abgar V's conversion around the middle of the first century A.D., Abgar VIII (176–213) is known to have been a Christian from the testimony of Sextus Julius Africanus, who visited his court.[2] The Roman conquest of Edessa in the year 216 brought the short reign of his successor, Abgar IX, to an end and opened up new channels for free com-

[1] 'La Légende d'Abger', in *Dict. d'Arch. Chrét. et de Liturgie.*

[2] Burkitt, p. 26 et seq.; Fortescue, p. 32.

munication with the chief base of Christianity in Jerusalem. The Assyrians were, moreover, Aramaic-speaking Semites, and barriers of race and language were virtually non-existent between them and their Jewish Christian brethren in the Holy City. Meanwhile, their familiarity with such Eastern religions as Zoroastrianism, which merged into Mithraism in the first century B.C., brought them numerous concepts which stood parallel to some of the basic ideas and tenets in the genesis of Christian thought. Mithras' god, who vanquished evil and ascended to heaven as well as the Babylonian worship of Marduk, who was unjustly killed and rose again triumphantly, are parallels to the Passion and the rise of Jesus from the dead. Again, the idea of supernatural birth was not unknown to Mesopotamian cults. Baptism and purification were practised by the priests of Mithras, who also consecrated bread, water and wine for the faithful. The high moral code of Mithraism compared favourably with Jesus' teachings. So striking was the similarity in the sacraments of both religions that a great church father like Tertullion found it necessary to explain Mithraism as a diabolical parody of the real faith intended to mislead the human race into error.[1] If we bear in mind the social standards governing the nations under the yoke of Rome as against the enfranchising nature of Christian teachings, which brought a message of hope and the fatherhood of God to downtrodden men, we can well perceive the relative ease with which the new faith found its way to the hearts of the Edessene people.

Historic Origins

The historic origins of the East Syrian or Assyrian, and later the Nestorian,[2] church are as enthralling as its legends. These abound in patristic literary monuments which have left their mark on the march of time. Between Tatian and Rabbula, there are decades that shine with the early bishops and saints of Edessa. From the *Diatessaron* to the *Peshitta*, we see how the Syriac Scripture was formulated for all generations. In the schools of Nisibis and Edessa, there are bulwarks of faith and a spiritual home for the pioneers who

[1] L. Patterson, *Mithraism and Christianity* (1912); A. d'Alès, 'Mithraisme et christianisme' in *Revue pratique d'apologétique*, III, 462–9, 519–28; H. Le Clercq, *Manuel d'archéologie chrétienne* (Paris, 1907), pp. 126–8; F. Cumont, *Textes et monuments figurés relatifs aux mystères de Mithra*, 2 vols. (Brussels, 1896–9); Emhardt and Lamsa, pp. 38–9.

[2] The 'Church of the East' is actually the official title of the church, otherwise the Nestorian or Nasṭūriya of the mediæval Arabic sources (see above p. 239 n. 1). The examples quoted by Badger, *Nestorians and their Rituals*, I, 178, on the use of the word by the Nestorians in 1609 coupled by the much older use of the term by Arab writers. See also Adeney, p. 484 n. 1.

spread Christianity in Osrhoene and in Persia. The persecutions and triumphs of the Syrian fathers in those remote parts of Asia took place at a time when the West was seriously involved in the decisive movement of the œcumenical councils. But it is hard to make any precise appraisal of the real interest or even awareness of the East in that movement before the Council of Ephesus in 431. Indeed, it was at Ephesus that one first sees the dividing line between East and West, Syriac and Greek, Semitic and Byzantine, Diophysite and Monophysite, Nestorian and Orthodox. Until then the East and West Syrians never severed relations and never wavered in their communion and mutual responsibilities.

Of the truly memorable names that stand out of those dim beginnings, we hear of Bardaisan and Tatian in the ante-Nicene period. Of noble descent, Bardaisan[1] was born in 154 and educated with King Abgar VIII (176–213). He became a celebrated writer and a true representative of Syriac philosophy. After his conversion to Christianity, he was ordained deacon by Hystasp, bishop of Edessa, in 179 A.D.; but when he turned to metaphysical and astrological polemics, he was anathematized by Bishop Aqai as a heretic and was forced to flee to the neighbouring Armenia around 216 – the year of the Roman conquest of Edessa. It is believed by some writers that he became a dualist gnostic and a follower of Valentinus.[2] Eusebius asserts that he later turned against the Valentinians, though 'he did not completely clean off the filth of his ancient heresy.'[3] Bardaisan developed an Oriental doctrine of astrological[4] fatalism. He held that Christ's body was a mere phantom and repudiated the idea of the resurrection. A man of great literary ability, he wrote numerous important works including a powerful *Dialogue with Antonius Concerning Fate*, and he is to be regarded as the father of Syriac hymnology. His hymns were, however, pervaded with his doctrines; but their beauty gained for him many followers for centuries to come. The apocryphal Acts of St Thomas[5] the Apostle are ascribed to circles under his influence. Bardaisan, sometimes described as 'the last of the Gnostics', left behind him a school which revived Syriac literature and philosophy at his death in 222.

Another contemporary of Bardaisan was Tatian, who, like him, made a monumental contribution to Syriac religious literature and also like him was accused of heresy. A native of Assyria of pagan birth, Tatian went to Rome after 150 A.D. where he was converted to Christianity before 165. He studied

[1] The fullest biography of Bardaisan is given by the Jacobite patriarch of Antioch, Michael the Syrian (1166–99), in his famous *Syriac Chronicle*. See Burkitt on 'Bardaisan and his Disciples' in *Early Eastern Christianity*, pp. 153–92.

[2] For example, Fortescue, p. 34.

[3] *Hist. Eccles.*, IV, xxx.

[4] See 'Bardesanes' in F. L. Cross, *Oxford Dictionary of the Christian Church* (Oxford, 1957).

[5] *Acta Thomae*, composed in the third century and containing some of the most beautiful hymns of the early Christians, such as the 'Hymn of the Soul'.

under Justin Martyr and appears to have succeeded him as a great teacher and Christian apologist. Then he fell under the spell of Valentinus and Gnostic philosophy, which made him unpopular in Rome. He laid the foundations of a new Gnostic sect known as 'Encratites,' or Abstainers, who dismissed marriage, meat and wine as sinful. His sect became conspicuous for the use of water instead of wine in the Eucharist. On account of growing suspicions towards him among the Roman ecclesiastical authorities, he was forced to retire to Edessa, where he was welcomed as a great Syriac mind by his native countrymen. He wrote in Greek his *Oration to the Greeks*, in which he combined the defence of Christian purity with a vehement deprecation of Greek civilization, which he regarded as incompatible with the teachings of Jesus. His real fame, however, rested on his contribution to Syriac religious literature, notably in the *Diatessaron*, a word which meant 'harmony'. Tatian then composed a life of Jesus, which he collated from the four Gospels, thus harmonizing, so to speak, a selection to form a continuous story. Until that time the Syrians had no full texts of the New Testament in Syriac, and so the *Diatessaron* was generally adopted in their churches as their canonical Scripture. Bishop Palūt, who perceived this irregularity, at once reacted with the introduction of a new Syriac version of the Four Gospels separately (*Evangeliōn da-Mēpharreshē*), which did not win general approval, and people continued the use of the *Diatessaron*. The task of substituting the final Syriac New Testament for both the old version of the separate Gospels and the *Diatessaron* was reserved to Bishop Rabbula in the early years of the fifth century. He made his final revision thereof in what is known as the *Peshitta* (a word literally meaning 'simple' or 'plain' version of the Syriac Vulgate). This comprised the current text of the Gospels according to the Antiochene tradition, together with the First Epistle of St Peter, the First Epistle of St John and the Epistle of St James as well as the Acts and Pauline Epistles, but excluding the four lesser Catholic epistles and the Book of Revelation.[1]

Bishop Rabbula of Edessa (421–35) was thus one of the most vigorous Syrian teachers in the defence of orthodoxy. Although the substitution of the *Peshitta* for the *Diatessaron* must be regarded as his enduring contribution to Syrian and Assyrian Christianity, Rabbula's role in the field of the reorganization of the Church as a whole was prominent in his day. As a staunch orthodox, his opposition to Nestorian irregularities and innovations remained unabated throughout his life. The canons which bear his name form an elaborate document intended to control the rules of matrimony and the order of society. They provide us with a true contemporary picture of the Mesopotamian church and society in the early decades of the fifth century. Burkitt gives a full analysis of those canons together with supporting excerpts from

[1] The Epistles omitted are 2 Pet., 2 and 3 John, and Jude. Burkitt, pp. 39–78; W. Wright, *Short History of Syriac Literature* (London, 1894), pp. 3–13, 47–9.

their original text.[1] On the whole, although a Syriac-speaking church leader, Rabbula voiced the teachings of Western orthodoxy and of Greek religious philosophy. It was in his lifetime that the seeds of an imminent split between the East and West Syrians were sown, but the open rupture came only in the reign of Ibas, his unorthodox successor.

Before entering into the details of the Nestorian controversy, however, a survey of the major events in the period separating Tatian from Rabbula appears to be inevitable for an understanding of the development of Eastern Christianity. In addition to Alexandria, Rome, Constantinople and Antioch as the traditional centres of Christian learning and orthodox religious thinking, we must remember that in the East, Edessa was also making strides as the rising centre of Syriac theology and letters. When Nisibis fell to the Persians in 363 A.D., its leading minds moved to Edessa. Foremost among these was St Ephræm the Syrian (ca. 306–73), often surnamed the Great for his sanctity, scholarship, unwavering orthodoxy and immense contribution to Syriac religious literature.[2] Born in Nisibis of parents whose Christianity is sometimes contested, he became a monk and is said to have been at Nicæ with his spiritual father, James, bishop of that town. He became an inveterate enemy of Arianism, which he combated at Edessa and elsewhere. Some sources speak of his doubtful visits to the Desert Fathers in Egypt as well as to St Basil the Great of Cæsarea in Cappadocia. His works in Syriac are monuments of Biblical erudition. Exegesis and asceticism as well as hymnology were the chief fields in which he worked. In fact, it may be argued that he was the true father of Syriac literature. Some of his works were translated into Greek, Armenian and even Arabic[3] at early dates.

Edessa was thus gradually growing into a stronghold of Syriac tradition while Antioch was increasingly hellenized, although both continued to abide by the resolutions of Nicæa until the opening decades of the fifth century. In fact, there were no real signs of open cleavage between the two great centres of eastern Christianity on matters of doctrine until the year 431 at the first Council of Ephesus. The appearance of Nestorius, bishop of Constantinople, on the scene of events, remote as that may seem from Edessa, proved to be the parting of the ways between the East and West Syrians. Nestorius was originally a monk of Antioch and a pupil of Theodore of Mopsuestia. He became famous for his ability in preaching and for his melodious voice in reciting the holy liturgy. Emperor Theodosius II's choice finally fell on him for the see of Constantinople. The Antiochian took to his new ditues with zeal

[1] Burkitt, pp. 143–52. The full title of the Canons of Rabbula is 'Commands and Admonitions to Priests and to Sons of the Covenant Living in the Country'.

[2] Burkitt, p. 55 et seq.; Fortescue, p. 35.

[3] St Ephræm was very popular with the Arabic-speaking monks at the Monastery of St Catherine in Mt Sinai. The Expedition of 1950 microfilmed some forty Arabic MSS. with citations from him. See list in Atiya, *Arabic MSS. of Mt Sinai*, p. 86.

and started purging the capital of heresies and heretics, unaware of what lay in store for him as the future arch-heretic of his own times. The problems of Christology which had already troubled the fifth-century world broke out again in a somewhat casual manner when a priest of Constantinople by the name of Anastasius, whom Nestorius had brought with him from Antioch, repudiated in one of his sermons the description of the Virgin Mary as *Theotokos*, that is, mother of God. The Greeks became disturbed and questioned his assumption, but Nestorius defended his man. In his defence, he began to elaborate on the subject of the relations of Jesus, the man born of Mary, and the word of God dwelling in him. This led him into the completely unorthodox assertion of the two persons: Jesus the perfect man without sin who is son of Mary in the flesh, on the one hand, and the divine word of God or the *Logos* settled within him, on the other. Thus the thesis of the two separate, not composite, natures of Jesus arose, perhaps unwittingly, but with vehemence. The fortress of orthodoxy at the time was Alexandria, and at its head was Cyril, a patriarch of greater theological knowledge, ability and resourcefulness than probably any cleric in his day. Synods both in Alexandria and in Rome decided against the new heresy in 430 and deposed Nestorius. The emperor sought to resolve the dilemma by summoning an œcumenical council at Ephesus[1] in the following year. A total of 198 bishops were convened there under the presidency of Cyril, with strong representations from Alexandria, Rome, Jerusalem, Thessalonica and Ephesus. Nestorius himself came with sixteen bishops and an armed escort under command of an imperial commissioner by the name of Candidian. John of Antioch and his suffragan bishops were however delayed *en route*; and so he dispatched a special envoy with a message to Cyril to hold the Council without waiting for his delegation. John's personal sympathy for Nestorius was known to Cyril, who accordingly decided to hurry the council business before his arrival to save him from embarrassment with a friend. Nestorius refused to appear before the council and was condemned, excommunicated and deposed. In the meantime, he met with forty-three rival bishops in a synod at his own house and issued a similar verdict against Cyril and the rest of the bishops. John and his thirty bishops later reached Ephesus to face these decisions, which no doubt annoyed them, though John was eventually persuaded to side with Cyril's viewpoint. Failing to establish peace between the rival parties, Theodosius II and his sister Pulcheria were led to accept the Council verdict. Cyril was allowed to return to Alexandria, Nestorius was exiled to the Libyan oases, and a new bishop of Constantinople by the name of Maximian

[1] Hefele (standard Fr. trans.), II, 1, 219–356; Landon (summary account), I, 254–65. M. Jugie, *Nestorius et la controversie nestorienne* (Paris, 1912), passim.; L. Duchesne, *Early History of Church*, Vol. III, pp. 218 et seq.; Fortescue, p. 54 et seq.; Vine, *Nestorian Churches*, p. 28 et seq.; Wigram, *Assyrian Church*, p. 135.

(431–4) was appointed in his place. Nestorius suffered a great deal in his exile. He was seized by the wild Blemmyes from the south, then removed to Panopolis, where the imperial governor of the area allowed him to stay. He tried to defend his name by a work which he called *The Bazaar of Heracleides*,[1] thus using a *nom-de-plume* to save the book from destruction, since anything bearing his own name would automatically have been burnt by the authorities. He died on the eve of Chalcedon and was interred in a place unknown.[2] His chief legacy to posterity was not limited to Nestorian Christology. It extended to the establishment of the Nestorian church, which espoused his teachings though he himself had no hand in founding it.

Bishop Rabbula of Edessa, who upheld the cause of orthodoxy in that church, died in 435 and was succeeded by Ibas (435–57), whose sympathy for Nestorius can be traced to his translation into Syriac of the works of Theodore of Mopsuestia, who had himself been the teacher of Nestorius and the chief source of his theological doctrine. Ibas fell under Theodore's spell, and though he never professed open Nestorianism, he remained technically in the Nestorian camp against the other Syrian Monophysites. This explains why the second Council of Ephesus[3] of 449, under Egyptian influence and the presidency of Dioscorus, patriarch of Alexandria deposed him, while Chalcedon[4] in 451 reversed the decision by reinstating him and excommunicating Dioscorus. It is doubtful whether these judgments affected the position of Ibas at home, where the Syrians were evenly divided between the so-called Nestorian and Monophysite parties. However, after Ibas's death in 457, the Monophysites had the upper hand in Edessa under Nonnus, his successor. The leader of the other faction, Bar Ṣaumā, who had previously been excommunicated by the so-called 'Robber Council', fled to Nisibis in Persia beyond the boundaries of the Roman empire. That date proved, therefore, to be a landmark in defining the frontier separating the Syrian Monophysites from the Syrian Nestorians. While Monophysites looked to Antioch within the empire, the Nestorians segregated themselves in Kurdistan and upper Mesopotamia within the orbit of Persian domination. Finally, Nestorian

[1] Surviving Syriac text ed. P. Bedjan (Paris, 1910); French tr. F. Nau (Paris, 1910); English tr. G. R. Driver and L. Hodgson (Oxford, 1925).

[2] Possibly Panopolis (modern Ikhmīm) in Upper Egypt.

[3] The chief object of this council was to consider the allegations against Eutyches, a Greek monk who taught that the two natures were separate before the Incarnation, then became united into one indivisible and divine nature afterwards. He was acquitted and reinstated in a boisterous meeting hurried before the arrival of the Latins. Pope Leo described that council as nothing better than a gathering of robbers (*latrocinium*), hence it became famous as the 'Robber Council', Hefele, I, 2, 554–621; Landon, I, 265–8; Vine, p. 50; Duchesne, III, 279 et seq.

[4] Hefele, II, 2, 649–880; Landon, I, 134–48; R. V. Sellers, *The Council of Chalcedon – A Historical and Doctrinal Survey* (London, 1953); *Das Konzil von Chalcedon*, ed. A. Grillmeier and H. Bacht, 3 vols. (Würzburg, 1951–4).

scholarship became extinct at Edessa when Emperor Zeno (474–91) ordered the closing of the Edessene School and the expulsion of all Nestorians from his realm. The Church later confirmed his decision at the fifth Œcumenical Council of Constantinople (553), which condemned both the person and the writings of Theodore of Mopsuestia, the original fountainhead of Nestorian teachings. Thus Nestorianism became illegal in the empire, and Edessa suffered a deadly blow from which it never recovered with the disappearance of Nestorian scholars and technicians from the area.

Nestorians in Persia

At this point the origins become clearer, and the frontiers between the Monophysite or Jacobite and the Nestorian or East Syrian Churches begin to narrow. It is true that in those early days there were Monophysites in Persia who mingled freely with the expelled Nestorians. The metropolitans of Seleucia-Ctesiphon were Jacobites who looked for leadership to Antioch within the Roman territory. Their allegiance to a hellenized patriarchate outside Persia was disastrous for their Church and offered the incoming Nestorians a chance for expansion at their expense. One of their bishops, Babowi by name, was seized in treasonable correspondence with Zeno, to whom he complained of being under the yoke of an impious sovereign, meaning the Sassanid king, Firooz. He paid for his folly with his life. Firooz crucified him, and under the influence of Bar Ṣaumā, bishop of Nisibis, the Monophysite priests of Persia were massacred. In 484 at the Synod of Beth Lapat or Laphat (the Persian *Jundishapur*), the Nestorian prelates under Bar Ṣaumā's leadership blessed the memory of Theodore of Mopsuestia and condemned all other doctrines, Monophysite and orthodox, of all churches under Roman rule. It is interesting to note that the same synod legalized marriage of priests and bishops. Bar Ṣaumā himself inauguarated this policy by marrying a nun. He missed becoming metropolitan of Persia with the death of his friend King Firooz and the accession of a more moderate king, Balash (484–8), who overlooked the intriguing Bar Ṣaumā and appointed Acacius (485–96) in his stead. The new prelate was not violently Nestorian in his approach, and he is said to have once declared, while on a visit to Constantinople, that he only participated in the banning of Monophysitism without attacking orthodoxy and that he was planning to excommunicate Bar Ṣaumā. The monks of Persia saved him from the ordeal by assassinating the bishop of Nisibis in 493, whom Acacius outlived by only three years.

Bar Ṣaumā's tempestuous life left him little time for literary activities, and his remains are few. Only fragments of the Acts of the Council of Beth

Lephat of 484 are known to exist, together with a number of funeral orations, hymns and a liturgy. Acacius too had a limited output. He composed homilies on faith and fasting, and wrote treatises against the Monophysites. For King Kavadh, he translated into the Persian language a book on the faith by Oseus, or Eliseus, bishop of Nisibis. Assemani places it among orthodox letters, but Chabot doubts its purity of doctrine. The patriarch was indubitably Nestorian in profession. In his discipline and canons, he authorized episcopal matrimony and blessed the marriage of priests and deacons beyond a shadow of doubt, even after ordination. He allowed monks to rescind freely in order to raise families.[1]

Confusion continued in the Nestorian Church in the reigns of the successors of Acacius for nearly fifty years. The period begins with an almost illiterate[2] patriarch, Babai II (497–502) who was followed by others among whom we find rival prelates excommunicating each other. Nevertheless, it would be a mistake to describe the period as an age of total darkness. In this formative period of transition, the Church reached maturity under the hegemony of the Persian kings and declared its complete independence of the West when Babowi assumed the title 'Patriarch of the East' in 498, thus raising the stature of his see to equality with and independence of Antioch, Alexandria or Rome. Meanwhile, the school of Nisibis assumed the place of the ancient school of Edessa and made a considerable advance under the able headship of Nerses, whom the Nestorians called the 'Harp of the Holy Ghost' and the 'admirable doctor' while the Monophysites referred to him as Nerses the Leper.[3] The chronicler ʿAbd-ʾIshūʿ ascribes to him 360 metrical poems of seven to twelve syllables each. They embody a fine historical commentary on the Books of the Ecclesiastes and the Prophets from the Old Testament. His hymns and homilies are known. He attacked Bar Ṣaumā in his work *Corruption of Customs*. Some of his writings found their way not only into the Nestorian but also into the Catholic liturgies.[4] That school became the great Nestorian educational centre and the nursery of noted patriarchs and prelates of future generations.

The Nisibene school was a kind of *cœnobium* where students, though not always monks, led a quasi-monastic life. Its rule insisted on celibacy and enforced regularity, residence and work. Theology, philosophy and canon law were taught by able church doctors. Labourt notes that here the Nestorian metropolis saw the birth of the earliest theological university on record, a phenomenon which aroused Justinian's admiration and surprise.[5] Since the Nestorian graduates of Nisibis were the teachers of the Arabs, who

[1] J. B. Chabot, *Littérature Syriaque* (Paris, 1934), pp. 51–2.
[2] Fortescue, p. 82.
[3] Labourt, pp. 279–310; Wigram, pp. 238–40; Vine, p. 54; Fortescue, p. 82.
[4] Chabot, pp. 50–51.
[5] Labourt, p. 301.

transmitted the heritage of Greece to the West in the later Middle Ages, it is not difficult to appraise the debt of the great schools of Europe to Nisibis.[1] To this school, the Nestorian Church owed its real reformers, of whom Mar Abā, patriarch of the East from 525 to 533, was a prominent figure. Travelling widely in his see, he strengthened the doctrine of his church and exterminated abuses by holding synods everywhere, finally earning the crown of martyrdom in Shapur II's persecution of the Christians.[2]

The Chronicler ʿAbd-ʾIshūʿ ascribes to him the only revised Nestorian Syriac Bible, complete from the Edessene and Alexandrian Greek texts as against the usual Syriac Simple Version or Peshitta. Among other works he also wrote a commentary on Genesis, Psalms, the Proverbs and the Pauline Epistles, in addition to a series of homilies and the Syriac version of the Liturgy of Theodore of Mopsuestia, still in use in the Catholic Chaldæan branch of the Nestorian Church.[3] By the end of the sixth century Nestorian doctrine became permanently established in its definitive form for all generations. Its greatest mouthpiece was Mar Babai, surnamed the Great to distinguish him from his namesake, Patriarch Babai II. He was abbot of the monastery of Mount Izala (569–628) and was a theologian of considerable merit. His *Book of Union* appears to have settled the final version of Nestorian beliefs, and his words incorporated in the Nestorian divine office for early morning from Advent to Epiphany may be quoted here as a clear and concise expression to the East Syrian Christology: 'One is Christ the Son of God, worshipped by all in two natures. In his godhead begotten of the Father without beginning before all time: in his manhood born of Mary, in the fulness of time, in a united body. Neither his godhead was of the nature of the mother, nor his manhood of the nature of the Father. The natures are preserved in their *qnume*,[4] in one person of one sonship.'[5] Until the present day, the Nestorians refrain from using the term *Yaldath Alaha*, the Syriac equivalent of the Greek *Theotokos*, and instead refer to the Virgin as *Yaldath M'shikah* – bearer of Christ.[6] Mar Babai's influence was very great on the whole church as he administered its offices during a patriarchal interregnum after the stormy reign of Sabr-Ishūʿ (590–604). It was an age of mixed feelings and policies toward Christians. Finally, when a successor was anointed patriarch in the person of Yeshuyab II (628–43), the Church left its troubles behind, and the new prelate embarked for the first time in history on a missionary programme for China, to be dealt with later in these pages.

[1] Wigram, p. 167.
[2] Labourt, pp. 163 et seq.
[3] Text pub. P. Bedjan (Paris, 1895); cf. Chabot, pp. 53–4.
[4] Syriac with Arabic equivalent *Aqnūm*, meaning nature, description of person. The original formula is 'two *qyāne*, two *qnūme*, one *parṣufā*', that is, 'two natures, two persons, one presence'. The word *parṣufā* is a corruption of the Greek.
[5] H. J. Sutcliffe, 'The Church of the East', in *Orthodoxy*, VI (1954), 259–60.
[6] Wigram, pp. 287–9. On the Creed of the Assyrian Church, see the same, pp. 290-3.

It is not easy to define precisely the extent of the Nestorian Church in Persia under Sassanid rule, nor is it possible to provide an accurate description of its territorial organization or enumerate its various ecclesiastical provinces and sees. Assemani[1] and Le Quien[2] attempted this difficult task in their antiquated but scholarly works, and a modern historian[3] of the Nestorian Church summed up the consensus of their views. The place names referred to by these authors are not clear, nor is the table of contents submitted by them final. Nevertheless, the material may be quoted here as a general guide to the constituencies of an expanding hierarchy. It will be seen, however, that this is limited mainly to the western part of the Persian empire, including upper and lower Mesopotamia between the Tigris and Euphrates. The eastern part, which is even more formidable in its dimensions, is treated lightly and out of proportion, we must assume, through lack of sources.

First, we have the patriarchal see, located at the ancient capital Seleucia-Ctesiphon. Then the province of Susiana, consisting of four bishoprics at Jundishapur, Susa, Ahwaz and Suster, all owing direct allegiance to the patriarch. Other provinces under the jurisdiction of a metropolitan with bishoprics included the following sees: (1) Patriarchalis, with a metropolitan at Kashkar and one bishop at Ḥīra; (2) Nisibis, with a metropolitan at Nisibis and a bishop at Bakerda; (3) Teredon, with a metropolitan at Baṣrah, a bishop probably at Destesana, and a church if not a bishopric at Nahr-al-Marah; (4) Adiabene (modern Ḥaydab situated between the Tigris and the Zab rivers), with a metropolitan at Erbil and bishops at Honita and Maalta; (5) Garamæa, with a metropolitan at Karkha and bishops at Sciaarchadate and Dakuka; (6) Khurāsān, with a metropolitan at Merv or Marw; (7) Atropatene, with a metropolitan at Taurisium; (8) Rawardshir, Rayy and Herāt, originally bishoprics, later metropolitan centres. Finally there seems to have been a number of other bishoprics not yet assigned to metropolitans. These were Maiperkat, Nineveh, Singara, Drangerda, Iṣfahan, Nishapur and Segestan south of Herāt.[4]

This is roughly the general picture of the Church at the time of the collapse of the Sassanid empire and the rise of the Muslim caliphate. Later in these pages, a similar account of the Nestorian dioceses under Arab rule will be made for purposes of comparison. Meanwhile, it will be seen that the Church continued to gather such strength as to lead to one of the most amazing missionary movements in the Far East. At one moment the whole of Asia beyond the Euphrates and Kurdistan became the parish of the Nestorian patriarch. This movement, already begun before the disappearance of

[1] Joseph Simonius Assemanus (Yūsuf Samʿān al-Samʿāni), *Bibliotheca Orientalis*, 3 vols. in 4 (Rome, 1719).

[2] M. Le Quien, *Oriens Christianus in Quatuor Patriarchatus Digestus*, 3 vols. (Paris, 1740).

[3] Vine, pp. 56–9.

[4] Ibid., p .57.

Persian rule, was continued with much vigour in Islamic times at least until the Tartar avalanche swept off almost all vestiges of material and spiritual civilization from those parts of Asia in the later Middle Ages. This story will be treated separately in some detail but cannot be explained without a brief survey of the source of strength of the Church as a whole. The backbone of Nestorian expansion lay with its monastic rule, which furnished the church with a great army of dedicated men ready to penetrate unknown regions and expose themselves to every peril to spread the faith in the far East.

14 • EXPANSION OF THE NESTORIAN CHURCH

With the stabilization of Nestorian doctrine and a firm hierarchical organization in Persia, the church began to look around for opportunities for expansion. This was made possible by both the external and the internal circumstances and conditions which accompanied the development of the Nestorian church and people. In the first place, the settlement of the Nestorians in Persia beyond the closed frontier of the Roman empire saved them from the encroachments of both Jacobite and Orthodox elements which flowed from Antioch and Constantinople. Nor were they involved in the doctrinal controversies which arose between the Monophysites of the ancient patriarchates of Alexandria and Antioch in one camp, and the Melkites who adhered to the Chalcedonian decisions and remained in the following of Constantinople and Rome. Even during local persecutions, they lived in relative peace and were allowed a normal growth without religious interference from outside. In fact, the tendency to exaggerate the gravity of religious persecutions in the East has to be re-considered in the general framework of the eastern state, where the whims of a despot or dictator resulted in the persecution of Christian and non-Christian alike without discrimination. On the other hand, the remaining frontiers of Persia, mainly looking eastward, lay open before the Nestorians with immense horizons of hope for evangelization and expansion. Seleucia-Ctesiphon was a natural meeting place of mercantile caravans from Arabia, Central Asia, India and China. It was here that the Nestorians became acquainted with people from all the countries of the East, and through this acquaintance began to work amongst these people. The bewildering success of their missions was made possible by a series of important internal factors. They combined with their enthusiasm for their faith a monastic system and a hierarchy ready for action and self-sacrifice. Moreover, they were extremely modern in the orientation of their missionary enterprise. Wherever they installed a new bishopric, a school with a library and a hospital with medical services were included in the project. The Nestorians were exceptionally noted for their technical ability, their learning and their medical skill. Like the modern missionary, they combined educational and medical services and religious work with great effect amongst the nations of the East. The wide expansion of the Nestorian church has bewildered scholars whose literary output on the subject has been tremendous.[1] A new appraisal of the glorious past of that Church has to be made, and, in the face of the many centres of its activity, the emergence, progress and extinction of Nestorian Christianity in each area must be considered in turn.

Arabia

The Arabian peninsula, long closed to all Christians and only re-opened to oil technicians in our lifetime, happened to be one of the earliest fields where the Nestorians launched their missionary enterprise. In reality, Christianity was not unknown in Arabia even before the advent of Nestorianism.[2] In 225, a bishopric was in existence at Beth Katraye, the country of the Qaṭars in south-east Arabia, opposite the islands of Baḥrain. Christianity had found its way to the tribes of Ḥimyar, Ghassān, Taghlib, Tanūkh, Ṭayy and Quḍā'a long before Islam; and an Arabian queen by the name of 'Maria' was a Christian who invited a Bishop Moses to come and live with her people. As early as 380 A.D., Ḥīrah and Kūfah contained numbers of Christians.[3] Nestorian Christianity is said to have come into Arabia from Persia as a result of Sassanid Christian persecutions, notably in the reign of Shapur II (310–79), when Christian emigrants found a haven of peace among the Arabs in adjacent provinces from 339 onwards.[4] Authentic knowledge from Syriac sources of the progress of Christianity in central and south Arabia is in *The Book of the Himyarites*,[5] written in 932 but containing references of great value to earlier periods, especially the sixth century. The

[1] For bibliographical material on the subject, see above (p. 242 n. 1) in addition to shorter accounts to be found in the general church histories by Fortescue, Kidd, Vine, Wigram and others. The older works of Assemani and Le Quien are still indispensable.

[2] On the Buhaira or Bahira legend, see R. Gottheil, *A Christian Bahira Legend* (New York, 1903), consisting of reprints from the *Zeitschr. fuer Assyriologie*, XIII–XVI, with Syriac and Arabic texts and English tr. See also Th. Wright's old work, *Early Christianity in Arabia* (London, 1855); H. Charles, *Le Christianisme des arabes nomades sur le Limes et dans le desert Syro-mésopotamien aux alentours de l'hégire (Paris, 1936)*; F. Nau, *Les arabes chrétiens de Mésopotamie et de Syrie du VIIe au VIIIe siècle* (Paris, 1933); and Louis Cheiko's Arabic work on Christian Arabic poets, *Shu'arā' al-Naṣraniya*, 2 vols. in 6 pts. (Beirūt, 1890–1), which is a monumental work of compilation, although his views have to be accepted with caution. A more recent survey in Arabic may be found in Asad J. Rustum, *The Church of the City of God, Great Antioch*, Vol. I (Beirūt, 1958), pp. 390–402.

[3] Stewart, pp. 50–4; L. E. Browne, *The Eclipse of Christians in Asia* (Cambridge, 1933), p. 13, quoting the Arab geographer ibn Ḥauqal.

[4] Vine, p. 59.

[5] Ed. and tr. Axel Moberg (Lund, Sweden, 1924).

main theme of the book revolves around the great massacre of the Arab Christians of Najrān and Ḥimyar by a Jewish Arab king, Masrūq, in 523 and the Abyssinian expedition of 525 to save them. It ended in the defeat of Masrūq, who drowned himself in the Red Sea.[1] It is said that there were six bishops in Arabia during the fifth century, of whom the bishop of Ḥirah owed ecclesiastical allegiance to the Nestorian metropolitan of Kashkar.[2] There were also churches at Ṣanaʿa, Aden and Dhafar as well as monasteries and schools at 'Marotha' and 'Jemana'. The reign of the Christian King Abraha al-Ashram[3] in the second half of the sixth century in Yemen revitalized Arabian Christianity. He built a cathedral at Ṣanaʿa. Arab Christians were usually followers of the 'Church of the East', though some were also under the influence of the Jacobite church in Syria. The current legend is that the Prophet Muḥammad learnt his first lessons about Christianity from a Jacobite monk – some say a Nestorian – by the name of Sergius Baḥīra.[4] However, in the course of the seventh century, the rise of Islam in Arabia swept both Christianity and Judaism from the peninsula, though we hear from Nestorian sources of isolated cases of Christian activities, such as a Nestorian synod held in 676 in southern Arabia with the Patriarch Georgius (660–80) presiding. Stray nomads such as Banu Ṣāliḥ clung to Christianity as late as 779, when the Caliph al-Mahdi wished to impose Islam upon them, and 823, when al-M'amūn persecuted them. We must assume, however, that by the ninth century at the latest all vestiges of Nestorian Christianity were stamped out of Arabia.[5]

Central Asia

Although we hear that Christianity was first introduced among the Gilanian tribes south-west of the Caspian, as well as Gog and Magog, by Aggai, who was Addai's disciple in 120–40 A.D.,[6] we must assume that this belongs to the realm of legend. Again we read of bishops of Rayy, Iṣfahan, Segestan, Nishabour, Herāt and Marw as signatories at a church council convened by the Catholicos in Seleucia-Ctesiphon in 424. The first instance on record which

[1] Stewart, pp. 57 et seq.

[2] Vine, p. 59. The others are the 'bishops at Kūfa, Beth Rahman, Perath Messenes, Beth Katraye and Najrān'.

[3] Th. Wright, pp. 92–100; Stewart, p. 68.

[4] Masʿūdi uses 'Buḥaira', diminutive of 'Baḥr', i.e. lake, but Gottheil (op. cit., p. 189, n. 1) shows this merely to be the Aramaic word meaning 'elect'.

[5] Vine, p. 125.

[6] The Syriac 'Doctrine of the Apostles', written in 250 A.D., makes similar reference to these early conversions; Mingana, 'Early Spread of Christianity', in *John Rylands Bulletin*, IX, 303; cf. Stewart, p. 77.

may be accepted as historical dates in the year 498, during the reign of Patriarch Acacius (485–96), when the tolerant Kavadh I (488–531) was ousted from the throne of Persia by the usurper Djamasp (496–8) and fled to Turkestan with Nestorians in his retinue. Among his companions were the bishop of Arran, four presbyters and two laymen who set to work to evangelize the Turks with considerable success. They were reinforced by a number of physicians, scribes and skilled artisans who helped to raise the cultural standards of the people, meanwhile extending the Gospel to them. The story runs that the presbyters worked for seven years in the area and that the laymen remained until 530. It is difficult to know what happened after that year, although Christianity must have persisted until an unnamed king of the Turks wrote in 781 to Patriarch Timothy (778–820), asking him for a metropolitan to administer to his people, who became Christians with him. Thomas of Margā speaks of the selection of eighty monks by Timothy and the ordination of bishops who were sent to the East to preach the Gospel. Shabhalishu's name is mentioned on the occasion as one of Timothy's envoys, for he knew the tongues spoken by Turks, Tartars and Mongols. Timothy named a metropolitan of Turkestan to be stationed at Samarqand with two bishops at Bu<u>kh</u>āra and Ṭa<u>sh</u>qand. The Nestorians then pushed toward Lake Baikal in the north-east, converting tribes of Tartar stock such as the Keraits, Uighurs, Naimans and Merkites, possibly in the course of the tenth and eleventh centuries. About 1077 ʿAbdishūʿ, metropolitan of Marw in <u>Kh</u>urāsān, wrote to the catholicos to inform him of the miraculous conversion of a king of the Keraits along with 200,000 of his people to Christianity.[1] Marco Polo (1265–1323) saw a church at the Kerait capital of Karakorum, and we begin to hear about the vast Christian kingdom of Prester John in Central Asia in the twelfth and thirteenth centuries. Both king and priest, Prester John also had the titles of 'Unc Khan' or 'Owang Khan'. It is suggested that 'Owang' is not dissimilar to 'Joannes',[2] and it is sometimes even identified as Jenghiz Khan,[3] who was not as hostile to Christians as Timur Lane. In Central Asia, the nomadic nature of the inhabitants rendered the frontiers of countries so mobile that we encounter both Mongols and Turks in the same territory. This accounts for the uncertainty of Prester John's frontiers, which were moved by travellers from Central Asia to China. The legendary nature of the story is shown by the fact that his empire was later identified with India and even Abyssinia. Although our knowledge of Nestorian Christianity in Central Asia in the later Middle Ages is meagre, recent archæological discoveries in the province of Semiryechensk in southern Siberia, now within the Union of Soviet Socialist Republics, prove

[1] Episode in Bar Hebræus quoted by L. E. Browne, pp. 101–2.

[2] Fortescue, p. 107.

[3] Article on 'Prester John', in *Encyclopædia Britannica* (14th and other edns., 1932 etc.)

beyond doubt that Christians must have been numerous in Turkestan until the fourteenth century. Christian cemeteries were found in the neighbourhood of the villages of Great Tokmak and Pishpek, near Lake Issiq Kōl. Many of the graves had stelæ with dated Syriac inscriptions ranging from 1249 to 1345. To quote a few examples, a stela of 1255 indicated the tomb of Chorepiscopos (that is, Bishop) Ama; and another of 1272 denoted that of Zuma, who combined at one and the same time the titles of priest, general and famous amīr, the son of General Gawardis. An inscription of 1307 reveals the grave of Julia, wife of the Chorepiscopos Johanan, thus demonstrating the laxity in observance of clerical celibacy in those remote regions. Other stelæ mention the priest Sabrishūʿ in 1315, Shlila, a celebrated commentator and religious teacher in 1326, and Pesoha, an eloquent preacher in 1338.[1] Other inscriptions name a woman, 'Terim the Chinese', a priest 'Banus the Uigurian', several laymen called 'Kiamata of Kashghar', 'Tatta the Mongol', and 'Shah Malik son of George of Tus'. This provides a clear demonstration of the great ethnic mixture of Christians, to whom the faith lifted all barriers between Syrian, Turk and Mongol in Central Asia.[2] The Crusaders dreamed of an alliance with those distant Christians under the leadership of the imaginary Prester John, who might descend on the Holy Land and help in saving it from increasing Muslim pressure. Western missionaries to the Far East, who traversed Central Asia and encountered Nestorians everywhere, wrote about Prester John and his immense realm in Cathay. John of Monte Corvino, the first Latin archbishop of Khān Bāliq, did so in 1305. It was not until Timur Lane (1336–1405) overran Transoxonia, together with Central and Western Asia, that Nestorian Christianity was obliterated from those regions.[3]

China

The romance of Nestorian Christianity in the Far East is one of the greatest revelations of modern scholarship. The Syriac *Breviarum Chaldanicum*[4] states that 'by St Thomas the Chinese also with the Ethiopians have turned to the truth,' that 'St Thomas has flown and gone to the Kingdom of the Height among the Chinese', and that 'the Indians and the Chinese . . . bring worship in commemoration of Thomas to Thy name, Our Saviour'. These

[1] Stewart, pp. 211–13; Vine, pp. 164–7.

[2] Stewart, p. 206.

[3] Ibid., p. 136 et seq.; Vine, pp. 61–2, 127–30 and 164–7; Kidd, *Eastern Christendom*, pp. 420–3.

[4] Ed. P. Bedjan, 3 vols. (Paris, 1886), III, 476 and 478; cf. Moule, *Christians in China*, pp. 11 and 26; Atiya, *Crusade in Later Middle Ages*, pp. 234–5.

statements, which trace the introduction of Christianity into China to the age of the Apostles, cannot be accepted as historical. Nevertheless, the Nestorians must have reached China in the early Middle Ages. The first recorded mission is known to have taken place during the patriarchate of Yeshuyab II (628–43), or more precisely, around the year 635. This has been proved by a great stone monument[1] which Jesuit missionaries discovered in 1625 at Si-ngnan-fu in the province of Shensi in Middle China. Its object is set out in the opening phrase of a long inscription in Chinese: 'Eulogy on a Monument commemorating the propagation of the Luminous Religion (i.e., Christianity) in the Middle Kingdom, with a preface to the same, composed by Ching-Ching a priest of the Ta-ch'in monastery, Adam priest and Chorepiscopos and papas (pope) of Zhinostan.'[2] After a very interesting outline of Christianity and the Bible, it is stated that the 'polished emperor' Tai-Tsung (627–50) received with honour in 635 a certain A-lo-pen, a Persian monk of high virtue who 'carried the true Scriptures'. The emperor read his books and commanded that they should be made known throughout the realm. Three years later (638), a decree was published ordering the local officials of the I-ning-gang quarter to build a monastery for this holy man and twenty regular monks. Before the end of the century the new religion had spread in ten provinces though with varying fortunes in successive reigns. The inscription notes that the stone was erected in 781 during the days of Catholicos Hanan Shua, the exact date of whose decease in 779 did not reach them until the completion of its consecration. It ends in Syriac script with the names of 128 persons, comprising priests and a metropolitan named Adam. On the whole, the Nestorians encountered no serious opposition to the preaching of Christianity in China during the seventh and eighth centuries. It was in the ninth century that this suffered, together with other foreign religions, its first deadly blows, when the Emperor Wu-tsung (840–6) decreed the return of all priests and monks to secular life. Although Christianity declined afterwards, it was never really obliterated from China until the late Middle Ages. This is clear from Syriac and Chinese sources which are confirmed by accounts of Arab travellers. To quote one example, Abu Dulaf, a poet at the Samanid court of Naṣr II b. Aḥmad of Bu<u>kh</u>āra (913–42), was enjoined by his master in 942 to accompany a Chinese embassy back to its native country. Later he wrote an interesting account of his travels in which he recorded that he had met Christians and seen churches in several towns of China.[3] In 1076, two Syrian monasteries were to be found in China – one at Sianfu and

[1] Saeki, *Nestorian Monument in China*, passim.; Stewart, p. 167 et seq.; J. Foster, *The Church of the Tang Dynasty*, pp. 91 et seq.; Moule, pp. 27 et seq.; Vine, pp. 130–5; K. S. Latourette, *History of Christian Missions in China* (New York, 1929), pp. 51–60; Fortescue, pp. 106–8; Kidd, pp. 420–3.

[2] C. E. Couling, *The Luminous Religion*, p. 49.

[3] Atiya, p. 236.

another at Chengtu.[1] Though no explicit and continuous record is available of subsequent metropolitans of China, we at least know that about 1093 the Patriarch Sabaryeshūʿ III appointed one Bishop George to Sestan and then transferred him to the see of Khatai (Cathay!) in North China. In 1266, Bishop John of the diocese of Hami, or Kamul, in China was present at the consecration of Patriarch Denha I[2] (1265–81). There were three Nestorian churches in the city of Iamzi (Yang-Chau-fu); and a Nestorian Christian called Mar Sargius who ruled over the province of Kian Su in China[3] in the years 1278–80. He was appointed to an office in Kublai Khan's household, and in 1281 built as many as seven monasteries. At the time the inhabitants of Chin-kiang-fu included 215 Christians.[4] At the close of the thirteenth century, we find a man of Chinese extraction on the throne of the Nestorian patriarchs in the person of Yahballaha III (1280–1317). The son of a Uigar archdeacon, born in Koshang in North China in 1245, and bearing the Syriac name of Morkos or Mark, was elevated to the see of Cathay and was subsequently elected patriarch while on pilgrimage at Jerusalem in 1280. Excellent physicians, technicians, scribes and artisans, the Nestorians were in demand at the Mongol court. Rabban Ṣaumā, a Uigar born in Peking, who became metropolitan of Khān Bāliq, was sent by the Mongol khan on a diplomatic mission to Europe lasting from 1287 to 1288. He visited Constantinople, Rome, Paris and Bordeaux and conferred with the Emperor Andronicus II (1282–1328), King Philip IV of France (1285–1314) and Edward I of England (1272–1307) as well as Pope Nicholas IV (1288–92). Chinese sources and both John of Monte Corvino and Marco Polo testify to the existence of Nestorians in China during the fourteenth century. There were twenty-three Christian families in Chinkiang about 1333 and three Nestorian churches at Yangchow in the early decades of the century.[5] With the advent of the Roman Catholic missionaries, the position of both Nestorian and Latin Christians was weakened by their quarrels in the face of the incoming Muslim. Then the Ming dynasty took control of China from the hands of the tolerant successors of Kublai Khan in 1369, and a wave of merciless persecution of alien religions began. It ended in the total extinction of Christianity in China by the turn of the century, while Timur simultaneously carried out the same destructive mission in Central Asia.

One relic of Nestorianism in the heart of Asia is said to be the survival of its ritual in a debased form in the Lamaism of Tibet. The striking resemblances with Lamaist Monasticism, the use of holy water, incense and vestments of a similar character to Nestorian practices, must be traced to the days of the Nestorian missionary in the high Middle Ages. It has sometimes

[1] Vine, p. 135.
[2] Stewart, pp. 189–90.
[3] Ibid., p. 193.
[4] Browne, pp. 104–5.
[5] Moule, pp. 145 et seq.; Latourette, pp. 64–5; Vine, pp. 167–8.

been suggested that Jesus came to Central Asia, from where He carried back those Buddhist teachings known to be identical with Christianity from Tibetan Lamaism. Since Buddhism did not reach Tibet until 640, it is unnecessary for the historian to waste his time refuting a baseless argument. Of more interest is the fact that an officiating lama recalls a Nestorian bishop celebrating the Nestorian liturgy.[1]

Other Places

The most enduring Nestorian contribution to the planting of Christianity in Asia undoubtedly took place in Southern India, where the Church of Mar Thoma is still a remarkable organization. Though it has changed obedience and is even divided, its origins at any rate must be associated with Nestorianism. A special section of this study will be devoted to that ancient church. We are left with the impression that Nestorian missionary activities in the Middle Ages knew no bounds in Asia. Apart from penetrating the Asiatic mainland in every direction, they preached the Gospel in such obscure places as the little island of Socotra in the Indian Ocean, some distance from the shores of Arabia and Africa. The Alexandrine explorer of the sixth century, Cosmas Indicopleustes, mentions the existence of Christians on that island. On two occasions we read of the consecration of a bishop of Socotra first in the catholicate of Enos (877–84) and then in the reign of the Patriarch Sabar-Ishūʿ III (1057–72). Again, Bishop Kyriakos of Socotra was present at the consecration of Yahballaha III in 1282 at the city of Baghdad.[2] The Portuguese also found their isolated settlement on the way to India and forced them to become Uniates in the fifteenth century.

Under the rule of the caliphate, Nestorian ambitions extended from eastern to western Asia and even to the strongholds of Monophysitism and Orthodoxy from which they had been barred by the Roman empire. Their missions therefore followed the Arab conquerors into Syria, Cyprus and Egypt, and the first Nestorian metropolitan of Damascus was nominated in the seventh century. Twice there is mention of a Nestorian bishop in Egypt in the middle of the eighth and eleventh centuries. Another bishopric at Tarsus seems to have been in existence until the middle of the fifteenth century. Jerusalem, too, normally had a Nestorian bishop who attended to the needs of pilgrims of his rite.[3] Yet it would be a mistake to over-rate the importance of their attempts in those regions. There was no continuity of

[1] L. A. Waddell, *The Buddhism of Tibet* (London, 1895), pp. 9, 421–2; cf. Fortescue, p. 109; Stewart, p. 252.

[2] Fortescue, pp. 104–5.

[3] Vine, pp. 125–26.

succession in any of those bishoprics, and the numbers of Nestorians was never considerable in any of those countries. Even in Jerusalem, which was raised to a metropolitan see in 1065, the Nestorians suffered from frequent interruptions, and their archbishops disappeared completely from the city after 1616. The few Nestorian converts in the Levant had either relapsed to their old creeds or became Uniates, as in the island of Cyprus.

Conclusion

Let us recapitulate the state of Nestorian expansion at its height, say in the year 1000, in order to see the magnitude of this achievement. The metropolitan dioceses under the ecclesiastical jurisdiction of the patriarch of the Church of the East were at least twenty in number with several bishoprics within each province. Traceable material concerning the twenty provinces may be summed up as follows:[1]

(1) Patriarchalis, with a metropolitan at Kashkar and bishops at Ḥīrah, Anbār, Karkha, Na'amania, Buazicha, Badaria, Tirhana, Kosra, Ocbara, Wāsiṭ, Rada and Naphara
(2) Jundishapur, with a metropolitan at Jundishapur and bishops at Susa, Ahwāz and Suster
(3) Nisibis, with a metropolitan at Nisibis and bishops at Bakerda, Balada, Arzun, Gesluna, Mardin, Amida (modern Diyarbekr), Maiperket, Ḥarran and Raqqa
(4) Teredon, with a metropolitan at Baṣrah and bishops at Ubullah, Destesana and Nahr-al-Marah
(5) Moṣul, with a metropolitan at Moṣul and bishops at Nineveh, Beth-Bagas, Haditha, Dasena, Nuhadra and Urmia
(6) Adiabene, with a metropolitan at Erbil and bishops at Maalta, Zuabia and Caftoun
(7) Garamæa, with a metropolitan at Karkh and bishops at Dakuka, and Buazicha – distinctive dioceses from those in the province of Patriar chalis
(8) Ḥalwan, with a metropolitan at Ḥalwan and a bishop at Ḥamadan
(9) Fars, with a metropolitan at Rawardshir and bishops at Shiraz, Shapur and Astachar, and on the islands of Socotra, Catara, Masamig, Drin and Ormuz
(10) Khurāsān, with a metropolitan at Marw or Merv and a bishop at Nishapur

[1] The following list has been compiled by Vine, pp. 123–4, with additional material from the same author, pp. 119–20.

(11) Atropatene, with a metropolitan at Taurisium and bishops at Marāgha and Achlat
(12) Herat, with a metropolitan at Herat and a bishop for Segestan
(13) Arran, with a metropolitan at Bardaa
(14) Rayy, with a metropolitan at Rayy and a bishop at Iṣfahan
(15) Dailam, with a metropolitan at Mukar
(16) India, with intermittent metropolitans at various places
(17) China, with metropolitans at Sianfu and numerous undefined bishoprics
(18) Turkestan, with metropolitans at Samarqand and numerous undefined bishoprics
(19) Damascus, with a metropolitan in Damascus
(20) Jerusalem, instituted as bishopric in 835 and raised to a metropolitan see in 1065

There is little doubt that however impressive this list may appear, it must be regarded as still incomplete. Assemani's estimate of the thirteenth century puts the metropolitan provinces of the Nestorians at twenty-five with an average of eight to ten episcopal sees for each province, thus totalling 200 to 250 Bishoprics.[1] These are figures in which any church could take pride. But destiny had a grim fate in store for the Nestorian church. By the end of the fourteenth century the Mongol hordes had overrun Central Asia and the Middle East, leaving behind them a trail of terror and burned cities. Timur Lane, who was himself a Muslim, spared neither Muslim nor Christian in his conquests. Even Baghdad was levelled to the ground. With the exception of the Malabarese church in southern India, all the missionary labours of centuries outside Persia went with the wind. The Nestorian church began a new chapter of decline.

[1] Assemani, *Bibl. Orient.*, III, 2, 630 et seq. cf. Fortescue, p. 108.

15 • THE NESTORIANS AND THE CALIPHATE

First Three Centuries

The Nestorian Church survived the frequent persecutions under the Sassanid empire until the seventh century, when the advent of the Arabs started a new era in its history. During the reign of Catholicos Yeshuyab II (628–44) the Muslim invaders seized Seleucia-Ctesiphon after the battle of al-Qādisiya in 637, and subsequently the whole empire succumbed to their armies. By the year 643, the Arabs had reached the Indian frontier. Yazdagird III, the last of the Sassanids, was a fugitive until he was assassinated by one of his own subjects at Marw in 652. With his disappearance from the scene, the caliphs became sole rulers of Persia with no rival native claimants. Under the Orthodox caliphs (632–61) and the Umayyads (661–750), Persia became a simple province in the vast Arab empire, whose seat of government was moved from Mecca to Damascus under the latter dynasty. With the coming of the Abbasids (750–1258), who founded their new capital, Baghdad, *Madīnat al-Salām* or the 'City of Peace', on the banks of the Tigris, the centre of authority shifted eastward back to Persia. Thus Persia began to recover its lost position in world events, and we must assume that the change had its impact on the Nestorians and their Church, though it is doubtful whether the new master meant any alteration in their political or social status. Under Islam, they continued to thrive as a special community in the same way as they had done under the Sassanids. Their status was defined in the Synod of Seleucia in 410 and was recognized by Yazdagird I (399–420). The Muslim rulers readily accepted the existing position of the Nestorians with all their rights and duties.

In the latter days of Sassanid rule, however, the Nestorians were subject to excessive taxation, the pretext being the Byzantine wars. Shapur II doubled his normal impositions, and Chosroes I exacted a poll tax from Christians *en lieu* of military service. The Arabs levied a land tax (*Kharāj*) and the poll tax (*jizyah*) in the same way as their predecessors. The Nestorians suffered political disabilites under both empires. On the other hand, Christians as a whole seemed to enjoy more favour with the Muslims than other conquered communities. Of course they shared with Jews and Zoroastrians the privilege of being *dhimmis*, or protected subjects. The Qur'ān makes it clear that Christians are next in religious kinship to the Muslims before all other races: 'Thou wilt certainly find nearest in affection to them that believe those who say, "We are Christians". This is because some of them are priests and monks, and because they are free from pride' (Sura V–85). They are described as the 'People of the Book' (i.e., the Bible) and also the 'People of the Covenant', that is, the 'Covenant of ʿUmar'[1] which granted them full protection. Scholars question the authenticity of this covenant and assume that Christians forged such documents at later dates for privileges with Muslim rulers. The Nestorian chronicler Māri states that the Nestorian Patriarch Yeshuyab II saw the Prophet Muḥammad, who gave him a document granting the Nestorian people certain privileges, and that the Orthodox Caliph ʿUmar confirmed its terms.[2] Again, the Caliph ʿAli accorded to the Nestorians a similar charter in recognition of their honourable behaviour with his army at Moṣul, where they provided his soldiers with food and water. The scrolls of Mount Sinai preserved in St Catherine's Monastery contain five copies of the so-called 'Covenant of the Prophet'.[3] The fact remains that early Islam respected Christianity and the clergy, and that the Caliphs treated Christians with remarkable tolerance. As to the Nestorians, Assemani states that within a couple of decades of the Arab invasion, the bishop of Adiabene wrote to say that the Muslims were not so unjust as they were thought to be, that they were not far removed from Christianity, and that they honoured the clergy and protected churches.[4] As late as the eleventh century, another Nestorian bishop, Eliya, metropolitan of Nisibis (1008–49), made a statement on the relations between Christians and Muslims in which he asserted that oppression of Christians was discountenanced by Muslim jurists.[5]

During the early centuries of the caliphate, the Christians enjoyed much better conditions than in the later Middle Ages. The Arabs loved justice and respected the conquered races' systems of government as well as the superiority of their cultures. Coming from an arid desert where cultural standards were limited to what the desert could offer, they sought for themselves a place in the superior civilizations of the peoples now under their rule. Unlike the Barbarians who wrecked the Roman empire, the Arabs did not barbarize the territories they conquered, but rather aspired to their intellectual attainments. In Persia they discovered the centres of Nestorian culture at Nisibis, Jundishapur and Marw or Merv, which they encouraged and utilized. These

[1] Text may be found in *Al-Mashriq Quarterly*, XII (1909), 681–2.

[2] Browne, pp. 41–2; Vine, pp. 89–90; Fortescue, p. 92.

[3] Atiya, *The Arabic MSS. of Mount Sinai*, p. 26.

[4] Assemani, III, 1, 131; cf. Fortescue, p. 92; Vine, p. 90.

[5] Browne, pp. 48–9.

schools furnished the state with an able body of administrative personnel, notably accountants and scribes. Physicians, teachers and interpreters were also supplied by the educated Nestorian community. The Nestorians knew how to make themselves necessary to the new regime. In spite of intermittent waves of repression, they flourished and sometimes gained enormous fortunes. It is unnecessary to give a full account of the persecutions, and thus bring out the darker side of a bright age. Each persecution, to be understood properly, has to be examined in the light of all its details. Some were due to the hatred of a Muslim bigot; others were caused by Christians intriguing among themselves. The pressure on Christians by ʿUmar II (717–20) was pre-eminently economic. The reign of Mahdi (775–85) was marked by one of the worst persecutions, including the persecution of Christian women. Hārūn al-Rashīd (785–809), on being told by a malicious courtier named Ḥamdūn that some Christians worshipped the bones of the dead in their churches at Baṣrah and Ubullah, ordered the churches to be destroyed. When the truth about these sacred relics was explained to him, however, he rebuilt them.[1] In the reign of al-Mutawakkil (846–61), the Nestorian Patriarch Theodosius was deposed and manhandled and disabilities were imposed on Christians, this time as the result of a pernicious intrigue by a Christian named Ibrāhīm ibn Nūḥ, who complained to the caliph against his catholicos out of jealousy.[2] Sometimes mob riots against the Christians occurred as in the case of the burning of a Nestorian church in the time of Patriarch John VI (1013–20).

As time passed and the number of Muslims in the countries of the Middle East became greater, a system of Christian disabilities developed in the official and legal circles. Though this system was not regularly applied, it seems instructive to outline it from a contemporary Arabic juridical source. The eleventh century writer al-Māwardi,[3] commenting on the Covenant of *Dhimmi* protection, elaborates the following thesis. A *Dhimmi* was bound by the contract of his protection to revere the Muslim Holy Scripture, refrain from uttering a falsehood against the Prophet Muḥammad, and never to speak ill of Islam as a religion. Furthermore, he was forbidden to approach a Muslim woman for marriage or illicit intent, to try to apostatize a Muslim or harm his person or property, and to assist an enemy of Islam or harbour a spy. All these obligations were inevitable. Others were commendable and included the use of a distinctive dress, the prohibition from erecting buildings higher than those of Muslims, from using church bells, from drinking wine and displaying a cross or a pig in public, from pomp and lamentation in

[1] Vine, pp. 93–4.

[2] Incident reported by Mari and Bar Hebræus in the *Syriac Chronicles*; cf. Browne, p. 54; Vine, p. 95.

[3] Cf. Browne, pp. 46–7, quoting Fagnan's version of al-Māwardi's 'Les statuts gouvernmentaux', pp. 305–6. See also Vine, pp. 99–100.

burial offices, and from horse riding. A breach of the items enumerated in the latter clause was legally punishable, though in practice considerable laxity was accorded by the rulers in their enforcement. The position of Christians in society was far from being despicable. As one commentator put it, they were highly respected and 'some of them are scribes of the sultans, and chamberlains of the kings, and physicians of the nobles, and perfumers and bankers'.[1] The great teachers of the early Abbasid times in Baghdad were Nestorians. The great academy of learning called the 'House of Wisdom' (*Dār al-Ḥikmah*) founded by Caliph al-Ma'mūn in 830, was staffed essentially by Nestorian scholars who mastered Syriac, Greek, and Arabic, and who were commissioned to translate the scientific and philosophical works of the Greeks. The pride of the age is the Nestorian Ḥunayn[2] b. Isḥāq (809–73) who is credited with the translation of a hundred works, although only a few have survived. Ḥunayn became the head of *Dār al-Ḥikmah* and received a stipend of five hundred gold dinars per month,[3] while al-Ma'mūn paid him in addition the weight in gold of the books translated by him. Ḥunayn was assisted and succeeded by his son Isḥāq, his nephew Ḥubaysh ibn al-Ḥasan, and ʿĪsa b. Yaḥya b. Ibrāhīm – all evidently Nestorian scholars. It was through these and others that the miracle of the Greek mind was transplanted into Arabic literature. Nestorian physicians, too, found their way to the caliph's palaces by winning their confidence through efficient and honest medical service. Caliph al-Manṣūr summoned Jurjis b. Bakhtīshū, a noted Nestorian physician, from the medical academy and hospital at Jundishapur to treat him for serious stomach trouble about 765. Afterwards this doctor settled in Baghdad, where he won great fame at Hārūn al-Rashīd's court. He established a family of medical specialists lasting six generations at a time when technical knowledge became a monopoly and was secretly passed from father to son. In fact, his own son Jibrīl b. Bakhtīshū was appointed as al-Ma'mūn's private physician and had free access to his palace. Ḥunayn b. Isḥāq, who combined with his duties as a

[1] Cf. Browne, p. 52.

[2] His full name is Abū Zayd Ḥunayn ibn Isḥaq al-Ibādī of Ḥērta (Arabic, al-Ḥīrah), usually called Joannitius by Latin writers. His apprenticeship in medicine started under Yaḥya or Yuḥannā b. Māsawayh, the Baghdad physician. But he broke away from him and went to complete his education in the territory of the Greeks and mastered their language and science. After rising in al-Mutawakkil's court, his downfall was precipitated by another Nestorian, Isrā'īl b. Ṭaifūrī. He died in 873 A.D. Though most of his works were in Arabic, he wrote in Syriac three books: one on the fear of God, a Syriac grammar and a Syriac dictionary used by later Syriac writers such as Bar ʿAlī and Bar Bahlūl in the ninth and tenth centuries. W. Wright, pp. 211–12; Chabot, p. 112.

[3] From the Latin *denarius*, the *dinār* was the standard gold currency weighing approximately 4 grams. It consisted of 10 or 12 *dirhams* (from the Greek *drachme*), a silver unit with a nominal value approximating 20 cents. Though somewhat arbitrary, the equivalent of the stipend quoted above must be about $1,000 in gold with a much greater purchasing power than that of our times.

great translator a knowledge of the medical arts, was similarly nominated as Caliph al-Mutawakkil's private physician. These men appear to have accumulated tremendous wealth[1] and were highly respected in society for their skill and integrity.[2]

While individuals thus gained position, fame and wealth during the first three centuries of Arab rule in Persia, the Nestorian church in general was not behind in its international activities and the expansion of its religious authority in the East. In reality, that age marked the peak of Nestorian history. Christians were tempted to claim full rights of equality with all Muslim fellow-citizens. The Caliph al-Muʿtaḍid (892–902) agreed to the appointment of a Nestorian as governor of the important region of al-Anbār in the neighbourhood of Bag͟hdad, the capital of the empire. This unprecedented decision vexed the Muslim population and incurred a great deal of jealousy and animosity towards the Christians. The rule of the 'Covenant of ʿUmar' had made it clear that Christians should not found new churches, though they were allowed to preserve and repair old ones. The Nestorians ignored this injunction and, in times of peace, took to building new and large churches. Cyprian, bishop of Nisibis, spent 56,000 gold dinars on a single church which he erected in 759 during the caliphate of al-Manṣūr (754–75).[3] This ostentation had detrimental repercussions on the position of Nestorians and the Nestorian church in later centuries. The progress made by the Christians is depicted in the ninth century by so celebrated an authority as al-Jāḥiẓ (d. 868/9), who accepts their wealth and power and praises their business ability, but revolts against their breach of earlier restrictions imposed upon them by the basic law of Islam.[4] While such attacks were intermittently launched against the Nestorians from without, the Church was gradually growing in wealth and worldliness from within. In the end, the elements of decay began to set in with disastrous consequences.

Beginning of Decline

When the caliphs discarded the old Sassanid metropolis of Seleucia-Ctesiphon and built their new capital Bag͟hdad between the years 762 and 766, the

[1] Jibril b. Bak͟htīshū (d.ca. 830) is said to have amassed a fortune of 88,800,000 silver *dirhems* in the reign of Caliph al-Ma'mūn. George D. Malech, *History of the Syrian Nation and the Old Evangelical-Apostolic Church of the East* (Minneapolis, 1910), mentions a case of treating the caliph's aunt for rheumatism, for which Hārūn al-Ras͟hīd rewarded him with 500,000 *dīnārs* (p. 275).

[2] P. K. Hitti, *Hist. of the Arabs*, pp. 309–14.

[3] Vine, pp. 102–3; Browne, p. 48.

[4] Cf. Browne, pp. 47–8.

Nestorian Patriarch Ḥananyeshū' II (774–9) considered it expedient to move the patriarchate in 775 to that city though still reserving the old title of Seleucia-Ctesiphon. As head of one of the richest and most influential communities in the Islamic empire, his position in the central administration became one of relative importance, sometimes through favour with the Caliphs themselves and sometimes through bribery and gifts. Spiritually, however, the patriarchal leadership was on the decline at a time when the church had reached the furthest limits of its extension in Asia. The patriarchs were beginning to look like civil servants as much as ecclesiastical dignitaries and were occasionally dispatched on diplomatic missions to Constantinople and Rome. The patriarchal throne was coveted by ambitious candidates who were ready to buy episcopal votes for large sums. Even in the latter part of the eighth century, signs of corruption could be detected in church matters. At the election of Timothy I (779–823), the candidate laid at the disposal of his electors heavy sacks to be opened after his success, presumably full of money. Timothy succeeded, and when his supporters opened the sacks they found them full of stones. He defended himself by retorting: 'The priesthood is not to be purchased for money'. The disappointed bishops became angry and wanted to replace him with his old rival Ephraem of Jundishapur. But it was too late, since he had procured the caliph's ratification of the original election, and he ably broke up the rebel forces. He proved, however, to be one of the most capable patriarchs of the Nestorian church. He loved learning and encouraged schools. He was in favour with Hārūn al-Rashīd. He reduced greatly the habit of marriage among bishops and fought heresies such as that of the *Mṣallians*. He had more than two hundred suffragans and entertained hopes of spreading Nestorianism westward by writing to invite the Maronites to join his church and accept his creed. At the time his aspirations seemed laudable, though they came to nothing. The length of his reign, more than forty years, enabled him to give the church that stability which it began to lose in the subsequent reigns. He was also a prolific writer. He left an astronomical treatise entitled the *Book of the Stars* as well as a correspondence numbering some two hundred epistles, an *Apology of the Christian Faith* in the form of a discussion with the Caliph al-Mahdi, many homilies, and an interpretation of the theology of Gregory Nazienzen.[1]

The church, however, became a prey to rivalry for the patriarchal throne, and this led to prolonged vacancies. Often it was won in the end by the highest bidder. Records of figures are incomplete but in the twelfth century at least three patriarchs were invested after the payment of considerable bribes. Yeshuyab V is known to have secured the patriarchate for five

[1] Chabot, *Littérature*, pp. 108–9. Half of his Epistles were published in text and French tr. by Braun (Paris, 1914).

thousand dinars in 1148.[1] That state was not altogether the outcome of external persecution; it was incurred by the internal condition of the church as well.

We have also to remember that the decline of the Nestorian church, especially in the twelfth and thirteenth centuries, was in one sense a reflection of the general decline characterizing the whole structure of the caliphate itself. In the ninth century the Caliph al-Muʿtaṣim (833–42) made his momentous decision to employ a bodyguard of Turkish slaves for the first time in Abbasid history. Like the Barbarian legionaries engaged by the Roman emperors, those Turks ended by wresting all power from the hands of the caliphs, who were thus rendered mere figure-heads and symbols of a great past that was no more. The Islamic empire was broken up into independent or semi-independent petty dynasties. Apart from Spain and the Shīʿite Idrīsids and Aghlabids of North Africa, who had no relations whatever with Baghdad, the Ṭūlūnids (868–905) and after them the Ikhshidids (935–69) in Egypt owed the Abbasid caliph a shadowy allegiance, while the Ḥamdānids (929–1003) in North Syria swung to Faṭimid rule (969–1171) soon after the establishment of their caliphate in Egypt. In the east, the situation was not much happier on account of the dismemberment of the provinces into another set of petty principalities. While the Ṭāhirids (820–72) planted their power in Khurāsān during the ninth century, the Ṣaffarids (867–903) wrested Sijistan in the same period, the Samanids (874–999) became independent in Transoxonia and parts of Persia, and the Ghaznawids (962–1186) became established in Afghanistān and pushed their rule over the Indian Punjab through the twelfth century, to quote only a few outstanding cases. The havoc which resulted from this patchwork was superseded by the rise of the formidable Mongol power which precipitated the final downfall of the Abbasid caliphate. The Nestorian church and people lived amidst all these tremendous upheavals, and the ensuing confusion necessarily told upon the administration of their community. Nevertheless, they survived the Abbasid caliphate itself and lived not too unhappily under Mongol rule, for the Mongols appeared in their turn also to favour the Nestorians. It is true that they must have suffered with everybody else from the devastations of the hordes of Jengiz Khan (1162–1227), who in the early decades of the thirteenth century left the flowering cities of Bukhāra, Samarqand, Balkh and Herāt depopulated and in ashes. Afterwards, Mangu (1251–60) the Great Khan decided in the opening year of his reign to incorporate China into his vast empire and to consolidate his rule over the whole continent of Asia. Thus he sent his two brothers at the head of two great armies, Kublai Khan to the east and Hulagu to the west. Kublai Khan (1260–94) succeeded Mangu as Hulagu inaugurated the Il-Khanate of Persia, which lasted to the four-

[1] Vine, p. 106.

teenth century (1258–1335). The details of these conquests and their repercussions[1] are much too complicated and involved to be treated here. Nevertheless, certain landmarks are worthy of special note owing to their direct bearing on Nestorian Christianity. It is said that Mangu Khan was almost a Christian himself. The extension of the *Pax tartarica* to China must have paved the way for Nestorian expansion into the Far East. In the West, Hulagu's sack of Baghdad and the final collapse of the Abbasid caliphate in 1258 was accompanied by some interesting events from the Nestorian viewpoint. Hulagu, of course, had a Christian wife – Dokuz Khatun[2] – and he was not averse to Christians. When the last caliph, al-Mustaʿṣim (1242–58), saw the end coming, he dispatched his wazīr, Ibn al-ʿAlqami, in the company of the Nestorian Patriarch Machicha II (1257–65) to seek less unfavourable terms of surrender. Though Hulagu refused to grant them audience, the incident shows how far the caliphs depended on the Nestorian catholicos. When the city was ruthlessly taken by storm, and the caliph and his retinue massacred together with an estimate of 800,000 dead, most of the Nestorians saved their lives by taking refuge in churches. Then as calm returned to the city, Christians were granted full freedom, and, what was more, the catholicos was given a palace where the caliph had kept his secretariat (*Dār al-Dawadār*). The patriarch moved into it and built a church there. Hulagu's successor, Abāgā (1260–5) was just as agreeable to the Christians of Persia as his predecessor, but they apparently abused the ruler's trust by taking the law in their hands. This is shown in an untoward incident of the reign of the Patriarch Denha I (1265–81), who smuggled an old Nestorian who had apostatized to Islam from Tekrit in 1268 and drowned him in the Tigris. This indiscretion bore its evil fruit later. Moreover, he rashly conducted processions in the capital under the protection of Mongol soldiers who manhandled the muslim spectators. These defiant acts of ostentation on behalf of the Christians, however, did not stop the internal confusion of the church hierarchy. The outrageous episode of the seizure and torture of the Nestorian Patriarch Yahballaha III (1281–1371) by the authorities on account of false accusations brought against him by two of his own bishops is a clear demonstration of the lamentable state of the church organization. When the Patriarch was acquitted and the Mongol Khan offered to kill his accusers, the saintly man disapproved and was content with their degradation and excommunication.[3] But the Mongol disgust with the Nestorian bishops remained, and the Il-Khans began to oscillate between Christianity and Islam in this period. In fact, the first western Il-Khan of Persia to adopt Islam openly was Aḥmad (1280–4). He was disowned by both Kublai Khan in the

[1] Howorth, *History of the Mongols*, Vol. III, pp. 154, 245–7, 265, 275, 396; Browne, pp. 146–78; Vine, pp. 141–69; Hitti, pp. 450–89.

[2] Howorth, I, 542.

[3] Browne, pp. 156–7.

east and his own successor Arghun (1284–91), who tended again to favour the Christians and sought alliance with the European potentates and the Roman pope through the famous mission of Bar Ṣaumā in 1287. The tradition of friendliness to the Christians persisted until the death of Baikhatu (1291–5), who left two claimants to his throne. The first was Baidū, a Christian at heart who rebuilt the ruined churches, and the second was Ghāzān (1295–1304), who slew his rival and seized the throne. On that occasion he publicly declared his final conversion to Islam in the same year. The position of the Christians was thus reversed. The patriarch was forced to leave the palace of 'Dār al-Dawādār', and the Arabs and the Kurds started to combat the Nestorians in 1295–6 without respite or deterrent. The turn of the century witnessed the renewal of Nestorian persecution with intense ferocity, even against the will of the Il-Khan. The massacre of the Christians assumed fearful dimensions in particular at the city of Marāghā.

The details of the Marāghā persecution are given in *The History of Yahballaha III.*[1] The patriarch was violently driven by the masses and subjected to much humiliation. One bishop was robbed and tortured. The monastery of St Thaddæus, where the relics of the saint rested, was destroyed. Yahballaha was saved only by payment of a heavy ransom and the intercession of Hayton, king of Armenia. But the movement had gone even beyond Ghāzān's power to control. In the following year (1297) Erbil became the scene of religious strife until Ghāzān raced to arrest the new outbreak. The patriarch was allowed to rebuild the Marāgha monastery and lead a life of precarious peace until the accession of Uljaitu (1304–16), who is said to have been brought up as a Christian in spite of his public profession of Islam, first in accordance with the Sunni rite, then changing to the Shīʿa, whereupon the populace changed his title from Khudabanda (Servant of God) to Kharbanda (Muleteer).[2] He was a vacillating and weak ruler, and the fact that he behaved mercifully towards the Christians and abolished the vexatious poll-tax was marred by his inept government. The thirteenth century ended and the fourteenth opened amidst the confusion and disintegration of the Il-Khanate of Persia. The reign of the last of the line, Abu Zaid (1316–35), was marked by another uproar at Āmid (Diyarbakr), where twelve thousand Christians were carried into slavery or slain and Bishop Mar Gregorios was beaten to death, while the magnificent Church of the Holy Virgin was burnt down (1317).[3] It is difficult to know how much of the damage is Nestorian

[1] Ed. under that title by J. A. Montgomery (New York, 1927), and by Wallis Budge under the title *The Monks of Kublai Khan* (London, 1928). Cf. Browne, p. 165.

[2] Browne, p. 168.

[3] The story is detailed in the *Syriac Chronicle* of Bar Hebræus. Assemani, III, ii, cxxxii–cxxxiiii, asserts that that bishop was Jacobite; cf. Browne, pp. 172–3. The identity of the church is, however, difficult to define, since both revered Mart Maryam though the Nestorians rejected the term *Theotokos*.

and how much Jacobite, though we must assume that at least part of it was Nestorian.

The continuous shrinking of the Nestorian church and the tendency towards a steady decline among the Nestorian people were accelerated in the fourteenth century by a much graver event. Timur Lane (1396–1405), who was not a Mongol and did not share with them that innate clemency towards Christianity, but who was a Muslim of the fierce Turkish stock of the Berlas tribe, established himself at Samarqand after usurping the throne of his Mongol master, Chagatay Khan. He then began one of the most bewildering and fearful careers of conquest in history. Between 1380 and 1387 he reduced to his sway Khurāsān, Jurjān, Mazandarān, Sijistān, Afghānistan, Fars, Azerbaijān and Kurdistān. He routed the forces of Toqtamish, Khan of the Golden Horde, in 1391, and in 1393 seized Baghdad together with the whole of Mesopotamia. Then he crossed to India, and after having overrun it, turned northwest to Anatolia and defeated the Ottoman Turks in the battle of Angora in 1402, and carried Sultan Bayezid I into captivity. Although the Timurid dynasty remained until about 1500, it had reached its widest expanse in Timur's lifetime. Timur wiped out whole cities even more ruthlessly than the Mongols. In Persia, for instance, he left a pyramid of 70,000 skulls on the ruins of Iṣfahan and another of 90,000 on the ruins of Baghdad. Amidst these misfortunes, both Muslims and Christians suffered equally. The Christians were no longer in favour. On the contrary, when identified they paid a great penalty for their faith.

The decline which had begun before Timur was thus increased. Witnesses had lost sight of older churches before the advent of Timur. The churches of Tirhana, Jundishapur, Balada, Dasena and Karkha had ceased to figure on records since 1318. Others, such as Beth Bagas and Gesluna, disappeared between 1318 and about 1360. After 1380, with Timur's invasions, churches were obliterated in the greater towns, including Baghdad, Moṣul, Erbil (Arbīl), Nisibis, Bakerda (Gezira), Taurisium (Tibriz) and Marāgha, which were strongholds of Nestorian Christianity, as well as other smaller towns such as Avadia, Urmia, Mardin, Amida (Diyarbakr) and Maiperkat.[1] Nestorian Christianity as a national and international organization crumbled under Timur's heels. Whole communities were massacred, others lost their ancient tenacity and entered the faith of the conqueror to save their skins, and the few survivors who retained their old religion fled from the open plains and cities and took refuge amidst the fastnesses of the Kurdistan mountains between Lake Urmia and Lake Van. Nestorianism was completely forgotten in China and Central Asia. It became a distant memory in its old home of Persia and Mesopotamia. The Nestorians sank into poverty, ignorance and seclusion until they were rediscovered in modern times.

[1] Vine, p. 159.

16 • THE NESTORIANS IN MODERN TIMES

Seclusion, Schism and Re-Discovery

Ever since the Timurid invasion of western Asia, the Nestorians had been gradually pushed out of the plains and central cities of Persia, Mesopotamia and Kurdistan to the only remaining places of safety, the Hakkiari mountain heights extending between Lake Urmia and Lake Van. Their flourishing communities were last heard of in 1551 at Taurisium (Tibriz) and in 1553 at Baghdad. The patriarchate had been moved from the city of the caliphs to Marāgha, east of Lake Urmia. Even in Nisibis, the ancient stronghold of Nestorian scholarship, they seem to have disappeared from the scene around 1556.[1] They occupied roughly the triangular area between the two aforementioned lakes with Moṣul at the head of the triangle. Their mountainous country, thus situated partly in Azerbaijan and mainly in Kurdistan, consisted of frontier territories between modern Persia and the Turkish empire comprising Mesopotamia. Wedged between two hostile states and surrounded by the wild Kurdish and Yazīdee tribes, they led a precarious existence for centuries and were segregated from civilization and the outer world to the extent that they were forgotten by other Christian nations and churches. In their long seclusion they fell an easy prey to ignorance and lost the ancient tradition of theological scholarship. Formalism became the distinctive feature of their religious practices. In their unremitting strife for survival, the leadership of their tribes had to be concentrated in the family which gave them their patriarch or catholicos, who grew to be not only their religious head but also a kind of theocratic prince to whom they resorted for arbitration in secular as well as religious troubles. The patriarchate thus developed into a peculiarly hereditary institution amongst the Nestorians. Since the patriarchs remained celibate, the crown consequently passed from uncle to nephew. That system, which in all probability worked satisfactorily during the early generations, had disastrous results in the long run. This was due to the fact that the patriarchal throne occasionally devolved upon children under the influence of their mothers or older sisters who

[1] Vine, p. 171.

handled the state affairs of the community. Ultimately the bishops also adopted the same hereditary procedure. In the course of the fifteenth century, the Nestorian people became restive about this state of things and some families decided to do away with that method of succession. Thus, when the Patriarch Shimʿūn bar Māmā died in 1551, a number of bishops, supported by a considerable section of the Nestorian community, wished to elect a more suitable candidate than his own nephew Shimʿūn Denha. A decision was reached in favour of a more mature monk, the *rabban* of Hurmizd Monastery by the name of John Sulāḳā[1] whose election started the first serious schism of the Nestorian church in modern history. Franciscan missionaries had already reached the Nestorian field by way of Jerusalem and evidently succeeded in convincing the new patriarch that he could strengthen his position if he were to accept the Roman profession together with confirmation by the pope. On accepting the proposition, he was taken by them to Jerusalem, where the Roman Catholic Custodian of the Holy Sepulchre furnished him with letters of introduction to the Holy Pontiff, and thence he went to Rome. Pope Julius III (1550–5) received him well and ordained him patriarch upon his declaring the Catholic profession in 1553. Afterwards he returned home hoping that the new pallium would help him in regaining the whole community of Nestorians to his side. He failed in the attempt and ultimately, perhaps through the plotting of his rival, was seized by the Turkish pasha of Diyarbekr and thrown into prison, where he was murdered. Nevertheless, the Uniate line was maintained by the election of Ebedyeshūʿ (1555–67) to succeed him; and he, too, received the pallium in due course from Pope Pius IV (1559–65). After the next two patriarchs, ʿAitallah and Denha Shimʿūn, who retained a shadowy allegiance to Rome, and their supporters became indifferent and the union, and relations with the Holy See became irregular. Fortescue[2] states that the last Catholic profession was submitted in 1670 by Mar Shimʿūn XII; and since then the Sulāḳa line reverted to its old Nestorianism except for one solitary and restless attempt to bridge the breach with Rome in 1770. Even in that early period of the union, it is doubtful whether the original Nestorian practices were changed beyond a formal submission to the Catholic profession and the receipt of the pallium from Rome.

The other line of succession began with Shimʿūn Denha, whose standards of morality appeared to be at the root of the schism. In 1607 and 1657 two of his successors, Elias VI and Elias VII, thought to disarm their Uniate opponents by declaring the Catholic profession in their turn and obtaining

[1] Assemani, *Bibl. Orientalis*, I, 523–34.

[2] *Lesser Eastern Churches*, p. 102. The dates of the patriarchs become quite hazy in the modern period, and we find lots of anomalies and contradiction in secondary literature on the subject.

a similar pallium. Curiously enough, the pallium was granted by the popes to both candidates, and accordingly there were two Uniate patriarchs – Elias at Moṣul and Shimʿūn at Urmia.[1] The two sat on the Nestorian throne and both were legally recognized by Rome.[2] So flimsy was the Romanist union that it grew more and more ineffective after Elias VII. In the middle of the eighteenth century, a certain archbishop of Diyarbakr called Joseph coveted that throne for himself and sought to buttress his claim by breaking away from the second line to start a third under Roman control and was accordingly granted papal confirmation and the pallium, too. With the return of the second line to papal allegiance, however, in 1826, the popes were persuaded to drop the third, which spontaneously disappeared from the scene of events in the course of the year.

From this narrative of confused developments, it may be deduced that the Uniate Chaldæan[3] line now in Moṣul paradoxically stems from the ancient Persian Church of the East, which had been the stronghold of Nestorianism against the West. Meanwhile the heirs to the Uniate line of Sulāḳa, at present in America, became the representatives of staunch resistance to Rome and the guardians of the old Nestorian doctrine. Apparently the former were politically the stronger of the two in Turkish times, since they were recognized by a special decree (firmān) from the Sublime Porte, whereas the others ruled only by the consent of the people with the approval and under the protection of the amīr of Kurdistan. Whenever the amīr withdrew his safeguard, for which the patriarch paid heavily, a wave of persecution invariably took place.

For some centuries the only approach to the Nestorians from the outer Christian world came from Rome; and Roman interests revolved around the chief aim of wresting the Catholic profession from him who sat on the throne in return for the pallium. Until the dawn of the nineteenth century the whole matter ended then, and the Nestorians remained where they had been before. The nations of the West were unaware of their very existence.

[1] His line apparently moved from Moṣul to Urmia in the seventeenth century and to Qudshanis in the eighteenth.

[2] This is a fact hard to explain, and the late Dom Fortescue (p. 103) leaves the question unanswered.

[3] The name 'Chaldæan' which is ethnic rather than religious was adopted to dodge the obvious contradiction in the use of the words 'Catholic Nestorian'. Chaldæans increased steadily, and in 1902 two Nestorian bishops and a group of 20,000 joined the Catholic Uniates. Attwater (II, 204) estimates the total of the community at 96,000. They also suffered great losses in the various massacres. Their head is the patriarch or *katholikos* of Babylon residing at Moṣul with ten bishops. He holds a seat *ex officio* in the Senate of Iraq. The Dominicans have been active amongst them since 1882. Chaldæan monasticism was reformed and revitalized by Gabriel Dumbo of Mardin, who founded a new order called the Antonians of St Hormisdas in 1808. The use of the Syriac liturgy is modified in conformity with their Uniate character. The chief contribution of the Catholic order, apart from education, is the suppression of the hereditary nature of the patriarchate.

Then suddenly came the age of re-discovery[1] of their little community as a revelation to a bewildered world. The story started with a certain Claude James Rich, then Resident of the British East India Company in Baghdad, who was not a man of religion but happened to be highly cultured and possessed of a very keen interest in archæology. He visited the ancient site of the Biblical city of Nineveh in 1820, and his report[2] on the area excited all manner of circles, both scholarly and missionary, in England and America. At long last he revealed to the English-speaking races the astounding facts about the Assyrians, who still conversed in a language similar to that spoken by Jesus and the Apostles and whose peculiar form of Christianity called for study and sympathy. A systematic archæological exploration was commenced by A. H. Layard.[3] On the religious side, however, the Nestorians were evidently and traditionally anti-popish and had neither icons nor crucifixes in their churches, only a simple and symbolic Cross. Their attitude towards the Virgin Mary was much akin to Protestant conceptions. Could they be the ancient 'Protestants of the East'? Hence ensued a deluge of missions and Protestant missionaries to those forlorn sons of a historic church in their God-forsaken abodes.

A brief survey of what happened will be of interest. The Rev. Joseph Wolff came to Kurdistan in 1820 and afterwards returned to England with a manuscript of the Syriac New Testament, which the British and Foreign Bible Society published and distributed amongst Nestorians in 1827. Hitherto the only copies of the Scripture were confined to the churches and the hands of dignitaries, a fact which explains the immense value of this initial contribution to the understanding of the Scriptures. Then the American Presbyterian Mission, composed of Messrs. Smith and Davies, arrived at Urmia in 1830, to be followed by Rev. Justin Perkins in 1834 and Dr Asahel Grant[4] in 1835. Others joined in the field at different dates without any enduring impression, such as the Danish Lutherans,[5] the Norwegian Lutherans and the Baptists.

[1] Fortescue, pp. 115 et seq., Vine, pp. 176 et seq.

[2] *Narrative of a Residence in Koordistan and on the Site of Ancient Nineveh*, 2 vols. (London, 1836).

[3] *Nineveh and its Remains*, 2 vols. (London, 1849).

[4] He is the author of the famous volume *The Nestorians, or, The Lost Tribes containing evidence of their identity, an account of their manners, customs and ceremonies, together with sketches of travel in ancient Assyria, Armenia, Media, and Mesopotamia, and illustrations of Scripture prophecy* (New York, 1841). The appeal of the discovery of the lost tribes of Israel naturally fired the imagination of the contemporary. French tr. Henriette Winslow, *Les tribus perdues* (Paris, 1843).

[5] They appear to have worked through a converted Nestorian by the name of Nestorius George Malech in 1893, who translated from Syriac a rather peculiar book written by his father, George David Malech of Urmia, entitled *History of the Syrian Nation and the Old Evangelical-Apostolic Church of the East, from Remote Antiquity to the Present Time* (Minneapolis, Minn., 1910) with much contradictory material and documents as well as a

The Russians, too, emerged on the scene as the supreme defenders of the whole of Eastern Christendom. As the arch-enemies of the Turks, the Russians continued to receive successive appeals from the Nestorians throughout the nineteenth century in the hope that the tsar might restore their freedom from their Ottoman oppressors by force of arms. As early as 1827, whole groups of Nestorian families crossed the Russian frontier and joined Russian orthodoxy. Towards the close of the century (1898) a Nestorian bishop with four priests appeared at St Petersburg and declared, on behalf of their nation, readiness to profess obedience to the Russian church in return for protection. The Russians responded by the establishment of an Orthodox mission centre, a printing press and a church at Urmia, together with forty parishes and sixty schools up and down the country. They claimed to have won some twenty thousand converts in 1900. Expectations ran high amongst the poor Nestorians, who awaited in vain the tsar's mighty battalions to come and deliver them from bondage. But the tsar's forces were not forthcoming, and, in disappointment, the orthodox converts relapsed to the old obedience.[1]

The truly lasting efforts amongst the Nestorians from the non-Catholic West belong primarily to the Presbyterians, who built schools, hospitals and welfare centres, and next, to the archbishop of Canterbury's Mission to the Assyrian Church. It is interesting to note the reaction of the Nestorians to these two new forces. Since the Presbyterians served and proselytized in the meantime, the Nestorian church looked with some disfavour and apprehension upon their activities. In contrast, the Anglican mission followed a different line of policy which is best represented by its chief exponent among the Nestorians, George Percy Badger, originally a printer who became an ordained minister and chaplain of the East India Company in the diocese of Bombay. Previously he had spent the years 1835–36 at Beirūt, where he acquired a knowledge of Arabic and became familiar with the Near East. He was accordingly chosen by Dr William Howley, archbishop of Canterbury (1766–1848), and Dr C. J. Blomfield, bishop of London, as delegate to the Eastern churches and especially to the Nestorians in Kurdistan for the years 1842–4. He revisited the region in 1850 and completed his valuable work on the Nestorians and their ritual.[2] From the very outset,

multitude of personal photographs without any value to the reader. The odd thing about N. G. Malech is that he combined with his Danish mission the dignity of archdeacon of the Nestorian church and a seat in a patriarchal committee.

[1] Fortescue, p. 119; Vine, p. 180.

[2] *The Nestorians and their Rituals: with a Narrative of a Mission to Mesopotamia and Coordistan in 1842–1844, and a Visit to those Countries in 1850; also, Researches into the Present Condition of the Syrian Jacobites, Papal Syrians, and Chaldeans, and an Inquiry into the Religious Tenets of the Yezeedees*, 2 vols. (London, 1852). The title of the book explains its chief contents. The second volume is devoted to the rituals. Badger's immediate predecessor

Badger made it clear to the Nestorian patriarch that Anglicanism, unlike Protestant missions, was there simply to help without any ulterior motives of proselytism. He had openly assailed the American Board of Foreign Missions in Constantinople, whose agents belonged to the Presbyterian, Independent, Dutch Reformed and other dissenting bodies, with 'their design to create schism' amongst the Christians of the East.[1] He equally disapproved of Roman tactics which had weakened the church of the East by splitting its membership into Uniate Chaldæans and the so-called dissident heretics. The English church was only concerned with educational help, the protection of a depressed people, and the reform of the old church from inside. The Nestorian patriarch was elated by these noble principles, and special favour was shown to the Anglicans. Unfortunately their mission led a fitful existence after Badger and was not stabilized until the 'eighties. Canon Maclean and his two companions, A. Riley and W. H. Browne, resumed work amongst the Nestorians in 1886. On account of the increasing influence of the Russian mission at Urmia, within the precincts of Persia, it was decided in 1903 to move the headquarters of the Anglican mission to Van, on the Turkish side of the frontier, during the tenure of Canon W. A. Wigram,[2] whose labours lasted from 1902 to 1912. The mission continued its good work without interruption until the First World War. Even the eloquent defence of the Roman Catholic position *vis-à-vis* the Nestorians by Adrien Fortescue[3] did not deter him from wishing 'the Anglican mission Godspeed in its noble work', of course with the additional hope that both Anglican and Nestorian might ultimately become Roman Catholic in the end.

The Last Phase

The political background of the western missionary enterprise amongst the Nestorians represents the beginning of the last phase in their pathetic history. Before the advent of the missionary, the Nestorians had lived a comparatively peaceful life with an equally primitive Kurdish neighbour. The outward appearance of the Nestorian and the Kurd was almost identical

after the memorable Wolff expedition was Mr Ainsworth, who also came to make inquiries in 1842 under the auspices of the Society for Promoting Christian Knowledge. He published another 2-vol. work entitled *Travels and Researches in Asia Minor, Mesopotamia, Chaldæa and Armenia* (London, 1842).

[1] *Nestorians and their Rituals*, I, 241–55, 267–98; P. E. Shaw, *American Contacts with the Eastern Churches, 1820–1870* (Chicago, 1937), pp. 95–100.

[2] Author of *The Assyrian Church, 100–640* A.D., often quoted in the foregoing pages.

[3] Op. cit., pp. 123–6.

in spite of the variance in religion, tradition and intimate private life. The Nestorian community was organized on a tribal basis under the headship of a *malik* for each tribe in its own village. The patriarch was the supreme head of the nation, and all chiefs owed him tacit allegiance in civil and religious affairs. Politically both the Muslim and Christian populations were subject to the Kurdish amīr of the region. The Kurdish amīr was accompanied by the patriarch on the same bench for mutual deliberations on legal issues involving Muslim Kurds and Christian Nestorians. It is extremely difficult to estimate the number of the whole community with any precision. The figure of 100,000[1] has been mentioned; and if so, the Nestorians must have suffered heavy losses in the ensuing massacres by the Turks, Kurds and Iraqis, respectively. However, at this moment, Kurdish affinity with the Assyrian was frequently described by the Kurds, who stated that only a hair separated them from one another, whereas a mountain stretched out between them and the Armenians. This does not imply that life in the Hakkiāri Mountains was uneventful. Mishaps continuously took place, but on a rather limited scale, and the wounds were soon healed by the leaders on both sides. In 1830 the Kurds attacked the Nestorians, whereupon representations in their favour were tendered by the European consuls to the Sublime Porte. The Sultan sent Rashīd Pasha to restore order and tranquility in Kurdistan, and the Turkish army withdrew in 1834.[2] Afterwards, when the Kurdish Amīr Nūr-Allah decided to visit Istanbul in 1840, he entrusted Mar Shimʿūn XVII Oraham with his civic powers and the guardianship of his *harem*.[3] It would appear that the harmony between Kurd and Nestorian was largely marred by the circumstances of the emergence of the Western missionary in the area with marked sympathies towards the native Christians and a promise of help which went beyond education and social welfare to political issues against the Muslim. Conscious of his superiority to his neighbour and

[1] Vine, pp. 183–4; Fortescue, p. 128, quotes three estimates from various sources, the highest by Silbernagl as 150,000, the lowest by Herzog and Hauck as 70,000 and a middle one at 100,000 by Cuinet (*La Turquie d'Asie* [Paris, 1892], II, 650), which is apparently acceptable to him. Cuinet puts the 19th-century distribution of Nestorians as 10,000 in Persia and 90,000 in Turkey, of whom 40,000 are *rayahas* or *Raya* (the Arabic *Raʿiyah*, or citizens) in the cities and 50,000 *ʿashīrah* (Arabic for tribe) Nestorians or tribal population in the mountain. This total number is accepted by D. Attwater, *The Christian Churches of the East*, II, 189–92. Owing to proselytization, massacres and steady emigration, their numbers have been considerably reduced in the Middle East. Attwater (II, 194) underlines the factor of reunion with Rome and gives one example of four members of the clergy with 200 Nestorians going over to Catholicism in 1923 at Ḥoms.

[2] Vine, pp. 187–9.

[3] P. Rondot, *Les chrétiens d'Orient* (Paris, 1955), pp. 161–2; see also ch. V, 'Christianity in Asia: Syrian and Assyrian', as part of a contribution by the author of these pages to a forthcoming publication on 'Modernism in the Arab World', a project subsidized by the Rockefeller Foundation under the general editorship of Prof. S. Ghorbal whose death later seems to have placed the publication in suspense.

becoming more aware of the glorious past of his church, the still immature Nestorian began to cherish a wider measure of enfranchisement from both Turk and Kurd and even entertained hopes of independence. The Kurd was therefore irritated and began to react by a show of hostility more than ever before, and the Turks were invariably on the Muslim side unless checked by foreign interference in Constantinople.

In reality, the first serious outbreak between Kurd and Nestorian occurred in the year 1843, when the hill tribes descended on the unsuspecting Christian villages under the generalship of a bigoted chief by the name of Badr-Khan of Bohtan, who aspired to assert his feudal lordship over all Kurdistan. The revolt, initially directed against Turkish rule, was soon deflected to a ferocious onslaught to exterminate the Nestorians as a first measure of unification and uniformity in Kurdistan. So poisoned was the whole atmosphere that even tolerant personalities like the aforementioned Nūr-Allah inevitably joined the movement. Both Grant[1] and Badger[2] were around at the time, and Badger gave refuge to the patriarch, whose life he had saved. The horrors of the ensuing massacre have been described as the worst since the ravages of Timur Lane. Only the firm representations of the British government persuaded the sultan to despatch the pasha of Moṣul at the head of an army to save the depleted numbers of the Nestorians from gradual extermination. It is said that the loss of life amounted to twenty thousand souls, including some Chaldæans. Several other thousands fled from Turkey to Russia in the Caucasus. Meanwhile, the Nestorian patriarch took to the habit of appealing to the Powers for protection. There appeared to be no way to bridge the gap which kept widening between Kurd and Nestorian.

The final tragedy of the Assyrians was precipitated by the circumstances of the First World War (1914–18) and its tragic aftermath. Having thus fallen out with their Kurdish neighbours beyond any repair, the harrassed Nestorians decided to descend from their Hakkiari Mountain retreat to the lower plains of Moṣul and to join the Allies against Turkey in the hope that thereby they might earn independence. Thus forty thousand of them discarded their old homes wholesale and their 'levies' volunteered to serve in the Dunsterforce with the British and the Russians. The hardships inflicted upon them in the rugged mountain paths must have equalled or even exceeded the Hakkiari massacres. The mortality especially amongst women and children was very high. The details of the complete picture are not yet entirely revealed, but they are in some way reminiscent of the exodus of the Jews from ancient Egypt through the Tīh Desert in Sinai, and of the Mormon trail from Nauvoo to the western frontier wastelands in 1846. During centuries of segregation from the rest of the outside world, the Nestorian outlook was

[1] *The Missionary Herald*, XXXIX (1843), 435 et seq.

[2] *Nestorians and their Rituals*, I, 256 et seq.

reduced to such limitation that they became incapable of coping with and integrating into the new order of Arab nationalism which had just broken away from the fetters of Turkish imperialism. Vain dreams loomed in their simple imagination of raising their tiny nation to the rank of independent statehood in the plains of Moṣul. In the fulness of hope for the revival of the old Assyrian nationality, they embarked on a suicidal career. In 1917 they lost their supreme leader, the Patriarch Mar Shimʿūn, XX Benyāmin,[1] who was assassinated by a fanatic Kurd on the Persian frontier. His successor, Mar Eshai XXI Shimʿūn, was only a child of thirteen who had to complete his studies at St Augustine's in Canterbury as a ward of the archbishop there. His patriarchal prerogative devolved on his older sister with her imperfect education at a minor missionary college, and with no means of effective communication with the tribal traditions of her nation. When the army levies were disbanded after the peace of Versailles, the derelict Nestorians virtually became homeless refugees on the banks of the upper Tigris and Euphrates Rivers under the British mandate in Iraq. Meanwhile, the ill feeling of the native Muslim towards the Christian was intensified by a series of untoward incidents in which the levies were involved. The fact that Britain was willing to help them in the League of Nations did not improve their relations with their Iraqi neighbours. At one moment, it was suggested that they might be removed as a whole to Canada,[2] but they preferred if possible to attain independence in their old homeland. With the end of the British mandate in 1933, and the return of the young patriarch from school in England, the sordid story of Nestorian strife was resumed with little or no respite. Mar Shimʿūn at once attempted to assume his ancestral quasi-tribal authority, both ecclesiastical and temporal, oblivious of the changes that had taken place in the new state of Iraq. The Nestorians apparently still lived in bygone days and refused to make any attempt towards integration in the general pattern of the new Iraqi nation. Their failure to cope with the situation ended in catastrophe.

When the Iraqi Minister of the Interior summoned the patriarch to Bag͟hdad in the course of 1933 and requested him to renounce the practice of civil authority and of acting as a state within the state, he refused and was

[1] He was only twenty-seven at the time of his assassination, and it is interesting to note that he was only seventeen at his accession to the patriarchal throne.

[2] Other projects for settling them in other countries were advanced. Brazil was willing to accept 20,000. Cyprus, French Sudan and British Guiana were also mentioned for partial settlement of their numbers. The French mandatory authorities in Syria agreed to accept 10,000 to be placed in the G͟hāb district in the upper valley of Nahr al-Kalb (the Orontes), provided the expense was met by contributions from Britain, Iraq and the League of Nations. This and all the other attempts came to nought, except for a few thousand Nestorians who somehow succeeded in finding their way inside the Syrian frontier and camped out in the district of Daīr al-Zor in the valley of the K͟hābūr River (Attwater, II, 191–2).

detained virtually as a prisoner in the capital. The Assyrian chiefs met at Moṣul and issued a severe protest against the government actions. The central administration responded by the issue of an ultimatum offering them the choice of abiding by the law of the land or freedom to depart from the country. One thousand armed men accepted the challenge and chose to cross the Euphrates into Syria in the summer of 1933. To their bitter disappointment, their entry was refused by the French in Syria, and they had to retrace their way to Iraq. A stray shot was fired on their arrival, and suddenly the armed forces of Iraq attacked the disorderly Assyrian refugees. Kurds and Bedouins joined the fray, which amounted to a general massacre. Moreover, many of the survivors were seized as rebels and shot in cold blood. The government indicted Mar Shimʿūm for the revolt and withdrew Iraqi citizenship from him by special act of parliament, whereupon he was deported to Cyprus. The tragedy extended to other Assyrians whose fate became an international scandal. From Cyprus the unhappy patriarch went to the United States of America, where he was invited by a relatively large colony of Assyrian emigrants to Chicago in 1940. In spite of the fact that he had become an American citizen, he rendered a state visit to the embassy of Iraq in Washington in 1948 to submit his loyal homage to the old home authority in the hope of repatriation, but without any positive response. The depleted number of the Nestorians in the Middle East is currently estimated at 30,000 of whom about 8,000 have succeeded in crossing the Syrian frontier and reside in the K͟hābūr Valley. The rest live around Bag͟hdad and Moṣul, shepherded by one metropolitan and a single bishop.

The fate of the Nestorians has been hard and pitiful. Their hopeless plight has been depicted from within by Syriac writers such as Abraham Yuhannan, whose story of Nestorian persecutions, already mentioned, is entitled *The Death of a Nation.*[1] Another significant book on their contemporary history by a younger Nestorian is *The Last Phase of Nestorian History.*[2] Whether this implies the end or the beginning of the end of Nestorianism remains yet to be seen. Although it is hard for the historian to issue a clear verdict in a case whose facts are not fully made public, a few remarks may help to elucidate some facets of a baffling position. Perhaps the root of the whole problem lay in the inability of the Nestorian to cope with the emergence of a new set of overpowering circumstances which tended to crush his very existence. Nestorian society had become petrified in its formalism, tribalism and narrow nationalism. It stubbornly refrained from lending itself to the inevitable process of minority integration in the formative years of the Iraqi nation. It

[1] Published in 1916 by Putnam of London and New York, even before the tragedy of the Nestorians reached its consummation in more recent years.

[2] Dissertation for which he obtained the degree of doctor of philosophy from Princeton University in 1957.

lacked the sagacity of wise leadership which seemed to be the only hope for steering a helpless little community to a haven of peace amidst tempestuous times and merciless events outside its control. In the first instance, it was hasty and foolish of the old patriarch to drag his people from their traditional homestead into the unknown on a wild goose chase for independence. It was equally wrong to discourage the integration of his tribes into the greater body politic of the Iraqi people, irrespective of religious or ethnic differences. To fan the flame of separatism and disaffection was criminal and insane. With all the goodwill and sympathy which the English people harboured for the Nestorians, the political creed of the state in England has always been to avoid the estrangement of a majority, in the defence of minority interests, however just these might be. Thus the patriarch had to pay the price of his folly. This by no means justifies the Nestorian massacres. At best, religious persecutions are sordid and utterly objectionable. No modern society can tolerate them over the years. On the other hand, it must be noted that Assyrian opinion itself has been sorely divided about the position and personality of the Nestorian patriarch. One Nestorian writer has overtly accused him of disloyalty to his people, irresponsibility, anarchism, opportunism and solid incompetence in qualities which undeservedly rendered the Assyrians unpopular in the countries of the Middle East.[1] In the United States, a new party of independent Assyrians has been launched at Chicago under the name of the American Assyrian Apostolic Church. The group is led by a relative of the present patriarch named the Reverend Sadok Mar Shimʿūn. Whether this is the beginning of a fresh schism in the shrinking ancient 'Church of the East', now in exile, depends largely on the progress of that movement amidst the American Nestorian congregations[2] and on the reaction of their fellow co-religionists in Iraq, Syria and elsewhere. Whatever the outcome of this fresh internal crisis may be, the Nestorian church will remain in exile a living symbol of a glorious career in the chequered history of Christianity in the East. Although those who owe it obedience have been reduced nowadays to an almost insignificant minority, few churches can claim for themselves the Nestorian evangelizing fire that swept all over the continent of Asia in the earlier Middle Ages. The splintering of the meagre residue of their one-time prosperous nation, even after the inroads of Protestantism, has left behind it three offshoots still existing to this day. The first is the Chaldæan church composed of Uniates who went to Rome but preserved the bulk of the original Syriac ritual. The second is the

[1] Quotation by Rondot, p. 169, from a publication of the 'Assyrian Liberation Committee in Syria'.

[2] These include one cathedral in Chicago and seven churches at Gary (Ind.), Flint (Mich.), Yonkers (N.Y.), New Brittain (Conn.), Philadelphia (Pa), Turlock (Calif.), and San Francisco (Calif.). See *Orthodoxy*, VI (1954), 271. Nestorians in the U.S.A. are said to be 25,000 (Attwater, II, 193).

Malabarese church of South India, which had become Jacobite long before the planting of Catholicism in the subcontinent by the Portuguese and the rise of the reformed Mar Thoma branch in later times. The third is the Mellusian 'Church of Trichur', consisting of a small body of Nestorians in the state of Cochin. The founder of the last sect was a certain Elias Mellus,[1] who apparently quarrelled with both Uniates and Jacobites in 1876 and thus decided to resuscitate the original Nestorian church in India. His party survived his decease until the Nestorian catholicos at Qudashānis in the course of 1907 ordained a Nestorian Archdeacon Abimelech as Bishop Mar Timotheus of South India and commissioned him to shepherd the Nestorian Indians, approximately 8,000 in number. The head of this symbolic minority styles himself Metropolitan of Malabar and the Indies.[2]

[1] Originally a native of Mardin, Turkey, by the name of Ḥanna (John), who became a Chaldæan priest under Patriarch Joseph Audo in 1864 before going to Malabar. He wrote an Arabic 'History of the Oriental Chaldæan Church', G. Graf, *Gesch. d. christlichen arabischen lit.*, IV, 112–13.

[2] Ibid., pp. 371–2; Attwater, II, 197–8.

17 • FAITH AND CULTURE

The Hierarchy

The questions of the Nestorian hierarchy and the ecclesiastical organization and administration of the church and community have inevitably been raised on various occasions in the course of the foregoing pages in the attempt to outline their general history across the centuries. The evolution of the hierarchical principles of the Nestorians has varied from age to age, and it would therefore be wrong to generalize in applying the same criteria throughout. Here it is planned to make a brief survey of clerical structure together with those traits and characteristics which have distinguished the Nestorians as a particular Christian sect in the last phase of their long story.

In common with all Christian churches, the Nestorian Church is headed by a patriarch or catholicos; but unlike them, the patriarch was vested with both spiritual and temporal authority over his people under Turkish rule. Whereas the Ottoman *millet* system within the Turkish empire gave patriarchs a measure of independence in handling the personal affairs of their communities, such as marriage, divorce and the like, while reserving the civil and criminal cases to the secular authority, it appears in the case of the Nestorians that all came under the tacit jurisdiction of the patriarch. He was generally called *ra'īs*, or supreme chief of his community; and under him, each tribe had its leader or *malik*, which literally stood for 'king' in Arabic and Syriac, though without the current meaning of the word. The principles of local government amidst the Nestorians were intensified by the circumstance of their dwelling in the seclusion of mountain fastnesses where communication with a central authority was exceptionally difficult. The exercise of a combined supreme jurisdiction over the tribal *malik* by the patriarch was retained at least in theory until the era of exile. In America, this prerogative has spontaneously come to an end.

Another special feature is the hereditary nature of the patriarchate from uncle to nephew, one which in modern history extended to the metropolitans and bishops. The patriarch's title is 'The Reverend and Honoured Father of Fathers and Great Shepherd, Mar Shimʿūn, Patriarch and Catholicos of the East.' In fact, the name Mar Shimʿūn with the Nestorians, like Mar Ignatius with the Jacobites, has become almost a distinctive title rather than a personal name. Sometimes a young child succeeded to the patriarchal throne by hereditary rights, and the affairs of state were conducted by his mother or his older sister during his infancy, with disastrous consequences to the community. A free election occurred only when the rightful family branch became extinct. On his accession, the patriarch was enthroned and consecrated by the chief metropolitan in the presence of the bishops with much pomp and ceremony.

The chief metropolitan emulated the same principles as his superior. He bore the name, or rather title, of Mar Ḥanānyeshūʿ (Mercy of Jesus) just the same as the patriarch was called Mar Shimʿūn. He, too, transmitted the dignity of his high ecclesiastical office to another member of his own family. In reality, the episcopal thrones as a whole became hereditary within the narrow lines of certain families. But the tradition of celibacy was generally observed by all higher dignitaries, although the records point to the existence of married bishops. Abstention from meat was promoted among higher clerics, and the historic tradition of the Nestorian hierarchy leaned towards austerity, though this has increasingly become a matter of personal temperament. In the last phase of Nestorian history in the Middle East, mention is made of seven bishops some of whom held only titular sees, besides the patriarch and the metropolitan, or *muṭrān*.

The lower clergy, as in all the other Eastern churches, are married. Unlike these other churches, however, the Nestorian Church approves of unlimited re-marriage of priests on the death of former wives. Those who take a monastic vow can obtain a dispensation to secede from monasticism without disgrace or difficulty. A priest is usually selected by his future parishioners, then confirmed and ordained by the bishop by the laying on of hands. The archpriest in the city and the *chorepiscopos* in charge of several parishes in the country have identical functions, and both exercise numerous episcopal duties in the absence of a bishop. The archdeacon is a kind of vicar-general in charge of diocesan finances and the landed property of the church. Usually each parish has several deacons, readers and clerks proportionate to its size and needs. From office to office, the Nestorians appear to have practised re-ordination. It is hard to know how much of all this still remains in the ranks of the exiled Nestorian Church, which is undergoing a steady process of adaptation to a new and strange environment in the New World.[1]

[1] Fortescue, pp. 126–37; Vine, pp. 183–5; Attwater, II, 192–4.

Monasticism[1]

The glory of the Nestorian church in mediæval times must necessarily be associated with the growth of its monastic order. The unknown heroes who carried the Gospel across Asia under the auspices of the Church of the East were self-denying members of the many Nestorian monasteries in Persia and upper Mesopotamia. The origin of monasticism among the Nestorians, or perhaps even more generally amongst the Syrians, is ascribed by tradition to Mar Augin,[2] a fourth-century pearl fisherman in the Red Sea at the ancient city of Clysma.[3] Legend clothes him in a garb of sanctity even before he decided to retire from the world to a Pachomian monastery, probably in the Thebaïd, and later to the wilderness of Scetis in the Nitrean valley. Evidently therefore, we must assume that he became a disciple of St Pachomius and that he transplanted his rule of cenobitic life to Persia and Syria around the middle of the century. It is said that he finally settled down in one of the upper valleys of Mesopotamia north of Nisibis with seventy companions, and that soon afterwards his followers numbered 350 monks from the entire Middle East.[4] Towards the end of his life he retired to Mount Izala, since famous for its Nestorian monastery, after blessing his original seventy companions who also discarded their abodes to found seventy other monasteries elsewhere. Thus Nestorian monasticism had its legendary beginning. It must, however, be remembered that at this stage monasteries were equally shared by eastern and western Syrians and that there was at first no distinction between monophysite and Nestorian foundations. Then, towards the end of the fifth century, as the Church was torn with factions and Nestorians became concentrated in Persia, monastic life suffered decline which may be demonstrated by the decisions of Bar Ṣaumā in the Synod of Beth Lapat or Laphat (484), where celibacy was disfavoured even among monks and nuns – a very curious and paradoxical inconsistency. One author, quoting Thomas of Margā, gives the picture of a monastic settlement as a village in the mountain where monks and nuns lived together and raised families with children.[5]

A true reform in monastic life in Persia came at the hands of Abraham of Kashkar (al-Wasīṭ),[6] who inaugurated a new era in the history of the movement. Born in 491 or 492 at Kashkar in lower Mesopotamia, he died in 586 at the advanced age of ninety-five years. He thus lived in the era of Nestorian reform and was a contemporary of its great Patriarch Mar Aba. Like

[1] The use of the word 'Nestorian' in connection with monasticism amongst the East Syrians is a matter of convenience rather than chronological accuracy, since the monastic rule in the area is much older than both the Council of Ephesus and the age of Nestorius.

[2] Also Awgin, or Eugenius.

[3] The Arabic al-Qulzum of mediæval times and the modern Suez.

[4] Labourt, pp. 302–15.

[5] Adeney, pp. 487–9.

[6] Labourt, pp. 315–21; Wigram, pp. 233–4.

him, he was a graduate of the School of Nisibis and studied under his namesake Abraham, an enlightened doctor and nephew of the outstanding Nestorian theologian Nerses. After spending some time in religious service in the region of Ḥirā on the eastern edge of Arabia, he went to Egypt, where he spent many years amidst the Coptic monks of the Scetis wilderness in the Nitrean Valley. Here he studied closely the rule of St Macarius the Great, a contemporary of St Pachomius. Then he visited Sinai, which teemed with recluses, and in all probability went to its Monastery of the Transfiguration (later St Catherine), only recently founded by Justinian in 525. He also undertook a pilgrimage to Jerusalem and the Holy Sepulchre before retiring to Mount Izala, where he introduced the rule of the Coptic monks among his native countrymen. His piety, good example and asceticism drew around him crowds of eminent monks and earned for him the title of 'Abraham the Great'. He was succeeded by able and saintly men who watched over the discipline of monastic life according to the rule of their master. His rule was enforced in his monastery in 571 and was strengthened by his immediate successor in 588.[1] Abraham had in his own lifetime designated his successor, who also was a saintly man and one of the prominent personalities of his time. This was Mar Dadishūʿ, who governed the community until nearly 620, or within a few decades of the Muslim Conquest. He was followed by another noted monk, Babai the Great, who ruled until 628. Eighty works are attributed to him, of which the most important is the treatise *On Union* embodying in systematic form Nestorian theology on the relation between the divinity and humanity of Jesus Christ.[2] The observance of celibacy became strict after his time. Though slightly modified, Abraham's rule was built on the model of the Coptic cenobitic traditions. Celibacy, chastity, poverty, fasting, silence, prayer, manual labour and study were essential conditions in Abraham's rule. At first the brothers prayed seven times a day, but later these were reduced to four. Meat and wine were forbidden, and they ate bread and vegetables at midday. Their dress consisted of a tunic, belt, cloak, hood and sandals; and they carried a Cross and a staff. After three years of cenobitic life, a monk had the right to retire to a solitary contemplative existence in the mountain. To distinguish themselves from their Jacobite neighbours, Nestorian monks wore a cruciform tonsure. Each monastery had an abbot, but he was subject to the local bishop who administered all monastic property. The strict obedience of monks to ecclesiastical authority provided the hierarchy with a powerful army of devotees who strengthened the Church and fearlessly penetrated the vast Asiatic continent in an attempt at large-scale evangelization. Even after the coming of the Arab, the monasteries remained the chief solace of the church for survival and sustained ex-

1 Chabot published fragments of his Rule in Rome, 1898; Chabot, *Littérature Syriaque*, p. 53.

2 Pub. by A. Vaschalde (Paris, 1915); cf. Chabot, *Littérature*, pp. 60–1.

pansion.[1] The number of monastic foundations increased in the sixth and seventh centuries. Mount Izala near Nisibis and Dorkena near Seleucis, where the Nestorian patriarchs had been buried for centuries, became the leading monastic centres. Other establishments of importance were at Tela, Baxaja, Haigla, Henda, Zarnucha, Camula, Anbar, Beth Zabda, Chuchta and Kuph.[2]

The Arab period was not devoid of monks who rose to fame. The best-known example is perhaps Thomas of Margā, the Nestorian historian[3] who entered the Monastery of Beth 'Abhe to the east of Moṣul in the year 832. Later he became secretary and pupil to Patriarch Abraham (837–50), who eventually made him bishop of Margā, then metropolitan of Beth Garmai to the north of Seleucia-Ctesiphon. He wrote a *Book of Governors*,[4] the history of his own monastery in which he incorporated a considerable mass of biographies of monks and material drawn from earlier monastic literature. The *Book of Governors* in the story of Nestorian monasticism became the equivalent of the *Lausiac History*[5] by Palladius in regard to the lives of the Egyptian fathers.

The annals of Nestorian monasticism, however, were not completely free from curious and rather degraded offshoots. The best-known example is the sect of the Msalleiani (Arabic=al-Muṣallīn, or 'praying men'), who became a source of trouble to the church and the nation for several centuries. Wigram[6] describes them as 'Christian Fakirs' and compares them to the later *dervishes* in Islam. We first hear of them in the middle of the fourth century, and they are known to have persisted at least until the twelfth. They were mendicant friars without affiliation to a monastery or an order. They held that the demon was innate in man, and only incessant prayer could drive him out of the body. With the departure of the evil spirit from a person, the Holy Ghost takes its place, giving rise to beatific visions and freedom from sin, accompanied by supernatural powers. Those who attained that stage became indifferent and invulnerable to church authority. Sometimes they were harmless mystics, but occasionally they proved to be a public nuisance and even committed unthinkable moral crimes under the cover of religion. From an early period Flavian of Antioch (ca. 449) exposed them and succeeded in banning them by synodal decision from western Syria. In the East, however, despite a sixth-century declaration by Patriarch Ishū'yahb I (582–96) that the church recognized no monk without a

[1] Labourt, pp. 321–4; Fortescue, p. 112; Wigram, pp. 233–5.

[2] Vine, p. 75.

[3] W. Wright, *A Short History of Syriac Literature* (London, 1901), pp. 219 et seq.; A. Baumstark, *Gesch. d. Syr. Lit.*, pp. 233 et seq.

[4] Syriac text and English tr. E. A. Wallis Budge, *The Book of Governors*, 2 vols. (London, 1893).

[5] See above.

[6] *Assyrian Church*, p. 236.

monastery, the members of this scandalous sect continued to rove among the Nestorians for several centuries afterwards.[1]

Concrete data on the monastic history of the Nestorians after Thomas of Margā's ninth-century chronicle become increasingly scarce, and it is difficult to paint an articulate picture of that great institution in later centuries. Nevertheless, judging by the achievement of Nestorian monks in Central Asia and China, the movement must have long persisted in strength and activity. Archæological discoveries and modern studies of the early attempts to establish the Nestorian mission throughout Asia prove this beyond a shadow of doubt to have been one of the brightest in the general history of Christianity. In fact, we must remember that the Nestorian church and its monastic order kept flourishing at least during the early centuries of the Abbasid caliphate and until the Mongol scourge loomed on the horizon and extinguished the flame of faith which those Christians carried to the heart of China. With Timur Lane's devastating conquests in the fourteenth century, the greatness of the Nestorian church becomes a thing of the past. Throughout modern history their monasteries have always been in ruins; and the monastic rule of the Nestorians has been reduced to an individual vow of celibacy by monks and nuns at home. The depleted church hierarchy still consists in principle of sworn celibates. But their scattered ranks are only a faint voice resounding faintly from ancient glories.

Rites and Liturgy

The Nestorians have proved to be very conservative in matters of faith, if not in the organization of the hierarchy. They accept the Nicæan Creed; but since Ephesus in 431, they have held fast to their own conceptions about the two natures of Christ and the *theotokos*. Unlike the Latins and like the Copts, the Nestorians have avoided the *filioque* in the Creed, as they considered the idea of the procession of the Holy Ghost from the Father as well as the Son

[1] The Msalliani or Messaliani were sometimes identified as Euchites or Euphemites who once disturbed the Monastery of Beth Abhē. They are also called Marcianites and Lampetians, so called after two of their leaders by the name of Marcian and Lampetus. A. Neander, *General History of the Christian Religion and Church*, English tr. J. Torrey, 9 vols. (London, 1851), III, p. 341, calls them 'the first mendicant friars'. In the later Middle Ages they appear to have mingled with the Bogomiles in the Balkans and even reappeared among the monks of Mt Athos. Adeney (pp. 490–2), rejecting somewhat the charge of immorality against them, tends to regard them as simple pietists, in some way allied to Puritanism and anticipating Quakerism. A special study of this subject with exhaustive references has been made by A. Vööbus, *Les Messalliens et les réformes de Barçauma de Nisibe dans l'église perse*, Contributions of Baltic University No. 34 (Pinneberg, 1947).

to be an innovation. On the other hand, the Nestorians, though holding the Virgin Mary and the Cross in great reverence, object to the use of the words 'Mother of God' and refrain from installing the Crucifix in their churches. Icons and images have no place in either the church or the home of a Nestorian, who nevertheless treasures saints' relics.[1] Avoidance of pictures, which they had in common with some Protestants, made the latter believe at first sight that Protestants were the 'Nestorians of the West' and that the Nestorians were the 'Protestants of the East' long before Martin Luther. Nevertheless, the Nestorians are highly liturgical in their services, and they appear to have developed their own liturgy from a relatively early date, first in Edessa, then in Persia, with a small measure of Antiochene features. Though Nestorian liturgiology is still far from being developed as a study, one cannot help being impressed by the liturgy's deep spirituality and primitive character.

The Church of the East uses three liturgies. The first is that of Theodore the Interpreter, from Advent to Holy Saturday; the second is that of Nestorius, used on the occasions of the Epiphany, the Memorial of the Greek Doctors, the Wednesday of the Ninevites and Maundy Thursday; the third and final one is that of the Apostles Mar Addai (St Thaddæus) and Mar Mari, who presumably brought it with them from Jerusalem, where St James the Less celebrated the first Christian offices (Qurbāna) in history. This last, used from Easter to Advent, remains the chief liturgy of the Nestorians and to the present day is kept in the old Edessene Syriac dialect stemming from Aramaic. The Nestorian liturgy is regarded as perhaps the most interesting feature or survival in that Church. This is not solely on account of the antiquity of its origins, but also because the Nestorians in their seclusion retained its primitive form without being exposed to the scholarly tampering of theorizing theologians. Its constituent elements do not betray the finally developed shape of the later Latin or Greek liturgies. Practically every occasion has a special office. While praying for the dead, they reject purgatory. They anathematize St Cyril the Great of Alexandria but sanctify the memory of Nestorius. Nestorians meet for prayer in the early morning and towards nightfall at the tapping of the *semantron*; but they are sparing with the celebration of the Holy Eucharist, which is regarded as a very special function, not necessarily associated with each Sunday liturgy. Whenever Holy Communion is offered, participants therein must fast from the previous midnight, while the celebrant and the deacon should start prayers on the eve of the appointed day and continue in the following morning until the afternoon for receiving the sacrament. Confession is not generally a requirement for participation in that solemn occasion. The 'holy leaven', regarded as one of the seven sacraments, is held to be literally

[1] Fortescue, p. 137, ascribes the absence of icons to Muslim influence.

in continuity of the Last Supper. The service of the Holy Eucharist begins with the elaborate process of making the holy bread in a special area opening into the nave within the church structure.

The Nestorians appear to recognize seven sacraments,[1] though they do not seem to be absolutely clear or stable about their nature. Baptism, marriage, the Holy Eucharist and holy orders are universally accepted. As to the remaining three sacraments, clerics seem to oscillate between various opinions which include the blessing of monks, the office for the dead, the oil of unction, absolution, the holy leaven, the sign of the Cross and the consecration of a church or altar.

Baptism is an important function with the Nestorians and is usually performed in stages. At birth the child is washed with water blessed by the priest in prayer. Then on the occasion of a great feast, baptism is carried out for the children of the community in an elaborate service. The Nestorian practices the threefold immersion with the child facing east, and this is followed by total anointing with holy oil.

Baptism and marriage services are also elaborate and are accompanied by much rejoicing. Cup, ring, cross, sacred relics, and coronation with colours are all used in the solemnization of matrimony.[2] However, divorce is permissible on numerous grounds. There are special services for ordination, for burial of priests, for burial of laymen, and for consecration of churches.

In regard to their calendar, the tradition is the use of the old style of the Julian reckoning for months, and the Era of the Greeks (i.e., the Seleucids) for years starting from 311 B.C. The ecclesiastical year begins on the first of December and is divided into nine periods of approximately seven weeks each, designated for the Annunciation, Epiphany, Lent, Resurrection, the Apostles, the summer, Elijah, Moses, and church dedication. They have four fasts of varying lengths: the longest lasts forty-nine days before Easter and is called the Great Fast; the shortest, Mart Maryam (Holy Mary), is only fifteen days in August; Wednesdays and Fridays are kept as fasting days throughout the year.[3] The total of fast days in the year has been reckoned at 172.

[1] According to Badger (II, 150), the seven sacraments are: (1) Orders, (2) Baptism, (3) Oil of Unction, (4) Oblation of Body and Blood of Christ, (5) Absolution, (6) Holy leaven, (7) Sign of the Cross. But Patriarch Timothy II (1318–60), according to Assemani (*Bibl. Orient.*, III, 1, 356 and III, 2, 240) gave the sacraments as follows: (1) Holy Orders, (2) Consecration of Church and Altar, (3) Baptism and Confirmation with Holy Oil, (4) Holy Sacrament of Body and Blood, (5) Blessing of Monks, (6) Office for Dead, (7) Marriage. Cf. Fortescue, p. 138.

[2] The whole service, rendered into English, appears in Badger, II, pp. 244–81. See also Brightman, *Liturgies Eastern and Western*, pp. 246 ff. For a comprehensive review of Nestorian liturgies, see A. J. Maclean, *East Syrian Daily Offices*, tr. from Syriac with Introduction, Notes etc. (London, 1894).

[3] Fortescue, pp. 147–9.

Ecclesiastical vestments of officiating Nestorian clergy are similar to those used by their Jacobite neighbours. These include the tunic (*Quthinā*), stole (*Urara*), girdle (*Zunāra*), chasuble (*Mapra*) without hood, and embroidered shoes. Bishops wear a small hood or embroidered amice (*Biruna*) over the head and carry the pastoral staff and cross. Outside the church, the clergy wear an ordinary, black turban, and of course all are bearded.[1]

Art and Architecture

If we go far back into the antiquity of Syrian Christianity, it will be difficult to distinguish what is Eastern from what is Western in its early culture. The saints of both East and West were the same and the theology identical. This applies to the spheres of art and architecture as well, and the foregoing remarks on the pre-Jacobite Church of Antioch may, in large measure, be taken to denote the nature of pre-Nestorian *motifs*. With the segregation of the Nestorians, the Church of the East Syrians began to look towards the East. In its greater days of expansion, the church expended its creative energy in fields other than art and architecture, where it tended towards practical simplicity. Later, as the church suffered from the Mongol invasions and the rise of the Turkish empire, it was impoverished and began to sink into oblivion and ignorance. These circumstances naturally had an impact on the art and architecture of the Nestorians. They had virtually no art comparable in any way to that of the Greeks or even that of the West Syrians. Besides their poverty and lack of artistic knowledge or interest, the Nestorians repudiated the use of icons and iconography. A Nestorian never tolerated an icon either in church or at home. They used simple crosses at the entrance of a church and over the altar, but they banned the crucifix from all parts of their religious buildings. Thus neither art nor sculpture was fostered by them, and their churches remained bare.

In architecture, Nestorian churches were also altogether unostentatious and invariably poor. As buildings they were recognizable from others only by the shape of a simple cross on the outer wall above the church entrance. That entrance was a mere aperture in the wall, quite narrow and very low so that anybody entering had to stoop down to gain access to the interior. As a rule its height was approximately three feet, and it has been suggested that the reason was to prevent the wild Kurd from housing his cattle in the Syrian place of worship.[2] Those familiar with the churches and monasteries in non-Christian countries of the East know of course that this was

[1] H. J. Sutcliffe, 'The Church of the East', in *Orthodoxy*, VI-8, 264–9; Fortescue, p. 151.

[2] Fortescue, p. 145.

deliberately done for reasons of defence to prevent hostile horsemen from storming the building. In the case of the old patriarchal church at Qudshānis, the entrance was reached by a ladder from outside, thus making access even harder. This led to a narthex or open court, partly covered, where the faithful left their shoes behind, though retaining their head gear in Oriental fashion as they went into the church itself. On excessively hot days the services were held in the court instead of in the church interior, which consisted of a sanctuary and a nave separated by a wall taking the place of the iconostasis but without icons. A large open doorway with a screen connected both parts. Outside the sanctuary there was a raised platform enclosed within a low wall for the choir and a lectern for the reading of the lesson as well as a table for Scriptural books and a simple Cross. The sanctuary had a single altar under a canopy, and the Eucharist was allowed only once a day in any church. The sanctuary walls had niches and cupboards for prayer books, the Holy Communion vessels, the holy oil and some sanctified leavened bread for re-use in baking a new loaf in keeping with established tradition. A baptistry room is generally situated next to the sanctuary with double access from the altar and the nave. This was also used as a vestry. The lower end of the nave opened into an enclosure with an oven for baking the holy bread. The call to prayer was made on the *semantron*, a wooden plank beaten with a hammer. The *semantron* is still used in the older Greek monasteries on Mount Sinai in Egypt and on Mount Athos in Greece.

Waning of Syriac Literature

Although the present work cannot possibly deal with all the literary achievements of the various communities of eastern Christians in their many languages, a few notes will be given on some facets of importance to the development of Christian thought. For the earliest times of Christianity, no writer can afford to overlook the special place which Syriac religious work occupied side by side with Greek, Latin and Coptic. Prior to the fifth century, when the christological controversies led to an open rupture between the Monophysite western Syrians and the Diophysite eastern Syrians, Syriac literature was neither Jacobite nor Nestorian but rather unified. It was essentially Biblical, homiletic and theological in character. Illustrious names such as Aphraates, Ephraem Syrus and Rabbula belong to that age. Many of the famous names in the literary annals of the Syrians were also historic figures and consequently have had to be treated in the course of the general history of Antiochene developments. This was the case in regard to the Jacobites after the fifth century with such names as Michael the Syrian and

Bar Hebræus. Now, in dealing with the Nestorians, it is fitting to follow up the phases which ended in the decline and fall of Syriac literature.

Since their separation, the Nestorians, or East Syrians, had been lured away from Syriac literature by the circumstances of living in the Persian empire, and by their tremendous missionary enterprise across Asia. Then with the advent of the Arabs, Nestorian scholars tended to become Arabicized, and their role in translating the great works of the Greek philosophers and writers in Syriac became a standing monument to Nestorian learning. It is true that the field of Syriac did not become utterly sterile under those circumstances. Even during the fateful years of the Arab thrust into Persia in the seventh century, we read of a certain Joseph Hazzaya, a Nestorian convert of Persian origin, who was seized by the men of Caliph ʿUmar (634–44) and sold into slavery. He regained his liberty in Kurdistan, where he established a monastery and distinguished himself in Syriac theological literature. Apparently he was a man of keen perception and a prolific author in Syriac. The mediæval register of Syriac manuscripts by ʿAbd-Ishūʿ ascribes to Hazzaya the fabulous number of 1,900 Syriac works, mostly lost. His new Syriac version of the *Paradise of the Fathers* by Palladius[1] was a contribution of the highest order.

Though persisting as a spoken language amongst the Nestorians throughout their history, Syriac began its steady decline as a literary language during the Arab period. Great Nestorian scholars of the time of the early caliphate such as Ḥunayn ibn Isḥāq and his school were bilingual, but they preferred in principle to write their best works in Arabic rather than Syriac. We almost reach the nadir of Syriac literature among the Nestorians in the course of the tenth century. The increase in output of Syriac grammars and lexicons at the time can only be explained by the pressing need for such treatises as a means of preserving the language. This phenomenon is demonstrated by the abundance of pure linguistic studies, especially during the tenth century or even the late ninth, when Arabic was in the ascendant at the expense of Syriac. Ishūʿ bar ʿAli, a disciple of Ḥunayn, in the ninth century laid the foundation of Syriac lexicons with numerous Arabic glosses. Bar Bahloul, the Arabic Abul-Ḥasan ibn al-Bahlūl, who taught in Ba<u>gh</u>dad in the tenth century, continued Bar ʿAli's work with many additions. Bar Maswai, better known in Arabic as Yaḥyā ibn Māsawayh (d. 857), composed his medical treatise both in Syriac and in Arabic. Grammatical works recurred frequently, and Elias bar Shinaia of Nisibis (d. 1049) wrote an 'Interpreter's Book' comprising an Arabic-Syriac vocabulary in addition to a Syriac grammar.[2]

[1] Chabot, *Littérature*, pp. 97, 100. Recapitulations of the same work were made later by Ḥanān-I<u>sh</u>ūʿ (Ananjesus) at the request of Patriarch Georges (658–80), which he enriched with material from St Jerome (pub. by P. Bedjan, Paris, 1877).

[2] Ibid., pp. 118–19.

The Nestorians had no such towering literary giants in later mediæval times as Dionysius bar Ṣalībi, Michael the Great and Bar Hebræus among the Jacobites. Nevertheless, we have to remember that the process of the disappearance of Nestorian Syriac literature was long and gradual. Nestorian writers of no special merit are to be found in every century until the thirteenth when Syriac literary productivity came to a standstill.

The ninth century was the dividing line after which the era of decline starts. We still meet with names of the older Syriac school. The Catholicos Timothy I (d. 823) is known to have written a lost astronomical treatise called the *Book of the Stars*. He left a great number of Epistles[1] which contain an apology of the Christian faith presented in the form of a discussion with the Caliph al-Mahdi (775–85). Apart from several homilies and an interpretation of Gregory Nazianzen, his most important work was a record of the acts of synods from 790 to 805. Other personalities included Ishūʿ bar Noun (Yashūʿ ibn Nūn), who became patriarch in 823 through the influence of Gabriel Bokhtyeshūʿ, private physician of the Caliph al-Maʾmūn. He compiled a Syriac grammar and some theological treatises. Thomas of Margā, later metropolitan of Beth Garmai, wrote in 840 his famous *Book of Governors*,[2] destined to become one of the chief sources of religious and monastic history of the Nestorians until his time. Ishūʿ-Dadh of Marw about the middle of the century compiled what is probably the greatest Nestorian Biblical commentary.[3] At the end of the century, Ishūʿ Denha, bishop of al-Baṣrah, wrote several treatises on logic, ecclesiastical history and a *Book of Chastity*.[4]

The tenth century relapses into decadence, and we find only a limited number of ascetic, theological or liturgical treatises by Elias, bishop of al-Anbar, George, metropolitan of Moṣul, Bar Bahloul and John bar Khaldoun. None of them rises to any great height, except perhaps the ascetic and mystical survey of the Nestorian monks by Bar Khaldoun. The eleventh century fares little better with very few names. Elias of Nisibis (d. 1049) left a chronicle besides the linguistic studies already mentioned. Abu Saʿīd ʿAbd-Ishūʿ bar Bahriz, metropolitan of Arbela and Moṣul, compiled the laws and legal decisions which took the place of Nestorian canon law. In the twelfth century, most Nestorians wrote in Arabic, except for a stray example such as Simeon Shankelāwi (or Shanklava), who left behind him a

[1] About 200, of which 60 are known and partly pub. by Braun with a Latin translation (Paris, 1914); cf. Chabot, p. 108.

[2] English tr. W. Wallis Budge (London, 1893); A. Baumstark, *Gesch. d. Syr. Lit.*, pp. 233–4; Wright, pp. 219–20; Duval, *Litt. Syr.*, pp. 206–7; Chabot, pp. 110–11.

[3] The Gospel part ed. Mrs Gibson (London, 1911); Chabot, p. 112.

[4] The history in 3 vols. was known to Michael the Syrian, but has been lost since. The last book pub. with French tr. J. B. Chabot, *Livre de la Chasteté* (Rome, 1896); cf. Chabot, *Litt. Syr.*, p. 113.

Syriac chronology and a Syriac treatise on the Nestorian Church hierarchy.[1]

The thirteenth century has a special characteristic amongst Nestorian writers, who took to composing their works in vulgar poetic form. Solomon of Khilāṭ or Akhlāṭ (on the shores of Lake Van in Armenia), later metropolitan of al-Baṣrah, wrote a book entitled *The Bee*,[2] a composition of mixed theological and historical material, in part legendary. George Warda of Arbela composed several hymns which were incorporated in Nestorian offices. More religious poetry was left by John of Moṣul and Gabriel Camsa towards the end of the century.

The only person to attain considerable eminence in matters of writing during that century was ʿAbd-Ishūʿ bar Berikha, who flourished under Yahballaha. He occupied the bishoprics of Sinjar, Shiggar and Beth Arabaye (Ṭūr ʿAbdīn) for five years, and in 1290 became metropolitan of Nisibis and Armenia until his death in 1318. ʿAbd-Ishūʿ, though incomparably short of Bar Hebræus' stature as a writer, will be found on the whole to occupy in Nestorian annals the same place as Bar Hebræus in Jacobite literature. Like him, he was destined to be the last really great author in the Nestorian line; but unlike him, most of his works have been lost. Nevertheless, all his writings are known through a complete list which he himself appended to his celebrated catalogue of ecclesiastical literature compiled in 1316. With all its shortcomings, this work is a priceless record of Syriac literature. It is the first known attempt at a comprehensive bibliography of all works written in Syriac, with special reference to those of Nestorian origin or authorship. It is classified in four categories: first, books of the Old Testament and some of the Apocrypha; secondly, books of the New Testament; thirdly, the Greek Fathers in the Syriac tongue; and fourthly, the Syrian Fathers including the Nestorian authors from the fifth century (with a few exceptions). Apparently he compiled it from the Syriac material available in the manuscript repository at Nisibis, and his dependence on that source of information alone may account for the omissions in his lists. On the other hand, he brings to light titles unknown elsewhere. Since the author was probably doing this for himself and his disciples and colleagues, who were familiar with those books, he did not take the trouble to assemble all the usual data which would render it a *catalogue raisonné*. He did not bother to analyse the contents of each book or even to provide the precise dates of each manuscript. He was equally lax in the matter of chronological order.[3]

[1] Chabot, *Litt. Syr.*, pp. 118–20, 128.

[2] Ibid., p. 137; Wright, pp. 282–3. Analysed by Assemani, *Bibl. Or.*, III, 1, 309–24, 'The Bee' appears in two European versions by J. M. Schönfelder (Bamberg, 1866) and W. Wallis Budge (Oxford, 1886).

[3] Chabot, pp. 14, 139; Wright, pp. 285–6. Assemani, *Bibl. Or.*, III, 325 et seq., gives extensive excerpts from it under the title 'Catalogus Librorum, Cap. CXCVIII – Ebedjesus Metropolita Sobensis'.

ʿAbd-Ishūʿs lost works comprise a Biblical commentary, a *Life of Our Lord on Earth*, a treatise called the *Scholasticus Against Heresies*, a book of the *Mysteries of Greek Philosophers*, a pretended *Letter from Alexander the Great to Aristotle on Alchemy*, and twelve discourses on all sciences together with some miscellaneous Arabic texts. Of the works still extant, *The Pearl* is his most valuable treatise on Nestorian theology and constitutes the official view of the sect.[1] Further, his codification of Nestorian canon law in his *Epitome of Synodical Canons*,[2] known briefly as *Nomcanon*, is the exact counterpart of a similar compilation by Bar Hebræus for the Jacobites. It contains both the civil and the ecclesiastical laws in consecutive divisions, together with the fullest account of the organization of the Nestorian church at the end of the thirteenth century. Later, in 1316, he developed what he called *Rules of Ecclesiastical Juridical Decisions*.

Conforming to the literary fashion of his time, ʿAbd-Ishūʿ composed several metrical and poetical works which gained wide popularity with his native countrymen. He wrote a discourse on the calendar in verse, and he even versified his catalogue. His most important poetical work is the *Paradise of Eden*, a collection of fifty theological and homiletic poems inspired by the Arabic *Maqāmāt*, or rhymed sessions of al-Ḥarīri, also fifty in number. Although he did not attain the literary heights of al-Ḥarīri's work, he demonstrated much ability and imagination in combining meanings with word and letter in the construction of poems and lines which could be read forwards and backwards yielding precisely the same text.[3] He finished the *Paradise* in 1290, but found it necessary to supplement it with additional explanatory notices as late as 1316. He also composed another set of twenty-two poems on the love of wisdom and knowledge.

Like Bar Hebræus in Jacobite literary history, ʿAbd-Ishūʿ was the last great figure in Nestorian literary history. After his day, Syriac was retained merely as a spoken language and a liturgical repository of Nestorian offices, with perhaps two solitary exceptions. These were the fourteenth-century canonico-liturgical treatise entitled *On the Sacraments*[4] by Patriarch Timothy II (d. 1328) and the anonymous *History of Yahballaha III*.[5]

[1] The Syriac *Margānīthā*, ed. with Latin tr. by Cardinal Mai (Rome, 1838), with some omissions. The complete text appeared at Moṣul in 1924.

[2] Analysed by Assemani, *Bibl. Orient.*, III, 1, 332–51.

[3] Analysed by Assemani, *Bibl. Orient*, III, 1, 325–32; text of 25 pub. P. Cardahi (Beirūt, 1889); cf. Chabot, *Litt. Syr.*, p. 141; Wright, pp. 287–8, A. Baumstark, *Gesch. d. Syr. Lit.*, pp. 323–5.

[4] Assemani, *Bibl. Orient*, III, 1, 572–80.

[5] Orig. Persian, with an early Syriac tr., this work ed. P. Bedjan (Paris, 1888); French tr. J. B. Chabot (Paris, 1897); cf. Chabot, *Litt. Syr.*, p. 142.

PART IV

THE ARMENIAN CHURCH

18 • INTRODUCTION

General Remarks

The story of the Armenian people and their Church is one of great tribulation and heroism. Although Armenian Christianity never attained the heights of universalism which characterized many of the ancient churches, it bears many unique features of which the Armenians have rightly prided themselves within their own frontiers. For one thing, Armenia was the very first kingdom in history to adopt Christianity as the official religion of both the state and the people at one and the same time. Its record of martyrs and saints, starting with the rest of the Christian world in antiquity, was replenished by a continuous chain of massacres which lasted until the twentieth century. In spite of their dispersion over all the countries of the Middle East and continents of the world, the Armenian people have preserved their own personality and retained their language and social and racial characteristics. The Armenian, much like the Jew or the Greek, has remained an Armenian above all other considerations. His tenacity had become proverbial, and perhaps the elements of language and religion were and still are decisive factors in the preservation of the race. Although small numbers of Armenians have become Protestant or turned to Rome, the bulk of the Armenian people as a whole has retained allegiance to the ancestral Eastern Church with its distinctive Monophysite character. It is estimated that at least three-quarters of the Armenians throughout the world are loyal members of their ancient native Gregorian Church.

The earliest geographical frontiers of Armenia stretched roughly from the Caucasas Mountains in the north to the Taurus Mountains in the south and from the Caspian Sea in the east to the Black Sea in the west. Tradition has it that here was the site of the Garden of Eden where, according to Genesis ii, 10 'a river went out of Eden to water the garden; and from thence it was parted, and became into four heads'. The fourth of those 'heads' or rivers was the Euphrates. That was, too, the land of Mount Ararat (17,000 feet high), where Noah's ark rested and life on earth was reborn. In this way, Armenia has therefore been closely associated with early Biblical tradition. In fact,

Armenians claim to possess still a fragment of the ark in one of their monasteries at Etshmiadzin, now within the southern borders of the Soviet Union. Wedged between Persia and Greece in antiquity, and amidst a host of belligerent powers in the Middle Ages, the country was harassed by Persian, Greek, Arab, Mongol, Egyptian and Turk until the last century, when the Armenian nation was menaced by complete extermination from its homeland. Originally, however, Armenians spread over parts of Kurdistan round Lake Van, western Anatolia and the upper Euphrates. To the north-east of the Euphrates, stretching towards the Caucasus and the Black Sea, was the country identified as Greater Armenia, whereas Lesser Armenia, or Cilicia, occupied the territories east of the river in the direction of the eastern Mediterranean. Its frontiers were very mobile and dependent on the force of the successive invasions from east and west, as will be seen presently from the historical survey of that much-battered nation. The main roads connecting the Iranian plateau with the Anatolian ports on the shores of the Mediterranean ran into the Armenian valleys and the country was consequently coveted by all those who aspired to control the commerce of the Orient and the politics of the ancient and mediæval worlds. From all this, we can realize how much the physical features of Armenia contributed to the shaping of its destinies.

The word 'Armenian' is of Greek origin, since the Armenians themselves call their nation 'Haikh' and their country 'Hayastan'. The father of the Armenian people, so runs the legend, was named Haik, a grandson of the Biblical Japheth. Racially they are an Indo-Aryan people, and their language with its ostensibly peculiar sounds and combinations of consonant formations has come to occupy a special place in the tree of Indo-European tongues. The Armenians number between three and a half and four millions.[1] About two and a half millions are almost evenly divided between Turkey and Russia,

[1] Fortescue, p. 396, puts the following estimates: 1,300,000 in Turkey; 1,200,000 in Russia; 50,000 in Persia; about one million in India, Egypt, Europe and America. L. Arpee, *History of Armenian Christianity, from the Beginning to Our Own Time* (New York, 1946), p. 307, is more restrained in his estimate of a total of two and one-half million, of whom 1,200,000 are in Soviet Armenia, 600,000 in Georgia and Azerbaijan, 120,000 in northern Caucasus and Greater Russia, about 100,000 in Turkey, half of whom are in Constantinople, 150,000 in Syria (including, of course, Lebanon); 100,000 in Persia; 150,000 in the United States of America; and 25,000 to 50,000 in each of France, Roumania, Bulgaria, Greece, Egypt, and Iraq; in addition to smaller Armenian colonies in Latin America, England, Belgium, Italy, Central Europe, Ethiopia, the Sudan, Palestine, India, Java and the Philippines. M. Ormanian, *The Church of Armenia* (London, 1955), p. 212, sums up with the following: Total Dioceses, 26; Armenian Church Members, 3,674,757; Parishes, 446; Churches, 417; Catholic Armenians, 51,349; Protestant Armenians, 29,667. Although the book was written in the first decade of this century, the above figures have been appended to the English translation on the basis of Armenian diocesan statistics in 1954. (References made in these notes to Fortescue, we mean Adrian and not E. F. K. Fortescue.)

and the rest are spread all over the Middle East, India, Europe and America. They are known for their extraordinary ability in business, their technical skill and indefatigable industry. Wherever they went, they generally grew rich and aroused economic jealousy among the natives.

It will be seen that, in spite of their precarious existence, the Armenians have made a real contribution to the civilized world in numerous fields.

The land in and on the fringe of Anatolia which they occupied before their dispersion was mountainous and thickly wooded, but intercepted by valleys and many arable plains. This accounts for the agricultural origins and ability in cattle-raising[1] which the Armenians were destined to lose under the relentless tide of invasion and this resulting tendency to emigrate to urban areas in other countries. Nevertheless, the isolation of the Armenian people in those remote valleys for many centuries imparted to them those national qualities which they appear to have retained throughout their subsequent history, even after their dispersion.

The general trends prevailing in Armenian Christianity have much in common with the rest of the ancient Oriental churches, especially the Coptic Church in Egypt. These trends may be summed up in its national character and its democratic organization. From the fourth century when the Armenians broke away from Cæsarea, their church declared thereby its determination to repudiate all control from Antioch, Constantinople or Rome. On the other hand, it never objected to any spiritual union with other sister churches in conformity with the basic features of primitive Christianity. Furthermore, we have to bear in mind that Armenian religious affairs were conducted by a hierarchy invariably elected by the Armenian people, who constituted the body politic of the church. The existence of secular councils to shoulder with the patriarchs the responsibility of deciding the policies of the community of the faithful outside purely doctrinal matters was a significant landmark, and the adherence of the church to the practice of allowing the congregation to participate in the selection of its own bishop may be regarded as a continuation from the age of Apostolic Christianity. The effects of a growing theocracy which were becoming more and more noticeable with the passing ages at Constantinople and Rome thus failed to influence the Armenian Church traditions.

The following chapters on Armenian Church history are compiled in the main from secondary writings, chiefly because of the linguistic difficulties of the sources. However, representative works of native Armenian scholarship have also been used, as well as Roman Catholic and Protestant accounts of this interesting story. One of the best spokesmen of these varied shades is Malachia Ormanian, himself an Armenian patriarch of Constantinople and a

[1] The Armenians are known for their wealth of cattle since remote antiquity, according to Herodotus; cf. F. Nansen, *Armenia and the Near East* (London, 1928), p. 233.

good historian whose works are now known in English and French.[1] Another is Leon Arpee, whose *History of Armenian Christianity*[2] marked the commemoration of the hundredth anniversary of Armenian Protestantism (1846–1946). The author, who is of course a Protestant, writes with affection though not uncritically about the church of his forebears. His chief sympathy, however, remains with the new denomination of his own adoption, and he tries continually to make a case for the Protestant minority. A third work, by Adrien Fortescue, is on the lesser Eastern Churches. Its scholarship is profound, but is frequently marred by bouts of Roman Catholic propaganda. Other writings quoted or studied in the course of constructing this brief survey of an intricate subject are mentioned in the footnotes; and it must be admitted that our dependence on the Armenian-speaking historians has been great in matter of documentation. After a brief survey of the historical background of Armenian Christianity, we shall analyse the origins and development of the church and its patriarchates and conclude with a general perspective of the present condition, organization and contribution of the hierarchy and faith of the Armenians.

The Armenian people long down-trodden, persecuted and massacred almost to the point of extinction at one moment, have re-emerged on the scene of Eastern Christianity as a nation whose tenacity, integrity and will to live and to succeed under the most untoward circumstances have commanded universal respect.

Historical Background

Like most of the nations of the Levant, the Armenians had a long history whose myth and legends are lost in antiquity. Here we are mainly concerned with the era of the appearance of Christianity in their midst, an era which coincides with the leadership of Rome. Being on the crossroads between East and West, between Persia and Greece at the outset, the country was first assimilated in the empire of Darius I (521–486 B.C.), then swallowed up by Alexander's world conquests (336–323 B.C.) and inherited by the Seleucids when Antiochus III defeated the Romans in the East in 190 B.C. At this point Armenia emerges as an independent state under a ruler of Greek extraction.

[1] This work appeared first in French in Paris in 1910, then in Armenian in Constantinople in 1911 (with 4 subs. edns.), and the first English tr. by G. Marcar Gregory pub. 1912. The second English edn. of 1955 (used here) prepared by the late Rev. Terenig Poladian, former Dean of the Armenian Theological Seminary at Antelias, Lebanon.

[2] Published by the Armenian Missionary Association of America. Arpee is a graduate of the Oberlin School of Theology, and his father was a converted Protestant missionary with the American Board Mission at Constantinople.

Its proximity to Persia, however, rendered it an easy prey to the expansionist policy of the Parthians until one of its kings, Dikran I, or Tigranes the Great, recovered Armenian independence from both Persia and the Seleucids in the early decades of the first century before Christ, only to succumb ultimately to the Romans in 66 B.C. For approximately five centuries afterwards, suzerainty over Armenia passed from the hated Persian to a loathsome Roman or was forcibly divided between them. In the end, the Roman Emperor Maurice (582–602) turned the whole country into a single province under Roman rule. During those unsettled and hard times we hear of native Armenian kings, famous amongst whom are Trdat II, who fled from the Persians to Rome in 261, and Arshak, whom the Persians carried into captivity in 364. However, the Arshakuni (Arsasid) dynasty in its precarious existence survived the Arab conquest in the seventh century when the country again became the object of dispute between the caliphate and the Byzantine empire. In their buffer state, the Armenians had fared ill with the Byzantines because of their repudiation of Chalcedon and their adherence to the principles of Alexandrine theology. Thus it mattered little to them whether they retained their allegiance to Constantinople on the one side or to Umayyad Damascus and Abbasid Baghdad on the Islamic side. Ultimately, an Armenian prince and patriot by the name of Ashot I succeeded in establishing the new Bagratuni dynasty in 856. Ashot the Great thus became 'king of kings' of Armenia, Georgia and the lands of the Caucasus. His title was ratified by the caliphs and confirmed by the Byzantine emperor, who deemed it wise also to offer him the crown.[1] The Armenians, who hated Greek autocracy as much as the Arab yoke, were able to hold their own in the face of both masters though they continued to be under titular Arab suzerainty until the very eve of the Crusades in 1071.[2] Then the appearance of the Saljūq Turks obliterated Armenian independence, and the kingdom of Greater Armenia on the fringe of the Caucasus has never since been fully restored.[3]

Actually, the never ending exodus of the Armenians from the old homeland began in that period; and although numbers of them emigrated to numerous neighbouring countries in the Levant, the major part of the nation crossed over to Cilicia towards the south and established a new principality of Lesser Armenia under Prince Reuben, a relative of the last Armenian king, whose successors were content with the title of baron and treated with the

[1] *Serapie Der Nessessian, Armenia and the Byzantine Empire – A Brief Study of Armenian Civilization* (Cambridge, Mass., 1945), p. 9.

[2] J. Laurent, *L'Arménie entre Byzance et l'Islam depuis la conquête arabe* (Paris, 1919), pp. 9 et seq., is perhaps the fullest account up to the year 886. See also René Grousset, *Histoire de l'Arménie dès origines à 1071* (Paris, 1947), pp. 296 et seq.

[3] Arpee, *Hist. of Christianity*, pp. 44–57 (Struggle with Persia), pp. 75–89 (Arab Domination); E. F. K. Fortescue, *Armenian Church* (London, 1872), pp. 17–41; A. Fortescue, *Lesser Eastern Churches*, pp. 383 et seq.

Crusaders from the West. They built a new capital by the name of Sīs in the north-east, inland from Adana. This phase of Armenian history is marked by fresh influences. In addition to the Byzantine and Turkish factors, their destiny was affected by the Latins from the west and soon afterwards by the Egyptian Mamlūks from the south as well as the Mongol hordes from the east. For the time being, the Cilician princes chose closer contacts with the Crusaders, even recognizing the sovereignty of Antioch and making attempts at union with Rome. In the end Leo I (1129–39), surnamed the Great, aspired to the royal crown, and in return for this, allied himself with Emperor Frederick Barbarossa, but Frederick was drowned in the River Saleph in Asia Minor before making him king. Frederick's son Henry VI (1190–7) carried out his father's pledge, and Armenia became a kingdom again. Meanwhile, the Byzantine Emperor Alexius III (1195–1203), who wished to preserve his traditional suzerainty over the Armenians, sent Leo II another crown with an invitation to come to Constantinople. Thus Leo's title became undisputed by East and West, and he was recognized as the greatest hero of Armenia since Dikran I. The new line remained in close contact with the Crusaders until the extermination of Latin dominion on the mainland was achieved by the Mamlūks when Sultan al-Ashraf Khalīl seized ʿAkka in 1291. The hostility to the Christians, however, survived the downfall of the Latin Kingdom of Jerusalem, and the Egyptian counter-crusade was directed against the kingdom of Armenia, which was situated on the northern border of Syria. In 1375, the amīr of Ḥalab (Aleppo) crushed the little kingdom and carried Leo VI,[1] the last of the Armenian kings in chains to the Citadel of Cairo. Later Leo was released on the condition that he should never set foot on Armenian soil. He died childless in Paris in 1393. His line thus became extinct and the title to his shadowy crown passed to the house of Lusignan in Cyprus.

After the withdrawal of Timur Lane from western Asia with Bayezid I as his captive in 1402, the Ottomans gradually extended their rule over the whole of Anatolia, including Armenian territories. The expansionist policy of the Turkish empire engulfed Syria and Egypt in 1516–17 and brought its frontiers into direct contact with Persia. Thus Armenia became again the battlefield of the Turco-Persian strife, more especially in the reign of Shah ʿAbbas (1586–1628). As a frontier country, it was perpetually devastated, and Persian encroachments resulted in new unspeakable horrors amidst the defenceless Armenians. In the eighteenth century one Armenian name shone like a meteor when a certain David led a rebellion for the liberation of his country which was again buried with him in 1728. The oppressed Armenians then appealed to Russia for protection, which was promised by the tzars from the reign of Peter the Great (1689–1725) onwards, but without concrete results until war broke out between the two empires and Russia annexed Transcaucasia

[1] Sometimes also styled Leo V.

as far as the River Aras in 1829. This brought a considerable section of the old territory of Greater Armenia including the Armenian holy city of Etshmiadzin within the realm of Orthodox Christianity. But this did not help the rest of the Armenians within the Turkish borders. They became the object of hatred and severe oppression. Meanwhile, Russian intervention aroused British fears and jealousy. They too posed as protectors of the Armenian people, but their vacillation between those two conflicting great powers had tragic results.

In fact, until the beginning of the nineteenth century the Armenians in Turkey had been living as all other Christian communities under the *millet*[1] system, but with even a greater measure of self-government. More privileges were acquired by the 'Hatti Sherif'[2] of Gulhane in 1839 and the Constitution of 1863, which assured Armenians of a semi-independent state within the framework and under the sovereignty of the Turks. Armenian youth, on the other hand, aspired to complete independence from Turkey and started plotting inside the country and abroad to realize that aim. At the time of the accession of Sultan ʿAbdul-Ḥamid in 1876, the 'Armenian Question' was a burning one, and the sympathy it received in Europe fanned more trouble. The inclusion of a protection clause for Christians in Turkey by Britain in the Berlin Treaty of 13 July 1878 encouraged the revolutionary youth even against the advice of the older generation and the church hierarchy. Underground societies were formed, of which the most celebrated was the 'Hunchak'[3] National party, started in Paris in 1885, and exciting circulars were published abroad and smuggled into Turkey in order to arouse public opinion. Special printing presses were set up on foreign soil for the publication of fiery appeals in Armenian. Even Catholic minorities took part in this movement, and their activity was demonstrated in the Armenian publications of the Mekhitarist fathers in Venice. The sultan was infuriated by all these clandestine movements, and he tried to play off Britain against Russia in regard to the tzarist expansionist policy in Armenia. Thus he acceded to Britain's claim to the title of protector of the sultan's Christian subjects in Asia Minor and even granted Britain the right to occupy Cyprus in return for impeding further Russian penetration into Armenia. This is the Cyprus

[1] The Arabic word *millah*, religion. Thus each Christian community was organized as a separate entity with the patriarch at its head aided by secular and ecclesiastical councils under Ottoman rule. The origin of this system is the so-called 'Covenant of ʿUmar', according protection to non-Muslim subjects known as *D̲h̲immis*, also in Ottoman times as *Rayah*, which is the Arabic *raʿiyah* or subjects. On that Covenant, see A. S. Tritton, *The Caliphs and their Non-Muslim Subjects* (Oxford, 1930), pp. 5–17. A Summary of the *millet* system is given by Sarkis Atamian, *The Armenian Community* (New York, 1955), pp. 26–7.

[2] The Arabic *al-k̲h̲aṭṭ al-Sharīf*, i.e., the noble or holy script of a Turkish *Firmān*.

[3] Meaning bell or clarion, the Hunchakian Party was socialist in character. See analysis of its constitution in Sarkis Atamian, pp. 94–100.

Convention, whose repercussions are still felt to the present day. The situation thus became highly complicated with opposite pressures on the Sublime Porte from outside and the continual danger of an explosive revolt among the Armenians from within. The sultan decided to resort to the summary methods of a real tyrant in solving the problem. During 1894, the state complacency led in the first place to a Kurdish attack on the Armenians in the Sasūn region near Diyarbekr, and the Turkish army moved to the area officially to quell the movement, but actually it took to burning several Armenian villages and killing the inhabitants. The young Armenians in the capital responded by their underground activities. In 1895 the sultan gave the signal for the bloodiest massacre, in which about 80,000 Armenians perished at Trebizond and in the adjoining Armenian provinces.[1] Then Hunchak incendiaries immediately answered by setting fire to the Ottoman Bank in Istanbul in 1896; and though the culprits were saved by deportation through diplomatic interference, innocent Armenians in remote places suffered the consequences. In two days 6,000 Armenians lost their lives. The election of the Patriarch Malachia Ormanian in the same year ushered in a period of respite through his wise and conciliatory policy towards the Sublime Porte and the Kurdish tribes. Thus general amnesty was proclaimed, and an uncertain peace reigned for a few years, to be broken again in 1905 with the Cilician massacre in which 20,000 Armenians perished.[2]

The final chapter of the Armenian tragedy under Turkey occurred during the First World War. Armenian leaders declared their loyalty to the sultan and Armenian recruits joined his fighting forces. Turkish doubts, however, resulted in the maltreatment of their contingent which was soon disbanded. The Turkish government, moreover, made the serious decision of mass deportation of the Armenians from Anatolia to Syria and Iraq. It is said that one third of the Armenian population was forced to leave their homes in Turkey, another third escaped and remained in the country, and the other third was simply massacred during 1915.[3] In the following year Russia em-

[1] See 'The Hamidean Massacres (1894–7)', in Sarkis Atamian, pp. 130–54; also M. C. Gabrielian, *Armenia – A Martyr Nation* (New York, 1918), pp. 250 et seq.

[2] Arpee, pp. 244–50, 252–65, 293–308.

[3] Gabrielian, pp. 298 et seq.; A. J. Toynbee, *Armenian Atrocities – The Murder of a Nation* (London, 1915), with a speech by Lord Bryce in the House of Lords; H. A. Gibbons, *The Blackest Page of Modern History – Armenian Events of 1915* (London, 1916). F. Nansen, *Armenia and the Near East* (London, 1928), p. 307, quotes a cypher telegram from the Minister of Interior (Ṭalaʿat Bey) to the Police Office at Aleppo, the text of which, if not a forgery, is distressing: 'It has already been reported that by the order of the Committee the Government have determined completely to exterminate the Armenians living in Turkey. Those who refuse to obey this order cannot be regarded as friends of the government. Regardless of women, children, or invalids, and however deplorable the methods of destruction may seem, an end is to be put to their existence without paying any heed to feeling or conscience.' The same functionary, however, issued subsequent orders for sparing children under five, since they could be brought up as good Turks, thus reminiscent of old Janissary tradition.

barked on the conquest of Turkish Armenia on the grounds of the liberation of its people from the yoke of the Turk. Their manœuvres were interrupted by the upheaval of the Bolshevik Revolution towards the end of 1917, and the Cossacks in the Caucasus abandoned the Armenians, who continued to fight single-handed the superior forces of the enemy. With varying fortunes in an unequal battle, the Armenians, who dreaded the Turks, succeeded by sheer determination and desperate fighting in saving their capital Erivan. Meanwhile, the armistice of 11 November 1918 brought operations to a standstill and gave the Armenians a breathing-space until the British police arrived in the Caucasus.

The details of subsequent events which determined the future of the Armenian people fall within the realm of purely political history. It is sufficient here to outline the salient factors at play in the whole drama. While Britain openly favoured self-determination for the Armenian people, their police force in control of the Transcaucasus failed to keep the peace in the area. They inadvertantly weakened the Armenian cause by disbanding most of its troops and by the shipment of its arsenal to the armies engaged in fighting the Russian counter-revolutionaries. Thus while Woodrow Wilson and the Allies were re-instating a new Armenian Republic on paper extending from Trebizond to Van, and while the Treaty of Sèvres recognizing Armenian independence in 1920 was being signed, the real issue for all practical purposes was in the course of being decided by the armies of nationalist Turkey and Soviet Russia in the field. In the tug-of-war between them, the Turks again managed to massacre some 30,000 Armenians.[1] After the stabilization of Russia and the advance of Russian troops inside Azerbaijan, the real peace was re-established by the signing of the Treaty of Moscow in 1921 laying down the Armenian frontiers without the regions from Trebizond to Van.

The beginnings of Armenian independence within the framework of Soviet Socialist Russia was achieved in two successive stages. First, in 1922 Armenia, Georgia and Azerbaijan were united in a single state named Transcaucasian Soviet Federated Socialist Republics. Second, when the aforementioned federation was dissolved in 1936, its three members became members of the Union of Soviet Socialist Republics, and Armenia had its new constitution as such. In 1928 the Armenian Communist Party numbered 61,245 out of a total population of 1,147,000. In 1939 the Armenians in Russia as a whole reached 2,151,884, of whom 1,025,000 remained inside the Armenian Soviet Socialist Republic. The actual area of the Republic is 11,506 square miles instead of 40,000 square miles stipulated in the Treaty of Sèvres.[2] It is centred around

[1] Arpee, *History of Armenian Christianity*, p. 305, says that in February, 20,000 perished at Marash and in October, 10,000 more at Hadjin.

[2] Figures taken from the article on Armenia in the *Encyclopædia Britannica* (1957 ed.).

Lake Sevan with Erevan as the political, and Etshmiadzin as the religious capital.

Against this background of a long and confused series of events, we have to review the development of Armenian Christianity and the rise of the ancient native church of Armenia. The one characteristic which stands out from any survey of Armenian history is the individualistic personality of its people. The mystery surrounding the Armenians is due to a widespread ignorance of their history, though interest in their fortunes has been accelerated in recent years by the gruesome massacres of that unhappy nation. Throughout the successive phases of their long history, the Armenians preserved their own special character and civilization and refused absorption by any alien master, even at the risk of extermination.

19 • ORIGINS AND DEVELOPMENT OF ARMENIAN CHRISTIANITY

Pre-Gregorian Christianity and the Age of Legend

The earliest chapter in the history of Armenian Christianity is rather vague on account of the absence or the scarcity of source material on the first three centuries. The Armenians had a spoken language but they had not yet developed an alphabet by which to record their native annals. At the opening of the Christian era, the Armenians had been under the influence of Persian religious tradition, though the Asiatic conquest of Alexander the Great also left its Greek impression on their modes of worship. Thus we find elements of Zoroastrianism and Mithraism combined with numerous Hellenic myths in Armenia[1] at the time when the Apostles attacked paganism amidst the peoples of the old world. It is conceivable that Armenia, because of its close proximity to Palestine, the fountain head of the faith of Jesus, may have been visited by the early propagators of Christianity, although it is difficult to define the extent of the spread of this new religion among its inhabitants. Orthodox Armenian historians, such as Ormanian,[2] labour to make a case for the continuity of Apostolic succession in their Church. To him the 'First Illuminators of Armenia' were Saints Thaddæus and Bartholomew whose very shrines still stand in the churches of Artaz (Macoo) and Alpac (Bashkale) in south-east Armenia and have always been venerated by Armenians. A popular tradition amongst them ascribes the first evangelization of Armenia to the Apostle Judas Thaddæus[3] who, according to their chronology spent the years 43–66 A.D. in that country and was joined by St Bartholomew in the year 60 A.D. The latter was martyred in 68 A.D. at 'Albanus'.[4] According to Armenian tradition, therefore, Thaddæus became the first patriarch of the

[1] Arpee, pp. 7–8, gives examples of survivals of the ancient religion in the customs and superstitions of the Armenians.

[2] *Church of Armenia*, pp. 3–7.

[3] To be distinguished from Judas Iscariot, occurring in Matt. x: 3 and Mark iii:18, sometimes also 'Lebbæus', believed to be one of the Brethren of Our Lord and author of the Epistle of Jude, often identified as 'Addai, one of the Seventy', who figured in the Abgar legend.

[4] Identified by Ormanian (p. 3) as 'Albacus', that is Albac or Alpac.

Armenian Church, thus rendering it both Apostolic and autocephalous. Another tradition ascribes to the see of Artaz a line of seven bishops whose names are known and the periods of whose episcopates bring the succession to the second century. Furthermore, the annals of Armenian martyrology refer to a host of martyrs in the Apostolic age. A roll of a thousand victims including men and women of noble descent lost their lives with St Thaddæus, while others perished with St Bartholomew.

It is interesting to note that the apocryphal story of King Abgar and Our Lord was reiterated by some native writers as having occurred in Armenia in order to heighten the antiquity of that religion amongst their forefathers.[1]

Though it is hard to confirm or confute the historicity of these legends so dear to the hearts of Armenians, it may be deduced from contemporary writers that there were Christians in Armenia before the advent of St Gregory Illuminator, the fourth-century apostle of Armenian Christianity. Eusebius of Cæsarea (ca. 260–340 A.D.) refers to the Armenians in his *Ecclesiastical History* on two occasions. First, he states that Dionysius of Alexandria (d. ca. 264), pupil of Origen, wrote an Epistle 'On Repentance', 'to those in Armenia . . . whose bishop was Meruzanes'.[2] On a second occasion, speaking of Emperor Maximin's persecution of 311–13, he says that 'the tryant had the further trouble of the war against the Armenians, men who from ancient times had been friends and allies of the Romans; but as they were Christians and exceedingly earnest in their piety towards the Deity, this hater of God [i.e., Maximin], by attempting to compel them to sacrifice to idols and demons, made of them foes instead of friends, and enemies instead of allies'.[3] Although this second episode must have occurred in the lifetime of Gregory the Illuminator, there is no doubt as to the antiquity of the first reference to the Armenians.

Further, if we believe the argument advanced by Ormanian and other native Armenian historians about a second-century quotation from Tertullian, it must be admitted that Christianity was not unknown in that region at that early date. This seems to be the case as we read of the Persian persecutions of Christians in Armenia by Artashes (Artaxerxes) about the year 110 A.D. and by Chosroes about 230. It is possible that the Persian tyrant almost blotted out the Christian religion from Armenia, where he exerted every effort to introduce Mazdaism in its place.

[1] The Armenian writers are Lerubna of Edessa and Moses of Khoren, in V. Langlois, *Coll. des historiens anciens et modernes d'Arménie*, 2 vols., (Paris 1880), I, 315–26, 326–31, and II, 93–100; also A. Carrière, *La Légende d'Abgar dans l'hist. d'Arménie de Moise de Khoren* (Paris, 1895); English tr. of Moses of Chorene, *Hist. of Arm.*, in *The Ante-Nicene Fathers*, VIII, 702–7.

[2] *Hist. Eccles.*, VI, xlvi. Meruzanes (or Mitrozanes), identified by Ormanian (p. 6) as Mehroojan, successor of the aforementioned bishops of Artaz.

[3] Op. cit., IX, viii. Duchesne, III, 366, thinks that Eusebius had in mind Lesser, not Greater, Armenia.

Armenian Christianity was, however, still in its infancy, and some writers think that it was neither orthodox nor apostolic, but rather Ebionite or Judaistic in character.[1] Armenian heterodoxy regarding the humanity and deity of Our Lord approached adoptionism, an early heresy which asserted that the sonship of God was not actual but merely adoptive. This stream of thought appears to have infiltrated into Armenia from Antioch, more especially in the days of its metropolitan, Paul of Samosata, in the course of the third century.[2]

The unsettled mind of the Armenians about their creed, and the oscillation between paganism and Christianity in Armenia was soon to be stabilized by the historic apostle of Armenian Christianity and the real founder of Armenia's church, Gregory surnamed the Illuminator. Before his time this religion was still unrecognized and often combated not only by foreign pagan invaders of that country but also by its own Armenian rulers. Until then, we must assume that no systematic evangelization had been practised in Armenia, and only stray preachers emerged on the scene of events from three main centres, that is, Jerusalem, Cæsarea and Edessa.

St Gregory the Illuminator

The historic role of the Church of Armenia began with the life and work of its real apostle, St Gregory, surnamed the Illuminator,[3] towards the end of the third and at the beginning of the fourth century. The country had fallen under the Persian yoke and the Sassanid emperors ruthlessly laboured for the spreading of their Mazdaitic religion about the middle of the third century. Thus many Armenians took to flight from the face of their oppressors to other adjacent countries. Amongst these were two youths worthy of special note. The one was the son of the Armenian King Khosrov, assassinated by a member of his family called Anak who was himself killed in turn by royal courtiers. His name was Trdat or Tiridates. The other was Anak's son and his name was Gregory. Both were of aristocratic descent. The first went to Rome where he was brought up in the Western pagan tradition, while the second [i.e. Gregory] stopped at Cæsarea in Cappadocia and there received his initiation in the tenets of the faith from the early Christian divines of its early church. Afterwards Khosrov's son recovered his father's lost throne in 287 A.D. with the aid of Emperor Diocletian the inveterate enemy of Christianity,

[1] F. C. Conybeare, *The Key of Truth* (Oxford, 1898), pp. xc et seq.; cf. Arpee, p. 8.

[2] A. von Harnack, *History of Dogma* (New York, 1957), p. 173; Arpee, pp. 9–10.

[3] Loosavoritsh in Armenian, also called 'St Gregor Partev', i.e., St Gregory the Parthian, denoting his origin. Ormanian, p. 8. He lived from approx. 240 to 332 A.D.

and he subsequently became Trdat II. Meanwhile, Gregory also returned to the homeland after the expulsion of the Persians and immediately started preaching Christianity to the pagans amidst his native countrymen. It did not take long before King Trdat II discovered him and at once arrested him as the son of his father's assassin, and as the enemy of his pagan gods. After having suffered great tortures, Gregory was ultimately cast into a dungeon of the Artashat (Artaxata) Fortress in the province of Ararat. He spent approximately fifteen years in that pit and was secretly fed by a widow to whom he owed his survival. During that period, the Armenian king inflicted an unremitting persecution upon his Christian subjects, and many of them earned the crown of martyrdom at his hands. Amongst his victims was a group of thirty-seven virgins including St Gayane[1] and St Hripsime, still commemorated by the Armenian Church on 5 October every year. The story runs that the latter virgin was extremely beautiful and that she captivated the king, but his approaches to her were met by scorn. After her martyrdom, he became incensed by his own cruelties and was haunted with the idea that he was demoniacally turned into a wild boar.[2]

The historian of the reign of Trdat II, who was the royal secretary and who wrote under the *nom de plume* Agathangelus,[3] provides us with the details of what happened afterwards, leading to the final and total adoption of Christianity as the state religion in the kingdom of Armenia. The story, which falls largely within the realm of legend, is interesting in its general significance. The writer speaks of two divinely inspired visions. First, the king's sister Khosrovitookhd[4] told her brother that she had dreamt of a man with a radiant face who informed her that the persecution of Christians must cease and that St Gregory must be summoned to show them the only way to relieve the king from his affliction. The king accepted her advice, and the saint was brought from the pit. Through his prayers, the king's health and sanity were restored, and he was subsequently baptized with all his household. The second vision[5] came to St Gregory while he was meditating once at midnight. As in a dream, he witnessed the sudden opening of the firmament like a pavilion, and the Lord descended from heaven surrounded by cohorts of winged figures, and the earth shone with resplendent light. Calling Gregory by his name to watch the miracles He was about to reveal to him, the Lord struck the earth with a golden hammer, and an immense pedestal of gold

[1] She was the abbess of a community of nuns in the old capital Vaghashapat. Ormanian, p. 9.

[2] The name Trdat, or Tiridates, literally meant 'gift of the Wild Boar God'. Arpee, p. 16.

[3] The main source of Trdat's reign was written by his own secretary under the pen name Agathangelus. See Agathange, *Histoire du règne de Tiridate et de la prédication de Saint Grégoire l'Illuminateur*, in *Coll. des historians anciens et modernes de l'Arménie*, ed. V. Langlois, I, 105–200.

[4] Op. cit., I, 150–52.

[5] Op. cit., I, 156–59.

emerged in the midst of the town, on which arose a column of fire with a cloud as its capital surmounted by a shining cross. Three other columns, red as blood, also surmounted with luminous crosses rose around the bigger column, evidently on the spots where the bodies of the said saints were laid to rest. The four crosses formed an arch on which stood a grand edifice with cupola, and on top he saw a golden throne with a fiery cross. From this wondrous edifice flowed abundant streams that flooded the plains beyond, and there were also innumerable altars of fire with crosses resembling the stars in the firmament. Then tremendous flocks of black goats crossed the water and became white lambs which multiplied in numbers. Suddenly half of them crossed the water again and turned into wolves which attacked the lambs and the scene was one of bloody carnage. The lambs had wings and joined the Lord's cohorts and fire descended on earth and devoured the wolves. The earth trembled as the day broke, and the vision ended.

It is said that St Gregory built an image of the mystical temple he saw in the place of the great column amidst the town of Vagharshapat, the name of which he changed to Etshmiadzin, that is, 'the Only-begotten has descended'.[1] This is the famous legend of Etshmiadzin, which appears to be apocryphal in character. The large gold column presumably represented Armenian primacy carrying its independent church, the other columns the souls of the martyrs, the black goats and white sheep the Armenian population before and after its evangelization, and the wolves its persecutors.

With the baptism of the king and the members of his court, it may be assumed that the progress of Christianity became a rapid process under the sponsorship of the state. Gregory was nominated by the king as catholicus of the Armenian Church and sent to Cæsarea for consecration by the Metropolitan Leontius and his bishops about the year 301. The pomp of the procession in his escort shows the aristocratic origin of the Church and the close ties with royalty which marked its subsequent history. The saint rode the royal golden chariot drawn by rare white mules with a body-guard of mounted satraps and their armed followers. On his return from the ordination offices, the king in person together with all his royal family and dependents left the capital and pressed onward to meet him on the way, and the two processions were united at the foot of Mount Nbad on the bank of the upper Euphrates, where mass conversions took place. Thus Christianity became the state religion for the first time in history, some dozen years before the recognition was given to the new religion in the Roman empire by the 'Edict of Milan' in 313. The Armenians to the present day pride themselves in this achievement.[2]

The next phase in St Gregory's life after his consecration was the task of

[1] Fortescue, *Lesser Churches*, p. 399.
[2] Arpee, pp. 15–20; Ormanian, pp. 8–10.

completing the Christianization of all his people and the organization of the Armenian church. Supported by the king's men, he set out systematically to destroy the ancient idols and either to pull down pagan temples or to transform them into churches. Bands of heathen priests such as the Albianos family were ordained priests of the new church after receiving baptism. The temple of Anahit in Yeriza became the monastery of St Karapak.[1] The temples of Tyr at Erazamuyn, Anahita at Artashat, Barsamina at Tortan, Armazd at Fort Ani, Nana at Til, Mithra at Pacarij and numerous others surrendered their vast property and estates to the Christian Church. The triple temples of Vahagn, Anahita and Aphrodite at Ashtishat, where past monarchs made their customary sacrifices, were completely destroyed, and the cathedral of Etshmiadzin was erected on their site and sanctified by the placing in its shrine of relics of John the Baptist which St Gregory brought back with him from the city of Cæsaria.[2] The king in person frequently accompanied the saint in his onslaughts on the strongholds of paganism. So impressive was St Gregory's work that posterity soon turned him into a legendary personality. It was mentioned that he baptized four million persons within the short span of seven days, which is clearly a flagrant exaggeration but points to the fact of mass conversions. The diocese of St Gregory extended approximately from Amid to Nisibis, and the contention is that he ordained about four hundred bishops within his jurisdiction.[3] That Armenia became pre-eminently a Christian country within the saint's lifetime ending about 325, is a matter beyond any doubt. On the other hand, the complete obliteration of paganism from the country in those days, a thesis supported by eager Armenian Church historians, must be received with great caution. The pagan priesthood in Armenia was wealthy, strong and militarized. It was not so easily exterminated at least in distant border districts. The saint wisely adopted a policy of ordaining bishops from among the sons of pagan priests as a measure of political sagacity. The burial of a certain Mooshegh about 378 was performed with full pagan rites, according to the historian Faustus of Byzantium.[4] Nevertheless, it must be admitted that at the close of his episcopacy, he had accomplished more than most of his contemporaries. He left behind him a well-organized church and Christianity as the religion of the state and the people of Armenia. It is interesting to note that in its latter pagan days, Rome was so alarmed at the progress of wholesale conversions to Christianity in Armenia that Emperor Maximianus the Dacian (286–305) decided to wage war against the Armenians to stop this outrage, unaware that his own throne was soon destined to be occupied by a Christian.

One problem of major hierarchal importance stemmed from St Gregory's

[1] A. Abrahamiam, *The Church and Faith of Armenia* (London, 1920), p. 19.

[2] Arpee, pp. 17–18.

[3] Fortescue, pp. 399, 401.

[4] Fr. tr. Langlois, *Coll. des historiens*, I, 298; cf. Fortescue, p. 401.

reign. Since he was consecrated by the metropolitan of Cæsarea, the Greeks chose to advance the view at a later date that the Armenian catholicos automatically became a suffragan to the see of that city. Again the Latins contend that Armenia gained her status as an autocephalous church, not from Cæsarea, but through the good offices of Pope Sylvester I (314–35), who granted the Armenians special licence to that effect, thus implying obedience to Rome. The Armenian view, put forward with the patriarchal authority of so distinguished a writer as Ormanian,[1] may be summed up here as shedding light on the official policy of this august and ancient church. In the first instance, Armenian church historians insist in principle on the Apostolic origin of their church, founded by St Thaddæus and St Bartholomew. The succession was never broken until the advent of St Gregory, who received his episcopal staff from Leontius of Cæsarea personally and without abrogating the Apostolic tradition. On the other hand, the Roman theory must be repudiated, since Sylvester's alleged licence was an apocryphal invention at the time of the Crusaders. Armenia Major had been outside the pale of the Roman empire and as such its ecclesiastical development could not have been influenced by Rome. The see of Armenia, like that of Persia or Ethiopia, grew independently outside Roman jurisdiction. Furthermore, if we study the subject of ecclesiastical relations of the sees in existence before the Council of Nicæa, it will be seen that none of them meddled in the affairs of the others. Advocates of the Byzantine or Roman viewpoint build up hypothetical arguments of no historic validity.

Perhaps the real weakness of the Armenian Church during the catholicate of St Gregory was due to the fact that Christianity was more of an aristocratic than a popular religion. The catholicos was a militant prelate who moved around the country with a great retinue supported by the king's battalions. He and his bishops were princes of the church and great feudal lords, since they laid their hands on the vast estates of the old pagan hierarchy. Actually the people as a whole had no access to the Christian religious literature which was either in Greek or in Syriac. The two languages were alien to the Armenian-speaking public in spite of the great efforts which Gregory exerted in the foundation of schools to bridge the gap of ignorance in those two spheres. This weakness was destined to vanish in the fifth century through the labours of other great Armenian ecclesiastical patriots. In those early days, however, it is not inconceivable that existing circumstances still permitted the survival of heathen superstitions among the unlettered Armenians.

As the great saint approached the end of his life, he chose his second son, Aristakes, who was celibate, to succeed him and actually ordained him. Aristakes was at the Council of Nicæa in 325, the year in which Gregory subsequently retired to die in the seclusion of his hermitage. At that time,

[1] *Church of Armenia*, pp. 11–13.

married bishops and church magnates could be found in the hierarchy, but the danger of a hereditary patriarchate loomed in Armenia as a result of popular favour for St Gregory's family. Aristakes reigned from 325 to 333 and was succeeded by his older married brother Vrtan (333–41) and his son Hoosik (341–8), another married man whose own sons refused ordination. Thus the patriarchal throne temporarily went to a collateral relative, Pharan of Ashtishat (348–52), to be resumed by a grandson of Hoosik, Nerses (353–73), whose reign was a definite landmark in Armenian history. After him the Gregorian line of succession was interrupted and went to the house of Albianos, of pagan priestly origin but converted to Christianity by Gregory himself. The Albianos successors who became mighty collaborators in the evangelization work also proved to be real rivals of the Gregorian line in its traditional claim to the patriarchal throne.[1]

The Judaistic colour of the Armenian hierarchy was evident from the outset. The Armenians claimed descent from Abraham, and the early Armenian patriarchs led a married life like the Jewish patriarchs. Bishops, too, followed the example of the heads of their church and their dioceses became hereditary. Perhaps the other curious feature accruing from this Ebionite tendency was the relative complacency towards polygamy. King Arshak III in the second half of the fourth century had two wives, namely Pharandzem and Olympia,[2] although it is unhistorical to make any generalization from isolated cases, and we must remember that Patriarch Nerses retired to a monastery in protest against such practices.

St Gregory's memory has been cherished by all Armenians to the present day. They have numerous celebrations commemorating his birth, persecution, incarceration, release and the translation of his relics. The last feast, occurring on 30 September, is observed also by the Byzantines and Jacobites as well as the Roman Catholics.[3] Where the saint was interred at Thortan on the upper Euphrates, a church and a monastery were built as standing monuments of the Apostle of Armenian Christianity.

[1] Faustus, I, 253; cf. Fortescue, pp. 402, 407. He murdered Olympia later to take more wives and set up a more complacent anti-catholicos to suit his purposes, and the schism came to an end only with the king's death in the Persian wars in 367.

[2] The immediate Albianine successors to the catholicate were Sahak (373–7), Zaven (377–81) and Aspoorakes (381–6); Ormanian, p. 14. Early Armenian chronology is still somewhat indefinite and subject to historical discussion; cf. Fortescue, p. 402, n. 1.

[3] The Catholics celebrate it on 1 October, the date fixed by Pope Gregory XVI for 'S. Gregorius, patriarcha Armeniæ, martyr, vulgo Illuminator', cf. Fortescue, p. 400, n. 2, where he rejects the papal injunction by saying that 'he was neither a patriarch nor a martyr'.

Fourth-Century Reform and the Armenian Bible

In order to understand fully the role which the Armenian Church played across the ages in Armenian life and civilization, we must remember that Christianity was the state religion and that the state in those early days was founded on a feudal basis with a semi-barbarous royalty. The Church with its vast spiritual power and its immense economic resources was therefore the chief beneficent factor in the community, especially at moments when it was blessed with an enlightened shepherd. This feature, which accompanied the ancient Armenian Church throughout its life even after the disappearance of Armenian kings and Armenian independence, was no more outstanding than in the reign of Gregory's great-great-grandson Nerses (353–73), a fourth-century prelate who rightfully earned the title of 'the Great'. Once the bulk of the task of the evangelization of the whole of Armenia was at least officially completed during the catholicate of Gregory and his immediate successors, the next natural phase was the final organization of the church order and the surveillance over the common people's immediate needs, both spiritual and material. The Church made its headquarters almost from the beginning at Ashtishat in the province of Taron, which became the ecclesiastical capital of Armenia as a parallel to Vagharshapat or Etshmiadzin, the state capital and royal residence. In this way the Church retained its independence from the state and acted on its own initiative. The feudal princes between themselves invariably resorted to Ashtishat for arbitration over their differences, which sometimes extended to the crown itself.

In the year 365, Nerses summoned a holy synod at Ashtishat, to which he invited the nobility along with the bishops, for the settlement of outstanding uncertainties as to the law of the land, and for the introduction of pressing reforms. This council first regulated marriage relationships and forbade the prevailing custom of marriage between first cousins whereby the nobles sought to preserve their feudal estates from dissipation. It also tried to stamp out the vestiges of pagan superstitions and customs still prevailing, such as wailings and self-disfigurement over the dead, the invocation of spirits and the use of amulets. Afterwards the council attended to a number of civilizing reforms. Special aid, in kind from the country and in cash from urban districts, was to be levied for the establishment of hospitals for the sick, refuges for lepers, homes for the blind, asylums for orphans and widows and hostelries for travellers.[1] Moreover, monasteries on the cenobitic model, then spreading from Egypt to the Byzantine empire and western Asia were to be built for housing stranded ascetics and hermits. In accordance with one estimate, a total of two thousand new establishments, large and small, was

[1] Arpee, p. 21.

reached in that age. The good work was momentarily arrested by a new Persian onslaught against Armenia and the vain Sassanid attempt to reintroduce Mazdaism amongst the people, as well as the lamentable attitude of the Armenian kingship in the disreputable reigns of Arshak III and his son Pap, both of whom met with violent ends.

The tempestuous reign of Pap, however, accidently gave the Armenian Church a new departure. The king, who set himself the task of undoing Nerses' reforms after, according to some reports, having poisoned the great prelate, nominated a new catholicos to his liking by the name of Yusik II from the rival house of Albianos. Fearing differences with Cæsarea over his ordination, he decided to have him consecrated by the Armenian bishops at home in the late seventies of the fourth century. This event marked the breach with Cæsarea and the resumption of ecclesiastical independence in Armenia. When the succession to the see of Ashtishat finally reverted to the Gregorian line by Sahak I's consecration in 387, the new catholicos confirmed the breach and was enthroned at home.

Sahak's long reign lasted from 387 to 439 with some interruption, exile and schism clouding the spiritual progress of Armenia at times, but without real bearing on the tremendous advance which took place in this age. Hitherto, Armenian had been a language of numerous and varying local dialects, but entirely without a recorded religious and secular literature, and even without an alphabet. The Church was completely dependent on Greek in the western regions and Syriac in the eastern Armenian provinces, but the bulk of the people understood neither of those two languages. Hence a device had to be made to bring the significance of the liturgy and church readings in a foreign language to the congregation. Two orders of a peculiar nature were incorporated in the church service: the readers (*Vendzanogh*), who read the Scriptures and other material, and the interpreters (*Thargmanitsh*), who translated the readings into Armenian for the native congregation. This was the position towards the end of the fourth century, and catholicos Sahak, who realized its disadvantages, sought the means for the removal of such confusion. By a happy coincidence, he found aid and solace in his plight in the person of a gifted Armenian to whose genius the whole Armenian literature owes its very existence. This was a cleric by the name of Mesrop whom he ordained in 396. A former secretary to the king, he became a disciple to the catholicos, who commissioned him to embark on a special mission to combat paganism and heretical teachings in the distant parts of the country. It was during his early travels that he must have felt the need for an Armenian Bible in people's hands as the first weapon to extirpate irregularities and heathen superstitions. Thus, on his return to Ashtishat, he raised the crucial question of the creation of an Armenian alphabet with the catholicos, who summoned a special council to give its blessing to the project, which the reigning King Vramshapooh joined with state support. Finally the new alphabet was designed by Mesrop in thirty-six letters at Balahovit (Paloo) at the dawn of the fifth century and approved by Sahak and the Church. Later in the twelfth century the number of letters was increased by two, bringing the definitive alphabet to thirty-eight. This event may be regarded as second in importance in Armenian annals only to the introduction of Christianity. Apart from providing the means whereby the whole literature of the Armenians was placed on record, it brought home the Bible and the liturgy to the Armenian people and helped in the obliteration of paganism from the country. Moreover, a standard authorized Armenian Bible was destined to become a unifying influence on the multitude of varied local dialects and consequently prevented the two sections of the nation under Persian and Greek rule from falling apart.

Accordingly, the next step after the invention of the alphabet was the authorizing of a translation of the whole Bible into Armenian.[1] To this end, a team of one hundred interpreters trained by Sahak and Mesrop were appointed to help the latter in the great task during the year 404. The commission began by translating the Old Testament from the Greek Septuagint with collations from the Syriac Peshitta. The members were scholars conversant with both Greek and Syriac. The initial experiment was successfully executed by Mesrop in Solomon's Proverbs. The final text of the whole Bible was completed before the end of 433. The Armenian Bible contains in addition to the canonical books some of the Apocryphal literature drawn from the old Alexandrine Greek texts as well as the Syriac sources.[2] Those were years of great pressure from Persia, and Mesrop and his companions reacted to the futile and successive efforts of the Sassanid usurpers to supplant Christianity with Zoroastrianism or Mazdaism by spurring on the work on the Armenian Bible. Meanwhile, the church established parish schools everywhere to train young Armenians to read the Scriptures in the new script.

Then followed the translation of the Holy Liturgy of St Basil, the rituals of baptism and confirmation, the services of church consecration as well as the marriage and funerary offices. Armenian texts formerly transliterated in Greek or Syriac characters were recopied in Armenian. Lives of the saints and a number of leading texts from the Greek patristic work gradually enriched the growth of Armenian literature. Though faithful on the whole to the letter of the prayer books, the translators gave the Armenian liturgy a special colour by means of the adoption of long-standing hymns (*sharakan*) of the Armenian people reflecting their own folk music, presumably inspired

[1] Ormanian, pp. 17–19; Arpee, pp. 33–43; Archdeacon Dowling, *The Armenian Church* (London, 1910), pp. 104–13; E. F. K. Fortescue, *Armenian Church*, pp. 137–49.

[2] Archdeacon Dowling gives an interesting analysis of the Books of the Armenian Bible. E. F. K. Fortescue, pp. 143–9, quotes in English tr. the text of the apocryphal Epistle of Paul to the Corinthians. For Armenian translations of both Bible and Liturgies, see K. Sarkissian, *A Brief Introduction to Armenian Literature* (London, 1960), pp. 13–30.

by the immortal hymnal of their great neighbour St Ephraem in the original Syriac.

Although Mesrop's Armenian Bible is sometimes regarded as being more impression than expression, more interpretation than translation, comparisons with modern authorized versions demonstrate beyond doubt that the fifth-century text is almost identical with our own.[1] The Bible was another powerful influence on the people of Armenia, to such an extent that subsequent attacks on them, if they undid the political structure, were never able to suppress Christianity. The ensuing Persian wars culminating in the tragic battle of Avarayr[2] in 451, and the rise of the great patriot Vahan Mamiconian to the position of leadership amongst his people, proved to the Sassanids the futility of their efforts in Armenia. Thus Yezdegird II (438–57) proclaimed religious freedom in Armenia and even confirmed Mamiconian in the governorship of the country. At this point, both governor and catholicos moved into Dwin as their new and common capital for closer action in times of danger.

The Armenians and Chalcedon[3]

The Armenians were probably unaware of the œcumenical council convened at Chalcedon in October of the year 451, although it is said that ten Armenian bishops were there.[4] Armenia was involved in desperate fighting for her life, and the church was in a merciless phase of persecution by the Persians which culminated in the martyrdom of its Catholicos Hovsep in 454. Even if the Armenians were informed and invited, it would hardly be conceivable for them to be in a mood to respond to the summons from the Emperor Marcian (450–7), who had forsaken them to the forces of darkness. The role of the Armenians with regard to the decisions made at Chalcedon had to be deferred to more peaceful days. Finally with the return of relative peace to the Church, and the proclamation of religious liberty in the later decades of the fifth

[1] Arpee gives interesting examples of the Armenian and English translations in parallel columns. Differences are more perceptible in the Old than in the New Testament.

[2] R. Grousset, *Hist. de l'Arménie*, pp. 203–7; Arpee, pp. 49–53. The Persians in the field were 300,000, the Armenians only 66,000. The losses were 3,544 Persians as against 1,036 Armenians. Elephants were used by the Persians. Unending guerilla war followed the defeat of the Armenians, whose spirits nevertheless remained high.

[3] For sources of important Council, see above under Copts. On Armenia and the Council, see Ormanian, pp. 24–6; Arpee, pp. 124–5; Fortescue, pp. 411–14.

[4] Fortescue, p. 411; F. Tournebize, *Hist. politique et religieuse de l'Arménie* (Paris, 1910), p. 87. These were possibly the members of the delegation sent to court aid from Constantinople and were unheeded by Marcian; Ormanian, p. 27. They could therefore hardly be described as representatives of the Armenian Church at the Council.

century, the Armenian Church felt herself in a position to deliberate on the reversal of the decisions of the second Council of Ephesus (449), which she had already recognized as canonical. The formula advanced by the Patriarch Cyril of Alexandria on the burning problem of the Christology of Jesus, that He had 'one nature united in the incarnate Word', was then shifted at Chalcedon to Leo's definition in his famous *Epistola dogmatica* to Flavian of Constantinople that the Lord was 'in two natures, without confusion, without conversion, without severance, and without division'. Thus the Catholicos Babguen (490–516) summoned a general synod of all Armenian, Georgian and Caspio-Albanian bishops in 506 at Dwin for a decision on the subject. It was held that the Chalcedonian terms savoured of Nestorianism and they unanimously voiced the Ephesian profession of the faith. Hence Armenia asserted her historic stand in the camp of the eastern Monophysites.

Behind the Armenian deliberations were certain conditions that must be borne in mind. The great clash between East and West, between Alexandria and Rome, though theological in character, had also a political background. Hitherto, the Alexandrian school of theologians had led former œcumenical councils. This was contrary to Roman ideas and to the growing spirit of theocracy at Constantinople. Hence we note from the very beginning that the papal delegates, Paschasinus and Boniface, arrived with explicit orders that the presidency of the next council should be given to the Romans and that any decision contrary to their beliefs should be regarded as invalid. The Armenians, like the Copts, must have felt that behind all that, was a question of Roman control over the Christian Churches; and their reaction to this could not be favourable. The hesitancy in Constantinople swang them to the other side. Although Marcian approved of the council decisions, a number of his successors remained in doubt. Basiliscus objected, Zeno issued the *Henoticon*, which approached Monophysite formulas, and Anastasius as late as 491 refused to acknowledge the authority of Chalcedon. Amidst these protests, the Armenians could not but retain their pre-Chalcedonian profession. Their traditional hostility to Nestorianism and Nestorians, as well as their unwillingness to discard their ecclesiastical and national independence from Greeks and Romans alike were decisive factors against the creed of Chalcedon.

The political impact of these decisions was far-reaching. The breach with Cæsarea, coupled with that of Chalcedon, resulted in the ecclesiastical isolation of the Church of Armenia. Its original profession of the faith was henceforth jealously guarded and continuously re-affirmed by the successors[1] of Babguen. The Synod of Dwin in 554 was convened by Nerses II (548–57) to renew Armenian allegiance to the decrees of Ephesus. Thus the foundations of

[1] His immediate successors, Samuel of Ardzke (516–26), Mooshe of Ailaberk (526–34), Sahak II of Ooghki (534–9), Kristaphor of Tiraridj (539–45) and Ghevond of Erast (545–548), in turn made these affirmations; Ormanian, p. 28.

Armenian faith were solidly laid for all future generations. The national Church has remained imperturbable in her adherence to the old profession. When the Catholicos Ezra acceded to the persuasions of Emperor Heraclius for union with the Greeks in 629, the Synod of Manzikert in 651 repudiated Chalcedon and condemned Ezra's action exactly two hundred years after the Council of Chalcedon. Finally, Armenia was saved from further temptation of union with the Greeks by one of the greatest upheavals in human annals – the Arab Conquest and the rise of the Islamic empire in the Middle East.

20 • TIMES OF TRIAL

The Caliphate

The Arab invasion of Armenia in the seventh century opened another era of paradoxes in Armenian Church history. The Arabs who wrested the country from both the Persians and the Greeks established a different policy of government. They found it more expedient to rule the new territory through the greater feudal princes who paid homage to the new master together with the annual *Kharāj* or tribute. The Byzantine empire, which had steadily been losing ground to the advancing Muslim armies, struggled to retain at least western Armenia within the imperial fold; and again this division of the country between the two different traditions of East and West enfeebled the position of the nation politically but not ecclesiastically. The Church was the only universal factor in the national life of Armenia, whether Arab or Greek. The Arabs, unlike the Greeks had no special quarrel with the church. Under Arab protection in accordance with the Covenant of ʿUmar, the Church felt itself in a better position when arguing with the Greeks about the Chalcedonian doctrines. The Armenian prelates could freely expound their Monophysitism undisturbed by Byzantine interference. On all possible occasions, the Armenian Church asserted its historic repudiation of Chalcedon and refused union with Constantinople. The outstanding example of this adamant position was demonstrated at the Synod of Manzikert of 726 held jointly with the Syrian bishops, under the presidency of the famous Armenian Catholicos Hovhannes Otzun, surnamed the Philosopher. Hovhannes, or John, Otzun was a man of great learning. He wrote numerous theological treatises and introduced disciplinary reforms in the church. He was also an able diplomat and seized every occasion to obtain privileges for his people. The most-quoted story about his encounter with Caliph ʿUmar II (717–20) is that he decked himself with the richest ecclesiastical vestments to meet the suzerain of his country. When the caliph asked him whether Christ taught his people to dress simply, the catholicos requested a moment's seclusion with him and then revealed to him a tunic of goat wool which he wore next to the skin concealed underneath his dazzling robes. The caliph remarked that no human flesh could endure such austerities without Allah's will and expressed readiness to grant the holy man whatever he asked. Hovhannes requested religious freedom for his people and exemption of churches and clergy from taxes. The request was approved and all Armenian prisoners of war were also freed by order of the caliph.[1]

In accordance with the terms of the Covenant of 'Umar, subject Christian communities were allowed to retain their religious foundations existing at the time of the conquest, but they had to refrain from building new ones or restoring older establishments. This rule was certainly not observed in Armenia. During the reign of King Ashot Bagratuni in the ninth century, his daughter Miriam, wife of Vasak Gabour, prince of Siounie, engaged in the building of one church in the province of Taron, forty churches and convents in the province of Siounie, and many others in the province of Ararat.[2] Stone was used in the erection of those magnificent edifices with their beautiful domes, arches and vaults. Older churches were restored and embellished with icons and mosaics. In matters of doctrine, the Church continued to reject all approaches from Byzantium. When Photios (858–67), the spirited patriarch of Constantinople, again revived efforts for the reunion of the Armenians, he was rebuffed outright by the Catholicos Zaccharias in a letter of 862 which repudiated Chalcedon as contrary to the spirit of the first three œcumenical councils. The Synod of Shiragavan in the same year reiterated old definitions of the united nature of Christ against the 'lies' of the Greeks.[3]

It would, however, be an error to assume that the Armenians had lived a life of complete freedom from violence under Arab suzerainty. Instances of excesses are indeed very numerous, and it would be idle to attempt a survey of Muslim–Armenian encounters from the seventh century onwards. On several occasions, the catholicoi had to undertake the hazardous journey to the capital of Islam to plead in person at the Caliph's court on behalf of their people. In the patriarchate of Hovhannes V (898–929), Dwin the ecclesiastical capital was sacked by the Arabs, and the seat of the catholicos was transferred to Van and afterwards to Ani, the political metropolis of Armenia. The successive heads of the Church in that period became wandering catholicoi, and the whole community was rent asunder by schism and heresy. Amid their tribulations however, Armenians did not waver in their loyalty to their historic doctrines, and any catholicos who leaned towards understanding with the Greeks was invariably deposed by the national bishops. As to the spread of the Paulician heresy[4] with its fanatical tendencies and

[1] Arpee, pp. 78–9.

[2] J. Laurent, *L'Arméenie entre Byzance et l'Islam* (Paris, 1919), pp. 45–50. Details are provided p. 45, n. 6.

[3] Arpee, pp. 132–3; Laurent, pp. 309 et seq.

[4] Arpee, pp. 101–19, devotes a whole chapter to the heresy. See also Ormanian, pp. 38–9.

esoteric cult, this was suppressed and pursued without mercy by the authorities of both Church and state.

As Arab influence grew weaker in Anatolia and upper Mesopotamia, the Saljūq Turks embarked on their expansionist policy in the area, while the Byzantine empire attempted to recapture some of its lost possessions in western Asia. Thus Armenia again became the bone of contention between the old and the new powers. Finally the battle of Manzikert, north of Lake Van in Armenia, took place in 1071; and the Saljūq leader Alp Arslan routed the Byzantine forces and seized the Emperor Romanus Diogenes as a prisoner of war. When the unhappy captive recovered his liberty by the payment of a heavy ransom, he returned to his capital to find Michael Ducas on his throne, a usurper who blinded his predecessor and threw him in a worse prison to die in oblivion. After Manzikert, Armenia was at the mercy of a ruthless foe.

Unlike the Arabs who had ruled Armenia by proxy, the Saljūq Turks came to stay as permanent settlers and rulers in the land. Also unlike the Arabs, they were extremely bigoted and destructive in their maraudings amongst the Armenian Christians. The Bagratid dynasty and the kingdom of Armenia underwent rapid distintegration at their hands. After the fall of Ani, confusion swept over the Church and the state. The wandering catholicoi were compelled to keep changing their residences from Ani to Theodosiopolis, Sebastea, Tarentia, Tavplur, Zamanta or elsewhere. As to the Armenian nobility, every man lived for himself alone in an effort to carve out a principality of his own at the expense of the dying central government. The displaced Armenians emigrated in great numbers to the regions of Edessa, the Anti-Taurus, and the Cilician mountains. An Armenian adventurer named Philaretus established himself in Edessa in 1083, and was succeeded by another called Thoros in 1090. Gabriel held Melitene (Malaṭiya). A robber-baron by the name of Kogh Vasil seized Raban, Kaisun, and Rumqalʿa in the valley of the upper Euphrates. We also hear of an Armenian duke of Vaspuragan bearing the Arabic name of Abul-Gharīb[1] ruling at Tarsus from 1072 and extending his conquests to Mopsuestia, Adana and the forts of Baberon and Lambron. More enduring than all these petty principalities was the appearance of a prince of Bagratid origin named Reuben, who finally succeeded in founding the new Reubenian dynasty of the kingdom of Lesser Armenia by seizing a number of Cilician mountain fortresses from the Byzantine garrisons of Asia Minor in 1080, that is, less than two decades before the advent of the Crusaders from Europe and the inauguration of a new chapter in Armenian political and ecclesiastical history.

[1] Arpee, p. 134.

The Crusades

The age of the crusades was simultaneously the age of the kingdom of Lesser Armenia which developed in Cilicia with Sīs as its capital. Two successive dynasties ruled the new kingdom, first as barons then as kings: the Reubenian dynasty from 1080 to 1219 and the Hethoumian dynasty from 1226 to 1375. Both dynasties were extremely friendly with the Crusaders in spite of their occasional belligerency and menacing attitude. Both had common interests in combating the Turk and both shared the same antipathy towards the Greek. This led to a movement of *rapprochement* between them and their Latin neighbours. This relationship was sealed by a succession of marriage alliances. Even before the foundation of the kingdom of Jerusalem, Baldwin married Morfia, daughter of the Armenian Prince Gabriel of Edessa; and the daughter of Constantine I (1095–9),[1] second in the Reubenian line, was united with Jocelyn I of Courtenay, lord of Turbessel and later of Edessa. Leo II received his royal title for Armenia from Emperor Henry VI and Pope Celestine II, and Cardinal Conrad of Wittelsbach later placed the crown on his head at the cathedral of Tarsus in 1199. Still more, when the Reubenian line was about to become extinct, since Leo had no male successor, the king married his daughter Zabel, or Isabel, to the Latin Philip of Antioch, who was elevated to the throne of Armenia in 1219 on condition that he should become Armenian in faith and order. When later he failed to fulfil these promises, the Armenian nobles removed him from the throne and took his life, then they married Zabel to an Armenian, Hethoum I (1226–69), founder of the Hethoumian line. The new line was, however, closely associated with the Latins in the Holy Land. The prince of Antioch, Bohemond VI, was Hethoum's son-in-law, and King Ochen (1308–20) married a daughter of Hugh III de Lusignan, king of Cyprus.

In the circumstances of these intimate political and even military alliances between the rulers of Armenia and the Crusaders, the Armenian Church necessarily fell under Latin influence throughout the Cilician period. The catholicos ultimately moved to Sīs, the new Armenian capital, and worked more closely with the kings. This steady approach towards Rome, it has to be observed, was dictated by political expediency rather than dogmatic conviction, and was usually led by the head of the Church while the majority of bishops and the clergy, who came to be known as the 'Band of Eastern Divines',[2] clung to the old Armenian ecclesiastical loyalties. The outward acquiescence of the Church as a whole was a matter of temporary convenience, for the Armenians looked to the West for possible aid. Even before the

[1] Strictly speaking, the earlier Armenian kings are described in the European sources as 'barons of Armenia'.

[2] Ormanian, p. 51.

outbreak of the Crusades, the Armenians had sent a bishop to Gregory VII (1073–85) to court his sympathy for the holy war and secure his support for the Armenians and their Church.[1]

The first serious approach between Armenians and Rome took place in the catholicate of Gregory III (1113–66), who visited Cardinal Alberic, the papal Legate at Antioch, in 1141 and participated in the Council of Jerusalem in 1142, then exchanged gifts and delegations with Popes Lucius II (1144–45) and Eugenius III (1145–53). Those amicable encounters, however, did not yield any official agreement on the profession of the faith. Meanwhile, Gregory's brother and immediate successor in the catholicate, namely Bishop Nerses 'the Graceful', later Nerses IV (1166–73), conceived the idea of widening the circle of negotiations for a greater union of Greeks, Romans, Syrians and Armenians. He discussed his universal project with the Greek governor of lower Cilicia, who took the matter to the Emperor Manuel I Comnenus (1143–80). Negotiations dragged along without any ostensible result till the end of Nerses' reign, since the emperor insisted on the acceptance of the Chalcedonian formula. The next catholicos, Gregory IV (1173–93), summoned the Armenian bishops to a council at Rhomkla, which attempted a compromise without adherence to the Greek proposals at the time of Manuel's death in 1180, while the internal conditions of the empire distracted the authorities from the resumption of negotiations.

The Armenians were thus constrained to depend upon the Latins under the influence of King Leo II (1187–1219) and at the risk of local schism in the church, more especially after Leo's coronation in 1199. The king had his nominees supported by the local Cilician bishops, whereas the Eastern Divines elected an anti-catholicos in defiance to the state. The movement of union with Rome came to an open declaration during the catholicate of Constantine I (1221–67). He was a contemporary of Leo II and Hethoum I, both of whom were staunch Latin allies. From that time, catholicos after catholicos declared the profession of the faith in accordance with the Roman creed. A party of 'Unitors' had been formed to work on the people of Cilicia; while Benedictine[2] missionaries established a formidable branch of their order to complete the Romanization of the national Armenian Church. Those who retained their anti-Chalcedonian tradition elected another national patriarch, and thus in that period there were two rival patriarchs, one Uniate at Sīs, and another Monophysite at Aghthamar. This dual arrangement of the Church remained in force until after the collapse of the Cilician dynasty.

[1] S. Runciman, *A Hist. of the Crusades*, 3 vols. (Cambridge, 1951–4), I, 202–3.

[2] Both movements are linked chiefly in the person of the Dominican friar Bartholomew of Bologna, who founded a Catholic monastery at Maragha around 1317. He was accompanied in his work by a Franciscan from Sicily called Peter of Aragona. Their original plan of preaching the Gospel to the Muslims in the Holy Land was diverted to the proselytization of the Armenians. Arpee, pp. 157–60; Ormanian, p. 56.

Fifteen patriarchs reigned over Sīs, all evidently Uniate, from Gregory VII to Gregory IX (1294–1441). A desperate attempt was made to bring an Armenian delegation to the famous Council of Ferrara-Florence (1438–9), and after much ado, Joachem, bishop of Aleppo, and three Armenian doctors of theology arrived at Florence two months after the adjournment of the council and the departure of the Greek delegates. Then Pope Eugenius IV received their submission separately and, three months later, issued the bull *Exultate Dei*[1] whereby he declared the Armenian Church reunited with Rome after nine hundred years of isolation and error. This shadowy union was never ratified by the Armenian synod, and the gap separating Armenia from Rome widened. The national clergy summoned the newly elected Patriarch Gregory IX at Sīs in 1439 to appear at Etshmiadzin. It is said that he had Uniate leanings[2] and preferred to remain where he was. So he declined the invitation and gave them permission to elect another. In 1441, a great synod of seven hundred bishops, clerics and Armenian nobles met at Etshmiadzin and elected as catholicos Kyrakos of Virap, who represented a new departure in their Church history.

The Five Patriarchs

The upheavals in Armenian national existence incurred by the waves of invasion and persecution to which the people were subjected in mediæval and modern times rendered the stability of the patriarchal see an impossibility. After the disintegration of the Bagratine monarchy, the catholicos was a wandering prelate except during the age of the Reubenian–Hethoumian dynastic settlement in Cilicia, when the centre of the Church moved from Rumqalʿa to Sīs. Thus the confused circumstances in which the Armenians had lived, together with a succession of schisms in the hierarchy, produced a peculiar position in the catholicate with five recognized patriarchs in five ecclesiastical capitals. How did this arise? When the city of Ani was destroyed by the Arabs in the tenth century,[3] the patriarchal residence and property were confiscated and the Patriarch Hovhannes V (898–929) had to seek another home. In those unsettled times, the feudal nobles carved out little local kingdoms of their own which they defended independently with

[1] Date of the bull, 22 November, 1439; cf. Arpee, p. 163.

[2] Fortescue, p. 416.

[3] Details of Ani and its splendid mediæval remains (now chiefly in ruins) are in H. F. B. Lynch, *Armenia – Travels and Studies*, Vol. I: *The Russian Provinces*, and Vol. II: *The Turkish Provinces* (London, 1901), I, 334–92. More modern material may be found in Sirapie Der Nessessian, *Armenia and the Byzantine Empire* (Cambridge, Mass., 1945), pp. 55 et seq.

their own military resources. The patriarch found refuge with one of those petty princes, the king of Vaspuragan,[1] and established his headquarters in a monastery on the small island of Aghthamar in Lake Van in the year 927. Schism followed, and the ecclesiastical adherents to the throne of Ani elected another patriarch until Khatshik I (973–92) restored the union at Ani in 991. Then Sīs emerged as a capital in the kingdom of Lesser Armenia and superseded other capitals as a patriarchal see. Its swing towards Rome in the age of the Crusades, however, led to the revival of the see at Aghthamar until Kyrakos of Virap was elected at Etshmiadzin. Later Aghthamar territory was contracted to almost titular dimensions, with only two dioceses which were completely wiped out in the course of the massacres, while Sīs with thirteen dioceses returned to the mother church.[2] The patriarchate of Sīs or Cilicia was eventually deported with most of its congregations during the First World War. Consequently, the patriarch took up his headquarters at Antelias in Lebanon with the help of the Near East Relief Organization.[3] In any case, at the end of the Middle Ages, we find three patriarchs in Armenia.

According to Ormanian,[4] himself a patriarch, the explanation is given that a system of patriarchal coadjutors came into existence whereby the acceptance of the principles of several patriarchs, besides satisfying ambitious prelates, helped to simplify procedures amidst the segregated and far-flung communities of Armenians. The problem of seniority was solved for centuries by a tradition highly regarded by the Armenian hierarchy. The right arm, the famous Holy *Adj*, or *Atsh*, in Armenian, of St Gregory the Illuminator was a precious relic treasured by the chief prelate in the Armenian Church and carried with him throughout his peregrinations. In the ceremony of patriarchal consecration, the Holy *Adj* is held over the head of the consecrated. It has therefore been admitted that the patriarch who owned the relic was 'The Supreme Catholicos-Patriarch of All Armenians', often designated also as 'Minister of the Right Hand and the Throne of St Gregory the Illuminator'.[5]

[1] Arpee, p. 85. Also called king of Van, other kings known to exist are those of Ani' Kars and Goorgarq; Ormanian, p. 37.

[2] Ormanian, pp. 118, 119.

[3] Ibid., pp. 80–1. Comparative tables of the dioceses before the First World War (App. II, p. 207) show the catholicate of Cilicia to comprise a total of fifteen dioceses, of which two are abbacies mainly in Anatolia. Statistics of 1954 (App. III, p. 211) show Cilicia to have only four dioceses: one in Lebanon, two in Syria, and one in Cyprus, but none in Turkey.

A brochure entitled *The Catholicate of Cilicia – Her Place and Status in the Armenian Church* (An official publication of the Catholicate at Antelias, Lebanon, 1961), pp. 14 ff., asserts that in the Armenian Church there are two catholicates – Etshmiadzin and Cicilia – and two patriarchates at Jerusalem and Constantinople. Etshmiadzin exercises jurisdiction over the two patriarchates and all other sees in the world except Cilicia whose traditional independence is maintained.

[4] Op. cit., p. 58.

[5] D. Attwater, *The Christian Churches of the East*, II, 250–1.

The two remaining patriarchates of Jerusalem and Constantinople owe their creation to a set of special circumstances. Jerusalem always had an Armenian metropolitan, the custodian of the holy places and sites within Armenian jurisdiction. Associations with the Holy City and the Holy Sepulchre lent him glamour in the eyes of Armenian pilgrims, and the first mention of the patriarchal title in Jerusalem was in 1311 when the Armenian Bishop Sergius[1] journeyed to Cairo and obtained permission from the Mamlūk Sultan al-Nāṣir Muḥammad in his third reign (1309–40) to assume the dignity of patriarch. But nobody elected him, and the title disappeared until the eighteenth century. It was in the reign of John Golod (1715–41), patriarch of Constantinople, that the title was granted to the metropolitan of Jerusalem in recognition of his support.[2] When the new patriarch of Jerusalem started to ordain bishops for his own diocese, he was forbidden to do so by the catholicos of Etshmiadzin, who insisted that that prerogative together with the power of consecrating the holy chrism should be reserved to those enthroned at Etshmiadzin and Sīs only. Originally the nominee of the General Assembly of the patriarchate of Constantinople, with the approval of the Sublime Porte, the patriarch of Jerusalem is now elected by the General Clerical Assembly of St James in the Holy City. His prestige has been enhanced by the foundation of the Theological Seminary of St James' Monastery in the City. This institution, which dates from the reign of Patriarchs Eghishe Doorian (1921–30) and Thorgom Gooshakian (1931–9), has produced many notable graduates administering to Armenian communities in many parts of the world and especially in the United States of America.[3]

As to the patriarchate of Constantinople, it apparently emerged at the time of the Ottoman Conquest. Constantinople is known to have had a considerable Armenian colony with a bishop in Greek times. When Muḥammad the Conqueror seized the city in 1453, he established the *Millet* system whereby the religious administration of the Christian communities was entrusted to their respective patriarchs. The sultan invested the Greek Patriarch Gennadius Scholarius with these powers over his Greek and other Orthodox Diophysite subjects in the Balkans. Later he acted similarly with regard to the Armenian Bishop Hovacim, whom he called from Brusa to take up residence in Constantinople in 1461 and assume the same jurisdiction with regard to the Monophysite Christians. Ormanian claims that the Armenian patriarch actually administered for the Armenians, Syrians, Chaldæans, Copts, Georgians and Abyssinians.[4] Doubtful as the assertion is, the fact remains that the Armenians were in favour with the sultans for centuries. The *Millet* system gave the patriarchs wide jurisdiction over all religious, educational and social matters including marriage, inheritance, benevolence,

[1] Arpee, p. 165.
[2] Ibid. p. 238.
[3] Ormanian, pp. 82–3.
[4] Op. cit., p. 61.

wakfs (trusts), census and all like powers entrusted to Shaikh al-Islām with regard to Muslims. Roman Catholics, even those who were converted natives, did not enjoy these privileges and were generally regarded as foreigners. Their recognition as a separate entity came only as late as the year 1830 with the creation of a Roman Catholic patriarchate having the same prerogatives as others. Both patriarchates, however, were reduced to a small fraction of their original membership during the hard years of massacres and deportations.[1]

In this way arose the suffragan patriarchates of Aghthamar, Sīs, Jerusalem and Constantinople, with Etshmiadzin at the head before the First World War. Aghthamar has since been dropped, and Sīs became the catholicate of Cilicia in exile. The Œcumenical Catholicos of All Armenians has under his own direct rule the province of Ararat, now called Erevan, together with sixteen other dioceses mainly in the Soviet Union and Iran, and a few more in the Old World and the New.[2] Within the fortified walls of the patriarchal residence stands a monastery, a printing press, a substantial theological seminary, a library, and a hostel for pilgrims who contribute freely to that ancient sanctuary.[3]

Coming of the Missionary

Since the collapse of Armenian independence and the dispersion and impoverishment of Armenian communities, the history of the Church became a sorry tale wrapped in the darkness of ignorance, separatism, superstition and formalism. Its annals consist of endless quarrels,[4] so demoralizing to the

[1] The statistical tables furnished in Ormanian's Appendices II and III, pp. 205–6, 212, reveal the following figures: before the First World War, the patriarch of Constantinople ruled over fourteen archbishops, twenty-seven bishops, six abbots, one prelate and two archpriests, and the Armenian Church members were 1,390,000 apart from 58,500 Catholics and 25,500 Protestants. In 1954, the tables show the patriarch with no other dioceses outside Istanbul, a membership of 100,000 in addition to 6,000 Catholics and 3,500 Protestants.

[2] The list consists of four dioceses in Russia and three in Persia and one in each of the following: Iraq, Greece, Bulgaria, Roumania, France, Egypt (also Ethiopia and the Sudan), North America (U.S.A. without California, but with Canada, Cuba and Mexico), California, South America (Argentina, Uruguay, Brazil and Chile). Armenians of the Soviet Union are said to be 2,745,000. Ormanian, App. III, p. 211.

[3] Dowling, *The Armenian Church* (London, 1910), pp. 20–2. Writing before the World War I, Dowling states (p. 21) that people referred to the catholicos of Etshmiadzin as 'his majesty'. Fuller description of Etshmiadzin at the dawn of the twentieth century is given by Lynch, I, 228–315.

[4] This turbulent temper of the Armenian clergy is noticeable even in the earlier periods where Ormanian devotes one chapter (pp. 29–32) to 'A Succession of Quarrels' and another (pp. 33–6) to 'A Return to Quarrels'.

congregation which began to suffer from defection at the coming of the missionary.

The most remarkable feature in Armenian Church history during the eighteenth century was the reappearance of the Catholic missionary under the protection of France and the French ambassadors at Constantinople. The bishops of Mardin and Aleppo were tempted to proclaim union with Rome and were punished by the native church for their secession. In fact, the Catholic missionary movement employed two opposite policies. The first was one of coercion in which the French ambassador used his influence to incarcerate the obstinate Patriarch Avedik of Tokat, then had him exiled to the island of Tenedos, from where he was abducted for trial and condemnation by the Inquisition in France in 1711.[1] In the second place, the Catholic missionary continued a peaceful attempt at proselytism and managed to win over one of the most enlightened Armenian ecclesiastics, Mekhitar of Sebastia (Sivas), who envisaged the establishment of a new monastic order in 1712 to serve Armenian education. By the year 1717, he realized the hopelessness of his plight at home and decided to retire to Venice in response to a papal invitation. He was followed to Italy by a number of Armenian admirers who formed the nucleus of the Mekhitarist religious order settled on the island of San Lazaro in the Venetian lagoons. The new order devoted its attention to scholarly work in the field of Armenian philology and letters. Even Ormanian,[2] who does not conceal his opposition to Catholic infiltration, offered the Mekhitarists of Venice and Vienna his grateful homage for their outstanding service to Armenian culture. Pope Leo XIII founded the Armenian College at Rome in 1883, thus displaying a sustained interest in the attraction of Armenians to the fold of Rome.[3]

Meanwhile, the Catholics decided to establish their proselytizing agency in Lebanon for two reasons: first, the Christians of Lebanon were essentially uniate Maronites; and secondly, the Armenians of Cilician origin who emigrated to Syria or remained in Turkey had had numerous historic ties with Roman Catholicism since the Crusades. It was thus that Abraham Attar inaugurated his monastic Antonian Society and met with some initial success. With two bishops and a handful of priests, they founded a Catholic patriarchate of Armenia and elected Abraham Ardzivian to the new dignity in 1740, and Pope Benedict XIV confirmed this creation in 1742. The latest occupant of that see is Cardinal Agajanian,[4] a man of unusual learning and

[1] Ormanian, pp. 67–8.

[2] Ibid., p. 68. The organization consists of about one hundred monks, of whom eighty are ordained priests with two abbots in Venice and Vienna, both titular archbishops; Attwater, I, 186.

[3] A. Fortescue, *The Uniate Eastern Churches*, ed. G. C. Smith (New York, 1923), p. 41; Attwater, I, 185.

[4] Raised to the cardinalate in 1945, his full title is 'Patriarch of the Catholic Armenians and Catholicos of Cilicia'. Attwater, I, 184–5.

ability, whose name was discussed as a possible candidate in the papal election of 1958. The impact of Catholic educational pressure in the eighteenth century gave the Armenian hierarchy their first rude awakening, and the Armenian abbot Vardan of Baghesh spurred on the cause of theological scholarship in his monastery of Amlordi. Of his pupils two became patriarchs of Constantinople and a third attained to the Jerusalem patriarchate.[1]

The nineteenth century saw three events of major importance in Armenian ecclesiastical circles. The first was the steady secularizing of Armenian Church administration. A mixed commission of theologians and laymen was set up to resolve the burning problems with the influential Roman element. The discussions dragged on for some years, and eventually the Ottoman authorities made a decision to establish a new Roman Catholic *millet* in 1830, which was the second major event. The third was precipitated by the second: the Protestant nations decided to join the race of proselytizing in Armenia. The first missionary of the American Board arrived in Turkey in the following year when the Reverend William Goodell was transferred from Malta to Constantinople with the aim of quickening the reform movement in the national Armenian Church and of rescuing it from formalism.[2] In the same year the Anglicans also dispatched the Reverend George Tomlinson for an exploratory visit to Athens and Constantinople with letters of commendation from the archbishop of Canterbury and the bishop of London to the patriarchs and bishops of the Eastern churches. The lines of policy pursued by the Presbyterians and the Anglicans were totally different, though both were in agreement on educational and social service. Whereas the missionaries of the American Board went forth with the object of proselytizing the Armenians, the Anglican intentions of helping the churches of the East to attain reform from within were clearly expressed in Mr Badger's report considered elsewhere.[3] The Presbyterian mission actually succeeded in attaining the *millet* status by 1847. This was a clear indication that, at that time, they too had won such numerical strength and political influence as to justify their own establishment as a separate entity. Though the mother church excommunicated all who attended Protestant gatherings, which enfeebled the Armenian nation, the Patriarch Ormanian ended his statement by

[1] Ormanian, pp. 68–9. These are Hovhannes Kolot and Hacob Nalian of Constantinople and Gregory Shkhthayakir of Jerusalem. Arpee says little or nothing about the Catholic contribution to Armenian education and progress, but he elaborates the cause of Protestant missionary work.

[2] F. E. Shaw, *American Contacts with the Eastern Churches, 1820–1870* (Chicago, Ill., 1937), p. 86. On the Protestant evangelical movement, see also Arpee, pp. 266–92; J. Richter, *A History of Protestant Missions in the Near East* (New York, 1910), pp. 104–80; R. Anderson, *History of the Missions of the American Board of Commissioners for Foreign Missions to the Oriental Churches*, 2 vols. (Boston, 1872), I, 386–426 and II, 1–77.

[3] See under Nestorians.

saying that 'they at any rate served in procuring for her certain advantages as regards her relations with the western world'.[1] Neither the Armenians nor the Greeks showed ingratitude for the philanthropy and educational services of the Protestants but both seemed to be justly alarmed at the increase in the number of proselytes. The Anglican Church and the Church of Scotland were sympathetic to the Armenian patriarch, and one can even read between the lines of some of Bishop Southgate's dispatches the uncertainty of the wisdom of building up a new sect. Many far-sighted missionaries deplored the idea. The Reverend J. D. Paxton, writing from Beirūt to a fellow missionary in Smyrna on 9 January 1837, said: 'The plan embraces the idea of not separating persons from those corrupt Churches, but keeping them in them, not pulling down or injuring those Churches, as it is called, but working in them, purifying them and reforming them.'[2]

It has already been mentioned that the Russians appeared on the scene of events amongst the European powers *vis-à-vis* the Ottoman empire and the Armenian question in the eighteenth century. The tsars wanted to pose as the chief defenders of the Armenians. This seemed to be one way for the settlement of their difficulties owing to the contiguity of their frontiers and the possibility of easy emigration from Turkey to Russia. This project of escape was fostered by Archbishop Hovsep Arghoutian, so highly patronized by Catherine II (1762–96) and Tsar Paul (1796–1801) that they raised the whole of the archbishop's family to the rank of Russian aristocracy. Thanks to the collaboration of the Armenian prelates and people, Etshmiadzin and Erevan were annexed by the Russians, a vital step which brought the head Armenian catholicate within the Russian orbit. Thus in 1836 the imperial administration issued a set of laws called the *prolojenye* for regulating the relations between the state and the patriarchate. This arrangement promised relief to the Armenians and non-interference in their ecclesiastical affairs, but apparently these promises were not kept in later years. The *prolojenye*, however, invested the clergy with church administration in contrast to the spirit of the Ottoman laws which increased lay control of the affairs of the patriarchate of Constantinople.[3] In Russia a Supreme Spiritual Council replaced the old Armenian synod with its mixed character. But the real secularization of the Armenian Church came into full effect with the rise of the Soviet Union after

[1] Op. cit., p. 72.

[2] Shaw, *American Contacts*, p. 106. The letter was addressed to the Rev. Josiah Brewer and was used by Arthur C. Coxe in a sermon at Hartford, Conn., in October 1846 while speaking on behalf of the Protestant Episcopal Mission at Constantinople.

[3] These laws made the following provisions: (1) in 1841 a chief council was entrusted with the financial administration; (2) in 1847, an administrative council consisting of fourteen ecclesiastics and twenty laymen was formed; (3) in 1853, an educational commission sprang from the general council for the supervision of public instruction. Finally, these separate regulations were incorporated in a comprehensive statute on constitution for the Armenians in 1860. Ormanian, pp. 73–4.

the First World War. That was of course the general tendency of the time, and the Armenian Church was not singled out for special treatment.

The later era was one of massacres and dispersion of Armenians in Turkey, and the European and American missionaries who were under the diplomatic protection of their own states played a prominent part in alleviating the sufferings of those harassed people. Many of them displayed numerous acts of heroism in conducting under their sponsorship columns of refugees outside the Turkish borders. Others offered refuge to hunted victims. In spite of the exotic look of both Catholic and Protestant church organizations with their Armenian proselytes, their many services to the people have been enormous. The American Board alone in its ninety-six years of service in Turkey before the First World War spent around twenty million dollars on the Turkish missions, including Armenian, Syrian and Greek work.[1] The Armenian awakening within both Church and nation owes much to the beneficent work of the missionary in the fields of education, social service and medical care.

[1] Arpee, pp. 274–5. Of this sum two millions were invested in lands, buildings and equipment. The English Mission in fifty years also contributed more than $540,000, of which $335,000 were spent in Asia Minor and European Turkey.

21 • ARMENIAN FAITH AND CULTURE

General Character

The bulk of the Gregorian church of the Armenians, it has been shown in the course of the foregoing pages, has remained Monophysite and unwavering in its anti-Chalcedonian temper. On this dividing line rested its ecclesiastical strife with Byzantium and Rome, as well as the repudiation of Greek and Syriac, the adoption of Armenian in all religious celebrations, and the invention of a special alphabet leading to the translation of the Bible and all liturgies into Armenian which made that Church self-sufficient and strictly national in character. This closed the Armenian fold round the Armenian people, and it is extremely doubtful whether anybody from another nation including even fellow Monophysites could have joined the Armenian Church, which was strictly a national institution. The reverse also took place, since, as has already been mentioned, smaller fractions of the Armenian people allowed themselves to become Roman Catholic or Protestant, and these somehow looked rather exotic amidst the homogeneous nature of the people as a whole.

The Armenian Church thus became identical with the Armenian people across the ages. The faith of the Armenian as symbolized by the church was the chief cohesive factor that gave the native even in exile the sense of solidarity and individuality. The conservatism of the church also kept its first principles and philosophy impregnable to change. This is one of the outstanding characteristics of all the ancient Eastern churches; and though it has kept them alive in the past and impervious to the elements of so-called 'progress', it has ensured their permanency in a changing world. The blood of Armenian martyrs sealed the attachment of that unhappy nation to the church and made the two appear identical. There is no nation in history with so much martyrdom throughout its annals as the Armenian. The Armenians accept the dogmatic teachings of the first three œcumenical councils, but as a rule they look with disfavour upon an increasing number of dogmas.[1] The Armenian does not believe that eternal salvation is an

[1] In his work, Ormanian (pp. 92–4) makes a case for the limitation of dogmas and

inherent faculty of his church alone. He tolerates other churches and other systems of thought and doctrine. Unlike the Roman Catholic, and to a large extent the Greek as well, the Armenian promotes the principle of *unitas in necessariis*; but beyond the essentials, the way of salvation is not closed to members of other churches. This liberal attitude towards others, it has been argued, led to Catholic and Protestant inroads amongst the Armenians.[1]

The Armenian Church, like most of the ancient Oriental churches, preserved in its doctrines and habits a remarkable touch of democracy in spite of its formalism and aristocratic origin. The part played by the laity in its synods, the secular participation in the election of the priesthood, and the obligation of the catholicos to abide by national and conciliar decisions are features of a democratic character which can be traced to the organization of primitive Apostolic Christendom. The Armenians do not believe in the infallibility of the catholicos. Instances have been quoted of catholicoi who either resigned or were deposed for a variety of causes including error, inefficiency or disharmony with the nation. Ecclesiastical authority was shared between the clergy and the congregation. This intertwining of those two elements and the identification of the Armenian people with their church gave the whole of Armenian civilization that predominantly religious impression detected without difficulty in their literature, art and architecture.

Liturgy and Armenian Rites

The holy liturgy of the Armenian Church belongs in the main to the family of Greek rituals.[2] Presumably, it was first compiled from a Greek version of

---

defends the Armenian view about the first three councils as against the seven councils recognized by the Greeks and the twenty of the Latins. Adrien Fortescue attacks his theory by a method and in a language somewhat unbecoming to a scholar of his calibre. It is clear from the course of Fortescue's arguments that he often goes out of his way to launch a merciless onslaught on anything that does not agree with the Roman Catholic teaching. He is systematically anti-Oriental, anti-Greek, anti-Anglican and anti-Protestant; cf. *Lesser Eastern Churches*, p. 425, n. 1.

[1] Op. cit., pp. 99–101.

[2] F. E. Brightman, *Liturgies Eastern and Western*, Vol. I (Oxford, 1896), includes the following under sect. IV, The Byzantine Rites: (1) The Byzantine Liturgy of the Ninth Century (pp. 309–44); (2) The Liturgy of the Presanctified of the Ninth Century (pp. 345–52); (3) The Modern Liturgy of S. Chrysostom (pp. 353–99); (4) The Prayers of the Modern Liturgy of S. Basil (pp. 400–11); (5) The Liturgy of the Armenians (pp. 412–57). Archbishop Tiran of the Diocese of North America edited *The Divine Liturgy of the Armenian Apostolic Orthodox Church* (New York, 1950) and *The Analysis of the Divine Liturgy* (repr. from above, 1952). The old English tr. published together with the Armenian text by Vardapet Isaiah Ashdvadzadourian's *Liturgy of the Holy Apostolic Church of Armenia* (London, 1887) is still useful. Another anonymous translation of *The Divine Liturgy of the*

St Basil's liturgy extant in the church at Cæsarea in Cappadocia, where St Gregory the Illuminator spent his youth and received his knowledge of the tenets of Christianity. In the meantime, the Armenian Church could not escape the Syrian influence of its neighbour Antioch where the Syriac Liturgy of St James also had its impact on the Armenian rites. Finally the text was revised by the same doctors who translated both Bible and liturgy into the Armenian tongue. In subsequent centuries, however, it was further amplified from Greek and Latin sources.[1] The liturgy of St John Chrysostom provided the Armenians with additional material, whereas during the Crusades, the latinization of Cilicia must have imparted numerous features to the Armenian liturgy, of which some have been retained. There is only one recognized Armenian liturgy at present, essentially Greek in character, but constituting a bridge between the Western and Eastern liturgies with its composite constitution. It is celebrated on Sundays and great festivals as well as on Saturdays if there is sufficient congregation.

Like most of the ancient liturgies, the Armenian consists of three principal parts. The first part is the introduction, where the celebrant is vested, then proceeds with his assistants to the chancel before the sanctuary, washes his hands and receives absolution from another priest after confession and before stepping inside the sanctuary as the curtain is drawn. The second is the liturgy of the catechumens, reminiscent of the early days when paganism and Christianity were still intermingled, and those who were not yet baptized were allowed to attend this part only. It begins with the *Trisagion*[2] and ends with the Nicæan Creed and the anathematization of Arians and Macedonians.[3] The third part is the liturgy proper, or the 'Great Entrance' of the consecration and communion. This is essentially the Byzantine Anaphora, and it ends with the celebrant descending to the middle of the church where he repeats a prayer from St John Chrysostom, then in accordance with the unrevised Roman rite sings the last Gospel from St John which he follows with the benediction. Then he enters the sacristy to take off the vestments and emerges for the distribution of the blessed bread. On the whole, the Armenian liturgy is recognized as one of the most beautiful of the ancient Oriental rites.

The church vestments used by the Armenian priesthood in officiating are

---

Holy Apostolic Church of Armenia (Cope and Fenwich [sic], 1908). See also F. C. Conybeare, *Rituale Armenorum* (Oxford, 1905); A. Torossian, *The Divine Liturgy according to the Rites of the Holy Apostolic Church of Armenians* (New York, 1933); E. F. K. Fortescue, *The Armenian Church* (London, 1872), pp. 225 et seq.

[1] Ormanian, pp. 143 et seq.; Dom Gregory Dix. *The Shape of the Liturgy* (3rd edn.; Westminster, 1947), p. 547; A. Fortescue, *Lesser Eastern Churches*, pp. 441 et seq.; E. F. K. Fortescue, pp. 150 et seq.; D. Attwater, II, 255–7; Dowling, pp. 116–28.

[2] The Greek 'thrice holy'. This is the Eastern chant 'Holy God, Holy and mighty, Holy and immortal, have mercy upon us'.

[3] Sect of followers of Macedonius (d. ca. 362), who defended the theology of Arius.

rich, varied and impressive. They include practically everything Greek and Roman except the Western chasuble. Bishops wear the Roman mitre and priests the Byzantine crown while celebrating liturgies. Other episcopal features adopted from the Catholics since the Crusades are the crozier and ring. From Byzantium again, bishops and higher prelates have the *Panagia* medal, the *omophrion* as the equivalent to the Latin pallium, the sandals and the *epigonation*. The last is usually reserved for the catholicos during whose consecration a great veil is placed on his head. In daily life, the clergy wear the usual black cloak with wide sleeves and a round cylindrical black cap with a conical top. Celibates use the veil as a special mark of distinction from secular clergy.

Armenians alone amongst the ancient Oriental churches use unleavened bread[1] for holy communion, and they mix no water with the wine. The vessels used on the altar are almost entirely Byzantine. The altar is square with several retables in degrees or steps mounting rearward under a canopy. The altar is covered with cloth and lace, and on it are placed candlesticks, liturgical books, communion vessels, sacred relics and occasionally a tabernacle. Two veils hang between the apse and the chancel and between the chancel and the nave, to be drawn at times in the service according to usage. The Armenians have no iconostasis, since most of their icons are placed on a screen in the apse behind the altar. They reject the use of statues, but maintain the seven sacraments, though extreme unction has been dropped. Baptism by complete and horizontal immersion of infants is the Armenian practice, but sprinkling is not held invalid in special cases of absolute necessity. They celebrate Christmas on January 6 (Theophany). Their fasting days total 157 a year.[2] The Armenians reckoned their days of saints in accordance with the old style of the Julian calendar until 1924, when they adopted the Gregorian calendar.[3] They do not believe in purgatory, though they pray for the dead.

The structure of the Armenian church is peculiar and distinctive. It can be recognized by the central dome, which is really a tower with a great cone on top of it. Inside the church, the chancel is raised on a platform and is separated from the nave by a railing. The apse or sanctuary area is again elevated by three steps above the chancel and is reached from the sides by two small entrances. Behind the apse is a closed area reserved for the treasure with two doors in the wall to the right and the left of the sanctuary.

[1] This is also the usual practice in the Maronite Church, but the Maronites are, of course, Uniates.

[2] S. M. Gregory, *The Land of Ararat* (London, 1920). A. Fortescue, p. 438, states that the Armenians have 160 fast-days and 117 abstinence-days in the year.

[3] This came into force by the encyclical of the Catholicos Gueorg V dated 9 November 1922. The patriarchate of Jerusalem and a few other dioceses in the Soviet Union have chosen to retain the use of the Julian calendar. Ormanian, p. 157 n.

Hierarchy[1]

We have already examined the developments leading to the emergence in Armenia of the five catholicates or patriarchates, of which four have survived, with Etshmiadzin as the supreme centre and head of the whole of the Armenian Church throughout the world. Those are the highest dignitaries in the church hierarchy. They are usually selected from amongst the high-ranking bishops. The term archbishop is also used in the Armenian church, but it is merely titular. The sole prerogative of an archbishop is simply that of summoning the bishops of a given area to a council if there is a compelling need for it. Two of the above-mentioned patriarchs also carry the title of catholicos, those of Etshmiadzin and Sīs, now better known as the catholicate of Cilicia. Both can consecrate the chrism and ordain bishops, whereas those of Constantinople and Jerusalem cannot. Yet we find that the patriarch of Constantinople before the era of the massacres ruled over forty-five dioceses, Sīs thirteen, Aghthamar two (which disappeared completely at a later date), Jerusalem five, and Etshmiadzin six in Russia together with the foreign provinces of the dispersed Armenians in other distant lands. The supreme authority of the last-named is perhaps pre-eminently doctrinal. The principle of decentralization is recognized by the Armenian Church, and each bishop exercises his local prerogative independently within the framework of ecclesiastical tradition. His authority over the clergy of his diocese is absolute, and his judgments in such matters as marriage and divorce are final. The Armenian Church allows divorce in cases prescribed by its canon law. But we must continually bear in mind that the exercise of authority is undertaken in collaboration with local councils which are partly clerical and partly secular. Below the bishop is the *Vartapet*, a monastic prelate of superior religious knowledge with ability to teach and preach. Sometimes he is a widowed priest of unusual ability. Vartapets are a peculiar feature in the Armenian hierarchy. They are the equivalent of the archimandrites in the Byzantine church. Bishops are usually chosen from the ranks of vartapets.

Until the end of the fourth century, the church was ruled by married prelates. The first nine catholicoi were married and transmitted the catholicate to their own sons. The bishops did the same until Sahak I the Great (d. 439) succeeded in the enforcement of celibacy on the higher clergy. It is difficult to say when married prelates completely disappeared from the picture, but at least they were checked in the fifth century. The lower clergy were allowed to marry. A deacon should have a wife before his ordination. He then may become a priest and in some cases an archpriest when he

[1] Ormanian, pp. 111–21, 125–39; Dowling, pp. 77–95; A. Fortescue, pp. 427–32; E. F. K. Fortescue, pp. 125–32.

administers a number of churches. If he loses his first wife, he may have a second on condition that he abstain from the exercise of sacerdotal duties.

To sum up the scale of the hierarchy as given by Patriarch Ormanian,[1] there are eight grades: (1) clerks (*dpir*); (2) deacons (*sarkavag*); (3) priests (*kahana* or *eretz*); (4) archpriests (*avagueretz*); (5) archimandrites or doctors (*vartapets*); (6) bishops (*episcopos*); (7) patriarchs (*patriark*); and (8) catholicos.

In addition to these principal offices, Ormanian indicates four other classes of minor clerks – the *ostiarius* or verger, the reader, the exorcist and the acolyte, no longer separately conferred. The sacristans and precentors participating in church services and receiving minor ordination wear a long buttoned-up vestment while assisting in church, but they use ordinary lay dress outside in daily life. As a rule, regular priests are selected from the precentor class. A priest cannot change his church without a new election by the members of his new parish. Candidates must be fully acquainted with the Armenian liturgy as well as ecclesiastical matters. They should be known for their exemplary life, and they cannot be ordained without the consent of their wives. Armenian priesthood has in many cases been sustained in the same families for numerous generations. The priests depend for their maintenance on the liberality of the parish members. Offertories and alms, as well as the proceeds of fees from the functions of baptism, betrothal and marriage, funerals, special mass celebrations, and the usual blessing of homes at Christmas and Easter are divided by the clerical members attached to each church.

At the outset of the First World War, the married Armenian clergy were reckoned to be about four thousand and the celibate nearly four hundred, including all bishops. Apparently these numbers were greatly reduced after the massacres and deportations.[2]

Literature

Armenian literature was born in the pale of the Armenian Church. This explains its pre-eminently religious character. Special mention has already been made of the invention of the Armenian alphabet by Mesrop (d. 440) in the catholicate of Sahak I the Great (387–439). The impact of that event on Armenian life and letters has been indicated, and the work of the commission of a hundred interpreters formed under Mesrop for translating the Bible, liturgy and patristic literature has been outlined. Those early translations were made in the purest classical Armenian. The text of the Old Testament from the Greek Septuagint and the New Testament from the Syriac Peshitta

[1] Op. cit., p. 147. [2] Ormanian, p. 150.

has been described as 'the queen' of all Biblical versions.[1] It is the beginning of what is known as the 'golden age' of Armenian literature extending from the fifth to the twelfth century, during which some fifty writers of considerable reputation left their mark on the history of their nation. The second phase, known as the 'silver age' of Armenian literature, covers the period from the twelfth to the seventeenth century.[2] In both ages, however, the ecclesiastical writers were the real makers of Armenian literature. Throughout that lengthy span of time Ormanian notes only four or five instances of lay authors worthy of any mention.[3]

The early age witnessed the Armenian versions of many works of Church Fathers such as, Ignatius of Antioch, Athanasius of Alexandria, Epiphaneus of Cyprus, Basil of Cæsaria, Gregory Nazianzen, Gregory of Nyssa, John Chrysostom and Ephraem the Syrian. The Mekhitarists of Venice have already published four volumes of the Armenian version of St Ephraem, which is still incomplete. The old masters did not overlook the Greek philosophers, notably Plato, Aristotle and Philo of Alexandria. Yet this did not deter the Armenian fathers from a critical outlook on ancient Greek writers and their heathen philosophy. Eznik tried to do this in his *Refutation of the Sects*, where he attacked paganism and Greek philosophy as well as Mazdaism and the Manichæan heresy. The historical literature of the age includes Josephus on the Jewish wars, Eusebius' *Ecclesiastical History*, Faustus of Byzantium, Zenobius' *History of Taron*, Elijah the Vartapet's *History of the Armenian Wars with the Sassanids*, Moses of Khoren's *History of Armenia*, Goriun's *Life of Mesrop* and a host of other works.[4] Apart from translations, a school of native Armenian authorship gradually came into existence. The Catholicos John of Otzun (717–28), surnamed the Philosopher, was a theologian of great merit who wrote a treatise *Against the Phantasiastæ*, a sect of Armenian heretics which flourished under Arab

[1] Cf. Arpee, p. 33.

[2] Ormanian, pp. 173–5.

[3] These include from the ninth century Shapuh Bagratuni, who wrote a history of his times now lost, and prince Gregory Magistros (d. 1058), of Arshakuni origin, who made a rhymed abridgment of the Bible, thus setting new style for future generations in Armenia. From the later period may be quoted a physician called Amir Tolvath and an official named Yeremia Keomurtjian. Ormanian, loc. cit.; 'Armenian Literature', in *Encyclopædia Brittannica*; J. Laurent, *L'Arménie entre Byzance et l'Islam*, p. 140, n. 7, mentions also 'le noble Moucathl de Venan' without specifying his dates or works. A. Sarkissian, *Armenian Christian Literature*, pp. 31 ff. deals only with samples of religious literature.

[4] A considerable number of the ancient Armenian texts have been tr. into French and pub. in three main source collections: V. Langlois, *Collection d'historiens arméniens*; Brosset, *Collection d'historiens arméniens*, 2 vols. (St Petersbourg, 1874–6); *Recueil des historiens des croisades, Documents arméniens*, 2 vols. (Paris, 1869–1906). On general Armenian literature see Sukias Sumal, *Quadro della Storia Litteraria di Armenia* (Venice, 1829); C. F. Neumann, *Geschichte der armenischen Literatur* (Leipzig, 1836); F. Nève, *L'Arménie chrétienne et sa litterature* (Paris, 1886); Ormanian, pp. 173–8; Arpee, see following notes below.

protection.[1] *The Book of Lamentations* by Gregory of Nareg[2] (ca. 1002) has been described as the 'Armenian Thomas à Kempis' "Imitation of Christ".' The Catholicos Nerses IV, 'the Graceful' (1166–73), was thus surnamed from his early monastic days on account of the grace and elegance of his poetry. His most famous composition is that entitled *A Lamentation in Romance*,[3] a devotional poem in four thousand lines. Nareg and Nerses are unanimously considered the most illustrious and most popular writers in the history of Armenian literature.

In the latter period, there seems to have been a marked decline in style. The general tendency among writers was to concentrate on history. Notable examples in the thirteenth century include Kyriakos of Ganzak, who wrote on the Tartars; Vahram's rhymed *Chronicle of the Cilician Kings*; and Vartan's *World history*. From the fourteenth century there are Archbishop Stephen Oberlian's *History of Siunik*, Sembat's *Chronicle*, and Hethoum's *Chronography* and story of the Tartars. For the rest may be mentioned Thomas of Medsoph's fifteenth-century *History of Timur Lane*, Araqil of Tibriz's seventeenth-century *History of the Persian Invasions* (1602–61), and the Catholicos Abraham of Crete's eighteenth-century *History* of his own times. The earlier period is noted for one of the most important Armenian theological compendia by Gregory of Datev (d. 1410),[4] whose *Book of Questions*, finished in 1397, is still recognized as the Armenian *Summa theologiæ*. Gregory was a pupil of another theological writer of fame, John of Orton (d. 1388), who had written Biblical commentaries, homilies and Monophysite tracts. The pupil surpassed the master and became the Thomas Aquinas of his church.

The Armenians were among the first Oriental peoples to avail themselves of the printing press for the publication of Armenian religious literature. The earliest record of a printed Armenian book is in 1513 at Venice. Then the Catholicos Michael I (1567–76) sent Abgar of Tocat to Venice to help with the printing of church books. After the printing of the Armenian Psalter in 1566, Abgar transferred the press to Constantinople, where he

[1] That tract first published by the Mekhitarists of Venice in 1833. An English version found in App. II in Arpee, *Armenian Christianity*, pp. 325–54. The tract is written mainly as a defence of Armenian Christology.

[2] 'The Book of Nareg', written in his own monastery and essentially addressed to the monks, is a devotional work professing the renunciation of the flesh. Arpee, pp. 165–70, compares its material not only with the 'Imitation of Christ' but also with St Augustine's 'Confessions' and Calvin's 'Institutes'.

[3] It is also known by the first line in the poem: 'Jesus, the Father's Only Son'. Nerses is also the author of a prayer comprising a spiritual appeal for every hour of the day and night, translated into thirty-five languages since 1690. He is also the chief composer of the Armenian hymns of the Armenian *Horologion*. Arpee (pp. 170–4) likens him to Bernard of Clairvaux, his contemporary; Latin tr. of his works by Capelletti (2 vols.; Venice, 1833).

[4] Arpee, pp. 175–86, gives an analysis of his work. Evidently, Gregory was influenced by St Thomas Aquinas, whose *Summa* had been translated into Armenian about 1330. He directed the theological Seminary of Siunik for a time, Ormanian, p. 57.

printed the Calendar, Hymnal, Horologion and Missal two years later. Abgar's rightful successor was John of Anqara, who cast a new type in Rome in 1637. In the meantime, the Convent of New Julfa established its own press and published several volumes. Consequently Armenian printing extended from Venice and Rome to Amsterdam in 1666 in Europe, and from Constantinople to Etshmiadzin in Turkey in 1729. The first edition of an illustrated Armenian Bible was produced in Amsterdam in 1666 by Bishop Voskan. In the following century John Golod (1715–41) issued more than ninety volumes of Armenian religious classics, including Gregory of Datev's *Book of Questions*, while the Mekhitarists founded their press in 1729 and rendered substantial services to Armenian letters.[1]

In recent times Armenian literature has undergone a radical change. First of all, it has departed from the classical style, which began to disappear from ordinary usage at the end of the Middle Ages. Secondly, it has been secularized, with new creations in modern Armenian comprising fiction, poetry and other works by laymen. Perhaps the most significant feature in modern literature is the development of Armenian journalism. There are scores of Armenian newspapers and reviews published in all parts of the globe. The press, being a powerful instrument in the preservation of national sentiment in modern times, has found an important place amongst Armenians throughout the world.

Art and Architecture

Monumental paintings and mosaics, though not unknown in Armenia, do not play such a great role in interior church decoration as in Byzantine foundations. The two fragments of mosaics found in the ruins of Zwarthnots and Dwin are of no consequence, but the tenth-century wall paintings of scenes from the life of Our Lord at the cathedral of Aghthamar are a standing testimony to the interest of the Armenian artist in that work.[2] For a fuller appreciation of Armenian painting, however, the student must turn to miniatures preserved in Armenian manuscript treasures.

Although the evolution of the Armenian miniature must have been quite early, it is certain that the end of the ninth century witnessed among the monks of Datev men who were 'incomparable in their skill as painters and

[1] S. M. Gregory, *The Land of Ararat* (London, 1920), pp. 43–59; Arpee, pp. 142–4; Ormanian, pp. 99, 176–7.

[2] Serapie Der Nessessian, *Armenia and the Byzantine Empire – A Brief Study of Armenian Art and Civilization* (Cambridge, Mass., 1945), pp. 110–13, and Plate XVII (1). Miss Der Nessessian's excellent work deals with architecture (pp. 55–83), sculpture (84–109) and painting (110–36).

scribes'. The Etshmiadzin Gospel[1] of 989 shows some affiliation with Byzantine decorative art, though other Gospels reveal unmistakable influence from early Syrian schools of a somewhat inferior quality. Miss Der Nessessian[2] sees in the Erevan Gospel[3] illustrations of 986 a degree of resemblance to the figures found in the Panopolis (Akhmīm) textiles from Upper Egypt as well as bird designs with rings around their slender necks from Sassanian silver plate and material. The decorative *motif* thus orientalized in the tenth century becomes distinctly Armenian in the Jerusalem Gospel,[4] written for King Gagik in the eleventh century. It contains a miniature representing the monarch with his queen and his daughter Miriam seated in a cross-legged posture on a low couch decked with a rug of geometrical pattern and a cloth with birds and elephants in medallions. The impact of artistic progress in Greater Armenia on the Cilician school is very considerable from the twelfth century to the end of Armenian independence. The Venice Gospel[5] prepared in 1193 for Nerses the Graceful and Hethoum of Lambron as well as the Gospel of Lwów in 1198, both written partly at Skevra and partly at Milidj, show even more refinement, elegance of pattern and variegated colour schemes.

The peak of the Armenian art of the miniature must have been attained in the course of the thirteenth century and the opening decades of the fourteenth. The names of Thoros Roslin and Sargis Pidzak are cited as founders of two eminent schools at that time in this field. Thoros worked mainly for the Catholicos Constantine I (1221–67) at Hromkla, and the Freer Gallery codex[6] in Washington ascribed to one of his pupils is one of the finest examples of thirteenth-century craftsmanship. The vitality and animated gestures presented in the miniatures in the Freer Gospel[7] of the entry of Our Lord into Jerusalem and the dance of Salome are new departures from the old rigid iconography. Sargis is regarded as one of the most prolific painters in the next century, since at least fifteen manuscripts are known to have been illuminated by him. He follows new techniques of simple Eastern *motifs* and uses heavier forms and geometrical designs in harmonious and pleasing compositions. The Descent from the Cross in the Jerusalem Gospel (no. 1973)[8] is one of his most striking creations. Apparently Sargis touched the highest peak of Armenian artistic genius; and, after his age, decline began in

[1] Op. cit., p. 115. [2] Op. cit., p. 116.

[3] Erevan, No. 81.

[4] Jerusalem, No. 2556. Gagik's reign covered the years 1029–64, but he lived to 1080 after the seizure of his kingdom by the Byzantine emperor.

[5] Venice, No. 1635; cf. Der Nessessian, p. 121, also Plate XXIV (1).

[6] Prepared for an Armenian prince called Vasak. Of the same school, another codex in Jerusalem (No. 2568) is dedicated to a son of Hethoum I bearing the same name Vasak; cf. Der Nessessian, p. 124. [7] Op. cit., Plate XXIX (142).

[8] Cf. Der Nessessian, pp. 129–30, Plate XXVII (2).

the art of the miniature. Although scribes continued to produce illuminated manuscripts in the region of Lake Van and at the city of Melitene (Malaṭiya) in Cilicia as late as the seventeenth century, long after the spread of printing, the creative spirit of the older Armenian masters became a thing of the past.

In addition to painting, the mediæval Armenian artist also demonstrated his unusual skill in the special department of sculpture which was pre-eminently architectural. Every Armenian ecclesiastical structure from the earliest days was embellished with a blind arcade on its *façade* as well as sculptured bands around all its openings. In most cases, the tympanum was fully carved with varied figures or *motifs*. The Armenian church with its exterior decorative sculpture stood in perfect contrast to the austerity of its Syrian counterpart on the southern periphery of Asia Minor. Sculpture in the more general sense of statuary never struck root in Armenia. Oriental ecclesiastics, more particularly since the iconoclastic period, discouraged the erection of statues or busts within churches; and the Armenians concentrated on sculpture in the form of bas-relief and haut-relief on the exterior of the walls of their religious structures. By the end of the ninth and the beginning of the tenth century, the Armenian sculptor mastered that art, and his genius displayed its creative faculties in the unique example of the cathedral of Aghthamar, erected on Lake Van between 915 and 921.[1] Friezes of animals of all description, vine and pomegranate scrolls animated with figures, hunting scenes, and complete Biblical cycles are represented in life-like reliefs on the walls. The crowned image of the founder of the church, King Gagik occupies the centre of a vine scroll on the eastern *façade*. Like his aforementioned miniature, here he is also seated in a cross-legged posture. In one hand he has a cup, while with the other he plucks a bunch of grapes. Moreover, each of the four *façades* has a large relief of an evangelist holding his Gospel in one hand and blessing with the other; and each stands exactly under the central gable of his side of the roof.

The important scene on the western *façade* consists of the figures of Christ and of the king on either side of the central window. Christ carries a Gospel on the left arm and his right hand is raised in benediction. Above His halo is inscribed in Armenian: 'I am the light of the world'. The king, sumptuously robed, offers a model of the church, which he carries in hand. Between them

[1] The best account in English of a detailed description of the Aghthamar cathedral decorations is given by Serapie Der Nessessian, pp. 90–96. Since then, she has also published an even more comprehensive work on the subject entitled *Aght'amar Church of the Holy Cross* (vol. I of the Harvard Armenian Texts and Studies, Cambridge-Mass., 1965), superbly and fully illustrated with all the artistic details of that extraordinary church. Another similar profusely illustrated publication of Turkish origin appeared by M. S. Ipşiroğlu, *Die Kirche von Achtmar, Bauplastik im Leben des Lichtes* (Berlin u. Mainz, 1963). References here have already been made to Der Nessessian's original work of 1954. See sample in Plate XVIII of this volume.

two smaller figures of angels hold a medallion with a beautiful Armenian cross in the middle.

The eastern wall has a representation of Adam and the Creation. Four figures of saints flank the central window and are generally identified as the Apostles St Thaddæus and St Bartholomew, who first introduced Christianity into Armenia, St Gregory the Illuminator, and St Thomas, whose relics were interred on that spot according to the Apocryphal Acts.

The reliefs on the two remaining walls have representations of the prophets and patriarchs of the Old Testament as well as an early Christian cycle with Christ enthroned between two archangels. Two richly dressed figures on the south *façade* are defined by an inscription as 'St Harmazasp Prince of Vaspuragan, Lord St Sahak brother of Harmazasp, martyrs and witnesses of Christ.' Defeated by the Arabs in 786 the two princes were imprisoned and martyred, as they refused apostacy to Islam.

A study of comparative archæological remains seems to point to Egypt as the fountain-head of the early Christian cycle represented on the walls of Aghthamar.[1] Neither Syrian nor Mesopotamean nor Roman examples have any bearing on the Aghthamar carvings whose prototypes have been preserved in two funerary chapels of the Christian necropolis of al-Bagawat in the Egyptian oasis of al-Kharga. Both chapels have been dated as fourth or early fifth century. That the cycle descended from early Egypt seems corroborated by the type of groups of mounted saints which are represented on both structures. Furthermore, Armenian knowledge of Egyptian sources is proved by the Etshmiadzin fifth- or sixth-century stone engraving of St Paul and St Thecla in conversation while sitting cross-legged on stools. Their names are inscribed in Greek or perhaps even Coptic. The same occurs at al-Bagawat and, what is even more interesting, also on textiles from Antinoë. The use of the crocodile hunt as a decorative *motif* inside a ninth-century architectural frame found in the Queen Mlk's Gospel,[2] written at the monastery of Varag near Van, supports the thesis that the Armenian artist was informed about the scenes and purport of Egyptian cycles. Another point of interest is that, though early Coptic church exteriors were only sparsely decorated with reliefs, ancient Egyptian temples were, on the contrary, completely covered with them; and it is possible that Armenian artists visiting Egypt witnessed their splendour and tried to imitate the master builders of antiquity.[3]

Equally fascinating and even more surprising is the influence of the Sassanian rock-tomb engravings of Taq-i-Bostan on the Aghthamar decorative

[1] Op. cit., pp. 94–5.

[2] Preserved in the Mekhitarist Monastery Library of San Lazaro, No. 1144; cf. Der Nessessian, pp. 95, 115, 131 and Plate XX(1).

[3] The whole argument is Miss Der Nessessian's, and we only add the last remark tentatively.

scheme. King Gagik's portrait is a true imitation of a Persian ruler from those engravings. Other portraits of martyrs, saints and princes follow the same *motif* of Persian figures from that period.[1] On the other hand, the artistic interchange with the East in the department of sculpture is reversed after the Arab conquest. The Arabs whose creative contributions were limited to their language and religion sought for themselves a place in the loftier cultures and civilizations of their conquered territories. Accordingly, the caliphs, notably in Umayyad and Abbasid times, patronized the artistic skills found in their new provinces and availed themselves of the services of all manner of local craftsmen, the Armenian included. It was in this way that the Armenian sculptors shared in the process of influencing the development of Arabic *motifs* together with the Copts of Egypt and the Syrians in Syria and Mesopotamia. The bands and friezes of geometrical interweaving and interlacing adopted by the Islamic world in the ornamentation of mosques and pulpits as far as North Africa and Spain[2] bear unmistakable signs of all those influences, and the Armenian played his part.

The sphere in which Armenian civilization appears to have made staggering strides on the road of progress with immense contributions outside its borders was in ecclesiastical architecture. The discarded cathedrals and churches which still stood at the end of the nineteenth century were photographed and fully described by Lynch,[3] the great traveller, in his monumental work. Then in the early years of this century, excavations were made by scholars and archæologists in eastern Armenia under Russian rule.[4] The facts thus revealed provided the eminent art historian Strzygowski[5] with the material for a startling hypothesis in which he traced the origins of numerous fundamental features in Byzantine architecture to the Armenians and even contended that western Europe owed them much in the shaping of the art of the Middle Ages and the Renaissance.

Without going too far into the details of Strzygowski's technical arguments, it may be helpful to summarize the substance of his hypothesis. The

[1] Der Nessessian, op. cit., pp. 95–6. See also reproduction of Khosru Parviz in a hunting scene at Tag-i-Bostan in J. Strzygowski, *L'ancien art chrétien de la Syrie* (Paris, 1936), p. 148.

[2] Der Nessessian, p. 103, mentions the carvings on pulpits of the Great Mosque at Algiers and the Mosque of Qayrawan in Tunisia and the open-work window slabs of the Great Mosque of Cordoba, Spain, as examples closely allied with the geometric designs of early Christian and Byzantine monuments.

[3] *Travels*, I, 370–92, contains details and pictures of the cathedral at Ani, the Church of St Gregory, the Chapel of the Redeemer, the Church of the Apostles, and the Monastery of Khosha Vank – all in the ruins of the city of Ani. The cathedral church of Agthamar at Van appears in II, 126–44, together with a survey of other churches at Erzrum and elsewhere.

[4] Excavations were made by Father Khatshik Tatian at Zwarthnots and by Prof. Marr and the Armenian architect Thoramanian at Ani. Cf. Der Nessessian, p. 56.

[5] J. Strzygowski, *Die Baukunst der Armenier und Europa*, 2 vols. (Vienna, 1918); idem, *Origin of Christian Art* (Oxford, 1923); idem, *L'ancien art chrétien de la Syrie* (Paris, 1936).

core of his idea is that the erection of the dome on a square bay or on four columns at the corners of a square, so characteristic of both Byzantine and European architecture, was discovered and perfected in western Asia by early Armenian architects. This mode of construction can be traced back to the primitive timber house in central Asia, where the roof of the square building was domed by the process of continuous corbelling. In other words, the builder deposited timber beams across the angles of the square and consequently across the angles of the octagon and so on until the base of the dome was formed. When this system reached Iran, where timber was scarce, *adobes* were used and they substituted the arch and the squinch for the corner beams. At this point the Armenians took over but it is difficult to fix dates, although St Gregory the Illuminator's vision speaks of four columns, arches and a dome in the fourth century. However, the fact remains that in the seventh century, highly developed stone churches were to be found in Armenia with domes resting on polygonal or cylindrical drums and covered with large conical roofs.

From the simple niche-buttressed and domed square, as in the fifth-century church of St Hripsime at Vagharshapat, Armenian architects developed the domed multifoil plans and cruciform churches of which the cathedrals of Ani and Aghthamar are examples of unusual splendour. In practically every case, the interior structure of the Armenian church is concealed within an outer form of a different description. The vaulted ceilings and domes are invariably encased in a gabled roof and cone-shaped towers. The uniform rectangular or circular *facades* often have a completely different arrangement inside. The apse is often buried in the thickness of the massive walls, and a simple rectangle masks a complex set of circles or semi-circles. The Zwarthnots[1] example is the reverse, since there the outer circular wall surrounds a quatrefoil of columns on three sides and a walled niche forming the apse in the east. Four massive piers at the four angles of the niches joined by tremendous arches carry the central dome inside its low-coned roof. This plan, according to Strzygowski, was adopted with minor variations in the 'Red Ruin' of Philippopolis in Bulgaria as well as the church of St Lorenzo in Milan, while the quatrefoil is found further west in Biella and Galliano in North Italy and Montmajeur in France.[2] Macler has also noted the great resemblance between some of the churches of France and those of Armenia. The twelfth-century church of Saint-Nectaire-le-Haut in the Auvergne and the eleventh- to thirteenth-century Church of Notre-Dame-du-Port at Clermont-Ferrand[3] were both planned on models from the East and bear much resemblance to the churches of Armenia. The cross-ribbed vaultings

[1] See diagram and plans in Der Nessessian, pp. 65, 67, 69, 74, and Plates II, III, IV and V.
[2] Cf. Der Nessessian, p. 76.
[3] F. Macler, *Trois conférences sur l'Arménie* (Paris, 1927), p. 126, Plate XIII.

so vital to Gothic structures were to be found in Armenia long before the Gothic style emerged in Europe.

Apparently the Byzantine civilization was the medium through which Armenian creations travelled indirectly to the West. Armenian craftsmen had been in Constantinople from an early date. Armenian immigrations to the empire from the ninth century are historically established. Moreover, emperors of Armenian extraction such as John Tzimisces must have surrounded themselves with Armenian courtiers who transplanted Armenian styles to their new environment. The records show that Trdat, the Armenian architect of the famous cathedral of Ani, was selected for the work of restoring the dome of St Sophia when it was impaired by the earthquake of 989. A stone slab with the carving of an ornamental cross found at Mistra has a Greek inscription reading: 'Joseph the Armenian, from Greater Armenia.'[1] The consensus of facts indicates surely some measure of the Armenian contribution to civilization beyond its own frontiers.

[1] Der Nessessian, p. 109. This is the type known in Armenia as *Khatshk'ar*, reproduced by the author in Plate XVII(2). Its intricate geometrical *motif* must have been adopted widely in the Islamic East, as it is seen in many mediæval mosques, and the design recalls the tent work still existing in Egypt.

PART V

THE ST THOMAS CHRISTIANS OF SOUTH INDIA

22 • HISTORICAL SURVEY

Malabar and Its People

The country where the ancient St Thomas Christianity spread in southern India from time immemorial extends roughly between the River Ponnani in the north and Cape Comorin, which is the tip of southern India. On both east and west, it is flanked by the heights of the Anamullay Mountains and the Arabian Sea. Within this area two hundred and fifty miles in length and about fifty miles in width, a rolling terrain of rich agricultural soil with unusually plentiful water forms the joint province known as Travancore-Cochin, Malayalam speaking, pepper-producing, and largely though not exclusively Christian. The country is inhabited by nearly a million Christians, originally unified in a single church until the coming of the Portuguese, who forced an alien Roman form of Christianity upon them and inaugurated the first of a series of schisms and confusions intensified by the well-meaning Protestant teachers who, in turn, started proselytizing natives under British rule and a British resident in control of the government until the independence of the Indian subcontinent. Allegedly of East Syrian origin, chiefly pepper merchants, who settled down amongst the natives and expanded through evangelization and integrating in the people of the land, these Christians succeeded in making themselves indispensable to both the rulers and the community, and held a high place in the new homeland by their industry, ability and integrity.

The thesis that these Christians were discovered by the West when Vasco da Gama landed with his Portuguese contingents on the shores of Goa is of course erroneous. The existence of Christians in Malabar had been known from a very early date. It is said that the great Egyptian scholar, Pantænus, later head of the Catechetical School of Alexandria, 'was appointed as a herald for the Gospel of Christ to the heathen in the East, and was sent as far as India' according to the testimony of the ecclesiastical historian Eusebius.[1] If the India here mentioned coincides with our conceptions, Pantænus must have reached it just before the end of the second century and, according to

[1] *Hist. Eccl.*, V, x.

the same historian, found that others had preceded his coming, 'for Bartholomew[1] [sic], one of the Apostles, had preached to them and had left them the writing of Matthew in Hebrew letters, which was preserved until the time mentioned'.

Whatever the authority of the Eusebian statement, the historicity of the relations between that part of India and some of the countries of the Middle East is established in antiquity beyond doubt. Two trade routes to India were frequented by seagoing craft from Egypt by way of the Red Sea[2] and from Mesopotamia by way of the Persian Gulf; and it is normal that ideas and new ideals should travel in the wake of trade. Moreover, a small Jewish group of residents had existed in Malabar from a very early date, indicating this interchange between southern India and the Semites of Syria and Palestine.[3]

The early period of the history of Christianity in India is shrouded in the mist of brief references and indefinite arguments. Perhaps the first reference to a church in Malabar is made around the middle of the fourth century in the story of Theophilus the Indian.[4] At the Council of Nicæa held in 325, a certain 'Bishop John the Persian of the Churches of the whole of Persia and great India' appeared together with a delegation of East Syrian bishops from Edessa and Nisibis.[5]

Probably the most generally accepted testimony is the one recorded by the noted traveller, geographer, merchant and later monk of Mount Sinai, Cosmas Indicopleustes, who wrote a *Christian Topography* of his eastern navigations between 520 and 525 during the reign of Emperor Justinian. He affirms the existence of a Christian church in inner India with clergy, a congregation of believers and a bishop of 'Kalliana', identified as Quilon in Travancore.[6]

In Europe itself, news of the Malabarese Christians was brought by Marco

[1] A native historian and former secretary of a former Syrian metropolitan of Malabar, the late E. M. Philip, in his *The Indian Church of St Thomas*, ed. with suppl. by his son E. P. Mathew (Kotteyam, South India, 1950), pp. 55–6, belabours the argument that Bartholomew is only a corruption of the Syriac Mar-Thoma or Barthoma.

[2] J. G. Milne, *History of Egypt under Roman Rule* (London, 1924), pp. 24, 56, 260, shows the resumption of the Indian trade under Nero (54–68), Antonius Pius (138–61) or Marcus Aurelius (161–80), and Diocletian (284–305). Pliny estimates the value of imports from Arabia and India at one hundred million sesterces around the end of the first century.

[3] L. W. Brown, *The Indian Christians of St Thomas* (Cambridge, 1956), p. 62, refers to a tradition that a Jewish colony settled in the first cent. in the Periyar valley, in Quilon, and in Muziris, receiving fourth-century privileges with the Christians, as recorded on copper plates. Philip (pp. 20–1) mentions a place called Jews' Hill near the Paluyar Church where a Jewish synagogue had been in existence before.

[4] Brown, p. 66.

[5] Ibid., p. 67. See also note by E. O. Winstedt to his edn. of *The Christian Topography of Cosmas Indicopleustes* (Cambridge, 1909), pp. 344–6.

[6] Winstedt's edn. p. 119; J. W. McCrindle's edn. (London, 1907), pp. 118 et seq. Cf. Brown, pp. 68–9; C. R. Beazley, *The Dawn of Modern Geography*, 3 vols. (London, 1897–1906), I, 192 et seq., 273 et seq.; Sir Henry Yule, *Cathay and the Way Thither*, 3 vols. (London, 1913), I, clxxi; Philip, pp. 83–8.

Polo, who visited India in the last decade of the thirteenth century. It was at that time that Pope Innocent III inaugurated his missionary enterprise to the Far East, and the first emissary to stay a whole year (1291) in Malabar on his way to China was John of Monte Corvino. He was followed by a Dominican friar named Jordanus, who came twice to India – first in 1319 and again in 1328 after his ordination as bishop of Quilon by the aspiring Avignonese Pope John XXII (1316–34). In the meantime, Oderic of Udine came in 1321 to Quilon and Mylapore to gather relics of other friars martyred by the Muslim rulers of southern India in 1302, and met numerous Nestorian families in that district. Another friar, John of Marignolli, reached Quilon in 1348 and left a detailed account of the area as the world's foremost pepper mart, chiefly owned by the St Thomas Christians. So widely diffused were the reports of that Christian community within the confines of the Indian subcontinent that Pope Eugenius IV (1431–47) dispatched a special embassy to its ruler with an epistle extending apostolic benediction to him. The Italian merchant-adventurer Nicolo di Conti encountered a thousand Nestorians of St Thomas at Mylapore in 1440, a few years before the advent of Vasco da Gama.[1]

The Christian people of Malabar, who were brought into more direct contact with Europe after the Portuguese invasion, were allegedly Syrian settlers accepted by the original indigenous natives with whom they mixed and lived at ease. Their economic system and prosperity were based on agriculture and commerce. While producing crops for their own livelihood, they sold their pepper produce for export from the earliest times. However, the face of Malabar and its rural economy is rapidly changing in this modern age on account of its steady industrialization and the progress of western education and European ways of life.

The St Thomas Tradition

The congregations of South Indian Christians have always prided themselves on a long-standing tradition that their Christianity is apostolic and that it was introduced into Malabar by the Apostle Thomas, after whom they call themselves. The literary origin of this tradition is found in the apocryphal *Acts of Judas-Thomas*[2] ascribed to the famous Edessene writer Bardesanes (154–222)

[1] Yule, II, 141, 342 et seq.; Brown, pp. 82–5; Philip, pp. 101–3; Cardinal Eugene Tisserant, *Eastern Christianity in India*, English tr. E. R. Hambye (London, 1957), pp. 19–23; Atiya, *Crusade in the Later Middle Ages*, pp. 248–52, 254–5.

[2] The sources of the St Thomas legend are enumerated by Brown, p. 64, including mainly H. Hosten, *Antiquities from San Thome and Mylapore* (Calcutta, 1936); A. E. Medlycott, *India and the Apostle Thomas – An Enquiry with a Critical Analysis of the 'Acta Thomæ'* (London, 1905); J. Dahlmann, *Die Thomas-Legende* (Freiburg, 1912); J. N. Farquhar,

towards the end of the second or the beginning of the third century. It is said that a certain Abbanes, a trade envoy to Syria was commissioned by the Indian King Gondophares to seek an able architect from that country to build a palace for him. The tradition states that he was directed by Our Lord Himself in a Jerusalem market to St Thomas, who accompanied him back to India. There St Thomas agreed with the king to undertake that task in winter instead of during the usual summer building season. At heart the saint really contemplated a celestial and not a material palace. As he squandered the royal funds in giving to the poor, the king seized him and put him in prison. At that time the king's brother, Gad, died and at his burial witnessed the untold splendour of the celestial palace promised by the saint, then miraculously came back to life to recount his wondrous vision. The king and his brother therefore released the saint and accepted baptism at his hand. The remaining parts of the *Acts* contain even more fabulous miracles until in the end, the Apostle committed the church to the care of a deacon named Zenophus (or Xanthippus) and went away to preach the Gospel in other parts where he earned the crown of martyrdom. After his burial, a Syrian co-religionist transported his body back to Edessa without the knowledge of the local king, who eventually wanted to try to cure his sick son by means of the saint's relic. Upon opening the grave, they found the body to be gone, but earth from the tomb performed the miracle and healed the ailing prince, and the whole royal family was converted to Christianity.

Two schools of thought have arisen in regard to this apocryphal tale. The first impulse of the scholar was to refuse outright the whole episode as altogether unhistorical. Such was the reaction of the old school.[1] More recent thought has tended not to discard the idea of St Thomas's apostolate to India, though still repudiating the legendary nature of the *Acts*.[2] It has already been pointed out that the sea route to South India was well used in Roman times for the purpose of the pepper trade, and that Roman gold and

---

The Apostle Thomas in North India and *The Apostle Thomas in South India*, in *The John Rylands Bulletin* (Manchester, 1926 and 1927); J. Charpentier, *St Thomas the Apostle and India* (Upsala, 1927); F. C. Burkitt, 'Three St Thomas Documents', in *Kērala Society Papers* (1932); Metropolitan Juhanon Mar Thoma, *Christianity in India and a Brief History of the Mar Thoma Church* (Madras, 1954), pp. 1–5; K. K. Kuruvilla, *The History of Mar Thoma Church* (Madras, 1951); T. K. Joseph, *South India's St Thomas*, (Cennanūr, 1952). See also Tisserant, pp. 2–6; Philip, pp. 24–47; and the older works by G. M. Rae, *The Syrian Church in India* (Edinburgh, 1892), pp. 27–61, and T. Whitehouse, *Lingerings of Light in a Dark Land . . . The Syrian Church in Malabar* (London, 1873), pp. 12–23; S. G. Pothan, *The Syrian Christians of Kerala* (New York, 1963), pp. 3–36.

[1] Rae represents this viewpoint, and his work is attacked by native writers such as Philip (p. 47).

[2] These include Medlycott, Dahlmann and Farquhar; cf. Tisserant, pp. 3–5, who accepts the new arguments.

silver coins[1] from the early centuries of our era have been discovered in Malabarese soil. Syrians had reached India, which is almost identical in the literature of the East Syrians with our modern India.[2] Moreover, startling numismatic evidence has established the existence of both King Gondophares and his brother Gad as historic figures and not simply legendary characters. Their names have been found on excavated coins and in a Gandhara inscription fixing their rule as about 19–45 A.D. in Scytho-India in the Indus valley.[3] Vestiges of St Thomas Christians are said to persist in secret in parts of northern India, for example at Tatta near the mouth of the Indus. It is thought that the Apostle was driven from the Indian Parthian empire by the descent of the Kushan invaders in the year 50 A.D. and that he sailed to the island of Socotra, whence he reached South India on a passing trade ship. Bishop Medlycott[4] contends that the climatic conditions specified by the *Acta Thomæ* apply more to South India than to the Punjab, and that the court life of Gondophares befits a maharaja's household more than a Parthian royal palace. We may conjecture that St Thomas the Apostle could have joined an already existing colony of Jews, Greeks and Syrians at Muziris-Cranganore on the shore of Malabar.[5]

Whatever the outcome of these arguments, it is clear that Christianity was planted in Malabar at a very early date, certainly before the end of the second century, as testified by Pantænus. Then in 295, the *Chronicle of Seert*[6] states that David, bishop of the Arabs, decided to leave his see at Baṣrah in order to devote himself to missionary work in India. The dubious story of the participation of Bishop 'John of Persia and great India' at Nicæa in 325, the appearance of Theophilus the Indian at Constantinople shortly afterwards, Emperor Constantius' (337–40) mission to the eastern lands comprising India, the mass Syrian emigration to India under the leadership of Thomas the Canaanite, a merchant sponsored by the eastern catholicos in 345, Ishūʿ Dad's colophon to his *Commentary on Romans* mentioning Daniel the Indian priest[7] – all these and

[1] More than a thousand coins of Tiberius, 450 of Augustus, and smaller quantities of Claudius, Nero and Trajan have been uncovered in hoards in South India; cf. Brown, p. 61.

[2] A. Mingana, 'The Early Spread of Christianity in India', in *The John Rylands Bulletin* (Manchester, 1926), pp. 11–14; cf. Brown, p. 47.

[3] Tisserant, p. 3; Brown, p. 47; Medlycott, pp. 4–15, where he also published a special plate with specimens of the Gondophares coins.

[4] *India and the Apostle Thomas*, pp. 75–9.

[5] Tisserant, pp. 5–6; Mingana, pp. 77–8, states that the Thomas tradition is not confined to the Malabar Christians and that Hindu legends mention that a foreigner by the name of Thomas opposed all the Vedas and converted to his 'Buddha' faith many prominent people. Rae, pp. 131–53, mentions 10,000 Indian Jews, of whom a considerable number lived in Cochin from Roman times.

[6] *Chronique de Seert, Histoire Nestorienne inédite*, ed. Mar Addai Scher, in *Patr. Or.*, IV, 236; cf. Mingana, p. 18, Tisserant, p. 7; Brown, pp. 66–7.

[7] Tisserant, p. 10; Brown, p. 68; Fortescue, *Lesser Eastern Churches*, pp. 356–8.

other scattered references only confirm Cosmas Indicopleustes' fifth-century statement that a regular Christian church had been long in existence in southern India. The fierce persecutions inflicted on the Persian Christians during the long reign of Shapur II (309–79) in his vast empire[1] comprising Mesopotamia was a chief factor which precipitated the transplantation of considerable groups of East Syrian refugees to Malabar in the course of the fourth century.

Pre-Portuguese History

It may safely be assumed that the Syrian church of St Thomas emerged on the scene of history with close ties and contacts with the East Syrian see of Seleucia-Ctesiphon at a date not later than the middle of the fifth century. Subsequent gleanings tend to prove that these ties grew stronger with the progress of time. In the reign of the Nestorian Catholicos Sabar-Ishūʿ (596–604), the *Chronicle of Seert* records that Marutha, the future maphrian of Tekrit, received gifts from India and China. In the reign of Ishūʿ Yahb (650–60), the catholicos reprimanded the metropolitan of Rewardashir in southwest Iran for irregularities, prominent amongst which was his recalcitrance in maintaining episcopal succession in the see of India.[2]

Perhaps the most significant events on record in subsequent centuries were the two waves of East Syrian emigrants to India under the leadership of Nestorian prelates. The first wave in the eighth century occurred about 774 when Bishop Thomas and a group of companions with their families from Mesopotamia landed on the shores of Kērala. Again in the ninth century around the year 840, Mar Sabar Ishōʿ (Sapor) and Mar Peroz (Parut), two Nestorian bishops, followed in Bishop Thomas' footsteps with more Syrian emigrants and settled down in the district of Quilon. The local rulers of the region granted both groups charters inscribed on two sets of copper plates, now in possession of the Mar Thoma Church at Tiruvalla. The inscriptions are in Old Tamil and bear signatures of witnesses in Kufic Arabic characters and a kind of Persian in Hebrew script.[3] They conferred on Christians a lofty place in their caste system. The metropolitans were thereby invested with both the civil and ecclesiastical jurisdiction over the whole community of St

[1] Labourt, *Christianisme dans l'empire perse*, p. 46 et seq.; Fortescue, pp. 45 et seq.

[2] Tisserant, p. 14; Brown, p. 69.

[3] Tisserant, pp. 15–16; Brown, pp. 74 et seq.; Philip, pp. 57–62; Rae, pp. 154 et seq.; Pothan, pp. 32–33, has published good reproductions of the plates. Plate IX has Kufic and Plate X Hebrew inscriptions side by side with the native scripts. Full textual translation of the plates is given in App. I and II, pp. 102–5. App. III (p. 106) gives the Indian astronomers' computation of the dates of the plates as 216 and 230 A.D., in which case the Arabic must be regarded as a later interpolation.

Thomas. Only criminal cases were reserved to the Hindu administration. The two prelates appear to have been unusually active, without being disturbed by the mild rule of their tolerant masters. They made conversions to Christianity, built churches, and erected open-air crosses carved in relief on granite slabs. The motif is generally Syrian Nestorian. The Velliapally Cross at Kottayam stands beneath a rounded arch with Pahlevi inscriptions.[1]

So strong did the Christians of St Thomas become that, at a given moment, they aspired to independence and set up a line of Christian rulers of their own which the rajahs of Cochin eventually suppressed shortly before the advent of the Portuguese. Their metropolitan resided at Angamali near Cranganore and was assisted in the discharge of his office by an archdeacon named by the Nestorian catholicos from the influential Palakomatta family. Upon the metropolitan's decease, the archdeacon assumed all his responsibilities and petitioned the said patriarch for a new substitute.

It is not possible to paint a comprehensive picture of this fascinating and largely unknown chapter in the story of ancient Indian Christianity during the Middle Ages. The source material for this dark period which existed in the Nestorian repositories of Mesopotamia and in the old records of the Indian churches was destroyed by the Mongol hordes on the one side and by the Portuguese invaders on the other. In fact the vandalism of the Mongol invasions of the Middle East was only surpassed in this sphere by the repercussions of the Synod of Diamper in 1599. That act of faith simply led to the obliteration of all Indian records, since it was decided to burn all religious manuscripts tainted with the heresy of Nestorius. Thus the historic records of Malabarese church history passed out of existence. Cardinal Tisserant, however, registers a couple of minor but interesting references bearing upon the later mediæval history of that church. The first dates from the fourteenth century, when a copyist named Zaccharias bar Joseph bar Zaccharias made an allusion to the Catholicos Yahballaha III (1281–1317) and to Mar Jacob, bishop of India, in 1301.[2] The second occurs in a Vatican codex,[3] apparently from the early sixteenth century, in Chaldaic script with Arabic and Syriac texts. It was brought to Rome from the East by Andrew Scander after a mission in the years 1718–21. This unusual document outlines what may be described as the last glimpse of Mesopotamia. The author notes that the Metropolitan See of India had been vacant for a long time, and that the Christians of St Thomas finally selected a delegation of three to go to the catholicos of Seleucia-Ctesiphon to request the consecration of a new metropolitan for Malabar. One of the delegates died *en route*, but the two others reached their destination. They were immediately ordained by the patriarch himself, and

[1] Rae, pp. 114–30. [2] Op. cit., p. 17.

[3] MS. Vat. Syr. 204; cf. Tisserant, pp. 24–5. Tisserant, an Orientalist himself, was previously curator of the Vatican Oriental MSS.

then he sent them to the historic monastery of Mar Augin to look for candidates. Their choice fell on Mar Thomas and Mar John, whom the catholicos readily consecrated, and they were joyfully received in Malabar. Afterwards Mar John retraced his steps to Mesopotamia with tithes and free offerings from the congregation. Meanwhile, he petitioned the new Catholicos Mar Elias V (1502–3) to appoint more Syrian prelates for the Indian diocese. Again the monks of Mar Augin furnished Mar Yahballaha as metropolitan with two suffragans – Mar Denha and Mar Jacob.[1] Such was the position of the Indian hierarchy at the time of the Portuguese conquest.

The Portuguese and Romanism[2]

Vasco da Gama rounded the Cape of Good Hope for the first time and, under the guidance of an Arab pilot named ibn Mājid, he succeeded in traversing the Arabian Sea and in landing on the shores of southern India near Calicut in 1498. This opening up of the direct sea route to India and the Far East by the Portuguese was almost as important an event in Western history as the discovery of America by Christopher Columbus in 1492. It was certainly a turning-point in the annals of the Indian Christians of St Thomas. So popular was the advent of those Portuguese fellow-Christians with their native co-religionists that Vasco da Gama made his second voyage to India in 1502. This time, however, his forces had a mixed reception by the natives who happened to include other elements beside the Christians. While his men were being ambushed by the Muslims in the region of Cochin, the Christians sent him a deputation with the sceptre of their suppressed kingdom – a red rod with silver decorations and three silver bells on top – to be taken to the king of Portugal as a friendly gesture. He evidently accepted it as a symbol of voluntary submission, while they wished thereby to gain a new ally in their bickerings with non-Christian neighbours. Originally, all that mattered for the Portuguese was to assure their monopoly of the pepper and spice trade which they had wrested from the intermediate Egyptian hands. In the end, they

[1] It is interesting to note that the Malabarese Jacobites advance the theory that their church became Nestorian only at the hands of this later set of bishops, that their hierarchy had previously stemmed from the Jacobite line, and that the Church recanted to the Jacobites on the first possible occasion of revolting against Romanism in 1653. The depletion of the mediæval sources since the burning of their records after the Synod of Diamper in 1599 makes it difficult to verify this thesis. For this Indian viewpoint, see Philip, pp. 124–58.

[2] Brown, pp. 11 et seq., 92 et seq.; Tisserant, pp. 27–100; Rae, pp. 187 et seq.; Philip, pp. 106–23, 167–72; Fortescue, *Lesser Eastern Churches*, pp. 363–7. Tisserant's work contains the fullest bibliography of the sources of the period (pp. 39–42, 108). Pothan, pp. 40 ff.

embarked on a new colonial career by the gradual conquest of southwestern India, with Goa as their capital. This resulted in a closer association with the Christians of St Thomas, who were unaware of the depth of the denominational differences separating their churches as well as the totalitarian religious imperialism of Rome.

The tragedy of the Indian church began with a parallel religious invasion by the Jesuits and the appointment of a pious but bigoted Augustinian hermit, Alexis de Menezis, as Latin archbishop of Goa in 1598. He was invested with vast powers and was determined to exterminate all traces of Nestorianism and heresy from that church and to impose Roman Catholicism by every possible means on those Eastern Christians. In the meantime, the old Syrian bishops who temporized with the new invaders died one after the other and were momentarily replaced by new ones who proclaimed the Roman profession of faith and submitted to the pope. Those who were tempted to recant were subjected to inhuman torture by the Inquisition, which had been extended overseas to India on the recommendation of one of the greatest and most saintly missionaries to the Far East, St Francis Xavier. Catholic pressures reached their height in the Synod of Diamper,[1] skillfully engineered by Menezis so that the representatives who assembled in 1599 gave way to the Roman dictates. The errors of Nestorius were condemned, celibacy was imposed on the priests, unconditional submission to the Holy See was declared, the Inquisition was recognized, and what was a calamity for the church historian, the older books and records – all suspected of heretical colour – were committed to the flames. The only privilege conceded to the Church was the continuance of the use of the Syro-Chaldæan language in the celebration of the liturgy, which was purged of all non-Roman elements, and the usual canonical pronouncements of conformity were introduced. The Synod led to the complete Romanization of the whole community, and Jesuit missionaries spread into most churches to indoctrinate the faithful and revile the old order. The Portuguese armies were strongly behind them, and the archbishop freely bribed the rajahs of Cochin to keep out of religious affairs.

In theory, the papal triumph in Malabar was sweeping, final and irrevocable. In practice, there was a different story to tell. The older Syrian ways and customs were far too deeply rooted to be abolished without resistance, and native adherents were only driven underground. The more open dissidents entrenched themselves inland behind the mountain fastnesses and secretly communicated with the Eastern patriarchs – Coptic, Jacobite and Nestorian alike – to consecrate a bishop to rule among them in defiance of Catholic impositions. This became extremely difficult since the Latins closely guarded

[1] T. Whitehouse, pp. 107–23; Rae, pp. 225–55; Brown, pp. 32 et seq.; Tisserant, pp. 56–68; F. E. Keay, *A History of the Syrian Church in India* (London, 1938), pp. 45–50; Philip, pp. 118–23.

all the seaports against such infiltration. Meanwhile, a Jesuit was appointed as Latin bishop of the Syrians in the diplomatic person of Francis Roz (1599–1624), who attempted to draw the recalcitrant flock to the fold by relegating some of his temporal power to the Indian archdeacon from the influential Palakomatta family, in keeping with former usages. But this proved to be only a gain to the natives, who nevertheless persisted in stirring up trouble for the Jesuits and Catholic prelates. Their abomination of the new regime was even intensified by an untoward event which inflamed public opinion. The Coptic patriarch of Alexandria consecrated a Syrian Jacobite priest called ʿAṭallah as Syrian bishop of India under the name Ignatius and he succeeded in reaching his diocese by landing at Surat in 1652 and proceeding to Mylapore, where the news of his arrival excited the natives, but the Jesuits soon arrested him. He was dispatched to Goa, where he was tried by the Inquisition as a heretic and burnt in 1654.

The position of the Jesuits became precarious as the Christians of St Thomas seceded and were in open revolt against their harsh rule. Meanwhile the competition of the Dominican missionaries weakened them in the eyes of the Holy See. Pope Alexander VII therefore decided to send a new Carmelite mission to bring the disaffected Indians back to Roman obedience. The first mission reached Malabar in 1657. It was reinforced by another in 1661 at a time when the Portuguese star was declining and the Dutch was rising. Quilon was captured by the Dutch in that very year, and in the following Cranganore fell. Cochin became Dutch in 1663 and the Indians of the South were able to breathe more freely under their rule. The Dutch at once ordered all the Catholic missionaries and Jesuit priests out of Malabar. Father Joseph, the Jesuit bishop of the Syrians, who apparently had brought eighty-four parishes back to Rome as against thirty-six remaining loyal to the old native church, was also told to leave the country; and he did so after a hurried consecration of the first native successor, Chandy Kattanar, who took the latinized name of Alexander de Campo with the title of bishop of Megara.[1] Nevertheless the Dutch were hailed by the native Christians on the whole as their saviours from the Portuguese yoke. The Catholic missionary under the protection of Portuguese arms was the first to sow the seeds of permanent schism and dissension among the Indian Christians of St Thomas.

Schisms, Confusions and Solutions

The subsequent period was one of great confusion in church ranks. We have to remember that the Indian Christians had been in a different position from

[1] Brown, p. 107.

the rest of Eastern and Western Christians with their doctrinal broils supported by racial and national aspirations. The Indians were not interested in theological definitions and did not care or perhaps even understand the network of causes at the root of the quarrels between Romanist, Jacobite and Nestorian. All that mattered to that distant congregation was Christ and a canonical succession of bishops to ensure the religious care of the faithful without impairing their local native way of life. This had been ensured in the past by an unwritten usage whereby the Syrian foreign bishop usually concentrated on the religious functions, whereas the civil responsibilities rested upon his native archdeacon. The Jesuits, on the other hand, had a different and totalitarian approach which the Carmelites could not mitigate, and accordingly the whole way of life of the Indians was dislocated from its older channels. A considerable section of the Indian community, even before the end of Portuguese rule, yearned for a return to the old system with an eastern bishop. In 1653, when the infuriated crowds failed to rescue Bishop Ignatius, the old ʿAṭallah the Syrian consecrated by the Coptic patriarch, they marched to the Mattanchari Church in Cochin and at its ancient Cross swore a solemn oath to cast off the Roman yoke, to expel the Jesuits, and to seek a bishop from one of the churches of the East. This is the famous Coonen Cross Oath.[1] Meanwhile assemblies were held in which the archdeacon was chosen as temporary head of the Church and consecrated bishop by twelve priests. He took the name of Mar Thoma I, and so started a new line of bishops bearing the same name. Thus at the coming of the Dutch, the Church was split between those who retained the Catholic profession under Bishop Chandy and those who reverted to the Syrians and Mar Thoma.

The position of the Catholics, however, was further weakened at the beginning of the new political regime by the appointment as coadjutor and future successor to Chandy of a certain Raphael, a half-caste, of mixed Portuguese and Asiatic parentage. This unwise step necessarily alienated many followers who considered the action humiliating to their social rank and honour. In the meantime, Mar Thoma's petitions to the Eastern churches brought forth a new Syrian Jacobite bishop, Mar Gregorios, who was received in Malabar with great joy in 1665, and who of course began by anathematizing the pope of Rome, the Romanist adherents, the Synod of Diamper and the whole Catholic profession. Although some doubt has been expressed about this confirmation of Mar Thoma's irregular consecration, it seems inconceivable from their amicable relations and their joint conduct of ecclesiastical affairs that the primate refrained from laying hands on him.[2] On the other hand, the

[1] Rae, pp. 256–61; Brown, pp. 100–1, Philip, pp. 159–72. Philip (p. 162) mentions that the oath was taken while the crowd seized a rope tied to the Cross, thus binding themselves thereby as a sacred vow.

[2] Brown, p. 112, suspects this on account of Mar Thoma's opposition to the advent of Jacobite bishops in 1678 and the absence of documentary evidence.

Dutch-Portuguese Concordat of 1698 seems to have alleviated the constant pressures on the Catholics by giving permission to one bishop and twelve Roman priests to enter southern India in return for papal toleration of Hungarian Protestants.

The picture became further complicated by the arrival of more foreign episcopal pretenders. In 1676, a certain Mar Andrew emerged on the scene as a papal nominee to the Romano-Syrian Indians. He was disowned by the Carmelites, and his career ended when he was drowned in 1682. A third faction of enduring importance arose with the coming of Mar Gabriel, whom the Nestorian patriarch sent in 1708 to recapture the Indian church. It is stated that forty-two Roman parishes sided with him, though the Catholic missionaries later recovered ten of them.[1] Since the death of Mar Gregorios in 1672, the Jacobites had other bishops to succeed him, but on the death of Mar Basilios, as evidenced by Mar Thoma's letter to the Jacobite patriarch in 1720, the succession was interrupted and the flock was endangered by the Nestorian heresy. The Mar Thoma line aimed at the reunification of the Indians under one ecclesiastical authority. Since this could be enforced by the support of the secular authority, they appealed to the Dutch for help, which was not forthcoming since all the factions were equally heretical in the eyes of the foreign ruler of the land. Mar Gabriel's death at about the end of 1730 did not usher in the re-establishment of peace. The Nestorians survived, though in a small group mainly drawn from the Syrian Catholics who were themselves at one time also torn asunder by the sudden revival of Mesopotamian relations and a claim over the Syro-Malabarese Catholics by the Syro-Chaldæan patriarch of Babylon. Nestorian succession, however, was maintained as late as 1952 when the exiled patriarch Shimʿūn XXI in the United States of America consecrated a Nestorian by the name of Mar Thoma as Metropolitan of Malabar and of India. This archbishop rules a community of approximately five thousand Nestorians in Trichur at the present time.[2]

As to the Jacobites, they succeeded in obtaining new foreign bishops of a poorer quality than the late Mar Gregorios, and a quarrel soon arose between them and their native colleagues, followed by protracted litigation and vacillation between Catholicism, orthodoxy and even Anglicanism for the solution of their problems and the restitution of their authority. This is a complex story and a dreary chapter in the annals of Indian Christianity, exemplified in the bewildering career of Mar Dionysios I towards the end of the eighteenth and the beginning of the nineteenth centuries. A Jacobite by birth and

[1] Le Quien, *Oriens Christianus*, II, 553, 589; cf. Brown, p. 116, n. 3. Mingana, *Early Spread of Christianity*, pp. 36–42, quotes the latter Syriac documents on Nestorianism in India.

[2] Tisserant, pp. 119–20 and notes. The translator (p. 120, n. 1) thinks that their number is decreasing on account of intermarriage with the 15,000 Syrian Catholic inhabitants of Trichur.

consecration, Mar Dionysios temporarily became a Catholic in 1799 without effect, then, while reverting to Jacobitism, discussed possibilities of union with the Anglican Church after 1800, and was able to live in a friendly spirit with Mar Dioscoros, the Jacobite patriarch's Syrian nominee for Malabar in 1807.[1]

Before the close of the eighteenth century, the political picture underwent a radical change which had tremendous impact on the course of events in Indian church history. The English finally replaced the Dutch in the south, and British residents were appointed for the administration of Travancore and Cochin. Without antagonizing the Syro-Malabarese Catholics, the first two residents were religious-minded Anglican Protestants who aimed at the settlement of the lamentable state of affairs in the native Jacobite church by helping it to reform itself from within. To achieve this purpose, Colonel Munro, the first Resident, thought that in addition to the enforcement of discipline the priests (*Kattanars*) must be armed with adequate religious education and the people should have direct intelligent access to the Scriptures.[2] It occurred to him to resort to the Church Missionary Society for aid in these fields without impairing the ancient customs, liturgies or traditional organization of the Church. In other words, the missionary was invited for purposes of edification without proselytization, a perfectly acceptable proposition to the Indian hierarchy. The first English missionary, Thomas Norton, arrived in 1816 and was followed by others[3] who were permitted by the metropolitan to preach in the Jacobite churches. The Resident encouraged the return of the clergy to married life in accordance with the Jacobite way and even offered the first wedded priests material assistance.[4] The old Malayalam text of the New Testament by Dionysius I, found inadequate, was revised and published in 1830. A college was inaugurated in which both Syriac and Malayalam were taught.

In spite of the fact that the Church Missionary Society strictly avoided interference with native church policies and usages, a new seed of dissension was unintentionally sown amidst a small group of reformist Syrians led by Abraham Malpan,[5] a Kottayam College teacher and vicar of Maramon, who became known to future generations as the prime founder of the Reformed Church of Mar Thoma. Abraham and his companions fell under the influence

[1] Brown, pp. 124 et seq.

[2] Ibid., pp. 132 et seq.; Rae, pp. 281–303.

[3] Norton was immediately followed by Benjamin Bailey, Joseph Fenn and Henry Baker; Brown, p. 133.

[4] Ibid., p. 133, n. 3. A present of 400 rupees was made to the first Kattanar to marry. Subsequently forty-one Kattanars followed the same example, and the bishop suggested the substitution of a small monthly aid of ten rupees to each instead of a lump sum. The Kattanars were miserably poor and depended for their livelihood on funeral and wedding fees, which were very small, certainly insufficient to raise a family.

[5] *Malpan* means teacher, as *Kattanar* means priest.

of Protestant ideas; but, unlike the minority of Syrians who openly repudiated the old profession and became Protestants, they were determined to remain in the church and to reform it. Abraham tried, therefore, to keep the outward forms of worship according to the Jacobites, but otherwise composed a Malayalam version of the liturgy which he freely modified in conformity with Protestant tenets.[1] The reigning Metropolitan Mar Dionysios IV was alarmed at these uncanonical aberrations and excommunicated the whole group. Realizing that his teachings were doomed without episcopal support, Abraham hastened to send Mathew his nephew to the patriarchal court at Dair al-Zaʿfarān in Ṭūr ʿAbdīn where, after some training, he was consecrated by Patriarch Ignatius Elias II as bishop under the name of Mar Matthew Athanasius in 1842, despite Mar Dionysios' warnings. He became the first of a Mar Thomite line with varying fortunes. When exposed, he and his followers were excommunicated and expelled from the church and church property. As a new sect, they began to build their own churches independently. They do not have images, do not venerate saints or pray for the dead, do not accept the teaching of the Eucharistic sacrifice, and pray in the vernacular instead of in Syriac. During English rule they were in communion with the Anglican Church of South India.[2]

After the new schism the remaining Jacobite hierarchy lived in comparative peace until another quarrel broke out over the patriarchal prerogative with its financial implications, and this was further aggravated by an existing schism in the mother church. To consolidate his position in the Indian diocese, the Patriarch Ignatius ʿAbdallah Saṭṭūf came to Malabar in person in 1909. Apparently the Indian prelates held different views on the right of the patriarch to draw interests on a church investment, which seems to have angered him to the extent that he excommunicated Dionysios VI and replaced him with another metropolitan, Mar Kurilos (Cyril). This signalled another split in Jacobite lines with immense consequences. Whereas some accepted the patriarchal sentence and became identified as the 'Patriarch's Party', others remained faithful to the old metropolitan, and an association of them met in committee and declared the excommunication inoperative. They formed

[1] He also broke the statue of a church father in the Church of Maramon as idolatrous and suppressed an annual festival which the folks observed in his honour. This is known as the Reform of 1012 [1837]. Brown, pp. 140–1.

[2] On the Mar Thoma separation, see Juhanon Mar Thoma, Metropolitan of Mar Thoma Syrian Church, *Christianity in India* (Madras, 1954), pp. 44 et seq.; F. E. Keay, *A History of the Syrian Church in India* (London, 1938); Brown, pp. 140 et seq.; Tisserant, pp. 147–51; G. M. Rae, *The Syrian Church in India* (Edinburgh and London, 1892), pp. 304–26; Philip, pp. 244 et seq. Archbishop Juhanon and Bishop Mathew in a call to the churches of India (Juhanon Mar Thoma, *Christianity in India*, App. I, p. 75) describe the Mar Thoma Church as 'a bridge Church, preserving in it the best features of Eastern traditional forms of worship and the Reformation principles of Luther and the Western Protestant Churches'.

the 'Metran's Party',[1] later identified as the 'Catholicos'[2] Party'. It happened at the time that the Ottoman government had deposed the former Jacobite patriarch Ignatius ʿAbdul-Massīḥ, who was of course a citizen of Turkey. Since his deposition by the Turks could not necessarily be held as binding on the Indians, Dionysios was constrained to regard his successor as an anti-patriarch and decided with his party to invite the older prelate for a counter-visit to India. ʿAbdul-Massīḥ readily accepted the invitation, came to Malabar in 1912, and declared his antagonist's decisions void. He confirmed Mar Dionysios and excommunicated Patriarch ʿAbdallah's nominee, Mar Kurilos. He consecrated more new bishops of his own and, what was much more serious, elevated Mar Ivanios to the dignity of catholicos, thus recognizing the local autonomy of the Church of St Thomas without its separation from Antioch. This also meant that the catholicos was empowered to consecrate bishops at his discretion.

The position of all these schismatic sections and sub-sections was even more complicated by the special circumstances of the racial division of the Malabarese people into Northists (*Nordhists*) and Southists (*Suddhists*), each with their distinctive leanings cutting across the varying religious parties and shades including even the Uniate branch.

In the meantime, litigation in the high courts was pursued by all rivals to establish the validity of their positions and their rights to handle the property and financial interests of the Church. In 1931, Lord Irwin, viceroy of India,[3] invited the Jacobite Patriarch Elias III Shakar (1917–32) to visit the country in the hope of settling this tangle of problems and differences. The patriarch responded by coming, but he died in Malabar and was buried in one of its churches[4] without accomplishing the reconciliation. Mar Dionysios followed him to the grave two years later. Effectively he remained the real ruler of the church until his decease. Afterwards, the new catholicos went to Ḥomṣ to see Patriarch Ephraem I, but again failed to come to a compromise with him. On his return to Malabar in 1934, a new Constitution of the Syrian Church was declared by the party in order to invalidate the *status quo* of its national autonomy.[5] This seems to have altered the legal outlook on the whole position, since the courts showed a tendency to consider this recent step as the foundation of a new church.

Although the final verdict in this protracted litigation is not yet clear, it

[1] The Arabic *Muṭran.* Both words derived from the Greek, signifying 'metropolitan'.

[2] The use of the word grew with the tendency towards local independence from Antioch, and could be taken as a revival of the old institution of the eastern maphrianate. The word 'maphrian', however, has not been used in this case.

[3] Brown, p. 156.

[4] Buried in Manjanikkara; ibid., p. 156.

[5] Comprising 127 articles, the Constitution made no direct reference to the patriarch and stipulated recognition of the catholicos; Brown, p. 156.

must be remembered that church life itself was not seriously affected by those differences. The clergy carried on their functions undisturbed by excommunications and counter-excommunications. The strife between the parties, though bitter at times, never actually assumed the dimensions of schism within the Jacobite Church as in the previous cases of the Syro-Malabar Catholics or the Mar Thomites. Continuous efforts have been exerted to restore peace between the prelates whose differences did not touch the faith but were restricted to administration, finance and autonomy. Rumours that the sustained efforts had come to fruition were circulated when the bishops of both parties came to the place known as the Old Seminary in Kottayam in December 1958 and sealed their reconciliation with a thanksgiving service celebrated in church in the presence of representative laity of the Orthodox Syrian Church. Apparently an agreement was signed by the bishops as well as by the priests and lay delegates from parishes. By the terms of this treaty, the reunited Indian Church of Kērala became autonomous with its own synod of bishops under the presidency of the catholicos. For all practical purposes, the catholicate replaces the patriarchate in Indian ecclesiastical affairs. The link between the two offices has been summed up in the exchange of notification whenever the patriarch or catholicos is deceased or newly elected. If the patriarch is present at the investing of a new catholicos, he shall officiate at the ceremony; but beyond that, his jurisdiction ends.[1]

Parallel to the conciliatory movement within the Syrian church in the last few decades, there has been a growing tendency towards œcumenicity. This tendency may be seen in three places. In the first place, within India itself, vague and undefined attempts have been conceived to bring the Jacobite, Mar Thoma and Anglican churches of Travancore and Cochin into a confederacy.[2] This idea was fostered at the Alwaye Union Christian College, and

[1] The news of the reconciliation as well as these particulars have been conveyed to me from India by the Rev. Father V. C. Samuel, who sent me a copy of his article, 'A New Era for the Orthodox Syrian Church', to appear in the February number of the *South Indian Churchman*. It will be interesting to read the document signed and watch its outcome both in Kērala and in Antioch.

[2] Archbishop Juhanon Mar Thoma, in his interesting *Christianity in India*, p. 71, sums up what he describes as the sad spectacle of the division of the once united St Thomas Christians of Malabar into seven communions: (1) The Nestorians of Trichur; (2) The Roman Catholics, comprising the Romo-Syrians, the Latinized Christians, and the Catholics of Syrian Rite who went to Rome from the Jacobite Church with Archbishop Ivanios in 1930; (3) The Jacobite Syrian Church in communion with Antioch; (4) The Independent Syrian Church of Malabar, known as Thozhyur Church of Kērala and founded in 1770, in communion with the Mar Thoma denomination; (5) The Anglican Church, now the united Protestant Church of South India; (6) The Orthodox Syrian Church, revising the catholicate of the East in Malabar on the authority of the order of Patriarch ʿAbdul-Massīḥ; (7) The Mar Thoma Syrian Church. An almost identical summary is provided by Pothan, p. 52, who states that the present head of the original Syrian Church, His Holiness Moran Mar Basalious, resides in Kottayam, while Archbishop Juhanon Mar Thoma's headquarters are at Kērala. The Church Missionary Society of South India has

subsequently conferences were held for discussing this purpose by representatives of the three organizations, but the conferences were impeded by the disaffection within the Jacobite Church. The Kērala Council of Church Union in the summer of 1936, however, mapped out the foundations of approach amongst the three church organizations on a federal basis. Each church would retain its own system of administration, its hierarchy and clergy, its profession of faith, and its own local traditions. The central federal body would control educational, cultural and missionary activities.[1] In the second place, the increasing emancipation of the Church in South India from Antiochene administrative influence is accompanied by a cry from the Indian Syrian Christians for closer spiritual ties with their Eastern Christian brethren abroad, whether Jacobite, Coptic or Armenian from the Monophysite camp. In the third place, the South Indian churches have consistently looked up to world œcumenicity with unreserved zeal and have joined the World Council of Churches. It is interesting to note that the Indian delegate of the Jacobite Church to the Evanston assembly in 1954 seized the opportunity to convene with the delegates of the Coptic, Armenian and even Greek churches in the hope of establishing some sort of intercommunion and mutual understanding. The new situation developing in the Orthodox Syrian Church in India is a combination of that nascent spirit of nationalism which pervades the whole of the Indian subcontinent and a resurgence of traditional piety and profound attachment to ancient Christianity.

---

a Moderator who lives in Madras. Fortescue, *Lesser Eastern Churches*, p. 375, adds yet another small Christian chiliast sect called the Yoyomayans, founded in 1874 by Justus Joseph, a Brahmin convert with the title of *Vidvan Kutti*, that is, the Learned Person. According to the 1931 census, the Christians in Travancore-Cochin are about 63 per cent of the total population. Nearly two million, the majority remains Roman Catholic (1,109,334), whereas the Jacobites were 363,721, the Mar Thomites 142,486, and both Anglicans and other Protestants 291,799. Keay, pp. 106–7. According to the *Catholic Directory* of 1956, quoted by Cardinal Tisserant (p. 139), the total of Roman Catholics in that year was 1,171,235. The same work (p. 154) gives the present total of the Jacobites as approximately 700,000.

[1] Keay, pp. 113–17. M. A. Varki, principal of Alwaye Union Christian College, called for a 'federal union' similar to that of the United States of America with a common head and a common assembly to be elected in addition to the separate heads of churches with their local assemblies.

23 • SOCIAL AND RELIGIOUS LIFE

Social Setting

Before the Western advance the Christians of Malabar led a simple life based on agricultural economy and trade, while the Church remained the centre of their social and religious life. After the coming of the Portuguese, their defenceless society was exposed to forcible apostasy and merciless plunder by one invader after another; and their survival, even in the disunited form now prevailing, must be ascribed to their strong social mettle and a profound sense of piety. At the outset of the nineteenth century, precisely in the year 1818, the first British resident, Munro, said in an address to the Madras Government on the St Thomas Christians: 'Notwithstanding the misfortunes which they suffered and the disadvantages of their situation, they still retain, however, some of the virtues by which they were formerly distinguished. They are remarkable for mildness and simplicity of character, honesty and industry; their pursuits are confined to agriculture and trade; and, although they have lost the high station and elevated sentiments which they once possessed, yet they are still respected on account of their integrity and rectitude of conduct.'[1]

Geographical factors, the remote origins from which they stemmed, and the historic development of their society across the centuries combined to give their community that special character which distinguished their own pattern of life. Entrenched between the Ghat Mountains and the Arabian Sea with an ample supply of water throughout their country, the St Thomas Christians were able to remain intact within an area where they evolved their mode of life in their scattered villages and became self-sufficient with their agricultural produce, in the meantime enriching themselves with trade in the excess pepper and spices at their disposal. Although they came to Malabar at first as immigrants and foreign merchants, they ultimately became integrated into Dravidian native stock, using Malayalam for common speech and Syriac only in ecclesiastical functions. Apparently they fulfilled a much needed

[1] Address quoted at greater length by T. Whitehouse, *Lingerings of Light in a Dark Land*, pp. 11–12.

requirement in Malabar by activating foreign trade. Moreover, they attained a high reputation as technicians and useful artisans, thus recalling the qualities which endeared the Syrian missionary to the hearts of the Asiatic races wherever he went to preach the Christian Gospel. It was on account of these attainments that they were not only accepted in the new society of Hindu, Brahmin and Nayar, but also granted a high station in their caste system and treated with the greatest respect. They enjoyed numerous privileges[1] and both their bishops and their bridal parties were allowed to use the processional ornaments usually restricted to the rajas. Silk umbrellas, flagstaffs, and men with wooden swords and shields covered with leopard skin could be seen in Christian processions. A bridegroom might ride an elephant or walk under a canopy with bands of musicians while lanterns lined the way and triumphal arches were erected for the occasion. Furthermore, in common with the Nayars from whose lines the rajas arose, the Christians enjoyed hereditary titles and were often recognized for military skill. Cases of intermarriage with Nayars are reported, and Nayar and Christian children received education together. Christians regarded themselves and were generally accepted as a caste, equal to Nayars and standing immediately after Brahmins. It is interesting to note that while Christians sent free offerings to the temples, the Hindus participated in Christian feasts and sought cures from their ailments by votive gifts to Christian saints and churches.[2]

Two main factors are to be found at work in the formation of the folk customs of the Christians of St Thomas – the one of native Hindu origin, and the other being the Church and Christian religious traditions. These combined influences are best represented on the occasions of birth, marriage and burial celebrations. Until recent times, astrology was practised at birth and omens were guarded. Rules about pollution after birth and death were also observed, and the problem of the outcast and untouchability[3] has not yet been completely eradicated from popular habits notwithstanding the sustained influence of Christian tenets. The ceremony of the first rice-feeding of a baby at the age of six months is performed by the Hindu in the temple and by the Christian in church with a lighted candle, never extinguished by mouth-blowing which would be sacrilege to the Indian goddess of fire. On the other hand, the priest or a male substitute usually utters aloud the phrase 'Jesus Christ is Lord'[4] in a child's ear at birth. Baptism is a formal function

[1] Brown, p. 170, mentions sixteen privileges in Iravi Korṭṭan's plate, and even seventy-two granted by Ceruman Perumal.

[2] Brown, pp. 167 et seq., devotes a considerable part of his work to a study of the social life of the community and furnishes first hand knowledge and data which have made the present chapter possible.

[3] Brown, p. 174, mentions that the value of fasting was lost upon touching an outcaste, and that landowners returning from the fields with outcaste labour usually changed clothing and bathed for purification.

[4] Ibid., p. 185, *Maron Yesu Masiha*; Pothan, p. 62.

whence the child became a *Nasrani*, or Nazarene. A boy was generally announced with more noise and rejoicing than a girl.

Christian betrothals and marriages are very solemn occasions. As a rule they are regarded as the common affair of the whole family and must be considered in council. Like the rest of the non-Christian Indians, however, child marriage has been common; and a girl became fit for betrothal at the time of piercing the lobe of her ear[1] for wearing a ring. The priest appears in most stages of the deliberations as a central figure, and a dowry equivalent to the girl's inheritance is usually fixed. The wedding is celebrated in church after mass (*Qurbana*), but the procession homeward is similar to that of the Hindus. A lamp denoting Christ's witness must hang in front of the altar during the celebration. The girl is loaded with jewels, both her own and others borrowed for the occasion, and she wears a gold flower tied to her hair. The bridegroom wears a gold chain with a pectoral cross, though in earlier days a crown was used in keeping with the traditions of the Eastern churches at the time of the wedding. Like Brahmins, a certain number of threads are taken from the wedding bridal cloth to be spun in what is known as *Minnu* and tied round the girl's neck by her bridegroom as the priest declares them man and wife. This *Minnu* must be kept and replenished throughout the husband's lifetime. During subsequent festivities and banquets, the lamp of Jesus' witness must be kept burning.

Towards the end of life the Syrian, like the Hindu, prefers to retire from the world for quiet meditation. Usually this takes place at the age of sixty-four. Last unction and sacrament are received just before the coming of the end. After death, the corpse is washed and dressed by servants, since relatives are prohibited from touching it. Then it is placed on a bed facing east with burning incense underneath while mourners squat on matting around the departed until the body has been taken to church for the funeral service, which is not attended by women. The family of a deceased person remains under pollution after burial until, like Brahmins, they bathe in the river on the occasion of the first feast to follow. Meanwhile, requiem *Qurbanas* are officiated throughout the first forty days after death. A similar function is celebrated on the anniversary of the decease, and on this occasion alms are given and special sweetmeats are distributed.[2]

Syrians respect old age. The grandfather of a family remains the centre of authority, and family ties are strong. Apart from sharing the superstitions

[1] Brown, p. 187. Usually at the age of six or seven, whereas the boys married at ten to twelve. The custom was strictly preserved by the Jacobites until 1890. Since then it has been fast disappearing. Further interesting details on betrothal and marriage are given by Pothan, pp. 64–72.

[2] Pothan, pp. 73–6, surveys the ceremonies at death. Bishops are buried in a seated posture from the Indian custom of the burial of a *sanyasi*, and the tomb is filled with flowers, incense and earth before sealing. Ibid., p. 90.

and customs of their Hindu neighbours, the South Indian Christians also have some of their own. Most interesting amongst these is the use of a book entitled *Palpustakam*,[1] composed of forty-nine Syriac adages preserved in churches for consultation about the future in regard to cases of marriage. After muttering the Pater, Ave and Credo, the priest signs the Cross and calls on someone to choose a number not exceeding the aforementioned. The corresponding statement in the book tells the fortune and provides the required advice. In bygone days they practised the ordeal of fire and water, somewhat similar to the usages of mediæval European feudal society. The accused could prove his innocence by holding hot iron, otherwise by thrusting hands in boiling oil, or by swimming clear across a crocodile-infested river. All these older cults or customs, however, have changed or are rapidly changing in a modern society with the progress of education.

Education and the Bible

Perhaps the greatest curse of Indian Christianity at the dawn of modern history was the lack of education and the spread of superstition. Neither the Portuguese nor the Dutch made any serious attempt to alter these lamentable conditions. In the church, the ignorance of the *Katanars* (priests) was phenomenal, and this was further aggravated by the use of Syriac, a foreign language, in the celebration of the holy liturgy and in Bible readings. The root idea of Resident Norton's decision to call upon the Church Missionary Society for help in the Travancore-Cochin area was the crying need for the education of Jacobite religious leaders as the sole means towards a better understanding of the faith. With the approval of the *Metran* (metropolitan), he insisted on teaching both the *Katanars* (priests) and the *Shamashes* (deacons) Syriac and Malayalam. Joseph Fenn accordingly became active as a teacher and as a preacher in the Old Seminary founded in 1813 at Kottayam. Mar Dionysios agreed to accept for ordination as *Katanars* only candidates who had obtained certificates from the seminary. In 1838, missionary funds were allotted to the Church Missionary College as well as to the high school opened at Kottayam for the education of Christians irrespective of denomination. A girl's school came into existence at Tiruvalla. Schools multiplied in numerous parishes and the new educational policy was most favourably received by native Christians. The English system was implemented with considerable results, and the college instruction soon rose to the level of granting degrees.[2]

[1] Brown, pp. 201–2. The text of the forty-nine adages may be found in English in App. IV to Pothan's work pp. 107–10. For Syrian belief in omens, see Pothan, pp. 95 ff.

[2] Ibid., pp. 133, 160; Juhanon Mar Thoma, pp. 38–9; Philip, pp. 222 et seq., 297–306.

In 1921, the Alwaye Union Christian College was inaugurated with an eye on the promotion of Christian unity in the district of Travancore. With the growth of sectarian tendencies in already existing institutions, the new college was conceived as a free centre for students of all persuasions, though without promoting 'undenominationalism'. Starting with only seventy students, its enrolment reached 359 in the year 1937 with 257 boarders living together in residence despite differences of creed. The college council was composed of Jacobite, Mar Thomite and Anglican members. Its teaching body was recruited essentially from its own alumni.[1]

The Roman Catholics in Malabar did not long lag behind the Protestant missionaries in the furtherance of education. By 1942, the Syrian Carmelites succeeded in maintaining sixteen schools, half of which were boarding institutions. In the field of higher education, the University College of the Sacred Heart was opened at Therava, a suburb of Ernakulam, after the Second World War. Still more recently, the Syrian Carmelites also founded two more university colleges at Iranjilakuda and Calicut in the dioceses of Trichur and Tellicherry respectively. Cardinal Tisserant mentions the building of a large house at Bangalore by the same order for theologians and philosophers.[2]

In this general atmosphere of progressive movements, the Jacobite Syrians had their awakening; and in spite of their internal strife, disaffection and prolonged litigation between parties, they have managed to accomplish a fair share in the education of their community. In the field of theological studies, the catholicos founded a Jacobite seminary at Kottayam, while the patriarch's supporters decided to establish a similar seat of religious learning at Alwaye. The total enrolment in both institutions, according to Philip,[3] amounted in recent years to eighty-five seminarists with fifteen professors. With the reconciliation in the church, it may be assumed that their unification will render them stronger. The same author mentions the existence of monasteries and nunneries under the auspices of the patriarchal delegate, with some seventy aspirants destined to enrich the spiritual life of the community. In the meantime, that delegate took under his own patronage the Sunday School Association, which celebrated its silver jubilee in 1946, while the catholicos also furthered a similar movement called the Sunday School Samajam. The total number of schools on both sides amounted to 480, with 3,600 teachers and some 50,000 pupils.[4]

Again in secular education, the Jacobite Syrians were active in two directions. In the first place, they founded a great number of vernacular primary, secondary and high schools in most parishes throughout the whole archdiocese. In the second place, for the purpose of special instruction, they created more than forty English high schools with some 770 teachers and

[1] Keay, pp. 108–10.
[2] Tisserant, p. 135.
[3] *Indian Church of St Thomas*, pp. 430–2.
[4] Ibid.

an enrolment of about 18,500 pupils. Accordingly, illiteracy has been greatly reduced in Malabar. The 1941 census shows literacy to have reached 26.5 per cent in Cochin, and 12.2 per cent in the Indian subcontinent.[1]

On the whole, the Syrians of South India have gone a long way on the road of modern education in recent years. Many of them, including Jacobite *Katanars*, have attained the highest degrees from English and American universities in both theological and secular studies. Brown[2] notes that the Finance Minister of the free Republic of India as well as the Chief Secretaries of Mysore and Travancore were of late all Syrian Christians.

Notwithstanding his objection to sectarian leanings and denominational favouritism on the part of the missionaries, a native Jacobite historian[3] records the gratitude of his co-religionists for two material advantages accruing from missionary labours. One was the spread of English education, and the other was the publication of the Bible in the vernacular (Malayalam). At one time, the conservative Indian clergy protested against the use of the Malayalam Bible, not only in the churches, but also in private homes. At present, their position has been altered. Whereas the Mar Thomites have abolished the use of Syriac altogether, the Jacobites allow a bilingual system in services and even the Syriac Bible lections are rendered into Malayalam for the congregation. Consequently, greater attention has been paid in recent times to the revision and publication of the Malayalam Bible.[4] The Jacobites have now at least four printing presses equipped with Syriac, English and Malayalam characters for the publication of religious literature comprising as well a number of periodicals devoted to ecclesiastical affairs. The publishing centre at Pampakuda has produced numerous editions of bilingual Anaphoras and liturgical books.[5] These concessions by the church authorities have made the resumption of evangelical work possible for Jacobite missionaries who laboured amongst the depressed heathen and untouchable classes. Several missionary associations have been founded for this purpose. Foremost among them is the Society of the Servants of the Cross, claiming in 1950 to have won over 18,733 converts to Christianity, together with 1,032 school pupils. The society was founded in 1924. Several other voluntary organizations are known to exist, but they have had more modest results.[6] The indigenous

[1] *Indian Church of St Thomas*, pp. 430–3. [2] *Indian Christians of St Thomas*, p. 160,

[3] Philip, pp. 297–8.

[4] Early edns. 1811, 1818 and 1830. Tisserant, p. 146.

[5] According to Tisserant, pp. 185–6, the Jacobites published: (1) Ritual of the sacraments; (2) Ritual of extreme unction; (3) Ritual of the funeral of a priest; (4) Ritual of the funeral of lay people; (5) Ordinary office (*Shim*) for the week. The Catholics have published two missals, Malayalam Mass, Ordinary office (*Shim*), three books of rubrics and the divine office in Malayalam for the laity, and a Malayalam translation of episcopal consecration.

[6] Philip, p. 430, mentions also the Evangelistic Association of the East, with fifty mission stations in Travancore and Cochin as well as seven in North Malabar, where

missionary, however, has necessarily been hampered in his noble pursuits by the lack of funds; and hopes have often been expressed for financial reinforcement from benevolent foundations abroad.

The Hierarchy

The question of the Jacobite hierarchy of Malabar in history was a simple one. Whenever the metropolitan died, the archdeacon assisting him took charge of his secular responsibilities and sent a notice to the patriarch of Antioch with the request for a new archbishop. The patriarch then selected a successor, usually a native Syrian monk, consecrated him and sent him to Malabar, where the people received him with great joy. Sometimes he also sent a suffragan with the archbishop, and later this suffragan was chosen from the celibate Indian clergy. While the foreign metropolitan dwelt on the spiritual needs of his flock, the secular matters within his jurisdiction were entrusted to his Indian advisor and archdeacon. His chief duties were the ordination of the clergy and the receipt of the tithes and free offerings which he habitually shared with the patriarch.

The patriarchal visitations of South India, otherwise known as the see of Malankara, became rather frequent after the latter part of the nineteenth century, with immense consequences on the organization of the hierarchy. During his visit to Malabar in the years 1875 and 1876, the Patriarch Peter III (1872–95) of Antioch divided the country into seven dioceses whose bishops were directly answerable to the patriarchal throne in both their spiritual and temporal functions without the intermediacy of a superior metropolitan. These were the dioceses of Kottayam, Quilon, Tumpaman, Niranam, Cochin, Angamali and Kolanceri. His bureaucratic policy was upheld by his successors until the high-handed action of the Patriarch ʿAbdallah Saṭṭūf in 1909 forced the excommunicated native Bishop Mar Dionysios to avail himself of the offices of his antagonist, the ex-Patriarch Ignatius ʿAbdul-Massīḥ, who came to India in 1912 and created the catholicate of the East, thus laying the legal foundation for the autonomy of the Syrian Jacobite Church of Kērala. The mounting political differences between the followers of the patriarch and of the catholicos for nearly fifty years have apparently been resolved in the reconciliation of 1958 by the complete enfranchisement of the Indian hierarchy.

---

voluntary workers attend to the needs of 700 families with seven churches, two chapels, four Gospel houses, one English middle school and one medical dispensary. Eight more minor associations claimed 8,000 converts in 1950. According to Cardinal Tisserant (p. 155), the Jacobite missionary societies working amongst the low-caste people claim to have converted approximately 15,000 souls between the two world wars.

It looks as if henceforth the generally acclaimed catholicos will resume all the patriarchal prerogatives in the see of Malankara which retains allegiance to the principles rather than to the person of the patriarch of Antioch.[1]

All bishops must be monks. Owing to the absence of regular monastic foundations in the accepted form in Malabar, however, the bishops are selected and consecrated from the class of celibate priests called *Rambans* who live like anchorites in solitude. Secular priests, on the other hand, marry prior to their ordination. According to Eastern church usage, if they lose their wives after ordination, they cannot re-marry. Like the Jacobites, they can be elevated to the dignity of *Chorepiskopoi* or rural vicars disposing of episcopal duties without being regular bishops.[2]

The priest (*Katanar*) is highly revered by the Indian community in spite of his relative poverty. He depends for his livelihood on the fees raised from the ceremonies of baptism, marriage and death as well as whatever free offerings as may be forthcoming on the occasion of feasts and saints' days. In public life, the priest precedes all laymen. He walks at the head of a procession, occupies the central seat of honour at any gathering, and opens a banquet after blessing the food. As a rule he is accompanied by the deacon (*Shamashe*) and retainers in the village, but not in town. The charge of ignorance, always brought up against the Jacobite clergy in the past, is steadily vanishing. At present, it is not impossible to find *Katanars* with the highest educational attainments from Western universities and theological institutions.[3]

In addition to the aforementioned classes of the Jacobite hierarchy, it appears that their settlements outside southern India and in the greater cities such as New Delhi, Calcutta, Madras, Bombay and elsewhere have made it necessary for the Church to establish its own places of worship in those localities with their *Katanars* or to borrow the Anglican churches for their meetings. A special bishop at large is consecrated for the purpose of shepherding this diaspora.[4] Moreover, owing to the sharp differences between the Southists and the Northists, and on account of the dispersion of the Southists in several dioceses, it was decided in the course of 1909 to establish the extraterritorial diocese of Knanaya under the care of a kind of itinerant bishop.[5]

[1] Father Samuel explains to me that the only link remaining between the catholicos and the patriarch is the notification of the survivor of the two whenever one of them died. The catholicate, for all practical purposes, is equal to the patriarchate. If the one is present at the elevation ceremony of the other, he has the right to officiate. Thus is defined the flimsy ties of Antioch and Kērala.

[2] Philip, p. 387, states that the married clergy consist of the *chorepiscopos*, *sovooro* (archdeacon) and *kasiso* (elder). Lower grades comprise the deacon, subdeacon, reader and so on.

[3] Brown, pp. 146, 181–2; Tisserant, pp. 154–5; Attwater, II, 240–1.

[4] Tisserant, p. 155.

[5] Attwater, II, 240.

Faith and Rites

It would be redundant to dwell at any length on the faith of the Christians of St Thomas, since they strictly follow the Jacobite teachings of the Syrians under Antioch treated elsewhere. They use the Nicene-Constantinopolitan Creed without the *filioque*. They reject the Council of Chalcedon (451) and accept the authority of the first three œcumenical councils only. They acknowledge the seven sacraments, namely, baptism, confirmation, confession, the Eucharist, ordination, matrimony and unction of the sick. They practise triple immersion in baptism. Their liturgy is the old liturgy of St James in Syriac with the prayers of the *Theotokos* (Mother of God) and the complete Eastern *Trisagion* comprising the debatable clause 'who wast crucified for us'. Nevertheless, they have numerous distinctive features which give their church a special colour and personality of its own. For a true picture of the church and community, it is essential to outline the salient peculiarities which characterize the St Thomas Christians in their historic setting.

Perhaps the most striking feature in Malabarese Christianity is that it was transmitted across the centuries to posterity through prayer and communal worship rather than systematic theology and Biblical polemic. They celebrated the holy liturgy and heard the Bible read to them in a foreign language of which they knew little. On the other hand, the entire lay community participated with religious devotion in the performance of the impressive drama of the Eucharist. In the villages, people began to flock to churches on Sundays before daybreak. Leaving their sandals on the porch, the men went to the north side of the nave, the women with covered heads went to the south side; and while the preparatory prayers and hymns were in progress, the church filled with the faithful. In an Indian church, even more than most of the Eastern rites, the laity takes a very active part in the celebration of the liturgy. Without its collaboration in the hymns and responses, the liturgy, except in cases of *requiem*, is regarded as incomplete and imperfect. To the South Indian, the church is the very centre of spiritual comfort and the meeting place of all the families living in a given area. Church-going on all possible occasions is a binding duty. To him, Christianity is a complete mode of life. His interest is not focused on the doctrinal formulas which marked the religious struggles between East and West; but, perhaps as an Indian, he is more concerned with the devotional aspect and mystical philosophy of religion. This particular quality may help in the understanding of the conversion of the St Thomas Christians from Nestorianism to Romanism and Jacobitism.

The Syrian word *Qurbana* for the Eucharist denotes to the Indian mind what it means literally, that is, offering. It is strictly speaking, sacrificial in character and conception. Brown[1] suggests that it stands in parallel to the

[1] *Indian Christians of St Thomas*, p. 295.

Hindu ancestor sacrifices. Moreover, their festivals are also marked with the Hindu paraphernalia, although the main feature remains the Christian *Qurbana*. On a festive occasion, the villagers flock to the churches during the preceding evening which is reckoned to begin the day according to the Indian church calendar. After praying and singing some hymns, the congregation marches out in procession around the church, carrying crosses, censors, flags, umbrellas, canopies and the insignia of aristocracy, making a great noise to demonstrate their joy. Afterwards they get together at the foot of the large stone cross in the churchyard where the priest resumes open-air prayer and offers incense before the crowd retraces its steps to the church. The priests together with the deacons and church elders then participate in a festive evening with a banquet. The following morning, after the celebration of the *Qurbana* and the delivery of a sermon on the saint's life which they commemorate on the day, another procession takes place. Money offerings are placed in a vessel underneath a cross; and sometimes special cakes are brought by the members, received by the priests, and redistributed after Mass.

The holy bread for the Eucharist is leavened and the use of a little oil and some salt in the dough is permitted. As a rule, it is prepared and baked on charcoal embers by the priest or a deacon very early on the day of the *Qurbana* celebration. In bygone days, when real wine was unknown, the Indians of St Thomas soaked raisins in water and used the juice as a substitute in the Eucharist.

The veneration of the cross by the Syrian Indians is very great. The towering stone crosses invariably erected in all churchyards are the material symbols of that veneration. The oath taken at the Coonen Cross in 1653 vouches for the solemnity of the occasion. Christian homes, workshops and even some of their implements are marked with crosses. The chief decoration of the church interior is the cross. The clergy, both high and low, use a small silver cross of Eastern design with a silk handkerchief hanging from it in blessing the congregation. People make the sign of the cross freely and frequently in private and public prayer and on solemn occasions.[1]

In regard to fasting, they observe exactly the same rule as their Jacobite brethren in Syria with a difference as regards the degree of austerity in the fulfilment of this duty. It is true that in modern times, the Indian Christian has become less rigid than his ancestors; but on the whole the Indian viewed the fast with solemnity as an important religious obligation. Apart from completely avoiding animal products, they refrained from drinking toddy and

[1] Brown, p. 279, seems to think that this usage is parallel to the Hindu custom of signing with a cross the palm of the hand of a man to whom one speaks, as well as the Hindu custom of signing themselves with a swastika at the morning devotion. The great veneration of the Cross, however, is general in Eastern Christendom, and a more likely proposition is the parallel with the Nestorians, who use no other decoration in their churches than a simple Cross, not a Crucifix.

chewing betel – the equivalent of modern smoking. The Indians were scandalized in the seventeenth century on noticing that the Portuguese ate fish during Lent. To obliterate all animal traces from their daily living, they plastered the floors of their houses and changed their kitchen utensils. The older generation habitually broke the fast only once after sunset. The Wednesday at the middle of the great fast as well as the fortieth day and Maundy Thursday are three occasions on which the Indians customarily hold general family reunions for the commemoration of the Last Supper. Brown[1] says that they prepared a special kind of unleavened black loaf crossed in the middle with a palm leaf to be broken into thirteen parts for distribution by the head of the family together with a special drink made of coconut milk, molasses and plantain to replace wine. Vows to fast for a year were not uncommon, and some pious old folk fasted forever. Of course, complete abstention from food or drink was obligatory before communion. A priest celebrating the *Qurbana* also avoided talking to non-Christians or riding a vehicle driven by one of them. Apparently the idea of Hindu and caste pollution lay behind this.

The Christians of St Thomas used to interpret the resurrection on the Day of Judgment literally in the corporal rising of the dead. Accordingly, they abhorred the Indian custom of cremation of human remains. It is stated that older people who lost a tooth guarded it closely for burial with their bodies after they died, so that when they came to life again on the Last Day, the tooth would be replaced and the body remain intact.[2]

Clerical vestments are identical with those of the Jacobites, save for a few minor innovations under the influence of Rome and the West. Perhaps the more noticeable feature of alien origin is the episcopal crown which is a peculiar combination of the Roman mitre and the Syrian Crown. According to some native church historians, a priest in full vestments is supposed to represent a two-winged angel, and the bishop a six-winged seraph.[3] The ringing of bells and the clashing of cymbals is customary as an accompaniment to church chanting.[4]

The church has been the throbbing heart of the religious and social life of the community from antiquity. The Malabarese countryside is dotted with parish churches with their peculiar ecclesiastical architecture. On closer examination, however, the interior is found to retain the main characteristic divisions of a Jacobite church in Syria: nave, chancel slightly raised and bordered with a low railing, a sanctuary elevated one or two steps upward and east from the chancel and comprising a high altar and two side ones for concelebration. The exterior, on the other hand, presents a different picture. With its gabled roof, usually in three successive stages or grades, the highest

[1] Op. cit., pp. 277–8.
[2] Brown, p. 295.
[3] Philip, p. 396.
[4] Fortescue, p. 378.

to the east in the shape of a square tower with a pyramidal top, the church is built in the midst of a considerably open yard. Like an Indian temple, that space is walled and has four entrances in the middle of the four sides facing the four cardinal points. The door of the church itself, always to the west, opens up into a long vestibule or narthex lined with seats or benches. At the end of this vestibule, a substantial door leads to the nave, a kind of hall without aisles or columns. The ceiling reaches its highest point in the east over the sanctuary. The whole is dimly lighted by a few small windows, and the congregation depends essentially on candles during the service.

Pre-Portuguese churches, either in stone or woodwork, are rather rare. Cardinal Tisserant mentions a Buddhist temple transformed into a Christian church at Thiruvancode in Travancore, as well as a Jacobite church at Chengannur probably dating from the thirteenth century.[1] The Indians do not use images or crucifixes, but a simple cross and only a few icons or wall paintings. Stone lintels and arches are sometimes moulded with peacocks and crosses in the current motif of Malabar.[2] Portuguese influence is more apparent in some churches than others. Specimens of older crosses bear much resemblance to Syrian originals with Pahlevi inscriptions prior to the advent of the Portuguese. A baptismal font in the Syro-Malabar church of Epadally has a frieze of lotus flowers below the rim and sits on four Asiatic lions at the base.[3] This is unmistakably due to the influence of pre-Portuguese Hindu art. Another font at the Katutturutti church also shows the Hindu influence in decoration.[4] Stone lamp-posts of Hindu type are also seen in the Cennanur churchyard.[5] Still more common are the open-air crosses on carved stone bases of some size, while others are hewn in relief on slabs bearing traces of both Syrian and Hindu arts.

The impact of local motifs and manners on the art and religious life of the Syrians of Malabar has imparted a romantic colour to their ancient form of Christianity. Their religion has been tainted by a multitude of superstitious practices, but these are rapidly receding before the tide of modern education. Instances of these taints have been given, and even more can be named such as sorcery,[6] exorcism[7] and a curious adaptation of the picturesque ceremony

[1] *Eastern Christianity in India*, Plates II(2) and III(1).

[2] Brown, p. 203.

[3] Tisserant, Plate III(2).

[4] Brown, Plate V(a).

[5] Ibid., Plate V(b).

[6] Ibid., p. 201. Brown mentions a book of sorcery entitled *Parisman*, which was condemned by the synod of Diamper. Another is the 'Book of Destiny' or 'Lots' (*Vapustakam*) which, when opened haphazard, provided the solution of a problem by the picture or passage to strike the eye at first.

[7] Ibid., p. 280. In cases of hysteria or mental disturbance, evil spirits were blamed. They were driven out by burning a palm Cross and infusing its ashes in water to be taken by the sick person on Hosanna Sunday. A prayer book was placed under his pillow to prevent recurrence. If the fit recurred, the priest exorcised the spirit by placing an open Gospel on the sick person's head and reading a text while signing the Cross on the forehead. All

of the washing of the feet,[1] annually performed by Eastern bishops on Maundy Thursday, but with a totally different interpretation. If we are able to overlook these accretions (and who can pretend complete freedom from the influence of superstition?), the profundity of their natural and historic piety begins to shine. Paradoxically speaking, the observer may well wonder whether the advent of the proselytizing emissaries of other creeds, both Roman and Protestant, from the West, as well as the free use of Malayalam have enhanced the cause of religion and brought those simple people nearer to God. Whereas the old way with the Syriac medium brought faith home to the Syrian through worship and communicated the Bible lections through folk music and song,[2] the modern way with its strong appeal to the enquiring mind seems to have disturbed the long established peace of a people living under the Lord.[3]

---

present recited the Creed. Sometimes the word 'faith' in Syriac is written by the priest on paper to be burnt and the ashes given to the patient in water to drink. Also charms of the Lord's Prayer in Syriac were tied to the arm in a small silver or gold container.

[1] Brown, pp. 276–7. Brown describes in detail the ceremony, usually performed by a wealthy person. Nine bearded men were made to bathe on a Saturday, first in oil, then in water. The rich sponsor then presented them with new clothing and took them to church for the Sunday *Qurbana*, in the celebration of which they participated with three priests, making a total of twelve in all – the number of the Apostles. The three priests also received new vestments. Afterwards, the men were taken in the priests' company to the sponsor's home, and at the threshold they again washed their feet in two basins before proceeding barefooted on strips of cloth to special benches in the yard. Here the sponsor poured water on the old men's feet, collected it in a large brass plate and dried their feet with a cloth tied to his waist. The water gathered from the last washing of the feet in the plate was handed to a priest who carefully poured it in a bottle without losing a drop and returned it to the sponsor. A feast for the twelve men was followed by the feeding of twelve children. The bottled water worked medical miracles, relieving mothers in pain at child-birth and healing diseased limbs.

[2] Ibid., p. 280. Brown states that he was told by old men that, before the publication of the Malayalam Bible and the spread of education, children used to learn Bible stories in the form of songs. On further Indian Syrian rites and ceremonials, see Pothan, pp. 77–90.

[3] Pothan, p. 101, closes his work with the following significant appeal: 'The motto borne on the crest of the old state of Travancore was "Charity is our Household Divinity". The people of Kērala can do no better than adopt the theme of that motto, and earnestly strive to cultivate charity, both in thought as well as in deed.'

PART VI

THE MARONITE CHURCH

24 • PRELUDE

In recent times, the Maronite church has become the chief bulwark of Roman Catholicism in the Middle East. It constitutes a solid block of Roman Christians occupying the major part of Lebanon at a focal point in Greater Syria. It is highly organized, and its hierarchy is composed of highly educated men, at least in its upper strata. With the passing of years, the Maronite congregation has cultivated a growing affinity towards Rome and begun to look West rather than East. Therefore, the expediency of surveying its history amidst the family of ancient Eastern churches which are neither Roman nor Greek in character might be questioned. Notwithstanding the fact that many notable Maronites, including distinguished members of the clergy,[1] have written lengthy treatises to exculpate their church from ever having been outside the pale of the Roman commonwealth, the historical facts leave no doubt as to the purely Eastern origin of Maronite Christianity. As will be seen from the following chapter, the process of Romanization started modestly with the Crusades for purposes of expediency rather than conviction. Even some of the most fervent Latins[2] in Rome never conceal the

[1] There are numerous examples of this tendency. The Maronite patriarch Stephan al-Duwayhi (the Latin Aldoënsis, 1630–1704) wrote an Arabic 'History of the Maronite Community' (*Tārīkh al-Ṭā'ifah al-Mārūniyah*), (Beirūt, 1890), where he defended Maronite loyalty to Rome from the earliest times. Then also the Maronite priest of Cyprus, Michel A. Ghabriel, *Histoire de l'Église Syriaque Maronite d'Antioche* (in Arabic: *Tārīkh al-Kanīsah al-Anṭākiyah al-Suryāniyah*), 2 vols. in 3 (Ba'abda, Lebanon, 1900–4), is highly apologetic. Archbishop Yūsuf Duryān, who acted for the patriarch in the Egyptian diocese, wrote a book in Arabic in 1911 on the origins of the Maronite Community (*Lubāb al-Barāhīn al-Jaliyah*), where he tried to establish the continuity of Maronite obedience to Rome but ended up by saying that they were undeniably Catholic from the twelfth century (p. 346). In recent times, P. Raphael, *The Role of the Maronites in the Return of the Oriental Churches*, English tr. P. A. Eid (Youngstown, Ohio, 1946), depicts the Maronite disciples of the founder of the Maronite Church, St Maron, as the staunch advocates of the western Chalcedonian profession in the fifth century (p. 14). The same system is maintained by Bishop P. Dib, *L'Église Maronite jusqu'à la fin du moyen âge* (Paris, 1930), as well as the historian of Syria, Archbishop Yūsuf al-Dibs, especially in his work on the Maronites, *Al-Jāmi' al-Mufaṣṣal fī Tārīkh al-Mawārinah al-Mu'aṣṣal* (Beirūt, 1905).

[2] Al-Duwayhi's above-mentioned work contains extensive chapters (pp. 358 et seq.) in defence of Maronite loyalty to Rome and enumerates those who denied this in both East and West, including Maronite Patriarch Jibrā'īl ibn al-Qelā'ī, Arnoldus Albertinus and the

view that the Maronites, originally Monophysite, then Monothelete, finally joined Rome and became confirmed Catholics in the later Middle Ages or in more recent times. Nevertheless, the Maronite church has preserved many features which make it almost unique in the history of Roman Catholicism. In the first place, it has retained its local independence under a Maronite patriarch, locally elected and merely ratified by the Roman pope. The Maronites cherish this local autonomy which their leaders have persistently defended. In the second place, it has preserved its ancient Syriac liturgy, still commonly in use in all Maronite churches with minor emendations to ensure conformity with the Roman profession and papal obedience. In the third place, the lower clergy have continued their old family status as married clerks, though the custom has started to die out in recent times, in the higher ranks of the hierarchy. If a member of that church is asked whether he is a Catholic, his spontaneous response is that he is a Maronite. There can be no doubt that the Maronite church came into being as a member of the Antiochian Syrian group which gave rise during the later œcumenical movement to the Orthodox Church of Antioch, the Jacobite or West Syrian Church, the Nestorian or East Syrian Church and finally to the Maronites, whose patriarch to the present day carries the title 'Maronite Patriarch of Antioch and All the Orient'. It is therefore only right that an account of this august church should appear in these pages with all its ancient sister churches.

The Maronites are one of the most interesting minorities in the Middle East. As the descendants of the Phœnicians, they have preserved the basic traits of their great ancestors. Like the Phœnicians, they still are born successful traders; and like them, too, they have retained their love for overseas adventure. It is said that there are about 100,000 Maronites overseas in the Americas, Egypt, Cyprus and elsewhere. The Maronites, the majority among the people of Lebanon, have lent strength to the Maronite church in both the religious and the political life of the country. The Lebanese population in the year 1913 consisted of 414,800, of whom 329,482 were Christians including 242,308 Maronites. The rest were Druzes and Muslims of both the Sunnite

---

Jesuit Juan Battista as well as many others. P. Dib's work is largely apologetic at its inception, first in vindicating the Maronites from Monophysitism (pp. 51–61), and next from Monotheletism (pp. 63–143). Nevertheless, the Catholic authors of the West continue to treat the subject quite differently. D. Attwater, *The Christian Churches of the East* Vol. I, pp. 165 et seq., speaking of the Maronites, mentions their 'perpetual orthodoxy' as a sixteenth-century tradition, not sanctioned by earlier writings, now abandoned except by a few die-hards. R. Janin, *Les églises orientales et les rites orientaux* (Paris, 1926), also another Latin, repudiates that 'perpetual orthodoxy' of the Maronites as entirely belonging to the realm of legend (p. 552). On the Patriarch Stephen al-Duwayhi, see al-Dibs, *Al-Jāmiʿ*, pp. 361–68, and Graf, III, 361–78; Ghabriel, *Hist.* (Arabic), III, 495–540. The last contains a list of twenty works by al-Duwayhi (III, 538–40).

and Shīʿite creeds. Ten years later, however, with the extension of Lebanese frontiers beyond Tripoli and Sidon, the Maronite majority was somewhat affected. The people of Lebanon increased to 628,863, but the new addition was preponderantly Muslim.[1]

The nature of the country has rendered it a stronghold of the Maronite church. In the west, its border is the Mediterranean shore roughly from the Orontes to the Leontes Rivers, and the country extends inland to comprise two ranges of Lebanese mountains running parallel with the sea. A narrow wedge of plain or richly arable plateau lying between them, 110 miles in length and from six to ten miles in width, is the ancient Cœle-Syria (hollow Syria) now known as al-Biqāʿ from Arab times. Though spreading everywhere throughout the country, the Maronites and their church have always preferred the mountains which are Lebanon proper. Those rugged heights have proved to be a haven of peace to which their tribes together with others of Druze and Shīʿite origin fled from their persecutors throughout the Middle Ages and under Turkish dominion in modern times. As a rule, the Maronites style themselves the people of the mountain (*Ahl al-Jabal*), and the chief seat of the Maronite patriarchate has for many centuries been at Bkirki in the rocky ravines of the Qadisha Valley. In the twin chains of Lebanese mountains with their snow-clad crests, the fathers of that church built their numerous monasteries which became the strongholds of the faith and defied an endless succession of persecutions and invasions. It was here, too, that they preserved the light of learning from extinction in the darkest hours of their long and chequered history.

[1] P. K. Hitti, *Lebanon in History* (London, 1957), pp. 489–90; P. Rondot, *Les Chrétiens d'Orient* (Paris, 1955), p. 248. The latter provides an estimate of 793,000, consisting of 396,000 Christians, 330,000 Muslims, and 53,000 Druzes together with some thousand Jews and others. He argues that if the Armenians and the Druzes are removed from both sides, the Muslims will fall to 330,000 and the Christians will remain stationary at 358,000 – Mgr. Raymond Etteldorf, *The Catholic Church in the Middle East* (New York, 1959), pp. 100, 104, reports that the present population of Lebanon is 1,303,939, with 508,841 Muslims almost equally divided between Sunnites and Shīʿites, the rest being Christians of whom 37 per cent are Catholics. The Maronites are the largest Catholic group, amounting to 377,544 adherents. A. H. Hourani, *Syria and Lebanon – A Political Essay*, 3rd ed. (Oxford, 1954), p. 121, quotes the following figures from the 1932 census: 383,180 Muslims (175,925 Sunnites, 104,208 Shīʿites, 53,047 Druzes), and 392,544 Christians, of whom 226,378 are Maronites and the rest belong to other creeds.

25 • ORIGINS AND DEVELOPMENT

St Maro and the Age of Legend

The early history of Christianity in Lebanon is somewhat obscure. Unconfirmed reports put it that St Peter the Apostle himself was the first to sow the seeds of the new faith amongst the Phœnicians, whom he affiliated to the ancient patriarchate of Antioch. Although not unlikely, this contention must remain in the realm of mere conjecture. Another legend of great interest is that one of the early pontiffs of the see of Rome was of Lebanese origin. This was St Anicetus, who became Pope about 157 A.D. and earned the crown of martyrdom between 161 and 168 A.D.[1]

The earliest irrefutable tradition of Christianity in the Lebanese mountains can be traced only as far back as the fourth century when St Maro,[2] also written St Maron, (350–433) espoused the monastic life and retired to live as a recluse on the banks of the Orontes between Apamea (Afamiyah) and Emesa (Ḥomṣ). It is said that eight hundred[3] new monks joined his community and, under his leadership, began to preach the Gospel in the surrounding country. The personality of this great Christian is established beyond all doubt by authentic references in the contemporary sources. St John Chrysostom mentioned him as a solitary priest in one of the epistles dated 404 A.D. Theodoret (ca. 393–ca. 485), bishop of Cyrrhus, a native of Antioch and a renowned writer, also referred to his great sanctity and good work. Apparently, Theodoret was well acquainted with some of St Maro's disciples.[4] After his death, the community of his followers constructed a church over his tomb, destined to become an important sanctuary, and ultimately a monastery arose around it. This became the focal centre whence the early Christian missionaries sallied in all directions to complete the

[1] Raphael, p. 12.

[2] Yūsuf al-Dibs, Maronite archbishop of Beirūt, *al-Jāmiʿ al-Mufaṣṣal fī Tārīkh al-Mawārinah al-Muʾṣṣal* (Beirūt, 1905), pp. 3–13; Michel A. Ghabriel, *Histoire de l'Église Syriaque Maronite d'Antioche*, I, 84–137.

[3] Raphael, p. 13.

[4] Amongst them were St Jacob the Solitary, Saint Limné and a holy woman called St Domnina; Dib, *Église Maronite*, p. 40.

conversion of their people. It was enriched by a continuous stream of donations. The monastery had indeed suffered much destruction in the Persian wars, but Justinian included it in his vast project of restoration and foundation of ecclesiastical buildings throughout the Byzantine Empire.

A landmark in its pre-Arab history is related to the reign of the Byzantine Emperor Heraclius. After his successful crusade against the Persians prior to the advent of Islam, the emperor visited the site of the monastery in 628 to discuss with the monks of St Maro his new ideas about mending the rifts in Christendom. Heraclius succeeded in winning them to the new doctrine of Macedonius, which he reckoned to be a potent factor in exterminating the Monophysite schism stemming from Chalcedonian differences. That was the doctrine of Monotheletism, according to which the will of Jesus Christ, both divine and human, was defined as one and indivisible. Evidently the Monophysites, who believed in the single or rather united nature of Jesus, were not attracted by the new doctrine, and the orthodox Western group later condemned it as a heresy. But the Syrians of Lebanon remained adamant in their Monotheletic profession and gradually segregated themselves from both the orthodox and Jacobite sections of the population. Monotheletism grew in the long run to be identified with their national and religious aspirations. In reality, it would appear that two decisive circumstances helped in the process of freeing their Church from Western influences, the one general and the other particular. First, the Arab Conquest put an end to the Christian persecutions of heretical groups emanating from Byzantium. Secondly, during the first decade of the eighth century, serious differences led to the exile of the patriarch of Antioch to the city of Constantinople, and the Lebanese Christians resolved to elect their own national patriarch, who assumed the title 'Patriarch of Antioch and the East' which he holds to the present day. Thus we see the 'Maronite' church emerging as the personification of a nation from both the political and religious angles.

St John Maron and the Maronites

If the fourth-century St Maro was the apostle of Lebanese Christianity, it may be argued that St John[1] Maron (Yuḥanna Mārūn) of the seventh and

[1] Assemani, *Bibl. Orientalis*, I, 496–520; Al-Duwayhi, pp. 70 et seq.; Janin, pp. 552–3; Bernard G͟hobaira al-G͟hazīri, *Rome et l'église Syrienne-Maronite, 517–1531* (Beirūt and Paris, 1906), pp. 50–9; Ṭubia al-ʿUnaysi, *Silsilah Tārīk͟hiyah lil-Baṭārikah al-Anṭākiyīn* (on the Maronite Patriarchs of Antioch; Rome, 1937), p. 14; al-Dibs, *Al-Jāmiʿ*, pp. 63–138; Ghabriel, *Histoire* (Arabic), I, 244–494. The last publication contains a Syriac text of some of the Saint's epistles on heresies of his time together with an Arabic translation (I, 337–408 and 409–40).

eighth centuries, often confused with his predecessor, was the real apostle of the Maronite church and the founder of national and ecclesiastical Maronitism. There is hardly any original contemporary material on the life of the new hero, but the story of the times may be gathered from later mediæval literature, presumably derived from more ancient records which disappeared in the successive massacres and destruction of Maronites and their foundations across the centuries. The monks of the old St Maro Monastery were situated too near to Antioch, the patriarchal seat, to enjoy autonomous peace. St John Maron led his flock to the mountain fastnesses and to isolated villages for safety. Ultimately he became their patriarch-elect from 685 to 707. During his reign, the Maronites fell prey to both the Greeks and the Arabs, who fought one another continuously in Lebanon, and neither spared the inhabitants of the land. In 694, the Greeks sacked the Monastery of St Maro and killed some five hundred monks of the Maronite settlement.[1] The Arabs later completed the destruction of the ancient establishment, and St John Maron had no choice but to entrench his patriarchate and his Maronite mountaineers in the rugged valley of Qadīsha. There they remained impervious to western influences until the Crusades. Maronite historians tend to accept the view that the church and the nation became identified with him in name and it would therefore be erroneous to use this new title before his time.[2]

The last Umayyad caliph, Marwān II (744–59), selected a puppet patriarch of Antioch by the name of Theophylactus bar Qanbara, who procured his master's authority to chastise the unruly Maronites with the help of Muslim soldiers.[3] By the first half of the tenth century, it may be assumed that the Monastery of St Maro, which had been the cradle of Maronite Christianity, disappeared from existence as a religious foundation. Nevertheless, the famous Arab geographer, historian and traveller al-Masʿūdi, writing about 950 on the subject of the Maronites, states that they had once possessed a huge monastery in the valley of the Orontes with three hundred monastic cells and considerable wealth including much gold, silver and jewels. He then says that its destruction was precipitated by the Arabs and the caliph's oppression. Al-Masʿūdi knew that the Maronites were then Monotheletes and that they differed from the Melkites, the Nestorians and the Jacobites, and that they were very numerous in Lebanon.[4]

It is very diffcult to provide any detailed account of the Maronite Christians during the Arab period prior to the Crusades. Although they occupied

[1] Al-Duwayhi, pp. 80–1.

[2] This is the view advanced by the older author Jibrā'īl ibn al-Qelāʿī, who wrote in 1494 and was accepted by al-Duwayhi, pp. 87–8.

[3] Dib, pp. 146–51; Duryān, pp. 159–61.

[4] *Bibliotheca Geographorum Arabicorum*, ed. J. de Goeje (Leiden, 1894), VIII, 153; Bernard Ghobaira al-Ghazīri, pp. 48–9. Yūsuf Duryān, pp. 207–9; Dib, p. 42.

fortified positions in the Lebanese mountains, they also engaged in trade and navigation. Members of the Syrian communities piloted ships for the Arab armies and the merchant marine. Others served in the administration of the caliphs and sultans. Some even served in the armed forces, and both the Muslim and the Christian learned to live side by side under the tolerant rule of the caliphs, except on occasions where the caliph's agents rather than the caliph incited revolt by their local exactions. The revolt of Lebanon in 759–60 spread from the mountainous district of Monaitra to the plains of al-Biqāʿ. The Lebanese mountaineers were encouraged in their abortive uprising by the temporary irruptions of Byzantine troops in the area.[1]

In the meantime, while gradually establishing their national individuality in the isolated mountains of Lebanon, the Maronites made a steady expansion in the surrounding country. Their life in the mountains did not lend itself to the foundation of big cities, and a kind of feudalism arose in the smaller villages, where the church became a great force in the religious and economic existence of the people. Numerous monasteries and churches were erected and supported by vast feudal estates. Nevertheless, considerable numbers of Maronites from Lebanon could be found in the outlying cities. Johannes Wirzburg, the eleventh-century pilgrim, found them established in Jerusalem.[2] A substantial group of Maronites obeyed the rule of a Maronite bishop, Thomas of 'Kaphartab', and in 1140 a Maronite chief by the name of Simon seized ʿAntab, north of the aforementioned city. Again in Cyprus, the Maronites had appeared from the ninth century and built their own foundations. They owned a monastery on that island in the first half of the twelfth century. The Maronites were on friendly terms with the Nestorians of Iraq and Persia, and this afforded them an opportunity of conducting their business at Baghdad and other Eastern cities of the Arab empire.[3]

The Crusades and Romanization

It was during the age of the Crusades that the Maronites were brought into direct contact with the nations of the West and with the Church of Rome. Like the Armenians, the Maronites appear to have welcomed the Crusaders as co-religionists and helpers against the ravages of some of their Muslim rulers. From the beginning of the movement they seem to have thrown in their lot with the invaders. They knew the mountain paths, valleys and gorges of the Holy Land, and consequently they became valuable guides to

[1] H. Lammens, *La Syrie – Précis historique*, 2 vols. (Beirūt, 1921), I, 114–17, 131–2.
[2] Al-Ghazīri, pp. 72–3.
[3] Dib, pp. 166–77; al-Ghazīri, pp. 74–84.

the first Crusaders in a strange land.[1] At a later date, their able archers served as an auxiliary force on the side of the Crusaders.[2] Marriage between the Western settlers and the native Christians produced that new mixed race known as the 'Pullani' in the histories of the Holy War, and most of these must necessarily have included the Lebanese people. Some of the inhabitants of the new county of Tripoli were Maronites.[3] Their clergy adopted a number of Latin usages hitherto unknown in the Eastern churches, such as wearing the mitre and the ring, and many native Maronites freely attended the Latin churches of the Crusaders. Then in the course of the year 1182, we are told by the famous historian of the Holy War, Archbishop William of Tyre, that by divine inspiration forty thousand Maronites descended from the mountain *en masse* to abjure their ancient heresy of Monotheletism and offer obedience to the pontiff of Rome in the presence of Amaury, the Latin patriarch of Antioch. If we regard these as having consisted solely of men, as might be expected in the social traditions of the East in those days, the total membership of the Maronite community in the twelfth century may well be envisaged as possibly exceeding one hundred thousand men, women and children.[4] The Dominican pilgrim and crusading propagandist Burchard reiterates a similar assumption in 1283 by asserting that the Maronites could furnish the Christian host in the Holy Land with forty thousand combatants;[5] and as late as 1336, after the extermination of Latin domination of the Holy Land, another propagandist, a German Dominican by the name of Wilhelm von Boldensele (alias Otto von Neuhaus), wrote that he received assurances that the Maronites would fight with the Western Christians in the next Crusade against the Mamlūks.[6]

The opening of the road to Rome by the Crusades is confirmed in a report by the Maronite prelate and the first real historian of the Maronite Church, Jibrā'īl ibn al-Qelāʿi (d. 1516),[7] who wrote in 1494 that there had been an

[1] Dib, p. 184; Lammens, I, 248.

[2] Archbishop Duryān in his historical account, *Nubdhah Tārīkhiyah* (3rd edn.; Beirūt, 1919), pp. 77 et seq., shows emphatically the bellicose nature of the Maronite mountaineers and their skill in archery.

[3] S. Runciman, *History of the Crusades*, 3 vols. (Cambridge, 1951–4), II, 294, 322.

[4] Dib (p. 185) is of the opinion that the group was all men, since William of Tyre, *A History of Deeds Done beyond the Sea*, English tr. E. A. Babcock and A. C. Krey, 2 vols. (New York, 1943), II, 458–9, adds that they were brave men, *viri fortes*: 'They were a stalwart race, valiant fighters, and of great service to the Christians in the difficult engagements which they so frequently had with their enemies.'

[5] Cf. Dib, p. 186.

[6] Atiya, *The Crusade in the Later Middle Ages* (London, 1938), p. 161.

[7] Jibrā'īl was the first great author in Arabic on the history of the Maronites up to his time, and was a theological and homiletic writer as well as a poet of some merit. His poetry was quoted by al-Duwayhi (p. 368). A Franciscan himself, he studied in Rome and later became Maronite bishop of Cyprus. He died in 1516. Most of his works, still in manuscript, are preserved in the Maronite School in Rome and in the Vatican. Graf, I, 6–7; II, 43; III, 309–33; al-Dibs, *Al-Jāmiʿ al-Mufaṣṣal*, pp. 310–12; Kamal S. Salibi,

exchange of fifteen letters between the popes of Rome and the Lebanese patriarchs, of which nine have been known to exist in modern times.[1] In reality, since their early conversion to Catholicism, we note that the Roman see worked hard on the Maronites. Patriarch Jeremiah al-'Amshīṭī was persuaded to go to Rome in person and to attend the Lateran Council of 1215. On his return to Lebanon, the reigning Pope Innocent III dispatched in his company a papal legate to secure from his congregation a solemn declaration of the profession of the faith according to the rites of Rome. Moreover, Franciscan and Dominican missionaries[2] came to Lebanon, to be followed later by members of the newly founded Society of Jesus, while Maronite students were invited to the Vatican. In 1584, Pope Gregory XIII dedicated the Maronite College (Collegium Maronitarum) to receive them in Rome.[3] The most illustrious amongst its graduates was undoubtedly Joseph Simonius Assemani (Yūsuf Samʿān al-Samʿānī, 1687–1768), originally a native of Tripoli, whose contribution to Oriental scholarship was phenomenal. In addition to his monumental *Bibliotheca Orientalis*,[4] he was largely responsible for the introduction of the ancient Syriac liturgies to the Western mind.[5] He handled most of the Vatican manuscripts in Syriac, Arabic, Hebrew, Persian, Turkish and Ethiopic while pursuing his researches on the Eastern Churches.

Notwithstanding all these fervent approaches, and in spite of the persistent apologetics of Maronite authors, it would be an error to consider that the Romanization of the Maronite people became complete in the course of the Middle Ages. The majority of the Maronite people were unaware of the real significance of communion with Rome and continued to worship in Syriac according to their older traditions. Then the reconquest of the Holy Land, completed in 1291 by the fall of Acre to the Mamlūk Sultans, must have consequently severed the relations between Rome and the Maronites. We do hear of an occasional Latin mission to Lebanon, such as that of the Franciscan Lewis de Ripario, who was enjoined by Pope Calixtus IV in 1475

Maronite Historians of Mediæval Lebanon (Beirūt, 1959), pp. 23–87, 236–8, 239. Salibi deals mainly with ibn al-Qelāʿi (d. 1516), al-Duwayhi (d. 1704) and Ṭannūs Shidyāq (d. 1861).

[1] Dib, p. 197.

[2] Ibid., pp. 197 et seq.; al-Ghazīri, pp. 84 et seq.

[3] Janin, p. 554.

[4] *Bibliotheca Orientalis Clementino-Vaticana in qua Manuscriptos Codices Syriacos, Arabicos, Persicos, Turcicos, Hebraicos, Samaritanos, Armenicos, Æthiopicos, Græcos, Ægyptiacos, Ibericos et Malabaricos, Jussu et Munificentia Clementis XI Pontificis Maximi Ex Oriente conquisitos, comparatos, avestos, et Bibliothecæ et Vaticanæ addictos Recensuit, digessit a spuriis secrevit addita singulorum auctorum vita,* Joseph Simonius Assemanus Syrus Maronita, 3 vols. in 4 (Rome, 1719–28).

[5] Al-Dibs, VIII, 553–68, and *al-Jamiʿ*, pp. 473–87; Graf, III, 444–55; Hitti, *Lebanon*, pp. 405–6.

to go to the Maronite patriarch with gifts of processional and pastoral crosses as well as an embroidered mitre.[1] But the tie with Rome was rather flimsy and even Monotheletism seemed to persist in the fifteenth century. Only in 1445 did Elias, the archbishop of Cyprus, and his congregation abjure that heresy.[2] Apparently, the Maronites were represented at the Council of Florence (1439) by a Latin Franciscan Friar John from Beirūt who submitted patriarchal letters to Pope Eugenius IV (1431–47) reassuring him of adherence to Rome. Nevertheless, as late as 1445 it was found necessary for Archbishop Elias of Cyprus and his Maronite congregation to abjure the heresy and proclaim submission to Rome. The circumstances of the diplomatic exchanges at the time of the Council of Florence and afterwards led to suspicions on the part of the Muslim governor, whose soldiers stormed and burnt the Convent of Meifūq where the patriarch resided. Many were killed in the encounter and the patriarch fled for refuge to the forbidding heights of the Qadīsha Valley in 1440, where he established his seat at the monastery of Qannūbīn,[3] still in use to the present day. So isolated was the Maronite patriarchate that when Simon ibn Ḥassān al-Ḥadathi was elected to the dignity in 1492, it was necessary for ibn al-Qelāʿi and Francesco Suriano, the Franciscan superior of the Holy Land and apostolic vicar of the East, to write two years later (1494) urging him to apply for the pallium and confirmation from Rome.[4] Actually the position of the Maronites in the Roman fold did not reach any substantial stability until the sixteenth or perhaps the seventeenth century. After the Fifth Lateran Council (1512–17), the patriarchs' direct contact with Rome was almost uninterrupted. Examples of Maronite envoys to the pope at every succession with the usual letters of submission were met with reciprocal approval, as is evident from the chronicles,[5] although on the whole the church clung faithfully to its Oriental and traditional practices. Educational missions to the Maronite College in Rome became more frequent. A prominent early example was Germanos Farḥāt, who became archbishop of Aleppo (1670–1732) and who founded the Maronite order of the Aleppine Antonian monks at Ehden.[6] Another

[1] Dib, pp. 223–4. [2] Janin, pp. 554.

[3] From the Latin *cœnobium* and the Greek *κοινοβιον*, formed of two words: *κοινος* [= common] and *βιος* [= life]; hence the place of living in common as distinct from 'hermitage', where anchorites and recluses led a completely segregated and ascetic life.

[4] Al-Duwayhi, pp. 135–7; al-ʿUnaysi, p. 31; Dib, pp. 234, 248–50.

[5] These examples become too numerous to be quoted in detail in this survey. See al-Duwayhi, pp. 148 et seq.; al-ʿUnaysi, pp. 33 et seq.

[6] Apparently he was a theological and moralist writer in Arabic and a poet of no mean merit. For details on his life and work, see Graf, III, 406–28; and al-Dibs, VIII, 571. On the interesting subject of Maronites educated in Rome, see Graf, III, 299–512; Yūsuf Elias al-Dibs, *Tārīkh Sūreya*, 8 vols., (Beirūt, 1893–1905), VII, 300 et seq. and VIII, 526 et seq.; idem, *Al-Jāmiʿ al-Mufaṣṣal*, passim., which is usually regarded as a ninth continuation volume to his 'History of Syria'. It comprises the substance of the Maronite data spread all over the original work which he concentrated in this single volume. The older work

scholar of repute was Casiri, a native of Tripoli whose original name in Arabic was Mikhā'īl al-Ghazīri (1710–91). Educated in Rome, he became librarian of the famous Escorial Library in Spain and catalogued some eighteen hundred Arabic manuscripts in its rich collections.[1]

Both Casiri and Assemani participated in the famous Lebanese synod held in 1736 at the Monastery of Saiyidat[2] al-Luwayzah (Our Lady of the Little Almond Tree) at the mouth of the Dog River (*Nahr al-Kalb*), which proved to be decisive in Romano-Maronite relations and discipline. Thirteen Maronite bishops came to this reunion which was an important landmark in Maronite Church history. Casiri represented the bishop of Tripoli, and Assemani arrived with a Latin pontifical encyclical which he translated into Arabic to serve as the basis for the ensuing discussions. Abuses were exposed, former decisions of other pro-Roman synods were affirmed, both the *filioque* and the Latin catechism were finally accepted, and the council approved of the insertion of the papal name into the Syriac liturgies, monastic life was organized on firm discipline by the total prohibition of cohabitation of monks and nuns in the same convents, and clerical marriage was strictly limited to the lower ranks. Moreover, the council made a resolution for the revision and codification of the law of personal family status, thus introducing orderly procedure in matters of matrimony, blood kinship and inheritance. This legal work was later resumed by a Maronite monk of Aleppo by the name of ʿAbdallah Qarʿali[3] (d. 1742), who was buried in the Luwayzah Monastery. However, in order to give its resolutions popular and civic support, the gathering was also attended by a strong delegation of the important Lebanese feudal families, notably the al-Khāzin Shaykhs who had been acting as French consuls-general from the time of Louis XIV.[4] The synod thus turned into something of a general council, or national assembly, according to Oriental usage. The implementation of the synodal decisions, however, was frustrated by a lamentable rift in the lines of the hierarchy

---

by De La Roque, *Voyage de Syrie et du Liban*, 2 vols. (Amsterdam, 1723), is still useful on early missions. De la Roque visited the historian Patriarch al-Duwayhi at the Monastery of Qannūbīn in 1690. Cf. Hitti, *Lebanon in History*, p. 406 nn.; Attwater, I, 167.

[1] *Bibliotheca arabico-hispana Escurialensis sive Librorum omnium MSS. quos Arabice ab auctoribus magnam partem Arabo-Hispanis compositos Bibliotheca Cœnobii Escurialensis complectitur, recensio et explanatio opera et studio Michaelis Casiri*, etc., 2 vols. (Madrid, 1760–70). Ghazīri died in Madrid on 12 March 1794. Graf, III, 475–6; al-Dibs, *Al-Jāmiʿ al-Mufaṣṣal*, pp. 490–1; Hitti, *Lebanon*, p. 406.

[2] Al-Dibs, *Tārīkh Sūriye*, VIII, 573–6; Hitti, *Lebanon*, p. 406.

[3] Graf, III, 400–6.

[4] See letter addressed to Abu-Nofal Nādir al-Khāzin by Louis XIV (1643–1715), king of France. The letter is dated 1659 and has been translated into Arabic by al-Duwayhi, *Maronite History*, pp. 233–4. It has also been reproduced by Duryān, *History* (pp. 175–7) where other communications are also quoted (pp. 173, 178, 194 et seq.).

and by rivalry for the patriarchal throne in those decades.[1] Consequently, a series of synods was summoned by the successive patriarchs for the ratification of the aforementioned decisions. This culminated in the Synod of Ghosta[2] in 1768 during the reign of Yūsuf Stephan, but this synod also was shrouded in darkness by the patriarchal support of Hindiyah (*alias* Ḥinna ʿUjaymi), a nun of the Sacred Heart and a curious visionary who claimed to be hypostatically united to the second person of the Trinity and became extremely conspicuous among the common people. The patriarch was eventually suspended and summoned to Rome to answer for his errors.[3] Strictly speaking, the state of anarchy in which Lebanon found itself immersed, coupled with incessant Christian persecutions, was reflected in the Maronite Church and patriarchate; and it may be assumed with some reservation that the final stabilization of ecclesiastical status within the framework of Roman Christianity but with the retention of a degree of Eastern doctrine and traditions came about in the long reign of Patriarch Paul Mubārak Masʿad (1854–90).[4] He was an old pupil of the College of Rome, where he became conversant with Latin and Italian in addition to Syriac and Arabic. He assisted personally at the eighteenth-century celebrations commemorating St Peter and St Paul in 1867. He held a synod at Bkirki in 1856 which was commended by the holy see, but he preferred to send four Maronite bishops to attend the Vatican Council without going himself for fear of pontifical pressures on him to renounce his local historic privileges. He wrote several treatises of a theological character and seems to have compiled new material for the continuation of Duwayhi's famous history. Al-Dibs[5] attempted to procure this material and edit it, but the patriarch finally answered that he was unable to locate it. Though the loyalty of the Maronites to Rome became incontestable in every detail, the Church continued to cherish several Eastern ways and traditions. The patriarchs settled down at Qannūbīn in winter, and Bkirki is their summer resort to this day.

A concluding remark to elucidate the paradox of the Maronite position *vis-à-vis* Rome appears to be of topical importance at this juncture. In spite

[1] This started with the election of Simon ʿAwwād, a graduate of the College of Rome and archbishop of Damascus in 1716, to the patriarchal dignity, and of Ṭubya al-Khāzin, archbishop of Aleppo, as antipatriarch; and the difference was settled by Pope Benedict XIV in 1743 in favour of the former candidate. Al-ʿUnaysi, pp. 51 et seq.

[2] The deliberations and decrees of that synod have been published in a brochure in Arabic on Maronite synods entitled '*Al-Mājāmiʿ al-Mārūniyah*' (Beirūt, 1904), pp. 18–38; al-Dibs, VIII, 577–80.

[3] Al-ʿUnaysi, pp. 55–7; al-Dibs, VIII, 526–39. On Ḥinna ʿUjaimi, see vol. I of the following important collection of original documents on Maronite history ed. Paul Massad and Nassīb Wehaiba al-Khāzin, *Documents inédits*, 3 vols. (Achkouth, Lebanon, 1956–8).

[4] Al-Dibs, *Tārīkh Sūriye*, VIII, 753–8; idem, *Al-Jāmiʿ*, pp. 551–7; al-ʿUnaysi, pp. 69–70; Ghabriel, *Hist.*, II, 2, 788–801.

[5] *Tārīkh Sūriye*, VIII, 757; also *Al-Jāmiʿ* p. 555.

of all the fervent apologetic literature by Maronite writers and the outspoken protests of Maronite ecclesiastics to establish the unbroken allegiance of their Church to Rome, it will be noticed that no Maronite was willing at any time to give up completely the acquired independence of their isolated mountain domiciles, and the prelates were eager to avoid the renunciation of their local traditional prerogatives in accordance with the habits prevailing in all the remaining Eastern Churches from high Christian antiquity. They preserved Syriac as the religious language and have never given up the use of the ancient Syriac liturgy of their forefathers, though they amended and incorporated minor sections to harmonize it with Roman rites. In reality, until some time in modern history, perhaps the seventeenth century (some say the eighteenth), they continued to use Syriac as the spoken language of their community. It would not be erroneous to accept the assertion that the Maronites retained their local independence in their invulnerable mountain heights until roughly the middle of the last century. This paradox of a theoretical subservience to the West and Rome together with a marked tendency towards social and religious independence and separatism may be illustrated in the majority of writings by Maronite authors, and it may be helpful to quote the works of a modern Maronite prelate by way of illustration. Yūsuf Duryān, titular archbishop of Tarsus and Maronite vice-patriarch for the diocese of Egypt, who wrote a book already quoted to prove the unwavering allegiance of his church to Rome since the fifth century,[1] also wrote a short historical account of the Maronite people in which his thesis is the establishment of the idea that they had become independent in the Lebanese mountains from time immemorial.[2] The Maronites will be more understood only when viewed against this background with all its complicated and contradictory circumstances.

[1] *Labāb al-Barāhīn al-Jaliyah* (see above).

[2] See especially the concluding chapters (pp. 262–315) of his work. Full title: *Nubdhah Tārīkhiyah fi 'Aṣl al-Ṭā'ifah al-Mārūniyah wa-Istiqlāliha bi-Jabal Lubnān min Qadīm al-Dahr ḥatta al-'ān* (Historical Account of the Origin of the Maronite Community and its Independence in the Mountain of Lebanon from the oldest time to the Present) (Beirūt 1919). Duryān has greatly utilized Duwayhi's older history.

Maronites and Druzes: Massacres of the Sixties

The story of Lebanon in modern times is pre-eminently that of Maronite and Druze. While the Maronites became concentrated mainly in the northern regions of the Lebanese mountains, the Druzes chose the southern heights in the district of Ḥaurān, where they led their own peculiar life in seclusion and obscurity, though the two elements overlapped in numerous areas. While it would be irrelevant here to enlarge upon the nature of Druzism,[1] it might help towards an understanding of their position among Muslims and Maronites to follow briefly the story of this strange community across the ages. According to a seventeenth-century myth, Druzes posed as descendants of Godefroy de Bouillon and the first Crusaders; but that tale has been discredited beyond a shadow of doubt. Druze origins should be traced to the reign of the Fatimid Caliph al-Ḥākim (996–1021), who was proclaimed a human incarnation of deity by his confidant Muḥammad ibn Ismāʿīl al-Darāzi.[2] Although Darāzi was killed in 1019, his doctrines found a powerful exponent in Hamzal al-Labbād (the furrier) al-Zuzāni, a Persian scholar who systematized Druze theology into an esoteric cult. The propagation of Druzism in Syria was the task of another disciple, said to be of Christian Syrian origin, namely al-Muqtanā Bahā'-al-Dīn (d. after 1042). His life and work occurred only a few decades before the advent of the

[1] B. Carra de Vaux, *Les penseurs de l'Islam*, 5 vols. (Paris, 1921–6), V, 56–78; see also article 'Druzes' by him in *Encyclopedia of Islam*, I, 1075–7; Hitti, *Lebanon*, pp. 257–65. Their literature, guarded in strict secrecy, was largely seized by the Egyptians when Ibrāhīm Pasha invaded Syria in 1834. The first insight into their religion as revealed by this literature was made possible by the old French scholar Sylvestre de Sacy, *Exposé de la Religion des Druzes*, 2 vols. (Paris, 1838). See also P. K. Hitti, *The Origins of the Druze People and Religion*, with extracts from their sacred writings (Columbia University Oriental Studies, Vol. XXVIII, New York, 1928).

[2] The word *Darazi* is possibly another form of *Tarazi*, i.e. tailor. The Druzes derived their name from him as the founder of their sect, though Druzism was not entirely new, since it could be regarded as an extreme form of the Ismāʿilite doctrine, in turn stemming from the Shīʿite heterodox Islamic creed as against Sunnite orthodoxy. Imām Ismāʿīl (d. 760) formulated his new doctrine in the eighth century.

crusaders. This last great commentator on Druzism, to whom we owe most of the secret literature seized in the Egyptian campaign of 1834, was ʿAbdallah al-Tanūkhī (d. 1480), whose tomb is still frequented by his co-religionists at ʿAbāyh in Lebanon. Druzism is a religion revealed to the 'sages' or the 'scholars' (*ʿUqqāl*, wise men) and concealed from the 'ignorant' (i.e., *juhhal*); and sages who attain excellence in piety rise to the rank of perfection or godliness (*ajāwīd*). High priests usually take vows of celibacy and hold their religious reunions on the eve of each Friday in the seclusion of their places of retirement (*Khilwahs*). They do not recognize al-Ḥākim's death and contend that, as the last incarnation of God, he voluntarily disappeared in a state of temporary occultation (*Ghaybah*) and will reappear at the appropriate time in conformity with the Mahdist theory. According to Bahā' al-Dīn, this religion theoretically became a closed circle allowing no departure of the faithful or incorporation of new elements from the unfaithful who had already proved themselves unworthy of its truth. This trait, together with the rule of blind obedience of its membership to the supreme chief of the community, may explain many events in their history. Otherwise, their code of ethics was strict, and all were pledged to the defence of every member of their clan. The good were reborn in human forms and the wicked returned to the world as dogs. Their unity gave them great strength, and they comprised in the main the tribes of Tanūkh, Maʿn, Arslān and Janbalāṭ which exist to the present day. Socially, the Druzes proved to be friendly with the Maronites and often participated in their religious ceremonies and venerated Christian shrines. At one time, the Maronites obeyed Druze princes, such as Fakhr-al-Dīn II of Maʿn, whose domain extended from Antioch to Ṣafad in Palestine between 1590 and 1635. On the other hand, instances of conversion from Druzism to Maronitism are not infrequent. The outstanding case is that of the great Shehābi dynasty, whose leaders kept oscillating between the two faiths until they ended in the Maronite camp by adopting Christianity. Other local families and amīrs followed their example, notably the Bellāma house.

In the middle of the picture of modern Lebanon, the rule of the great Amīr Bashīr II al-Shehabi (1788–1840) was both a stabilizing factor and a vanguard of modernization of the country. He fought the battle of freedom for Lebanon and dexterously played its foreign invaders against one another. He was exiled four times from his homeland, but persisted in his defiance to the encroachments of the Turkish sultan's agents on traditional Lebanese autonomy. Deeply impressed by Muḥammad ʿAli's reforms in Egypt, he tried to apply the same progressive methods of modernization to Lebanon. He sent promising native young men to study medicine in the newly founded school of medicine at Qaṣr al-ʿAiny in Cairo. His magnificent mountain residence called Bayt al-Dīn (House of Faith) with its tremendous structures, beautiful architecture, artistic decorations and an aqueduct for the conveyance of a continuous water supply from the snowy peaks is in itself a standing monument to the man's imagination and forceful personality. The historian of Lebanon[1] sums up his many-sided character in the following words: 'Christian in Baptism, Moslem in matrimony, Druze through convenience rather than conviction, Bashīr, in the tradition of his house and its predecessor, followed a liberal and enlightened religious policy.' The Maronite Church was particularly favoured in his reign, though the Druzes were not frustrated. Maronite clergy thus lived in perfect peace and harmony with their Druze neighbours. In Bayt al-Dīn, Bashir erected a Maronite chapel side by side with the original Muslim mosque. He encouraged education without reserve, while the modest Maronite seminary rose to the status of a full-fledged college at ʿAyn Waraqah.[2] One of its graduates, the historian Yūsuf al-Dibs (1833–1907), archbishop of Beirūt and one of the greatest historians of Syria founded the even more important Madrassat al-Ḥikmah[3] (School of Wisdom) in 1874 on a Western model in his diocese.

The enduring legacy of Bashīr's reign in Lebanon was twofold – first, it opened, though perhaps unwittingly, the country to foreign influence; and secondly, it strengthened the peace between Maronite and Druze. Bashīr's alliance with Muḥammad ʿAli of Egypt and his campaigning side by side with his son Ibrāhīm Pasha against the Turks in Syria during the 1830's ultimately precipitated foreign interference in Lebanon by England, Austria, Russia and France. As to the peaceful co-existence of Druze and Maronite in his reign, it unfortunately proved to be short-lived. Two main factors contributed to the rupture of a neighbourly relationship between the members of the two communities. In the first place, the disappearance of Bashīr during his last exile from the country and his death abroad in 1850 left a vacuum of power. Consequently, Lebanon suffered utter confusion and the Turkish governors did everything in their power to encourage this state to the verge of anarchy. In the second place, the Sublime Porte at Constantinople issued an order to Lebanese citizens to surrender all arms to the authorities as a necessary measure for the re-establishment of order after the withdrawal of Ibrāhīm Pasha and the Egyptians from Syrian soil. What happened in reality was that the Turks carried out this order literally in regard to the Christians and overlooked its application to the Muslim population. While thus systematically disarming the Maronites, they even armed the Muslims in general and the

[1] Hitti, *Lebanon*, p. 417. [2] Al-Dibs, VIII, 604–5.

[3] Ibid., IX, 574–6; Hitti, pp. 460–1. According to his own account, Archbishop al-Dibs spent a total of 30,000 French *livres* on its construction and endowed it with lands amounting to 100,000 cubits, together with houses rented for 15,000 piastres. He appointed as its first principal his own brother, a graduate of ʿAyn Waraqah, whom he had sent to Paris in 1875 for completing his studies and who returned to Lebanon in 1880.

Druzes in particular. This favouritism was accompanied by the steady sowing of the seeds of separatism between Christian and non-Christian, which became one of the most flagrant issues of the time. Meanwhile, the internal politics of the Maronites and their Church were none too felicitous. Disaffection became rampant amidst the Maronite feudal aristocracy, and great social changes were imminent. The people of Lebanon were rising to throw off the yoke of feudalism. The lower clergy who were recruited from the poorer classes threw in their lot with the populace, whereas the hierarchy took sides with the conflicting feudatories. The Turks took care to fan trouble, and the Druzes, who had been rebuffed by Ibrāhīm Pasha, began to consolidate. The moment was ominous, and the Maronites did nothing to evade local clashes with their restive Druze neighbours, especially where their villages intermingled. The Christian village of Dair al-Qamar, the native home of Camille Shimʿūn, last president of the Lebanese republic, was set on fire and destroyed by the united Druze clans in 1841 as the result of shooting the partridge of a Druze and subsequent family strife.

Hitherto, Lebanon under the Turks had had its local native Lebanese lord. In 1842, the last of the Shehābi's was dismissed, and the sultan placed in his stead a Hungarian renegade by the name of ʿUmar Pasha al-Nimsawi (the Austrian), who had apostatized to Islam. ʿUmar occupied Bayt al-Dīn in the heart of Lebanon where he could stir up mischief on the spot. In the meantime, the country was split into two provinces north and south of the road between Beirūt and Damascus with two sub-governors, a Christian for the north and a Druze over the south. This arrangement was entirely unworkable and led to more trouble, since the Druze south included 17,350 Maronites[1] and even more than that number of other Christian denominations. These were consequently at the mercy of a Druze master who was in favour with the Turks. In 1845, both Christians and Druzes started burning one another's vulnerable villages. The incident of Dair al-Qamar and the incendiaries of 1845 were but modest heralds of the reign of complete anarchy ending in open revolt and sweeping massacres in 1860. This untoward infamy has been known as the 'Massacres of the Sixties' (*Maḏhābiḥ al-Sittīn*). Their fury lasted from April to July of that year, and innumerable horrors were inflicted upon those largely disarmed Christian villages. Within a period so limited and an area so restricted, an estimated twelve thousand Christians perished and the damages amounted to some four million pounds sterling.[2] Religious institutions did not escape. Churches and monasteries were left in rubble heaps, and their congregations either fled for their lives or were shot dead. The flames of revolt touched Damascus, where Turkish duplicity resulted in an attack on the rich and populous Christian quarter in the Syrian capital. It is stated that here some eleven thousand lost their

[1] Hitti, p. 435.

[2] Ibid., p. 438.

lives, and only the chivalry of a certain ʿAbd al-Qādir, himself an Algerian refugee from French rule in North Africa, saved the remaining Christian citizens from extinction. A total of one hundred thousand refugees from Lebanon and adjacent Syrian cities were rendered homeless, and the signs of famine and epidemics were menacing.

At last, the conscience of the Western world was awakened, and France took the lead by calling then the other powers to end this tragedy. Without awaiting the outcome of negotiations for common action, a French expedition landed on the shores of Lebanon in order to restore order and re-establish security. Meanwhile, the Sublime Porte appointed its minister of foreign affairs, Fouad Pasha, as extraordinary commissioner for Lebanon to deal in conjunction with an international body of representatives of the Powers in settling the position and in punishing criminals. Some 111 soldiers were shot, a few civilians were hanged, others were imprisoned or deported, ʿAbd al-Qādir was decorated, and an indemnity of a million and a quarter pounds was imposed on the Druzes and shouldered by the Ottoman treasury, only to be suspended after partial payment.[1]

During the following year, a new constitution for Lebanon was proclaimed at the Turkish capital. France, England, Austria, Prussia and Russia were amongst its signatories with the Ottoman government. The autonomy of Lebanon was recognized internationally under a Christian governor (*Mutaṣarrif*) whom the sultan nominated for a renewable term of five years. Assisted by a council of twelve members elected by the various religious communities and including five Christians, the new chief executive owed responsibility to the Sublime Porte. In this way, the unity of Lebanon was restored, but the impotence of its Turco-Lebanese administration and the dwindling of the Maronite feudal aristocracy since the Shehābi days opened the road to ecclesiastical prestige and power as the only remaining alternative. It was thus that the Maronite hierarchy rose to the status of leadership and the patriarch became the most powerful personality, not only in the church, but also amidst all his people. Around the church organization, therefore, most of the social, political and religious reforms were conducted during the later decades of the nineteenth century and even at the beginning of the twentieth.[2]

[1] Al-Dibs, VIII, 647–61, 667–75, 685–7. The contemporary account of an eyewitness of those events, Colonel Churchill, *The Druzes and the Maronites under Turkish Rule from 1840 to 1860* (London, 1862), contains most of the details of these events, and the book ends with an eloquent exhortation (p. 283) to his Christian readers, to Christian peoples, and Christian emperors and kings for supporting a sacred cause desecrated by the monstrous Turk.

[2] Hitti, *Lebanon*, pp. 433 et seq.; Lammens, *Syrie*, II, 150–90.

The Church, Independence and Nationalism

The new constitution remained in force until the fateful years of the First World War. During that time, a great wave of sympathy towards the Christians of the Middle East and notably the Maronites of Syria swept through many countries of the West, especially France and the United States of America as a result of the Massacres of the Sixties and the subsequent events. Pliny Fisk and Levi Parsons, the great pioneers of Protestant Christianity in Syria and Lebanon, sailed from Boston on the *Sally Anne* in 1819 to find the area stricken with poverty, disease, ignorance and superstition under the Turkish yoke, and the Rev. Isaac Bird and the Rev. Wm. Goodell arrived at Beirūt in 1823. The patient and charitable work which they and their successors in the field carried out in Lebanon was phenomenal. Its consummation in the development of the American University of Beirūt, the first really modern university in the Middle East, has been a fine landmark in the modernization of Lebanon.[1] Daniel Bliss, who transformed the old Syrian Protestant College founded at Beirūt in 1866 into the present American University and became its first president, laid down the enlightened policy of that institution in the much-quoted words: 'A man white, black or yellow; Christian, Jew, Mohammedan or heathen, may enter and enjoy all the advantages of this institution for three, four or eight years; and go out believing in God, in many gods, or in no God. But it will be impossible for any one to continue with us long without knowing what we believe to be the truth and our reasons for that belief.'[2] In the meantime, the French Catholic organizations and their work in Lebanon proved a worthy peer of the service rendered by the Protestant mission. In reality, those Catholic bodies had more direct access to the Maronite Church. The Jesuit seminary founded at Ghazīr in 1846, was moved to Beirūt to become the solid base of the French Jesuit University of St Joseph in 1875. The schools, orphanages, benevolent societies and monastic establishments for both men and women were potent instruments of westernization. Suddenly, we find Lebanon emerging from mediæval obscurity into the limelight of modernism; and the Church, it must be remembered, was the focal point through which the good work was effectively carried out.

The influence of the ecclesiastical hierarchy on the Modern nationalist movement in its formative years was also tremendous, since Lebanese Christians as a whole tended to identify their native homeland with the

[1] Daniel Bliss, *The Religions of Modern Syria and Palestine* (New York, 1912) pp. 312–35, containing interesting chapter on the influence of the West in general; see also Hitti, *Lebanon*, pp. 452–69.

[2] *The Reminiscences of Daniel Bliss* (New York, 1920), p. 215; Hitti, *Lebanon*, p. 454.

Maronite Church. The agonies of Lebanon at the hands of the Turkish command in the war years proved to be more devastating than the horrors of the Massacres of the Sixties. The death toll, it is said,[1] reached 100,000 out of a population of only 450,000. Monasteries situated at strategic points on mountain heights were evacuated of their inmates and turned into military fortifications. The historic monasteries of St Isaiah (Mar Ishʿiya) and St John (Mar Yuḥanna) al-Qalʿah were amongst them. Whole villages were completely depopulated. Prelates were disbanded. The Maronite bishop of Beirūt was exiled and met his end in Anatolia; and the patriarch feigned illness and sent a substitute when summoned to receive an imperial *firmān* at Beirūt. Christians and Muslims, suspected of nationalist subversion, were subjected to great rigours; and on 6 May 1916, fourteen victims were executed in Beirūt and seven others in Damascus on account of their Arab or French sympathies. The horrors of Ottoman oppression were ended only with the advent of General Allenby's allied armies and the Arab troops under the command of Sharīf Ḥusayn's son, the future King Fayṣal I, in September 1918. The events which followed from Woodrow Wilson's famous declaration of the principle of self-determination to the Peace of Versailles, the establishment of the French mandate in Lebanon and the British in Palestine, and subsequent struggles leading to the proclamation of Lebanese independence on 23 May 1926 – all these and other details of the highest importance in the political annals of Lebanon and the Middle East can only be mentioned in passing. Throughout these national upheavals, however, the Church was the most prominent factor, and its influence on the course of events was monumental. The Maronite patriarch at the time, Buṭrus Elias Hoyek,[2] who died in 1932 after a career of very great eminence, was not only a prelate of note but also a national figure of distinction. He went to Paris at the head of a Lebanese delegation during the Peace Conference to plead for the independence of his country. He exchanged notes with Clemenceau, who gave him a written assurance of granting a satisfactory solution to his aspirations. Then at a later stage Hoyek's negotiations were effective in ending the French mandate, and Greater Lebanon was given new life as a republic on 23 May 1926. Its new constitution accepted the principles that the president of the republic must be a Maronite, the Prime Minister a Muslim Sunnite, the chairman of the Chamber of Deputies a Shīʿite, the Minister of Defence a Druze.

Hoyek was succeeded by Patriarch Anṭūn ʿArīḍah, a man of indefatigable

[1] Hitti, *Lebanon*, p. 486.

[2] Archbishop Yūsuf Duryān, *Nubdhah Tārīkhiyah*, pp. 477–522; Al-Dibs, *Tārīkh Suriya*, VIII, 761–3; idem, *Al-Jāmiʿ al-Mufaṣṣal*, pp. 559–61; Al-ʿUnaysi, pp. 71–3; Ghabriel, *Histoire*, II: 1, 841–73; P. Rondot, *Chrétiens d'Orient* (Paris, 1955), pp. 257–8. He visited Rome several times, was friendly with the Holy See, and was universally respected by all people of different nationality or religion.

energy, courage and great devotion. His vigilance over the independence of his country has been commended by both Muslim and Christian political leaders. Within recent memory, during the unfortunate events of 1958, when the political revolt to depose President Camille Shimʿūn began to take on a religious colour, the present Maronite patriarch, Bolus al-Maʿūshī, who had spent part of his early career in the priesthood in the United States of America, managed to save the worsening situation by proclaiming the Church on the side of the Arab commonwealth of nations and states, and he disowned the president, who was instrumental in calling for Western military interference. The patriarchal remonstrances undoubtedly sealed the political doom of the Maronite president, who had to retire from the arena of national leadership and international politics.

27 • ORGANIZATION, FAITH AND CULTURE

The Hierarchy

The Maronite Church reflects in the organization of its hierarchy a number of historic factors which have given it its special character and personality. Of Eastern origin and tradition, it has acquired numerous Western features, thus rendering it a Janus-headed edifice and a bridge between the East and West. The position of the Maronite 'Patriarch of Antioch and the East' – his official title – represents this unusual amalgamation of the doctrines stemming from Roman and Syrian sources. He is elected for life by all the Maronite bishops and archbishops convened in synod. He should not be less than forty years of age and he must obtain two-thirds of the votes in the synod. Then he is consecrated by the laying on of hands, the oldest of the bishops officiating on the occasion. The clergy and the congregation of the faithful are expected to offer him homage and obedience after the election. Meanwhile, a notice is sent to the holy see in Rome together with a profession of the faith for due confirmation by the pope, who presents the patriarch-elect with the pallium as well as the ring, staff and a pectoral cross. He is expected to report to the papal *curia* in Rome every decade from the time of his election. The patriarch, on the other hand, maintains most of his pre-Roman prerogatives. As a rule, his selection is not subject to papal scrutiny, although his confirmation has grown in modern times to be a condition of the stability and legality of his position. He is vested with full powers to nominate all his Maronite archbishops, bishops and titular bishops or *chorepiscopoi*. He summons the holy synod at least once in three years, consecrates the chrism, issues final verdicts in cases of appeal from the lower courts in matters of personal status, and controls the original text and secondary versions of the liturgies. He alone can grant absolution from certain grave sins such as apostasy, the use of consecrated sacramental vessels in sorcery, the attempt to assassinate a bishop, or the expulsion of a priest from his parish. His name figures in all public prayers immediately after that of the holy pontiff. He wears a small black turban, very similar to that worn by the Nestorian patriarch. His official residence was fixed in later mediæval times at the monastery of Qannūbīn in the heights of the Qadīsha Valley, still in use for the summer, while Bkirki, some twenty miles north-west of Beirūt, became the patriarchal seat in winter. If the pope nominates a patriarchal coadjutor accepted by the synod with the right to future succession, that prelate becomes patriarch *ipso facto* without any need for elections at the decease of the occupant of the throne.[1] The dioceses of Jibayl (the ancient Byblos) and Baṭrūm are reserved for the patriarch and are administered on his behalf by a titular bishop. Moreover, part of the episcopal tithes is granted to the patriarchate by all the bishops to help in its maintenance; and additional funds from the West and Maronites overseas are often regarded as essential for balancing the patriarchal budget.

Next to the patriarch in dignity are the archbishops and bishops, whom he designates in synod. The title of archbishop or metropolitan is merely honorary. Otherwise, both prelates are identical in character. Episcopal dioceses were defined and fixed in the Synods of Luwaizah in 1736 and 1818.[2] A bishop is not allowed to leave his diocese without special dispensation from the patriarch. He is usually consecrated by the patriarch with the assistance of two bishops. He watches over the spiritual welfare of his flock, administers the ecclesiastical property, receives the tithes, and applies the laws of personal status. He is assisted by an archdeacon in ecclesiastical and legal matters, and by an *economus* in the financial and secular administration. From among the bishops, moreover, the patriarch appoints two vicars in residence to help him in both the spiritual and the temporal affairs of the church. A third patriarchal vicar is nominated as head of the Maronite church in Egypt, an honour which Archbishop Duryan, the Maronite historian, held in the early decades of this century.

The parochial priests (*Kh̲ūris*) are almost entirely secular and married, contrary to Latin tradition and in keeping with the pre-Roman Eastern usages. They are selected by the congregation, but the bishop, who consecrates them, has the right of veto. Generally, they are not highly educated, but they must be proficient in Arabic and Syriac and have some theological knowledge. They are poorly endowed and most of them practise a secular vocation to supplement their earnings. There are 500 parishes with 780 churches and about 600 secular priests altogether.[3] They administer the sacraments, except confirmation, and perform baptism, marriage and death rituals. The clerical profession in towns has occasionally been reinforced with priests from the ranks of the monastic or, according to the Catholic definition, the regular clergy.

[1] Janin, pp. 555–7; Attwater, I, 169–70.

[2] Al-Dibs, *Al-Jāmiʿ al-Mufaṣṣal*, pp. 492–6, 565–6.

[3] This estimate is quoted by Janin, p. 560. Attwater, I, 171, mentions a thousand secular priests and considers that number insufficient.

Rites and Liturgies

Since the Maronites are Antiochene Syrians by origin and Roman by conversion, their rites and Liturgies present a chequered patchwork of both Oriental and Catholic. Although their modern churches are entirely identical with those of the Latins, they still possess a number of ancient churches bearing such Syrian features of the pre-Roman days as the altar-screen or iconostasis. In addition to bells adopted from the Catholics, they also reserve the use of the Syrian cymbals to mark time, and the resultant unusual noises surprise the Western visitor. Although the objects employed in the liturgies are identical with those of the Roman church, the celebrant blesses the congregation with the small Syrian cross from which a long silk handkerchief hangs. Their vestments are also a curious mixture of both the Syrian and the Latin, especially Syrian in the ranks of the lower rural clergy. Syrian embroidered cuffs as well as the Roman mitre and crozier are used by bishops. The ordinary dress is a purple cassock under the black gown with wide sleeves for the patriarch, violet for bishops and black for the lower hierarchy. The head gear consists of a round flat cap, but the bishops and patriarchs wear the Syrian *Masnafto* or cap under a black turban.[1]

The Maronite liturgy is essentially the old Syrian Liturgy of St James the Less, first bishop of Jerusalem, still in use in Syriac amongst the Jacobites. It is recited in the Aramaic dialect of Syriac, though it has been subjected to such emendations and interpolations as to bring it in line with Catholic traditions. These alterations were not binding until the national synod of 1736 issued its definitions of the faith and enforced all the details of Latin origin. They have in common with the Syrians and Chaldæans no less than fourteen anaphoras, of which two are certainly Romanized versions – the Anaphora of the Catholic and Roman Church Mother of all Churches, and the Anaphora of St Peter Prince of the Apostles. The Anaphora of St John Maron is their own, and that of Marutha of Tekrit is East Syrian. They have the Liturgy of the Presanctified on Good Friday, exactly like the Latin rite. Concelebration is not unusual in monastic churches and in large cathedrals. They pray for the pope, the patriarch, the diocesan bishop, and for all the faithful, living and deceased. The Gospel is read in Syriac or in Arabic. The lesson and other prayers delivered in Arabic have their rubrics in Garshūni or Syriac letters.

The Divine Offices are identical with the Syrian except for Lauds and were confirmed by the synod of 1736. Seven in number, they are the Night Office, Matins, Third, Sixth and Ninth Hours, Vespers and Compline. Unleavened bread is used in the Eucharist. Marriage ceremonies are per-

[1] Janin, pp. 541 et seq.; Attwater, I, 173 et seq.

formed in Arabic and according to the Syrian customs, though with Roman additions. Infant baptism is practised by the Maronites according to Eastern customs, though they also use the Roman method of baptizing by infusion or pouring the baptismal water over the head of a person rather than complete immersion. They do not however give communion to an infant at his baptism as do the Latins. The ceremony of extreme unction is largely derived from Roman ritual.[1]

The Maronite church has used the Gregorian calendar since the year 1606. Maronite feasts, twenty-three in number, comprise those of Syrian origin, that of St Maron and a few others which they have adopted from the western Catholic Church, such as the Feasts of the Blessed Sacrament, of St Joseph, Rosary Sunday and the Name of Mary.[2]

Fasts have been regulated by the synod of 1736. All Wednesdays and Fridays are days of abstinence except between Christmas and Epiphany, and the Fridays before Lent, Easter and Pentecost, as well as June 24 and 29 and August 6 and 15.[3] Lent lasts seven weeks before Easter and is called the Great Fast in the East. Abstinence until midday is recommended, though the fast is broken on Saturdays and Sundays except on Holy Saturday and feast days within those dates. Other fasts include four days before the Apostles' Day (25–28 June), eight days before the Assumption (7–14 August), and twelve days before Christmas (13–24 December). On the whole, fasting obligations amongst the modern Maronites are much less lenient than in the other Eastern churches.

Like the Latins, they cover all icons and statues with dark cloth during Passiontide. They perform the ceremony of the washing of the feet in common with the churches of the East on Maundy Thursday. The patriarch also consecrates the holy chrism on that day. Midnight liturgies are celebrated on the eves of Christmas, Epiphany and Easter.

Monasticism

Monastic rule has had an uninterrupted history amongst the Maronites who, in common with the rest of the Syrian churches, espoused its cause from the earliest times. St Maro of the fourth century was probably the first to embark on a celibate life with its vows of chastity, poverty and obedience which his numerous followers must have maintained. St John Maron, the founder of

[1] P. Dib, *Étude sur la Liturgie maronite* (Paris, 1919); Prince Maximillian of Saxony, *Missa Maronitica* (Ratisbon, 1907). English tr. of the liturgy are extant by Father Joseph Gorayeb (Buffalo, N.Y., 1915), Father Peter Sfeir (Detroit, 1936), and Attwater's *Eastern Catholic Worship* (1945); Cf. Attwater, *Christian Churches of the East*, I, 175.

[2] Janin, p. 551; Attwater, I, 176. [3] Janin, p. 551.

the Maronite church in the seventh and eighth centuries favoured the sanctity of monastic life for the clergy. Monasteries multiplied in Lebanon. The patriarch-historian, al-Duwayhi (1630–1704),[1] enumerates twenty-one convents of ancient standing in his day. Al-Dibs (1833–1907) follows him with a statement of other new foundations century by century.[2] A modern estimate provides the number of seventy-two fully-fledged monasteries comprising about 750 monks and more than 500 ordained regular priests in addition to forty-two residences for one or two resident monks charged with overseeing landed estates.[3] Monastic rule in the Maronite church had been either in keeping with the Oriental tradition of great austerity or rather lax where each monk extemporized his own way of living. That was the state of Maronite monasticism when Stephan al-Duwayhi, the father of Maronite history and the first serious historian since Jibrā'īl ibn al-Qelāʿi, succeeded to the patriarchal throne of Qannūbīn in 1670. He was an enlightened man and a great reformer whose reforms touched the monasteries. At the beginning of the following century, he established a new monastic order on the Western models which he had seen during his student days in the Maronite College at Rome. His new Rule of St Anthony, as he named it after the great Coptic patriarch of all monks in the wilderness of the Red Sea, stabilized the monastic vows as four instead of the traditional three. Thus to obedience, chastity and poverty, he added humility as a new factor in the life of a model monk.[4] The new rule sponsored by the Maronite patriarch became very popular, and a real renaissance in the church began to bud in his own lifetime. The organization absorbed already-existing monasteries, and monks so multiplied in numbers that it was eventually necessary to split their settlements under different rules. This movement was inaugurated by the Patriarch Jibrā'īl al-Belauzawi, who succeeded Stephan al-Duwayhi in 1704, and who died in the following year. It was actually during his long episcopate at Aleppo that he founded the Monastery of St Isaiah (Mar Ishʿiya), where he confirmed al-Duwayhi's rule and endowed it with his accumulated fortune. Then, within a few decades, Maronite monasticism was re-organized in 1768 in two orders to meet the needs of expansion – the rural or Baladite Antonians[5] and

[1] *Tārīkh al-Ṭā'ifah al-Mārūniyah*, pp. 264–5.

[2] Al-Dibs's accounts, spread over his greater 'History of Syria', are recapitulated in his work on the Maronite Church (*Al-Jāmiʿ al-Mufaṣṣal*), though again under centuries from the twelfth (pp. 200 et seq.), the seventeenth (399 et seq.), the eighteenth (502 et seq.), and the nineteenth (567 and 579 et seq.) He often mixes churches and monasteries.

[3] Attwater, I, 171.

[4] See al-Duwayhi's *History*, p. 268, where the editor, Rashīd al-Shartūni, has added an interesting account of Maronite monasticism (pp. 362–77) to the author's time; and also al-Dibs, *al-Jāmiʿ*, pp. 361–7, on al-Duwayhi's life and work.

[5] R. Etteldorf, *The Catholic Church in the Middle East*, p. 101, estimates their actual number at 450 monks with their main monastery at Koziah, 21 other contemplative monasteries and 13 houses for parish work and teaching.

the Aleppine Antonians[1] pertaining to Aleppo where the aforesaid Jibrā'īl inaugurated the movement. Apparently this took place in the reign of the Patriarch Yūsuf Stephan (1767–1808), whose fame rests on the celebrated case of Hindiyah or Ḥinnah ʿAjami. This was a nun of Aleppo who commanded great popular appeal for her sanctity and was supported by the patriarch in spite of her claim that union with the manhood of Jesus was normally resultant from receiving holy communion. Reference has been made to the inquiries held by order of the Roman pontiff in this connection, the summons of the patriarch to Rome to answer for his action, and the ultimate written surrender of Hindiyah on every detail of her doctrine. What matters here is that she became the head of a considerable organization of nunneries, received substantial gifts from the faithful, and even bought whole convents where she housed the increasing female followers of her Order of the Sacred Heart.[2]

In fact, the seventeenth century saw a great increase in female celibacy. The nucleus of this movement came into being in 1718 with St George's Convent. Before the end of the century, there were about ten others.[3] More emerged in the nineteenth century under the indigenous Society of the Maryamat (i.e., Maries), whose fuller title was the Congregation of the Sisters of the Sacred Hearts of Jesus and Mary. From 1853, it even began to incorporate several already-existing orders and specialized in the care of orphans and in female education. In 1931, the Maryamat are said to have had some 266 sisters, 51 schools and 5,777 girl students.[4] In 1895, the patriotic Patriarch Buṭros Hoyek also founded the Sisters of the Holy Family for educational purposes. They numbered eighty nuns in nineteen houses. A total of 450 sisters belonging to Maronite congregations is the latest estimate.[5] On the whole, the educational services of the monastic foundations, both secular and ecclesiastical, male and female, to the Maronite community have been very great. Patriarchs and bishops, men of learning and of irreproachable sanctity, have been recruited from their seminaries.

Maronite monasticism produced many saints even in her darkest hours, men who preserved the Eastern ideals of their mother church in spite of her increasing closeness to western Catholicism. They made their monasteries

[1] Ibid., pp. 101–2, estimates them at 100 monks with their monastery at Luwayzah and twelve houses in Lebanon. The Antonians of Mar Ishʿiya also have 100 members with their head monastery at Decouane, thirteen other contemplative monasteries and ten houses, mostly engaged in parish work.

[2] Al-Dibs, pp. 446–60.

[3] Ibid., pp. 446–60, 507–10.

[4] Janin, p. 565. Hitti, *Lebanon*, p. 448, states that in 1914 they had 6,000 girls in 30 schools. Bikfaiya was their headquarters, and apparently they merged with another female celibate organization at Zaḥlah.

[5] Etteldorf, p. 102. This number excludes several hundreds of Maronite sisters enrolled in the inter-ritual Catholic congregations in Syria.

homes of piety and learning, and they handed the torch of Syriac and Arabic scholarship to subsequent generations. As early as 1610, a Maronite student from Rome introduced for the first time in the annals of the Middle East the art of printing, whereby a press equipped with Syriac and Arabic characters was established at the old Monastery of St Anthony (Mar Anṭūnyus) of Qazḥāya.[1] This claims precedence over the famous Bulāq Press, founded in Cairo in 1820. Because of the tenacity of these obscure sons of the Maronite Church, the humble Maronite nation was able to survive its gigantic oppressors from the Byzantine Empire to the Ottoman Caliphate.[2]

Maronite Culture

The progress of Lebanese culture was inevitably intertwined with the Maronite Church. Its structure proved, as has already been mentioned, to be the rock on which national, social and religious reform became effective. The religious character of those sturdy mountaineers, who fought valiantly for their existence against the poverty of their soil and the hostility of the natural elements, constituted the very basis of their salvation as a unit. Hence, throughout their long history their civilization must be viewed in its spiritual setting. It would be a false assumption to contend that Lebanon produced figures who changed the course of history, religion or creed. Nevertheless it made its modest contributions to the march of events. These would appear small when seen against the wider world background, but great when considered within the limited dimensions of a minute community. Their monastic system which had started with two of the great saints of the East, St Maro and St John Maron, never ceased to yield men of modest stature but of saintly qualities. Even within living memory, the Maronite Church produced Charbel Makhlouf (d. 1898), a monk of the Monastery of Our Lady of Meifūq, and later of the Monastery of Annaya, whose brilliance in theology and in Syriac and Arabic letters did not deter

[1] Hitti, *Lebanon*, pp. 456–7. *Qazḥaiya* is a Syriac word meaning 'treasure of life'. The first book to be published in the same year was the Psalter in Garshūnē, i.e., in the Arabic language but printed by Syriac characters. The example of Qazḥaiya was followed by other monasteries such as that of St John the Baptist (Mar Yūḥannā al-Ṣābigh) at D-hūr al-Shuwayr in the Lebanese mountain where printing was practised in 1733.

[2] In his eloquent and piquant style, Edward Gibbon, *Decline and Fall of the Roman Empire*, ed. J. B. Bury, V, 156–7, says: 'Yet the humble nation of the Maronites has survived the empire of Constantinople, and they still enjoy under their Turkish masters, a free religion and a mitigated servitude.' Of course, Lebanon was still under the Turks in Gibbon's lifetime (1737–94), and the Massacres of the Sixties occurred in the following century. Hitti, *Lebanon*, p. 249, quotes the same sentence, though in a different variant of which the origin is unknown to us.

him from becoming a Maronite successor of St Anthony as an ascetic recluse. His bed was oak leaves strewn over the bare ground, his pillow was a block of wood rolled in an old cloth, his garment was a rough hair shirt, his single daily repast was boiled or raw vegetables only rarely flavoured with oil, and he spent his days in manual labour and his nights in meditation and prayer. His tomb at Annaya has become the modern shrine of Maronite pilgrimage, and Rome is said to be investigating his case for canonization.[1]

Unlike the Syrian Jacobites in their better days when they were still identified as the original Antiochene church, the Maronite genius did not express itself in stone similar to St Simeon's or the defunct towns of northern Syria. The art and architecture of the Maronites has been modest and does not deserve much space here. They usually built their monasteries at forbidding heights on fortified promontories as havens for refuge and defence. This was all that mattered to them and few thought of embellishment and decorative *motifs*. The gigantic mountain setting with its rugged beauty and its aged cedars were their real pride. In modern times, as they progressed towards westernization, their churches became modest replicas of the ordinary European model, and thus lost even their Eastern personality.

The period *par excellence* when Lebanon and its Maronite society leapt into speedy modernization was the nineteenth century. This process was made possible by the existence of two spiritual agencies from the West – the one Catholic and essentially French, the other Protestant and consisting of the American missionary. Nevertheless, it would be wrong to contend that the Maronites had had no contacts whatever with Europe prior to that age. In fact, the impact of the West on Maronite society had certainly been preceded by the impact of Maronites on some aspects of European scholarship. Even before Gregory XIII's dedication of the Maronite College (*Collegium Maronitarum*) at Rome in 1584, Maronite students had made their appearance in the Catholic capital, and one of their early numbers was Jibrā'īl ibn al-Qelāʿi (d. 1516), theologian, historian and later Maronite bishop. Since the founding of the Maronite College, however, the door of Europe was opened to other Maronite scholars who eventually became 'the educators of Europe'[2] in Orientalism. This forgotten chapter is one of the most fascinating facets of Maronite annals.

The first modern Syriac grammar to be composed in Latin (*Grammatica linguæ syriacæ*) was the work of a Maronite student in Rome, where it was published in 1596. Its author was Jurjis ʿAmīrah[3] (d. 1644), who rose to the dignity of the Maronite patriarchate in 1633. Under the same title, another Syriac grammar was written and published at Rome in 1636 by another

[1] Etteldorf, pp. 88–90; Jules Leroy, *Moines et monastères du Proche-Orient* (Paris, 1958), p. 144. [2] Leroy, p. 149.
[3] Al-Dibs, *Al-Jāmiʿ al-Mufaṣṣal*, pp. 353–6; Graf. III, 338–9; Hitti, *Lebanon*, p. 403.

Maronite, Isḥāq al-Shadrāwi (the Latin Sciadrensis), who went to Rome at the age of twelve, travelled in Italy and France, became bishop of Tripoli in 1660, and was active in international politics between Lebanon and France.[1] We have to remember that the Maronite community was bilingual in the seventeenth century, and scholars from Lebanon were therefore proficient in both Syriac and Arabic.[2] They were certainly especially fitted for the introduction of Syriac into European Orientalist circles.

Whereas the aforementioned scholars returned to Lebanon, others of even greater fame preferred to remain in Europe. Jibrā'īl al-Ṣahyūni,[3] the Latin Sionita (1577–1648), taught at the *Collegium Sapientiæ* in Rome, then occupied the chair of Semitic languages at the *Collège Royal* in Paris at the request of King Louis XIII. He was largely responsible for the first polyglot Bible published in Paris including the Syriac and Arabic versions. He published one of the earliest Arabic grammars (*Grammatica arabica maronitarum in libros quinque divisa*, Lutetiæ, 1616). Then in collaboration with another compatriot from the College of Rome, Yūḥanna al-Ḥaṣrūni (Hesronita), he edited the Arabic text of Idrīsi's *Geography* (*Nuzhat al-Mushtāq fī Dhikr al-Amṣār wal-Aqṭar*), written in 1154, together with a Latin translation of part of it (*Geographia Nubiensis*, Parisiis, 1619). Sionita was succeeded in the Paris chair by Ecchellensis, Ibrāhīm al-Ḥāqili[4] or al-Ḥaqilāni (1605–64), a native of Ḥāqil in the Jibayl district of Lebanon, who was also educated in Rome and published an Arabic grammar (*Breveis institutio linguæ arabicæ*, Romæ, 1628), A Syriac grammar (*Linguæ syriacæ sive chaldaicæ perbrevis institutio*, Romæ, 1628), and many texts of a literary and theological nature from Arabic and Syriac. He died in Rome, and his books, sixty-four in number, were deposited in the Vatican Library and listed by Assemani in the first volume of his *Bibliotheca Orientalis*. The names of both Sionita and Ecchellensis are inscribed on the entrance of the *Collège de France*, the old *Collège Royal*. Ḥāqili's nephew, Murhij ibn Namrūn or Nirūn, Faustus Naironius (1630–1711),[5] born in the neighbourhood of Qannūbīn in the Qadīsha Valley, became interpreter for the Congregation for the Propagation of the Faith and professor of Oriental languages in Rome. Besides working on the Syriac and Arabic New Testament, he wrote a Maronite history (*Dissertatio de origine, nomine, ac religione Maronitarum*, Romæ, 1679). Maronite scholarship reached its peak in the illustrious careers of Assemani (Yūsuf Samʿān al-

[1] Al-Dibs, p. 373; Graf, III, 347–50; Hitti, pp. 403–5.

[2] Travellers report the use of Syriac as the Lebanese vernacular in numerous places. De Chasteuil in 1632 heard Syriac spoken at Ḥaṣrūn and Ihdin, De la Roque at Bisharri and al-Ḥadath in 1688, and even in 1810 the Swiss Burckhardt reported that 'many Maronites' spoke Syriac. Hitti, p. 404.

[3] Al-Dibs, pp. 382–3; Graf., III, 351–3; Hitti, p. 404.

[4] Al-Dibs, pp. 383–6; Graf., III, 354–9; Hitti, pp. 404–5.

[5] Al-Dibs, pp. 386–8; Graf., III, 359–61; Hitti, p. 405.

Samʿānī, 1687–1768) and Casiri (Mikhā'īl al-Ghazīri, 1701–91), to whose works allusion has been made.[1] It is no exaggeration to claim that these pioneers of Orientalism laid down the modest foundations of Syriac and Arabic, if not Semitic, studies in Europe and awakened the Western mind to the importance of the theological and liturgical heritage of Eastern Christendom for the first time in modern history.

Although the influx of Maronite students in Europe continued, the brilliance of its old school began to subside as the West reversed the tide by sending to Lebanon in the nineteenth century multitudes of missionaries and teachers. The decline of the Turkish caliphate and the loosening of the Ottoman grip over the Syrian province as a result of growing Western interference in Lebanese affairs after the Massacres of the Sixties brought Europeans and especially the French to the Maronite people. The culmination of Catholic French public educational and missionary enterprise in Lebanon was reached in 1875 with the establishment of the famous University of St Joseph in Beirūt, its confirmation by the pope in 1881, and its endowment with an annual subsidy from the French Ministry of Education to start schools of medicine and pharmacy in 1883. The university also had faculties of philosophy and theology, but both were surpassed by its faculty of Oriental studies. There is little doubt as to the immensity of the contribution of this last faculty to the field of Arabic scholarship where the Western canons of research and editing of manuscripts were introduced into the Middle East on a systematic basis. In conjunction with the Catholic University, the Catholic Press, founded in 1853, received a great impetus from scholars who provided it with some of the finest texts, hitherto unknown in the area, for publication.

One of the most prolific examples of the joint efforts of the university and the press is represented by the career of Louis Cheikho (1859–1928), a Chaldæan native of Mārdīn who became a Jesuit and occupied the chair of Arabic in the Jesuit University for many years. His output is staggering in quantity if not always in quality. He was one of the greatest manuscript hunters of all time, and his researches in the European repositories brought to light the jewels of Arabic literature. Harassed by the wealth of material before him, and eager for publication without respite, his work is sometimes assailed for its lack of the critical spirit of our time. Nevertheless, it is hard to minimize his impact on Arabic research. Indeed, if he achieved nothing beyond the editing of the Catholic University review *Al-Mashriq*[2] (The Orient) and the publication of the nine volume literary compendium *Majānī al-Adab fī Ḥadā'iq al-ʿArab* (Gleanings of Letters from the Orchards

[1] Vide supra, pp. 399 ff.

[2] *Revue catholique orientale* (bi-monthly from 1898, monthly from 1908, and quarterly from 1934).

of the Arabs),[1] he would have done enough to justify a place among the builders of Arabic scholarship in modern times. Under his editorship, *Al-Mashriq* became one of the leading organs in the development of Arabic literature, history, science and religion. *Majānī al-Adab* is still reckoned the finest book of extensive selections of Arabic literature. Cheikho's monumental history of Christian Arabic poetry from pre-Islamic times is unique and indispensable, if not definitive and invulnerable.

Although we are not here concerned with the literary history of Lebanon and the Maronites, it may be noted that the Catholics realized the importance of journalism in the cause of social and religious reform. Khalīl al-Khūry of al-Shuwayfāt was perhaps the editor of the first Lebanese journal, *Ḥadīqat al-Akhbār* (Garden of News), founded in 1859 and ranking third in Arabic press precedence – the other two being Muḥammad ʿAli Pasha's *Al-Waqāʾiʿ al-Miṣriyah* (The Egyptian Events), started in 1828, and *Mirʾāt al-Aḥwāl* (Mirror of Present Conditions) of Rizqallah Ḥassūn of Aleppo in 1854. The Jesuits, too, published *Al-Bashīr* (Missionary, or Herald) to counteract the earlier Protestant *Al-Nashrah* (The Review) of 1866.[2]

The impact of Protestant Christianity on the cultural and religious awakening of the Maronite community cannot be overlooked. The American University of Beirūt was founded on the basis of the Syrian Protestant College in 1866 and has rendered immeasurable services to all the nations of the Middle East regardless of faith, the Maronites included. Established earlier, in 1833, the Mission Press at Beirūt has since developed from hand printing to electrically powered equipment producing 3,000 pages per hour and a catalogue of over 500 publications. Outstanding amongst its output is the Arabic Bible, started by the Rev. Eli Smith (1802–57) and completed in 1864 by Dr Cornelius V. A. van Dyck (1819–95) with the help of Lebanese scholars including Buṭrus al-Bustānī (1819–83) and the poet Nāṣif al-Yāziji (1800–1871) as well as Shaykh Yūsuf al-Asīr (1815–89). Bible editions of the Mission Press in seventy-two forms have attained a total of well-nigh two and a half million copies and one and a half billion pages of Scriptures, Commentaries and other categories of purely religious literature. Protestant Lebanese scholars were worthy peers of the Romanized Maronites. Bustāni's Arabic encyclopædia[3] (*Dāʾirat al-Maʿārif al-ʿArabiyah*) and his Arabic lexicon[4] (*Muḥīṭ al-Muḥīṭ*, i.e., Circumference of the Ocean) are monuments of learn-

[1] Published Beirūt, 1882–3, it has been re-edited at least sixteen times.

[2] Hitti, *Lebanon*, pp. 464 et seq.

[3] He issued six volumes of this work in his lifetime (Beirūt, 1876–82), and his son Salīm issued five others in collaboration with Sulaymān al-Bustāni (Beirūt, 1883–1900). A new edition of the work has been resumed by the Lebanese State University in recent years.

[4] In 2 vols. (Beirūt, 1870), it has a condensation in two smaller volumes published Beirūt, 1869. Cf. Hitti, *Lebanon*, p. 462.

ing. Even outside Lebanon, graduates of Protestant colleges made literary history. Ya'qūb Ṣarrūf and Fāris Nimr issued the famous monthly review *Al-Muqtaṭaf* (Gleanings) first at Beirūt in 1876, whence they transferred it to Cairo and inaugurated their daily newspaper *Al-Muqaṭṭam*, both becoming extinct in 1952 after a glorious career. Jirji Zaydān (1861–1914), another emigrant to Egypt, was a great pioneer in the field of writing on the history of Muslim civilization and Arabic literature,[1] and his literary monthly review *Al-Hilāl* (The Crescent) survives to the present day.

[1] *Tārīkh al-Tamadyun al-Islāmī* (History of Muslim Civilization), 5 vols. (Cairo, 1902); *Tārīkh al-'Ādāb al-'Arabiyah* (History of Arabic Letters), 4 vols. (Cairo, 1911). He also wrote a series of historical novels illustrating the genesis of Arab and Muslim history in all its phases.

PART VII

THE VANISHED CHURCHES

EPILOGUE

28 • THE VANISHED CHURCHES

Introductory

Although the majority of the Eastern churches have survived the tremendous impact of the successive upheavals which have filled their world with sword and fire throughout their long and chequered history, some were unable to withstand those shocks and completely vanished from existence. The present volume has been limited to the surviving churches rather than to including the vanished ones. Nevertheless, we may be justified in adding a few brief notes on those ancient institutions as a reminder of their past glories. In the course of our survey of the history of the Jacobite and Nestorian churches, occasional reference was made to Christian communities in the Arabian peninsula, in the diocese of Baṣra, and in the Nestorian sees of Central Asia, Mongolia and the heart of China. All are now gone, and we tried to unravel some of the archæological and literary evidence proving their existence in the past. Other churches elsewhere suffered the same fate in spite of their former vitality and magnitude.

As we now review the map of Eastern Christianity, we note that the early Church struck root in three main centres where, after a period in which the faith and theological scholarship flourished beyond every expectation, simply vanished from the world altogether. These were the see of Carthage in North Africa on one side, the Pentapolis or Cyrenaica on the other and the kingdom of Nubia in the upper reaches of the Nile Valley beyond the First Cataract. The historian has to explain their extraordinary rise and their extraordinary disappearance. Of the three churches, Carthage has of course left a most indelible mark on the progress of Christian theology and learning. Curiously, however, it met its doom before the other two centres.

Some writers link Carthage and the Pentapolis too closely and almost identify them as one organization, since both were geographical twins with racial kinship in the wider unit of North Africa. On closer scrutiny, this is found to be unjustifiable. Whereas Cyrenaica looked eastward to Alexandria, Carthage looked rather to Rome. But we must be careful not to exaggerate or even suggest any Carthaginian ecclesiastical subjection to Roman authority in those early times. It is extremely difficult to define the first sources of the introduction of Christianity in the Western region of North Africa and to say whether it came from the West or the East or perhaps from both. In those early centuries, we find that most of the writings of the Fathers were in Greek; and Latin influences of North Africa as a whole were quite meagre. In fact, Greek was invariably the ecclesiastical language in use in Italy and even at Rome itself. Cyrenaica, on the other hand, was attached to the see of Alexandria by the terms of the sixth Nicæan injunction of 325 A.D.

Those two sections of North Africa, however, had much in common. Both were meeting places of races and cultures. In addition to the original natives, better known as Berber since the Islamic invasion of the seventh century, there were Phœnicians, Greeks, Jews, Romans, and Egyptians. Greek influence was stronger in Cyrenaica, while the Phœnician impact long outlived Phœnician dominion in Carthage. This racial and cultural mixture of the North African may be at the root of that religious renaissance which left behind it a monumental heritage of Christian scholarship.

Carthage[1]

This is not the place for the intricate survey of the details of Carthaginian Christianity and the organization of the North African Church. Our aim is to establish the importance of that phase in early Christian annals, and this is best done by enumerating some of the immortal names associated with it,

[1] Interest in North Africa started at a fairly early date, as may be seen from the works of E. A. Schelstrate, *Ecclesia Africana sub primate Carthaginiensi* (Paris, 1679); M. Leydecker, *Historia ecclesiæ Africanæ*, 2 vols. in 1 (Ultrajecti, 1690); T. Ruinart, *Historia persecutionis Vandaliæ* (Venice, 1732); F. Munteri, *Primordia ecclesiae Africanae* (Hafniae, 1829). The following is a selection of modern scholarship: J. Mesnage, *Le Christianisme en Afrique*, 3 vols. (Paris, 1915); H. Leclercq, *L'Afrique chrétienne*, 2 vols. (2nd ed.; Paris, 1904); G. Bardy, *L'Afrique chrétienne* (Paris, 1930); C. Cecchelli, *Africa Christiana, Africa romana* (Rome, 1936); J. P. Brisson, *Gloire et misère de l'Afrique chrétienne* (Paris, 1949); idem, *Autonomisme et Christianisme dans l'Afrique romaine de Septime Sévère à l'invasion vandale* (Paris, 1958); S. A. Donaldson, *Church Life and Thought in North Africa A.D. 200* (Cambridge, 1909); E. Buonaiuti, *Il Cristianesimo nell'Africa romana* (Bari, 1928); R. Höslinger, *Die alte afrikanische Kirche* (Vienna, 1935); E. Wieland, *Ein Ausflug ins christliche Afrika* (Stuttgart and Vienna, 1900); J. Lloyd, *The North African Church* (London, 1880); A. Schwarze, *Untersuchungen über die äussere Entwicklung der afrikanischen Kirche mit besonderer Verwertung der archäologischen Funde* (Göttingen, 1892); Mgr. Toulotte, *Géographie de l'Afrique chrétienne – Maurétanie* (Montreuil-sur-Mer, 1894). G. P. Groves, *The Planting of Christianity in Africa*, 4 vols. (London, 1948–58), I, 55 ff.; Ch.-André Jullien, *Histoire de l'Afrique du Nord*, 2 vols. (Paris, 1952–6), I, pp. 289–322, for full bibliographical references; Ch. Diehl, *L'Afrique byzantine, Histoire de la domination byzantine en Afrique, 533–709*, (Paris, 1896), still retains its value for general background of the pre-Arab period.

men whose life and work have moulded Christian thought for all time. To Carthage belongs the honour of producing Tertullian, St Cyprian and St Augustine of Hippo.[1] Each of them was a towering personality in the age in which he lived. In those three, the Christian Church found some of its most inspired confessors, defenders and interpreters.

Tertullian[2] was the son of a proconsular centurion resident at Carthage. Born in paganism at that city around 160 A.D., he was imbued with all the knowledge of his time and probably received part of his education in Rome. But he was a true Carthaginian and became a Christian in his native city, where he wrote most of his works. A lawyer by vocation, he turned his gift of eloquence to the defence of the Christian martyrs and the Christian faith. That was the age of Roman persecutions, the intensity of which is vividly depicted by Tertullian in his famous dictum: 'If the Tiber reaches the walls, if the Nile does not rise to the fields, if the sky does not move or the earth does, if there is famine, if there is plague, the cry is at once: "The Christians to the Lion!" '[3] Then occurred the passion of St Perpetua and St Felicitas together with a few others thrown to the wild beasts by order of Emperor Septimius Severus in the amphitheatre of Carthage on 7 March 203 within sight of Tertullian, who recorded the event. The North Africans therefore had their martyrs for Christ in common with the faithful elsewhere. In the course of his defence of Christian communities, Tertullian fortified the persecuted souls by his proverbial formula: 'Seed is the blood of Christians' (*Semen est sanguis Christianorum*) thus assuring them that their numbers will multiply beyond description.

Tertullian was a very prolific theologian and writer, the true Origen of the North African Church. Though he wrote several treatises in Greek in keeping with the spirit of the times, he was the first Church Father to inaugurate writing in Latin, which he used in the majority of his later works. To him also we owe the first use of the word 'Trinity', a creation of his lucid logic in the definition of the unity of God as he defended orthodoxy against Gnostic teachings. He drew the main lines of Western theology in parallel to Origen in the East. He was probably the first Christian theologian to apply the principles of the growing science of psychology to religious thought in a treatise entitled *De anima*. His unlimited fervour for the faith led him to espouse the rigorist cause of Montanism. Apart from its prophetic character, that doctrine enforced all manner of restrictions in fasting, forbidding flight from persecution, and the necessity of a second baptism for those who apostatized. He even fell out with Pope Calixtus I over teaching forgiveness

[1] The modern city of Bona, or Bone.

[2] For the many edns. and tr. of Tertullian's works as well as the innumerable studies written about him, see Quasten, *Patrology*, II, 246–340.

[3] Tertullian, *Apology*, ed. with English tr. by T. R. Glover (The Loeb Classical Library, London, 1953), pp. 182–3.

in case of mortal sin. Tertullian went to the extent of accusing the Catholic Church of lack of spiritual discipline. He became extremely ascetic in his living habits. He fought idolatry and heresy in all its forms, whether Gnostic, Manichæan or Marcionist. Though never canonized, he must be regarded as one of the most illustrious ante-Nicene Fathers of the Church. Subsequent generations continued to build on his illuminating trinitarianism and Christology after his death about 220 A.D.

The next great name of the African Church was St Cyprian[1] (d. 258), a man of a different character from Tertullian. Born a pagan and educated in rhetoric, he ultimately became a Christian a couple of decades after the death of Tertullian, with whose works he was thoroughly acquainted. Following in his footsteps, he became an ascetic and was elected bishop of Carthage only two years after his conversion about 248 A.D. He fled from the Decian persecution in 250, and on his return the question of rebaptism flared up again. He felt strongly about Roman laxity in this regard and was supported by numerous African church councils in the principle of enforcing baptism on heretics and schismatics. He wrote a fair amount, but his works generally reflect the practical nature of his pastoral office. He dealt with the conditions of reconciliation of apostates, alms-giving for indulgence, and the relations between the episcopate and church unity. He also wrote in praise of celibacy. He discussed such subjects as the ministry and the sacraments. Amongst his numerous epistles, those addressed to Stephen, bishop of Rome, are of exceptional interest. Their aggressive tenor has been used in refuting the traditional assumption of Roman supremacy over Carthage. Cyprian led a rather stormy life both within the church and outside. He was pursued by the imperial agents until in the end he surrendered himself and was martyred in 258.

Approximately a century after Cyprian's martyrdom, the genius of the African Church reached its peak in the emergence of the person of St Augustine of Hippo (354–430) whose life and work became one of the greatest landmarks in the development of Christian theology. St Augustine was a native African, born of a pagan father and a Christian mother. Educated at Carthage, he moved from rhetoric to philosophy and entertained serious doubts about Christianity. He lived for fifteen years with a woman to whom he was not married. He became a Manichæan for some nine years, during which he had many puzzling problems for which Faustus, his teacher, failed to give him the solution. Afterwards he migrated to Rome, where he taught rhetoric for a living, then moved to Milan, where he fell under the spell of St Ambrose. First he became a neo-Platonist, thereby opening his mind to the teaching of Christ. In the end, he found solace in reading the life of St Antony who provided him with the only solution of the prob-

[1] For bibliographical survey, cf. Quasten, II, 340–83; Jullien, I, 317.

lems of his turbulent spirit. In 386 he decided to retire to the seclusion of Cassiciacum for some months of meditation before accepting baptism in the following year. Subsequently he became a monk and returned to his birthplace in North Africa, the Numidian village of Thagaste, where he established a monastic community with some of his old companions in 388. At a later date, when he visited the city of Hippo, he seems to have profoundly impressed its inhabitants. Thus they took him by force to their old Bishop Valerius who elevated him to the priesthood and made him his episcopal coadjutor. On the decease of that prelate around the year 396, Augustine succeeded to that dignity and retained the title of Bishop until his death in 430 while the Vandals were hammering at the gates of Hippo.

Augustine[1] wrote against all the heresies of his time and refuted his old Manichæism as well as Arianism. His influence on Christian theology seems to have surpassed all his predecessors. Towards the end of his days, he became particularly involved in the Pelagian controversy and appears to have defended the doctrine of predestination. But of course the two great works which make him one of the foremost writers of any age are his *Confessions* and the *City of God*. The *Confessions* are in the nature of a penetrating autobiography which he brought down to 387, the year of his mother's death. He then outlines his own literary activity to 427 in his unfinished *Retractationes*. Altaner[2] sums up Augustine's position in Christian antiquity in these words: 'The great Bishop of Hippo combined the creative power of Tertullian and the intellectual breadth of Origen with the ecclesiastical sense of Cyprian, the dialectical acumen of Aristotle with the idealistic enthusiasm and the profound speculation of Plato, the practical sense of the Latin with the agile intellect of the Greek.' Few works have contributed as much as the *City of God* to the shaping of Christian thought in the Middle Ages. After the fall of Rome to the ungodly hordes of Alaric in 410, men's Christian hope and faith were shocked beyond recognition. It seemed as if the end of the world and all Christian civilization was imminent, and man's belief in the religion of Christ, to which some attributed that great calamity, was shaken. For thirteen years (413–26) Augustine laboured to weather the vehement onslaught on the faith and formulate his vindication of Christianity in the *City of God*. This work has indeed turned out to be a philosophy of history and of religion which, in the words of Pope Leo XIII,[3] 'set forth so clearly

[1] The Augustinian bibliography is of course fabulous in dimensions. One of the best selections of original edns., translations and other works on the numerous facets of Augustine's life and work may be found in B. Altaner, *Patrology*, tr. 5th German edn. Hilda C. Graeff, pp. 487–534; Jullien, I, 317–18.

[2] Patrology, 492.

[3] Encyclical letter on the Christian Constitution of States, *Immortale Dei*, dated 1 November 1885. *Nicene and Post-Nicene Fathers of the Christian Church*, ed. P. Schaff, II, iii (Grand Rapids, Mich., 1956).

the efficacy of Christian wisdom and the way in which it is bound up with the well-being of States, that he seems not only to have pleaded the cause of Christians of his own time, but to have triumphantly refuted the false charges for ever'. The Kingdom of God, the celestial Jerusalem, was the eternal kingdom which no earthly ravages or heathen human intellectualism could impair; and its only visible form on earth was the Catholic Church. It was in this way that Augustine was able to substantiate all the elements of patristic thought in the service of Catholic Christianity more effectively than any of his predecessors.

If the North African Church had produced no creative writers beyond Tertullian, Cyprian and Augustine, it would have more than justified its lofty place in Christian antiquity. But North Africa contributed even more in a smaller way through the works of other minor authors to whom little space can be allotted in a brief essay. Of these one was the famous rhetorician and teacher Arnobius of Sicca,[1] who lived from 253 to 327 and was a Christian convert from pagnism. Another was Lactantius,[2] also a teacher of rhetoric and a contemporary of Diocletian (284–304). After Christianity had become the state religion, the Emperor Constantine the Great nominated him in 317 to a tutorship of his son Crispus at Trèves in Gaul. He was then advanced in years and his death occurred soon afterwards about 320.

There is little doubt that under the *Pax romana* and after the termination of the age of persecution, Christianity continued to flourish and penetrated the distant regions of Africa, Numidia and Mauretania. Carthage, in addition to its illustrious theologians, had its own councils convened for settling local differences of doctrine, notably the Council of Carthage in 390, intended to deal with the growing Donatist schism[3] in the country. This schism, which seems to have persisted until the coming of Islam, started in the early fourth century on the pretext that the consecration of one bishop of Carthage named Cæcilian was performed by Felix, whom the hierarchy knew to be a '*traditor*' who had surrendered the Holy Scriptures to the persecutors of Christians. Hence, seventy of their bishops elected a rival bishop in the person of Majorinus in 312. After the peace of Constantine and the death of Majorinus about 315, Donatus, who had led the movement, succeeded him and consecrated many local bishops in villages and farms in order to gain numerical superiority over his rival. The Donatists were both rigorists and nationalists at the same time, and they leaned on the authority of Cyprian to support their independence from Rome. Even the weight of St Augustine's disapproval of the Donatist tendencies proved to be without avail.

The position became even worse after the Vandal invasion in the fifth century. The Vandals were Arians by confession and substituted their Arian

[1] Quasten, II, 383–92. [2] Ibid., pp. 392–410.
[3] References on Donatism, see Jullien, I, 318–19.

priesthood for both Catholic and Donatist. In fact, Catholicism might have been completely extinguished from Africa, had it not been for the premature death of King Huneric at the end of 484. It is interesting to note that, while using Latin for diplomatic and legal purposes as a written language, the church liturgies were celebrated in the Vandal or Germanic vernacular under Vandal rule. Thus another element of confusion was added to the list which the native Berbers could not digest, and Christianity remained only skin-deep with pagan superstitions still surviving in Berber tradition.

The return of the province of Africa to Byzantine rule under Justinian meant a new form of persecution for Arians, Donatists, Jews and pagans. The imperial Christianization of the Berber chiefs hardly touched the lower members of their clans, and the Gospel only proved to be a cheaper mode of holding the threads of authority than armed force was in the remote outposts of Byzantine Africa.[1] Thus the stage began to be set for the impending Muslim upheaval.

The Pentapolis

Cyrenaica, the Pentapolis or the five towns – namely Cyrene (Shaḥḥāt), Apollonia (Marsa Goua), Ptolemaïs (Ṭolmeta), Berenice (Beng<u>h</u>āzi) and Barce (Barqa) – was wedged between Tripoli and the Egyptian province of Mareotis in the western desert. It had more to do with Egypt than with the North African province of Carthage and beyond. Both its geographical setting and the fact that it formed the terminal station of the caravan routes reaching it from the heart of the desert, made it attractive to the Greek and Jewish settlers and traders who linked the area more closely with the eastern Mediterranean and, more especially, with the Egyptian metropolis of Alexandria. All this paved the way for the spread of Christianity in the area at one and the same time as Egypt. Indeed, the apostle of Egyptian Christianity was a native Jew of Cyrene, St Mark the Evangelist, who came to Alexandria by way of the Pentapolis and, after planting the new faith in Egypt, himself returned to Cyrene to work on his fellow-citizens on more than one occasion. Ecclesiastically, therefore, from the very beginning the Pentapolis was tied to the Egyptian capital, and the Council of Nicæa ordained that it should be subject to the see of Alexandria. The Coptic patriarch to this day carries the Pentapolis in his title as a province of the see of St Mark.

Thus we must assume the continuous flow of ecclesiastical and missionary

[1] Leclercq, *L'Afrique chrétienne*, II, 214 ff.; Lloyd, *North African Church*, 314 ff.

personnel between those two countries in much the same way as between Carthage and Rome. The overwhelming Greek element in Cyrenaica also facilitated communication between the two groups, since Greek was the *lingua franca* of both. Most of the leading clerics in the Pentapolis were educated in Alexandria, formerly in the Museion and later in the Christian Catechetical School. Though the data as to the extent of the interchange between the two churches are not yet fully available, it would appear beyond doubt that it was active. The example of Arius, the heresiarch of Alexandria, is sufficient testimony to Libyan infiltration in the hierarchy at the metropolis. On the other hand, Alexandrine culture, both philosophical and theological, in the Pentapolis is best represented by Synesius of Cyrene,[1] bishop of Ptolemaïs, whose name has come down in history as one of the Fathers of the Eastern Church.

He was born of pagan parents of great wealth in Cyrene about 370. After receiving all the education offered at Cyrene, he moved to Alexandria, where he attended the classes of the last of the pagan neo-Platonists, Hypatia, at the Museion. He was captivated by the spell of her teachings and became her neo-Platonist disciple. He continued to cherish her memory with the deepest of reverence, even though he became a Christian and she died a pagan, stoned by his own co-religionists. From Alexandria, he went to Athens for more knowledge, but to his disappointment found there no more teachers and no more philosophy. So he returned to his native country, where his fellow-citizens commissioned him to go to Constantinople and plead with the emperor on their behalf for tax relief. The success of his mission made him popular with his own people. Afterwards, he went back to Alexandria, where he received his wedded wife from the hands of the Patriarch Theophilus (385–412). This is sufficient proof that he became a Christian, though there is no evidence to show that he was baptized as late as 410. It was in that year that his people wanted to demonstrate their gratitude to him for the success of his mission to Byzantium and for organizing their defence against Berber inroads from the south by electing him to the episcopate.

Synesius was a married man and a confirmed neo-Platonist, and he was unwilling to give up either for the proffered privilege. Thus the clergy and the people of Ptolemaïs appealed to the patriarch, who was not unaware of his stature and sincerity, and he readily granted their request. Until the end of his life, about 414, Synesius was the true leader of his people, not only in matters of religion, but also in public justice, administration and defence. He was a lover of mankind and an outstanding horseman, he used the bow and arrow skilfully, and was a church builder. The visitor to the Pentapolis can still witness the archæological remains of some of his churches which

[1] Quasten, *Patrology*, III, 106–14; W. Bright, *The Age of the Fathers*, 2 vols. (London, 1903), II, 141–4.

were turned into self-contained fortresses whenever an attack came from the Berber marauders.

Together with his practical instincts in war and peace, he was able to compose religious hymns and homilies, though he clung to his neo-Platonist philosophy to the last. He had his sense of humour and found time to write a treatise in praise of baldness. He is, however, better known to us by a collection of 156 epistles written between 399 and 413 and addressed to all manner of people, from the pagan Hypatia to St Theophilus the Patriarch. They are a rich source for the social life and geographical lore of the period. They deal with private affairs, official transactions, ecclesiastical business, and some even betray the element of syncretism in his treatment of matters of philosophy and theology. Synesius was probably the greatest personality in the whole of the history of the Pentapolis. He was also described as one of the three pillars of the church of St Mark, the two others being Isidore, the priest of Pelusium, and Shenute of Athripe, abbot of the White Monastery. Isidore guarded the eastern gate, Shenute the southern, and Synesius the western gate while Alexandria stood in the midst of the three.

On the whole, the Pentapolis followed Alexandria in all phases of its development during the Christian period. It was subjected to the same wave of persecution, and one of its bishops, Theodore, succumbed in the reign of Diocletian, and figures on the Coptic *Synaxarium*. Even in matters of heresy, there were the same divisions within Cyrenaica when two of its local bishops, Theonas of Marmarica and Secundus of Ptolemaïs, stood solidly behind Arius. It is interesting to note that the third-century heresy of Sabellianism or Subordinationism, which made distinction between the Son and the Father, the Logos and the Creator of the Logos, arose from a discussion by Sabellius, bishop of Ptolemaïs, and was opposed by two other bishops from the Pentapolis, by name Amon and Euphranor.

One fact remains clear about Cyrenaican Christianity. It seemed to be almost entirely concentrated amongst the Greek population, who fought the Berbers from the southern Sahara as a race of marauders whom they never truly cared to convert or civilize. Thus the Berbers remained outside the pale of the Church with their own pagan practices. When the Arabs came on the scene, the Greeks emigrated, and the two remaining nomadic races met with better understanding. This in part accounts for that sudden disappearance of Christianity from the Pentapolis and the spread of Islam after the advent of the Arabs.

Nubia

As already shown in the course of our discussion of the Coptic missionary enterprise, Christianity was introduced into Nubia by way of Egypt at an early date. Nubia had been open to Egypt since the eleventh dynasty (2100–2000 B.C.) during the Middle Kingdom. Egyptian civilization and Egyptian religion had been accepted by the Nubians. Numerous Egyptian temples were built in the area, especially in the reign of Ramses II. No greater example could be found than the formidable rock-hewn temples of Abu Simbel, which were destined to be submerged by the rising Nile water behind the Aswān High Dam, had they not been saved by a consorted effort of the civilized world. Still further up the Nile, under the ægis of ancient Egyptian civilization, the Meroïtic culture developed in the area of Meroë, and valuable remains have been recovered from the region of Shendi through modern excavation.[1] It is not as strange as it might seem that the Egyptian Christian missionaries followed the beaten road to Nubia without great difficulty. In fact, a closer enquiry would show that the kings of Nubia themselves pleaded with the Egyptian Church to send special heralds to preach the new Gospel at their courts.

One may safely assume that before the end of the sixth century,[2] Christianity had penetrated all three Nubian kingdoms extending south of Syene (modern Aswān) into the lower and central Sudan. The first of these was the kingdom of the Nobadæ, between the First and Second Cataracts. The second was the kingdom of the Makorites, across the Third, Fourth and Fifth Cataracts round the great bends of the Nile River with Meroë as its capital just north of present-day Shendi. The third was the kingdom of the Alodæ (the Arabic *ʿAlwa*), around the confluence of the White Nile and the Blue Nile and comprising the Jezira between them with its capital Soba, just a few miles south of Khartoum on the banks of the Blue Nile. Of course the frontiers of these kingdoms were rather fluid, although the inhabitants had many common characteristics and all seemed willing to follow the religious

[1] See above, chapters on Coptic Missionary and on Coptic Art.

[2] U. Monneret de Villard, *Storia della Nubia Cristiana* (Orientalia Christiana Analecta, No. 118; Rome, 1938), pp. 130 ff.; Groves, I, 106 ff.; J. S. Trimingham *Islam in the Sudan* (Oxford, 1949), pp. 48 ff., 67 ff.; E. A. Wallis Budge, *The Egyptian Sudan*, 2 vols. (London, 1907), I, 64 ff.; idem, *A History of Ethiopia, Nubia, and Abyssinia*, 2 vols. (London, 1928), I, 103 ff.; F. L. Griffith, *Christian Documents from Nubia* (British Academy Proceedings, London, 1928), pp. 117–46; ibid., *The Nubian Texts of the Christian Period* (Abhandlungen der Königl. Preuss. Akademie der Wissenschaften, Jahrgang 1913. Phil.-Hist. Classe. Nr. 8. Berlin, 1913); Zāhir Riāḍ, *The Church of Alexandria in Africa* (in Arabic; Cairo, 1962), pp. 147–93. Another study in Arabic has also appeared under the title *Islam and Nubia in the Middle Ages*, a thesis pub. by Mosṭafa Muḥammad Misʿed (Cairo, 1960), pp. 42 ff.

example of Egypt from the ancient gods to Christ. Unlike the Greeks in Cyrenaica and the citizens of Carthage and other North African towns who kept Christianity as the aristocratic religion and did not care to plant it amongst the Berbers, the Egyptians displayed the greatest eagerness to convert the Nubians and to help them develop their own Christianity from within. This particular feature may help in understanding why Nubian Christianity managed to persist much longer than North African Christianity after the advent of the Muslim invaders.

Preliminary archæological research has confirmed the spreading of the Gospel widely into Nubia. Mention has been made of the findings of Christian antiquities in the Meroïtic excavations in the Sudan. Furthermore, it has been established that no less than fifty monastic and church buildings of note have been located between Aswān and Sennār on the Blue Nile. This magnificent revelation has been the contribution of Somers Clarke,[1] who made an archæological and architectural survey of every one of those monuments. It would be a grave error to say that Clarke had accumulated all the details of a complete inventory of all monuments of Nubian Christianity. All that may be asserted here is that he has led the way for further discoveries in a field where our knowledge has only touched the surface.[2] As late as the thirteenth century, the historian of the Coptic churches and monasteries, Abu Ṣāleḥ 'the Armenian', puts on record that the northern Nubian kingdom of the Makorites, or Makurra, comprised seven bishoprics and numerous monasteries and churches, while the southern Nubian kingdom of the Alodæ, or ʿAlwa, had some four hundred churches. Even allowing for exaggeration, this indicates the degree of the progress of Christianity in Nubia, a fact confirmed by some Islamic geographers of mediæval times. Some place names, proper names, and even common words with a Christian or Coptic connotation are said to have survived in Nubian usage to the present day. The story of Bishop Longinus, already mentioned in previous pages, could not have been a solitary episode, and there is reason to believe that the ascetic monks of Egypt were not deterred from their pious pursuits beyond the southern frontier of their own country.[3] Another point which must be made clear in this connexion is that Nubian Christianity and Axumite or Ethiopian Christianity were isolated and without much interaction between them. Both of them were initiated from Egypt, and Ethiopia received its evangelists by the Red Sea route while Nubian Christianity travelled upstream along the Nile Valley. The latter thus had greater access to the mother church. It was not until the Copts became deeply involved in their

[1] *Christian Antiquities in the Nile Valley* (Oxford, 1912), pp. 34 ff. See also Monneret de Villard, *Nubia Cristiana*, pp. 158–68.

[2] On the problem of evangelization, see Monneret de Villard, pp. 53–70.

[3] Cf. Groves, I, 107; Trimingham, p. 69.

own local troubles long after the Arab Conquest that this relationship frittered away and the Nubians were left to themselves, a forlorn Christian group to be gradually engulfed in the rising sea of Islam.

Advent of Islam: Beginning of the End

It is needless here to dwell on the rise of Islam in the seventh century or even to attempt a full review of its bewildering but inevitable conquests of the Asiatic and African provinces of the Byzantine empire. However, the logical sequence of the Arab Conquest of Egypt in 640–42 was a further thrust westward into the Pentapolis and North Africa, which the Arabs designated as *Barqa* and *Ifrīqiya,* in order to safeguard the fairest of all their acquisitions against surprise attacks from those Byzantine bases. Their campaigns started as mere raids of intimidation by ʿAmr ibn al-ʿĀṣ himself but it was soon discovered that they could be conducted for permanent occupation. The first real actor in that drama was ʿUqba ibn Nāfiʿ, an aggressive and impulsive warrior who sallied through Cyrenaica to Ifrīqiya where he was superseded by the more diplomatic freedman Abu al-Muhājir Dīnār, who aimed at conciliating the Berbers by offering them Islam, equality and participation in the war with their common enemy, the aristocratic Byzantine. It took the Berbers some time to comprehend Arab policies and to accept the generous offer; and they were pacified only after numerous struggles associated with the names of the Lawāta tribe, a Berber leader called Kusaila, and a Berber priestess (al-Kāhina) whose extermination made the *rapprochement* between the native Berber and the Arab a possibility. This, in addition to the rising maritime supremacy of the Arabs, sealed the fate of the last Roman strongholds in Africa. Carthage had fallen into their hands in 698. Other centres soon succumbed and the leading Christian townfolk emigrated *en masse* to Spain, Sicily, Italy and Byzantium in much the same way as the Melkite Orthodox Greeks did after the Arab conquest of Egypt. With their emigration, Christianity began its precipitous decline in Africa.

Let us review the causes and factors at work behind this sudden disappearance of the Christian Church in Africa.[1] In the first place, the Church which gave the world such luminous names as Tertullian, Cyprian, Augustine and Synesius remained embedded in the towns and its sons never really cared to undertake any enduring missionary enterprise amidst the Berber tribes. In Cyrenaica they were repelled and at Carthage they were shunned. After Chalcedon (451) and the inauguration of systematic persecution of the Monophysites, the situation worsened and Egyptian vitality was exhausted in

[1] Z. Riāḍ, pp. 66–73; Groves, I, 78 ff.; Leclercq, II, 274 ff.; Lloyd, pp. 374 ff.

local squabbles rather than devoted to any attention to the diocese of the Pentapolis. The Berbers with their superstitious mythology were thus kept outside the pale of Christian civilization.

In the second place, socially the Christians were urban and sedentary, and the Berbers were nomadic like the Arabs. The very mode of Berber life fitted much more readily with that of the Arabs, but never with that of the Greeks and Romans identified with Christianity.

In the third place, the Arabs extended the privileges of the Covenant of ʿUmar to the North African tribes, while offering them the new religion with full equality. As a matter of fact, the Arabs invited Berber co-operation in their Spanish military venture, and that policy persisted even after the fall of Visigothic Spain in 711.

In the fourth place, the waves of emigration to and from North Africa altered the racial balance of power in the region. Whereas the Christians departed after the advent of the Arabs, we find that another tide of emigration took place in the other direction from Arabia. Barqa and Ifrīqiya seem to have captivated Arab imagination, and whole tribes began to pour into the vacuum created by the disappearance of the Greeks and the Romans. The adventures of Banū Hilāl and Banū Sālim, which are still an object of Arabic folklore, are representative examples of that movement of Arab clans and families toward the west. Apparently they became merged in the native Berber population after a short transitional period.

In the fifth place, we note that most of the heterodox parties amongst the Arabs took to the west, where they pursued a missionary career among the Berbers. The Khārijites inaugurated this movement. The Shīʿites followed later and became so strong as to establish their own caliphate, known as the Fatimid caliphate, which conquered Egypt from the west in the tenth century and built up a vast empire in the Near East.

In the sixth place, it must be remembered that the whole economy of Cyrenaica and North Africa was pre-eminently founded on slavery and the slave trade, and Islam came to offer full enfranchisement to armies of slaves in the provinces of Africa with a promise of equal brotherhood as the price of conversion.

Last but not least, was the burden of Byzantine taxation, which seems to have been on the ascendancy. Though it would be an error to contend that that burden was curtailed under Islam, the Berbers encountered a promise of Arab leniency, and realized that they were treated no more harshly by the new masters than by the old.

It is therefore no wonder that the Berber tribes found it more to their advantage to accept the new situation readily and to settle down with the invaders on a footing of social equality. They even offered a helping hand in the task of exterminating the Church which they regarded as a symbol of past humiliation. It took little time and effort to accomplish that mission, since the Church was already on the edge of bankruptcy.

The picture becomes somewhat different when we look at Nubian Christianity and its stand *vis-à-vis* the coming of Islam.[1] Here, resistance proved to be more tenacious, and the native church survived as long as the independent kingdoms were able to last. The first onslaught in Nubia occurred in 651–2. ʿAmr's successor, ʿAbd-Allah ibn Saʿd ibn Abi al-Sarḥ, managed to attain Dongola, but soon found it more expedient to retire from the field with a favourable treaty than to follow a wild-goose chase. In sum, he safeguarded Muslim interests in Nubia and wrested a promise of payment of an annual tribute known as *Baqṭ*, amounting at that time to 360 slaves.[2] These were the conditions which recurred with regularity throughout the next six centuries. On the other hand, we read of counter-attacks from the Nubian side every time the news reached their king that the Coptic patriarch in Egypt was abused or subjected to extortionate imposts together with their northern brethren. About a century after the conclusion of the said treaty, Kyriakos, king of northern Nubia (744–68), invaded southern Egypt for that very purpose. The episode appears to have been repeated on other recorded and unrecorded occasions. In 854, the Baga tribes suspended the tribute and invaded Egypt. In 963, a similar incident occurred. In 969, the Fatimid caliph sent an embassy to George, king of Nubia, to invite him to accept Islam and to render the annual tribute. The king treated the embassy generously and sent his tribute with a refusal of conversion. Caliph al-Ḥākim insisted that the patriarch should not contact the king of Nubia without the knowledge of the governor for fear that he might cause the king to invade Egypt.[3]

In reality, systematic inroads into Nubia from Egypt did not begin to assume serious dimensions until the period of the Crusades and the rise of Saladin.[4] Crusade propagandist literature frequently refers to the possibility of consorted action with the Christians of Nubia against the Islamic empire. These references recur in the later mediæval period, and we find them in the works of Marino Sanudo and Ludolph von Suchem as late as the middle of the fourteenth century.[5] But the tide of the southern invasion had begun. While Saladin's armies were invading Barqa in 1172–3, he dispatched his own brother Shams-al-Daula Tūrān Shah to the south, where he played havoc in the kingdom of the Makorites (Maqurra), seized Ibrīm – the Roman Primis – and left there a Kurdish garrison, though the Christian kingdom as a whole remained intact and independent.

The real catastrophe of Nubian Christianity occurred during Mamlūk

[1] Trimingham, p. 69.

[2] Treaty quoted by Lane-Poole, pp. 21–3, and Trimingham, pp. 61–2.

[3] Lane-Poole, pp. 41, 88, 105, 129, 143.

[4] Monneret de Villard, pp. 196 ff.

[5] Atiya, *Crusade in the Later Middle Ages*, p. 121.

rule. The story started in 1272 when King David refused to pay the usual *Baqṭ* tribute to Sultan Baybars (1260–77). Accordingly, he sent two expeditions in 1275 and 1276 which played off one Christian pretender against another and secured a treaty whereby the Nubians should pay a poll-tax of one gold dinar for every adult male to retain his Christian faith. Other expeditions followed during the reign of Sultan Qalā'ūn in 1287 and 1289, ending in the occupation of the important town of Dongola. Qalā'ūn's son al-Nāṣir Muḥammad repeated the campaigns in 1315 and 1316, and his men placed on the throne a nephew of King David called ʿAbdallah ibn Sanbu,[1] who apparently apostatized to Islam though the bulk of the population was still Christian. New complications arose with the emergence of a Muslim principality at Aswān led by Banū Kinz and the gradual opening of Nubia to Muslim Arab settlers, notably of the Juhayna tribe. The Coptic Church in Egypt was engrossed in its own local troubles and became unable to exert a direct pastoral influence on the Nubian people, who were spiritually isolated. More Muslim inroads are recorded in the years 1365, 1378, 1385 and 1397.[2] The confusion was accentuated by Arab dissensions when the Hawwāra Arabs exterminated the rule of Banū Kinz and destroyed Aswān in 1412. In the meantime the Fung and Shilluk negro peoples descended on the kingdom of ʿAlwa from the upper reaches of the Nile and seized the capital, Soba.[3] While Dongola was turned into a stronghold of Arab and Islamic influence, a Fung kingdom of Sennār arose around the Blue Nile beyond Soba, and the Christians were caught between two fires in the late Middle Ages. Nevertheless, it would be a mistake to minimize the length of the transitional change from Christianity to Islam in Nubia. Portuguese reports in the sixteenth century indicate the survival of Christians in Nubia, but they were doomed beyond saving, although they clung to the faith surprisingly longer than any of the other vanished churches of North Africa. In the end came the final extinction of the early church, not only in Carthage and the Pentapolis, but also in Nubia.

[1] Trimingham, p. 70.
[2] Somers Clarke, pp. 10–11.
[3] Trimingham, p. 79.

29 • EPILOGUE

At this journey's end, it is fitting to ponder over the causes of survival of the most ancient Christianity of the East in the midst of a surging sea of Islam. This phenomenon becomes all the more of a miracle when we realize that a Christian had little to gain from either society or state by staunchly maintaining the religion of his forefathers, whereas Islam spontaneously removed his disabilities and offered him limitless social preferment and material privilege. In the meantime, we must not forget that Islam was only another monotheistic religion, a good religion where the change of profession, though discountenanced by and distasteful to his co-religionists, did not really throw a long shadow of shame on an apostate.

The sources of this miracle of survival may be classified as partly internal and partly external. First and foremost among the internal sources is perhaps the profound spirituality of those churches. Watered by the blood of myriads of their martyrs, their spirituality was further confirmed by the racial consciousness and individuality of those historic communities. Within the walls of that fortress of the faith, the eastern Christian was able to preserve the purity of his race from pollution through intermarriage with the ceaseless waves of conquerors from outside. Initially a way of worship, faith in the end became a comprehensive way of life and a symbol of an old culture for the isolated Christian in the old homeland. He was the bearer of a torch which he was determined to hand over to posterity and keep aglow.

Though long unrecognized, the external factors in the picture of Christian survival in the East seem to be of equal importance. When we regard the expanding majority of Muslims against a shrinking minority of Christians, it is not inconceivable to envisage the possibility that, at many critical moments in the past, the majority might have exterminated the minority in an age addicted to violence. On the whole, historic facts appear to indicate a different outlook. The Christian was not only accepted, but also revered by his Muslim neighbours. There was no humiliation in being a Christian in the eyes of a Muslim, and it was equally honourable for the Muslim to be a Muslim in the opinion of the Eastern Christian. It is unhistoric to read more than is necessary in the periodic Christian persecutions in Islamic times. Strictly speaking, sporadic use of force invariably emanated from the personal whims of an abnormal monarch, and was occasionally steered against Muslims and Christians without discrimination and with similar brutality. Mob violence, on the other hand, flared up at times; but this was usually restricted to the big city and was often stirred by foreign influence. That state of affairs, it must be remembered, was in keeping with the tenor of life itself in the framework of mediæval society. Without exaggerating Christian liberties, which were foreign to the age, it would appear that the survival of Christianity in the East was ensured at least in part by the acceptance of its Islamic environment. It is wrong to minimize the importance of this external factor, and antiquated conceptions must be modified in the light of new knowledge.

The churches under review in this volume are pre-eminently of apostolic origin, and their contributions to the shaping of Christian theology in the earliest formative centuries of the faith have never been in question by either friend or foe. Their cities were great repositories of religious scholarship and their saints were legion and legendary. Jerusalem, Antioch, Alexandria, Nicæa, Ephesus, Nisibis, Edessa, Damascus and a whole host of other towns, now changed in character or lying in ruins, were once seats of the most illustrious patriarchs and prelates whose stories are little known or still unstudied. Names of men like Ignatius, Origen, Antony the Great, Athanasius, Pachomius of the Thebaïd, Cyril I, Ephraem the Syrian, Gregory the Illuminator, Jacob Baradæus, Bar Hebræus, ʿAbd-Ishūʿ, Mar Jahballaha, and hundreds more mentioned in the foregoing pages were architects of capital events or whole systems of thought and action in the annals of mankind. The panoramic galaxy of those immortals, scarcely clarified in Western scholarship, has even been forgotten by their own kin and native communities. As a matter of fact, our knowledge of almost all aspects of Eastern Christianity is still in its infancy and calls for endless scholarly endeavour.

Apology has been sought and justified as to the state of oblivion in which the Eastern Christian found himself concerning his own glorious early heritage. Like a soldier in the field, he had little time to sit back for introspective reflection and literary productivity. Even with Muslim acceptance, he continued to live in the hazards of a permanent struggle for survival until the emergence of the modern age of religious tolerance. With the progress of liberalism and enfranchisement of the mind in our day, like all other communities, the Christians of the East have gained enough respite to look into the annals of their notable forbears of whom they have the right to pride themselves. Nevertheless the gulf between the immensity of their heritage and the paucity of their modern literature is still lamentable. With growing reassurance from within, and increasing interest in their communities from outside, this situation has just started to show signs of a change.

In fact, one of the remarkable features of our time is the growth of sympathy with and understanding of the Eastern Christians amongst the children of their ancient adversaries in the West. The current œcumenical movement has been the scene of these epoch-making developments in the history of modern Christianity. After centuries of isolation and separatism, the churches of the East have at long last sent official delegations to the World Council of Churches. Furthermore, they are now permanently represented on its Central Committee and are playing their role in the deliberations of world divines. While raising the morale of these eastern communities, this type of recognition is steadily bridging the gap which has separated East and West since the disaster of Chalcedon in 451 A.D.

Equally impressive is the momentous struggle taking place within the Vatican Œcumenical Council against Roman traditionalism. That council is rightfully regarded as the greatest Catholic assembly ever convened since the Council of Trent (1545–63) and the turbulent times of the Counter-Reformation. Besides the Eastern uniate minority bishops within the council, the major ancient churches of the East have despatched their own observers to witness the progress of its deliberations from outside. Here problems of the highest interest to the Eastern Christian have been raised in the Council *schema*. In addition to the recognition of episcopal collegiality which restores the ancient Eastern usage of fraternal authority to all bishops in harmony with the pope and the Roman *curia*, whole groups of prelates have insisted on the discussion of such subjects as religious liberty, co-operative fellowship with all Christians of other denominations, and even a deferential attitude towards the ways of members of other faiths – Muslims, Jews, Hindus and Buddhists alike.

It may be well at this juncture to remind the reader of a basic principle in the primitive structure of Eastern Christianity. While upholding the greater issues of unity and universality of the Apostolic Church round the person of the Christ, the Eastern Christians insisted on recognition of the local autonomy of each church within its own ecclesiastical confines.[1] Moreover, intercommunion between churches and the exchange of prelates from lands

[1] It is interesting to note that the patriarchal dignity in the East, whether orthodox or Catholic, is still regarded as a summit in the universal hierarchy. When Pope Paul VI recently decided to create a group of new cardinals, including uniate patriarchs, there arose strong opposition in the eastern ecclesiastical circles to the acceptance of the title. Archbishop Elias al-Zughby, patriarchal *nuncio* of the Catholic Church of Antioch in Egypt and the Sudan, voiced that trend in the Synod by actual resignation from the position of *nuncio* as a protest against the installation of his patriarch Maximus IV al-Sayegh in the cardinalate which implied subservience to the Pope who himself was only the patriarch of Rome, otherwise *primus inter pares*.

far and near were established canonical usages in Eastern Christian jurisdiction. The example was set from antiquity by the ancient sees of Antioch and Alexandria where the patriarchal dignity was open to candidates from both sources on one and the same footing. A Copt, namely Paul the Black,[1] was elected Patriarch of Antioch (564–81), while Ephraem the Syrian was enthroned in Alexandria[2] (975–78) and acclaimed by the Copts as consecrated father of their Church and community. Even the unsuccessful but interesting preferment of the Jacobite Isodorus[3] to the episcopate in the Coptic hierarchy within living memory (1897) is another illustration of the validity of that ancient custom.

Although the matters of religious liberty and the implementation of the decree *De œcumenismo* are still in abeyance within the Vatican Œcumenical Council, there is no reason for doubting the seriousness of papal authority in pursuing every possible means of building bridges of understanding and co-operation with other churches. One concrete demonstration of this revolutionary departure from the rigidity of Roman traditionalism has occurred as these lines are being written (18 February 1965) in the visit of so eminent a personality as Augustin Cardinal Bea to the seat of the World Council of Churches at Geneva. The eighty-three-year-old Cardinal, who is the head of the Secretariat for Christian Unity in the Vatican has officially announced that the 'Holy See greets with joy and fully accepts' the council invitation to Rome 'to explore together the possibilities of dialogue and collaboration'. This is perhaps the beginning of the first bridge over the fearful hiatus which has existed for centuries between the Catholic Church and the 214 member churches represented in the World Council comprising the Greek Orthodox, Anglican, Protestant and Eastern denominations. A joint committee is contemplated to review what the Cardinal termed as causes of tension between the churches. The hitherto uncompromising attitudes of ecclesiastical authorities over mixed marriages, religious liberty and proselytization will be re-considered. Collaboration in the fields of philanthropy, social and international affairs, programmes bearing on various systems of theology and œcumenism, and that common interest in the missionary endeavour must be promoted.

As a matter of fact, the *schema*[4] of the Second Vatican Council goes even

[1] See above under Jacobite Church, Chapter 9, p. 185.

[2] See above under Coptic Church, Chapter 5, pp. 87–8, note 4.

[3] See above, Chapter 6, p. 111.

[4] Though the Vatican Œcumenical Council proceedings are still in progress, the growth of literature on the subject is continuous. The following is a selection of works written on the subject. U. Betti, *La constituzione dommatica 'Pastor Æternus' del Concilio Vaticano II* (Rome, 1961); P. Palazzini, *Alta vigilia del Concilio Ecumenico Vaticano II* (Rome, 1961); Y. Congar, H. Küng, and D. O'Hanlon (eds.), *Council Speeches of Vatican II* (London and New York, 1964); J. A. Mackay, *Ecumenics: The Science of the Church Universal* (Englewood

further, at least in theory. In one chapter as already stated, it speaks of human dignity and forbids religious discrimination between members of faiths other than Christianity. It unfolds terms of a loving and brotherly way towards all mankind for 'He who does not love does not know God.' (I John, iv, 8).

Throughout all these salutary *rapprochements* between East and West, and between organs Catholic and non-Catholic, one novel feature of special importance to this study has become more ostensible than ever before. This is the greater attention and regard accorded to the Oriental churches, whether African or Asiatic. In recent years, all have expressed apprehension over the fate of a subject in which they share a common interest, that is, the missionary endeavour in Africa and the whole East. The gravity of the position has been unmitigated by contemporary political developments amongst the resurgent nationalist sentiments of newly created states where the white missionary has been rightly or wrongly indentified with the former colonialist.

An African diplomat by the name of Milton Obote, premier of Uganda, once said: 'We would avoid difficulties by having more African clergymen; after all churches are international. White missionaries have done good work, but their era is finished.' The educational, medical and social services of the Western missionaries, Catholic or Protestant, were valued by the natives and all went well in Africa and the East until two factors precipitated the decline of the movement. In the first place, there was the temptation of the missionary to pursue the easy way of proselytism in the folds of fellow Christians from the ancient Eastern churches. The inevitable consequence was separatism in the ranks of Christians before the doubting non-Christian and this was certainly no service to the missionary cause. In the second place, this predicament was further intensified by the state of new nations, long under the yoke of the white colonialists with whom the missionary was spontaneously repudiated.

These emerging paradoxes of our time call for constructive solutions to save the noble missionary movement from frittering away into bankruptcy. Courageous thought and drastic action in Mission Board policies are our only hope for dealing effectively with a difficult situation. If the native eastern churches rather than the European religious envoys were the accepted channels through which the native of our day could be reached with impunity, then two steps would appear commendable in our procedures. First, the drive towards proselytism must be arrested once and for all in order to strengthen the churches of the East by a systematic avoidance of separating their sons from their ancient professions. Little good can accrue

---

Cliffs, N.J., 1964); Douglas Horton, *Vatican Diary – Vatican Council II*, 1962 and 1963 (Boston, 1964); M. Novak, *The Open Church – Vatican II, Act II* (New York, 1964).

from manœuvres against those remaining timeless bridges to the peoples of the East. Subsequently, all duties incumbent upon western missions should be gradually relegated to the clerics of the original ancient churches whose presence in the former mission fields could not be held as unsavoury to the Afro-Asian communities. But the Eastern churches are at best too limited in their means to cope with those vast responsibilities. Unless the Boards see a way towards replenishing their thin resources from accumulated funds in America and Europe, the chances of keeping up the labours of generations of the faithful are slim.

From all this, the need for consorted action and a united front, if not union, of the churches of Christ is paramount and now seems to be universally upheld in principle, though the realization is still more of a dream than a reality. Sustained efforts, a deluge of goodwill, and the placement of Christ above denominationalism are bases from which future generations can begin. Within the limited fold of Eastern Christianity, which is the chief object of our enquiry, there is one speck of light on the horizon which must never be extinguished. A dialogue between the Chalcedonians and the anti-Chalcedonian delegates to the World Council of Churches has been recurring for the lifting of ancient barriers. This healthy approach has culminated in the grouping of representative professional theologians of Eastern orthodoxy at Aarhus in Denmark (August 1964) to discuss 'our' differences. These consisted of seven members of Greek rite and nine from the East – Coptic, Ethiopian, Syrian, Indian and Armenian. Their illuminating deliberations have given birth to 'An Agreed Statement'[1] of the highest interest. While rejecting monophysitic Eutychianism and diophysitic Nestorianism, they unanimously re-asserted the Cyrillian formula of 'the one *physis* or *hypostasis* of God's Word Incarnate' – the Greek *mia physis Theou Logou sesarkomene*[2] – thereby quietly shelving the disagreement of Chalcedon. Nevertheless, it would be an error to interpret this felicitous step as a reunion of the East. The role of political, sociological and cultural factors at play in the creation of tensions and factions in the past cannot be effaced overnight. But, as the statement puts it, 'They could not, however, continue to divide us.' Perhaps the dawn is breaking and the circle may widen until all men of good faith re-discover their common Father.[3]

[1] Unofficial consultation between theologians of Eastern Orthodox and oriental Orthodox Churches. Minutes and papers of the Consultation held at the University of Aarhus, Denmark (11–15 August 1964). Mimeographed text ending with 'An Agreed Statement', pp. 33–4.

[2] This subject is studied in detail from the Coptic angle in a thesis presented to the Theologische Fakultät der Christian-Albrechts-Universität zu Kiel (October 1963) by a young Coptic theologian, Karam Naẓīr Khella, under the title: *Dioskoros I von Alexandrien: Theologie und Kirchengeschichte* (444–54), 2 vols., still in manuscript.

[3] Since writing this volume, a new 'Conference of the Orthodox Oriental Churches'

(*Continuation of Footnote 3*)
was convened at Addis Ababa from 15 to 21 January 1965. It was attended by the Patriarchs of those churches and inaugurated by Emperor Haile Selassie. Delegations from the Coptic, Syrian, Armenian, Ethiopian and Indian Churches were present, and the general trend of the Council was conciliatory. As to the Roman Catholic Church, the Council expressed the desire to maintain a dialogue for closer understanding, though Chalcedon (451) remains as a dividing line in the historic picture. Regarding the World Council of Churches, cordial relations were mentioned, but difficulties with member churches arise from proselytization which should cease. A Standing Committee of eight members from Alexandria, Antioch, Ethiopia and India was selected to pursue the Council decisions in the interim period.

SELECT BIBLIOGRAPHY

The present list is limited to works or collections of a general character which refer to numerous churches or varied communities. Though strictly selective and of necessity incomplete, the list is intended as a mere guide to wider studies on a subject of unusual breadth. Our listing is arranged alphabetically within each of the following categories: Bibliographic and Literary Studies, Dictionaries and Encyclopædias, General Collections of Original Source Materials, General Histories of the Church (Western, Eastern and Patrology), and Atlases and Maps. Reference to works mentioned in this bibliography will be limited to names of authors or general titles of collections. More specialized books or studies dealing with a single subject or church are given fuller bibliographic citation in the footnotes but are not listed here. Other bibliographical works of a more comprehensive nature, both Eastern and Western, may also be utilized. I have enumerated the essential ones elsewhere (cf. The Crusade – Historiography and Bibliography [Oxford, 1962], pp. 79–83).

Bibliographic and Literary Studies

O. BARDENHEWER, *Geschichte der altkirchlichen Litteratur*. 5 vols. 2nd ed. Freiburg, 1913–32.

A. BAUMSTARK, *Geschichte der syrishen Literatur, mit Ausschlusz der christlich-palästinensischen Texte*. Bonn, 1922.

H. G. BECK, *Kirche und theologische Literatur im byzantinischen Reich*. Munich, 1959.

S. J. CASE et al., *A Bibliographical Guide to the History of Christianity*. Chicago, 1931.

U. CHEVALIER, *Repértoire des sources historiques du moyen âge*. (1) *Bio-bibliographie*. 2 vols. Paris, 1877–86. Supplément 1888. 2nd ed. 1905–7. (2) *Topo-bibliographie*. 2 vols. Paris, 1894–1903.

G. GRAF, *Geschichte der christlichen arabischen Literatur*. 5 vols. Vatican City, 1944–53. (Studi e Testi, 118, 133, 146, 147, 172.)

A. VON HARNACK, *Geschichte der altchristlichen Litteratur bis Eusebius*. 2 vols. Leipzig, 1893–1904.

W. KAMMERER, *A Coptic Bibliography*. Compiled by W. K. with the collaboration of Elinor M. Husselman and Louise A. Shier. Ann Arbor, 1950. (University of Michigan General Library Publications.)

K. KRUMBACHER, *Geschichte der byzantinischen Litteratur von Justinian bis zum Ende des oströmischen Reiches* (527–1453 A.D.) 2nd ed. Munich, 1897.

K. E. MOYER, *A Selected and Annotated Bibliography of North Africa and the Near and Middle East*. Missionary Research Library, Union Theological Seminary. New York, 1957. (In mimeograph.)

L. J. PAETOW, *A Guide to the Study of Medieval History*. Revised ed. prepared under the auspices of The Mediæval Academy of America, Cambridge, Mass., 1931. Kraus reprint, New York, 1959.

A. POTTHAST, *Bibliotheca historica medii ævi*. Wegweiser durch die Geschichtswerke des europäischen Mittelalters bis 1500. Berlin, 1862. Supplement 1868. 2nd ed., enlarged and improved, 2 vols., Berlin, 1896.

A. PUECH, *Histoire de la littérature grecque chrétienne depuis les origines jusqu'à la fin du quatrième siècle*. 3 vols. Paris, 1928–30.

Revue d'histoire ecclésiastique. Louvain, 1900 ff. (Most comprehensive register of works publ. in the twentieth century on Christianity. For other periodical material, see bibliographical citations in guides to mediæval studies.)

Dictionaries and Encyclopædias

Perhaps the most comprehensive attempt in modern times is the *Encyclopédie des sciences ecclésiastiques*, published by Letouzy of Paris under the following categories: (1) F. Vigouroux, *Dictionnaire de la Bible*, 5 vols. (Paris, 1895–1912) with supplement by L. Pirot, 6 vols. (Paris 1928–60) and more fasc. in progress. (2) A. Vacant, E. Mangenot and E. Amann, *Dictionnaire de théologie catholique*, 15 vols. (Paris 1899–1962). (3) F. Cabrol and H. Leclercq, *Dictionnaire d'archéologie chrétienne et de liturgie*, 15 vols. in 30 (Paris, 1907–1953). (4) A. de Meyer and E. van Cauwenbergh, *Dictionnaire d'histoire et de géographie ecclésiastique*, 15 vols. (Paris, 1912–62). (5) A. Villien, E. Magnin and A. Amanieu, *Dictionnaire de droit canonique*, 39 fasc. (Paris, 1924–60).

The following is a selection of other encyclopædic works alphabetically arranged under editor or author.

W. E. ADDIS and T. ARNOLD, *Catholic Dictionary*. 6th ed. rev. T. B. Scannell. London, 1903.

J. S. BUMPUS, *Dictionary of Ecclesiastical Terms. Being a History and Explanation of Certain Terms used in Architecture, Ecclesiology, Liturgiology, Music, Ritual, Cathedral Constitution*, etc. London, 1910.

F. L. CROSS, *The Oxford Dictionary of the Christian Church*. London (Oxford University Press), 1957

G. H. DEMETRAKOPOULOS, *Dictionary of Orthodox Theology*. New York, 1964.

Encyclopedia of Islam, 1st ed., 4 vols. and Suppl. (Leiden, 1913–33); rev. 2nd ed. in progress, Leiden, 1945 ff.

J. HASTINGS, *Encyclopedia of Religion and Ethics*. 13 vols. Edinburgh, 1917–27.

P. HÉLYOT, *Histoire des ordres monastiques, religieux et militaires, et de congrégations séculaires*. 8 vols. Paris, 1711–21.

C. G. HERBERMANN and others, *Catholic Encyclopedia*, 17 vols. including Index and Supplement. New York, 1907–22.

J. J. HERZOG, *Realencyklopädie für protestantische Theologie und Kirche*. 24 vols. 3rd ed. D. A. Hauck. Leipzig, 1896–1913.

S. M. JACKSON and others, *New Schaff-Herzog Encyclopedia of Religious Knowledge*. 12 vols. New York, 1908–12.

S. MATHEWS and G. B. SMITH, *Dictionary of Religion and Ethics*. New York, 1921.

J. MCCLINTOCK and J. STRONG, *Cyclopedia of Biblical, Theological and Ecclesiastical Literature*. 12 vols. including Suppl. New York, 1867–91

J. P. MIGNE, *Encyclopédie théologique, ou série de dictionnaires sur toutes les parties de la science religieuse*. 50 vols. in 53. Paris, 1844–49. Supplemented by: (1) *Nouvelle encyclopédie théologique*. 52 vols. in 53. Paris, 1851–55. (2) *Troisième et dernière encyclopédie théologique*. 67 vols. Paris, 1855–73. The whole series of three sets is completed in a total of 172 vols.

M. S. and J. LANE MILLER, *Harper's Bible Dictionary*. 3rd ed. New York, 1955.

G. MORONI, *Dizionario di erudizione storico-ecclesiastica da S. Pietro sino ai nostri giorni*. 109 vols. including 6 vols of Indices. Venice, 1940–79.

W. SMITH and S. CHEETHAM, *Dictionary of Christian Antiquities*. 2 vols. London, 1875–80.

W. SMITH and H. WACE, *Dictionary of Christian Biography, literature, sects and doctrines*. 4 vols. London, 1877–87.

General Collections

O. BARDENHEWER et al., *Bibliothek der Kirchenväter: Eine Auswahl patristischer Werke in deutscher Übersetzung.* 61 vols. and 2 Indices. Munich, 1911–1930. Second Series, 20 vols., 1932–9.

J. BOLLANDUS, *Acta Sanctorum.* Begun in Antwerp, 1643. 65 vols. completed to November 10. Supplemented by *Analecta Bollandiana* inaugurated by the Bollandists in Brussels, 1882. See also *Bibliotheca Hagiographica Orientalis* which is an adjunct to the *Acta Sanctorum* prefaced by P. Peeters and published in Beirūt, 1910.

Centro Francescano di Studi Orientali Cristiani, *Studio Orientalia Christiana. Collectanea. Studi, Documenti, Bibliografia.* 9 vols, Cairo, 1956–64.

J. B. CHABOT et al., *Corpus scriptorum christianorum orientalium.* Paris, Rome, Leipzig and Louvain, 1933 ff. Texts and translations of source materials from Arabic, Armenian, Coptic, Ethiopic, and Syriac.

B. GEYER and J. ZELLINGER, *Florilegium patristicum, tam veteris quam medii ævi auctores completens.* 44 vols. Bonn 1906 ff.

R. GRAFFIN, *Patrologia Syriaca.* 3 vols. Paris, 1894–1926.

R. GRAFFIN and F. NAU, *Patrologia Orientalis.* 30 vols. Paris 1907–63. Includes Arabic, Armenian, Coptic, Ethiopian, Greek, Georgian, Slav, and Syriac source materials.

É. GUIMET, *Annales du Musée Guimet.* 33 vols. Paris 1880–1909.

C. J. VON HEFELE, *Conciliengeschichte.* 7 vols. Freiburg, 1855–74. 2nd ed. in 6 vols. (1873–90) continued by J. A. G. Hergenröther who completed vols. VIII–IX (1887–90). English tr. W. R. Clark, *History of the Christian Councils*, vols. I–V (to 787 A.D.), Edinburgh, 1871–96. Authorized standard French tr. H. Leclercq, *Histoire des Conciles*, 11 vols. in 22, Paris, 1907–52.

H. HYVERNAT, *Bibliothecæ Pierpont Morgan codices coptici photagraphice expressi.* 56 vols. in 63. Rome, 1922.

INSTITUT FRANÇAIS D'ARCHÉOLOGIE ORIENTALE, *Bibliothèque des études coptes.* Cairo, 1900 ff.

KIRCHENVÄTER–KOMMISSION DER PREUSSISCHEN AKADEMIE DER WISSENSCHAFTEN, *Die griechischen christlichen Schriftsteller der ersten Jahrhunderte.* Leipzig, 1901 ff.

K. LAKE (ed.), *The Apostolic Fathers.* With English tr. 2 vols. (The Loeb Classical Library, gen. ed. T. E. Page et al.) London, 1912.

E. H. LANDON, *A Manual of Councils of the Holy Catholic Church.* 2 vols. Rev. ed. Edinburgh, 1903.

J. D. MANSI et al., *Sacrorum conciliorum nova et amplissima collectio.* 31 vols. to 1590 A.D. Florence and Venice, 1759–98. New ed. and continuation, vols. 32–53, Paris, 1901 ff.

A. J. MASON, *Cambridge Patristic Texts.* Cambridge, 1899 ff.

J. P. MIGNE, *Patrologiæ cursus completus.* (1) Series Latina, 217 vols. and 4 Indices, Paris, 1878–90. (2) Series Græca, 161 vols., Paris, 1857–66. Index to the Græca by T. Hopfner, 2 vols., Paris, 1928–36. Also earlier Indices by F. Cavallera, Paris, 1912.

A. RABBATH, *Documents inédits pour servir à l'histoire du christianisme en Orient.* 2 vols. Paris, 1910.

A. ROBERTS and J. DONALDSON, *Ante-Nicene Fathers,* Translations of the Fathers to A.D. 325. 10 vols. New York, 1885–7.

P. PAUL SBATH, *Vingt traités philosophiques et apologetiques d'auteurs arabes du IXe au XIVe siècle.* Cairo, 1929.

P. SCHAFF, *Select Library of Nicene and Post-Nicene Fathers of the Christian Church.* First Series, 14 vols., New York, 1886–9. New Series, ed H. Wace and P. Schaff, 14 vols., New York, 1890–1900.

SOCIETY FOR THE PROMOTION OF CHRISTIAN KNOWLEDGE, *Translations of Christian Literature* – Series I: Greek Texts; Series II: Latin Texts; Series III: Liturgical Texts. London 1918 ff.

For shorter selections of illustrative material from the sources, see B. J. KIDD, *Documents Illustrative of the History of the Church to 461 A.D.* 2 vols., London, 1920–3; J. C. AYER, *A Source Book of the Ancient Church History,* New York, 1913; and H. BETTENSON, *Documents of the Christian Church,* Oxford, 1944.

General Histories of the Church

J. ALZOG, *Manual of Universal Church History.* Tr. from 9th German ed. by F. J. Pabisch and T. S. Byrne. 4 vols. Dublin, 1879–82.

C. BARONIUS, *Annales ecclesiastici a Christo nato ad annum 1198.* 12 vols. (Rome, 1588–1607). Ed. by J. D. Mansi, 38 vols. (Lucca, 1738–59). Apparatus 1 vol., 1750. Index 4 vols. (1757–9). New Ed. with all continuations, 37 vols. (Bar-le-Duc & Paris, 1864–83). Originally intended to be in 50 vols.

L. DUCHESNE, *L'histoire ancienne de l'Eglise chrètienne,* 3 vols (1906–10, placed on the Index in 1912). *Standard edition: Early History of the Christian Church, From its Foundation to the End of the Fifth Century.* Eng. tr. by Claude Jenkins. 3 vols. 7th ed. London 1950–1. See also: L'Église au sixième siècle (1925).

C. FLEURY, *Histoire ecclésiastique.* Continued by J. C. Fabre and indexed by Rondot. 36 vols. & 4 indices. (Paris, 1691–1720, 1726–37, 1769–74). English version by J. H. Newman, 3 vols. Oxford, 1842–4.

A. FLICHE and V. MARTIN (eds.) *Histoire de l'église depuis les origines jusqu'à nos jours.* 25 vols. Paris, 1934 ff.

J. A. G. HERGENRŒTHER, *Histoire de L'Église.* French tr. P. Bélet. 8 vols. Bibliothèque Théologique du XIXe siècle. Paris, 1880 etc.

K. S. LATOURETTE, (1) *A History of the Expansion of Christianity.* 7 vols. New York, 1937–45. (2) *A History of Christianity*, (New York, 1953).

H. H. MILMAN, (1) *History of Christianity to the Abolition of Paganism in the Roman Empire.* 3 vols. London, 1840. (2) *History of Latin Christianity.* New ed. 9 vols. London, 1883.

C. F. R. DE MONTALEMBERT, *Histoire des moines d'Occident depuis S. Bénoît jusqu'à S. Bernard.* 7 vols. Paris, 1860–77. English tr. with Introduction F. A. Gasquet, *Monks of the West*, 6 vols. London, 1896.

J. L. VON MOSHEIM, *Institutiones historiæ ecclesiasticæ antiquæ et recentioris.* Helmstedt, 1764. English tr. A. Maclaine: *An Ecclesiastical History, Ancient and Modern*, 6 vols., Philadelphia, 1797–8; also J. MURDOCK: *Institutes of Ecclesiastical History*, 3 vols., New York, 1832.

J. A. W. NEANDER, *Allgemeine Geschichte der christlichen Religion.* 6 vols. Hamburg, 1823–52. Tr. by J. TORREY, *General History of the Christian Religion and Church* (to 1430 A.D.). 9 vols. London, 1847–55.

P. SCHAFF, *History of the Christian Church.* New ed. 7 vols. New York, 1882–1910.

General Histories of the Eastern Churches

W. F. ADENEY, *The Greek and Eastern Churches.* Edinburgh, 1908.

J. S. ASSEMANI, *Bibliotheca orientalis Clementino-Vaticana, in qua manuscriptos codices Syriacos, Arabicos, Persicos, Turcicos, Hebraicos, Samaritanos, Armenicos, Æthiopicos, Græcos, Ægyptiacos, Ibericos, et Malabaricos . . . recensait.* 3 vols. in 4. Rome (Sacred Congregation for the Propagation of Faith), 1719–28.

D. ATTWATER, *The Christian Churches of the East.* 2 vols. Milwaukie, Wisconsin, 1948–61. Vol. I – *Churches in Communion with Rome.* Vol. II – *Churches not in Communion with Rome.*

C. DECLERCQ, *Les églises unies d'Orient.* Paris, 1934.

J. FINEGAN, *Light from the Ancient Past, The Background of the Hebrew-Christian Religion.* 5th. ed. Princeton, 1951.

ADRIAN FORTESCUE, *The Lesser Eastern Churches.* London, 1913.

F. HAASE, *Altchristliche Kirchengeschichte nach orientalischen Quellen.* Leipzig, 1925.

R. JANIN, *Les églises orientales et les rites orientaux.* Paris, 1926.

B. J. KIDD, *The Churches of Eastern Christendom, from* A.D. *451 to the Present Time.* London, 1927.

M. LEQUIEN, *Oriens christianus, in quatuor patriarchatus digestus; quo exhibentur ecclesiæ, patriarchæ cæterique præsules totius Orientis.* 3 vols. Paris, 1740.

J. M. NEALE, *A History of the Holy Eastern Church:* I. – *General Introduction,* 2 pts.; II. – *The Patriarchate of Alexandria,* 2 vols. London, 1847–50.

P. RONDOT, *Les chrétiens d'Orient.* (Cahiers de l'Afrique et l'Asie, IV.) Paris 1955.

B. SPULER, *Die morgenländischen Kirchen.* Leiden, 1961. (Handbuch der Orientalistik, Erste Abteilung, Band VIII, Abschnitt 2.)

A. P. STANLEY, *Lectures on the History of the Eastern Church.* London, 1907.

G. VRIES, *Oriente cristiano ieri e oggi.* Rome, 1950

W. DE VRIES, *Rom und die Patriarchate des Ostens.* Frieburg/Munich, 1963.

Patrology

B. ALTANER, *Patrology.* Tr. from 5th German ed. Hilda C. Graef. Edinburgh –London, 1960.

O. BARDENHEWER, *Patrology: The Lives and Works of the Fathers of the Church.* Tr. from 2nd German ed. (Freiburg, 1894) T. J. Shahan. St Louis, Miss., 1908.

J. QUASTEN, *Patrology.* 3 vols. Westminster, Md., 1951–60. (For more secondary literature, see same, I, pp. 5–9.)

Atlases and Maps

CH. BACHATLY, *Map of Christian Egypt.* (Publ. Soc. of Coptic Archæology.) Cairo, 1955.

C. F. BUCKINGHAM, *Atlas of the Arab World and the Middle East.* London, 1960.

CAROLUS A SANTO PAULO, *Geographia sacra, cum notes, animadversionibus lucæ Holstenii.* Amsterdam, 1704.

G. DROYSEN, *Allgemeiner historischer Handatlas.* Bielefeld & Leipzig, 1886.

H. W. HAZARD, *Atlas of Islamic History.* Princeton, 1954.

K. HEUSSE and H. MULERT, *Atlas zur Kirchengeschichte.* Tübingen, 1905.

E. MCCLURE, *Historical Church Atlas.* London, 1897.

O. MEINARDUS, *Atlas of Christian Egypt.* Cairo, 1962.

R. L. POOLE, *Historical Atlas of Modern Europe from the Decline of the Roman Empire*. Oxford, 1902.

N. J. C. POUNDS and R. C. KINGSBURY, *An Atlas of Middle Eastern Affairs*. New York, 1963.

R. ROOLVINK, *Historical Atlas of the Muslim Peoples*. Harvard University Press, 1957.

K. VON SPRUNER and TH. MENCKE, *Handatlas für die Geschichte des Mittelalters und neueren Zeit*. 3rd ed. Gotha, 1880.

ALI TANOGLU and others, *Atlas of Turkey*. Istanbul, 1961. (Publications of the Faculty of Letters, University of Istanbul.)

S. L. TERRIEN, *Lands of the Bible*. London, 1958.

F. VAN DER MEER and CHRISTINE MOHRMANN, *Atlas of the Early Christian World*. English tr. and ed. by Mary F. Hedlund and H. H. Rowley. London, 1958.

G. E. WRIGHT and F. V. FILSON, *The Westminster Historical Atlas to the Bible*. Philadelphia, 1945.

SUPPLEMENTARY BIBLIOGRAPHY

The following works have appeared since the first publication of this book.

ABDELSAYED, GABRIEL. "The Coptic Americans: A Current American Contribution." *The New Jersey Ethnic Experience,* ed. by Barbara Cunningham. Pp. 120 ff. Union City, New Jersey, 1977.

ADAMS, WILLIAM Y. "Architectural evolution of the Nubian Church, 500–1400 A.D." *Journal of the American Research Center in Egypt.* Vol. IV (1965), pp. 87–139.

D'ALBANO, GIACOMO. *Historia della Missione Francescana in Alto Egitto-Fungi-Etiopia, 1686–1720,* ed. by P. Gabriele Giamberardini. Cairo, 1961.

ARBERRY, A. J., ed. *Religion in the Middle East: Three Religions in Concord and Conflict.* 2 vols. (See Vol. I, Part 2 "Christianity") Cambridge, 1969.

ARRAS, VICTOR, ed. & trans. *De Transitu Mariae Apocryphe Aethiopice.* Corpus Scriptorum Christianorum Orientalium (CSCO), Scriptores Aethiopici, T. 67–68. Louvain, 1973.

ATIYA, A. S. *The Copts and Christian Civilization.* The 42nd Annual Frederick William Reynolds Lecture at the University of Utah. University of Utah Press, 1979.

ATIYA, A. S. "Ḳibṭ." *Encyclopaedia of Islam,* 2nd ed. Leiden, 1979.

BAGATTI, FR. BELLARMINO. *The Church from the Gentiles in Palestine, History and Archaeology.* Jerusalem, 1971.

BAUER, J. C., *et. al. The Westminster Dictionary of Church History.* Philadelphia, 1971.

BECK, EDMUND. *Des Heiligen Ephraem des Syrers Sermones I.* (CSCO, Scriptores Syri, T. 131.) Louvain, 1970.

BECK, EDMUND, ed. & trans. *Des Heiligen Ephraem des Syrers Sermones.* 7 vols. (CSCO, Scriptores Syri, T. 130–31, 134–5, 138–39, 148) Louvain, 1970–73.

BECK, EDMUND, ed. & trans. *Des Heiligen Ephraem des Syrers: Hymnen auf Abraham Kidunaya und Julianos Saba.* (CSCO, Scriptores Syri, T. 140–41) Louvain. 1972.

BEETHAM, T. A. *Christianity and the New Africa.* London, 1967.

BETTS, R. B. *Christians in the Arab World—A Political Study.* Athens, 1975.

BILANIUK, PETRO B. T. *Studies in Eastern Christianity.* Ukranian Free University, Monograph no. 25. Munich & Toronto, 1977.

BLEEKER, C. J. and G. WIDENGREN. *Historia Religionum: Handbook of the History of Religions.* 2 vols. Leiden, 1969–71.

BLUM, GEORG GŬNTER. *Rabbula von Edessa: Der Christ, Der Bischof, der Theologie.* CSCO, Subsidia, T. 34. Louvain, 1969.

BÖHLIG, A. and WISSE, F. *The Gospel of the Egyptians.* Leiden, 1975.

BOWIE, LELAND. "The Copts, the Wafd, and Religious Issues in Egyptian Politics." *The Muslim World,* Vol. LXVII, No. 2 (April 1977), pp. 106–26.

BURMESTER, O. H. E. *The Horologion of the Egyptian Church; Coptic and Arabic Text from a Mediaeval Manuscript.* Trans. and Annotated. Cairo, 1973.

BURMESTER, O. H. E. *The Egyptian or Coptic Church: A Detailed Description of her Liturgical Services and the Rites and Ceremonies Observed in the Administration of her Sacraments.* Cairo, 1967.

CERULLI, ENRICO, ed. & trans. *Les vies éthiopiennes de saint Alexis l'homme de Dieu.* 2 vols. CSCO, Scriptores Aethiopici, T. 59–60. Louvain, 1969.

CHAKMAKJIAN, HAGOP A. *Armenian Christology and Evangelization of Islam.* Leiden, 1965.

COLBI, SAUL P. *Christianity in the Holy Land, Past and Present.* Tel Aviv, 1969.

DALMAIS, I. H. *La Liturgie d'Antioche: Rite Syrien et Rite Chaldéen.* Tours, 1967. (Work translated from A. A. King, *The Rites of Eastern Christendom.* 2 vols. Rome, 1947–48.)

DAMANHŪRI, SHAYKH. *On the Churches of Cairo (1739).* Arabic text and English trans. by M. Perlman. Berkeley, Los Angeles, & London, 1975.

DAUMAS, FRANÇOIS, & A. GUILLAUMONT. *Kellia I, Kôm 219.* Fouilles de l'Institut Français d'Archéologie Orientales, Tome XXVIII, fasc. 1 and 2. Cairo, 1968.

DESSARRE, EVE. *L'Afrique Noire Chrétienne.* Paris, 1960.

VAN DONZEL, E. J. *La Porte de la Foi: Apologie Ethiopienne du Christianisme contre l'Islam à partir du Coran.* Introduction, Texte, Critique, Traduction. Leiden, 1969.

DRAGUET, RENÉ. *Les Cinq Recensions de l'Ascéticon d'Abba Isaïe.* 4 vols. (CSCO, Scriptores Syri, T. 120–23) Louvain, 1968.

DRAGUET, RENÉ, ed. *Commentaire du Livre d'Abba Isaïe (Logoi I–XV) par* Dadiso Qatraya (VIIe *s.).* 2 vols. (CSCO, Scriptores Syri, T. 144–45) Louvain, 1972.

DRESCHER, JAMES, ed. & trans. *The Coptic (Sahidic) Version of Kingdoms I, II (Samuel I, II).* 2 vols. (CSCO, Scriptores Coptici, T. 35–36) Louvain, 1979.

EGAN, GEORGE A., ed. *Saint Ephrem: An Exposition of the Gospel.* (CSCO, Scriptores Armeniaci, T. 5) Louvain, 1968.

FARAG, FARAG ROFAIL. *Sociological and Moral Studies in the field of Coptic Monasticism.* Leiden, 1964.

FIEY, J. M. *Jalons pour une Histoire de l'Église en Iraq.* (CSCO, Subsidia, T. 36) Louvain, 1970.

FREND, W. H. C. *The Rise of Monophysism.* Cambridge, 1972.

GARITTE, GÉRARD, ed. & trans. *Expugnationis Hierosolymae A. D. 614.* 2 vols. (CSCO, Scriptores Arabici, I. 26–27) Louvain, 1973.

GARSOIAN, NINA G. *The Paulician Heresy: A Study of the Origin and Development in Armenia and the Eastern Provinces of the Byzantine Empire.* Paris, 1967.

HADDAD, WILLIAM W. "Christian Arab Attitudes towards the Arab-Israeli Conflict." *The Muslim World,* Vol. LXVII, No. 2 (April 1977), pp. 127–45.

HAGE, WOLFGANG. *Die Syrisch-jakobotische Kirche in frühislamischer Zeit.* Wiesbaden, 1966.

HAMMERSCHMIDT, ERNST. *Symbolic des orientalischen Christentums.* Stuttgart, 1966.

HAMMERSCHMIDT, ERNST. *Äthiopien, Christliches Reich zwischen Gestern und Morgen.* Weisbaden, 1967.

HAYMAN, A. P., ed. & trans. *The Disputation of Sergius the Stylite against a Jew.* 2 vols. (CSCO, Scriptores Syri, T. 152–53) Louvain, 1973.

HECHAÏMÉ, CAMMILLE. *Louis Cheikho et son livre 'Le Christianisme et la Litterature Chrétienne en Arabie avant l'Islam'.* Etude critique. Beirut, 1967.

HESPEL, ROBERT, ed. & trans. *Sévère d'Antioche: La Polémique Antijulianiste.* 5 vols. (CSCO, Scriptores Syri, T. 124–27, 137) Louvain, 1968.

HOLWECK, F. G. *A Biographical Dictionary of the Saints.* St. Louis, Mo., 1924.

HUSSELMAN, ELINOR M. "The Martyrdom of Cyriacus and Julitta in Coptic." *Journal of the American Research Center in Egypt,* Vol. IV (1965), pp. 79–86.

HUSRY, KHALDUN S. "The Assyrian Affair of 1933." *International Journal of Middle East Studies,* Vol. V, No. 2 (April 1974), pp. 161–76; and Vol. V, No. 3 (June 1974), pp. 344–60.

ISAAC, EPHRAIM. *The Ethiopian Church.* Boston, 1968.

JARRY, JACQUES. *Hérésies et Factions dans l'Empire Byzantin du IVe au VIIe Siècle.* Cairo, 1968.

KAMIL, MOURAD. *Coptic Egypt.* Cairo, 1968.

KASSER, R. *Kellia 1965.* Recherches Suisses d'Archéologie Copte, I. Geneva, 1967.

KAWERAU, PETER. *Die Jakobitische Kirche in Zeitalter der Syrischen Renaissance.* Berlin, 1960.

KENYON, FREDERIC G. *Our Bible and the Ancient Manuscripts.* London, 1940.

KENYON, FREDERIC G. *The Chester Beatty Biblical Papyri.* 14 vols. London, 1933–58.

KERSCHENSTEINER, JOSEF. *Der Altsyrische Paulutext.* (CSCO, Subsidia, T. 37) Louvain, 1970.

KING, NOEL Q. *Christian and Muslim in Africa.* New York, 1971.

KUR, STANISLAS. *Actes de Marḥa Krestos.* 2 vols. (CSCO, Scriptores Aethiopici, T. 62–63) Lovain, 1972.

LINDSEY, R. L. *A Hebrew Translation of the Gospel of St. Mark: Greek-Hebrew Diglot with Eng. Introduction.* Jerusalem, 1969.

LITTLE, DONALD P. "Coptic Conversion to Islam under the Bahri Mamlūks, 692–755/1293–1354." *Bulletin of the School of Oriental Studies* (University of London), Vol. XXXIX, Part 3 (1976), pp. 552–569.

MAC DERMOT, VIOLET. *The Cult of the Seer in the Ancient Middle East: A*

Contribution to Current Research on Hallucinations Drawn from Coptic and Other Texts. Berkeley and Los Angeles, 1971.

MACLAGAN, EDWARD. *The Jesuits and the Great Mogul.* New York, 1972.

MAHFOUD, GEORGES-JOSEPH. *L'organization monastique dans l'église maronite.* Bibliothéque de l'Université de Saint-Esprit, Kaslik, Jounieh, 1967.

EL-MASRI, IRIS HABIB. *The Story of the Copts.* Middle East Council of Churches. Cairo, 1978.

MÉCÉRIAN, JEAN. *Histoire et Institutions de l'Église Arménienne: Evolution Nationale et Doctrinale, Spiritualité.* Beirut, n. d.

MEYENDORFF, JOHN. *Byzantine Theology: Historical Trends and Doctrinal Themes.* New York, 1974.

MOMIGLIANO, ARNALDO. *The Conflict between Paganism and Christianity in the Fourth Century.* Oxford, 1963.

Le Monde Copte: Revue Trimestrielle de la Culture Copte. Ed. Pierre de Bogdanoff. Paris, 1976 f.

MONTET, PIERRE. *Egypt and the Bible.* Leslie R. Keylock, trans. Philadelphia, 1968.

MOORE, ELINOR A. *The Early Christian Church in the Middle East.* Beirut, 1968.

MOORE, ELINOR A. *Some Soldier Martyrs of the Early Christian Church in East Jordan and Syria.* Beirut, 1964.

MŬLLER, C. D. G. *Grundzŭge des Christlich-Islamischen Ăgypten von der Ptolemăerzeit bis zur Gegenwart.* Darmstadt, 1969.

NAG HAMMADI. *The Facsimile Edition of the Nag Hammadi Codices.* 14 vols. Leiden, 1972 f.

NEIMAN, DAVID and SCHATKIN, MARGARET, eds. *The Heritage of the Early Church: Essays in Honor of the Very Rev. Georges V. Florovsky.* Rome, 1973.

DA PALERMO, ILDEFONSO. *Cronaca della Missione Francescana dell' Alto Egitto: 1719–1739,* ed. Gabriele Giamberardini. Cairo, 1962.

DE PAOR, MAIRE and LIAM. *Early Christian Ireland.* London, 1964.

PELLIOT, PAUL. *Récherches sur les chrétiens d'Asie Centrale et de l'Extrême-Orient.* (Oeuvres Posthumes) Paris, 1973.

RAHNER, K., ed. *Encyclopedia of Theology: The Concise Sacramentum Mundi.* New York, 1975.

RAHNER, K., *et. al.,* eds. *Sacramentum Mundi: An Encyclopedia of Theology.* 6 vols. New York, 1968–70.

RAYMOND, E. A. E. and BARNS, J. W. B. *Four Martyrdoms from the Pierpont Morgan Coptic Codices.* Oxford, 1973.

RICCI, L., trans. *Vita di Walatta Piēṭros.* (CSCO, Scriptores Aethiopici, T. 61) Louvain, 1970.

ROBINSON, JAMES M., general ed. *The Nag Hammadi Library.* New York, 1978.

RONCAGLIA, MARTINIANO P. "La chiesa copta dopo il Concilio di Calcedonia (451): Monofismo reale e monofismo nominale?" *Instituto Lombardo di Scienze e Lettere* (Milan, 1968) pp. 493–514.

RONCAGLIA, M. P. *Histoire de l'Église Copte.* 6 vols. Beirut, 1966f.

AS-SADAMANTI, BUTRUS. *Introduction sur l'herméneutique.* Edition critique avec introduction et traduction par P. Van Den Akker. Beirut, 1972.

SADER, JEAN. *Le De Oblatione de Jean de Dara.* (CSCO, Scriptores Syri, T. 132) Louvain, 1970.

SALIB, CYRILLE. *La Liturgie des Sacrements du Baptême et de la Confirmation.* Trans. into French from Coptic. Cairo, 1968.

SAMUEL, ATHANASIUS YESHUE. (Metropolitan Mar.) *Anaphora: The Divine Liturgy of St. James the First Bishop of Jerusalem, according to the Rites of the Syrian Orthodox Church of Antioch.* Trans. from the original Syriac. Hackensack, New Jersey, 1967.

SAUMAGNE, CH. *Saint Cyprien, Èvêque de Carthage, "Pape" d'Afrique* (248–*58*). Paris, 1975.

SAWIRIS IBN AL-MAKAFFA'. *History of the Patriarchs of the Egyptian Church* (*See above* p. 25, n. 1) Vol. III, Parts 1, 2, and 3; Vol. IV, parts 1 and 2, ed. and trans. Antoine Khater and O. B. E. Burmester. Cairo, 1968–74.

SCHNEIDER, MADELAINE, ed. and trans. *Actes de Za-Yohannes de Kebrān.* 2 vols. (CSCO, Scriptores Aethiopici, T. 64–65) Louvain, 1972.

SCHOLER, D. M. *Nag Hammadi Bibliography 1948–69.* Leiden, 1971.

SIDARUS, ADEL G. *Ibn ar-Rāhibs Leven und Werk: Ein Koptisch-arabischer Enzyklopädist des 7/13.* Jahrhunderts. Freiburg, 1975.

SMITH, W. and WACE, H. *A Dictionary of Christian Biography, Literature, Sects and Doctrines: Being a Continuation of 'The Dictionary of the Bible.'* 4 vols. New York, 1974.

Studia Orientatia Christiana: Collectanea-Studi, Documenti, Bibliografia. Edizioni del Centro Francescano di Studi Orientali Christiani. 13 vols. Cairo, to 1969.

THOMSON, ROBERT W. ed. *Athanassiana Syriaca—Part III: De Incarnatione Contra Arianos, contra Appolinarium I, de Cruce et Passione; quod Unus sit Christus; de Incarnatione Verbi; ad Jovianum.* 2 vols. (CSCO, Scriptores Syri, T. 142–143) Louvain, 1972.

TILL, WALTER. *Koptische Heileigen-und Martyrerlegenden: Texte, Übersetzungen and Indices.* 2 vols. Rome, 1936.

VERGOTE, JOSEPH, A. L. "Der Manichäismus in Ägypten." *Manichäismus.* (Darmstadt, 1977), pp. 385–99.

VERGOT, JOZEF. "La Valeur des vies grecque et coptes de S. Pakhôme." *Orientalia Louvaneiensia Periodica,* Vol. VIII (1977), pp. 175f.

VOLKOFF, OLEG V. *D'ou vint la Reine de Saba?* Cairo, 1971.

VÖÖBUS, A. *Syrische Kanonessammlungen: Ein Beitrag zur Quellenkunde.* 2 vols. (CSCO, Subsidia, T. 35, 38) Louvain, 1970.

VÖÖBUS, ARTHUR, *History of the School of Nisibis.* (CSCO, Subsidia, T. 26) Louvain, 1965.

VÔÔBUS, A. *The Pentateuch in the Version of the Syro-Hexapla.* (CSCO, Subsidia, T. 45) Louvain, 1975.

VÖÖBUS, A. *The Synodicon in the West Syrien Tradition.* (CSCO, Scriptores Syri, T. 161) Louvain, 1975.

VÖÖBUS, A. *Handschriftliche Überlieferung der Mēmrē-Dichtung des Ja'qōb von*

Serūg. 2 vols. (CSCO, Subsidia, T. 39–40) Louvain, 1973.
WASSEF, CÉRÈS WISSA. *Pratiques Rituelles et Alimentaires des Coptes.* Cairo, 1971.
WATERFIELD, ROBIN E. *Christians in Persia.* New York, 1973.
WYON, O. *An Eastern Palimpsest: A Brief Survey of the Religious Situation in Turkey, Syria, Palestine, Transjordania, Egypt.* London, n.d.

PLATES

I

II

III

IV

V

VI

VII

VIII

IX

X

XI

XII

XIIIa

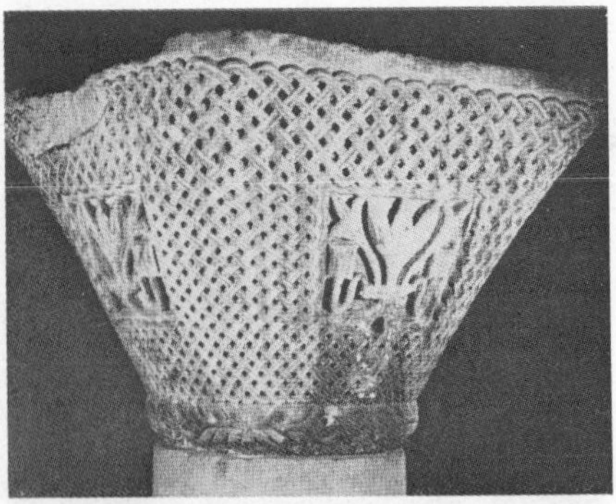

b

c

e

XIV

XV

XVI

XVII

XVIII

XIX

INDEX

The abbreviations used in this index are: Patr. = Patriarch, b. = ibn, Bp = Bishop, Archbp = Archbishop, and Emp. = Emperor. Space economy has been observed in grouping entries dealing with a general subject in common. Minimum explanatory notices are inserted, and these can easily be identified by reference to the text of the book. Book titles and foreign terms are reproduced in italics.